INDUSTRIALRELATIONS

IN CANADIAN INDUSTRY

INDUSTRIAL RELATIONS
IN CANADIAN INDUSTRY

RICHARD P. CHAYKOWSKI, Editor
QUEEN'S UNIVERSITY

ANIL VERMA, Editor
UNIVERSITY OF TORONTO

DRYDEN

A Division of Holt, Rinehart and Winston of Canada, Limited

Toronto Montreal Orlando Fort Worth San Diego Philadelphia
London Sydney Tokyo

Canadian Cataloguing in Publication Data

Main entry under title:

Industrial relations in Canadian industry

Includes index.
ISBN 0-03-922877-0

1. Industrial relations—Canada. I. Chaykowski, Richard P. (Richard Paul), 1958– . II. Verma, Anil.

HD8106.5.153 1992   331'.0971 C91-095672-3

Editorial Director: Scott Duncan
Acquisitions Editor: Donna Muirhead
Developmental Editor: Brenda Hutchinson
Editorial Assistant: Yolanta Cwik
Director of Publishing Services: Steve Lau
Editorial Manager: Liz Radojkovic
Editorial Co-ordinator: Sandy Walker
Production Manager: Sue-Ann Becker
Production Assistant: Denise Wake
Copy Editor: Beverley Beetham Endersby
Interior Design and illustrations: Loates Creative Design
Cover: Dave Peters
Typesetting and Assembly: Loates Creative Design
Printing and Binding: Best Gagné Book Manufacturers

   This book was printed in Canada on acid-free paper.

1 2 3 4 5   96 95 94 93 92

Dr. Richard P. Chaykowski is Assistant Professor of Industrial Relations at the School of Industrial Relations at Queen's University. He received his Ph.D. from Cornell University in Industrial and Labour Relations. From 1988 to 1990 he was a Queen's National Scholar at Queen's University. He has been a Visiting Professor at the Centre for Industrial Relations at the University of Toronto and Visiting Scholar at the Sloan School of Management at the Massachusetts Institute of Technology. He is also currently a Faculty Associate of the Centre for Resource Studies at Queen's University.

His general areas of interest include the theoretical and empirical analysis of industrial relations and human resource issues, labour economics, and comparative economic systems. The range of his published research has included investigations of the factors that give rise to alternative collective bargaining outcomes, issues associated with the implementation of pay equity, the impacts of technological change on the organization of work and employee skills, and the determinants of employee compensation. He has recently turned his attention to the transformation of industrial relations systems at the industry level.

Dr. Anil Verma is Associate Professor of Industrial Relations and Human Resource Management at the University of Toronto, where he holds a joint appointment at the Faculty of Management and the Centre for Industrial Relations. His primary research interests are in the area of management responses to unionization, participative forms of work organization and the contribution of human resource management policies such as employment stabilization practices, profit/gain sharing and other innovations in industrial relations to Canadian competitiveness in international trade.

Professor Verma consults with a wide range of businesses, unions, and government agencies and has been a speaker at many national and international conferences. He has published over thirty articles in research journals and books. He has taught previously at the University of Saskatchewan, the University of California, Los Angeles, the University of British Columbia, and worked in the steel industry as an engineer for five years.

He earned a B. Tech. in electrical engineering from I.I.T., Kanpur (India), an M.B.A. from the University of Saskatchewan, Saskatoon (Canada), and a Ph.D. in management from the Sloan School of Management, M.I.T., Cambridge, MA (USA).

Foreword

Thomas A. Kochan*

This collection of essays on Canadian industrial relations breaks considerable new ground in the analysis of the dynamics of national industrial relations systems. Too often, commentaries that seek to make general statements about such systems are either mired in descriptive detail and lacking any clear analytical framework or prone to oversimplified generalities about so-called national features or trends that miss the diversity or variability within the system. I am pleased to see that, as readers will discover, the editors of this volume and the authors who have contributed to it have avoided both of these problems.

Moreover, this book should serve as a warning shot over the bow of Canadian managers, labour leaders, and government officials. For, if the editors are correct, failure of the parties to engage in more conscious self-appraisal and action will lead to declining equity and efficiency in Canada and a slow erosion of the competitiveness of the economy of Canada and the standards of living of its citizens.

In this brief foreword, I wish to highlight what I see as some contributions this volume makes to the literature. The fact that the subject matter of these essays spans the spectrum of theory and method, policy analysis, and practice is a tribute to the breadth of the work.

The application of the strategic-choice model in a systematic fashion within ten key sectors of the Canadian economy demonstrates the usefulness of a common analytic framework. Individually, the authors are able to test and modify the model while describing the key developments within a particular sector. As a whole, the book provides a detailed analysis of both the variability or diversity inherent in any large modern economy such as Canada's and the raw materials needed to expand and further develop the model. In taking this approach, the book builds on the unit and method of analysis John Dunlop (1958) used in developing and presenting his classic industrial relations systems model. The value of this combination of a single model and in-depth analysis of multiple sectors is that it avoids two common pitfalls of macro studies of industrial relations—the tendency to overgeneralize on the basis of one sector's experiences or visible cases and the tendency to get buried under mountains of detailed but noncomparable data that cannot support theoretical generalizations or predictions.

The authors also extend and challenge the strategic-choice model and show how it must be adapted to cope with the differences between the U.S. and Canadian

* Thomas A. Kochan is Leaders of Manufacturing Professor and George Maverick Bunker Professor of Management at the Sloan School of Management, Massachusetts Institute of Technology.

industrial relations systems. For example, they note that more attention needs to be given to the role of industry- or sector-wide institutions. This need is clear in the steel industry (Chapter 3), where the parties have attempted to use tripartite, industry-wide efforts to introduce change.

Another important modification noted here is that of giving greater emphasis to the role of union power as a determinant of the degree and type of change experienced in an industry. Unlike their U.S. counterparts, Canadian unions have served to limit the dominance of management as the driving force in introducing and shaping the direction of change. Thus, in Canada, as in other countries where union membership and political influence remain strong, the strategic choices of unions take on greater importance. Understanding the forces that affect union strategies remains, however, an underdeveloped area of research.

Finally, the editors and a number of the authors emphasize the importance of public policy in shaping the direction and the pace of change in industrial relations. This emphasis is most clearly illustrated in the comparison of changes in unionization in construction across the western and eastern provinces (Chapter 5). The repeal of a law in Saskatchewan that restricted the growth of nonunion shops led, as Joseph Rose puts it, to the "collapse" of collective bargaining and union membership in that province, while union membership grew in the provinces of Quebec and Ontario. The challenge, therefore, in these latter two provinces is to demonstrate that equivalent improvements in productivity, flexibility, and dispute resolution can be achieved through transformations in labour–management relations. Thus, by highlighting the effects of industry-level institutions and the effects of differences in the strength and strategies of labour in the economy and society, and discussing more fully the role of public policies, the authors have expanded the scope and power of the strategic-choice model as a framework for analyzing national industrial relations systems.

In their concluding chapter, the editors stake out a strong theoretical position and, in doing so, offer a warning to Canadian policy makers and practitioners. They argue that failure of the industrial relations system to transform practices more fully and more quickly will result in a less competitive Canadian economy, especially in international markets or in the emerging Canadian–U.S.–Mexican trading bloc. They argue that competitiveness could perhaps be achieved by following several different paths, but that different choices would result in significantly different outcomes for the standard of living of Canadian workers and the future of unions and worker representation. Thus, the authors clarify the efficiency and equity consequences of different choices and paths of transformation that have been, at best, implicit or only partially explicated in previous presentations of the strategic-choice model.

Specifically, I take the analysis presented in the final chapter to suggest the following predictions:

1. The traditional industrial relations system is not well suited to the contemporary economy of Canada. Adherence to traditional practices and principles will

result in declining performance of the economy. But, because competitive pressures will continue to build, the slow evolutionary pace of change will continue to erode union strength and membership. Failure of the parties to take more conscious and aggressive action to transform more fully industrial relations practices will lead to a continuation of a slow and uneven evolution away from many features of the traditional industrial relations system, but will not be sufficient to produce the fundamental changes in the system needed to enhance competitiveness.

2. In environments where unions are weak, a "management dominance" path of transformation will not only continue but, if competitive pressures increase, likely escalate. This path of transformation may enhance the competitiveness of firms by lowering costs. However, this strategy will come at the expense of union membership and will ultimately reduce the standard of living of Canadian workers. Thus, the management-dominance model predicts potential efficiency gains at the cost of reduced equity.

3. The strategic-alliance path to transformation, however, is predicted to do a better job of enhancing efficiency and equity while preserving a stronger role for union and worker representation. But, for this path to be viable, a more proactive and public vision and strategy on the part of labour leaders and government policy makers than has been the case to date is required.

These are strong propositions, ones that are worth consideration and debate among practitioners and policy makers, and further testing by researchers.

The argument that labour leaders and government policy makers will be pivotal actors in determining the pace and direction of change is particularly interesting, especially given the recent electoral successes of the New Democratic Party (NDP) in Ontario, British Columbia, and Saskatchewan. These provinces will serve as laboratories for all to see whether labour-led transformations of public policy and private practice will result in further evolutionary transformations to a more efficient and equitable economy or in an effort to return to the status quo of a previous era. If the strategic-choice model is valid at this level of policy analysis, then the policy debates that will make the most difference lie well beyond the traditional issues of union certification, dispute resolution, and incomes policy. Rather, the issues are the pace and nature of privatization, industry deregulation, trade policies, training, human-resource development and adjustment, and the degree to which governments actively encourage diffusion of industrial relations innovations and transformation strategies.

Thus, the editors highlight the importance of reaching a clear long-run vision of, and conscious industrial relations strategy and economic policy on, these issues in Canada. However, this strategy and vision must go beyond the traditional boundaries of our field to be broadly based and integrated with the views of economic policy makers and industry regulators. Debates over the future of industrial relations must, therefore, transcend the traditional domains of industrial relations policy makers.

Finally, this book offers insights on how we might move on to the next level of development and testing of the strategic-choice model, namely, international comparisons. If this or any other model is to be used for international comparisons, the same type of cross-industry data will be needed before reaching broad generalizations about changes in any given national system. I would go a step further and suggest that what is needed is an examination of firms that follow different competitive and industrial relations strategies. To do otherwise would fail to capture the diversity within systems and fail to test an even more challenging theoretical hypothesis recently advanced by Richard Locke (1992). He argues that the diversity within industrial relations systems may, in certain cases, be greater than the diversity across systems; that is, the strategic choices of the parties may lead to predictable and common outcomes that call into question the very utility of the concept of a national industrial relations system. Editors Chaykowski and Verma and the other contributors to this volume provide a valuable example of how this and other challenging propositions might be developed and tested in a carefully contructed international and comparative research project. I look forward to a decade of debate over these and other propositions that this type of careful comparative analysis can support. The editors and authors are to be commended for making this initial contribution to theory, method, and policy analysis. In the meantime, this book should provide considerable food for thought and debate in the Canadian industrial relations community for many years to come.

Cambridge, Massachusetts
October 1991

REFERENCES

Dunlop, John T. 1958. *Industrial Relations Systems*. New York: Holt, Rinehart and Winston.

Locke, Richard. 1992. "The Demise of the National Union in Italy." *Industrial and Labor Relations Review*, Vol. 45, No. 2, pp. 229-249.

Preface

The industrial relations literature in Canada has tended to concentrate on developments and outcomes in various political or economic regions, on jurisdictions, or on other industrial relations outcomes at macro levels of analysis. Complementing this research are a growing number of micro-level studies aimed at particular firms or unions, or other specific institutions relevant to industrial relations. However, there has been virtually no systematic study of developments at the industry level. The objective of the "industry studies" project was to produce a volume of studies that focussed on changes in industrial relations in a cross-section of Canadian industries.

While the selection of industries is by no means exhaustive, we hope that it will provide the reader with a representative view of Canadian industrial relations developments. A number of key industries we wished to include in this volume, were perforce omitted; the lack of previous research at this level made it difficult to synchronize all the efforts it would have taken to cover additional sectors such as forestry, petroleum, paper, and health. It is our hope that the research reported in this volume will encourage and stimulate further research at the industry level.

As the research program proceeded, we decided to convene a working conference at which the papers could be presented in a forum that would facilitate peer review and direct feedback on the papers from both researchers and practitioners. The Industrial Relations in Canadian Industry conference, held at Queen's University on April 25–26, 1991, offered the researchers an opportunity to present their work and obtain constructive comment at a formative stage in their research. We thank all participants of the conference from industry and academe for their contributions to the development of the papers. We are grateful to the Social Sciences and Humanities Research Council, the Industrial Relations Centre at Queen's University, the Centre for Industrial Relations at the University of Toronto, and HBJ-Holt for the financial support without which this conference would not have been possible.

Since its inception in 1990, we have both worked on all aspects of this project jointly, and our efforts and written work reflect this partnership. The entire project has benefited from the informal and formal feedback provided by numerous colleagues. In addition to the co-operation of our contributors, we are particularly appreciative of the feedback and help received from Roy Adams, Bryan Downie, Tom Kochan, Pradeep Kumar, and Morley Gunderson.

We are grateful to the School of Industrial Relations for generous institutional support at all stages of the project. In particular, we appreciate the assistance of Barbara Gibson, Mary Joan Edwards, and Liann Joanette in conference support and manuscript preparation, and Angela Zezza in background research. Finally, we would like to acknowledge the enthusiastic support, throughout the project, of Donna Muirhead, our editor at HBJ-Holt.

Richard P. Chaykowski
Anil Verma

PUBLISHER'S NOTE TO STUDENTS AND INSTRUCTORS

This textbook is a key component of your course. If you are the instructor of this course, you undoubtedly considered a number of texts carefully before choosing this as the one that would work best for your students and you. The authors and publishers spent considerable time and money to ensure its high quality, and we appreciate your recognition of this effort and accomplishment. Please note the copyright statement.

If you are a student, we are confident that this text will help you to meet the objectives of your course. It will also become a valuable addition to your personal library.

Since we want to hear what you think about this book, please be sure to send us the stamped reply card at the end of the text. Your input will help us to continue to publish high-quality books for your courses.

LIST OF CONTRIBUTORS

Pankaj Chandra
Faculty of Management
McGill University

Richard P. Chaykowski
School of Industrial Relations
Queen's University

Bryan M. Downie
School of Industrial Relations
Queen's University

E.G. Fisher
Faculty of Business
University of Alberta

Michel Grant
Department of Administrative Sciences
Université du Québec à Montréal

Alex Kondra
Faculty of Business
University of Alberta

Pradeep Kumar
School of Industrial Relations
Queen's University

Noah M. Meltz
Centre for Industrial Relations
University of Toronto

Allen Ponak
Faculty of Management
University of Calgary

Joseph B. Rose
School of Business
McMaster University

Terry Thomason
Faculty of Management
McGill University

Mark Thompson
Faculty of Commerce and Business
Administration
University of British Columbia

Anil Verma
Faculty of Management and
Centre for Industrial Relations
University of Toronto

Peter Warrian
University College
University of Toronto
and Canadian Steel Trade and
Employment Congress

Joseph M. Weiler
Faculty of Law and Nemetz Centre
for Dispute Resolution
University of British Columbia
and Associate Counsel, Heenan Blaikie

Harris L. Zwerling
Faculty of Management
McGill University

CONTENTS

1. Adjustment and Restructuring in Canadian Industrial Relations: 1
   Challenges to the Traditional System
      Richard P. Chaykowski and Anil Verma

2. Industrial Relations in the Canadian Automobile Industry   39
      Pradeep Kumar and Noah M. Meltz

3. Industrial Relations in the Canadian Steel Industry   87
      Anil Verma and Peter Warrian

4. Industrial Relations in the Canadian Mining Industry: 141
   Transition Under Pressure
      Richard P. Chaykowski

5. Industrial Relations in the Construction Industry in the 1980s   187
      Joseph B. Rose

6. Industrial Relations in the Clothing Industry: 220
   Struggle for Survival
      Michel Grant

7. Labour Relations in the Canadian Textile Industry   244
      Terry Thomason, Harris L. Zwerling, and Pankaj Chandra

8. Restraint, Privatization, and Industrial Relations in the   284
   Public Sector in the 1980s
      Mark Thompson and Allen Ponak

9. Industrial Relations in Elementary and Secondary Education: 323
   A System Transformed?
      Bryan M. Downie

10. Canada's Airlines: Recent Turbulence and Changing Flight   358
    Plans
       E.G. Fisher and Alex Kondra

11. Industrial Relations in the Canadian Telephone Industry   405
       Anil Verma and Joseph M. Weiler

12. Canadian Industrial Relations in Transition   448
       Richard P. Chaykowski and Anil Verma

Key Word Index   475

Name and Author Index   488

ADJUSTMENT AND RESTRUCTURING IN CANADIAN INDUSTRIAL RELATIONS: CHALLENGES TO THE TRADITIONAL SYSTEM

Richard P. Chaykowski
Anil Verma[1]

*T*he system of industrial relations in Canada that took shape during the three decades following the Second World War began to change in significant ways in the 1980s. The extent of the change is subject to debate. Some observers see the system as altering only at the "margin" (Thompson 1987), whereas others see a more substantial "transformation" taking place. Most experts agree, however, that the conduct of industrial relations has changed in important ways in the last decade. Some modifications in public policy, in approaches to human-resource management, and in industrial relations practices that began to show up sporadically in the 1980s appear to be gathering momentum in the 1990s.

The pressures for change are numerous.[2] International competition has intensified in recent years, in part because of the shifting loci of manufacturing from the industrialized to the newly industrializing countries, and in part because of the trend toward lowering tariff barriers to trade. These developments have at once compelled and encouraged the Canadian government to allow rapid and substantial restructuring of the economy. The Canada–U.S. Free Trade Agreement (FTA) is but one example of attempts to facilitate restructuring of the Canadian economy. Talks began in 1991 to negotiate a North American free-trade zone across Canada, the United States, and Mexico. Some sectors, such as transportation and communications, have also been deregulated, essentially to facilitate restructuring for greater efficiency and competitiveness. In the same spirit, the federal and some provincial governments have begun privatizing a number of hitherto publicly owned enterprises. These restructuring initiatives are driven to some extent by rapid advances in the technology of production. Lastly, demographic develop-

ments in the labour force, increases in the participation rate of women, immigration, and demands for employee voice, human rights, and privacy in the workplace, have contributed to pressures to change industrial relations and
human-resource management policies and practices.

The system of collective bargaining that developed in Canada in the 1950s
under the Wagner Act "model" relied on a growing domestic market and tariff
protection against imports that seriously threatened domestic industry. Within
this context, unions adopted a strategy to "take wages out of competition" by organizing all major employers in a given industry and to bargain for annual increases
in wages and benefits that were only indirectly linked to productivity improvements. The success of this system gave Canadian workers one of the highest standards of living in the world by the end of the 1970s. However, in the 1980s, our
industrial relations system began to respond to the requirements of a larger and
external political economy—the global marketplace. As a result of external market forces, wages in many industries could no longer easily be taken out of competition, and firms could not pass compensation increases on to consumers in the
form of higher prices.

This book examines the parties' responses to the pressures for change experienced in a number of selected industry sectors over the last ten years. The authors
examine competitive pressures in each industry and identify the different
responses of the parties. In order to set the stage for each of the industry studies
that follow, this chapter first discusses the analytical framework guiding the analysis in the next ten chapters, then provides an overview of the Canadian economy
and the industrial relations system as a whole. The generalization of the Canadian
experience presented in this chapter is intended to complement the subsequent
treatment of individual sectors whose experiences are unique to themselves.

A Framework for Understanding Change

The Dunlop (1958) systems framework is a useful device for describing the actors
and the context of industrial relations in the 1980s. The foundation for the following chapters is a combination of Dunlop's systems framework and the strategic-
choice model (Kochan, Katz, and McKersie 1986), used to capture the dynamics
of the change process. In this section, we first outline the basic features of the
strategic-choice framework, then discuss its suitability to the Canadian context.
We conclude that modifications may be necessary to make the strategic-choice
framework useful in the Canadian situation. Lastly, we address the issue of adopting the industry as the level of analysis.

THE STRATEGIC-CHOICE FRAMEWORK

An effective industrial relations system must meet the goals and aspirations of all parties to the system (Dunlop 1958). The simultaneous pursuit of equity and efficiency, therefore, has often been cited as the ideal for industrial relations systems (Barbash 1964). In practice, it may be argued, a greater emphasis was put on equity during the 1950-80 period, as evidenced by the growth of collective bargaining and labour laws. The emphasis in the post-1980 period appears to have swung in favour of efficiency. The challenge for Canada is to make the transition from a traditional system that, in general, was relatively insulated from external demands to a system that will enhance Canadian competitiveness in international markets without surrendering the guarantees of equity and fairness on the job that were gradually, and with difficulty, developed over a century.

This challenge confronts most industrialized economies. The issue is therefore of great importance to policy makers in government, business, and labour, not only in Canada, but in other countries where the past development of collective bargaining has been guided largely by internal rather than external demands. The dynamics of transition are also theoretically significant. So far, this theory has lagged behind events. The Inter-university set of studies of the 1950s (best known through the summary report, *Industrialism and Industrial Man* [Kerr et al. 1964]) explored the underlying logic of industrialization, and industrial relations as a sub-system emerging from that process. That study presented a good explanation of the process by which industrial relations systems developed in industrializing nations and grew to a level of maturity characterized by the type of system that prevailed in Canada in the 1970s. However, it does not provide much guidance on the current transition of the Canadian (and other) industrial relations systems.

The most important recent theoretical development addressing this issue is the strategic-choice framework proposed by Kochan, Katz, and McKersie (1986). This framework was derived inductively from developments in U.S. industrial relations over the 1950-80 period. In this study, the authors argue that the U.S. industrial relations system underwent a "transformation" during this period, and that this transformation was achieved largely through the growth of a parallel nonunion system that forced collective bargaining to reform itself in significant ways, even as the nonunion system supplanted collective bargaining in every sector of the economy. The U.S. experience illustrates one of the strategies (i.e., permitting growth of a nonunion sector) that can be used as a policy instrument to facilitate large-scale restructuring of workplace.

For Canadians, learning from the U.S. experience is problematic. During the first 60 years of this century, the evolution of the Canadian industrial relations system paralleled that of the United States. However, since the 1960s, their paths have diverged (Meltz 1985, 1990b). Union density, the most widely discussed aspect, is currently almost twice as high in Canada as in the United States (Chaison and Rose 1991). In addition, the Canadian labour movement appears to be more militant, and Canadian legal provisions that are in general more favourable to unions appear to be more strictly enforced (Meltz 1990b). [In the 1980s, Canadian employers generally did not emulate U.S. practices of union avoidance and substitution (Verma and Thompson 1990). Thus, the events of the 1980s by themselves do not suggest that the U.S. framework for understanding change applies to Canadian developments.]

Yet, some observers have suggested that Canadian developments may lag behind those in the United States (Troy 1991). With the implementation of the FTA, Canadian firms now face their U.S. competitors more directly. This situation certainly harmonizes competitive pressures on both sides of the border. Whether these pressures will result in similar responses by the parties remains to be seen. In other words, will the Canadian industrial relations system experience significant changes similar to those found in the U.S. trend, will it continue the patterns of the last half-century, or will it develop in a new direction unique to the Canadian context?[4] What is needed is an understanding of how management and unions respond to these pressures.

But the strategic-choice framework is more than a description of developments in U.S. industrial relations. As a theoretical approach, it can be useful in situations that differ from the U.S. pattern. Several features of this framework explain Canadian developments. Further, the framework suits the analytical task of this volume, namely, to understand the dynamic processes that characterize the evolution of mature industrial relations systems and to inform policy makers (and the concomitant debates). Our intent has not been to adopt this framework *in toto*, but to use it as a starting point for our analysis. It is only natural, and therefore expected, that we will adapt and change some aspects of the framework as we develop our analysis.

According to Kochan, Katz, and McKersie (1986), the strategic-choice framework was proposed to add more dynamics to industrial relations theory.[5] Although open to different interpretations (Chelius and Dworkin 1990), at its core the framework proposes the following:

1. Industrial relations decisions are made at three levels: business, collective bargaining and the workplace.
2. Effective strategies are those that act in concert at all three levels.
3. Parties face a number of alternative choices in adopting a suitable strategy.

Strategic choices are defined as the choices that each party makes to achieve its objectives *through concerted actions over a period of time*. Critics charge that almost anything a party does could be construed as strategic (Lewin 1987), a criticism that is somewhat incomplete despite its validity. To be defined as "strategic," the actions must form part of a pattern or a system of behaviour.

Since "strategy" plays a key role in this framework, it is important to understand the various connotations of this term. Taken from military usage, it refers to concerted campaigns to achieve a major goal. Such campaigns are generally planned and executed from a high level within the organization. Since a strategy is intended to accomplish major goals, it generally takes time to execute fully, and its outcomes typically have significant impact. In wars, successful strategies decide winners and losers; in industrial relations, they may determine a firm's competitiveness. Thus, strategic behaviour in industrial relations can be thought of in terms of decisions that are: (a) designed to achieve a major goal; (b) planned and executed from a high level in the organization; (c) executed over a relatively long period of time; and (d) likely to have significant impact on the parties.

As is true of all new terms, unless the term's implications are well understood, its newness may simply be a matter of semantics rather than of substance. One implication of strategic behaviour in industrial relations is that the parties act simultaneously at three levels to implement and co-ordinate strategy. The traditional system (as described by the systems framework) was focussed almost exclusively on the collective-bargaining process, the contract, and its administration. Such matters as capital investment in the firm and employee involvement in the quality of production were traditionally considered to be outside the purview of industrial relations decisions. Strategic decisions (or choices) required that parties abandon an exclusive focus on a collective-bargaining process that was limited to wages and benefits and that embodied only circumscribed references to the external environment. Strategic choices forced the parties to view investment and other market-related decisions as part of industrial relations decision making; it has also forced the parties to rethink the central role of rank-and-file workers in the industrial relations process.

Although many aspects of the Canadian industrial relations system, such as union density, law enforcement, and collective-bargaining outcomes in the 1980s, are at variance with the U.S. experience, the strategic-choice framework can be used to advantage. Strategic *choice* suggests that there will be variation in outcomes; that is, not every firm, union, or government facing similar pressures will make the same choices. Indeed, Canadian managers, public-policy makers, and union leaders have made choices in the 1980s different from those of their U.S. counterparts. An analysis of these differences and their consequences would help further explain the strategic-choice framework itself. It would make a valuable contribution and offer an opportunity for others to learn from the Canadian experience. Further, a strategic analysis would reveal the tactics that Canadian parties are *not* fully exploiting for various reasons. By focussing attention on differences in strategic behaviour, this process of analysis may help policy makers.

We view the strategic-choice framework, which is central to this book, as an augmentation of the Dunlop systems framework rather than as an alternative paradigm. As mentioned above, the systems framework guides the organization of our material. The traditional system described by Kochan, Katz, and McKersie (1986) corresponds to the dominant industrial relations system that developed through the 1960s and 1970s in Canada. But the emergence of a "transformed" system, as occurred in the United States in the 1980s, has not yet been seen in Canada. Many of the factors shaping the Canadian system, and hence the process by which changes are implemented, are equally profound but significantly different. Strategic choice is essentially used to explain the dynamic process that led to unprecedented changes in Canadian industrial relations in the 1980s.

In considering the progression of the industrial relations system in Canada in the concluding chapter, we suggest a model that consists of various stages in the evolutionary paths of development that can vary across industries. Specifically, the initial stage is characterized by the "traditional" system, which dominated prior to the 1980s throughout North America. Clearly, the industrial relations system of some industries essentially remains in this state. However, under external and internal pressures for change (e.g., foreign competition, deregulation, or advances in technology), the conduct of industrial relations in a number of industries has begun a process of transformation. The key issue is the type of system that will emerge to replace the traditional one. Whereas, in the United States, the growth of the nonunion system brought pressures for transformation, such has not yet materialized as the overall pattern in Canada.

Many firms and unions that have been experiencing intense pressures, and in some cases economic crisis, confront the issue of choosing the direction in which changes to their union–management relationships will occur, a choice that will in turn shape the course of change in whole industries. Industries may move toward a nonunion system, either immediately or gradually over the long run, or may become characterized by more highly developed relationships between firms and unions, including strategic bargaining and alliances, and joint initiatives. These alternative paths offer significantly different implications for the development of industrial relations systems in various industries, and consequently for the entire system. In the concluding chapter, we revisit this model in greater depth, in light of the benefit of the results of the industry studies, with a view to assessing the status and nature of the transformation of Canadian industries.

INDUSTRY AS THE LEVEL OF ANALYSIS

Each of the following chapters describes developments occurring in a particular industry. We have chosen the industry as the level of analysis for this book for a number of reasons. This level of analysis has attracted only limited attention in Canada in the past. To our knowledge, the only other systematic and contemporary effort made to examine individual Canadian industries was undertaken by the Woods Taskforce on Industrial Relations in 1968. Most of these task force studies were never published as public documents and, hence, are unavailable to most researchers. Thus, the studies in this book fill an important gap in the literature.

There are, however, more compelling reasons to study industrial relations at this level. The competitive forces that we mentioned earlier have focussed considerable policy attention at this level. First, international trade agreements are frequently specific to certain industries, for example, the Auto Pact (Chapter 2), the MultiFibre Arrangement (Chapters 6 and 7), and the "Open Skies" agreement (Chapter 10). Such agreements reflect the fact that trade policy is best managed at this level. Measures at the level of the whole economy are averaged across industries and are therefore aggregate and of limited use in this regard. Measures at the level of the firm can be misleading because of the large variance in performance at this level, even within the same industry.

Not only trade agreements but public policy designed to facilitate industrial restructuring is also frequently focussed at the industry level, sometimes taking the form of subsidies or incentives directed to certain weak sectors. Government also consults business and labour leaders at this level, particularly in matters of trade policy. Technology, which is an important determinant of productivity and, therefore, of economic growth, is often common to a sector, but different across sectors, making analysis at the industry level germane.

In regard to industrial relations policies, several factors support the choice of the industry as a focus of analysis. Some sectors have their own industrial relations legislation, such as construction (Chapter 5) and education (Chapter 9). Historically, unions formed within industry sectors because they wanted to take wages out of competition. Although unions are now organizing across industries, most large unions still remain identified with specific sectors. One outgrowth of unions taking wages out of competition has been pattern bargaining. Although no formal studies of this phenomenon have been undertaken, anecdotal evidence suggests that these patterns spilled across industry boundaries—for example, an automobile agreement may be emulated in rubber, or a steel agreement in mining—and that, since the 1980s, these cross-industry patterns may be breaking down. Reportedly, the basis for wage increases is now shifting to the ability of relevant product markets to pay. If such is the case, then the industry that essentially forms a product group is the appropriate level at which to examine trends in costs, productivity, and collective bargaining.

This is not to suggest that this level of analysis is the only appropriate one for study. Indeed, there are some shortcomings in pursuing this approach. The decentralized nature of bargaining in Canada makes it difficult to capture all developments at the industry level. Typically, the employer organization within the industry has little or no role in bargaining. The decentralization is also reflected within union organizations. Frequently, the national or regional office can only offer advice to the local, which must make all the collective-bargaining decisions. Some employee groups identify much more strongly with their occupation or profession than with the industry. The wages and working conditions of such groups as nurses, computer technicians, and clerical workers, to name a few, are determined at the occupational as opposed to the industry level. Industry-level analysis should, therefore, be seen as a complement to macro, regional, firm, and occupational levels of analyses, rather than as a substitute for them.

Canadian Economic Performance: An Overview

Canada's economic growth is an important determinant of domestic employment opportunities, and ultimately labour's share of national wealth. With the emergence of globalized markets, Canada's economic performance in relation to that of other major economies has become increasingly important. In this context, we discuss Canada's economic growth, trade, and productivity. In addition, various employment trends have significant industrial relations implications (e.g., for unions). Our discussion, therefore, also focusses on shifts in the employment mix that occurred as a result of industrial restructuring. Finally, while economic

Figure 1.1
Canadian Gross Domestic Product and Annual Change (%)

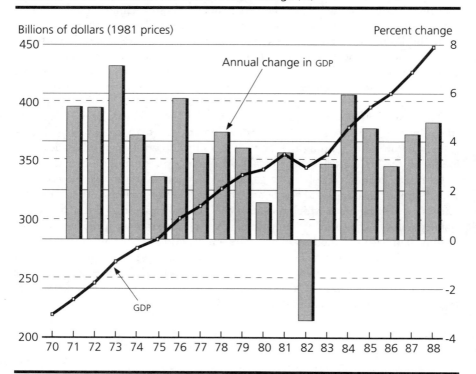

Source: Statistics Canada, *Canadian Economic Observer: Historical Statistical Supplement, 1988/89,*
            Catalogue 11-210 (Ottawa: Minister of Supply and Services, July 1989), Vol. 3 Table 1.3: Gross
            Domestic Product at 1981 Prices, Expenditure Based.
            International Monetary Fund, *International Financial Statistics Yearbook* 1990. Vol. XLIII:163
            (Washington, DC: IMF, 1990).

growth, trade, and productivity performance are important indicators of Canada's economic capability, two crucial factors underlying these indicators are the competitiveness of labour and public policy. Importantly, macroeconomic variables, such as interest rates, currency exchange rates, and price inflation, can often obscure underlying changes in firm-level costs and physical productivity.

ECONOMIC GROWTH

Canada's Gross Domestic Product (GDP) has doubled since 1970 and has increased by approximately one-third since the recession of the early 1980s (see Table 1.1 and Figure 1.1). Perhaps more importantly, the Canadian economy has grown rapidly relative to those of other major industrialized countries. In the period from 1978 to 1988, the annual growth of GDP in Canada has typically exceeded that of the United States and Germany. Although Canadian growth rates lagged behind those in Japan in the late 1970s and early 1980s, Canada's performance has improved in recent years (see Table 1.2).

However, in the 1980s, the growth in GDP has been uneven across industrial groupings. Increases in GDP have been greatest in the nongovernment-services sector,[6] followed by the manufacturing, fishing and forestry, and construction

Table 1.1
Canadian Gross Domestic Product, 1970–1988

Year	GDP (millions of dollars)
1970	219 498
1971	232 137
1972	245 441
1973	264 369
1974	276 006
1975	283 187
1976	300 638
1977	311 504
1978	325 751
1979	338 362
1980	343 384
1981	355 994
1982	344 543
1983	355 445
1984	377 865
1985	395 878
1986	408 143
1987	426 411
1988	447 779

Note: GDP is at 1981 prices and is expenditure based.
Source: Statistics Canada, *Canadian Economic Observer: Historical Statistical Supplement, 1988/89*, Catalogue 11-210 (Ottawa: Minister of Supply and Services, July 1989), Vol.3, Table 1.3.

Table 1.2
Percentage Change in Gross Domestic Product for Selected OECD Countries, 1978–1989[ab]

Year	United States	Canada	Japan	Germany
1978	5.2	4.2	5.2	2.9
1979	2.1	3.7	5.3	4.1
1980	-0.2	1.5	4.3	1.4
1981	2.0	3.0	3.7	0.2
1982	-2.5	-3.4	3.1	-0.6
1983	3.7	3.7	3.2	1.5
1984	6.8	6.1	5.1	2.8
1985	3.8	4.6	4.7	2.0
1986	3.0	2.9	2.7	2.3
1987	3.5	4.3	4.6	1.8
1988	4.6	5.5	5.7	3.7
1989	3.0	—	4.8	—

Notes: [a] Percent change over previous year.
        [b] Calculated from indexes.
Source: International Monetary Fund, *International Financial Statistics Yearbook 1990*. Vol. XLIII: 163. (Washington, DC: IMF, 1990)

Table 1.3
Canadian Gross Domestic Product by Major Industry, 1978–1988

	GDP (millions of dollars)						
	Agricult. & Related Services	Forestry & Fishing[b]	Mining	Manuf.	Constr.	Non-Gov't Services[c]	Gov't Services
1978	9 999	2872	17 940	60 057	21 222	160 435	20 884
1979	9 191	2805	20 272	62 309	21 440	167 868	20 973
1980	9 736	2854	19 720	59 518	22 527	173 965	21 146
1981	10 611	2873	17 511	61 709	25 094	180 025	21 715
1982	11 277	2567	17 028	53 755	25 109	175 803	22 326
1983	10 951	3090	18 123	57 230	24 667	181 140	22 659
1984	10 597	3305	20 606	64 598	23 111	191 713	23 012
1985	10 961	3401	21 493	68 237	24 443	201 500	23 219
1986	12 135	3511	20 954	70 025	25 029	209 313	23 574
1987	11 481	3771	21 896	73 799	26 453	218 258	23 585
1988	10 016	3869	23 751	78 117	28 182	228 167	23 794

Notes: [a] GDP is at 1981 prices and is at factor cost.
        [b] Fishing, trapping, logging, and forestry.
        [c] Transportation and storage; communications; finance, insurance and real estate; community, business and personal services; trade; utilities.
Source: Statistics Canada, *Canadian Economic Observer: Historical Statistical Supplement, 1988/89*, Catalogue 11-210 (Ottawa: Minister of Supply and Services, July 1989), Vol. 3, Table 1.16.

sectors. Growth in GDP in the government-services sector has been quite flat, particularly in the period since the recession of the early 1980s, whereas growth in mining has been modest during the latter 1980s. Nongovernment services and manufacturing are the largest sectors in terms of their contribution to GDP. The nongovernment-services sector is approximately three times the size of manufacturing (see Table 1.3).

TRADE

Canada's small open economy depends largely upon international trade for its economic prosperity. In 1987, exports and imports taken together comprised a much greater proportion of GDP in Canada (43.9 percent) than in the United States (15.3 percent) or Japan (16.0 percent). In contrast, Germany's exports and imports together (46.6 percent) constituted a percentage of GDP similar to that in Canada (see Figure 1.2).

Between 1971 and 1987, Canada's share of world exports declined slightly, as did that of the United States. In contrast, the share of world exports held by the European Economic Community (EEC) was steady, and the world export share of the Pacific Rim countries[7] increased (Economic Council of Canada 1990, Chart 1-5). Conversely, during 1971–87, both the Pacific Rim and the United States

Figure 1.2
Foreign Trade as a Percentage of GDP, 1987 and 1990

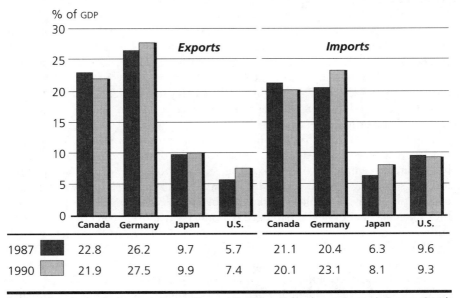

	Canada	Germany	Japan	U.S.	Canada	Germany	Japan	U.S.
1987	22.8	26.2	9.7	5.7	21.1	20.4	6.3	9.6
1990	21.9	27.5	9.9	7.4	20.1	23.1	8.1	9.3

Source: Organization for Economic Cooperation and Development (OECD), *OECD Economic Surveys: Canada* (Paris: 1990, 1991), Basic Statistics: International Comparisons.

became more important to Canada as export markets, whereas the EEC declined in importance (Economic Council of Canada 1990, Chart 1-6).

PRODUCTIVITY

Productivity is a key factor determining Canada's ability to compete internationally. Beginning in the late 1970s, Canada has experienced successive periods of lower average annual growth rates in capital, labour, and total factor productivity in the business sector than in the previous decades (Canadian Labour Market and Productivity Centre [CLMPC] 1991, Table IV-3).[8] Most disturbing is the failure of aggregate labour productivity to increase significantly in the past decade. Trends in labour productivity have varied across industries, with service-sector productivity growing less rapidly than productivity in the goods-producing industries (CLMPC 1991).

Various reasons have been offered to explain the slow productivity growth since the mid-1970s, including a deceleration in the shift in employment from the relatively low-productivity agricultural sector to high-productivity sectors; diminished output growth (which could itself create opportunities for increasing returns to scale that would allow the possibility of increased productivity); and reduced growth in the capital-to-labour ratio (CLMPC 1991). Ultimately, future wage increases, and hence an increase in the standard of living, will be related to productivity growth.

EMPLOYMENT

During the 1980s, the overall labour-force participation rate continued to increase. The male labour-force participation rate, which had remained at approximately 78 percent throughout the 1980s, declined to approximately 76.6 percent by 1988. In contrast, the female labour-force participation rate increased steadily; in fact, participation increased from approximately 50.4 percent at the outset of the 1980s to 57.4 percent in 1988 (McKitrick 1989, Table 14). The increase in the relative employment of women continues to be one of the most important labour-force trends of the 1990s.

Employment in both Canada and the United States grew steadily throughout the 1970s and 1980s. The general rapid expansion of the labour force in Canada has generated significant pressures on the economy to create jobs. Consequently, it is not surprising that one of the most significant macrolevel employment issues confronting Canadian policy makers has been the reduction of the persistently high unemployment rates, which have typically been above 8 percent in the 1980s and have consistently exceeded U.S. rates (see Figure 1.3). At the industry level, continued industrial restructuring and corporate downsizing, particularly in the basic resource industries and manufacturing, has exacerbated the unemployment problem. These developments have placed job security at the forefront of labour concerns and kept the unemployment safety-net issue high on the public-policy agenda.

From 1981 to 1986, the impact of trade and technological advances on the Canadian employment mix was significant (Economic Council of Canada 1990).[9] As a result, manufacturing employment has substantially declined, as has employment in primary industry. In contrast, service-sector employment (in particular, trade, finance and insurance, and business services) has increased dramatically (Economic Council of Canada 1990, Table 1-2).[10] The net result is a shift toward a services-oriented economy in which the production of many goods depends upon increasing service inputs. The implication for employment patterns is a steady shift toward services and away from the traditional industries (Economic Council of Canada 1991).

Throughout the 1980s, employment in goods-producing industries has been relatively steady; employment fell during the recession of the early 1980s and subsequently increased, but did not achieve the prerecession employment level until 1988. In contrast, employment in services increased throughout the 1980s, and dramatically in the latter half of the decade (see Table 1.4).

Figure 1.3
Labour Force and Unemployment Rate Annual Change (%)

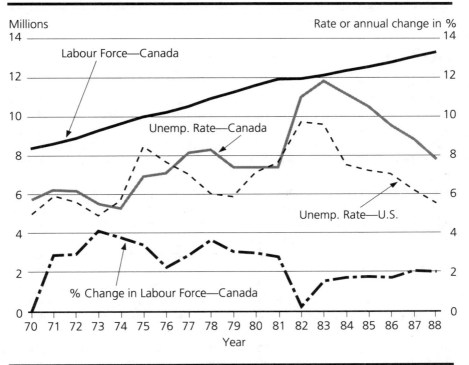

Source: Statistics Canada, *Canadian Economic Observer: Historical Statistical Supplement*, 1988/89, Catalogue 11-210 (Ottawa: Minister of Supply and Services, July 1989), Vol. 3, Table 2.1: Labour Force Summary and Table 13.1: U.S. Economic Indicators.

Table 1.4
Canadian Employment in Goods- and Service-Producing Industries, 1978-1990

| Year | Employment Levels by Industry | |
| | Goods-Producing Industry | Service-Producing Industry |
	(000s)	
1978	3443	6543
1979	3592	6803
1980	3638	7070
1981	3711	7290
1982	3376	7242
1983	3317	7359
1984	3404	7528
1985	3425	7796
1986	3477	8054
1987	3555	8306
1988	3696	8548
1989	3741	8744
1990	3626	8946

Source: Statistics Canada, *Historical Labour Force Statistics 1990,* Catalogue 71-201 (Ottawa: Minister of Supply and Services, February 1991), 172.

LABOUR COSTS

Since the production of internationally traded goods is a sizable source of employment in Canada, one of the major factors affecting the general competitiveness of Canadian industry is the cost of labour relative to its costs in other nations. At the close of the 1970s, both compensation per hour and unit labour costs in Canadian manufacturing were lower than similar costs in the United States, Japan, and Germany. However, by the latter half of the 1980s, hourly compensation for Canadian manufacturing workers had exceeded the hourly rate for workers in those other countries, and unit labour costs remained lower than similar costs in Japan and Germany, but had exceeded U.S. levels. Thus, in terms of both compensation per hour and unit labour costs, Canada had unambiguously fallen behind the United States (see Table 1.5 and Figure 1.4).

Since the United States is Canada's largest single trading partner, and since the FTA has further expanded the potential for trade between these two countries, the relative cost of Canadian versus U.S. labour has become a particularly important factor in Canada's drive to improve its competitiveness. According to one study, Canadian labour earnings as a percentage of earnings in the United States tended to increase in all industries from 1966 to 1976, but then declined slightly from 1976 to 1986 (Lendvay-Zwickl 1988, Table 2). Lendvay-Zwickl (1988) attributes the decline in relative Canadian earnings primarily to the decline of the Canadian dollar (see Figure 1.5). Commensurate with this decline in relative earnings since 1976, the average annual growth in Canadian manufacturing productivity lagged

Table 1.5
Labour-Cost Indicators for Selected OECD Countries, 1978–1989

	Compensation per Hour (U.S. dollars)				Unit Labour Costs (U.S. dollar basis)			
Year	Canada	U.S.	Japan	Germany	Canada	U.S.	Japan	Germany
1978	64.4	68.2	78.1	78.6	67.8	70.5	116.6	101.1
1979	71.0	74.8	83.1	83.9	72.1	76.9	111.5	113.5
1980	78.6	83.7	88.4	90.4	83.1	86.7	107.3	123.6
1981	90.4	91.8	95.0	96.2	88.9	93.8	113.8	104.3
1982	100.0	100.0	100.0	100.0	100.0	100.0	100.0	100.0
1983	106.1	102.6	103.0	104.4	99.0	97.7	102.5	94.5
1984	111.1	105.9	106.1	108.9	91.0	96.3	98.5	85.7
1985	116.8	111.1	110.9	115.1	88.2	96.8	97.0	84.5
1986	121.3	116.2	116.3	119.7	91.4	96.8	141.9	120.2
1987	125.6	118.9	119.0	125.2	98.7	94.3	156.9	155.8
1988	131.5	122.9	121.6	130.0	110.8	92.0	172.7	160.0
1989	141.3	127.7	129.5	135.9	122.8	92.6	161.0	149.9

Source: U.S. Department of Labor, *Monthly Labor Review* (Washington, DC: Bureau of Labor Statistics, June 1991), Table 50: Annual Indexes of Manufacturing Productivity and Related Measures, 12 Countries, 100.

Figure 1.4
Relative Earnings in Manufacturing: Canada/United States Ratios, 1970–1986

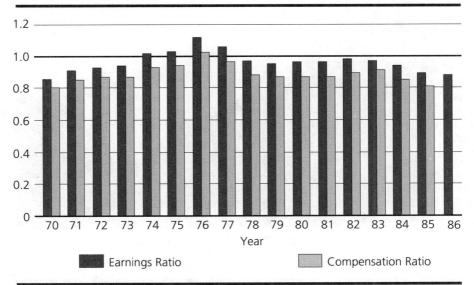

Year

■ Earnings Ratio   ▨ Compensation Ratio

Source: J. Lendvay-Zwickl, *How Well Do We Compete? Relative Labour Costs in Canada and the United States,* Conference Board of Canada Report 28-88 (Ottawa: Conference Board of Canada, February 1988), Table 6.

behind similar growth in U.S. productivity during this period. Furthermore, while the average annual *growth rate* of Canadian unit labour costs was *lower* than that of such costs in the United States from 1976 to 1986, the *levels* remained higher in Canada through to 1986. Several other trends suggest that Canada is entering a potentially difficult period in global markets. During the 1980s, productivity in Canadian manufacturing was finally surpassed by West Germany, Italy, and France; by 1988, most of the manufacturing industries in Canada had greater unit labour costs relative to those of their U.S. counterparts; and most measures of Canadian competitiveness in technology and science placed Canada at or near the lowest rank among Japan, the United States, West Germany, the United Kingdom, France, the Netherlands, and Sweden (Economic Council of Canada 1989).

Lendvay-Zwickl (1988, 11) concludes that growing international competition will continue to require that firms maintain competitive production costs, which will in turn demand that Canadian firms maintain competitive relative labour costs while striving for improved productivity. Thus, firms will need to develop human-resources practices and union–management initiatives that improve labour productivity and ensure that labour costs remain competitive. Freeman (1990)

Figure 1.5
Value of the Canadian Dollar (in U.S. dollars)

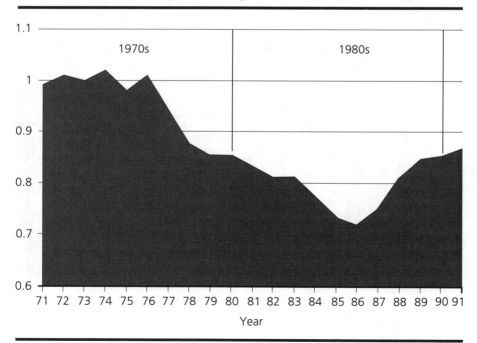

Note: *1991 figure is for Jan-Aug.*
Source: International Monetary Fund, *International Financial Statistics Yearbook 1991.* (Washington, DC: IMF, 1991).

points out that the waning unionization levels in Japan and the United Kingdom, and particularly the deunionization of the United States, will intensify pressures on Canadian labour institutions through foreign trade, the increasing international mobility of capital, and increased anti-union influences of U.S. business practices. One strategy for unions is to ensure that wage increases do not result in higher labour costs and to be responsive to employer initiatives that increase productivity and lower operating costs (Freeman 1990). For example, Kochan (1990) notes the potential for contingent pay schemes to facilitate a moderation in labour costs, yet recognizes that, to date, neither labour nor management appears to be interested in such schemes.

SHIFTS IN PUBLIC POLICY

In the past decade, Canadian policy makers have embarked upon a number of initiatives that have caused tremendous shifts in the composition of the Canadian economy, including the Canada–U.S. Free Trade Agreement, a privatization policy, and the deregulation of key economic sectors. The prospects are that each of these developments will continue to transform the economy, having important implications for the structure of the industrial base, employment patterns, and the fortunes of organized labour.

Exports and imports constitute a large proportion of Canadian GDP (approximately 43.9 percent in 1987), and the prospect is for trade to become an increasingly important source of future economic growth. Perhaps the most significant development in Canadian trade in the past several decades has been the implementation of the FTA in 1989. Given that the United States was Canada's largest single trading partner prior to the FTA, the further opening of the North American market would appear to be a natural extension of an already well-established and extensive trade partnership. With the FTA firmly in place, the country now faces the prospect of a North American trading bloc that includes Mexico.

For unions, which have generally opposed the FTA, the challenge will be to resist the potentially aggressive, anti-union industrial relations strategy common in the United States. Unions will also face management demands for contract settlements similar to those negotiated in the United States, which may include forms of variable compensation, such as profit sharing and lump-sum payments, as well as nonwage provisions that allow for greater employee involvement in quality and production decisions. So far, few unions have embraced such changes willingly.[11] There are further fears that economic pressures would undermine support for Canadian public policy, which in turn would compromise the basic framework of Canadian industrial relations (Coates 1991). Confronted with economic integration with a country that is rapidly becoming nonunion, Canadian unions will be seeking new strategies to avoid the same fate in Canada. Already strongly opposed to the FTA, labour leaders have, not surprisingly, also expressed opposition to a similar agreement with Mexico.

The 1980s witnessed a major thrust toward privatization of publicly owned enterprises and government-run services (Chapters 8 and 10). Key firms, including Air Canada within the federal jurisdiction and the Potash Corporation of Saskatchewan at the provincial level, have been privatized. Plans have also been developed for the privatization of Petro-Canada, once the key to Canada's oil industry strategy. Furthermore, extensive contracting-out of traditional government activities is well underway (Kumar and Coates 1989). Coates (1991) reports that, by the end of the decade, approximately eighteen crown corporations had been either sold or diminished.

In the transportation industry, the privatization of Air Canada has now been followed by moves to negotiate the status of "open skies" with the United States (Chapter 10). This policy is in accordance with the development of the North American trading bloc. The sale of Air Canada, whose public ownership once represented a cornerstone of federal transportation policy, is closely linked to the deregulation policy.

Deregulation in transportation has been followed by the announcement of plans for deregulating telecommunications (Chapter 11). The twin policies of privatization and deregulation have influenced both industrial organization and trade unions. For example, air transportation is now dominated by only two major carriers, with some prospect for only one major carrier to remain by the end of the 1990s (Chapter 10). Corporate reorganization usually results in employment loss, as well as changes in bargaining structure and collective-bargaining outcomes.

The immediate prospects for Canadian public policy are that these three major policy trends will continue: free-trade agreements will be expanded, more publicly owned corporations and government services will be privatized, and more industries will be deregulated. Each policy will place tremendous pressure on unions and firms to restructure. As firms try to improve efficiency by introducing new technology and increasing worker involvement, unions can be expected to resist attempts to lower labour costs and to erode employment conditions won through tough negotiations in the past.

Industrial Relations Developments

*I*n the past decade, the industrial relations landscape has changed in important ways as a result of the pressures outlined earlier. Changes in the composition of the labour market, shifts in employment, growth in services and high-technology sectors, and the decline of traditional manufacturing have, in turn, led to changes in union membership and density, and management strategies, and, consequently, in collective-bargaining outcomes. In additon, unions and firms have responded to changes in public policy and the legislative environment that have had major impacts at the workplace in the past decade.

LABOUR-FORCE DEVELOPMENTS

Two important developments that have had significant implications for unions are increases in the labour-force participation of women and the growth of part-time employment. By 1987, 80 percent of new union members were women, and they accounted for roughly 37 percent of total Canadian membership (Coates 1991). As female membership increased, unions have begun to address issues of particular concern to women, such as family-related leaves, childcare, and pay and employment equity. Women are increasingly better represented in the union hierarchy, as well as among professional staff. Giving women a greater role in the union in general, and particularly in those industries and occupations dominated by women, will become essential for the success of union-organizing campaigns in the future.

As a percentage of total employment, part-time employment has slowly but steadily grown over the 1980s. By 1988, part-time employment stood at 15.4 percent of total employment (McKitrick 1989). The modest but steady growth in part-time workers poses a significant challenge to unions in organizing these workers.

UNION DENSITY

Although membership grew steadily throughout the 1980s, overall union density has fluctuated; union density peaked in 1980, at 38.5 percent; then declined in the early 1980s, only to recover to 38.1 percent in 1985. Since then, density has declined, to 36.2 percent in 1990 (Table 1.6). However, these aggregate trends

Table 1.6
Union Membership and Density in Canada, 1978–1990

Year	Union Membership (000s)	Union Density[a]
1978	3278	38.4
1979	NA[b]	NA[b]
1980	3397	38.5
1981	3487	36.7
1982	3617	37.0
1983	3563	37.9
1984	3651	37.9
1985	3666	38.1
1986	3730	37.7
1987	3782	37.0
1988	3841	36.5
1989	3944	36.2
1990	4031	36.2

Note: [a] Union membership as a percentage of paid (nonagricultural) workers.
[b] Data not available (NA) for 1979.
Source: Labour Canada. 1990. *Directory of Labour Organizations in Canada 1990/91* (Ottawa: Minister of Supply and Services, 1990), Appendix II, Table 1.

mask significant underlying differences between industries in union density.

Between 1978 and 1988, union density declined in fishing, mining, and manu-facturing; it was relatively stable in construction, and increased in forestry. How-ever, density increased in most service-sector industries (see Table 1.7). While employment *growth* during the past decade has been great in the service sector, density *levels* in many individual service industries remain relatively low (Meltz, in press).[12] Therefore, the greatest potential for future membership growth remains in the private service sector.[13] Since the public service sector is now very highly unionized, it is unlikely that past growth rates in this industry will be matched in the future.

The unionization trend in Canada is somewhat at odds with those in a number of other industrialized countries in that unionization has not declined as substan-tially in Canada as it has in these countries. Union density in Canada increased slightly in the late 1970s, to a peak of roughly 38 percent in 1980, and remained at about this level in the early 1980s before marginally declining to 36.2 percent by

TABLE 1.7
Canadian Union Membership by Industry, 1968–1988

	Union Membership			Union Membership as a Percentage of Paid Workers		
	1968	1978	1988	1968	1978	1988
Agriculture	1 239	165	2 524	1.13	0.01	1.9
Forestry	44 391	28 536	29 355	63.4	40.2	47.3
Fishing and trapping	3 213	5 385	5 066	—	53.9	39.0
Mining	59 024	57 279	52 080	50.9	37.4	28.6
Manufacturing	748 552	857 845	762 673	43.7	43.0	36.8
Construction	214 435	272 505	308 106	55.0	53.3	52.8
Transportation, communications[a]	364 462	419 850	480 936	57.0	50.5	56.6
Trade	115 953	121 981	205 887	11.0	7.6	10.4
Finance, insurance, & real estate	7 913	12 687	22 010	2.6	2.3	3.4
Community, business, and personal services[b]	305 833	608 066	1 237 522	18.7	23.5	33.4
Public administration[c]	281 417	490 620	610 735	61.4	73.8	76.4

Notes: [a] Includes transportation, storage, communications, and other utilities.
[b] Includes both public- and private-sector industries (e.g., education, health and welfare, personal ser-vices and accommodation services).
[c] Includes federal, provincial, and local administration.

Source: Statistics Canada. *The Annual Report of the Minister of Industry, Science and Technology Under the Corporations and Labour Unions Returns Act. Part II - Labour Unions.* Catalogue 72-202. (Ottawa: Minister of Supply and Services). Various years.

1989 (see Table 1.6). Union density in Japan, Germany, and the United States has declined more substantially (Bean 1989).

UNION MEMBERSHIP

⎡Union membership in Canada reached 3.3 million in 1978 and increased to 4 million by 1990. In marked contrast, from 1978 to 1985, union membership increased only marginally in Japan, decreased slightly in Germany, and decreased precipitously in the United States (Bean 1989).⎤However, as was true for union density, these aggregate trends obscure important industry differences.

Between 1978 and 1988, the traditional union strongholds of manufacturing and mining experienced declines in union membership, while membership held steady in forestry and fishing, and increased slightly in construction. In contrast, over the same period, membership in the nongovernment-services sector increased significantly (from 1.16 million to 1.95 million). Specifically, union membership increased in each of transportation (by 14.6 percent); trade (by 68.8 percent); finance, insurance, and real estate (by 73.5 percent); and community, business, and personal services (such as health services and education) (by 103.5 percent). Union membership in the nongovernment services thus surpassed manufacturing membership, which declined from approximately 858 000 in 1978 to 763 000 in 1988. Between 1978 and 1988, membership also increased in public administration by 120 000 members (14.5 percent) (see Table 1.7).

Many of the largest private-sector unions in Canada experienced membership declines between 1982 and 1990, including the United Steelworkers of America (loss of 37 000 members), the International Brotherhood of Electrical Workers (6500 members), the United Brotherhood of Carpenters and Joiners (27 000 members), and the International Association of Machinists (4 800 members). Modest membership increases were accomplished by the Teamsters (7 000 members) and the Labourers' International Union of North America (1 800 members). Among the most successful unions were the Service Employees International Union, which increased by 10 000 members, and the United Food and Commercial Workers International Union, which added 34 000 members over this period (Coates 1991, Table 5).

A major challenge to many international (United States–based) unions is the continued decline in their membership levels in their traditional bases in manufacturing and primary industries. ⎡In 1988, internationals accounted for 33.2 percent of total union membership in Canada, national unions accounted for 53 percent, and government unions accounted for 13.8 percent; but in 1965, the internationals accounted for 67 percent of total membership (Statistics Canada 1988, Chart 1.1). The relative decline of international unionism resulted from both the modest decline of international union membership since the 1970s and, more importantly, the strong growth of national unions.⎤

Major contributions to national union membership in the late 1980s occurred following the formation of an independent Canadian union from the Canadian section of the United Auto Workers in 1986, the gaining of autonomy by the International Woodworkers in 1987, and the transfer of a Newfoundland local of the United Food and Commercial Workers Union to the Canadian Auto Workers in 1988 (Statistics Canada 1988). By 1988, international union membership stood at approximately 1.25 million, national union membership was approximately 2 million, and government unions accounted for roughly 0.5 million members (Statistics Canada 1988, Chart 1.2).

The growth of national unions may also be attributed to the successes of the public and private service-sector unions. In 1990, the two largest unions in Canada were the Canadian Union of Public Employees and the National Union of Provincial Government Employees, each with more than 0.25 million members. Both unions experienced rapid growth from 1982 to 1990, as did service unions, such as the Ontario Nurses Association.[14] The ascendancy of national unions in Canada has been closely tied to the growth of public-sector unions, but in the future the relative growth rates of international and national unions will likely depend on their relative abilities to organize workers in other economic sectors.

In many cases, the reaction to pressures to increase membership levels and the need to expand the membership base have resulted in the organization of members outside traditional jurisdictions. In the private sector, the United Steelworkers has organized fisheries, security guards, and taxi drivers; the United Food and Commercial Workers International Union has organized nursing homes; and Canadian Auto Workers now represents employees in the airline and railway industries. Notable among public-sector unions, the Canadian Union of Public Employees has organized employees in education, airlines, and longshoring. The commitment of financial and human resources to organizing workers has been a major union strategy (see Coates 1991).

THE DIVERGENCE/CONVERGENCE DEBATE

Of particular concern to Canadian unionists is the rapid deunionization of the United States. Given the close economic and social ties between Canada and the United States, the issue of whether or not Canadian trade union fortunes will ultimately follow those of their U.S. counterparts is controversial. Rose and Chaison (1985) suggest that two key factors underlying the divergence between the Canadian and U.S. labour movements are employer resistance to unions and the overall legal (policy) framework. Chaison and Rose (1991) extended this line of analysis by assessing the roles of market factors; the public-policy environment; employer resistance to unions; the organizing efforts of unions; and the social environment, including public opinion and values. Chaison and Rose (1991) conclude that, although product-market and labour-market structural changes have had a minor role in determining the differing union experiences in Canada and the United States, union organizing, employer resistance to unions, and particularly public-policy differences, constitute important influences on union growth patterns in the two countries.

In marked contrast to the view that substantive differences in the industrial relations systems in Canada and the United States have resulted in "divergent" union fortunes, Troy (1991) has forwarded the view that, although the systems may differ, the labour movements in the two countries are *converging* and will continue to do so. In this regard, an important distinction has been drawn between trends in union density in the private and the public sector. Troy (1991) argues that private-sector union membership and density are declining in both countries, whereas public-sector membership in both countries has grown.[5] Kumar (1991), in turn, concludes that public-sector unions have been the major source of union growth in Canada and the United States, and Canadian public-sector unions have displayed greater strength.

The central issue undoubtedly concerns the future direction of private-sector unionism in Canada. Aside from the direct relevance of these issues to the parties themselves, policy makers in Canada may be increasingly called upon to respond to trends in unionization rates by establishing policies that alter such factors as the legislative and economic environments.

LEGAL FRAMEWORK

As noted, public policy is a critical determinant of industrial relations developments and is typically cited as an important difference between Canada and the United States (e.g., Chaison and Rose 1991). Unions have long sought protective labour legislation, as well as legislation favourable to union organizing and collective bargaining through political means. The relationship between organized labour and the New Democratic Party (NDP) at both the federal and the provincial level of government has therefore been an important component of labour's strategy for social change. Consequently, the election of the NDP in Ontario in 1990 and the associated prospects for significant reforms for a wide range of labour-related legislation have redirected attention to the importance of this relationship.

While the basic legislative framework of industrial relations in Canada did not change, the breadth of existing legislation, particularly with respect to protective labour legislation, increased in the 1980s. At the federal level, the Charter of Rights and Freedoms and increased emphasis on employment equity have had a considerable impact on firms and unions. Major legislative developments also occurred in the areas of occupational health and safety (e.g., the Workplace Hazardous Materials Information System [see Chapter 4] and, in Ontario, the *Act to Restrict Smoking in Workplaces*, 1990), the regulation of pension standards (e.g., enactment of the *Pension Benefits Act* in 1990, the first such standards legislation in Prince Edward Island; Coates 1991), and reform of provincial Workers' Compensation programs in Ontario and Quebec. Compliance with labour (standards) legislation has, therefore, understandably had a direct impact on the human-resource practices of union and nonunion firms (Lendvay-Zwickl 1989, 1990).

However, one of the most important legislative developments during the 1980s has been the gradual accretion of pay-equity, or comparable-worth, legislation in most Canadian jurisdictions. This trend is in marked contrast to developments in the United States, where comparable-worth legislation has been enacted only in the public sector and in a limited number of states. The issue underlying such proactive legislation—the persistent male–female earnings gap—has become a major concern for firms and unions, and, hence, policy makers.

As of 1990, pay-equity legislation existed in seven provinces, including Quebec and Ontario, in addition to the federal jurisdiction. While most jurisdictions confine coverage to the public sector, the passage of Bill 154, *An Act to Provide for Pay Equity* (1987),[16] in Ontario applied pay equity to the private sector for the first time (Gunderson and Robb 1991, Table 1). Firms now face costs of implementing pay-equity plans as well as the harmonizing of pay equity with internal employment-equity initiatives. Unions also face issues related to the implementation of pay equity: concern exists that traditional seniority principles be preserved and that job evaluation not be used by employers to undermine bargaining as a determinant of wages (Weiner and Gunderson 1990).

Cumulatively, the active promulgation or revision of a broad range of employment-related legislation throughout the 1980s has expanded the agendas of industrial relations and human-resource specialists. Much of the legislative change has likely served to enhance employee rights in both unionized and nonunionized environments, thus reinforcing the view that an active public-policy environment is a key factor that distinguishes Canada from the United States.

Nonmonetary Changes in Collective Agreements

Although bread-and-butter issues such as wages and benefits continue to be the main concern for workers and management, pressures for restructuring have translated into changes in the type and structure of bargaining outcomes in collective agreements (Chaykowski 1990, 1991). A comparison of collective-agreement provisions over the 1981–91 period shows that, although significant changes did occur, they were not similar in magnitude or character to those reported in the United States.

Table 1.8 shows the percentage of collective agreements that contained selected provisions. Data for 1981 are drawn from collective agreements in Canada covering 200 or more workers in both federal and provincial jurisdictions (Labour Canada 1981). By 1991, Labour Canada had reduced the sample of collective agreements that it coded. The 1991 data cover collective agreements for 200 or more employees in the federal jurisdiction but 500 or more employees in the provincial jurisdiction. As a consequence, the 1981 data are not directly com-

Table 1.8

Collective-Agreement Provisions 1981–91 (as a percentage of contracts)

	1981[a]	1991[b]		
Provisions[c]	Total N = 2181	Private N = 603	Public N = 637	Total N = 1240
Employment and Job-Security Provisions				
• Contracting-out	38	53.1	32.3	42
• Part-time work	NA	29.7	79	55
• Job sharing	NA	1.4	12.7	7.2
• Work sharing	7.3	3.1	0.8	1.9
• Advance notice for technological change	29.4	47.8	50.5	49.2
• Employment guarantees	NA	5.0	16.6	11.0
• Training on the job	19	49.9	30.9	40.2
• Training—outside courses	11.3	19.9	38.9	29.7
• Apprenticeship	7.7	50.1	14.2	31.6
• Educational leave	29.6	16.9	44.4	31.1
Wage-Incentive Plans				
• Piece-rate incentives	5.5	9.6	0.6	5.0
• Group incentives	0.4	1.7	NA	0.8
• Productivity bonuses	6.6	2.5	0.3	1.4
• Profit sharing	NA	2.0	NA	1.0
• Other	3.3	2.5	2.2	2.3
• No provision	84.2	85.1	97.0	91.2
Cost-of-living adjustments (COLAS)	35.1	30.8	27.3	29.0
Labour–Management Co-operation				
• Labour–management committees	NA	33.0	60.3	47.0
• Joint committee—Tech change	11.0	17.2	20.3	18.8
• Joint committee powers in health and safety	45.5	33.4	18.9	25.9
• Quality-of-Working Life	NA	12.9	13.9	13.4
• Joint role in job evaluation	NA	44.5	44.1	44.2
Fairness and Equity				
• Anti-discrimination provisions	NA	32.3	40.8	36.7
• Affirmative-action plans	NA	4.3	5.7	5.0
• Sexual harassment	NA	11.8	35.8	24.1
• Equal pay for equal work	NA	3.6	3.9	3.8
• Equal pay for work of equal value	NA	2.7	11.0	6.9

Notes:

a *Source:* Labour Canada, 1981. Provisions in Collective Agreements in Canada Covering 200 and More Employees: All Industries (excluding Construction). (Ottawa: Minister of Supply and Services, March 1981).

b *Source:* Provisions in collective agreements covering 200 or more employees in the federal jurisdiction and 500 or more employees in the provincial jurisdiction. Data provided by Labour Canada on request. Note that the presence of a contract provision does not determine "favourableness" to the union (management).

parable to the 1991 data in Table 1.8. Both sets of data are presented, nonetheless, to give the reader some estimates of the prevalence of selected provisions in contracts. A number of provisions of interest coded in 1991 were not coded by Labour Canada in 1981. The 1991 data are further broken down by public and private sectors.

JOB SECURITY

In the area of job security, the Labour Canada collective-agreements file shows that, in 1991, 116 (or 11 percent) of all agreements covering 500 or more workers contained some form of employment guarantees. While this coverage is low, it strongly suggests that employment security is fast becoming a major concern on the collective-bargaining agenda. Contracting-out provisions, which mostly take the form of restricting management prerogatives, increased from 38 percent of all agreements in 1981 to 42 percent in 1991. Provisions for part-time employment, not coded in 1981, were found in 55 percent of the agreements in 1991. Job sharing where more than one individual performs a single job, could be found in 7.2 percent of the agreements in 1991. The incidence of providing advance notice for technological change increased sharply, from 29.4 percent in 1981 to 49.2 percent in 1991. The incidence of provisions for training, apprenticeship training, and educational leave increased during the 1980s. Thus, there were, clearly, some changes in the areas of creating flexible employment, as well as increasing employment security, either directly through guarantees or indirectly through advance notice and better training opportunities.

There were some major differences in these developments across the public and private sectors. Provisions on contracting-out and on-the-job training and apprenticeship were more likely to be found in the private sector; provisions on part-time work, job sharing, employment guarantees, outside training, and educational leave were more prevalent in the public sector.

INCOME SECURITY

In general, Canadian unions have in the past put greater emphasis on income security than on employment security. In the 1980s, there was greater pressure on unions to make better employment security a priority. They have partially accomplished this aim by linking job security more closely with income security in some instances. By 1990, there were clear positive trends in indexing of pension plans. For example, in 1988 Inco Limited negotiated a key agreement with the United Steelworkers that included pension indexing (Chapter 4).[17] Also in 1990, the Canadian Auto Workers began a trend to negotiate income-security provisions, including advance notice of plant shutdowns, layoffs affecting significant numbers of workers, and technological change (Chapter 2).

WORKPLACE FLEXIBILITY

The Labour Canada coding scheme does not include some other areas where movements in collective agreements have been reported. For example, in some industries, there is evidence of a reduction in the number of job classifications. At the national level, there are no data available on the extent of changes in collective agreements to increase flexibility in production. A survey limited to British Columbia, however, showed that roughly 62 percent of unionized workplaces had negotiated at least one change in their collective agreement to increase flexibility (Verma 1986). Among these were changes in hours of work, scheduling, work assignments, and subcontracting. These changes, favourable largely to managerial interests, were accompanied by others, favourable to worker interests, affecting job security (positively), sharing of information on technology, training, and worker involvement. B.C. industrial relations is characterized by a high level of unionization and a militant labour movement. It may be an overstatement, therefore, to infer that such adjustments took place widely across the country.

CONTINGENT PAY

There was some experimentation with wage incentive plans in Canada during this period, but the verdict of the parties appears to be against them. Most incentive plans declined in incidence between 1981 and 1991: piece-rate incentives from 5.5 to 5.0 percent, productivity bonuses from 6.6 to 1.4 percent, other plans from 3.3 to 2.3 percent. There was a small increase in group incentive plans, but it is most likely not significant. Overall, the percentage of agreements that had no such provisions increased from 84.2 to 91.2 percent (see Table 1.8). Since such plans have achieved a sizable following in the United States (Mitchell and Broderick 1991), it is clear that the Canadian pattern is distinctively different.

Gain-sharing and profit-sharing plans, too, have diffused to a very limited extent in Canada. One study found that such plans, broadly defined, grew from 2 percent of direct labour costs in 1957 to a little over 3 percent "recently" (Riddell 1987). However, recent high-profile agreements in some industries that include profit-sharing arrangements, such as mining (Chapter 4), may further encourage contingent pay schemes in certain sectors. According to Table 1.8, 1.0 percent of the agreements provided for profit sharing in 1991 and another 1.4 percent contained provisions for various types of productivity bonuses. There were no significant differences across the public and private sectors.

FAIRNESS AND EQUITY

In 1991, in Canada, there appear to be increases in provisions for preventing discrimination and sexual harassment, which could be found in 36.7 and 24.1 percent of the agreements, respectively. Affirmative-action plans were found in 5 percent of the agreements. This number is likely to grow during the 1990s. Equal-pay provisions may not increase much beyond 1991 levels, as they have been covered by law. In general, the public sector made greater progress in this area than did the private sector.

EMPLOYEE/WORKER INVOLVEMENT

In Canada, workplace innovations diffused further in the 1980s, but at a slow rate. An Economic Council of Canada survey found semi-autonomous work groups in 11 percent of the establishments surveyed, and quality circles in 14 percent of the establishments (Betcherman and McMullen 1986). In 1991, 13.4 percent of the collective agreements contained a provision for a joint Quality-of-Work Life (QWL) initiative (see Table 1.8). Labour–management committees were found in 47 percent of the agreements; joint committees on technological change were provided for in 18.8 percent, and on health and safety with certain powers in 25.6 percent of the agreements. In 44.2 percent of the agreements, some joint role in job evaluation, either through a joint committee or in some other form, was provided for. Although the private sector tended to have more joint committees on safety and health with powers than did the public sector (33.4 percent as compared to 18.9 percent), the overall incidence of joint committees in the public sector (60.3 percent) was much higher than in the private sector (33 percent).

In only a handful of cases in Canada have joint labour–management efforts in employee involvement and work reorganization been introduced. The best-known example is the Shell Canada plant in Sarnia, Ontario, which has successfully used a team-based work organization along with other innovations since 1975 (Halpern 1984). An excellent overview of such developments until the mid-1980s is provided by Mansell (1986).

In most organizations, innovations such as employee involvement diffused very slowly and tentatively in the 1980s, with the parties taking a much more cautious approach. In such companies as McDonnell Douglas, Inglis, MacMillan Bloedel, B.C. Hydro, and General Motors of Canada, among others, tentative steps were taken by one or both sides. Management was often not sure how quickly to proceed, given the ambivalence or possible opposition of their unions. Unions were, similarly, unsure of how innovation might impact on their political standing vis-à-vis their constituents or how it might affect collective bargaining. In a growing number of organizations, some innovations were considered and abandoned so completely that their revival on the bargaining agenda appeared unlikely in the near future. At other companies—for example, the Atomic Energy Corporation, Rockwell, and Colgate-Palmolive—worker-involvement initiatives have been tried and abandoned.

In the United States, after a slow start in the 1970s, workplace innovations were introduced rapidly in the 1980s. A survey by the American Management Association (Goodmeasure and Co. 1985) showed that employee-participation programs such as semi-autonomous work groups and quality circles were to be found in 28 percent to 36 percent of U.S. firms. At first, it was believed that a large majority of these programs were adopted in the nonunion sector. More recent surveys, however, suggest that the adoption rate is nearly the same in the union sector. In a survey of firms' strategic business units, Ichniowski, Delaney, and Lewin (1989) found that the incidence of employee participation programs in the union sector (49 percent) compared favourably with that in the nonunion sector (44 percent).

INDUSTRY-LEVEL JOINT COMMITTEES

Although industry-level joint committees have a much longer tradition, they received increased attention in Canada in the 1980s as a way of focussing on the mutual interests of labour and management. The theoretical assumption behind these initiatives, even if not fully stated, is that, if the parties can share a common view of the problems facing the industry, they will be able to proceed with needed reforms at the workplace. The Canadian Textile Labour Management Committee was formed in 1967 and has been active in the area of trade policies affecting the industry (Sexton, Leclerc, and Audet 1984; see Chapter 7). Similarly, the Canadian Steel Trade and Employment Congress was established in 1985 as a joint initiative of the United Steelworkers and the major steel companies (Chapter 3). Since 1987, it has also received funding from Employment and Immigration Canada's Industrial Adjustment Service (IAS) to operate adjustment programs for laid-off workers in the steel industry (*Worklife Report* 1990).

In the same spirit, the IAS has also signed agreements with the Canadian Automotive Repair and Service Council and the Joint Human Resources Committee of the Canadian Electrical and Electronics Manufacturing Industry (CEEMI), both formed in 1988. Both of these committees are primarily concerned with developing and implementing a strategy to improve the skills available to the industry (CEEMI 1989). While a full assessment of these initiatives is somewhat premature, some observers have already noted that sectoral-level co-operation has not necessarily spurred the consideration and adoption of innovations at the firm or plant level (Warrian 1990; Docquier 1989). It is possible that the newer initiatives of the 1980s need more time to percolate down to the firm level. However, it is also likely that sectoral initiatives facilitate innovations only in a very indirect way.

NATIONAL JOINT INITIATIVES

It is important to note that the 1980s saw a number of both private and public initiatives at the national level in which labour and management tried to arrive at broad understandings. After consulting with labour leaders, the Canadian Chamber of Commerce (1988) issued its report, *Focus 2000*, in which it affirmed its resolve to build a stronger relationship with the labour movement. In another initiative, the Niagara Institute (1987) assembled an impressive array of leaders from both labour and management, whose report, *The Search for a Better Way*, spells out a code of conduct for labour–management relations. While these initiatives may well have a positive impact on the firm-level adoption of innovations, it is simply too early to tell at this time. There is no doubt, though, that such inputs are important in that they send a positive signal to the labour and management community at large.

In the area of public policy, in 1988 the federal government initiated the Advisory Council on Adjustment to examine ways in which Canadians could not only withstand the shock of adjustment to the Canada–U.S. Free Trade Agreement, but also benefit from it. The council, under the chairmanship of Mr. A. Jean de Grandpré, in its much publicized report, *Adjusting to Win* (1989), recommended a series of measures to invest in labour skills, among other things. It urged a review of the nation's training and education infrastructure. It also recommended that the government should "shift the emphasis of government assistance toward employment promotion rather than income maintenance" (Advisory Council on Adjustment 1989, xix).

As a result of these recommendations, in 1990 the federal government initiated a number of task forces with the help of the Canada Labour Market and Productivity Centre (CLMPC) to develop a national training policy. The task forces, seven in all, completed their report by late 1990. In early 1991, the government announced its intention to set up a Canada Labour Force Development Board that will be managed at arm's length from the government by representatives from labour, business, the community, and educational institutions. The government also enacted Bill C-21, An Act to Amend the Unemployment Insurance Act, that transfers $800 million from the Unemployment Insurance fund to the newly created training fund. It is too soon to determine whether this initiative will breathe new life into Canada's training programs; funding by the federal government for training had decreased since 1984–85 (Meltz 1990a). It is clear, however, that the process of consultation followed by the government and the willingness to move training away from the political winds that blow on Parliament Hill are positive developments.

Conclusions

Among the numerous challenges to Canadian industry, the pressures created by growing international competition, which is likely to assume even greater importance as trading blocs are consolidated in North America, Europe, and the Pacific Rim, and the significant changes in federal public policy in such areas as privatization and deregulation, are at the fore. Unions and firms are seeking ways in which to adjust to the emerging economic and public-policy environment. Many private-sector unions, and particularly those with declining fortunes, have sought to move beyond their traditional membership bases and are also shifting the focus of their attention at the bargaining table to emphasize employment security, training, and retraining. The participation of major unions and firms in joint industry-level committees highlights the recognition among union and management leaders that co-operative efforts can facilitate needed reforms and innovations in industry. For their part, firms are keenly aware of the need to be "competitive." Aside from a heavy emphasis on applying new technologies and developing innovative products, many firms are accenting industrial relations and human-resource initiatives as components of broader strategies to improve productivity, lower costs, and thus enhance their competitiveness. In conjunction with programs to downsize work forces, firms have actively sought new initiatives in areas such as contingent-pay systems, lump-sum payments, and flexibility in the workplace in order to achieve improved cost competitiveness.

The industry studies themselves deal with a variety of issues. First, in what ways and to what extent have unions and firms responded to the emerging pressures? For example, have changes occurred, on the management side, with regard to union avoidance, or efforts to increase employee involvement, and have unions adapted their bargaining priorities, the focus of their bargaining efforts, or their structures? Second, to what extent has the influence of the nonunion component of the industry been growing relative to the unionized component, and has there been growth in the use of contracting-out, the establishment of nonunion plants, and the downsizing of unionized firms? Third, has the adoption of new technologies taken place in response to environmental pressures confronting the industry, and what have been the effects on the parties—and, in turn, the reactions of the parties—to such changes? Fourth, has the scope of bargaining altered from traditional areas of concern? Finally, have changes in work rules, job-security provisions, profit/gainsharing plans, employee participation, or training programs taken place in reaction to industrial relations developments in the industry?

A number of general industrial relations issues have arisen in the 1980s and 1990s at the industry level. Given the observation that many major unions have experienced membership declines in the private sector, the centrality of collective bargaining to industrial relations may be eroding in some industries. Consequently, the choices and strategies of firms and unions may have been transformed by economic pressures. Given that various industries have experienced different degrees of change, what explains any findings of relative stability or transformation in industry? To what extent have industrial relations and human-resource management in industry become competitive factors? Taken together, the industry studies will explore whether or not the conduct of human-resource management and industrial relations in the 1980s was different from that of previous decades and whether the roles of unions and the human-resource function have been altered.

The investigations in each industry will therefore shed light on the paradigm that the conduct of industrial relations has moved from being confined mostly to the traditional collective-bargaining system that characterized the immediate post–Second World War era to the adjacent levels of the workplace and the business-strategy levels.   Analysis at the industry level will also shed light on whether management and unions in a given industry have pursued strategic choices in response to the major labour-market, economic, social, and political pressures that may be at work.   That is, in the face of these environmental developments, has a "transformation" occurred across industries? A scenario of change or of the maintenance of stability in the industry may provide important lessons for policy makers among management, unions, and government.

Although further change is inevitable, it is far from clear what course the evolution of the industrial relations system in Canada make take into the turn of the century.   Much depends on the choices that the actors in the system make for themselves.   It is clear, however, that the prosperity of Canadian society depends a great deal on developing a system of industrial relations that will be responsive to external demands without compromising internally developed goals.

REFERENCES

Advisory Council on Adjustment. 1989. *Adjusting to Win: Report of the Advisory Council on Adjustment*. Ottawa: Minister of Supply and Services, 1989.

Barbash, Jack. 1964. "The Elements of Industrial Relations." *The British Journal of Industrial Relations*. 2: 66–78.

Bean, R., ed., 1989. *International Labour Statistics: A Handbook, Guide, and Recent Trends*. London: Routlege.

Betcherman, Gordon, and Kathryn McMullen. 1986. *Working with Technology: A Survey of Automation in Canada*. Ottawa: Minister of Supply and Services.

Canadian Chamber of Commerce. 1988. *Focus 2000: Report on the Task Force on Harnessing Change*. Ottawa: August.

Canadian Labour Market and Productivity Centre (CLMPC). 1991. *Quarterly Labour Market and Productivity Review* (Winter/Spring). Ottawa.

CEEMI (Canadian Electrical and Electronics Manufacturing Industry). 1989. *Connections for the Future: A Human Resources Strategy for the Canadian Electrical and Electronics Manufacturing Industry*. January.

Chaison, G.N., and J. Rose. 1991. "Continental Divide: The Direction and Fate of North American Unions." In D. Sockell, D. Lewin and D. Lipsky, eds., *Advances in Industrial and Labor Relations*, Vol. 5. Greenwich, CT: JAI Press Inc. 169–205.

Chaykowski, Richard P. 1990. "Union and Firm Preferences for Bargaining Outcomes in the Private Sector." *Relations Industrielles/Industrial Relations* 45/2: 326–55.

——. 1991. "The Analysis of Nonwage Bargaining Outcomes: Evidence from the Canadian Private Sector." In D. Sockell, D. Lewin and D. Lipsky, eds., *Advances in Industrial and Labor Relations*, Vol. 5. Greenwich, CT: JAI Press Inc. 235–89.

Chelius, James, and James Dworkin. 1990. *Reflections on the Transformation of Industrial Relations*. Metuchen, NJ: IMLR Press/Rutgers University and The Scarecrow Press, Inc.

Coates, Mary Lou. 1991. *The Current Industrial Relations Scene In Canada 1990, Industrial Relations in 1990: Trends and Emerging Issues*. Kingston, ON: Industrial Relations Centre, Queen's University.

Docquier, Gerard. 1989. "Forging New Management Relations—A Competitive Necessity?" Notes for remarks made to the Human Resources Section of the Canadian Pulp and Paper Association.

Dunlop, John T. 1958. *Industrial Relations Systems*. New York: Holt, Rinehart and Winston.

Economic Council of Canada. 1989. *Legacies: Twenty-sixth Annual Review*. Ottawa: Minister of Supply and Services.

——. 1990. *Transitions for the 90s: Twenty-seventh Annual Review*. Ottawa: Minister of Supply and Services.

——. 1991. *Employment in the Service Economy*. Ottawa: Minister of Supply and Services.

Freeman, R.B. 1990. "Canada in the World Labour Market to the Year 2000." In K. Newton, T. Schweitzer, and J. Voyer, eds., *Perspective 2000*, Proceedings of a conference sponsored by the Economic Council of Canada (December 1988), 187–98.

Goodmeasure and Co. 1985. *The Changing American Workplace: Work Alternatives in the 1980s*. New York: American Management Association.

Gunderson, Morley, and Roberta E. Robb. 1991. "Equal Pay for Work of Equal Value: Canada's Experience." In D. Sockell, D. Lewin, and D. Lipsky, eds., *Advances in Industrial and Labor Relations*, Vol. 5. Greenwich, CT: JAI Press Inc. 151–68.

Halpern, Norman. 1984. "Socio-technical Systems Design: The Shell Sarnia Experience." In J.B. Cunningham and T.H. White, eds., *Quality of Working Life: Contemporary Cases*. Ottawa: Labour Canada. 31–75.

Ichniowski, Casey, John T. Delaney, and David Lewin. 1989. "The New Human Resource Management in US Workplaces: Is it Really New and Is It Really Nonunion?" *Relations Industrielles/Industrial Relations* 44 (Winter): 97–123.

Kerr, C., J.T. Dunlop, F.H. Harbison, and C.C. Myers. 1964. *Industrialism and Industrial Man*. New York: Oxford University Press.

Kochan, T.A. 1990. "Looking to the Year 2000: Challenges for Industrial Relations and Human Resource Management." In K. Newton, T. Schweitzer, and J. Voyer, eds., *Perspective 2000*, Proceedings of a Conference sponsored by the Economic

Council of Canada (December 1988), 203–17.

Kochan, T.A., Harry C. Katz, and R. McKersie. 1986. *The Transformation of American Industrial Relations*. New York: Basic Books.

Kumar, Pradeep. 1991. "Industrial Relations in Canada and the United States: From Uniformity to Divergence." Queen's Papers in Industrial Relations 1991–2. Kingston, ON: Industrial Relations Centre, Queen's University.

Kumar, P., and Mary Lou Coates. 1989. *The Current Industrial Relations Scene in Canada 1989, Industrial Relations in 1989: Trends and Emerging Issues*. Kingston, ON: Industrial Relations Centre, Queen's University.

Labour Canada. 1981. *Provisions in Collective Agreements in Canada Covering 200 or More Employees in Federal and Provincial Jurisdictions, All Industries (excluding Construction)*. Ottawa.

Lendvay-Zwickl, Judith. 1988. *How Well Do We Compete? Relative Labour Costs in Canada and the United States*. Conference Board of Canada Report 28-88. Ottawa: Conference Board of Canada, February.

———. 1989. *Compensation Planning Outlook 1990*. 8th ed. Ottawa: Conference Board of Canada, October.

———. 1990. *Compensation Planning Outlook 1991*. 9th ed. Ottawa: Conference Board of Canada, October.

Lewin, David. 1987. "Industrial Relations as a Strategic Variable." In Morris M. Kleiner, Richard N. Block, Myron Roomkin, and Sidney W. Salsburg, eds., *Human Resources and the Performance of the Firm*.

Madison, WI: Industrial Relations Research Association. 1–41.

McKitrick, Ross. 1989. *The Current Industrial Relations Scene in Canada 1989, Industrial Relations in 1989: The Economy and Labour Markets Reference Tables*. Kingston, ON: Industrial Relations Centre, Queen's University.

Mansell, Jacquie. 1986. *Workplace Innovation in Canada*. Ottawa: Economic Council of Canada.

Meltz, N. 1985. "Labour Movements in Canada and the United States." In Thomas A. Kochan, ed., *Challenges and Choices Facing American Labour*. Cambridge, MA: MIT Press. 315–334.

Meltz, Noah. 1990a. "The Evolution of Worker Training: The Canadian Experience." In L. Ferman, M. Hoyman, J. Cutcher-Gershenfeld, and E. Savoie, eds., *New Developments in Worker Training: A Legacy for the 1990s*. Madison, WI: Industrial Relations Research Association. 283–307.

———. 1990b. "Unionism in Canada, US: On Parallel Treadmills?" *Forum for Applied Research and Public Policy*, 5/4 (Winter): 46–52.

———. In Press. "Unionism in the Private Service Sector: A Canada-US Comparison." In Jane Jensen, ed., *Canadian and American Labor Respond: Economic Restructuring and Union Strategies*. Philadelphia, PA: Temple University Press.

Mitchell, Daniel J.B., and Renae F. Broderick. 1991. "Flexible Pay Systems in the American Context: History, Policy, Research, and Implications." In Donna Sockell, David Lewin, and David B. Lipsky, eds., *Advances in Industrial and Labour Relations*, Vol 5. Greenwich, CT: JAI Press Inc. 95–149.

Niagara Institute. 1987. *Code of Conduct for Labour–Management Relations*. Niagara-on-the-Lake (October).

Riddell, Craig. 1987. "Wage Flexibility and Public Policy in Canada," Paper presented to the Pacific Rim Comparative Labor Policy Conference (June 25–26), Vancouver, B.C.

Rose, L., and G. Chaison. 1985. "The State of the Unions: United States and Canada." *Journal of Labor Research* 6:97–111.

Sexton, Jean, Claudine Leclerc, and Michel Audet. 1984. *The Canadian Textile Labour–Management Committee*. Ottawa: Labour Canada.

Statistics Canada. 1988. CALURA *Labour Unions*, Catalogue 71-202. Ottawa: Minister of Supply and Services.

Thompson, Mark, ed. 1987. *Is There a New Canadian Industrial Relations?* Proceedings of the 23rd Annual Meeting of the Canadian Industrial Relations Association, May 29–31, Winnipeg, Manitoba.

Troy, Leo. 1991. "Convergence in International Unionism Et Cetera: The Case of Canada and the US." Queen's Papers in Industrial Relations 1991–3, Kingston, ON: Industrial Relations Centre, Queen's University.

Verma, Anil. 1986. "Recent Changes in Workrules in Collective Bargaining in British Columbia." In *Proceedings of the Annual Meetings of the Canadian Industrial Relations Association*,

Winnipeg, Manitoba.

—— 1990. "A Comparative Perspective on the Strategic Choice Framework." In *Reflections on the Transformation of Industrial Relations*. Metuchen, NJ: IMLR Press/Rutgers University, and The Scarecrow Press, Inc.

Verma, Anil, and Mark E. Thompson. 1989. "Managerial Strategies in Canada and the U.S. in the 1980s. In *Proceedings of the Forty-first Annual Meetings*, Industrial Relations Research Association, Madison, WI. pp. 257–264.

Warrian, Peter. 1990. "Is the Wolf Coming to the Canadian Steel Industry in 1990?" Draft manuscript (April).

Weiner, N., and M. Gunderson. 1990. *Pay Equity: Issues, Options and Experiences*. Toronto: Butterworths; Ottawa: Minister of Supply and Services.

Worklife Report, The. 1990. "Community and Sectoral Approaches to Labour Market Policy" 7/3:1–17. Kingston, ON.

ENDNOTES

1. The authors names are listed in alphabetical order to reflect the equal contributions made. The authors gratefully acknowledge the helpful comments of Bryan Downie, Mary Lou Coates, Morley Gunderson, Noah Meltz, and Terry Thomason.

2. Kochan (1990) identifies the key developments confronting the Canadian industrial relations system into the twenty-first centruy: international competition; labour-cost reduction; strategic corporate restructuring; the Canada–U.S. Free Trade Agreement; the impacts of new technologies; and developments in the labour force, including the increased labour-force participation rate of women and the effects of immigration.

3. Such was particularly the case for the manufacturing sector, although this generalization applied in varying degrees to other sectors as well.

4. There is a very significant and growing debate over the future of the Canadian human-resource management and industrial relations system relative to the U.S. system. Essentially, the issue has become a question of whether or not the extent of unionization in the Canadian private sector has begun to decline, in essence following the U.S. trend, with a lag. Moreover, there is an issue as to whether the climate and outcomes of the industrial relations system in Canada may eventually follow U.S. outcomes. Refer to Chaison and Rose (1991), Kumar (1991), Meltz (1990b), and Troy (1991) for discussions of these trends as well as of the explanatory factors offered.

5. The discussion in this section is drawn from Verma (1990).

6. This sector excludes the public service, but includes education; health; transportation; communications; finance; insurance and real estate; community, business, and personal services; trade; and utilities. Crown corporations, though publicly owned, are also included in this group. This group is also referred to as nongovernment services elsewhere in this chapter, while the broader services sector is taken to include government services.

7. Includes Japan.

8. Specifically, the average annual percentage changes in productivities during the 1960–73, 1973–79, and 1979–88 periods were: total factor productivity, 2.0, 0.7, 0.2, respectively; labour productivity, 2.8, 1.5, 1.4, respectively; and capital productivity 0.5, – 0.7, – 2.0, respectively (CLMPC 1991, Table IV-3).

9. The results for this analysis rely upon the use of input-output tables (refer to Economic Council of Canada 1990, Appendix B).

10. The impact on education and health services was minor.

11. For example, Kumar (1991) discusses the opposition of Canadian unions, such as the Canadian Auto Workers, to contingent compensation schemes (e.g., profit sharing).

12. Union density levels vary considerably across individual service sector industries. In 1988, density levels were low in trade (10.4 percent), finance, insurance and real estate (3.4 percent); moderate in the services (such as health and education) (33.4 percent); but very high in both transportation (56.6 percent) and public

administration (76.4 percent) (see Table 1.7).

13. Refer to Coates (1991, 51) for a discussion of the industries with potential for future union organizing as well as the challenges to organizing.

14. The Service Employees International Union is an important example of a growing international union. Notably, its membership is rooted in the public-service sector.

15. Troy's (1991) analysis centres on the definition of the public sector in Canada. For example, Troy includes the education and health-services industries in the Canadian public sector, instead of under the normal "services" classification, since these industries are primarily publicly funded.

16. The law required wage adjustments to begin in January 1990 in the public sector, and in January 1991 in the private sector, depending on the size of the employer.

17. As further examples, Ontario Hydro and the Canadian Union of Public Employees, Canadian Airlines and the International Association of Machinists, and Stelco and the United Steelworkers each negotiated agreements with some degree of pension indexing (Coates 1991).

Chapter 2

INDUSTRIAL RELATIONS IN THE CANADIAN AUTOMOBILE INDUSTRY

Pradeep Kumar
Noah M. Meltz[1]

*T*he automobile industry is one of the key manufacturing industries in Canada, with significant input–output linkages to various sectors of the economy. Nearly one in every seven Canadian manufacturing jobs depends directly on the automobile industry (Taskforce 1983, 1), including more than 160 000 persons employed in its three branches: assembly of passenger cars, trucks, and vans; manufacture of motor vehicle parts and accessories; and manufacture of truck and bus bodies. In addition, the industry provides jobs for more than half a million workers employed in the sales and service of cars and trucks, and road transportation (1986 Census of Canada, unpublished tabulation). Motor vehicles and parts are major contributors to international trade, representing nearly one-quarter of Canada's merchandise exports and imports.

The industry is currently experiencing a fundamental restructuring in response to formidable international competitive pressures, especially from Japanese manufacturers. The increased imports from overseas and from plants established by foreign-based companies (termed "transplants") are offering strong competition to the Big Three (General Motors, Ford, and Chrysler). The Japanese challenge is particularly significant because of that country's higher-quality products and innovative human-resource policies and practices.

The competitive pressures and the emerging overcapacity in the industry have led the Big Three to restructure their production and management systems to enhance flexibility in compensation and work arrangements, and to form partnerships with workers and their unions in workplace organization and administration. These changes are designed to achieve cost and quality competitiveness. The dominant union in the industry, the Canadian Auto Workers (CAW), has been reluctant to support such management initiatives, although it has worked together with management on issues of mutual interest.

This chapter focusses on the restructuring of auto assembly operations and its implications for industrial relations in the 1990s. The chapter deals with five major subjects: a profile of the industry; the evolution of the industry in general, and of the vehicle assembly sector in particular; the divergence in labour relations between Canada and the United States; the reasons for the divergence; and the outlook for the 1990s.

INDUSTRY PROFILE

The Canadian automotive industry consists of three major components: assemblers of passenger cars, buses, vans, truck chassis, and tractors; manufacturers of motor vehicle parts and accessories; and manufacturers of truck and bus bodies, commercial and noncommercial trailers, and mobile homes. Motor vehicle assem-

Table 2.1
A Profile of the Automotive Industry, 1988

	Total	Assembly	Parts	Trucks and Bus Bodies
Number of establishments	1 001	28	630	343
Value of shipments ($ millions)	44 394	28 114	14 539	1 741
Percent in Ontario	93.4	94.2	96.5	54.3[a]
Number of employees				
Total	162 272	52 681	94 335	15 256
Production	134 250	41 351	80 317	12 582
Nonproduction	28 022	11 330	14 018	2 674
Per establishment	162	1 881	23	44
Value added (manufacturing)				
Total ($ millions)	11 944	4 954	6 356	634
Per employee	73 605	94 042	67 375	41 557
Average annual earnings				
Per employee				
Total	34 072	42 683	30 799	24 576
Production	32 282	41 188	29 184	22 793
Nonproduction	42 632	48 141	40 024	32 964

Note: [a] Estimate based on total value of shipments 1987; data 1988 not available.
Source: Statistics Canada, unpublished data.

Table 2.2
Economic Indicators of the Canadian Automobile Industry, 1961–1990

| Year | Value of Shipments | | Production (000s) | | | | | Capital Expenditures ($ Millions) |
	Actual $ Billions	Percent of Total Manufac- turing	Cars	Trucks	All Vehicles Total	Percent of Production North American	World	
1961	1.3	5.5	324	63	387	5.8	2.8	48
1962	1.7	6.6	425	81	506	6.5	3.0	57
1963	2.1	7.7	532	99	631	6.7	3.0	92
1964	2.4	7.8	560	111	671	7.1	3.5	144
1965	3.0	8.9	707	140	847	8.0	3.6	NA
1966	3.2	8.6	696	201	897	9.5	3.9	239
1967	3.6	9.3	714	226	940	9.8	4.1	187
1968	4.5	10.6	891	279	1170	11.7	4.5	145
1969	5.3	11.5	1035	317	1352	12.3	3.9	188
1970	4.6	10.0	923	253	1176	11.4	4.1	316
1971	5.9	11.7	1094	277	1371	11.4	4.1	163
1972	6.6	11.7	1155	320	1475	11.1	4.0	169
1973	7.8	11.7	1235	347	1582	12.9	4.2	174
1974	8.6	10.5	1143	376	1579	13.9	4.3	297
1975	9.4	10.6	1056	390	1446	12.5	4.2	234
1976	11.4	11.6	1143	501	1644	11.8	4.1	255
1977	13.5	12.4	1162	612	1774	12.3	4.2	438
1978	16.1	12.5	1131	656	1787	12.3	3.8	470
1979	16.7	11.0	945	635	1580	14.6	3.5	661
1980	15.1	9.0	847	528	1375	13.1	3.2	1106
1981	17.3	9.1	744	497	1241	15.6	3.5	1175
1982	19.0	10.1	802	449	1251	13.8	3.8	600
1983	24.7	12.8	969	547	1516	14.7	4.5	904
1984	33.3	15.4	1062	812	1874	14.2	4.3	849
1985	37.8	16.2	1091	856	1953	14.1	4.1	1495
1986	38.5	16.3	1073	793	1866	12.5	3.4	2835
1987	36.9	13.6	810	825	1635	13.9	3.7	2873
1988	44.4	15.1	1026	949	1975	15.2	4.3	3177
1989	44.5	14.7	1002	914	1916	15.2	4.3	2674
1990	42.8	14.5	1072	833	1905	14.1	4.5	1910

Sources: Statistics Canada, Motor Vehicle Manufacturers, Catalogue 42–209, Annual (Ottawa: Minister of Supply and Services).
Statistics Canada, Motor Vehicle Parts and Accessories, Catalogue 42–210, Annual (Ottawa: Minister of Supply and Services).
Statistics Canada, Truck Body and Trailer Manufacturers, Catalogue 42–217, Annual (Ottawa: Minister of Supply and Services).
Statistics Canada, Motor Vehicle Industries, Catalogue 42–219, Annual (Ottawa: Minister of

Table 2.2 (continued)

Supply and Services).
Statistics Canada, *Transportation Equipment Industries,* Catalogue 42–251, Annual (Ottawa: Minister of Supply and Services).
Statistics Canada, *Investment Statistics: Manufacturing Sub-industries and Selected Energy Related Industries Outlook,* Catalogue 61–214, Annual (Ottawa: Minister of Supply and Services).
Statistics Canada, *Canadian Economic Obseerver,* Catalogue 11–010, Monthly (Ottawa: Minister of Supply and Services).
Industry, Science and Technology Canada, *Statistical Review of the Canadian Automotive Industry: 1989,* (Ottawa: 1990), and *1983 Report on the Canadian Automotive Industry* (Ottawa: 1984).

bly and parts and accessories manufacture account for 96 percent of the total value of industry shipments and 91 percent of total employment (Industry, Science and Technology Canada 1990; Table 2.1); motor vehicle assembly, the focus of this essay, alone accounts for almost two-thirds of the value of shipments, although a larger number of workers are employed in the parts industry. Canada is the sixth-largest producer of motor vehicles in the world, accounting for 4.5 percent of worldwide production, and 14 percent of total North American production in 1990 (Industry, Science and Technology Canada 1991; Table 2.2).

STRUCTURE OF THE INDUSTRY

The automobile industry, especially motor vehicle assembly manufacturing, is highly oligopolistic, almost completely foreign-owned, and heavily unionized, with a sizable proportion of labour in value added, high levels of productivity, and extreme geographical concentration. The industry is dominated by the Big Three American multinationals (General Motors, Ford, and Chrysler) who account for over 90 percent of vehicle production, 41 percent of the value of parts production, and 50 percent of the industry employment. However, the new Asian-owned assembly operations, popularly known as "transplants," have begun to reduce the dominance of the Big Three. Honda of Canada, a subsidiary of the Japanese giant car manufacturer, began production at its Alliston, Ontario, plant in November 1986. Another Japanese transplant, Toyota Motor Manufacturing Canada, started producing at its Cambridge, Ontario, plant in November 1988. The South Korean–owned Hyundai Auto Canada's plant in Bromont, Quebec, came into operation in January 1989. The CAMI Automotive plant at Ingersol, Ontario, jointly owned by Suzuki of Japan and General Motors, started production in April 1989.

These four foreign "transplant" manufacturers, according to an estimate, assembled close to 160 000 cars between January and August 1990; their maximum production capacity is forecast at 460 000 vehicles, or 16 percent of total Canadian capacity (Roy 1991; Table 2.3). The production at the Big Three as well as at the new Asian manufacturers is heavily export oriented. More than four-fifths of the passenger cars and trucks produced in Canada are exported to the United States: the U.S. market accounts for almost 100 percent of the value of Canadian automotive exports and 82 percent of the imports (see Table 2.4).

Table 2.3
Asian Vehicle Assembly Transplants in Canada

Company	Location	Operations Start Date	Maximum Capacity	Employment At Maximum Capacity	Investment (approximate) in Millions of Dollars	Product
Honda of Canada Mfg. Inc.	Alliston, Ontario	November 1986	100 000	1400	400	3-door Civic (Hatchback)
Toyota Motor Mfg. Canada Inc.	Cambridge, Ontario	November 1988	60 000	1000	400	4-door 1.6-litres Corolla
Hyundai Auto Canada Inc.	Bromont, Quebec	January 1989	100 000	1000	450	Sonata
CAMI Automotive Ltd.	Ingersoll, Ontario	April 1989	80 000	2000	620	Suzuki
			120 000			Sidekick/Geo Tracker

Source: Francine Roy, "Recent Trends in the Automotive Industry," *Canadian Economic Observer* (January 1991): 4.1–4.14.

Table 2.4
Canadian International Trade in Automotive Products, 1966-1989

| Year | TRADE ($ Millions) | | | | TRADE BALANCE ($ Millions) | | |
| | Exports[a,b] | | Imports[b] | | | | |
	Total Canadian	Percent to U.S.	Total Canadian	Percent from U.S.	Total[b]	Vehicles	Parts
1966	1 048	84.5	1 636	90.9	(588)	103	(695)
1967	1 686	90.2	2 198	92.9	(512)	261	(784)
1968	2 673	92.0	3 094	92.0	(421)	561	(966)
1969	3 520	94.0	3 750	90.6	(230)	1075	(1272)
1970	3 521	92.8	3 454	88.7	67	1094	(1011)
1971	4 249	95.1	4 376	87.8	(127)	955	(1038)
1972	4 767	95.5	5 205	86.6	(438)	854	(1232)
1973	5 559	95.4	6 348	89.8	(789)	728	(1449)
1974	5 793	93.8	7 344	89.4	(1551)	645	(1984)
1975	6 519	90.6	8 422	91.7	(1903)	767	(2406)
1976	8 495	92.7	9 707	91.4	(1212)	1392	(2591)
1977	10 687	92.3	11 890	92.1	(1203)	2066	(3167)
1978	13 037	92.0	13 884	90.6	(847)	2505	(3287)
1979	12 467	91.7	15 814	91.8	(3347)	841	(4097)
1980	11 480	89.8	14 073	87.8	(2593)	1540	(4130)
1981	14 417	88.3	16 580	87.2	(2163)	2287	(4865)
1982	17 684	92.9	15 478	87.7	2206	6395	(4749)
1983	21 637	96.5	19 964	88.2	1673	6052	(4657)
1984	30 674	97.3	27 626	86.6	3048	9011	(6207)
1985	34 505	98.0	33 611	85.8	894	7672	(7078)
1986	35 363	97.5	35 249	83.2	114	7048	(7401)
1987	33 379	97.6	34 852	82.3	(1473)	4474	(6267)
1988	36 881	97.5	37 802	84.5	(921)	7086	(9488)
1989	36 309	97.5	36 061	81.7	248	8419	(8434)

Notes: [a] Canadian exports are derived from the counterpart United States Statistics of Imports.
            [b] Includes tires and tubes and re-exports.

Sources: Statistics Canada, *Motor Vehicle Manufacturers,* Catalogue 42–209, Annual (Ottawa: Minister of Supply and Services). Canada.
          Statistics Canada, *Motor Vehicle Parts and Accessories,* Catalogue 42–210, Annual (Ottawa: Minister of Supply and Services).
          Statistics Canada, *Truck Body and Trailer Manufacturers,* Catalogue 42–217, Annual (Ottawa: Minister of Supply and Services).
          Statistics Canada, *Motor Vehicle Industries,* Catalogue 42–219, Annual (Ottawa: Minister of Supply and Services).
          Statistics Canada, *Transportation Equipment Industries,* Catalogue 42–251, Annual (Ottawa: Minister of Supply and Services).
          Statistics Canada, *Investment Statistics: Manufacturing Sub-industries and Selected Energy Related Industries Outlook,* Catalogue 61–214, Annual (Ottawa: Minister of Supply and Services).
          Statistics Canada, *Canadian Economic Observer,* Catalogue 11–010, Monthly (Ottawa: Minister of Supply and Services).
          Industry, Science and Technology Canada, *Statistical Review of the Canadian Automotive Industry: 1989* (Ottawa: 1990), and *1983 Report on the Canadian Automotive Industry* (Ottawa: 1984).

The motor vehicle industry is heavily concentrated in Ontario. Except for General Motors's plant in Ste.-Thérèse, Quebec, the new Hyundai plant in Bromont, Quebec, and the Volvo assembly operations in Halifax, Nova Scotia, all light motor vehicles plants are located in Ontario. Ontario accounted for 86 percent of employment in motor vehicle assembly and 95 percent of vehicle parts and accessories manufacturing in 1986 (Côté 1989). The industry's work force is predominantly male and blue-collar, more so than the average for all manufacturing (Côté 1989). In 1988, 83 percent of employees were blue-collar production workers, and only 3 percent of the production work force and 17 percent of nonproduction employees were female.

Motor vehicle manufacturing is a high value–added industry, with significant labour input. In 1988, the total of wages and salaries in the industry was $5.26 billion, 47 percent of the value added; in motor vehicle assembly operations, $2.25 billion was spent on wages and salaries, 36 percent of total value added. In 1988, production workers in the industry as a whole earned an average annual income of $32 282, while those in auto assembly earned $41 188 or $17.0 an hour; nonproduction or white–collar workers earned an average of $42 632 versus $48 141 in assembly (see Table 2.5). According to the calculations made by the Automotive Industry Human Resource Taskforce, as much as 62 percent of the work force was unskilled; the proportion of unskilled was much higher in the assembly plant than in the auto parts work force. (Taskforce 1986, 120). However, the industry creates more value added per hour worked than most other manufacturing industries (Taskforce 1983). In 1988, value added per hour in motor vehicle assembly was 22 percent higher than the all-manufacturing average.

LABOUR RELATIONS CHARACTERISTICS

The automobile industry is heavily unionized, with almost all of the union members belonging to the Canadian Auto Workers (CAW). The CAW was formed in 1985, breaking away from the International Union of United Automobile, Aerospace, and Agricultural Implement Workers of America (UAW). While accurate estimates of union–density figures for the industry are unavailable, the percentage of workers covered by collective agreements ranges between 76 and 83 percent. According to Labour Canada estimates, 99 percent of the hourly rated production workers and 7 percent of the salaried employees in motor vehicle assembly manufacturing were covered by collective agreements in 1984. In the parts and accessories industry, collective–bargaining coverage was 90 percent for production workers and 9 percent for salaried workers (Kumar, Coates, and Arrowsmith 1986). The CAW estimates show that, of the 170 000 CAW members in 1990, 55.4 percent were in the motor vehicles industry, 26.4 percent in assembly, 11.9 percent in component parts and 17.1 percent in independent parts (CAW 1990). Based on these figures and employment estimates of Statistics Canada (Industry, Science and Technology Canada 1991), it appears that 61 percent of the automotive industry workers employed in vehicle assembly, truck bodies and

Table 2.5
Employment, Earnings, and Productivity in the Automotive Industry, 1961–1988

Year	Employees (000s)			Average Annual Earnings ($000s)			Productivity ($000s)	
	Total	Production	Non-production	All Employees	Production Workers	Non-production Employees	Value Added Per Employee	Real Domestic Product Per Employee
1961	50.2	35.3	14.9	NA	4.8	NA	9.2	11.7
1962	54.0	39.0	15.0	NA	5.3	NA	11.1	13.6
1963	62.5	45.8	16.7	NA	5.6	NA	12.4	14.6
1964	71.6	53.4	18.2	6.0	5.6	7.1	11.4	14.1
1965	81.7	61.3	20.4	6.5	6.2	7.5	12.4	16.0
1966	86.0	64.4	21.5	6.5	6.1	7.9	12.4	16.3
1967	85.4	63.9	21.5	6.7	6.3	8.1	14.7	18.8
1968	90.3	67.8	22.4	7.7	7.2	9.1	15.0	22.0
1969	97.7	74.6	23.1	8.0	7.5	9.7	17.4	24.8
1970	90.8	67.1	23.8	8.5	7.7	10.5	15.0	22.1
1971	102.5	78.7	23.8	9.2	8.5	11.7	17.6	25.9
1972	109.8	84.8	25.0	10.0	9.3	12.3	18.6	28.8
1973	122.6	96.1	26.5	10.8	10.1	13.4	19.3	30.8
1974	119.5	96.7	22.8	12.1	10.9	17.4	23.0	31.8
1975	110.4	85.1	25.3	13.0	12.2	15.7	23.4	34.6
1976	118.1	92.0	26.1	14.9	14.1	17.6	26.9	36.5

Table 2.5 (continued)

Year	Employees (000s)			Average Annual Earnings ($000s)			Productivity ($000s)	
	Total	Production	Non-production	All Employees	Production Workers	Non-production Employees	Value Added Per Employee	Real Domestic Product Per Employee
1977	123.4	97.0	26.4	16.5	15.7	19.6	31.6	37.8
1978	130.1	102.7	27.4	17.8	16.9	21.4	35.7	36.7
1979	129.6	102.7	26.9	18.7	17.5	23.2	37.1	34.6
1980	111.7	85.9	25.8	20.4	19.1	24.7	34.1	28.0
1981	113.1	88.0	25.1	23.0	21.8	27.2	40.9	31.2
1982	110.1	85.0	25.1	24.1	22.7	28.6	44.6	32.6
1983	120.9	95.9	25.0	26.9	25.5	32.2	60.0	42.5
1984	142.2	114.8	27.5	29.7	28.1	36.3	69.2	46.3
1985	152.7	124.6	28.1	30.8	29.5	36.8	76.4	47.3
1986	151.8	124.7	27.1	31.8	30.2	39.1	74.9	46.2
1987	154.0	NA	NA	32.7	NA	NA	68.9	44.1
1988	162.3	134.2	28.0	34.1	32.3	42.6	73.6	45.2

Sources: Statistics Canada, Motor Vehicle Manufacturers, Catalogue 42–209, Annual (Ottawa: Minister of Supply and Services).
Statistics Canada, Motor Vehicle Parts and Accessories, Catalogue 42–210, Annual (Ottawa: Minister of Supply and Services).
Statistics Canada, Truck Body and Trailer Manufacturers, Catalogue 42–217, Annual (Ottawa: Minister of Supply and Services).
Statistics Canada, Motor Vehicle Industries, Catalogue 42–219, Annual (Ottawa: Minister of Supply and Services).
Statistics Canada, Transportation Equipment Industries, Catalogue 42–251, Annual (Ottawa: Minister of Supply and Services).

Table 2.6
Chronology of Breakthroughs in Collective Bargaining Between the Big Three and the CAW

Paid vacation	1940
Union security	1945
Paid holidays	1948
Cost-of-Living adjustment (COLA)	1948 (effective 1950)
Annual improvement factor (AIF)	1950 (became 3% in late 1960s)
Pension	1950 (30 & Out any age—1976)
Medical/Hospital/Surgical	1954
Supplemental unemployment benefits (SUB)	1955
Optical, dental	1973
Health & safety committees	1973
Hearing aids	1976
Paid personal holidays (PPH)	1976 (extended in 1979)
Paid education leave (PEL)	1977
Video-display terminal protection	1981 (improved in 1982)
Paid maternity leave	1982
Childcare	1983 (expanded in 1987)
Legal services plan	1984
Income maintenance	1984 (beyond SUB)
Union counsellors	1984
Affirmative action	1984
Health & Safety—Company-wide co-ordinators	1986
Weekend worker	1986
Pension indexation (for future retirees)	1987
Worker security program	1990

Source: Canadian Auto Workers, *A New Decade—Challenging the Corporate Agenda: Our Response,* Report to the National Collective Bargaining and Political Action Convention, May 29–June 1, 1990 (North York, ON: 1990) and *C.A.W. Contract Reports (September 1990)* (North York, ON: 1990).

trailers, and automotive parts and accessories are unionized in 1990.[2]

The percentage organized is significantly higher among the production workers than among salaried workers. All production workers employed in the Big Three and CAMI, the new joint venture of General Motors and Suzuki, are covered by collective agreements. A small proportion of salaried workers, mostly clerical workers at Ford and Chrysler, are also unionized. However, the three Asian transplants—Honda, Toyota, and Hyundai—are nonunionized. Union coverage is lower in the vehicle parts sector than in assembly manufacturing (56 percent versus 67 percent, using the CAW estimates).

The CAW (Canadian region of the UAW prior to 1985) is very aggressive and innovative, with a strong and well-articulated social-unionism orientation. It has bargained hard for improved wages and benefits and campaigned vigorously for legislative changes, and for social and economic reforms to advance the well-being of workers. The union believes in incremental and evolutionary changes in workplace management through the collective-bargaining process and has achieved many significant breakthroughs over a period of 50 years (see Table 2.6). As Table 2.7 shows, these breakthroughs often occurred following prolonged negotiations and occasional work stoppages. In the 30 years of strikes that are chronicled, the average duration of strikes was 35 days, or 5 weeks, which is double the overall average strike duration for Canada](Coates, Arrowsmith, and Courchene 1989, 111). However, more than half of the strikes at Big Three plants lasted less than three weeks, the largest number lasting one to two weeks.

While opposed to direct participation in management decision making, the union has favoured active involvement with employers at the strategic policy level, and at the workplace level on issues of mutual interest. At the industry level, the president of the union was a co-chairman of the Taskforce on the Canadian Motor Vehicles and Automotive Parts Industry in 1983, and again of the Automotive Industries Human Resources Taskforce in 1985. At the workplace level, the union has been engaged in joint union–management initiatives at the Big Three in such areas as apprentice training, employee orientation, affirmative action, employee assistance and counselling, human-rights and literacy training, and health and safety.

Ⅼ The organizational structure of the union is highly decentralized, with an emphasis on rank-and-file participation in union decision-making through a network of policy councils, a system of in-plant representation, and extensive educational programs (Yates 1988). The union is also very active in organizing the unorganized. Since 1967, union membership almost doubled, from 90 800 to 160 400 in 1989 (Coates, Arrowsmith, and Courchene 1989), with over 90 percent, or 63 000 coming from new organizing (Herzenberg 1990, 178). In the four years, (1985 to 1988) following its breakaway from the parent organization (the UAW), the CAW organized 16 440 new members, 3769 in the motor vehicle industry alone. Throughout the 1960s and 1970s, the Canadian region's organizing successes received special mention in the UAW President's Report to Constitutional Conventions (Herzenberg 1990, 185).⊃

[Wages, benefits, working conditions, and workplace rules and regulations in the industry are established through collective bargaining every three years.] At the Big Three, labour–management relations are governed by two sets of collective agreements, the national Master Agreement and local agreements at various plant locations. The Master Agreement and local agreements are negotiated simultaneously, and are normally of three years' duration. The Master Agreement covers such basic matters as the recognition of the exclusive bargaining agent, union representation, management rights, grievance procedure and arbitration, general seniority rules, leaves of absence, hours of work and overtime, holidays and vacations, wage increases and cost-of-living allowance, and shift premium. The Master Agreement also includes provisions relating to the equitable distribution of overtime, bulletin boards, smoking, bereavement pay, work assignments, and mechanisms for resolving disputes arising from changes in production standards, outside contracting, and work by supervisory employees on hourly rated

Table 2.7
Major Work Stoppages at the Big Three, 1961–1990

Year	Date of Start & Termination	Length in Days	Number of Workers Involved	Number of Days Lost	Location	Company
1961	08-12-61 14-12-61	6	16 000	56 080	Oshawa	G.M.
1962	19-02-62 18-04-62	58	3 000	123 000	Windsor	Chrysler
1964	01-12-64 21-12-64	20	23 829	303 900	Various Locations, Ontario	G.M.
1965	28-01-65 08-63-65	38	6 000	162 000	Windsor	Chrysler
1968	24-01-68 05-02-68	12	8 675	65 070	Various Locations, Ontario	Chrysler
1968	07-02-68 29-03-68	50	23 626	831 830	Various Locations, Ontario	G.M.
1968	16-04-68 24-04-68	8	10 906	65 430	Various Locations, Ontario	Ford
1968	09-02-68 29-03-68	48	1 848	64 680	Ste-Thérèse, Quebec	G.M.
1970	14-09-70 18-12-70	95	23 500	1 598 600	Various Locations, Ontario	G.M.
1970	14-09-70 18-12-70	123	2 300	156 400	Ste-Thérèse, Quebec	G.M.

Table 2.7 (continued)

Year	Date of Start & Termination	Length in Days	Number of Workers Involved	Number of Days Lost	Location	Company
1971	19-01-71 27-01-71	18	14 270	76 530	Various Locations, Ontario	Ford
1973	15-09-73 24-09-73	9	11 250	56 250	Various Locations, Ontario	Chrysler
1973	23-11-73 10-12-73	17	15 000	165 000	Various Locations, Ontario	Ford
1982	05-11-82 13-12-82	38	8 815	224 780	Toronto/Windsor	Chrysler
1984	16-10-84 30-10-84	14	31 835	283 840	Oshawa & Others, Ontario	G.M.
1990	15-09-90 24-09-90	9	12 890	64 460	Various Locations, Ontario	Ford

Source: Labour Canada (unpublished special tabulation).

jobs. Also included in the Master Agreement are special provisions on skilled trades, including terms, eligibility, training, and rate schedules of apprentices, as well as the permissible ratio of apprentices to journeymen/journeywomen.

Employee benefit plans (e.g., pension, supplementary unemployment income-security programs, legal services) are enumerated in attached supplemental agreements, which are not subject to the grievance procedure. The Master Agreement also includes as appendices a number of memoranda of understanding and documents of company intent in the form of statements and letters. Local agreements are comprised of three separate agreements—a seniority agreement, a wage agreement, and a general agreement. These agreements include hourly wage scales for each skilled and unskilled job classification, and provisions relating to transfer rights, seniority groups and classifications, layoffs and recalls, distribution of overtime, and a number of local issues.

*E*volution of the Industry

*C*anada's automobile industry has undergone many structural changes since the establishment of the first car plant in Windsor, Ontario, by the Ford Motor Company of Canada in 1904, and subsequently the merger of the McLaughlin Motor Car and Chevrolet companies to form General Motors of Canada in 1918. Economic and industrial relations developments in the industry have been shaped by five key factors: (1) Canada's proximity to the United States, which has provided the market as well as the capital and the production technology; (2) the high level of foreign ownership and the domination of the industry by the big American multinationals; (3) the organization of workers into a single union, the UAW, and the innovative cross-border collective bargaining with common collective-agreement expiration dates; (4) international competitive pressures; and (5) government policy.

The economic and industrial relations developments in the industry can be divided into three periods: pre-1965, 1965–80, and the 1980s. The management and labour strategies followed in the 1980s set the stage for those in the 1990s.

THE PRE-1965 PERIOD

The pre-1965 period was characterized by considerable instability in the industry, with growing domestic demand for automobiles, static production, declining exports, and an increasing volume of imports. During this period, the industry was highly protected and beset with serious problems because of the high level of wages and prices, low productivity, and high unemployment (Taskforce 1983, 14–17).

While the industry was in a crisis resulting from serious competitive pressures during the 1950s and early 1960s, the foundations for a stable labour relations system were laid during the period, with the advent of multiyear collective agreements and co-ordinated bargaining in 1953 at General Motors of Canada. The system, which became a model for stable labour relations in the industry during the later 1960s and the 1970s, was inspired by the historic 1948 collective agreement between the UAW and General Motors Corporation in the United States. The three key elements of this model were: (a) the determination of *formulaic wage rules* in multiyear contracts, including an annual improvement factor (AIF), equivalent to the average long-term productivity growth (traditionally 3 percent), and a cost-of-living adjustment (COLA) clause, which provided roughly a 0.8 percent wage increase for every 1 percent increase in the consumer price index; (b) a *connective-bargaining* structure defining the connection between national- and plant-level bargaining, which led to a centrally imposed uniformity in wages and general contract provisions; and (c) a *job control focus* that linked worker rights and wage rates to narrowly and strictly defined job classifications and provided for contractual resolution of disagreements and grievances arising over matters covered by the contract (Katz 1985, 1987; Perusek 1988; Holmes and Kumar 1991).

The "competitive crisis" in the industry was resolved through rationalization of assembly and parts production at the Big Three and a sequence of adjustments in the tariff structure between 1963 and 1965, finally leading to the signing, in 1965, of the Canada-U.S. Automotive Products Trade Agreement (APTA), commonly known as the Auto Pact.

THE 1965–1980 PERIOD

The Auto Pact marked a turning point in the evolution of the industry, and ushered in an unprecedented era of growth in output, productivity, employment, and trade for both Canada and the United States. In its 1983 report, the Taskforce on the Canadian Motor Vehicles and Automotive Parts Industry summarized the performance of the industry under the Auto Pact as follows:

> The Auto Pact, despite any shortcomings, has brought positive results for both Canada and the United States. It has enabled the U.S. automotive companies to maintain the dominant share of the world's seventh largest vehicle market. For its part, Canada has gained substantially more production, expanded trade, increased productivity, a greater share of North American automotive employment, and lower consumer prices. (Taskforce 1983, 21)

The improved industry performance immediately following the signing of the Auto Pact was largely attributed to the process of rationalization and modernization. The Auto Pact created an integrated continental market for auto products and parts manufacturing by providing "free trade" in new vehicles and original equipment parts with safeguards for maintaining pre-Pact levels of Canadian production and employment. Among the key safeguards were: (1) vehicle and parts eligible to enter the United States free of duty must come from Canada and must have at least 50 percent North American content; (2) each designated manufacturer (that is, the companies making cars or trucks in Canada) must maintain a certain ratio between the net sales value of vehicles made in Canada and the net sales value of vehicles sold domestically; and (3) the amount of value added for all classes of vehicles made in Canada must be at least as great as the amount that was attained in the base year (Taskforce 1983, 17–18). Levels of production and consumption were set at the combined North American level rather than at the level of the individual economies.

A series of mergers followed the Auto Pact, resulting in horizontal integration in the form of oligopolistic concentration of the industry. Also, significant vertical integration of both parts and assembly production and consumption took place. For example, General Motors, the largest North American auto producer, assembled 737 000 vehicles (trucks and cars) in Canada in 1988, of which only 20 percent were sold in Canada, the remainder being exported to the United States. In the same year, GM of Canada imported about 400 000 vehicles from its U.S. parent for sale in the Canadian market (General Motors of Canada 1989). Similarly, over 70 percent of the parts manufactured by GM in Canada are shipped to the United States, and 75 percent of parts used in Canada are imported from the United States.

The international sourcing pattern of original equipment parts of major auto manufacturers provides an additional perspective on vertical integration. The U.S. purchases from in-house suppliers jumped from $17 million in 1965 to $454 million in 1970, and to $2.36 billion in 1979. Over the same period, Canadian purchases from in-house suppliers in the United States rose from $522 million in 1965 to $1.15 billion in 1970, and to $4.7 billion in 1979 (Industry, Science and Technology Canada 1990). The production rationalization was the reason for significant increases in Canadian auto industry employment, value added, productivity, trade, and investment during the period from 1965 to 1979 (Tables 2.4 and 2.5; Taskforce 1983, 21–32).

The Auto Pact also had a marked impact on labour relations policies and practices. The economic integration under the Auto Pact led to uniform management structures, as well as uniform wages and working conditions and work practices in the two countries through common collective agreements with the single union in the industry, the United Auto Workers (UAW). For example, GM of Canada became a part of the corporate Chevrolet-Pontiac-Canada (CPC) division. Chrysler management was also integrated. Only Ford remained an independent entity. Management personnel travelled south and north as a result of integration.

At the time of the introduction of the Auto Pact, Canadian wages were about 30 percent lower than the U.S. equivalents (in respective national currencies). The integration led to the demand for nominal wage parity by the UAW. The wage parity agreement between the Big Three and the UAW, signed in 1968, provided for the elimination of differences between U.S. and Canadian base wage rates (expressed in national currencies), and parity became a reality in 1975, following incremental adjustments. By 1975, the industry was fully integrated, with identical nominal wages and working conditions, common agreement-expiration dates, and integrated human-resource management and labour relations practices. Productivity in Canadian plants—about 35 percent lower before the Pact—caught up with that of U.S. plants, and, in some plants, surpassed the comparable U.S. levels (Taskforce 1983, 22).

The industrial relations climate on both sides of the border appeared to be stable, characterized by mutual accommodation, but within an adversarial labour relations framework where there were occasional confrontations on contract renewal and during the term of the agreement. Examples of working together include UAW acceptance of new technology in the manufacture of motor vehicles and automotive parts (Taskforce 1983, 122).

THE DEVELOPMENTS IN THE 1980s

The period from 1978 to 1982 marked another turning point in the evolution of the industry. The growth and prosperity of the North American industry following the introduction of the Auto Pact was shattered by a series of developments leading to a serious economic downturn and a competitive crisis in the industry. Plants were closed or only partly used, workers were laid off in large numbers or employed for only a short time, and capital investment declined drastically (see Tables 2.2 and 2.5). Vehicle production declined by 27.2 percent; parts production declined by 27.5 percent; imported vehicles doubled their share of the North American market, to 25 percent in 1981; and employment fell by 41.4 percent between January 1979 and May 1980 (Perry 1982, 3, 17–18).

There were two main reasons for the dramatic reversal in the fortunes of the industry. First, the industry was unable to cope with the rising fuel prices that followed the second oil price shock in 1979, leading to higher costs and prices and a shift in consumer demand toward small, fuel-efficient cars. The change in consumer preferences together with the high prices of North American–built cars resulted in a decline in demand for domestically produced vehicles and a rise in imports, particularly from Japan. The decline in demand was further intensified by the severe recession of 1981–82, the worst since the depression of the 1930s, reducing new car and truck sales in both Canada and the United States. Second, the industry faced a serious erosion of its international competitive position as a result of escalating production costs. The competitive challenge was particularly formidable from the low-cost, high-quality Japanese imports. It was estimated that "the Canadian vehicle manufacturer had, in 1981, a cost disadvantage in direct labour of about $1882 per vehicle compared to imports from Japan" (Perry 1982, 3). The cost disadvantage followed from three major factors: (1) the low exchange value of the Japanese yen against the Canadian and American dollar; (2) the high, and rising, compensation levels in Canada and the United States compared to those in Japan, resulting from contractual real wage increases, which had become a feature of post-

Table 2.8

New Motor Vehicle Sales in Canada—By Origin

Year	Total Units (in '000s)	Place of Manufacture North America (%)	Place of Manufacture Total Offshore (%)	Total Passenger Cars (in 000s)	Place of Manufacture North America (%)	Place of Manufacture Japan (%)	Place of Manufacture Other Offshore (%)
1965	831	90.7	9.3	709	89.4	0.4	10.2
1966	827	91.6	8.4	695	90.2	0.4	9.4
1967	815	90.6	9.4	679	89.1	0.8	10.1
1968	890	87.7	12.4	742	85.9	2.1	12.0
1969	918	85.9	14.1	761	83.9	5.1	11.0
1970	774	80.3	19.7	640	77.6	10.2	12.1
1971	940	78.9	21.1	781	75.9	13.7	10.5
1972	1066	79.2	20.8	859	76.1	13.6	10.3
1973	1227	83.0	17.0	971	80.6	11.5	7.9
1974	1349	87.8	12.2	943	84.5	9.3	6.2
1975	1317	87.1	12.9	989	84.5	9.7	5.9
1976	1292	87.1	13.0	947	83.8	10.7	5.5
1977	1345	84.4	15.6	991	80.5	13.6	5.9
1978	1366	86.4	13.6	988	82.5	11.5	6.1
1979	1396	89.1	10.9	1003	86.1	8.0	5.9
1980	1224	85.9	14.1	892	83.0	15.5	1.5
1981	1191	75.4	24.6	904	71.6	23.0	5.5
1982	921	71.3	28.7	714	68.6	25.0	6.4
1983	1081	75.6	24.4	843	74.1	20.9	5.0
1984	1284	77.8	22.2	971	74.6	17.6	7.7
1985	1530	74.5	25.5	1137	69.9	17.5	12.6
1986	1516	74.5	25.5	1095	69.5	18.6	12.0
1987	1534	72.9	27.1	1065	65.8	22.8	11.4
1988	1566	75.7	24.3	1056	68.6	23.1	8.3
1989	1484	74.0	26.0	988	68.3	24.2	7.4
1990	1318	71.4	28.6	885	65.5	27.2	7.2

Sources: Statistics Canada, *New Motor Vehicle Sales,* Catalogue 63–007, Monthly (Ottawa: Minister of Supply and Services).

Statistics Canada, *New Motor Vehicle Sales,* Catalogue 63–208, Annual (Canada: Dominion Bureau of Statistics.

Industry, Science and Technology Canada, *Statistical Review of the Canadian Automotive Industry: 1989,* (Ottawa: 1990), and *1983 Report on the Canadian Automotive Industry* (Ottawa: 1984).

war pattern bargaining in the North American auto industry; and (3) the marked difference between Japanese and North American productivity.[3]

The auto industry made a remarkable recovery after 1982, with a significant increase in output, employment, and sales, as can be seen in Tables 2.2 and 2.5. North American production of motor vehicles increased 65.6 percent between 1982 and 1990, more than 55 percent in Canada and 67 percent in the United States. Retail sales of motor vehicles went up 61 percent: 39 percent in the case of automobiles and 137 percent for trucks. Total employment rose by 13.6 percent in the United States and 47 percent in Canada (Industry, Science and Technology Canada 1991). The improvement in industry performance was attributable to a number of factors: the strong economic recovery in both the United States and Canada from the recession of 1981–82; a dramatic appreciation in the exchange value of the yen; a voluntary restraint agreement on Japanese car exports negotiated in 1981; and a serious restructuring of the industry. However, despite the increased sales of North American cars, the share of foreign imports of new passenger cars in Canada increased from 25 percent in 1984 to 35 percent in 1990 (see Table 2.8). The Japanese market share, following a decline from 25 percent in 1982 to 17.5 percent in 1985 on account of voluntary restraints on exports, rose to 27 percent in 1990 (Table 2.8; Industry, Science and Technology Canada 1990). There are many reasons why the number of imports, particularly from Japan, have continued to rise. The key reason is that, while the Japanese industry's advantage in wage costs has dissipated as a result of the appreciation of the yen, it continues to enjoy higher productivity and superior product quality when compared to the Big Three. In addition, Japanese manufacturers have invested heavily in North America in both vehicle assembly and auto parts plants to maintain and increase their presence in the North American market.

The Big Three responded to the Japanese challenge by significantly increasing capital investment in plant rationalization and modernization, and by taking a number of initiatives to restructure their production and management systems to regain flexibility and achieve price and quality competitiveness through cost cutting and productivity improvement. The rationalization process has led to the closing of fourteen plants since 1980, the opening of six new plants, and the conversion of four car assembly plants to the production of light trucks. The majority of remaining car assembly plants have been refurbished to accommodate new models and to substantially improve their productivity. All 27 truck plants owned by the Big Three remain intact because of increased truck sales and relatively low levels of import penetration (Industry, Science and Technology Canada 1989). Similarly, although Canadian plants comprise 16 percent of total North American Big Three capacity, no Canadian operations were closed in the 1980s.[4] In fact, Canadian capacity increased with the opening of Chrysler's new Bramalea plant in Ontario, and the expansion and modernization of General Motor's facilities in Oshawa, Ontario (Industry, Science and Technology Canada 1989). There is a general consensus that Canadian assembly plants survived the competitive pressures in the 1980s due, in large part, to a very advantageous product mix and the high quality of their products within each of the Big Three companies.

SETTING THE STAGE FOR THE 1990s

The drive for a higher-quality and lower-cost vehicle, beginning in the early 1980s, has led the Big Three to focus on the following initiatives, which are shaping North American labour–management relations in the 1990s:

1. accelerated use of computerized manufacturing technologies, such as CAD/CAM, robotics, programmable controllers, Automatic Guided Vehicles (AGVs), and automatic monorail systems to replace traditional assembly lines;
2. adoption of new management systems, such as statistical process control (SPS) and the Just-in-Time system of inventory management;
3. revamping the parts sourcing by enforcing tough new quality standards, consolidating the number of suppliers, subcontracting, sole-sourcing of components with preferred suppliers, and involving suppliers in product research and development;
4. joint ventures with Japanese and other foreign manufacturers to produce small cars;
5. rationalization of the management and the production work force through a new system of work organization transferring management decision making to worker teams;
6. contingent compensation to reduce fixed labour costs through lump-sum payments or bonuses, profit sharing, and pay for knowledge in lieu of standard wage increases;
7. cost cutting through two-tier or wage-progression systems, elimination of premium pay for weekend and shift work, alternate work schedules, etc.; and
8. the transformation of labour relations and human-resource management through flexible work arrangements, greater employee involvement in the management process and technological change, fewer job classifications, multiskilling, greater expenditures on training and retraining, and more information sharing with workers and unions. Another key element of this strategy is the management emphasis on "co-operation and partnership" with unions, to facilitate employment rationalization, reduction in absenteeism, and effective training and retraining.

The Big Three strategy of cost cutting through lower wages to new hires, contingent compensation, flexible work arrangements, new Japanese-style work organization, and co-operation and partnership with unions has become the major source of growing divergence in collective-bargaining approaches and outcomes between the two countries. Whereas the UAW has accepted this management strategy, the CAW remains skeptical of its purpose and impacts.

The new labour relations and human-resource management strategy pursued by the Big Three signals a fundamental change in collective-bargaining goals and approaches, and has had a marked impact on labour–management institutions and relationships. Two effects are particularly noteworthy. First, management has become an initiator of change, rather than being reactive to union demands, aggressively pursuing changes in compensation systems, work arrangements, work reorganization, and the nature and direction of union–management relations. Second, the focus of industrial relations activity has shifted from collective bargaining to the strategic-policy and workplace levels. Third, the partnership between the UAW and Big Three management has raised questions about the role and functions of the union in enterprise decision making. The UAW and other industrial unions that formed the Congress of Industrial Organizations in the 1930s always championed the adversarial role of a union in protecting and advancing the economic and social interests of workers against the owners of capital and the state. The role and functions of union and management were unambiguous in the labour relations system that governed collective bargaining and labour–management relations in the North American auto industry from the end of the Second World War to the early 1980s. Under this system, "there was an explicit agreement that it was the job of management to organize and direct work, the employees' obligation to follow instructions, and the unions' role to ensure that management carried out its function in accordance with the literal interpretation and administration of the rules contained in the contract" (Holmes and Kumar 1991, 8).

The new management strategy in the auto industry seeks to transform the role and function of the union from a "management watchdog" to a partner with management in the administration of the enterprise. While the UAW in the United States appears to have adjusted to this new role, apparently to save jobs, by participating in initiatives to make the industry competitive and prosperous, the Canadian union leaders are not convinced of the merits of "co-operation and participation" in management decision making. Instead, they believe in consensus building and working together on issues of mutual interest (CAW 1990; Kumar and Ryan 1988). It was this ideological divide that led to the split in the UAW and the formation of the CAW in 1985, and subsequently the shift in cross-border labour relations from uniformity to diversity. It is important to first understand the background of the UAW split in order to fully appreciate the nature and rationale for the divergence in collective-bargaining approaches and outcomes in the Canadian and U.S. automobile industry (Gindin 1989; Holmes and Rusonik 1990; Holmes and Kumar 1991).

The U.S.–Canadian Divergence in Labour Relations

*U*p to 1980, labour relations practices in the automobile assembly industry in Canada and the United States were similar, having the same terms and conditions

Table 2.9
Highlights of Collective Agreements between UAW/CAW and the Big Three, 1964–1990

U.S. (UAW)	CANADIAN (CAW)
1964–1979: During this period collective agreements at Big Three in both Canada and the United States showed few significant variations. Three-year contracts in 1964, 1968 (retroactive), 1970, 1973, 1976, and 1979 generally contained increases to the base rates, an annual improvement factor (AIF) of a defined percentage, a cost-of-living adjustment (COLA) to be folded-in over the life of the contract, and marginal increases in nonwage benefits, including: pensions, holidays, vacation, SUB, and health. Breakthroughs over this period included: optical and dental benefits, and health and safety committees in 1973; hearing aids in 1976; and paid education leave in 1977.	
Chrysler (November 1979): • Contract renewal • Wages and pensions frozen • 6 personal paid holidays (PPHs) lost	**Chrysler** (November 1979): • Under Single International Agreement, Canadians accept same pattern of concessions
Chrysler (January 1980): • Contract reopened • Wage freeze and 17 PPHs lost as a condition for loan guarantee from Congress • Profit sharing introduced • Total value of concessions $243 million	**Chrysler** (January 1980): • Canadian workers refuse to reopen contract and refuse to accept further concessions; single International Agreement to end in 1982
Chrysler (January 1981): • Contract reopened • $1.15 per hour wage cut (COLA) • 3 PPHs lost • One day's pay lost • Total value of concessions $622 million • Moratorium on plant closures • Ratified by 59% of members	**Chrysler** (January 1981): • Canadians agree to reopen contract and accept same package of concessions except the one day's pay; ratified by only 51% of members

Table 2.9 (continued)

U.S. (UAW)	CANADIAN (CAW)
Ford (February 1982) and **General Motors** (April 1982): • Contracts reopened • Wage, COLA, and pension freeze • Elimination of PPHS • Local work-rule changes allowed • Profit sharing introduced • Ban on plant closures	**Ford and General Motors:** • Canadians refuse to reopen contracts
Ford and General Motors (September 1982): • Contract renewals • Two-year contract • Wage freezes continued • Wide acceptance of new work practices	**Ford and General Motors** (September 1982): • Canadians forgo AIF, but receive small wage increase and retain both COLA and pensions • Shift to Canadian inflation-based COLA in 1984 • 3 PPHS retained • Local contracts not to open to change work-rules • Union rejects Quality-of-Work Life (QWL) program and profit sharing • Plant Closing Fund established
Chrysler (December 1982): • Contract renewals • Initial agreement, which included a freeze on wage and COLA, and reduction in job classifications • Final agreement averaged $0.75 per hour increase; reduction in "skilled" classifications; stock option plan	**Chrysler** (December 1982): • Average $1.15 per hour increase and COLA; union rejected changes in job classifications, stock option plan, and attendance control plan

Table 2.9 (continued)

U.S. (UAW)	CANADIAN (CAW)
Chrysler (August 1983): • Extension of 1982 agreement • 3% wage increase • $1.00 retroactive COLA • Pension parity with GM and Ford	**Chrysler:** • Same as United States
Ford and General Motors (December 1984): • Contract renewals • AIF and COLA given up • 2.25% increase in base wage in first year; lump sum payments in 2nd and 3rd year not folded into base rates • Job Opportunity Bank set up • SUB extended • Profit sharing continued • Ratified by 57%	**Ford and General Motors** (October 1984): • AIF restored as Special Canadian Adjustment (SCA) • COLA retained • New income security plan • Increase in paid holidays • Union rejected lump-sum payments and profit sharing • Ratified by 87%
	Split in UAW (1985)
Chrysler (September 1985): • Contract renewals • Talks initially collapse • Eventually settle for Canadian pattern, except do not achieve synchronization with GM and Ford contracts • Three-year contract	**Chrysler** (September 1985): • AIF restored • Regain parity with Ford and GM by end of contract • Two-year contract synchronizes contract renewal with GM and Ford in 1987 • Ratified by 94%

Table 2.9 (continued)

U.S. (UAW)	CANADIAN (CAW)
Ford and General Motors (September 1987): • Contract renewals • 3% increase in base rate; lump sums in 2nd and 3rd years • Expansion of Job Opportunity Bank and SUB • Plant-closure freeze • Profit sharing **Ford** (May 1988—U.S. only): • No increase in base rates • $1000 early settlement bonus • Three-year performance bonus—October 1988, 1989 • COLA folded-in • Profit sharing • Plant-closure freeze **Ford, General Motors and Chrysler** (September 1990): • Chrysler joins GM and Ford pattern • 3% increase in base rates in 1st year • 3% performance bonus in 2nd and 3rd years • COLA folded-in • Expand Job Opportunity Bank • Profit sharing	**Chrysler** (September 1987): • AIF and COLA retained • Indexed pensions—major breakthrough **Ford and General Motors** (September 1987): • Follow pattern set by Chrysler Canada • 3% increase in base rate in 1st year, $0.25 in 2nd and 3rd years • SCA folded-in **Chrysler, Ford and General Motors** (September 1990): • Chrysler joins GM and Ford pattern • 3% increase in base rates in 1st year, 2% in 2nd and 3rd years • COLA folded-in • New worker security program (one-year advance notice for plant closure) • Income-security plans to continue

Sources: John Holmes and Anthony Rusonik, "The Breakup of an International Labour Union: Uneven Developments in the North American Auto Industry and the Schism in the UAW," *Queen's Papers in Industrial Relations, 1990–2* (Kingston, ON: Industrial Relations Centre, Queen's University, 1990); *U.A.W. Contract Reports (September 1990)* (Detroit: Solidarity House, 1990); and *C.A.W. Contract Reports (September 1990)* (North York, ON: 1990).

of employment established through collective bargaining between the single union in the industry on both sides of the border (the UAW) and the Big Three. In the aftermath of the 1981–82 recession, the practices began to diverge, first with the Canadian refusal to accept profit sharing, then the creation of the CAW, and finally very different focuses in the subsequent rounds of bargaining.

The process began with the sharp downturn in demand for North American cars and the increase in Japanese imports after the 1979 oil price shock, which brought Chrysler Corporation to the brink of bankruptcy. The Canadian and U.S. governments provided financial assistance in the form of loan guarantees, and the UAW agreed to open up the collective agreement and grant wage and other concessions during the period from 1979 to 1982. In the aftermath of the 1981–82 recession, both Ford and General Motors also sought changes in compensation systems and work arrangements. Major demands by the Big Three automakers included contingent compensation (lump-sum payments and profit sharing), new forms of work organization, and "jointness" with management in workplace administration and organization. The Canadian region of the UAW was particularly opposed to introducing contingent compensation and thereby departing from the three-decades-old annual improvement factor (AIF), which provided an increase in base wages approximately equivalent to the increase in productivity in the industry. The Canadian leadership was also less enamoured than their U.S. counterparts with the new forms of work organization and jointness with management (Gindin 1989). The Canadians attempted to convince the UAW leadership of the long-run adverse implications of the concessions for the economic and social status of the workers, and for the representative role of the union, but were unsuccessful. The disagreements came to a head in 1984 when Canadians rejected the U.S. pattern negotiated at General Motors, staged a two-week-long strike, and were successful in achieving a more traditional settlement without profit sharing and lump sums. The Canadians later split, and formed the CAW in 1985. Since 1985, while the UAW has continued to follow the "new pattern" and become more deeply committed to partnership with management (see "Attachment C" in the 1987 National Agreement between General Motors and UAW; Herzenberg 1990), the CAW has become even more resolute in its opposition to the new management strategy.

As Table 2.9 shows, up to 1980, collective-bargaining outcomes for assembly plant workers of the Big Three firms were almost identical in the two countries. Since 1980, major divergences have arisen. The divergence in wage rates, employment security, work practices and work organization, and union–management relations, and their effect on the economic and industrial relations performance of the industry in Canada and the United States, are discussed below.

BASE WAGE RATES

The most fundamental collective-bargaining issue in the Canadian auto industry in the 1980s was contingent compensation in the form of lump-sum payments and profit sharing. As noted earlier, the Canadian region of the UAW vehemently opposed the lump-sum payments and profit sharing agreed to by the UAW in its collective agreements with General Motors, Ford, and Chrysler in the United States, and was able to negotiate a continuation of the long-standing annual improvement factor. Katz and Meltz (1991) examined the impact of profit sharing on auto workers' earnings in the United States and found that U.S. workers in assembly plants would have had much greater earnings had they not had profit sharing but an increase in base rate, as occurred in Canada. Assuming all other things equal, General Motors assemblers in the United States would have increased their cumulative pay by $13 402 between 1982 and 1989, Chrysler workers by $8721, and Ford workers by $1755. Only Ford workers have received any significant benefits from profit sharing, where bonuses have averaged over $2000 per year since 1984, compared to an average of $200 per year at General Motors and Chrysler (Holmes and Kumar 1991, Table 4).[5] By the fourth quarter of 1989, the base wage rate per hour was $2.09 higher in Canada (in Canadian dollars) than in the United States (in American dollars) for GM and Chrysler workers, and $2.08 for Ford (Katz and Meltz 1991; Holmes and Kumar 1991, Table 3).

EMPLOYMENT SECURITY

One of the reasons why the UAW did not oppose contingent compensation to the same extent as did the CAW leadership was the hope of achieving greater employment security and saving jobs (Herzenberg 1990). The UAW convinced its membership that the 1982 concessions pact would bring job security. The 1984 UAW contract with General Motors included an innovative $1 billion job-bank program (Perusek 1988). The job-bank program was further expanded in the 1987 and 1990 contracts. As a consequence of the UAW emphasis on job guarantees, the United States has more extensive employment-security provisions than Canada, including the Job Opportunity Bank, extended supplementary unemployment benefits (SUB), and a plant closure freeze since 1987. Layoffs are restricted, except as occasioned by market conditions, model change, or sale of a plant. The guarantees are, however, precarious because of continuing deterioration in market conditions and the accelerated pace of restructuring involving sale and closure of plants. The employment trends in the industry show that despite strong employment guarantees, assembly employment has declined on balance in the United States and increased in Canada (Industry, Science and Technology Canada 1991).

Job losses in the United States have been particularly heavy at the Big Three, where total employment since 1986 has declined by about 10 percent, largely as a result of cutbacks at General Motors (the company eliminated more than 100 000 jobs over the three-year period from 1986 to 1988). By contrast, employment in the Canadian subsidiaries of the Big Three increased slightly, from 72 637 in 1986 to 73 371 in 1988. Employment has remained steady at Ford Canada, declined at General Motors, and increased at Chrysler. Part of the employment decline in the United States is probably related to the older age of the factories, but part may also be related to the better performance of auto plants in Canada.

Canadian agreements provide for more income security (severance pay, pension indexing) than employment security, in addition to extended SUB, restrictions on outsourcing, and advance notice and consultation on plant closures and technological change available in both Canada and the United States. Workers are therefore less protected against layoffs in Canada than are their counterparts in the United States. The CAW has preferred income security to employment security in the belief that it is difficult for an enterprise to provide effective job security, and that, in the event of job loss, workers may be better off making their own decisions than having the employer decide for them.

WORK PRACTICES AND WORK ORGANIZATION

As part of their strategy to meet the increased foreign competition, the Big Three have embarked on a program to change work practices and work organization to provide management with greater flexibility in work scheduling, and to enhance employee involvement and participation in shop-floor decisions. Specific changes in work practices and work organization sought by management have included a reduction in the number of jobs classifications, provision for team systems of work, use of the pay-for-knowledge system for purposes of multiskilling, management discretion in the allocation and assignment of work, and flexibility in work schedules and shift work. Taken as a whole, the package of changes in work practices and work organization is designed to move toward a "world-class contract," as it is called at General Motors, or "modern operating agreements," as they are called at Chrysler. Whatever the nomenclature, the purpose is to improve flexibility and efficiency.

The results of a survey of plant practices at one of the Big Three conducted by Katz and Meltz (1989) show that the changes in work practices have been more widespread and favourable to management in the United States than in Canada. There are more job classifications in Canadian plants than in their U.S. counterparts (except for the skilled trades). Team systems are also less common in Canada, although flexibility in work rules has increased considerably. There is also a greater percentage of production workers in Canada than in to the United States who perform minor maintenance and have responsibility for inspection work. But, whereas changes in work organization and work practices have been formal in the United States, they have been more informal in Canada. The survey also points out that, in Canada, there has been a marked increase in informal employee participation and communication on productivity and quality issues. In the United States, however, participation has been more formal through contractual team concepts, employee-involvement mechanisms, and quality circles. The formal method gives little discretion to the union and is associated with a larger bureaucracy than is the informal method.

Table 2.10 contains some detailed comparisons of selected work practices in

Table 2.10
A Comparison of Assembly Plant Practices: United States and Canada, 1986

Practices	Assembly Plants—Canada			Assembly Plants—U.S.		
	Min	Max	Mean	Min	Max	Mean
1. Employee Participation and Communication						
a) meet on a regular basis in small groups to discuss production or quality problems.	10	100	50.0	0	100	50.7
b) track or are given statistical information on their work group's quality or productivity performance.	30	100	60.0	0	100	70.7
c) are given information on the competitive or economic conditions of the business on a regular basis.	30	100	66.0	0	100	90.7
d) attitudes are regularly assessed through surveys or are discussed regularly in group meetings.	0	50	20.0	0	100	27.9
e) receive formal training in group problem solving, decision making, and communications.	0	100	38.0	0	100	52.9
f) receive formal training in statistical process control techniques.	10	100	42.0	0	100	40.7
g) regularly utilize statistical process control techniques.	10	100	40.0	0	100	30.0
2. Orientation and Training						
How many hours of formal orientation typically are provided new production employees?	6	40	26.8	0	80	24.9
How many hours of formal training other than						

Table 2.10 (continued)

Practices	Assembly Plants—Canada			Assembly Plants—U.S.		
	Min	Max	Mean	Min	Max	Mean
orientation, on average, are provided:						
a) to new production employees?	8	40	33.6	0	104	26.4
b) to hourly employees already working in the plant?	8	40	33.6	0	160	31.1
3. New Technology						
Of those workers directly affected by new technology, what percent of workers or their elected representatives:						
a) discuss the new technology with management before the final design specifications are depicted?	10	100	68.0	0	100	26.4
b) discuss with management the way jobs or duties will be restructured by the new technology before the final decisions are made?	10	100	80.0	0	100	45.7
c) discuss the impact on jobs or employment levels after new technology has been selected or introduced?	0	100	78.0	0	100	77.9
d) are involved in planning and co-ordinating training for employees after new technology has been introduced?	20	100	84.0	0	100	55.0
4. Staff Levels						
How many company paid full-time union representatives function in your plant? (per 100 workers)	6 (0.25)	32 (1.47)	22.8 (0.82)	0 (0)	96 (5.20)	50.1 (1.47)

Table 2.10 (continued)

Practices	Assembly Plants—Canada			Assembly Plants—U.S.		
	Min	Max	Mean	Min	Max	Mean
How many salaried employees are there in the plant whose primary job is to interface on a regular basis with union reps? (per 100 workers)	6 (0.18)	8 (0.34)	7.4 (0.27)	5 (0.24)	36 (2.00)	19.4 (0.64)
How many levels of management exist in your manufacturing operation above the first line supervisors up to and including the plant manager?	3	4	3.6	3	6	4.8
How many first line supervisors are there? (per 100 workers)	83 (2.72)	200 (6.04)	123.6 (4.40)	41 (2.86)	590 (16.40)	207.7 (5.94)
5. The Organization of Work: Production/ Assembly Employees						
Employees are paid for the number of jobs they are able to perform rather than for the specific job performed on a given day.	0	0	0.0	0	100	20.7
Employees in a given work area are expected to learn the different jobs within their work area.	0	20	6.0	0	100	45.7
Employees are required to rotate across jobs in their work area sufficiently to maintain proficiency in those jobs.	0	20	6.0	0	100	27.1

Table 2.10 (continued)

Practices	Assembly Plants—Canada			Assembly Plants—U.S.		
	Min	Max	Mean	Min	Max	Mean
Employees in a given work area certify when their peers master new skill levels or job requirements.	0	0	0.0	0	90	6.4
Work assignments within a given work area regularly are made by employees (as a group) rather than by a supervisor.	0	10	2.0	0	90	20.0
Employees in a given work area regularly participate in training new workers in their area.	0	50	26.0	0	100	55.0
Employees in a given work area regularly maintain written records on:						
a) quality	10	30	20.0	0	100	29.3
b) costs	0	30	16.0	0	100	23.6
c) productivity	0	30	16.0	0	100	29.3
d) scrap	10	30	18.0	0	100	36.4
Employees have the responsibility to design, time, and lay out jobs in their work area.	0	20	6.0	0	100	20.7
Employees have the right to stop the line or production process to correct a problem.	0	10	4.0	0	100	40.7
Production/Assembly workers on occasion:						
a) set up and adjust their machines	0	10	4.0	0	100	26.4
b) perform minor maintenance	0	20	4.0	0	100	13.6
c) perform major maintenance	0	0	0.0	0	0	0.0
d) inspect their own work	20	100	70.0	0	100	75.7

Table 2.10 (continued)

Practices	Assembly Plants—Canada			Assembly Plants—U.S.		
	Min	Max	Mean	Min	Max	Mean
e) perform any necessary "repair" work;						
i) on their own work	20	100	56.0	0	100	52.9
ii) on the work of others	20	70	46.0	0	100	21.4
f) inspect the work of others	10	60	38.0	0	100	25.7
g) perform their own housekeeping	0	60	32.0	0	100	50.0

Notes: Min—Minimum observed response.
Max—Maximum observed response.
Mean—the average response, unless otherwise specified.
unl—unlimited. When specified as Min or Max, the most frequently reported response (mode) is reported.
Unless otherwise specified, most information is based on percentage of hourly rated workers.

Source: Unpublished results of the "North American Auto Plant Practices" survey conducted by Harry C. Katz, as referred to in Harry Katz and Noah M. Meltz, "Changing Work Practices and Productivity in the Auto Industry: A US–Canada Comparison," In *Industrial Relations Issues for the 1990s*, Proceedings of the 26th Conference of the Canadian Industrial Relations Association, June 4–6, 1989 (Quebec: Université Laval, 1989), Table 3.

assembly plants in Canada and the United States based on a survey conducted by Harry C. Katz (as reported in Katz and Meltz 1989). The figures show the same percentage of workers involved in regular meetings; more training, in general, and more statistical training, in particular, in Canada; more discussions in Canada on the introduction of new technology; a flatter organizational structure in Canada (fewer levels of management and fewer first-line supervisors per 100 workers), but more pay for job knowledge and greater responsibility for design, time, and layout of jobs, and greater freedom to stop the line in the United States. These results indicate that the United States is ahead in flexibility in some areas, but behind in the extent of discussions and training. These latter factors are likely to be among the reasons for the higher productivity levels in Canadian plants.

The slower pace and informal nature of changes in work rules and work organization since 1982 in Canada, as compared to the United States, is related to union approaches and strategies. In the United States, the collective agreements between the UAW and the Big Three have emphasized the need for work-rule changes and new forms of work organization as essential elements of the strategy to achieve competitive efficiency. In these contracts, the UAW has promised "to be responsible for innovative job assignments," to look seriously into drastically altering restrictive work rules, and to let employees open local agreements before their expirations (Perusek 1988, 330). This commitment was formalized in 1987 in the "Attachment C" (Memorandum of Understanding—Goals and Objectives of Job Security and Operational Effectiveness) of the National Collective Agreement between the UAW and General Motors Corporation (1987). The memorandum included an agreement to set up national and local job committees to "focus on cooperative efforts toward our common goal to improve the effectiveness of operations and remove barriers to improvements, increase job opportunities and fully utilize the workforce." Among the initiatives to be addressed by locals were the following: the establishment of a team concept and/or pay-for-knowledge wage structure; the examination of new forms of work organization, such as job assignments, relating to Just-in-Time or other quality-enhancement systems; a realignment in skilled classifications to a number of appropriate basic trades to support the needs of the operation or location; the implementation of skilled trades team concepts; and initiatives to reduce chronic absenteeism.

The Canadian Auto Workers has opposed formalization of a union role and commitment to changes in work practices and work organization. While supporting the introduction of new technology, the need for training and retraining, and importance of workplace improvements, the union has favoured evolutionary and incremental changes at the initiative of the locals. The CAW leadership's opposition to work-rule and work-organization changes stems from their belief that these changes are a form of "concessions" and have the potential for undermining the role of the union at the shop-floor level. The recently adopted CAW statement on reorganization of work (see Exhibit 2.1) acknowledges "the ambiguity of work organization issues that 'will not always be black and white' and emphasizes that union members will have to constantly analyze the implications of reorganization

EXHIBIT 2.1

CAW's Guidelines Concerning Its Relationship to Management

The workplace is changing, but the outcome of the changes is not predetermined. Much is new in the workplace, but what is not is that management has its agenda and we have ours. Management has articulated its program—packaged as the team concept—as empowering workers and reforming the workplace. The theme of industrial democracy is not new to us. Our union was born out of and continues to be built on demands for a more democratic workplace. And the barrier to workplace democracy continues to be management. Their obsession with getting more with less subordinates workers' rights and working conditions to a narrow preoccupation with reducing costs, reducing staff and eliminating any free time.

We reject managerial efforts, under whatever name, which jeopardize workers' rights, undermine workplace conditions and erode the independence of the union.

1. We reject the use of Japanese production methods which rigidly establish work standards and standard operations that limit worker autonomy and discretion on the job;
2. We reject the use of techniques such as Kaizening (pressure for continuous "improvement" where the result is speed-up, work intensification, and more stressful jobs);
3. We reject the introduction of alternative workplace structures and employees-based programs which purport to represent workers' interests while circumventing the union;
4. We reject efforts to shift compensation from wages to incentives and to individualize the rewards of productivity improvements;
5. We oppose the process of union nomination or joint appointees to new jobs created to perform company functions;
6. We oppose initiatives which undermine workers' solidarity like structures that require conformity to company determined objectives and divide workers into competing groups internally, nationally and internationally;
7. We oppose the use of peer pressure in company campaigns to discipline and regulate the behaviour of workers;
8. We oppose workplace reorganizations which threaten job security by subcontracting or transferring work outside the bargaining unit;
9. We oppose efforts to render workplaces so lean there's no place for workers with work-related, age-related or other disabilities;
10. We oppose efforts to involve and reward workers in the systematic elimination of jobs or the disciplining of other works; and
11. We oppose workplace changes that limit mobility, weaken transfer rights and erode seniority provision.

We support efforts to involve and empower workers, to increase worker dignity, to produce quality products with pride, to make jobs more rewarding and workplaces more democratic. These objectives will be achieved through *our own agenda for change,* our own demands around:

Exhibit 2.1 (continued)

—training
—technology
—improving jobs
—improving the work environment
—guaranteeing health and safety
—strengthening mobility rights
—strengthening affirmative action
—strengthening the union.

Source: Canadian Auto Workers, CAW *Statement on the Reorganization of Work* (North York,ON: CAW
Research Department, 1989).

in specific contexts" (Herzenberg 1990).   Notwithstanding its skepticism, the
union has accepted changes in work organization, including team work and consolidation of job classifications, at a number of assembly and vehicle parts plants.
The examples include General Motors's Ste.-Thérèse and Oshawa plants,
Chrysler's Bramalea plant, Ford of Canada's Windsor plant, CAMI, and Magna's
parts plant. "However, while work practices have changed they have done so without either the pay-for-knowledge wage structures or a significant erosion of seniority rights with respect to job allocations, and with little job rotation"(Holmes
and Kumar 1991, 37).

UNION-MANAGEMENT RELATIONS

The sharpest divergence between the CAW and the UAW has been in the nature of
union–management relationships.   Whereas the relationship in Canada continues
to be adversarial, with emphasis on incremental and evolutionary joint initiatives
for working together on issues of mutual interest, co-operation and partnership between union and management has become a norm in the United States.   The
UAW has clearly moved from its historical adversarial orientation to co-operation,
partnership, or jointness with management (Herzenberg 1990).   The shift is evident in a host of UAW activities, particularly at General Motors Corporation.
These include hierarchies of joint labour–managment committees under "Attachment C"; quality network councils ("dedicated to finding ways of improving quality"); a jointly administered Human Resource Center near Detroit for training and
education activities, and a wide array of other joint programs (e.g., substance-
abuse prevention and an absentee-control program).   The best example is the
UAW's direct involvement in the administration of General Motor's Saturn subsidiary.   The preamble to the Memorandum of Agreement between the corporation and the UAW states:

> Saturn and the Union . . . recognized the necessity of developing a co-
> operative problem-solving relationship between management and the
> Union.   With the understanding that this philosophy of total coopera-

tion offers an opportunity to forge a new relationship, and demonstrate that a competitive, world class vehicle could be manufactured in
the United States. (Memorandum of Agreement 1985, 1–2)

The CAW views the Saturn Model as potentially destructive for the union's role,
and remains suspicious of management initiatives toward union–management
co-operation and partnership. The union continues to espouse an adversarial
labour-relations culture with the conviction that the interests of labour and management are not inherently the same, particularly on economic issues. Robert
White, the president of the CAW, unambiguously articulates his union's relationship with management in the CAW *Statement on the Reorganization of Work*
(1989, 1):

> The CAW relationship with the majority of employers with whom we
> have collective agreements is very sound. At times we have similar
> objectives. But clearly the role of the union is to pursue the goals of
> the workers, including a more democratic workplace with more worker
> involvement and control, better wages, hours of work and benefits.
> Many times these goals conflict with employer interests. The state-
> ment also reaffirms our committment to building quality products and
> providing quality services. It in no way interferes with worker input to
> achieve these objectives . . . we will not, however, support manage-
> ment attempts to use the team concepts or quality circles, to manage
> the workplace by stress, to introduce speed up, or to encourage workers
> to discipline each other. We do not accept the inference that we are
> part of management's team.

However, within the adversarial framework, the union continues to expand its
participation in joint programs that it considers are of mutual benefit. Examples
of participation negotiated at the Big Three in Canada include the apprentice
training programs, health and safety, employee assistance and counselling, affirmative action, human rights, and literacy training. The union emphasizes strict adherence to the union agenda for protecting and advancing the interests of workers,
but is willing to discuss workplace changes whenever required.

INDUSTRIAL RELATIONS AND ECONOMIC PERFORMANCE

Although the nature of the union–managment relationship has diverged sharply
in the two countries, the performance indicators show a stable labour relations climate in the industry on both sides of the border. As Katz and Meltz (1989) show,
grievance rates and employee discipline rates—the two important indicators of industrial relations performance—are lower in Canadian plants than in their U.S.
equivalents. The Canadian absenteeism rate, another industrial relations performance indicator, however, remains higher.[6] Similarly, Katz and Meltz point out

that, despite the emphasis on adversarialism in Canada, compared with formal union–management co-operation and partnership in the United States, the incidence of consultation and discussion on new technology and related changes in production methods, training and retraining, and on productivity and quality issues, has been higher in Canada than in the United States (see Table 2.10). Katz and Meltz (1989) also note that Canadian plants, both assembly and component parts, are equally, or more, productive and efficient—in terms of labour productivity, number of supervisors per worker, and product quality—as the U.S. plants.

Explaining the Divergence

The pattern of divergence in collective-bargaining approaches and outcomes in the industry can be explained by differences in the economic and political environment, the bargaining processes, and union and management strategies (Gindin 1989; Holmes and Rusonik 1990; Holmes and Kumar 1991; Herzenberg 1990).

ENVIRONMENT

The differences between the American and Canadian economic and political environment in the 1980s partly explain why the UAW in the United States accepted the new management strategy of flexible compensation and work arrangements, new forms of work organization, and a commitment toward co-operation and participation, and the Canadians opposed it. First, while the Canadian industry is about one-seventh the size of the U.S. industry in terms of total North American output, and accounts for 16 percent of total industry employment, most Canadian plants are relatively new, more capital intensive, and highly modernized. They are rated highly in both efficiency and product quality. Canada has also enjoyed a labour cost advantage over the United States in hourly compensation costs attributable to a favourable exchange rate and lower health care costs because of Canada's publicly funded medicare system.[7] Second, the downturn in industry production and sales during the period 1978–82, as a result of the serious recession and the rising Japanese imports, was far more severe in the United States than in Canada. Employment at the Big Three in the United States was cut by one-third, from 1.0 million in 1978 to 661 000 in 1982. In Canada, over the same period, job losses at the Big Three totalled less than 15 000 or 20 percent of the total work force. Gindin (1989, 64) notes that the high level of layoffs at the beginning of the 1980s left U.S. auto workers particularly demoralized.

While the severity of job losses and noncompetitive costs may explain why the UAW accepted the management agenda in order to save jobs, differences in the nature of the labour movement and the political environment were also factors in creating the sharply different approaches and strategies adopted by union leaders in the two countries. In the United States, the labour movement is perceived as weak, isolated from other social groups, and lacking solidarity and a political voice (Kumar 1991). The Canadian labour movement in comparison, is relatively strong and united, and has close ties with the NDP and community and social groups (Kumar and Ryan 1988; Meltz 1990). Canadian unions in 1982 opposed "concessions" of any kind and demonstrated considerable solidarity in enforcing resolution. The CAW, in opposing the industry's corporate agenda of flexibility, was able to withstand the pressure, in part, because of the labour movement's solidarity. The UAW did not have these protections and the support needed to reject management's agenda. Not only could it not rely on the labour movement for support to fight "concessions," it also faced an unsympathetic, anti-labour government.

BARGAINING PROCESS

Bargaining processes and structures also differ in Canada and the United States. The bargaining agenda in the United States is dictated by the UAW staff, with little input from locals; in Canada, bargaining demands are formulated after extensive consultation with locals. Locals are less powerful in influencing the International Executive in the United States than in Canada, where locals have significant input into decision making through a network of policy councils (Yates 1988; Perusek 1988).

Bargaining in both Canada and the United States is conducted at two levels: co-ordinated bargaining for major economic and strategic-enterprise policy issues through a Master Contract, and bargaining at the local level for plant-level matters, such as job classifications, transfer rights, distribution of overtime, and work organization issues. The major difference is that, while in Canada both the Master and local agreements are negotiated simultaneously, in the United States they have been negotiated separately since 1982, when the UAW agreed to let employers open local contracts. In the past ten years, there has been a significant variation in work rules, work organization, and working conditions in the U.S. plants because of the whipsawing between locals. Canadian local agreements are relatively more uniform, with only a few exceptions, such as the GM plant in Ste.-Thérèse, Quebec, and the CAMI plant (Suzuki–GM) in Ingersoll, Ontario.

Another difference between the two countries relates to the negotiating process. In the United States, negotiations are conducted by the UAW staff; in Canada, elected officials on the bargaining committee are fully responsible for bargaining, with the assistance of the staff.

UNION GOALS AND APPROACHES

The CAW is a very strong, aggressive, and militant social union, with a young and dynamic leadership and well-defined economic, social, and political goals. In addition to hard bargaining for improved wages and working conditions, the union is actively engaged in legislative lobbying for better employment standards and greater worker protection, in social and political activities on working-class issues, and in building union solidarity and community alliances. The CAW leaders have close ties with the NDP, which is of particular importance since the election in the fall of 1990 of an NDP government in the province of Ontario, where most of the auto industry is located.

The CAW is viewed as a more democratic union than the UAW (Herzenberg 1990; Perusek 1988). It fosters greater internal democracy through its decentralized structures, and more automony to locals through a network of consultative councils at the regional, industry, and enterprise level. Through these councils, elected officials are able to wield greater influence in decision making (Yates 1988; Herzenberg 1990).

The union espouses an adversarial culture, and believes in an incremental and evolutionary approach to consultation and co-operation on restructuring. (For a detailed list of the CAW's guidelines concerning its relationships to management, see Exhibit 2.1.) While opposed to contingent compensation, new forms of work organization, and direct participation in management decision making, the union has favoured active involvement with management at the industry level. The union believes that QWL is primarily a management device to undermine the role of the union. It is pragmatic, however, and stresses the merits of an evolutionary and incremental change rather than dramatic solutions, and participates in joint programs (called "working together initiatives") on such worker issues as training, health and safety, drug and alcoholic abuse, affirmative action, and human-rights and literacy training. The union also has provisionally supported the team concept in both greenfield and old plants on an experimental basis.

Unlike the CAW, the UAW over the years, has become more singularly a business union, largely preoccupied with job-security issues to the neglect of organizing and sociopolitical activities (Herzenberg 1990). The UAW, in its quest to save jobs, has become increasingly supportive of management goals of flexibility through contingent compensation and new forms of work organization. The present leadership sees co-operation and partnership with management as the only way to save jobs and for the industry to compete internationally. In the process, the union has become more bureaucratic and its leadership somewhat removed from the rank and file, and highly defensive, leading to a growing dissension in the rank and file under the New Directions for Labour Movement, which is inspired by the Canadian experience (Herzenberg 1990; Perusek 1988).

MANAGEMENT APPROACHES

While the industry is dominated by the Big Three, management approaches appear to differ in the two countries. Although, in both countries, the emphasis is on restructuring through cost rationalization, higher productivity, and greater employee involvement, Canadian management appears more pragmatic regarding co-operation and participation issues. Unlike the U.S. management, which has actively pursued new patterns of human-resource management and joint participation of unions in facilitating employment rationalization and workplace organization changes, Canadian management has adopted an incremental, evolutionary, and informal approach to change. It is working together with the union on issues of mutual concern in the hope that the favourable experience will lead to an extension of participation activities (Curd 1988). Canadian management has not pushed the union into accepting new forms of work organization or contingent compensation schemes as long as the plants continue to show improved productivity and product quality.

IMPLICATIONS OF THE DIVERGENCE

It would appear from our analysis that, at least up to the beginning of the 1990s, social unionism and the adversarial union culture espoused by the Canadian Auto Workers (CAW) were not incompatible with the economic goals of efficiency and flexibility. Indeed, the experience leads us to conclude that social unionism can be not only more effective in terms of economic and social responses but also a viable approach to reconciling management's need for greater flexibility and labour's desire for employment and institutional security. The experience of the 1980s shows that, in the Canadian context, an incremental, evolutionary approach based on mutual recognition of each other's goals and objectives, and working together on issues of mutual concern, may produce more stable results than the discreet change from an adversarial system to a system of corporatism with formal co-operation and participation with management. Finally, the growing divergence in the labour relations systems of Canada and the United States indicates that there are no unique solutions to improvements in efficiency and product quality. The same bottom line could be achieved by different approaches and diverse institutional frameworks. For policy makers the lessons are that industrial relations problems, at least in this industry, can be solved with a mix of approaches particular to Canada, developed in Canada, and focussed on collective bargaining.

The Outlook for the 1990s

The medium-term outlook for labour relations in the automobile industry is clouded with many uncertainties. Public and private forecasts suggest that the industry is approaching a serious supply and demand imbalance. Retail sales of motor vehicles, passenger cars, and trucks, in both Canada and the United States, have been declining since 1988, partly as a result of the recession. There is also a growing realization that vehicle markets in both countries are approaching satura-

tion and that vehicle sales are unlikely to grow at more than 1 to 2 percent annually over the 1990s (Industry, Science and Technology Canada 1989). However,
the production capacity of both North American manufacturers and Asian transplants has been increasing. According to a federal government analysis, the total
North American vehicle production capacity increased from 13.5 million cars and
trucks in the 1988 model year to 14.3 million vehicles in 1990; up from 11.48 million to 11.89 million in the United States, and from 2.02 million to 2.41 million
in Canada. Most of this increase is attributable to the establishment of Asian
transplants in both countries and the Big Three expansion in Canada. Production
at the Big Three in the United States dropped markedly as a result of the closure
of six General Motors and Chrysler plants (Industry, Science and Technology
Canada 1989).

By 1993, the total North American production capacity is expected to be 15.58
million, 9 percent higher than in 1990 and 15 percent greater than the 1988 level.
In Canada, the total production of cars and trucks for the 1993 model year is estimated to be 2.59 million, compared with 2.41 million units in 1990 and 2.02 million in 1988. The federal Industry, Trade and Technology Canada (1989)
estimates suggest that at the current rate of import penetration (30 percent), there
will be between 1.0 million and 2.19 million units of excess passenger car production capacity by 1993. No overcapacity is forecast for truck production because of
continuing high demand and low levels of imports in this segment.

The overcapacity, at least over the short-term or medium-term horizon, is
bound to lead to lower rates of capacity utilization and/or plant closures, resulting
in major layoffs in Canada. The recent increase in temporary layoffs at Big Three
plants provides evidence of the growing divergence between capacity and the demand for vehicles. In December 1990, a total of 10 700 of 35 000 General Motors
of Canada and 2600 Chrysler Canada workers were reported on temporary layoff
(Roy 1991).

The overcapacity issue is likely to produce intense pressures on the Canadian
Auto Workers to modify its position on contingent compensation, new forms of
work organization, and union–management "co-operation" to improve productivity and product quality. The 1991 General Motors of Canada statement, asking
the union "to come up with plans to make the Oshawa line more competitive" to
avoid a possible transfer in 1995 of the production of Lumina and Regal models at
the No. 2 Oshawa, Ontario car plant to a recently upgraded Georgia plant, may be
a forerunner of the kind of pressures the union is likely to face. If the Oshawa
plant does not get a new car line beyond 1995, about 4000 jobs could be lost. Although General Motors of Canada has not yet made the threat, or demanded any
explicit concessions, the CAW knows that the company's intentions are serious
(*Globe and Mail*, July 5, 1991, B12). The persistent high value of the Canadian
dollar in 1990–1991 and the rising payroll costs of legislated programs (e.g., Canadian Pension Plan, Unemployment Insurance, worker compensation, and medicare), by eroding the Canadian labour cost advantage, are also expected to
reinforce demands for "concessions."

Rising levels of imports, particularly the captive imports, is another source of uncertainty facing the industry, and adding to the growing divergence between production capacity and demand for motor vehicles. The level of imports, especially in the passenger car segment, has remained high throughout the 1980s in spite of the industry restructuring and the arrival of Asian transplants. The share of foreign imports of new passenger cars has doubled, from 17 percent in 1980 to 34 percent in 1990.[8]

The final source of uncertainty is the free-trade agreement between Canada and the United States (FTA) that came into effect January 1, 1989, and the trilateral negotiations between Canada, Mexico, and the United States for a "North American Free Trade Zone" that began in early 1991. While the FTA removes the duty on automobiles entering Canada from the United States by 1998, and the U.S. automobile companies will no longer have to meet the sales/production ratios and the Canadian Value Added (CVA) percentages required under the Auto Pact, there will continue to be incentives to maintain Auto Pact standing after 1998. Under the FTA, the right to duty-free importation from third countries is restricted to the original Auto Pact members, so that the "transplants," with the possible exception of CAMI Automotive Inc., operate under less attractive conditions by being permanently excluded from the Auto Pact (MacDonald 1989, 10).

The FTA also terminates, by 1996, Canadian duty-remission programs designed to attract foreign investment and tied to the value added contained in production in Canada,[9] and enhances the Big Three's ability to move capital and production to the United States and other countries, thus adding to their bargaining power *vis-à-vis* the CAW.

The trilaterial negotiations for the free-trade pact between Canada, Mexico, and the United States are expected to strengthen the Big Three's economic power. The Big Three have made large investments in the Mexican automobile industry. Mexico has become an increasingly important source of imports, particularly of motor vehicle parts and accessories. Although the potential effects of a North American Free Trade Agreement (NAFTA) are still uncertain, the short-run impacts on the auto industry are likely to be minimal for two reasons. First, the volume of Mexican auto imports is still very low. And second, there is already a *de facto* free trade in automotive products between Canada and Mexico. Most Mexican auto imports are through the Big Three and, therefore, enter duty free under the terms of the Auto Pact and the FTA. Mexican exporters not covered by the Auto Pact or the FTA pay very little effective duty on exports to Canada (Investment Canada 1991, 16–20). Notwithstanding the *de facto* free trade in auto products between Canada, Mexico, and the United States, the NAFTA will further enhance the Big Three's ability to shift production from Canada to Mexico if Canada loses its labour cost advantage for any reason (e.g., due to a high exchange value of the Canadian dollar, poor productivity performance, or higher wage and benefit costs). The trilateral pact is also bound to add to the competitive pressures in an industry that has been losing market share to the imports for almost two decades, thereby increasing the likelihood in the 1990s of more plant closures or plant relocations to outside Canada.

In summary, the Canadian auto industry would appear to face more difficult economic prospects in the 1990s than in the 1980s, including overcapacity and heightened competition at home and abroad. While there may be some sizable investment in the industry in this decade, it seems less likely that the investment will be of the absolute and relative magnitude that occurred in the 1980s. That suggests new challenges for the industrial relations system. Within this competitive environment, employment in the industry may decrease rather than rebound after the 1990–91 recession, the way it did after the 1981–82 recession. The pragmatic approach the CAW has taken, focussing on contingent benefits in the form of enhanced severance and pension payments and reduction in working hours, is ideally suited to a contraction of the industry. How severe the employment contraction will be depends on the ability of the union and the companies to restructure their relationships to adapt to the competitive pressures. The issues for the future include whether the adversarial but pragmatic "working together" approach adopted by the CAW toward management of the Big Three auto firms, in a framework of social unionism, will endure in the intense competitive environment of the 1990s; whether the CAW will be able to withstand renewed employer demands for flexibility in compensation and work arrangements in the FTA and NAFTA environment; and whether the CAW will be able to provide the same level of benefits to its members in the 1990s as it did in the 1980s.

REFERENCES

Canadian Auto Workers. 1989. CAW *Statement on the Reorganization of Work*, North York, ON: CAW Research Department.

———. 1990. *A New Decade—Challenging the Corporate Agenda: Our Response. Report to the National Collective Bargaining and Political Action Convention*, May 29–June 1, 1990. North York, ON: Canadian Auto Workers.

Coates, Mary Lou, David Arrowsmith, and Melanie Courchene. 1989. *The Current Industrial Relations Scene in Canada: The Labour Movement and Trade Unionism Reference Tables.* Kingston, ON: Industrial Relations Centre, Queen's University.

Côté, Michel. 1989. "The Canadian Auto Industry, 1978–1986." In Statistics Canada, *Perspectives on Labour and Income*, Catalogue 75-001E. Ottawa: Minister of Supply and Services, Autumn. 7–18.

Curd, Frederick, Jr. 1988. "Labour Relations at General Motors of Canada." In P. Kumar, ed., *Industrial Relations Issues in the 1980s: Issues and Implications*. Kingston, ON: Industrial Relations Centre, Queen's University. 7–10.

General Motors of Canada. 1989. *1988: In Review*, Oshawa, ON: General Motors of Canada Limited.

Gindin, Sam. 1989. "Breaking Away: The Transformation of the Canadian Auto Workers." *Studies in Political Economy* 29:63–89.

Herzenberg, Stephen. 1990. "Towards a Cooperative Commonwealth? Labor and Restructuring in the U.S. and Canadian Auto Industries," Ph.D. Dissertation, Department of Economics, Massachusetts Institute of Technology.

Holmes, John and Anthony Rusonik. 1990. "The Breakup of an International Labour Union: Uneven Developments in the North American Auto Industry and the Schism in the UAW." *Queen's Papers in Industrial Relations*, 1990–2, Kingston, ON: Industrial Relations Centre, Queen's University.

Holmes, John, and Pradeep Kumar. 1991. "Divergent Paths: Restructuring in the North American Automobile Industry." *Queen's Papers in Industrial Relations*, 1991–4. Kingston, ON: Industrial Relations Centre, Queen's University.

Industry, Science and Technology Canada. 1989. *Restructuring in the North American Automotive Industry.* 2nd ed. Ottawa.

———. 1990. *Statistical Review of the Canadian Automotive Industry: 1989*, Ottawa.

———. 1991. *Statistical Review of the Canadian Automotive Industry: 1990*, Ottawa.

Investment Canada. 1991. *The Opportunities and Challenges of North American Free Trade: A Canadian Perspective*, Working Paper No. 7 (April). Ottawa.

Katz, Harry, and Noah M. Meltz. 1989. "Changing work practices and productivity in the auto industry: A U.S.–Canada comparison." Proceedings of the 26th Conference of the

Canadian Industrial Relations Association, Industrial Relations Issues for the 1990s, edited by Michel Grant, June 4–6, Université Laval: Québec, 388–396.

———. 1991. "Profit Sharing and Auto Workers' Earnings: The United States vs. Canada." *Relations Industrielles/Industrial Relations* 42/3: 513–30.

Katz, Harry C. 1985. *Shifting Gears: Changing Labor Relations in the U.S. Automobile Industry.* Cambridge, MA: MIT Press.

———. 1987. "Automobiles." In David B. Lipskey and Clifford B. Donn, eds., *Collective Bargaining in American Industry.* Lexington, MA: D.C. Heath and Company. 13–53.

Kumar, Pradeep. 1991. "Industrial Relations in Canada and the United States: From Uniformity to Divergence." *Queen's Papers in Industrial Relations, 1991–92.* Kingston, ON: Industrial Relations Centre, Queen's University.

Kumar, Pradeep, Mary Lou Coates, and David Arrowsmith. 1986. *The Current Industrial Relations Scene in Canada.* Kingston, ON: Industrial Relations Centre, Queen's University.

Kumar, Pradeep, and Dennis Ryan. 1988. *Canadian Union Movement in the 1980's: Perspectives from Union Leaders,* Research and Current Issues Series No. 53. Kingston, ON: Industrial Relations Centre, Queen's University.

MacDonald, Neil D. 1989. "Will the Free Trade Deal Drive a Gaping Hole Through the Auto Pact?" *Policy Options.* 10/1 (January-February): 10–17.

Meltz, Noah M. 1990. "Unionism in Canada, U.S.: On Parallel Treadmills?" *Forum for Applied Research and Public Policy.* 5/4: 46–52.

Memorandum of Agreement Between Saturn Corporation and the UAW (July 1985).

Perry, Ross. 1982. *The Future of Canada's Auto Industry.* Toronto: James Lorimer & Company.

Perusek, G. 1988. "The Internal Politics of the United Automobile Workers, 1967–1985," Ph.D. Thesis, University of Chicago.

Roy, Francine. 1991. "Recent Trends in the Automotive Industry." *Canadian Economic Observer,* January: 4.1–4.14.

Taskforce on the Automotive Industries Human Resources. 1986. *Automotive: Why People Count.* Ottawa: Supply and Services Canada.

Taskforce on the Canadian Motor Vehicle and Automotive Parts Industries. 1983. *An Automotive Strategy for Canada.* Ottawa: Minister of Supply and Services.

Yates, C. 1988. "From Plant to Politics: The Canadian UAW, 1936–1984," Ph.D. Thesis, Carleton University.

ENDNOTES

1. This essay is part of a research project undertaken by Harry C. Katz (Cornell University) and Noah M. Meltz under the International Motor Vehicle Program, Massachusetts Institute of Technology, and by Pradeep Kumar and John Holmes (Queen's University) under the U.S.–Canada Relationship Project, funded by the Donner Foundation and the Ontario Ministry of Labour. The authors are grateful to the participants of the Industrial Relations in Canadian Industry Conference, held at Queen's University in April 1991, for their helpful comments and suggestions based on the preliminary draft.

2. These estimates are similar to those from Statistics Canada's Labour Market Activity Survey in 1989. Based on survey data, 60 percent of all employees in the transportation equipment industry were unionized. The largest component of transportation equipment manufacturing is the automobile industry (Statistics Canada, unpublished special tabulation).

3. According to an estimate, the unit cost of producing a vehicle in Canada was nearly five times that in Japan in 1981 ($494 in Japan compared to $2376 in Canada, expressed in Canadian currency). Total hourly compensation in the Japanese auto industry ($9.32 Cdn) was about 38 percent less than the Canadian level ($15.02 Cdn). Similarly, the estimated person-hours per vehicle were 53 in Japan and 142 in Canada and the United States (Perry 1982, 35). According to Holmes and Kumar (1991), the "competitive cost crisis" was related to both the deficient corporate management strategy and the "inflexible" collective-bargaining system. They observe:

    > Throughout the 1950s and 1960s, the annual increases in base wage-rates had been financed out of sustained increases in labour productivity. Labour productivity growth, however, stagnated in the early 1970s and for over a decade showed no signs of recovery. Coupled with contractual annual real wage increases, which had become an entrenched feature of post-war pattern bargaining in the auto industry, the poor productivity performance led to rapidly escalating unit costs, further weakening the international competitiveness of North American auto-makers. (Homes and Kumar 1991, 9)

4   General Motors plans to close the Scarborough, Ontario, van plant in 1992, and there is some uncertainty about whether the recently refurbished Oshawa No. 2 car plant will remain in operation after 1995.

5   Katz and Meltz (1991, 520–21) report average profit sharing between 1984 and 1989 of $2154 at Ford, $538 at Chrysler, and $191 at General Motors. The difference between the figure for Chrysler shown here and that of under $200 indicated by Holmes and Kumar (1991) is attributable to variations in the designation of the lump-sum payments in lieu of profit sharing for 1985–88.

6   The differences in absenteeism rates are attributed, particularly in the case of General Motors, to the system of penalties and rewards in the United States. For example, the UAW–GM agreement in 1990 included an attendance control program focussing on: (1) counselling and other assistance after eight days of absences within twelve months; (2) a five-step progressive discipline procedure after sixteen absences, culminating in discharge at the fifth occurrence of absence; and (3) an attendance bonus award of

$600 a year for perfect attendance in the form of a Christmas Bonus. No such agreement provisions exist in Canada.

7   According to an estimate (Holmes and Kumar 1991), compensation per hour in 1986 in Canada (in U.S. dollars), was $16.34 ($22.71 in Canadian dollars), compared to $24.01 in the United States. Payroll costs in Canada (in national currencies) were $1.00 per hour higher, but benefit costs were $2.23 an hour less than in the United States. Differences in exchange value, however, accounted for over 80 percent of the compensation cost differential. Katz and Meltz (1991, 526) used exchange rates to calculate purchasing-power-parity earnings in the United States and Canada and found that earnings of Canadian workers in U.S. dollar terms were below those of auto workers in the United States in both 1982 and 1989, but the gap had narrowed from 15 to 9 percent at Ford and 6 percent at GM and Chrysler. The industry in Canada also enjoyed protection as a result of the built-in safeguards under the Auto Pact.

8   The captive imports—vehicles imported into North America by the Big Three—have accounted for a larger proportion of the overall increase in imports. They comprised 5.9 percent of the car sales and 2.6 percent of commercial vehicle sales in 1989 (Roy 1991). As Roy (1991, 4.12–4.13) points out: "The increase is attributable to a proliferation of new foreign models marketed by American companies in the past few years . . . . Some of the . . . captive imports are the Isuzu I-Mark marketed by Chevrolet as Spectrum; the Mercury Tracer assembled in Taiwan by Lio Ho, a Ford subsidiary; GM Lemans and Optima, manufactured in Korea by Dacwoo; and a number of Mitsubishi products made in Thailand for Chrysler." Mexico is another source of rising captive imports by the Big Three.

9   The duty-remission programs, which made possible the setting up of the Canadian plants of Toyota, Honda, Hyundai, and CAMI, allowed the company to import an amount of its products duty-free, based on the Canadian value added in the products it exported, with the amount related to their progress toward Auto Pact status. The FTA provides that existing remissions cannot be extended to additional recipients, or expanded, or extended where such remissions apply to goods imported from other countries and are tied to performance requirements on automotive and other goods. Duty remissions earned through parts exports to the United States are ruled out, and will be terminated by 1998. Under the FTA's new rules of origin, 50 percent of the direct production costs of any vehicle (70 percent requirement on the old Auto Pact basis) traded under the FTA will have to be incurred in Canada and the United States to qualify for duty-free treatment.

Chapter

3

INDUSTRIAL RELATIONS IN THE CANADIAN STEEL INDUSTRY

Anil Verma
Peter Warrian[1]

*I*n the early 1950s, the Canadian steel industry was a relatively inefficient producer and a minor player in the world market (Barnett and Schorsch 1983). Over the next twenty years, the industry expanded and modernized, assisted by a favourable tax regime and public policy that recognized the status of the sector as vital to Canadian postwar industrial development. By the late 1960s, Canadian firms were as competitive as their major U.S. counterparts in many product lines (Hogan 1983). During the 1970s—in retrospect, the golden era of the industry— the Canadian steel industry was the most profitable in the world, overtaking its U.S. counterpart in both productivity and profitability.

The 1980s brought an initial downturn, along with tougher competition from abroad, which intensified over the decade. Although the industry weathered the recession of 1981–83 reasonably well, several factors had conspired by the end of the decade to shake the industry to its very foundations. The U.S. industry went through large-scale restructuring to improve its productivity substantially. By the late 1980s, U.S. producers had gained better access to Canadian markets under the Canada–U.S. Free Trade Agreement (FTA), even as the rising value of the Canadian dollar made Candian steel less attractive to foreign buyers. More competition came from other offshore firms, particularly from those in Asia. By 1990, macroeconomic conditions turned unfavourable: high interest rates, a higher Canadian dollar, and a recession in 1990, all hampered the industry's ability to compete. In addition to these adversities, the industry withstood two major strikes in 1990— one at Algoma and another at Stelco—each lasting approximately thirteen weeks.

By 1991, the once-proud Canadian steel industry was under siege. Even as it faced the need to further upgrade its plant and equipment to maintain its competitive position, it had to cope with gloomy forecasts of declining domestic demand over the next five years. Given its high labour costs, the industry must continually improve productivity and seek specialized, high-value-added niches in the market to survive. Although some changes and restructuring took place during the 1980s in response to economic pressures, further restructuring is essential if the industry is to remain viable.

As the industry searches for a new competitive paradigm for the 1990s, it is clear that industrial relations and human-resource policies and practices will form a key part of any formula for success. The evidence lies in the pressures facing labour–management relations to respond to the challenge of a changing environment. Both parties must demonstrate that they can successfully make the transition from a system of workplace governance based on a low-trust relationship, which served them well, nonetheless, in the past, to one that will address the needs of a more demanding marketplace in the future. The ultimate success of the industry depends, in large measure, on the choices that the parties make about their relationship and the rules they jointly make to facilitate steelmaking in Canada.

This essay attempts to describe and understand the developments in the steel industry, in general, and to identify the role of industrial relations policies in the industry's successes and failures, in particular. Our hope is that this analysis will help identify the strategic choices that both labour and management face as they cope with difficult restructuring decisions.

This essay is organized into four sections. First, we provide an overview of the industry and discuss the North American economic and technological environment in which Canadian steel companies largely compete. In the next two sections, we describe each of the parties to the employment relationship and the process and outcomes of collective bargaining. In the last section, we discuss the emerging issues and implications for the industry of labour and management making certain choices in industrial relations and human-resource policies.

*T*he Canadian Steel Industry

STEEL FIRMS

In 1990, there were twelve companies making raw steel in Canada, of whom three were integrated iron and steel producers, i.e., producers extracting metal from ore. The three largest firms—Stelco, Dofasco, and Algoma—accounted for nearly 70 percent of the steel produced in 1990. On August 19, 1988, Algoma became a wholly owned subsidiary of Dofasco, leading to further concentration in the industry. Thus, the industry is, in fact, dominated by the two giants—Stelco

Table 3.1
Major Steel Companies in Canada: A Profile (1989)

Company	Primary Location	Ownership	Steel-making Process^a	Raw Steel Output (000 tons)	No. of Employees	Major Unions	Principal Products^b
Algoma Steel	Ontario	Dofasco	BF/BOF	2788	6 132	USWA	B,P,S,SH
Dofasco Inc.	Ontario	Widely held	BF/BOF	7242	22 500	NU	P,SH
QIT-Fer et Titane	Quebec	BP America	EF	277	2 000	CSN	I
Sidbec-Dosco Ltée.	Quebec	Prov. of Quebec	EF	1485	2 700	USWA	B,P,SH,S
Stelco Inc.	Ontario	Widely held	BF/BOF/EF	4729	16 147	USWA	B,P,SH,S
Sydney Steel Corp. (Sysco)^d	Nova Scotia	Prov. of Nova Scotia	EF	110	850	USWA	I,S
Atlas Stainless Steel	Quebec	Sammi (Korea)	EF	260	450	CNTU	B,SH
Courtice Steel	Ontario	Widely held	EF	149	285	USWA	I,B
Ipsco Inc.	Saskatchewan/B.C.	Widely held	EF	775.8^c	1 692	USWA	B,P,SH,S
Ivaco Inc.	Ontario	Widely held	EF	NA	4 881	USWA	B
Lake Ontario Steel (Lasco)	Ontario	Co-Steel Inc.	EF	750^c	800	USWA	B,S
Manitoba Rolling Mills	Manitoba	Canam Manac	EF	250	680	USWA	B,S
Slater Steels	Ontario & Quebec	Slater Industries Inc.	EF	250	640	USWA	B,s,Spring Steels

Notes: ^a BF—Blast Furnace; BOF—Basic Oxygen Furnace; EF—Electric Furnace; OH—Open Hearth Furnace
^b I—Intermediate products (ingots, billets, etc.); B—Bars and rods; P—Pipes and Tubes; S—Structurals; Sh—Sheets
^c Shipped tons
^d In 1989, Sysco was shut down for a six-month period to complete modernization of its plant.

Sources: Annual Reports; Financial Post Cards; Some data supplied by firms on request.

and Dofasco. Table 3.1 shows an overview of twelve major companies in the industry. Most of Canada's steel is produced in Ontario (80 percent) and Quebec (10 percent), with firms in Nova Scotia (Sysco) and the West (Ipsco) accounting for the rest (Litvak and Maule 1985).

A number of Canadian producers recycle steel by melting scrap in electric steel furnaces. The major producers in this category are: Sysco, owned by the Province of Nova Scotia; Atlas Specialty and Stainless Steels; Courtice Steel; Ipsco; Ivaco; Lasco; Slater Steels; Manitoba Rolling Mills; and Sidbec-Dosco, owned by the Province of Quebec. Sysco, an integrated producer at one time, phased out its open-hearth operations in 1990, switching completely to electric-arc furnace. At some companies, steel products are made from bars and sheets produced by the steelmakers. These include Cold Metal Products in Hamilton, Ontario; Laurel Steel in Burlington, Ontario, owned by Harris Steel; and Union Drawn Steel in Hamilton, Ontario. Most of these companies are much smaller than the "Big Two" in terms of output and employment.

The industry is, with the sole exception of Dofasco, almost completely unionized at the level of production and maintenance workers. Dofasco in Hamilton has no union, although a number of its subsidiaries are unionized. The dominant union in the industry is the United Steel Workers of America (USWA).

OUTPUT AND PLANT UTILIZATION

Table 3.2 provides an overview of the industry's aggregate performance over the years 1981–90. The 1981–82 recession was hard on the industry, causing a 22 percent decline in 1982 in iron and steel shipments, and a 19 percent drop in raw steel production. The picture improved gradually and steadily after 1982, reaching a peak of 14.689 million tons of finished steel in 1989. Raw steel production recovered to its prerecession levels of about 16 million tons by 1984, and grew steadily thereafter, to 16.9 million tons in 1989. Output declined again in 1990–91 with the onset of another recession.

Capacity utilization in the industry was very low in the early 1980s (see Table 3.3). In 1982, a recessionary low of 55.2 percent was reflective of the difficulties that steel industries in most of the Western countries experienced. Because further additions to capacity were avoided, plant utilization in the industry improved steadily after 1982, rising to a peak of 81.3 percent in 1989. This achievement compared favourably with other industrialized countries' performance.

In contrast to the decline experienced in the United States from 1960 to 1986, Canada's share of world steel consumption stayed fairly constant, at about 2 percent while steel production rose from 5 million tons in 1960 to 16.6 million tons in 1989. Howell et al. (1988) attribute part of the success of the Canadian industry to a favourable public policy and good communication between the industry and the government in the 1950s and 1960s. The Canadian steel industry, as a result, was very competitive on a world basis in the 1970s and the 1980s. The industry did not overbuild and so maintained high capacity-utilization rates over the

Table 3.2
The Canadian Steel Industry, 1981–90

	1981	1982	1983	1984	1985	1986	1987	1988	1989	1990
Raw Steel Production (000 tons)	16 135	12 965	14 030	16 058	16 019	15 419	16 118	16 235	16 901	13 430
Primary Iron & Steel Shipments (000 tons)	13 227	10 306	11 020	12 742	12 854	12 855	14 053	14 618	14 689	12 741
Employment[a] (000s)	55 800	52 051	47 412	48 719	47 503	46 461	46 694	44 110	44 740	44 349
Capital Expenditures (millions of dollars)	710	416.3	166.2	189.9	439.4	843.2	757.1	534.0	563.1	NA
Capacity (000 tons)	22 062	23 473	23 519	23 519	23 519	19 185	19 185	19 185	21 191	20 609
Capacity Utilization (%)	73.1	55.2	59.7	68.3	68.1	77.8	81.3	81.9	85.3	65.3
Exports (000 tons)	3 676	3 519	2 960	3 401	3 236	3 843	4 254	3 904	4 356	4 317
Imports (000 tons)	2 654	1 260	1 373	1 955	2 204	2 100	2 257	2 993	2 353	2 861
Apparent Domestic Demand (000 tons)	12 205	8 047	9 433	11 296	11 822	11 112	12 056	13 707	12 686	11 286
Imports as a % of Domestic Demand	21.8	15.7	14.6	17.3	18.7	18.9	18.7	21.8	18.5	25.4
Total Imports from the U.S. (000 tons)	955	490	587	583	563	501	688	1 007	1 087	1 694
U.S. Imports as a % of Apparent Domestic Demand	7.8	6.1	6.2	5.2	4.8	4.5	5.7	7.3	8.6	15.0

Notes: [a] Employment in the primary steel industry (SIC = 291) only. For employment in the total industry including pipe and tubes (SIC = 292) and wire and wire products (SIC = 392), see Figure 3.1.

Sources: Canadian Steel Producers' Association, Steel Facts, various years.

Table 3.3
Capacity Utilization in the Steel Industry

	1980 %	1986 %
Canada	80	75
Japan	70	65
European Community	NA	66
U.S.A.	73	64
O.E.C.D.	69	67

Source: Bernard Keeling, *World Steel: A New Assessment of Trends and Prospects* (London: Economist Intelligence Unit, 1988), 42.

whole demand cycle. Government assistance in Canada has been less than that in most other countries, the exceptions being that received by Sysco and Sidbec-Dosco (Howell et al. 1988, p 456).

EMPLOYMENT, PRODUCTIVITY AND LABOUR COSTS

Table 3.4 shows the relative costs of producing a ton of cold-rolled coil steel[2] over the 1960–90 period in the United States and Canada. These numbers suggest that, in the 1950s and the 1960s, productivity was similar in both countries, with Canada enjoying a marginal advantage. During the 1970s, however, U.S. mills began to fall behind under the weight of much higher wage increases and lack of new investment to replace old plant and technology. The result was a wide productivity gap by 1980 in favour of Canadian plants. In 1980, the average Canadian plant produced a ton of finished steel in 6.5 person-hours, as compared to approximately 9.9 person-hours in the United States. Comparative data indicate that Canadian plants were second only to the Japanese in productivity in 1980.

Since then, however, U.S. steel plants have made steady gains in productivity. As discussed later, these gains were achieved mainly through closing old plants, many of which used aging equipment based on old open-hearth furnace technology, and opening new mills that use cost-efficient electric furnaces. The industry,

Table 3.4
Production Cost of a Ton of Cold-rolled Coil (current U.S. dollars per ton)

	U.S.	Canada
1960	135	125
1970	180	160
1980	410	330
1990	435	435

Source: Economics Associates Inc.

Figure 3.1

Steel Industry Output and Employment 1971–1989

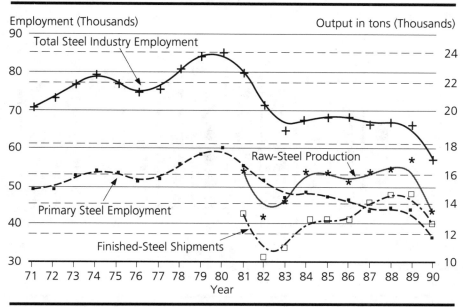

Source: Statistics Canada, *Employment, Earnings and Hours,* Catalogue 72-002 (Ottawa: Minister of Supply and Services, various years).

once mostly unionized, saw the growth of a sizable nonunion sector, which, by some estimates, is close to 60 percent of the total industry in terms of employment.[3] Where unions remained, many changes were made to the collective agreement to increase flexibility and reduce costs.[4] These measures brought the U.S. plants' productivity to Canadian levels by 1990: U.S. productivity had improved to about 5.6 person-hours for every ton of finished steel. Productivity in Canadian plants also rose to about 5.5 person-hours per ton. Some industry analysts hold that Canadian plants were still more productive than the U.S. plants in 1990 because these figures hide the fact that the U.S. plants have come to rely heavily on subcontracting, a practice that is still fairly limited in Canada. As we show later in discussing collective-bargaining outcomes, there is increasing pressure on Canadian plants to catch up with the shop-floor flexibility that the "born-again" U.S. industry has developed in recent years.

Employment trends in the primary iron and steel sector corroborate the competitive strength of the industry. As Figure 3.1 shows, employment grew nearly 20 percent during the 1970s, from 49 258 in 1971 to a peak of 60 451 in 1980. These gains are particularly impressive when compared with the substantial declines in industry employment in other industrialized nations. Bain (1992) reports that, over the 1970–88 period, Canada's loss of employment in the industry was the least among eight industrialized economies. Employment losses in Canada were

Figure 3.2
Average Hourly Earnings in Steel: Canada and the United States, 1980–1990

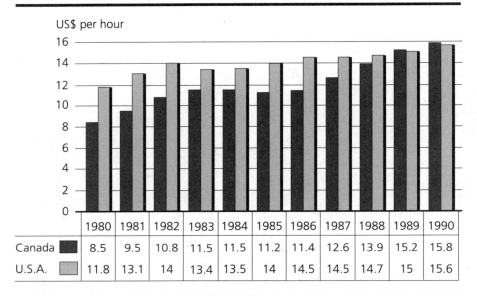

US$ per hour

	1980	1981	1982	1983	1984	1985	1986	1987	1988	1989	1990
Canada ■	8.5	9.5	10.8	11.5	11.5	11.2	11.4	12.6	13.9	15.2	15.8
U.S.A. ▨	11.8	13.1	14	13.4	13.5	14	14.5	14.5	14.7	15	15.6

Source: Statistics Canada, *Employment, Earnings and Hours,* Catalogue 72-002 (Ottawa: Minister of Supply
and Services, various years).

much lower (11.5 percent)[5] than those in Japan (39 percent), Sweden (33 percent), West Germany (45 percent), Belgium and Luxemberg (53 percent), the
United States (60 percent), and Great Britain (75 percent). Employment declined
gradually in the 1980s, to 43 000 in 1989. Most of the increase in output and decline in employment is directly attributable to higher productivity through the introduction of new technology and changed work practices.

Labour productivity in the United States grew at an annual rate of 7.7 percent
between 1981 and 1986. Similar figures apply for Canada (Canadian Steel Trade
and Employment Congress [CSTEC] 1989, 10), although Canada appears to have
had an advantage in wage rates, a key component of unit labour cost. During
1976–86, Canadian wage rates in primary metals were consistently lower than
those in the United States (Lendvay-Zwickl 1988, 19). As Figure 3.2 shows, average hourly earnings in Canada were lower every year between 1980 and 1988. In
1989 and 1990, Canadian hourly earnings exceeded those in the United States by
20 (US) cents per hour. Higher negotiated wages and an increase in the value of
the Canadian dollar contributed to sharp increase in hourly wage costs. In 1980,
labour costs were a smaller proportion of total production costs in Canada (24.5
percent) than in the United States (32.4 percent). By 1990, Canadian mills had
lost this advantage and these percentages became nearly the same: 30.6 percent in
the United States and 31 percent in Canada. According to one estimate,[6] even

though Canadian unit labour costs had risen faster over 1980–90 (from US$12.50 to US$24.50) compared to those in the United States (from US$18.50 to US$26.50), Canadian mills still enjoyed an advantage of US$2.00 an hour in 1990. The trend in 1991 was an upward pressure on Canadian costs driven in part by the high value of the Canadian dollar (see Chapter 1, Figure 1.5) and in part by higher wage settlements in collective bargaining.

FOREIGN TRADE

Though Canadian trade in steel in the 1980s increased gradually in volume and in value, the trends had a detrimental impact on the Canadian industry. As Figure 3.3 shows, Canadian exports to the United States rose gradually, from 2.4 percent of the U.S. market in 1983 to a peak of nearly 3.8 percent in 1987. This share of the U.S. market has since declined, to about 2 percent in 1990. In contrast, the U.S. share of the Canadian market, traditionally around 6 percent, declined at first, from 7.8 percent in 1981 to a low of 4.5 percent in 1986. It has risen every year since then, at first gradually, to 8.6 percent in 1989, and then quite dramatically, to 15.1 percent in 1990 (*Financial Post*, April 12, 1991). U.S. penetration of the Canadian market may have been facilitated by the two long strikes at Stelco and Algoma, but, in 1991, U.S. imports have continued to grow.

Figure 3.3
Canada and U.S. Market Shares in Each Other's Market

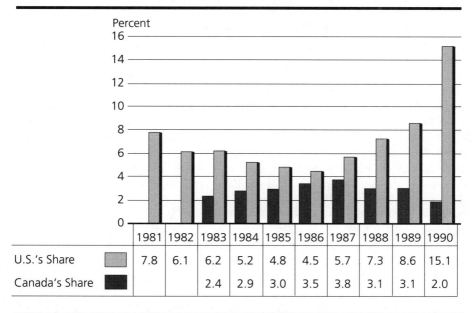

	1981	1982	1983	1984	1985	1986	1987	1988	1989	1990
U.S.'s Share	7.8	6.1	6.2	5.2	4.8	4.5	5.7	7.3	8.6	15.1
Canada's Share			2.4	2.9	3.0	3.5	3.8	3.1	3.1	2.0

Source: Canadian Steel Producers' Association, *Steel Facts,* various years.

Figure 3.4
Imports as a Percentage of Steel Consumption Canada and the United States

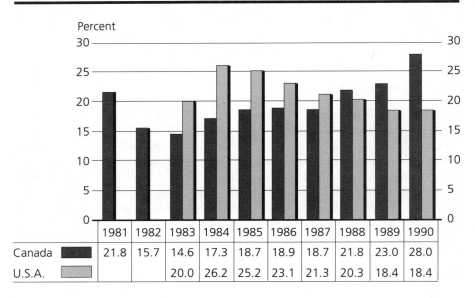

	1981	1982	1983	1984	1985	1986	1987	1988	1989	1990
Canada	21.8	15.7	14.6	17.3	18.7	18.9	18.7	21.8	23.0	28.0
U.S.A.			20.0	26.2	25.2	23.1	21.3	20.3	18.4	18.4

Source: Canadian Steel Producers' Association, *Steel Facts,* various years.

Total imports, including those from the United States also rose quite dramatically in 1990, to 24.5 percent of apparent domestic consumption (see Figure 3.4). In 1982 and 1983, this figure was closer to 15 percent although in two other years, 1981 and 1988, imports have been in excess of 20 percent of domestic consumption. For the 1981–89 period, imports averaged around 18.4 percent. The 1990 import penetration is thus a sharp increase, compared to the "normal" share of imports for the 1980s. In contrast, import penetration into the U.S. market was gradually reduced, from a high of 26 percent in 1984 to 18.4 percent in 1989 and 1990. The reduction was brought about largely through informal negotiations with foreign suppliers and later through voluntary restraint agreements (VRAs).[7]

Canada is a net exporter of steel products; in 1989, Canadian mills produced 16.9 million tons, imported 2.3 million tons, consumed 12.7 million tons, and exported 4.4 million tons (see Table 3.2). In 1989, 68.3 percent of Canada's steel exports were to the United States; however, Canadian mills buy $300 million worth of U.S. equipment and supplies annually and spend $1.19 in the United States for every $1 of steel sold there (CSTEC 1989, 14). Thus, in aggregate, the United States appears to have a net balance-of-payments surplus on its total steel and steel-related trade with Canada.

Under the Canada–United States Free Trade Agreement (FTA), import duties on steel will be reduced gradually over a period of ten years. The import duty on steel averaged 12 percent before the FTA. Canadian producers were not able to take advantage of declining import duties in the United States because of un-favourable macroeconomic policies during 1989–91. Apart from productive effi-ciency, Canadian industry's ability to compete in international markets depends on the value of the Canadian dollar. During much of the 1980s, Canadian produc-ers enjoyed a cost advantage because of the lower value of the Canadian dollar rel-ative to the U.S. dollar (see Chapter 1, Figure 1.5). This advantage was gradually lost by 1990, when Canadian producers also had to face high interest rates. The sudden increase in imports from the United States in 1990 is, at least in part, at-tributable to the relatively high value of the Canadian dollar and high interest rates.

The 1980s saw the gradual dilution of a Canadian steel market and the emer-gence of a North American steel market, thanks largely to the psychological and the economic impact of the FTA. During the 1981 strike at Stelco, Canadian steel production and consumption were similarly affected. However, during the 1990 strikes at Stelco and Algoma, Canadian consumption was much less affected be-cause U.S. producers moved in to fill the void with deep discounts. Moreover, the continued closure of steel-consuming industries in Canada during the 1990–91 re-cession made Canadian producers even more dependent on markets abroad. Stel-co, according to President Bob Milbourne, began, in 1990, to position itself as a supplier of 4 percent of the North American market rather than as a supplier of 30 percent of the Canadian steel market. For these reasons, Stelco started taking a more active role in the American Iron and Steel Institute (AISI) and dropped out of the Canadian Steel Producers Association (CSPA) whose protectionist lobbying efforts were not congruent with Stelco's goal of producing steel for the continental market.

TECHNOLOGY

Canadian firms have invested steadily in their plant and equipment to keep abreast of new technology. As Table 3.2 shows, capital expenditures were high ($710 million) in 1981, which capped steady spending in the mid to late 1970s. A recessionary slump occurred during 1982–84, followed by increasing expenditures in the late 1980s, although the spending level did not quite match the pace set in the 1970s. The effects of capital spending can be observed in two technological trends in the industry. First, there has been a movement away from open-hearth steelmaking toward basic oxygen furnaces (BOFs) and electric-arc furnaces. By 1990, there were no open-hearth furnaces left in the industry when Sysco replaced the last of its open-hearth furnaces with an electric-arc furnace. In 1990, 67 per-cent of Canadian steel output came from BOFs and the remainder (33 percent) from electric-arc furnaces (see Figure 3.5).

Second, the industry has rapidly moved toward continuous casting, a process that eliminates several steps (i.e., casting of ingots and successive hot-rolling) to produce a billet or slab. The yield of continuously cast steel is 17 percent higher than that of steel cast as ingots. Over 50 percent of world steel is continuously cast, with Japan at 93 percent (Keeling 1988). In 1981, roughly 32.6 percent of raw-steel production in Canada was continuously cast (see Figure 3.6). This proportion has grown steadily since (77.2 percent in 1990). At Stelco and Algoma, 90 percent of the steel output was continously cast in 1991 (Stelco 1989). At most other steel companies, close to 100 percent of the steel produced is continuously cast. The only company that is making slower progress on this front is Dofasco, where roughly 50 percent of the output was continuously cast in 1989.[8]

In 1990, Dofasco and NKK Corporation of Japan agreed to invest $240 million in a jointly owned, state-of-the-art, hot-dip galvanizing plant in Windsor, Ontario, expected to become operational by 1993. The new facility would coat cold-rolled steel supplied by Dofasco and NKK's U.S. affiliate, National Steel. The product would have the latest available technology and high value added for corrosion-resistant automotive body parts and other difficult applications. At Stelco, a zinc-coating mill (Z line) was installed during 1990 that would galvanize cold-rolled products for the auto industry. Stelco joined hands with Mitsubishi of Japan to form a strategic alliance over this investment that totalled $200 million. It is the first such facility in Canada capable of zinc-coating 72-inch-wide steel sheets to meet the high-quality needs of the auto industry.

Figure 3.5
Crude Steel Production by Process 1971–1990

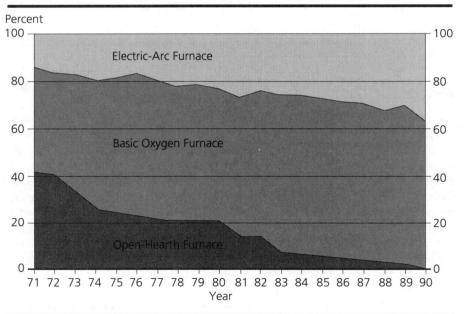

Source: Statistics Canada, *Primary Iron and Steel,* Catalogue 41-001 (Ottawa: Minister of Supply and Services).

Figure 3.6
Continuous-Cast Steel Production 1971–1990

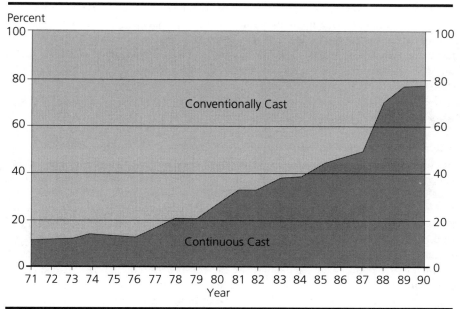

Source: Statistics Canada, *Primary Iron and Steel,* Catalogue 41-001 (Ottawa: Minister of Supply and Services, various years).

Canadian firms cannot afford to be complacent on the technology front, even though they have invested well in the past. There are new technologies on the horizon that will require further investments to keep the industry competitive. A new technology, used currently only by Nucor Inc., a United States-based min-imill, allows steel to be cast continuously as a thin slab (typically 1.5 inches thick), thus cutting down on the high-cost equipment normally employed to reduce thick slabs to thin sheets. At Nucor's plant in Crawfordsville, Indiana (annual capacity: 800 000 tons), it takes only $335 to produce a ton of finished-sheet steel, compared to $435 per ton using more conventional methods. Although the quality of Nucor's output is currently not as high as that obtained from more conventional processes, analysts expect that quality will improve gradually. Nucor is currently building a second such plant, expected to go into production by 1993. The thin-slab casting process currently accounts for 2 percent of the total U.S. output. It is expected to rise to 12 percent by 1995, and to 20 percent by the year 2000.

In Canada, Stelco, Dofasco, and a number of other steel companies have joined forces with universities and government laboratories in an all-Canadian effort named "Project Bessemer," designed to develop a new commercial process that would allow a hot-rolled strip coil (as thin as 0.1 inch) to be cast directly from a ladle of molten steel. This process, still some years away from the shop floor, is expected to achieve significant cost savings.

Another new technology has been dubbed "cokeless steel." This technology, currently being perfected in the laboratories, involves treating the iron ore so that it is reduced to steel at the level of small pellets. This process would replace blast furnaces, which require coke as a raw material, a process considered to be too inefficient and polluting for the future. Both of these technologies will require substantial new investments in capital.

STEEL: THE U.S. STORY

The preceding discussion hints at several competitive strengths and weaknesses of the U.S. steel industry. Since the Canadian industry's fortunes are closely linked to developments in the United States, it is important to understand the strategies that U.S. firms have pursued to stay profitable. According to some observers, the United States now has two distinct industries within the steel sector: the large mills and the minimills (Barnett and Crandall 1986; Crandall 1981). The larger U.S. steel companies have been reducing their productive capacity and employment by closing plants and divesting marginal operations. Faced with rising costs, declining prices, and excess capacity, the big companies reduced their capacity by one-third between 1975 and 1985.[9] Large producers, such as Kaiser, LTV, McLouth,[10] and Wheeling-Pittsburgh, have either exited the industry or gone into bankruptcy to reorganize. The large producers that remain in the business are not very profitable (Barnett and Crandall 1986).

In sharp contrast, the minimills have grown rapidly in size, more than doubling their output between 1975 and 1985 (Barnett and Crandall 1986). The minimill sector accounted for 20 percent of the total U.S. raw steel output in 1985, compared to 2 percent in 1960. Many minimills, such as Nucor, Chapparal Steel, and Florida Steel, have not only increased their capacity substantially but have been more profitable than the large producers. Initially, these mills produced a narrow range of products (typically in small cross-sections) for regional markets, using small-capacity furnaces. By 1990, many of them produced larger cross-sections for the broad market, using larger furnaces. By steadily improving their reach, the range of product offerings, quality, and costs, they not only took business away from the integrated producers but also displaced imports (Hogan 1987).

The success of minimills can be attributed to four major factors: product specialization, geographic specialization, efficient production processes' and a unique human-resource strategy. Most mills specialize in a narrow range of products. This specialization allows the mills to operate with higher efficiency because of the simplification of production and standardization of production-related services. Since the minimills use scrap as their raw material, they do not have to bear the cost of transporting large quantities of iron ore or coal supplies. They can locate closer to the customers, and thus enjoy considerable transportation-cost advantages over the integrated producer. Minimills can be found in remote locations (e.g.,

Plymouth, Utah, and Jackson, Mississippi) as long as there is a market for at least 200 000 tons of steel within a single product group.

In general, with this product range and plant size, minimills can run their plants more efficiently than can the large producers, and can implement new technologies more rapidly. Even when the processes are very similar, minimills can obtain better efficiency by reducing cycle times at various stages of production. This ability derives very clearly from the human-resource strategy of these mills, of which there are four key components. First, they tend to be located in smaller communities, away from large urban centres (where the large mills are located). These locations provide a triple advantage: they protect the minimill (at least initially) from taking on the big mills directly; they help the minimill avoid unions, because rural locations tend to be low in unionization; and they allow the employer to hire cheap labour, because prevailing wages in such areas tend to be low. Thus, operating nonunion and paying low (i.e., lower than industry average) wages are important parts of the competitive strategy. Second, the basic wage rate is designed to be two-thirds of total earnings. Thus, a third of an employee's earnings is variable rather than fixed, as it is for large unionized mills.[11] At Nucor, fixed wages comprise only one-third of total earnings for the typical worker. Another one-third of earnings comes in the form of incentive pay, based on meeting quality and production targets. The remaining third comes from profit-sharing bonuses, based on company's annual profits. The total compensation well exceeds that of other jobs in the area.

The third component of the strategy is to get younger, motivated workers who have no prior steelmaking experience and who have never been members of a union. The average age of workers at the industry leader, Nucor, was 34 years in 1991, compared to 43 years at Inland Steel, a large producer (Paré 1991). The ability of Nucor to turn farmers, store clerks, and even grandmothers into steelworkers is a matter of pride within the company (Preston 1991). Managers feel that such workers best respond to incentive pay and bonuses, such as profit sharing. Lastly, the strategy includes efficient forms of work rules and work organization, such as broadly defined jobs and work teams on the shop floor. At Chapparel Steel, every one of the 900 employees must make sales calls (Paré 1991). At Nucor, employees work in teams, and each can cover for a co-worker who may be late or absent from work (Ansberry 1991).

The success of this strategy was writ large on the productivity and profitability statements of the companies. Between 1984 and 1990, the minimills averaged a profit of roughly US$30 per ton compared to $15 per ton for the large mills (Paine Webber 1991, Chart 9). Similarly, while the most efficient large mills took about 4 person-hours to produce a ton of steel, Nucor's flagship plant in Crawfordsville, Indiana, could roll a ton of steel every 54 minutes. There is a dark side, however, to the minimill success story, particularly at Nucor, where the fatality rate between 1980 and 1990 was the highest of all mills in the United States (Ansberry 1991). Critics charged that the pressure to increase output had been so great that safety procedures were frequently ignored. The company contended that many of the accidents related to the construction phase of the plant that did not reflect on operational safety. It is a matter of record that Nucor has made a name for itself in completing the construction of the plant in record time, as well as in reducing cycle times at every stage of the production process (Preston 1991). In any case, the success of the minimill industry will likely continue to transform the U.S. and, indirectly, the Canadian steel industry.

Canada has not such growth in the minimill industry. Several factors preclude a similar development in Canada, at least for now. First, the geographical distribution of population in Canada is such that the strategy of locating in rural areas does not produce the same advantages as in the United States. New mills can not avoid unions by going into rural Ontario or Quebec, where most of the market lies. They could possibly do so by going to Alberta or Prince Edward Island, where unionization tends to be low, but these locations are far from the markets. Also, rural and far-flung locations do not produce the same degree of wage advantage in Canada because interprovincial variance in wages is much smaller than interstate variance in the United States (Verma and Thompson 1990). Canada's stronger and more militant unions make it difficult for a new mill to alter drastically the compensation structure such that most of the wage becomes contingent upon performance. Two Canadian companies, Ipsco and Lasco, are close to the U.S. minimills in terms of size, cost, and product strategies, although not in terms of human-resource strategy. Workers at both these companies are fully unionized.

A less-well-known development in the U.S. steel industry is the entry of Japanese steelmakers in U.S. plants in the 1980s. In 1991, there were 66 Japanese-owned or joint-venture steel plants in the United States with an investment of US$7 billion and employing 30 000 workers (Kenny and Florida 1991). Much of the Japanese investment has gone into building technology-intensive plants that produce value-added coated steel for automotive body parts. Many of these plants are unionized, and although wages are often comparable to those paid by other large U.S. mills, their collective agreements include fewer and more flexible work rules along with sharing plans, employee involvement, and team forms of work organization. An illustrative example is I/N Tek, a joint venture between Inland Steel and its Japanese collaborator, Nippon Steel, that produces cold-rolled sheets for the auto industry in its US$525 million, state-of-the-art plant in New Carlisle, Indiana. At I/N Tek, wages are comparable to those paid by the large U.S.–owned mills, but its productivity is much higher, thanks to a more flexible collective agreement and high-technology equipment that can cut up to five major steps from a conventional cold-rolling process.

O*rganized Labour in the Industry*

The United Steel Workers of America (USWA) is the dominant union in the industry in both Canada and the United States.[12] The union is an active and influential affiliate of the American Federation of Labor–Congress of Industrial Organizations (AFL–CIO) in the United States and of the Canadian Labour Congress (CLC) in Canada. The USWA has been one of the largest unions in North America since the Wagner Act (1935) came into effect. Its membership peaked in the mid-1970s, at 1.4 million. In the last fifteen years, its fortunes, linked closely to steel and allied industries, have fallen with the decline of these industries. Membership fell sharply through the 1980s, to 460 000 in 1989 (Kumar 1991).

In the 1980s, the union fared better in Canada than in the United States. While U.S. membership declined by nearly 73 percent during 1975–89, from 1.2 million to 321 000, in Canada the decline over the same period was closer to 27 percent, from 220 000 to 160 000. In 1980, there were 189 905 members in 851 locals, compared to 166 001 members in 727 locals in 1988 (Statistics Canada, 1990). The relative success of the Canadian steel industry contributed in good measure to the union's better performance.

In Canada, the union tried to diversify its membership to establishments outside the traditional base of the iron and steel industry. These efforts took on an added sense of urgency during the recession of 1981–82, when a sense of crisis prevailed in the industry. During the 1983–87 period, the USWA organized 40 000 new members in Canada. In Ontario alone, they organized 12 900 new workers during 1981–88 (Verma and Meltz 1990). During the 1980s, the union organized more workers in Ontario (District 6 of the USWA) than did any other union in the province. In particular, the union escalated its efforts to break into low-wage sectors filled by women and new Canadians, among them security guards and taxi drivers in Quebec, nursing-home workers, eastern Ontario seafood-processing workers, Saskatchewan insurance workers, Trail (B.C.) credit union workers, and Simon Fraser University employees. In 1985, the upholsterers' union merged with the USWA. Thus, the union has tried, and succeeded to some extent, in diversifying its constituency base in Canada.

In 1991, the typical member of the USWA worked for a small manufacturer or service-sector employer with fewer than 250 employees in the bargaining unit.[13] This profile is in sharp contrast to the mid-1970s, when the typical worker was employed by a large or medium-sized integrated steelmaker.

As an industrial union, the USWA has generally pursued egalitarian policies, both in collective bargaining and at the political level. In the steel industry, they usually negotiate wage increases that are specified in cents-per-hour rather than in percentages. The effect is to compress the wage spread, because fixed cents-per-hour increases mean larger percentage increases for workers with lower wages than for those earning higher wages. Wage compression is further exacerbated by cost-of-living adjustment (COLA) payments. Politically, the union is active in the left-leaning New Democratic Party (NDP), although they have traditionally taken a more neutral political position in U.S. politics. In the Ontario elections in the fall of 1990 that resulted in the first-ever NDP government for Ontario, five former and current steelworkers were elected to the legislature.

In collective bargaining, the union pursued a blend of traditional and innovative policies. While it opposed wage concessions in principle, wage freezes were negotiated in many cases during the 1980s. In general, the emphasis was gradually moved away from wage gains toward measures to enhance job and income security. The National Office advocated a pragmatic approach to restructuring and encouraged locals to examine new ideas without prejudice. One position paper (USWA 1990, 15), urged workers to consider "a partnership in which both union and the employer make commitments that they have previously not been willing to make." The basic elements of such a partnership may include consultation and involvement in decision making, two-way commitments that involve a process of give-and-take (*quid pro quos*) and union security. To address employer concerns about flexibility, the union negotiated reductions in the number of job classifications and agreed to multiskill classifications in many instances. Despite this line of thinking at the national level, the progress toward these policy objectives was slow during the 1980s. Although some of the blame for the slow progress in adopting such policies was attributable to employer hesitation over sharing more power with the union, the slow process of diffusing such principles within the USWA organization also contributed to the lack of progress on this front.

By the late 1980s, the union had developed a stated policy on gain sharing (USWA 1987; Delaney 1989). A number of locals had negotiated various forms of gain- or profit-sharing (or some combination of both) provisions by 1991. Among those of the large companies, Stelco's 1990 agreement (discussed below) contained a formula based on value added. The union also developed a policy statement (USWA n.d.)[14] on employee involvement that supported initiatives as long as they were implemented through the collective-bargaining process. This stand differs markedly from those of such unions as the Canadian Auto Workers and the Canadian Paperworkers, who have generally opposed employee involvement in any form (Verma and Gallina 1991).

In keeping with its historical tradition, the union also pursued a socialist agenda that sought reforms such as employment equity and rights for the handicapped and other disadvantaged groups. In 1985, the union started a "Humanity Fund" dedicated to humanitarian and development work overseas and at home. Subsequently, a drive began to negotiate worker and matching company contributions to the fund in collective agreements. At Stelco, the two sides agreed in 1987 to have employees contribute 40 cents a week, and the company to match employees' contributions, subject to a maximum of $1500 per annum. By 1991, more than 50 locals across the country had negotiated similar provisions with their employers.

Collective Bargaining

BARGAINING STRUCTURE

Although there has never been national industry-level bargaining in the past, USWA locals across firms have always attempted to "co-ordinate" their bargaining. In Ontario, and across the country, USWA locals at Stelco, Algoma, and other steel companies bargain at about the same time, with the intent of signing agreements only when each local is satisfied with the outcomes. Such co-ordination allowed the locals to ensure that their agreements were set in the same pattern. It may also have provided the unions with some leverage in bargaining, although this advantage is partially neutralized by consultation and "co-ordination" among employers. Since Algoma and Stelco have been competitors, they might be just as interested in a similar pattern as the unions, because patterned agreements would "take wages out of competition" in a growing market.

During the 1981 bargaining round, just as the Canadian economy entered one of the worst recessions since 1929, the pattern similarity between Stelco and Algoma broke down (Adams and Zeytinoglu 1987). Algoma workers (USWA Local 2251) settled, while Stelco workers rejected the contract and went on strike in support of their demands. Within Stelco, two groups of workers, at Lake Erie Works and in the fasteners and forgings plants, voted to accept a settlement and end the strike after 28 days. The strike continued for 125 days at the Hilton Works, the Edmonton plant, and the McMaster Works in Contrecoeur, Quebec. Although wages were not substantially different after the 1981 negotiations, the pattern had been broken. Stelco settlements were somewhat larger than those at Algoma. Wage increases at Stelco were $1.15, $0.25, and $0.30 in the following three years, as compared to increases of $1.00, $0.15, $0.15, respectively, at Algoma (see Table 3.5). Once this pattern was broken, increasing pressures were put on the union by employers to decentralize bargaining even further. At Stelco, the company had succeeded in obtaining different contracts for its various plants by 1990 (discussed below in greater detail).

Table 3.5
Wages and Wage Increases at Stelco and Algoma, 1981–1983

| | General Wage Increases ($/hour) | | | Typical Wages in 1981 ($/hour) | | |
	1981	1982	1983	Janitor	Crafts-person	Mill Operator
Stelco	1.15	0.25	0.30	10.39	12.74	14.62
Algoma	1.00	0.15	0.15	10.30	12.65	14.38

Source: Labour Canada, Collective Agreements. File.

Table 3.6

Average Hourly Earnings for Workers Paid by the Hour in Selected Industries (In Current Dollars per Hour)

Selected Industries	1971	1981	1985	1990	% Change 1971 to 1990	% Change 1981 to 1990
Steel	4.34	12.27	15.08	17.92	312.9	46.0
Forestry	NA	NA	16.49	18.43	NA	NA
Mining	4.18	12.96	15.90	19.88	375.6	53.4
Manufacturing	3.41	9.70	11.86	14.75	332.6	52.1
Durable	3.65	10.26	12.37	15.54	325.8	51.5
Nondurable 3.16	9.11	11.28	13.90	340.0	52.6	
Construction	5.04	14.07	14.09	17.64	250.0	25.4
Transportation, communication, and utilities	NA	NA	13.79	16.09	NA	NA
Trade	NA	NA	8.04	9.86	NA	NA

Source: Statistics Canada Labour Division, *Employment, Earnings and Hours,* Catalogue 72-002 (Monthly). Wages shown are for December.

INDUSTRY WAGES

As Table 3.6 shows, wages in the steel industry, although traditionally high compared to the rest of manufacturing, rose more slowly in the last twenty years than did those of most other industry groups. In 1971, steel industry wages were similar to those in mining, and higher than those in most industries except construction. By 1990, steel wages were still higher than those in manufacturing as a whole, but they had fallen behind wages in mining and forestry. The increase in steel wages over 1971–90 and 1981–90 was smaller than that in mining and manufacturing as a whole.

The traditional strength of organized labour in the industry was reflected in wage movements in the 1980s. According to a USWA (1989) study, wages adjusted for inflation (according to the consumer price index) fell in each of the years from 1984 to 1987. Real wages negotiated in the industry's major collective agreements also fell, but by a smaller amount. For example, real average weekly earnings declined by 1.2 percent in 1984, 0.7 percent in 1985, 1.4 percent in 1986, and 2.0 percent in 1987; the corresponding decrease in real wages negotiated in major collective agreements was 0.8 percent in 1984, 0.3 percent in 1985, 0.7 percent in 1986, and 0.4 percent in 1987. In 1988, average weekly earnings rose 0.9 percent but the increase in negotiated wages was lower. For the period 1984–88, average weekly earnings declined 4.35 percent in real terms, whereas real negotiated wages declined by only 1.8 percent.

STELCO

Until Dofasco acquired Algoma in 1988, Stelco, incorporated as the Steel Company of Canada in 1910, was the largest steel company in Canada. It is an integrated producer that extracts metal from ore in two plants in Ontario: Hilton Works in Hamilton, and Lake Erie Works in Nanticoke. It also operates two minimills that recycle scrap in electric furnaces: in Edmonton, Alberta, and Contrecoeur, Quebec. Besides hot- and cold-rolled steel sections, Stelco also produces steel products, such as fasteners, forgings, pipes and tubes, and wire and wire products, at several locations. Stelco is unique among Canadian steelmakers in the range of products, processes, geographical locations, and union status.[15]

Table 3.7 shows the operating results of the company between 1981 and 1989. The company enjoyed financial success in the 1980s, although recessions and strikes, among other factors, resulted in losses in 1982, 1983, and 1990. Steel production increased slightly over the 1980s, but employment fell, from a peak of 26 263 in 1981 to 16 147 in 1989. Some of this decline was attributable to productive new technology.

Technology and Productivity

Stelco's plants were generally considered to be modern, although there were some pockets of older equipment. Lake Erie Works, at 4500 tons a day, produced 30 per-

Table 3.7
Stelco Inc.: An Historical Overview

	1981	1982	1983	1984	1985	1986	1987	1988	1989	1990
Revenues (millions)	2 174	2 020	2 033	2 401	2 435	2 400	2 546	2 711	2 749	2 101
Profits[a] (millions) (loss)	83	(41)	(14)	48	85	54	63	98	94	(197)
Assets (millions)	2 910	2 758	2 769	2 803	2 905	2 915	2 804	2 856	3 078	2 521
Long Term Debt as % of Shareholders Equity	0.4	0.4	0.3	0.4	0.4	0.4	0.5	0.7	0.7	0.8
Return-on-investment%[b]	7.78	(1.77)	(0.08)	5.00	7.93	6.17	7.20	10.49	10.13	(11.70)
Semi-Finished Steel in 000's tons[d]	4 042	4 084	4 370	4 681	4 587	4 557	4 528	4 503	4 729	2 785
Shipment 000's tons	3 804	3 575	3 598	4 004	4 023	4 003	4 257	4 245	4 254	3 390
Revenue per ton ($)[c]	571	565	565	600	605	600	598	639	646	620
Operating profit per ton ($)[c]	29	(11)	(2)	20	36	27	32	45	49	(65)
Export (% of sales)	16	24	21	22	21	19	20	16	17	15
Capital Spending (millions)	210	163	45	32	136	274	244	123	160	130
Number of employees	26 263	22 104	19 519	20 612	18 773	17 768	16 960	16 207	16 147	14 348

Notes: [a] Profits before "extraordinary items."
[b] Net Income before tax deduction divided by Equity, Long term debt and Short term debt.
[c] Between 1984 and 1989, revenue per ton and operating profit per ton are calculated on amount shipped.

Source: Information provided by Stelco on request.

cent of Stelco's total steel output and employed 7 percent of total staff. It is one of the most technology-intensive modern plants in the world. Its fully automated computerized hot-strip mill was brought on stream in June 1983. Lake Erie Works was designed to meet the competition from more efficient offshore producers. It used fewer than half the workers required by a similiar manual operation. The average employee's age was 29, and all have a minimum of grade 12 education. Until Nucor's mill in Crawfordsville, Indiana, came on stream, Lake Erie Works was the lowest-cost manufacturer of hot-rolled products in North America. It hot-rolls a ton of steel in two person-hours, as compared to the four person-hours such production takes at the Hilton Works and the one person-hour at Nucor's mill (Milbourne 1990). Despite its technological advantage, Lake Erie Works will continue to be under pressure to lower its costs gradually to maintain its leadership position. As its markets continue to shift to south of the border, its products will have to bear additional freight costs, which, if not compensated by cost reductions elsewhere, will decrease its competitive advantage in the marketplace.

The two minimills in Edmonton and Contrecoeur are both considered to be reasonably competitive in their regional, focussed product markets (Milbourne 1990). The Edmonton mill produces some 250 000 tons a year of bar products. The Contrecoeur mill produces 300 000 tons a year of bars (for the market) and billets for rerolling at the Hilton Works.

The weakest link in Stelco operations is the oldest facility, the Hamilton Works, which is one of the last few multiproduct integrated steel complexes in North America. It produces between 2.0 million and 2.7 million tons of finished steel, using aging equipment (with one exception, the No. 2 Rod Mill, which has been upgraded to state-of-the-art technology) and infrastructure. The Hilton Works produces a ton of hot-rolled steel in four person-hours, as compared to two person-hours at Lake Erie Works and one person-hour at Nucor. At least one person-hour in extra costs at the Hilton Works is attributable to poor infrastructure, such as age and complexity of utility distribution, facility layout, and transportation equipment (Milbourne 1990). A further one person-hour difference may be attributed to poor productivity practices on the shop floor and poor labour–management relations, according to Milbourne (1990).

Because of customer demand for lower cost yet high quality,[16] Stelco invested about $1 billion in modernization over 1980–1990. About $250 million was spent to make Hilton Works a continuous-cast facility. These changes have helped the company reduce operating costs by $70 to $80 a ton over the last seven years. The company continued to remove obsolete equipment, such as old open-hearth furnaces and blast furnaces, and invest in new technology that would add more value to its products. As mentioned earlier, Stelco joined with Mitsubishi of Japan to invest $200 million in a zinc-coating mill (Z line), commissioned during 1990.

Labour Relations

The largest local at Stelco, Local 1005 of the USWA, was certified in 1944 after the introduction of PC 1003, the Canadian version of the Wagner Act. Union relations with the company are best described as arm's length; the two sides recognize each other's legitimacy but have not moved toward active co-operation. There have been strikes throughout the history of the relationship, starting with a strike in 1946 over wages and a 40-hour work week. In the last ten years, there were strikes in 1981 and 1990. Despite the breakdown of patterns across Stelco and Algoma, mentioned earlier, all of the Stelco locals negotiated jointly in 1981. For the 1984 round of bargaining, the union initiated a different strategy.[17] All the USWA locals at Stelco (there were seventeen locals in 1984) decided to form a joint negotiating committee, with which the company agreed to negotiate. Bargaining was to occur at three levels. A central negotiating committee discussed "all items which have a monetary consideration and those administrative proposals which are common to all Works and Locals." Joint regional committees discussed areas of interest common to plants within the same region. Lastly, local committees discussed issues specific to that local plant. Bargaining at this tiered, but somewhat centralized, structure at the firm level was not as smooth as the parties might have envisaged. They sought the assistance of a mediator to reach a settlement (without a work stoppage). Partway through the negotiations, it became necessary to appoint an oversight committee to review and co-ordinate the work across the three tiers of bargaining. The 1987 round produced separate collective agreements, but a co-ordinated bargaining process was used.

By the 1990 round of bargaining, Stelco had undertaken a reorganization of the company (discussed in note 15). In 1990, the company served notice on the union that it would not negotiate centrally at one table. The company successfully sought to separate its bargaining with the steelmaking locals (now part of Stelco Steel) and its bargaining with workers from the wire, pipe, and other finished-products operations (now part of Stelco Enterprises). For instance, Steffco workers at Gananoque negotiated a separate contract in 1990 that allowed for a wage freeze in exchange for further investment in plant and equipment. After the 1984 bargaining round, the company began to rethink its bargaining structure. In doing so, Stelco was motivated simultaneously by two factors. First, it was under pressure from the market to differentiate between more- and less-profitable product lines. These were compelling reasons, backed up by differential financial performance in various product sectors. These data were relentlessly brought up by finance industry analysts, whose opinions are influential in attracting investor interest in the company. Second, the company faced pressure from within its own ranks to decentralize bargaining and let each unit pay according to its ability rather than continue with a centralized structure leading to a corporation-wide wage.

BARGAINING OUTCOMES IN THE 1980s Since the 1978 settlement produced only a modest increase in wages at a time of high inflation, workers were "all fired up" to achieve a catch-up 1981 settlement. Local 1005 president, Cec Taylor, was elected on a platform of flexing union muscle in the 1981 bargaining round. Healthy company profits over the previous three years also encouraged this stance. After an impasse, a strike began August 1, which lasted till December 3,

1981. The union improved on the company's last offer, and negotiated a total increase in compensation of $7.82 an hour (Adams and Zeytinoglu 1987). There were no productivity-enhancing provisions or others that would allow for greater union–management consultation on productivity problems. In hindsight, it would appear that the parties placed themselves out of step with the developments that would follow the next year, and for the rest of the decade. A deep recession took hold in both U.S. and Canadian economies soon thereafter, forcing most firms to address productivity and quality issues in the context of their relationships and collective agreements.

In the 1984 round, the parties agreed to maintain COLA, but there was a wage freeze in the first year, a 25-cent-an-hour (about 2 percent) increase in the second year, and 30-cent-an-hour (about 2 percent) increase in the third year. But, unlike in previous agreements, the accumulated COLA was not folded back into the base rate. The company wanted a freeze on COLA and wages, and a profit-sharing scheme for the second and third years. The company proposal was rejected by the stewards by a vote of 45 to 23. Once again, no productivity- or quality-enhancing arrangements were agreed upon.

In 1987, the union agreed to a contract that froze base wage rates for three years, during which the only increases in pay would come from COLA payments. Some work rules were changed to give management flexibility on the shop floor. Work scheduling provisions allowed for the introduction of seven-day continuous operations at finishing plants when additional orders were secured. The employees affected would receive a one-time $5000 lump-sum payment in return for changing voluntary weekend overtime into scheduled work at regular pay. As described earlier, this agreement included the "Humanity Fund" provision.

Although the conduct of industrial relations in the joint ventures and partnerships is completely divorced from that of Stelco, it is likely that experience with labour elsewhere may influence its expectations from bargaining with the USWA. Some of the joint-venture plants in the United States are nonunion. Industrial relations and human-resource innovations in these plants, and their possible positive effect on profits, are likely to encourage management to seek similar arrangements within its steelmaking business.

SHARP TURN: THE 1990 BARGAINING ROUND The USWA did not take very kindly to the company's efforts to fragment bargaining. To the union, this was an attempt by the company to divide the workers and rule with a heavier hand smaller and weaker groups of workers. To the company, this was the most reasonable way to deal with the demands of the marketplace. By the first quarter of 1990, Stelco profits had vanished into a sea of red ink—a loss of $13.3 million versus a profit of $32.7 million a year earlier. In January 1990, Fred Telmer, a long-term Stelco employee, took over as the chairman of Stelco, Inc. Telmer's task in 1990 was to put the relations with the union on a "new" footing, one that was driven more by the demands of the market and to a lesser extent by past practice and workers' needs. Although he is well regarded for his "ability to talk and deal candidly with employees" (*Financial Post*, May 23, 1990), a confrontation with the union became hard to avoid. A good illustration of industrial relations in the post-decentralization era came from Steffco in 1990.

THE STEFFCO STORY   Steffco, a Stelco subsidiary created in 1988, produced nuts, bolts, and other fasteners for the North American auto industry. Stelco wanted to consolidate its money-losing fastener operations in one modern plant, and thus save the business and many of the jobs. The consolidated new plant would need new investments in plant and machinery, and would employ 500 workers, while the remaining 150 workers of the 650 in the older plants would be offered early retirement. The consolidation would lead to the closing in 1990 or 1991 of plants in Toronto, Burlington, and Brantford. Stelco wanted the USWA locals in Steffco to accept an agreement that would amount to a concessions-for-investment swap. If the locals did not accept this proposal, Stelco threatened to abandon plans to consolidate the business in the new $24.5 million plant in Brantford.

A three-year contract was signed on December 23, 1989, providing for the elimination of COLA after July 31, 1990, when the contract expired, and a wage freeze over the length of the contract. Operations were to be phased out, starting in Burlington in July 1990, in Toronto by end of 1990, and in Brantford (the old plant) by end of 1991. The union executive did not recommend this agreement to its members. With the company insisting that this was the only way to save jobs, the workers voted to accept the agreement. The USWA officials, especially those in the District 6 (Ontario) headquarters, felt betrayed by the company's attempt to exploit workers' fears to win a local ratification vote rather than to develop an understanding directly with the union.

After the Steffco experience, the USWA vowed a tough fight in its overall negotiations with Stelco Steel. Several other factors combined to produce a costly showdown. Within the company, John Allan, the Chairman, and Vic Harris, the Vice-President of Industrial Relations, a long-term Stelco hand, had retired. According to the union, bargaining was handed over to "neophyte" negotiators who tried to change the "game." The company proposed negotiating nine different agreements. The union insisted on common table negotiations on pensions, group insurance, and supplementary unemployment benefits (SUB). The company wanted cost-of-living increases, tied to productivity. The USWA calculated that steelworkers had lost about 86 cents an hour in earning power during the 1987–90 contract. It asked for a $3.00 per hour raise over two years, with another 4 percent to cover inflation resulting from the newly introduced goods-and-services tax (GST), indexed pensions, and restrictions on the number of contractors used. Underlying the impasse in bargaining was Stelco's attempt to tailor each contract to the economic realities of each operation, in contrast to the USWA's attempt to secure standard terms of employment for all its members at Stelco.

The talks broke down, and a strike started in August 1990, even as the industry was slipping into a recession. The strike lasted thirteen weeks and was characterized by each side using picket-line and legal tactics to neutralize the other.[18] Eventually the union gave up its demand for centralized bargaining on common issues, and nine separate agreements were signed. However, each local presented identical positions on common issues, even as they bargained separately. Thus, centralized bargaining was abandoned as a formal structure, although some aspects of it did influence the talks. Another seven plants belonging to Stelco Enterprises signed similar contracts after three months.

The 1990 agreement contained three new provisions that may set the tone for collective bargaining in the 1990s. First, there were considerable improvements in terms affecting employment security. A joint labour–management committee became empowered to examine all plans to subcontract work and to consider possible alternatives. Stelco must open its books to the union and back its case for subcontracting. Though its powers are to be exercised only through the grievance procedure,[19] the formation of this committee in itself could prove to be a major improvement in employment security, as it gives workers more input into decisions affecting employment. The agreement also permitted workers scheduled to be laid off to go for job interviews on company time. Severance pay was improved for laid-off workers to a maximum of one year's pay. Recall security was provided. Special early retirement provisions were established as an incentive. A 30-year employee could get up to 23 months' vacation pay before retirement, and indexed pensions, another new benefit, would, it was hoped, encourage many to opt for early retirement.

Second, an income-sharing plan based on value added was introduced. The union had successfully resisted profit-sharing proposals in the 1984 and 1987 talks (Adams 1988). It is designed to reward high-quality work during periods of high profitability. The plan is based on value added (the adjusted gross margin or AGM) beyond a historical benchmark at each plant. For example, at the Hilton Works, the benchmark is set at an AGM of 13 percent, the average AGM for 1987, 1988, and 1989. Each plant has its own benchmark. Any excess over an AGM of 13 percent is split 75/25 between the company and the workers. During 1991, Lake Erie Works paid out dividends under the plan in the first two quarters, paying the maximum allowable ($3.00 an hour) in the second quarter. Edmonton Works also made payments in both quarters; there were no payments at other sites. In the United States, many profit-sharing plans were offered in the context of concessions (Kochan, Katz, and McKersie 1986). In this case, it was not clear if the plan was a replacement for base-wage increases. Clearly, it would act as a safety valve, paying out dividends when profits are high.

Lastly, the agreement provided for indexed pensions, which, although not new in Canada (GM and Ford had negotiated these earlier in 1990), was a first for the steel industry. The plan aimed to compensate workers for up to 80 percent of inflation, and applied to both current and future retirees. Indexing would be funded out of pension surpluses, which, according to the agreement, belong to workers and not to the employer.

After the strike, the company recalled its work force very slowly. Some constraints were temporary, such as a $127 million renovation of a key blast furnace in Hamilton, which was completed in May 1991. Other factors were structural and, therefore, more worrisome. The company estimated that, during the strike, roughly 5 percent of its customer base had vanished. Some steel-consuming industrial plants had closed, and others had turned to imports. Together, the loss of these customers meant a reduction in demand of 400 000 tons for the Canadian steel industry.

Looking to the Future

The labour strife at Stelco well illustrates the problems and pressures generated by the restructuring of Canadian industry. The traditional industrial relations system, which relied on pattern bargaining and extension of a standard set of terms to all workers within the firm and, preferably, to the entire industry, became increasingly untenable. At the industry level, the failure of the USWA to organize Dofasco has made pattern bargaining, the hallmark of industrial relations in the auto industry, an unsustainable strategy. According to Bob Milbourne,[20] who became president of Stelco Steel in January 1991 and president and chief operating officer of Stelco, Inc., in May 1991, Dofasco's nonunion status causes large amounts of income transfer from unionized facilities to nonunion producers during every strike. "To understand our situation, imagine what it would be like if a major producer like Ford were nonunion in the auto industry."

Within the company, Stelco's productivity, costs, and profit margins vary a great deal across the integrated mills, minimills, and steel components, such as fasteners and forgings. The company, therefore, is searching for ways to tie compensation more directly to each operation and to move away from the notion that the Stelco name must carry a standard compensation scheme across its diverse operations. The income-sharing plan discussed earlier, with separate benchmarks for each plant, is a step in this direction. Stelco is also eyeing agreements made by the USWA at smaller mills, such as Ipsco, where the union has agreed to changes in the contract in return for new investments. Edmonton Works competes directly with Ipsco in some products, and Stelco is fearful that, unless the union allows similar changes to occur at Edmonton Works, Stelco would lose business to Ipsco. The union, though it has accommodated these business needs to some extent, is wary of management efforts to weaken its power. Clearly, it finds some of the company demands unjustifiable, and others difficult to accommodate within its political process and structure.

According to Bob Milbourne, the company, while clear about the need to develop compensation and other arrangements tied to the needs of each specific product line, will strive to improve relations with the union. In a speech, he acknowledged that Stelco's "five-year investment in employee relations, training, and attitudinal change, based on a commitment to secure, stable employment for the people in our manufacturing facilities was inadequate" (Milbourne 1990, 1). In an interview with one of the authors, he summarized Stelco's strategy:

Our lack of dialogue and development of a strategic agenda with the union have been our main failures. While we will continue to stress that the best business solutions can be developed only locally at each plant, we want to increase contacts with the union to develop an on-going dialogue and an agenda to make Stelco profitable and the employees better off. Clearly, we can not afford more incidents such as the PEP program in Contrecoeur (which was done in good faith but using the wrong approach) and the Steffco negotiations (which was deliberate on our part and which left the union with no room to manoeuvre).

Our current contract provides for more formal contacts with the union over contracting-out and pensions. These will be supplemented with active dialogue with the National and district-level union officers. For this reason, we hope to reactivate our membership within CSTEC, a seat which has not been occupied since our former chairman, John Allan, resigned his position in late 1989.

We find that the "one size fits all" type of approach to compensation and work rules was perpetuated by both company and union bureaucracies. In our attempt to facilitate solutions at the level of plant manager and the local union, we have eliminated the corporate industrial relations function starting in 1991. The argument of economies of scale is no longer as valid for centralizing a variety of functions, such as payroll, because technology (computers, etc.) allows us to obtain the same efficiencies at a more decentralized level.

By May 1991, when Stelco held its annual meeting, the company's troubles had mounted to such levels that its very existence was threatened. Stelco posted a loss of $196.7 million for 1990, a stunning reversal from a profit of $93.9 million in 1989. In March 1991, the company ended an unbroken 75-year record of dividends by suspending all further payments. Its common stock, which traded at around $21 a share in early 1990, dropped to around $8 in March, and slipped further to around $5 by early fall 1991. In the first half of 1991, Stelco lost another $79 million, though it was expected that its financial position would improve in the latter half of 1991.

Stelco's dramatic reversal of fortunes highlighted the competitive pressures under which Canadian steel companies will operate in the 1990s. First, companies in Stelco's position cannot hope to survive without active co-operation with its union. Industrial relations strategies, therefore, must be integrated with the overall business strategy of the firm. In his address to the shareholders at the annual meeting in May 1991, Chairman Fred Telmer proposed "making peace with the union" as one of the three components of his strategy to return the company to profitability. Second, firms need to restructure to move away from low-value-added products to high-technology, high-value-added products. The result may be the loss of jobs and heavy investments in training, but the ones that remain are likely to be more secure. Third, Canadian steel companies must look to the North American market rather than limit themselves to Canadian markets. According to Telmer, Stelco would aim at 4 percent of the North American market in the future, as opposed to its historical stance of supplying 30 percent of Canada's requirements.

At this meeting, Telmer also announced that the company will go back to its original organizational structure by dissolving the subsidiaries, Stelco Steel and Stelco Enterprises, and bringing all operations directly under Stelco, Inc.

DOFASCO

Founded in 1912, Dofasco was the second-largest steel producer until 1988, when it became the largest, following its acquisition of Algoma. It is also the most profitable company in the Canadian steel industry, and one of the most profitable among steelmakers in the industrialized West. Table 3.8 provides an overview of its operating results during the 1980s. Although Dofasco manufactured a wide range of products, it specialized in flat-rolling, putting out sheets and coated-steel products.

Because of its financial success, as well as its alternate employee relations paradigm, it provides a unique opportunity for comparison. Its employee relations policy—reflected in the corporate slogan, "Our product is steel; our strength is people"—is central to its corporate image. The philosophy of employee relations was instilled in the company by its founding chairman, Frank A. Sherman, a member of the founding family, whose Golden Rule for effective employee relations has been, "Treat others as you want to be treated yourself." As a nonunion company, it has relied on these simple principles, in addition to modern innovative human-resource practices, such as those of newer firms described by, among others, Foulkes (1980), Verma and Kochan (1985), and Verma (1985). Dofasco could have been described as an old-style nonunion company in 1991. It relied on close contacts with its employees, mixed with a benevolent paternalism that characterized the human-relations school of the 1920s. The main components of its human-resources strategy are its nonunion status; a set of policies aimed at open communications and close employer–employee contact; incentive programs, such as a suggestion scheme and a profit-sharing plan; and a set of "as if unionized" policies that recognize seniority; a grievance procedure, and other employee benefits negotiated by unions elsewhere. Each of these is discussed below.

Several attempts to unionize Dofasco workers over the years were unsuccessful.[21] Prior to 1938, when a profit-sharing plan was introduced, attempts to unionize were suppressed with a heavy hand—union sympathizers were either fired or laid off (Storey 1981, 11). Beginning with the profit-sharing plan in 1938, the company gradually evolved a set of employee-welfare policies that wooed rather than coerced workers away from unionization. For example, it curbed the powers of foremen to hire and fire, and gradually introduced a complaint procedure. It also promised, in 1946, that wages and major benefits, such as holidays and hours of work, negotiated at Stelco would be closely emulated at Dofasco, a promise that

Table 3.8
Dofasco Inc.: An Historical Overview

	1981	1982	1983	1984[a]	1985	1986	1987	1988	1989	1990
Revenues (millions)	1 768	1 486	1 606	1 926	1 994	1 935	2 163	2 982	3 908	3 250
Profits (millions)	169	64	120	181	170	136	154	222	218	(679)
Assets (millions)	2 052	2 023	2 175	2 204	2 673	2 789	3 060	4 872	5 091	3 401
Debt/equity ratio	0.9	0.9	1.1	0.3	0.2	0.3	0.3	0.6	2.2	2.8
Return-on-investment%	NA	NA	16.36	22.57	17.82	12.76	13.29	14.84	13.79	(18.8)
Raw steel production in net tons (000s)	4 258	3 626	3 700	4 468	4 373	4 035	4 048	4 989	7 242	5 746
Shipments in net tons (000s)[b]	3 223	2 682	2 858	3 319	3 258	3 421	3 411	4 388	6 019	5 015
Revenue per ton ($)[c]	415	409	562	580	612	565	634	680	649	646
Operating profit per ton ($)[c]	40	18	32	41	39	34	38	44	30	(118)
Exports (% of sales)	NA	NA	11	14	12	16	17	16	26	26
Capital spending (millions)	249	138	52	91	195	451	424	199	321	375
Number of employees	13 700	12 700	11 400	13 200	13 600	12 800	13 100	22 500	22 500	19 200

Notes: [a] Figures for 1984 have been adjusted for capital reorganization for 3-for-1 split, Jan., 1984.
[b] Shipments include flat rolled steel products, steel castings, semi-finished steel.
[c] Revenue per ton and operation profit per ton were calculated on amount produced.

Sources: Data supplied by Dofasco upon request.

the company has kept up to the present. These policies gradually reduced the need for the company to use a heavy hand in opposing unionization drives.

Communication and Contact

Dofasco's emphasis on communication and close contacts with its employees was reflected in "fireside chats" that all managers and supervisors were encouraged to hold with the employees. In general, this contact was made on a one-on-one basis, although some smaller departments would hold a weekly meeting. In recent years, the president began sending out a video newsletter (roughly once every six months, though this is not a stated goal) to keep workers informed about the company. In addition to in-house publications, special meetings are called to explain new technologies, investments, and reorganization plans.

There is a "visitation" program under which two full-time visitation officers call on employees who need help during illness or other family occasions, such as funerals. The company throws a huge Christmas party for all its employees every year. Thirty-five thousand employees and their families are taken by bus to a large warehouse, where each of them receives a gift and their families enjoy entertainment. It is a large undertaking, and has substantial symbolic value for the company and, it would appear, the employees. All employees receive a "Christmas Bonus" cheque, whose symbolic significance is important beyond its monetary value ($50). The company maintains a large recreational centre (Recreation Park) in Hamilton at its own expense, offering a range of recreational facilities to employees free of charge.

Suggestion Scheme

Dofasco has operated a suggestion scheme for employees for many years. Employees are encouraged to submit suggestions for improving any aspect of work. More than 4000 suggestions were received in each of the last two years: 4465 in 1989 and 4094 in 1990 (see Table 3.9). A small group of full-time staff processes all suggestions. About 40 percent of the ideas are accepted in any year. In 1989, 1739 suggestions were accepted; 1934 suggestions were accepted, for implementation in 1990. Employees receive a cash award based on the net savings obtained from im-

Table 3.9
Suggestion Scheme at Dofasco

	1990	1989
New ideas received	4094	4465
Ideas processed	4411	4344
Ideas adopted	1934	1739
% Adopted	43.8	40.0

Source: Data supplied by Dofasco upon request.

plementing the suggestion. There is an upper limit of $50 000 (tax paid), an amount that was paid out in one instance in the last two years.

Profit-sharing Plan

Dofasco's profit-sharing plan, introduced in 1938, became a key component of its human-resource strategy over the years. Some researchers have concluded that the plan was the most significant company policy that helped keep the company stay nonunion over the years (Storey 1983). The plan is open to all employees after two years of service. Upon joining, every member receives an orientation and a gift of welcome. Each employee contributes a maximum of $300 per annum, and the company contributes 14 percent of pretax profits (for the Hamilton operations only) to the plan. Half of the accumulations go to a profit-sharing fund that is essentially a pension plan for the employees. The other half of the fund is allocated to a deferred plan that may be left in with the profit-sharing fund for retirement savings or taken out in cash every year. Employees received a bonus in every year during the 1980s.

"As if Unionized" Policies

The company maintained a set of policies as if it were unionized. According to company officials, this plan was designed to provide many of the same services to its employees as workers received in a unionized workplace. The close proximity of Stelco's Hamilton Works clearly influenced these policies. For example, wages and major benefits closely follow developments in the union sector. Similarly, seniority plays a major role in personnel decisions such as promotion, transfer, layoffs, and recall. The company runs several employee-assistance programs such as counselling for alcohol and drug abuse, for vocational and rehabilitational needs, and for family-related problems.

A grievance procedure called an "open door" policy has been used by the company to encourage employees to discuss their problems. Every employee has the right to speak to his or her supervisor. If the problem is not resolved, the employee can consult with those in higher levels of supervision within their department, and then the director of personnel. The last step would be a meeting with the president of the company. It is the responsibility of the manager at each level to arrange a meeting for the employee to take the complaint to the next level. No statistics are kept on the number of complaints raised and settled at various stages. According to the company, "a few" go to the president every year, but most are resolved at lower levels.

There is also a program for reimbursement of tuition fees for any pre-approved programs of training or education. Initially, reimbursement was limited to courses closely related to a person's job. In recent years, the scope of courses eligible for reimbursement has broadened considerably. It is generous compared to many other such programs.

Job Security and Training

There was no formally stated policy of providing job security, though the company would appear to place a heavy emphasis on it. The only major layoff in the history of the company was in 1982 when some 2100 were laid off during the recession. All those who wanted to return (about 1900) were recalled within a year. The company has downsized operations in the 1980s, a procedure that was accomplished completely through attrition. To provide continuity of employment, the company reassigned workers and provided substantial training to ensure smooth transfers. Training was provided in-house in a wide range of areas, from trades training to quality control. The corporate head office established a training group within the human-resource function in 1990 to give training a strategic focus within the company. The effect of these practices was reflected in the long service status of the work force. In 1990, the average age was 41 years, and the average tenure 16 years.

Absenteeism

Dofasco maintained a relatively low level of absenteeism in its plants during the 1980s. The overall level was 4.9 percent (absent days as a percentage of total days worked) in both 1988 and 1989. Accountable absenteeism, defined as absence under employee control, such as non–work-related illnesses, totalled 2.9 percent in 1988 and 2.8 percent in 1989. Compensable absenteeism, defined as work-related injuries and illnesses and other absences out of employee's control, such as jury duty, added up to 1.8 percent in both 1988 and 1989. An absenteeism counselling program along the following lines was apparently effective: a verbal counselling followed the fourth incident of absence in any twelve-month period; the fifth incident incurred a written reprimand; the sixth incident resulted in a final warning, which could be written or include a suspension; the seventh incident could result in dismissal. Company officials were of the view that very few workers abused the system.

Future Directions

In 1991, Dofasco was exploring a number of new policy initiatives that would give it the profile of a more "modern" nonunion firm. For example, it had begun to involve employees in task forces structured to address specific problems of quality or other aspects of production. Some of these task forces were vertically integrated; others included employees from a given area of the shop floor. The frequency, role, and responsibilties were not formally defined. Each task force was formed on an *ad hoc* basis. No specific training was geared to task force members, although some members might have been exposed to in-house training that was conducted periodically.

In a new mill that was under construction at the time of this writing, the company was considering forming work groups on the shop floor. Its specific details were not yet decided. Similarly, the company was considering the use of pay-for-skill for certain maintenance groups.

ALGOMA

Prior to its acquisition by Dofasco in 1988, Algoma had been the third-largest fully integrated steelmaker and supplier of flat-rolled steel rails and structurals, and seamless tubes. Table 3.10 provides a summary of its operations during the 1980s. Both symbolically and substantively, Algoma became a paradigm for all of the industry's ills in 1991 when the company faced bankruptcy and, according to some analysts, even total closure. At the time of this writing, it was not clear what solutions would be found for the company. The ability of all the parties and stakeholders to find a way to make Algoma profitable once again will be a key indicator of the future of the Canadian steel industry. Although many of Algoma's troubles were specific to its own situation, there were others that it shared in common with the rest of the industry: the need to modernize technology, to make operations more profitable to pay for the cost of modernization, and to transform industrial relations in a way that it would become a key to productivity growth.

The company was founded in the 1890s by Francis Hector Clergue, an American who transformed Sault Ste. Marie in northwestern Ontario by building a steel mill, railway, foundry, pulp mill, and mining operations. Before its current crisis, the company had faced bankruptcy twice before: in 1903, and during the Depression in the mid-1930s. As Table 3.10 shows, the company was profitable in 1981, but had a difficult time recovering from the 1982–83 recession. It lost money in all the years between 1982 and 1986, returning to profitablity in 1987 and 1988. In 1989, it barely broke even; 1990 was a disastrous year in which it posted a loss of $108 million.

Its main products are steel slabs, flat-rolled products for the auto industry, plates and structural sections for the construction industry, and tubes used chiefly in the oil industry. In 1988, Dofasco became interested in buying Algoma as it would provide much-needed ingots and slabs for the existing hot mills and a new $465 million cold-rolling mill that Dofasco was building to become operational in 1992. Despite these attractions and the fact that, during 1978–88, Algoma made more money than it lost, there were several risks associated with the purchase. First, Algoma's mills were situated far from the markets, leaving Algoma with some of the highest transportation costs in the industry. Second, industrial relations were not such that customers could be assured of uninterrupted supply. Third, the structural products were vulnerable to lower-cost producers, and the tube division's prospects were tied to the fortunes of the oil patch. Dofasco decided to buy the company on the premise that Algoma, with a little help, could make money.

Dofasco paid $563 million for the company and invested another $222 million over the next two years, but did little to restructure the company to minimize its weaknesses (Fleming and Olive 1991). Rather than consolidate its operations by cutting back on unprofitable lines, it increased its output in 1988 and 1989. Dofasco made no changes in the top-management ranks and let the old team make all the decisions. Labour relations made little progress during this period. In

Table 3.10
Algoma Steel Corporation Ltd.: An Historical Overview

	1981	1982	1983	1984	1985	1986	1987	1988	1989
Revenues[a] (millions)	1 426	874	860	1104	1177	1093	1228	1384	1492
Profits[a] (millions) (loss)	165	(40)	(127)	(46)	(10)	(53)	31	73	8
Assets[a] (thousands)	1 718	1729	1668	1647	1784	1484	1572	1693	1858
Debt/equity ratio[b]	0.7	0.8	0.9	0.3	0.8	0.7	0.9	NA	1.1
Return-on-investment (%)[c]	NA	NA	(9.88)	0.01	2.38	(1.66)	8.41	12.94	4.91
Steel production net tons[a] (000s)	3 017	1899	2306	2528	2742	2422	2590	2529	2788
Shipment of steel products net tons[a] (approx—in 000s)	2 519	1472	1757	1951	2063	2032	2125	2132	2430
Revenue per ton[c*] ($)	NA	NA	489	566	570	538	578	649	614
Operating profit per ton[c*] ($)	NA	NA	(70)	8	25	(5)	NA	NA	NA
Exports (% of sales)[c]	NA	NA	22	36	18	18	20	18	27
Capital spending[a] (millions)	265	185	32	24	143	131	45	72	186
Number of employees[bd]	13 787	7100	8900	9000	9868	7700	8700	9206	6132

Sources: [a] Financial Post Cards, 1990.
   [b] Canadian Business, various years.
   [c] Globe and Mail Report on Business, various years.
   [d] Annual reports, various years.
   * Between 1984 and 1989, revenue per ton and operating profit per ton were calculated on amount shipped.

fact, they deteriorated to the point that a thirteen-week work stoppage[22] began on August 1, 1991. Apparently, the management was not in a great hurry to settle the strike (Fleming and Olive 1991). According to the union, "the company didn't even table a monetary package until after the strike deadline had passed." By January 1991, Algoma had begun to run out of cash, and faced the prospects of bankruptcy. On January 23, 1991, Dofasco announced that it would write off its $700 million investment and invest no more capital in the financially troubled Algoma. This action essentially left Algoma to manage its survival on its own resources. At this time, Algoma's debts, amounting to $817 million, had to be restructured if the company was to survive.

In summer 1991, the union proposed an employee buyout plan, which called for, among other things,[23] a fresh infusion of capital by Dofasco. Dofasco responded that it planned to have "no further direct financial involvement in Algoma" (*Financial Post*, August 2, 1991). Earlier, Algoma had obtained a bridge-financing loan of $40 million to buy time until October (a court-ordered deadline) to present a restructuring plan. The workers voted in June to take a 14.5 percent wage cut to raise $10 million as their share of the bridge loan.[24] Negotiations over the restructuring plan continued into September 1991.

The Algoma crisis raised a number of issues for the industry as a whole. In each case, the resolutions found would have implications for the industry's growth or decline in the 1990s. First, the critical role of industrial relations at a time of crisis was well demonstrated. The crisis pointed out that, if steel companies were to prosper, industrial relations would have to improve to the point that a joint process could manage the restructuring process without costly disputes. Second, it raised the issue of worker ownership. Some employee buyouts in the United States, such as at Weirton Steel (formerly a unit of National Steel) and Republic Engineered Steel (formerly of LTV), became reasonably profitable and stable after the change to employee ownership. Algoma faces much tougher business conditions than did these U.S. plants. In 1991, Canadian tax laws did not permit any tax advantages for such buyouts. Largely influenced by the Algoma case, the provincial government announced its intention in July 1991 to introduce a bill that would provide tax advantages for worker ownership. Of course, for a buyout to be successful, the business must be a viable one and, in Algoma's case, it might have to be a downsized, restructured operation. These issues would have to be resolved by the new owners. The question of whether such buyouts could prove to be a solution to the industry's problems, at least in some cases, remains unanswered for now.

Third, this case well illustrated the transition that the Canadian steel industry needed to go through to revive its profitability. Canadian manufacturers needed to move out of low-value-added products and into high-value-added items, which inevitably required infusions of new technology and capital. Algoma may well end up scrapping much of its operations and concentrating on a smaller core that is more technology intensive.[25] Last, Algoma's case brought to the surface the issue of a governmental role in steel's future. The productive and profitable 1970s capped two decades of favourable public policy and high priority for the industry's needs in areas such as investment and trade policy (Barnett and Schorsch 1983). By 1991, it appeared that the federal government had moved its priorities away from steel to other high-growth sectors. Could the industry rejuvenate itself without an actively sympathetic administration in Ottawa? Some analysts believed that it would be extremely difficult for the industry to return to its previous competitive strength without a better understanding of the industry's needs within government policy-making circles. Although the future remained uncertain in mid-1991, the Algoma crisis had helped illustrate the critical role that public policy could play in shaping the future of the steel industry.

THE CANADIAN STEEL TRADE AND EMPLOYMENT CONGRESS (CSTEC)

Over the years, the industry has faced two problems that have brought labour and management closer together. The first, and the more obvious, common problem has been the need to influence trade policy. Although both labour and management had lobbied the government in the past over trade issues, they had either done so separately or formed *ad hoc* alliances for the issue at hand. The second problem, less obvious in its appeal to both sides, has been one of cyclical and structural worker displacement and the need to assist employees in adjusting to the trauma of job loss. During the 1981–82 recession, the USWA set up a modest network of unemployment help centres to assist workers in relocating and retraining through government-funded programs. Subsequent experience and joint discussion[26] led to the formation of CSTEC, the Canadian Steel Trade and Employment Congress, in May 1985. It is a joint initiative of the USWA and the major steel companies.

On the trade front, it has lobbied the government with some success on monitoring imports and exports and targeting unfair competition from abroad. Its efforts have led to the removal of General Preferential Tariff on imports from South Korea, Brazil, Taiwan, and Romania. On the employment front, apart from lobbying efforts, it provides employment services for dislocated steelworkers. These services are organized under the HEAT (Helping Employees Adjust Together) program described below. CSTEC also conducts research on problems facing the steel industry, and publishes the findings occasionally in the form of reports.

The HEAT Program.

Soon after its third conference in November 1987, CSTEC lobbied the federal government to give it a more prominent role in the employment adjustment process within the industry. The government agreed to transfer its adjustment funds, normally spent under Employment and Immigration Canada's Industrial Adjustment Service (IAS), upto a maximum of $5000 per worker, to CSTEC to provide the same services. Subscription to the HEAT program is voluntary for the companies and local unions, who can opt out of HEAT and go directly to the IAS if they so wish. CSTEC, therefore, must sell the idea to steel companies to make HEAT viable. So far, all the major employers in industry are supporting it.

Under the program, after a layoff or plant closure is announced, workers and management approach CSTEC for adjustment assistance. A local labour–management committee is formed, which works with the help of CSTEC staff (or "facilitators") to assess the needs of the displaced workers and to draw up a plan for providing a range of services. These services may include some or all of the following: information on conditions in the relevant job market, training and counselling on starting your own business, relocation assistance, and personal financial planning and retraining. After three years' experience with HEAT, both labour and management representatives agree that it is an improvement over the earlier system that required each plant to go directly to the IAS. Managers at two companies that have used HEAT services, Sydney Steel and Greenwood Donald, felt that HEAT was better than going to the IAS because it involved less red tape and CSTEC provided specialized industry-specific expertise (*The Worklife Report* 1990). The USWA is very enthusiastic about the program because it helps them demonstrate their effectiveness in providing services to their members. Thus, at least at this level, it is likely that CSTEC and its programs like HEAT will continue to grow in size and importance to the industry.

In the three years from 1988 to 1991, HEAT provided services to 5000 workers in 22 steel plants around the country.[27] The largest group was semiskilled (65 percent), followed by labourers (13 percent), trades (7 percent), clerical (6 percent), technical (2 percent), and supervisors (7 percent). The educational level of this group was modest: nearly 45 percent of the displaced workers did not attain even a high school diploma; only 5.6 percent had obtained a university degree. At the end of the three years, 73 percent of the workers who came through HEAT had found employment. Another 4 percent were in training; 13 percent had retired or taken disbility leave; only 10 percent remained unemployed. Most workers (55.9 percent) increased their wages after taking HEAT's training and counselling; 20.5 percent suffered a small loss in wages of up to $1.50 an hour; 7.9 percent suffered moderate losses ($1.50–$3.00 an hour); 5.6 percent suffered large losses ($3.00–$4.00 an hour); and, 10.1 percent suffered substantial losses ($4.00 an hour and above). Of the occupational groups, the trades group suffered the smallest wage loss ($0.70 an hour); semiskilled and clerical workers suffered the largest losses (about $1.55 an hour); labourers suffered a loss of about $0.80 an hour. Since comparable data are not available for workers who did not go through the HEAT program, it is difficult to assess the differential impact of the HEAT program on these outcomes.

EMPLOYEE INVOLVEMENT

Greater employee involvement was tried by many companies in the 1980s as a key component of their restructuring strategy, although its use was more widespread in the United States than in Canada (Verma 1991; Verma and Kochan 1990). The steel industry began experimenting with employee-involvement programs, but the efforts, in general, were not central to the restructuring strategies. Also, it was more likely to be found in smaller companies than in the large mills. In neither the large nor the small sector, however, did employee involvement make a mark in the 1980s.

Stelco introduced a program (PEP—Performance through Employee Participation) for greater employee involvement at its McMaster Works in Contrecoeur, Quebec. This program was developed by Stelco and reviewed with the local union, which agreed to a trial implementation. The local union, according to the company, had shown some interest in getting more directly involved in issues such as productivity and the quality of workers' jobs on the shop floor. The program was based on workers' identifying problems and developing solutions to them in a fashion similar to a suggestion scheme. The program was intended to improve communication through a number of joint committees. Despite the program's being jointly sponsored at the site, Local 1005 in Hamilton, along with union officials from the National and District 6 offices, strongly opposed the program as it was not negotiated at the bargaining table. The local union in Quebec showed internal divisions, with some backing the Local 1005 position and others wanting to pursue an agenda tailored to the local situation. The dominant thinking within the union was that such local arrangements were creating internal problems for the union. The program was discontinued subsequently by the company.

Similar programs, such as one in LTV's Cleveland plant, have been introduced relatively more successfully in the United States under joint governance. In contrast to the PEP approach, Stelco is successfully introducing self-regulating work teams at its new highly automated zinc-coating line (Z line). The line, when fully operational, will employ 26 workers, within one job classification. Every individual is trained in all aspects of the line. Workers make all production-and-quality-related decisions on the job. Workers were sent to visit plants in Japan and the United States to study state-of-the-art production methods. The union supported the initiative in the hope that the Z line, with its promise of new investments and well-paid jobs, would become a model for the rest of the company to emulate. Although the Z line employed a tiny fraction of the Stelco work force, developments here could influence the makeup of the entire company and its relationship with the union.

Another illustrative example comes from Neelon Casting,[28] a small manufacturer of steel castings in Sudbury, Ontario, with about 300 employees in 1990. The company almost went out of business during the 1981–82 recession. After gaining some concessions from the USWA local, both sides agreed to introduce a highly participatory form of a Scanlon Plan[29] in 1984. Under the plan, weekly production meetings and monthly crew meetings were held to discuss ideas for continuous improvement. In 1985, the company successfully negotiated a five-year wage freeze. In 1986, with few gain-share payouts and discouraged by the concessionary agreement, workers voted to suspend the plan. It was revised and reinstated in

1987 with a two-thirds vote of the employees. Between 1987 and 1990, there were only two gain-sharing payments (payments are made monthly) under the plan. An assessment of the plan by the USWA[30] in 1990 revealed that, despite many frustrations and reservations, many workers supported the plan and made an effort to attend and participate in meetings held as part of the plan. In the last three years, roughly $16 million were invested in the plant, and employment had grown from 190 in January 1987 to more than 300 by the end of 1990.

At Lasco, a minimill located in Whitby, Ontario, the management began to talk to its USWA local as early as 1983 about the need for joint initiatives in improving quality and productivity.[31] Lasco had, in the past, produced steel for the auto industry, a market it had gradually left to concentrate on bars and structurals for the construction industry. The company wanted to re-enter the auto market because of the higher margins obtained on higher-value-added products. The auto industry, under severe pressure from imports to improve quality, had begun to insist that its suppliers guarantee near-zero-defect deliveries and implement some form of employee involvement to ensure such quality. In 1984, the plant management began to seek volunteers to participate in problem-solving task forces. Though union stewards volunteered to participate as individuals, the union was not asked and did not participate in the governance of the task force program. The task forces themselves were vertically integrated, with hourly paid employees usually outnumbered by higher-level employees. By 1990, their use had declined substantially after the company decided not to pursue the auto market. Some task forces were still constituted occasionally.

Both workers and union officials interviewed in late 1990 were of the view that the task forces were very much a management-run and -controlled activity. They viewed the idea positively, but were skeptical about the unilateral control of its process. The company had also introduced teams or crews on the shop floor. The crews generally had a supervisor to begin with, but were being trained to function as self-regulating teams. Over the years, the company had reduced the number of supervisors in relation to its work force.

Atlas Stainless Steels: Forging New Directions[32]

As a small specialty steelmaker, Atlas produces roughly 60 000 tons a year of stainless steel sheets and 200 000 tons a year of stainless steel bars in two Canadian plants, in Tracy, Quebec, and, Welland, Ontario. Formerly a subsidiary of Rio Algom, it was bought by the Sammi group, a large conglomerate from South Korea, in 1989. It has a U.S. subsidiary, Altech, that also produces stainless steel, in two plants in New York.

Labour strife had characterized the Tracy plant since it was built in 1962. Some work stoppages and violence took place during the construction phase itself. In the 1970s and the 1980s, the Tracy plant was no different from most other plants in Quebec. Its employees, represented by two USWA locals since inception—one for plant employees and another for office employees—struck their employer on numerous occasions. The most recent strike in the plant, in

1985, was lengthy (three months) and bitter. Earlier, a nine-month strike in 1979 had led to the plant workers switching their certification from the USWA to the Confederation of National Trade Unions (CNTU), the second-largest labour federation in Quebec. From 1962 to 1985, the Tracy plant reported to the head-quarters at Welland, Ontario. According to company and union officials, some of the strife in earlier years was linked to the perception that Tracy had to report to an "absentee landlord," namely, the head office in Welland. In 1985, Atlas decided to let Tracy form a separate division, complete with its own sales, finance, and personnel functions.

By the end of the 1980s, the plant appeared to be running out of steam. It needed an infusion of capital to upgrade plant and equipment, otherwise its viability would be threatened. Labour–management relations, however, were mired in a very traditional mould that, along with other factors, discouraged most potential investors. When its parent, Rio Algom, put it up for sale, there was a clear signal that Atlas was not a company with a great future.

At this stage, the Quebec government played a role in, first, attracting Sammi to buy the plant and, later, brokering a three-way agreement among the company, the union, and the government. Through the offices of the Minister of Labour, the government orchestrated a deal that guarantees new investments for the plant in exchange for labour peace. Although this *quid pro quo* forms the core of the agreement, it reaches into other areas to ensure that the deal would begin a new era of labour–management co-operation at the company. Specifically, the three-year agreement, signed on March 27, 1991, allows for the following:

1. The *Government of Quebec* will provide a loan guarantee of $100 million at favourable terms.
2. *Atlas Steel* will invest $300 million in new plant[33] and equipment over the next five years and guarantee to maintain employment at a level no less than its 1991 mark (410 bargaining-unit members) for the next six years. The company commits to hire most workers from the Sorel-Tracy region. It will refrain from locking out employees for the next six years.
3. The *union*,[34] a CNTU local, agrees to a no-strike commitment for six years. All other terms of the contract will be renegotiated after three years, at the expiry of this contract. If the parties fail to agree, the dispute will be submitted to binding final-offer (as opposed to item-by-item) arbitration on the entire contract.

Looking beyond the investment-for-peace swap, the government wanted to ensure that the plant embark on a new path toward competitiveness and self-sufficiency. The contract, therefore, commits the parties to work together to restructure the plant.

4. The government will meet every year with both parties to help them live up to the spirit of the agreement and to mediate any problems arising out of the contract.

5. Management and labour will form a joint committee that will oversee all aspects of the modernization plan.

6. The parties agree to collaborate on implementing a quality-improvement program that may involve new forms of work organization.

It is clearly too early to tell if these efforts at sowing new seeds will bear fruit. There are promising signs, though, that recommend this approach. Both labour and management representatives interviewed in mid-1991 expressed the belief that relations had greatly improved between them and there was a "new" spirit of co-operation since the contract was signed.[35] Beyond these "good" feelings and the contract itself, the real test of the renewed relationship lies in the parties' ability to reform the workplace to make it more flexible and productive through joint efforts. For example, the plant currently has no program to enhance worker involvement or to share savings from cost improvements suggested by workers or to foster greater teamwork on the shop floor. It is up to the joint committee set up under the contract to examine these and other relevant innovations for possible introduction and to negotiate the terms under which these may be implemented. If the parties successfully introduce further innovations through the joint process, they will reinforce the spirit that made the current agreement possible. The probability that Atlas will move rapidly toward competitiveness and self-sufficiency, in that case, will be high. If the parties fail in the joint process, the current agreement would appear to be an externally imposed requirement that the parties joined without enthusiasm. In that event, a few years down the road the government will have to intervene again to ensure the plant's viability.

The Atlas case demonstrates a possible model for the role of public policy in the restructuring process. Quebec's approach of brokering a deal and coaxing the parties to work together on restructuring issues is an innovative one. Although not completely new, it is an approach that is not currently very popular in other parts of the country. The success of the Atlas "experiment" in fostering a joint (bilateral) process will determine the effectiveness of using this approach to facilitate restructuring in the 1990s.

*F*uture Directions in Industrial Relations

OUTLOOK FOR THE CANADIAN STEEL INDUSTRY

The crisis in the steel industry in 1991 did not appear to be cyclical in nature. Though the recession was exacerbating some problems, the most serious threats to the industry were structural. Increased global competition was likely to hold prices down and reduce operating margins. Imports from the United States and other countries were capturing an ever-increasing share of the domestic market. However, exports could decline as the U.S. industry continued its trend toward improving productivity. By the end of this decade, the Canadian and U.S. economies would have become highly integrated. If Mexico joined the free-trade zone, it would bring additional competitive pressures to bear in certain products such as carbon steels and structurals. Production in less-developed economies was expected to increase sharply in the 1990s. China's steel production will grow by 47 percent by the year 2000, according to estimates by Paine Webber, a consulting firm that specializes in the global steel industry. These developments, combined with slow growth in developed economies, were expected to cause a decrease in Canadian raw steel output to less than 14 million tons by the year 2000.

The elements of a survival strategy in this environment will most likely include the following: Canadian producers will have to continue moving toward specialty products of high quality and away from large-volume, low-value-added products. In order to move to more technology-intensive production, Canadian mills will need continued investment in new technologies. These investments will be financed either by attracting new capital or through internal resources. In either case, there will be pressures to obtain higher quality, better customer service, and moderate costs.

SURVIVAL STRATEGIES AND THE INDUSTRIAL RELATIONS CONNECTION

Policy makers in the industry on all sides must decide if the prevailing system of industrial relations and human-resources policies can help them pursue a viable path toward survival and prosperity. The evidence in 1991 suggested major gaps between prevailing practices and the requirements of a successful competitive strategy. The parties were not able to avoid costly work stoppages in 1990 despite their experience in working jointly on issues of mutual concern (e.g., CSTEC). The steel industry remained, at the beginning of the 1990s, with one of the lowest investments in human capital. Lastly, there were only modest movements in collective bargaining in the 1980s toward creating a highly trained, committed, and involved work force that could work with management to provide high quality and service at low cost.

Investment in Human Capital

In the 1980s, Canadian steel companies made major investments in new technology, plant, and equipment. Even as this investment poured in, the work force was reduced by approximately 25 percent. According to the seniority rules, the majority of laid-off workers were younger and, hence, better educated. The industry now faces the 1990s with an older, less educated work force than in the 1980s. This fact is particularly worrisome at a time when firms will be increasing their reliance on new technologies and production methods. The CSTEC experience in placing laid-off workers illustrates the past underinvestment in human capital in the industry (Warrian 1990). The fact that steelworkers require major investments in time and expense to equip them to re-enter the job market successfully indicates that the steel industry has fallen behind in its investments in human capital. As the investment in physical capital increases, the need for better-trained workers will require higher investments in human capital as well. Recent studies reinforce the value of investments in workers, without which returns on investments in physical capital can not be realized fully (Kochan 1988).

Labour–Management Co-operation and the Task of Restructuring

Although the formation of CSTEC was not explicitly meant to improve labour–management relations at the plant or firm level, it was only natural for many to expect that the experience of the parties in dealing with each other at a centralized level would benefit the relationship at other levels. Many of the principal personalities are the same at both the industry and the firm level. In theory, then, one would expect that CSTEC's experience in a restructuring issue such as employment adjustment could facilitate new accommodations on flexibility and security within collective bargaining. Unfortunately, this did not happen to any significant extent in the 1980s. In a speech to the Canadian Steel Producers Association in 1989, Gerard Docquier, the Canadian director of the USWA, summarized his experience:

> In some relationships, I think it is fair to say that we understand each other better. . . . In others, however, the objective appears to be to keep the CSTEC relationship in a watertight compartment. Cooperation and communication on CSTEC issues; the law of the jungle at the bargaining table and the shop floor. (Docquier 1989)

Docquier saw two risks associated with the split-policy approach. First, it cuts short the gains that both parties can make in labour relations, flowing from co-operation at other levels. Second, it puts CSTEC itself at risk. It is diffcult for local leaders to understand why their national leaders are working co-operatively with management when there is so little give-and-take in bargaining and in the daily activities of the shop floor. Without some spillover of goodwill and co-operation from the centralized activities to relations at the firm or plant level, local enthusiasm for the centrally directed initiatives is likely to wane sooner or later.

REFERENCES

Adams, Robert M. 1952. *The Development of the United Steelworkers of America in Canada, 1936–51.* Monograph. Kingston, ON.

Adams, Roy J. 1988. "The 'Old Industrial Relations' and Corporate Competitiveness: A Canadian Case." *Employee Relations* 10/2: 3–7.

Adams, R., and I. Zeytinoglu. 1987. "Labour–Management Dispute Resolution in Canadian Heavy Industry: The Hilton Works Case." In T. Hanami and R. Blanpain, eds., *Industrial Conflict Resolution Market Economies. A Study of Canada, Great Britain and Sweden.* Deventer: Kluwer. 71–99.

Ansberry, Clare. 1991. "Hazardous Duty: Nucor Steel's Sheen Is Marred by Deaths of Workers at Plants." *Wall Street Journal*, May 10.

Bain, Trevor. 1992. *Banking the Furnace: Unions, Job Security, and Restructuring of the Steel Industry in Eight Countries.* Kalamazoo, MI: W.E. Upjohn Institute of Employment Research.

Barnett, Donald F., and Louis Schorsch. 1983. *Steel: Upheaval in a Basic Industry.* Cambridge: Ballinger Publishing Company.

Barnett, Donald F., and Robert W. Crandall. 1986. *Up From the Ashes: The Rise of the Steel Minimill in the United States.* Washington, DC: The Brookings Institution.

Canadian Steel Trade and Employment Congress (CSTEC). 1989. *Steel Trade Between the USA and Canada.* Toronto: January.

Crandall, Robert W. 1981. *The U.S. Steel Industry in Recurrent Crisis.* Washington, DC: The Brookings Institution.

CSPA. 1989. *Steel Facts 1988.* Ottawa: Canadian Steel Producers Association.

Delaney, Ken. 1989. "Developing a Worker's Agenda for Gainsharing." Paper presented to Wayne State University, Detroit, MI, March 23. Toronto: USWA Canadian National Office.

Docquier, Gerard. 1989. "Labour Relations in the Canadian Steel Industry—Are We Really Getting Anywhere?" Address given to the Canadian Steel Producers' Association, October.

Fleming, James, and David Olive. 1991. "Dofasco's Big Misadventure." *Report on Business Magazine*, June, 32–39.

Foulkes, Fred K. 1980. *Personnel Policies in Large Nonunion Companies.* Englewood Cliffs, NJ: Prentice-Hall Inc.

Heneault, Robert E. 1989. "The Competitive World—Is Canada a Fit or a Mis-Fit?" Industrial Relations Centre, Queen's University. Reprint Series No. 87. Kingston, Ontario

Hogan, William T., S.J. 1983. *World Steel in the 1980s: A Case of Survival.* Toronto: Lexington Books.

——. 1984. *Steel in the United States: Restructuring to Compete.* Toronto: Lexington Books.

——. 1987. *Minimills and Integrated Mills: A Comparison of Steelmaking in the United States.* Toronto: Lexington Books.

Howell, Thomas R., William A. Noellert, Jesse G. Kreier, and Alan M. Wolff. 1988. *Steel and the State: Government Intervention and Steel's Structural Crisis*. Boulder, CO: Westview Press.

Keeling, Bernard. 1988. *World Steel: A New Assessment of Trends and Prospects*. London: Economist Intelligence Unit.

Kenny, Martin, and Richard Florida. 1991. "How Japanese Industry Is Rebuilding the Rust Belt." *Technology Review*, February/March: 25–33.

Kochan, Thomas A. 1988. "On the Human Side of Technology." ICL *Technical Journal*, November: 391–400.

Kochan, Thomas A., Harry C. Katz, and Robert B. McKersie. 1986. *The Transformation of American Industrial Relations*. New York: Basic Books.

Kumar, Pradeep. 1991. "Industrial Relations in Canada and the United States: From Uniformity to Divergence." Working Paper. Kingston, ON: School of Industrial Relations, Queen's University.

Lendvay-Zwickl, Judith. 1988. *How Well Do We Compete? Relative Labour Costs in Canada and the United States*. Conference Board of Canada Report 28–88. Ottawa: Conference Board of Canada.

Lesieur, Frederick G. 1958. Editor, *The Scanlon Plan*. Cambridge, MA: M.I.T. Press.

Litvak, Isaiah A., and Christopher J. Maule. 1985. "The Canadian Aluminum and Steel Industries." In D.G. McFetridge, ed., *Technological Change in Canadian Industry*. Toronto: University of Toronto Press. 145–175.

Milbourne, R. J. 1990. "Stelco Steel— The Agenda for the '90s." Speech given to the Niagara Chapter of the American Iron and Steel Engineers, November 6.

Paine Webber. 1991. *World Steel Dynamics*. New York.

Paré, Terence P. 1991. "The Big Threat to Big Steel's Future." *Fortune*, July 15, 106–8.

Preston, Richard. 1991. *American Steel: Hot Metal Men and the Resurrection of the Rust Belt*. Toronto: Prentice-Hall.

Rayback, Joseph G. 1966. *A History of American Labor*. New York: Free Press.

Statistics Canada. 1990. *Corporations and Labour Unions Returns Act*, Catalogue 71–202. Ottawa: Minister of Supply and Services Canada.

Stelco. 1989. Annual Report. Hamilton, ON: Stelco.

Stieber, Jack. 1980. "Steel" in Gerald G Somers, ed., *Collective Bargaining: Contemporary American Experience*. Madison, WI: Industrial Relations Research Associations. 151–208.

Storey, Robert Henry. 1981. "Workers, Unions and Steel: The Shaping of the Hamilton Working Class, 1935–1948." Ph.D. Thesis, University of Toronto, Department of Sociology.

———. 1983. "Unionization Versus Corporate Welfare: The 'Dofasco Way.'" *Labour/Le Travailleur*, 12 (Fall): 7–43.

Sweeney, Vincent D. 1947. *The United Steelworkers of America: The First*

Ten Years. Pittsburgh: USWA.

———. 1956. *The United Steelworkers of America: Twenty Years Later, 1936 – 56.* Pittsburgh: USWA.

United Steel Workers of America (USWA). n.d. "Towards a Trade Union QWL Agenda." Policy paper of USWA National Office (Canada), Toronto, ON.

———. 1987. "Facing Management's New Workplace Strategies." Policy paper presented to the Canadian Policy Conference, United Steel Workers of America, Toronto, ON.

———. 1989. "Overview and Analysis." Prepared by Research Department, USWA National Office (Canada) for USWA Steel Conference, Toronto, June 13, 1989.

———. 1990. "Steel in Canada: A Strategic Overview." Paper presented to the Western Rolling Mills 1990 Conference, Vancouver, BC, November 23.

Verma, Anil. 1985. "Electric Cable Plant," in Thomas A. Kochan and Thomas A. Barocci, eds., *Industrial Relations and Human Resource Management.* Boston, MA: Little, Brown. 425–433.

———. 1991. "The Prospects for Innovation in Canadian Industrial Relations in the 1990s." Report made to Canadian Federation of Labour and World Trade Centres in Canada Joint Committee on Labour Market Adjustment. Ottawa: Canadian Federation of Labour.

Verma, Anil, and Mark Gallina. 1991. "Radical and Unionist Critiques of Direct Worker Participation." Paper presented to the *Third European Re-gional Congress of the International Industrial Relations Association,* Bari-Naples, Italy, September 23–26.

Verma, Anil, and Thomas A. Kochan. 1985. "The Growth and Nature of the Nonunion Sector Within a Firm." In Thomas A. Kochan, ed., *Challenges and Choices Facing American Labor.* Cambridge, MA: MIT Press. 89–118.

———. 1990. "Two paths to Innovations in Industrial Relations: The Case of Canada and the United States." *Labour Law Journal* 41(8) August: 597–601.

Verma, Anil, and Noah M. Meltz. 1990. "Union Organizing Activity in Ontario in the 1980s." In A. Ponak, ed., *Proceedings of the Annual Meeting of the Canadian Industrial Relations Association.* Victoria, BC: Canadian Industrial Relations Association. 465–474.

Verma, Anil, and Mark E. Thompson. 1990. "Managerial strategies in Industrial Relations in the 1980's: Comparing the US & Canadian Experience." In *Proceedings of the Forty-first Annual Meeting,* of the Industrial Relations Research Association. Madison, WI: Industrial Relations Research Association.

Warrian, Peter. 1990. "Is the Wolf Coming to the Canadian Steel Industry in 1990." Unpublished manuscript, Canadian Steel Trade and Employment Congress, Toronto, April.

Wilkinson, Paul. 1990. "A Description and Analysis of Workers' Perceptions of the Effectiveness of the Paton Plan at Neelon Castings."

Report made to USWA (Canada), Toronto, Ontario.

The Worklife Report. 1990. "The Canadian Steel Trade and Employment Congress." Vol. 7, No. 3, 9–10.

ENDNOTES

1   This manuscript has benefited greatly from the information and feedback provided by many individuals. While it is impossible to individually thank everyone who helped us, we are especially grateful to Roy Adams, Don Barnett, Reynald Bourque, Ken Delaney, Dennis Martin, Bob Milbourne, Bob Primeau, Don Wells, and participants at the Industrial Relations in Canadian Industry conference, among others, for all their help. Timely and able research assistance was provided by Joanne Sack, Frank White, and Angela Zezza. Financial support from the Social Sciences and Humanities Research Council and the National Centre for Management Research and Development is gratefully acknowledged.

2   Not only do production costs vary by the type of finished steel, i.e., sheets, bars, rods or coils, but the relative competitive advantage of Canadian mills also depends on the type of finished product. It is prudent, therefore, to compare productivity for a given product. Cold-rolled coils are chosen here for comparison because they are a key input for the automobile industry.

3   This rough estimate was made on our request by Don Barnett of Economics Associates Inc.

4   For a more detailed account of the developments in the United States, see Bain (1992), Barnett and Crandall (1986), and Hogan (1984; 1987).

5   These numbers, obtained from the OECD, are calculated on a somewhat different base than those cited in Table 3.2, which were obtained from Statistics Canada.

6   Provided by Don Barnett of Economics Associates Inc.

7   Perhaps because of the relatively low share that Canada has of the U.S. steel market, it has been relatively fortunate in not incurring major retaliation in the form of U.S. protectionism. Canada was not subject to Voluntary Restraint Agreement rules in 1984 (Howell et al. 1988, 459), despite the fact that, between 1982 and 1988, the U.S. Department of Commerce reached Affirmative Antidumping findings against Canada (all of which were terminated or revoked subject to agreement) in the areas of sheet piling, rebars, structurals, and bars and oil country tubular goods (OCTG). The department also set a no-injury determination in the area of rectangular pipe and tube, and set a countervailing duty in the area of OCTG. In addition, the United States did not impose import restrictions on Canada in the 1985–88 period because the situation was complicated by the impending negotiations of the free-trade agreement (Howell et al. 1988, 533).

8   This, however, had not been a major disadvantage because Dofasco rolled direct from ingot to hot-rolled steel, i.e., rolling without ever letting the steel cool down from the time it was poured. Most other manufacturers allowed the steel to cool down at some intermediate stage of finish. The steel then had to be reheated to be rolled again into a finished section. Nonetheless, there is pressure on Dofasco to cast more of its steel continuously.

9   According to Barnett and Crandall (1986), the large steelmakers made serious errors in forecasting demand and investing accordingly. In the mid to late 1970s, the industry forecasted that U.S. demand for steel would grow to 132 million tons of finished

steel output by 1983. Even as late as 1980, the industry worked on the assumption that demand would grow to 134 million tons of finished steel by 1988. At the peak of the business cycle in 1985, U.S. consumption was only 96 million tons, and production only 88 million tons. Barnett and Crandall (1986, 43) contend that, "had integrated steel makers known that there would be a decline in steel sales over the 1974–84 decade, they might have behaved quite differently. They might not have built many of their large new blast furnaces or basic oxygen furnaces. Nor would they have invested huge sums in iron ore mines and iron pelletizing facilities."

10   McLouth has since returned to profitability.

11   At large mills, the variable component of compensation comes from production incentive plans, which typically earn the worker 5 percent (at most 10 percent) of the base wage rate.

12   The USWA, formed in 1942, descends from an earlier organization called the Steel Workers Organizing Committee (SWOC) of the Congress of Industrial Organizations (CIO). For a more detailed description of the union's history, see Rayback (1966, 351), Adams (1952), Sweeney (1947, 1956), and Stieber (1980).

13   Based on union records.

14   See also USWA (1987).

15   Effective January 1, 1988, the company reorganized itself as Stelco, Inc., a holding company, with two wholly owned subsidiaries: Stelco Steel, the primary iron and steel operations, and Stelco Enterprises. Although this structure was abandoned later in 1991, it is presented here because it is useful in understanding the diverse operations at the company.

Stelco Steel included the steelmaking operations in four major locations: Hilton Works in Hamilton and Lake Erie Works in Nanticoke (both in Ontario); McMaster Works in Contrecoeur, Quebec; and Edmonton Steel Works in Edmonton, Alberta. Stelco Enterprises included four wholly owned strategic business units making finished steel products, such as wires, pipes, and drawn steel: Stelwire, Stelpipe, Steffco, and Canadian Drawn Steel. Stelco Enterprises also included joint ventures and partnerships including Moly-Cop Canada, Jannock Steel Fabricating Company, M.E. International, Kautex, and Torcad. Both Jannock and M.E. International are attempts by the company to diversify its interests outside the core steelmaking business. Robert E. Heneault, president of Stelco Enterprises, described the newly reorganized business units and joint ventures thus:

> Our four wholly owned business units manufacture, respectively, fasteners and forgings, pipe and tubing, wire and wire products, and cold drawn bars. These companies were formed from our various steel fabricating plants that existed prior to and at the time of our corporate restructuring, comprised of 13 plants located in Alberta, Ontario and Quebec. The largest of our joint ventures is the Jannock Steel Fabricating Company which operates plants throughout Canada as well as four recently acquired facilities in the United States. It is Canada's dominant supplier of culverts, grain bins, pre-engineered buildings, curtain wall, roof decking, and siding for commercial and farm buildings. Two

other joint ventures—Moly-Cop Canada and M.E. International—produce grinding balls and mill liners for the mineral processing industry. Moly-Cop is situated in Kamloops, British Columbia, and is thus strategically positioned to service the large copper and mineral properties that are located in that province. M.E. International is U.S.–based with two operating facilities, one in Minnesota and the other in Michigan. Torcad Limited is engaged in steel plating and finishing, roll preparation and chroming, and precision bar manufacturing with plants in Toronto, Mississauga, Grimsby, and Stoney Creek.

Our most recent joint venture involves merging one of our wholly owned business units—the Canadian Drawn Steel Company—with Bliss and Laughlin of Harvey, Illinois. The latter company, which also operates plants in Ohio and Georgia, is North America's second-largest producer of cold drawn bars. Perhaps our most interesting joint venture, however, was initiated at the beginning of this year when we became an equal partner with Kautex Werke of Bonn, West Germany, in the ownership of Kautex Canada, a Windsor-based enterprise That makes plastic fuel systems for the automotive industry utilizing sophisticated blow-moulding technology. This particular undertaking is interesting in as much as it represents our first manufacturing venture outside of steel. Market has already been established for a one-million-unit output, and we foresee growth beyond the initial plateau as well as elsewhere as Kautex moves into the production of other automotive parts."

For further details see Heneault (1989, 2–3).

In his address to the Annual General Meeting of the shareholders in May 1991, Chairman Fred Telmer announced that the company will go back to its original organizational structure by dissolving the subsidiaries, Stelco Steel and Stelco Enterprises, and bringing all operations directly under Stelco, Inc.

16   The auto parts industry, a major customer for steel producers, has pushed very hard for cost and quality. Materials account for roughly 70 percent of the value of finished auto parts.

17   Description of the 1984 bargaining arrangements is based largely on Adams and Zeytinoglu (1987), 81–83.

18   On August 14, 1990, the Supreme Court of Ontario rejected a request to grant an injunction against the USWA picketing a warehouse, owned by a numbered company, shipping Stelco inventory. There was violence on the picket line, property damage, and arrests.

19   If the committee is deadlocked on a decision, the dispute is submitted to the grievance procedure for resolution. Effectively, this means submitting all committee disputes to arbitration.

20   These and subsequent comments in this section attributed to Bob Milbourne come from an interview with Anil Verma, September 11, 1991.

21   For a detailed account of the attempts to organize Dofasco workers and the company's efforts to remain nonunion, see Storey (1981, 1983).

22 The union claimed that it had been locked out, while the company maintained that the union called a strike.

23 The union plan centred on new capital spending that would come from Dofasco and some of the banks. Workers were to take a 10 percent wage cut for five years to increase their equity from 15 percent in the first year to 70 percent of the company at the end of the five years. Employment was to be reduced by 1600 through early retirements (*Financial Post*, August, 2, 1991).

24 Others solicited to make a contribution to the bridge loan were the bankers, the company, and the provincial and federal governments. The Conservative federal government, given its ideological coolness to government bailouts, proffered advice but no money, although it did not rule out some participation in a final rescue plan.

25 The irony here may be that the technology-intensive tube mill may close. Although the mill is very efficient, the operations that supply liquid metal to the mill are not cost competitive.

26 More than 100 USWA and steel company executives met in Sault Ste. Marie in May 1985 to examine a range of issues facing the steel industry. According to a CSTEC brochure, "The conference was so successful they decided to continue their discussion of labour adjustment and trade issues via four working groups." Initially, they decided to form the Canadian Steel Trade Conference (CSTC), which grew from a fact-finding group into an organization. At the third conference, in November 1987, they decided to change their name from CSTC to CSTEC to better reflect the dual mandate.

   Although credit for successful formation of CSTEC must go to both parties, much of the initial enthusiasm and background work that generated the momentum for subsequent action came from Gerard Docquier, then Canadian National Director of the USWA.

27 This information is based on the results of an evaluation study conducted internally by CSTEC and made available to the authors upon request.

28 Although Neelon is not a steelmaker, this example is included here because it illustrates USWA's experience with and approach toward employee-involvement plans.

29 A popular form of gain-sharing plans. For more details on how the plan works, see Lesieur (1958).

30 See Wilkinson (1990).

31 This account is based on interviews with workers and union officials by Paul Wilkinson and Joanne Sack.

32 We are indebted to Professor Rey Bourque of Université du Québec à Hull and Mr. Pierre Marc Bédard, Directeur du Personnel et des Relations industrielles, Aciers Inoxydables Atlas, division de Sammi-Atlas Inc. for valuable assistance in obtaining data for this case study.

33 This investment would increase the annual production to 300 000 tons a year from the present 90 000 tons.

34 Le Syndicat des employés des Aciers inoxydables Atlas.

35   Efforts to improve labour–management relations go back to 1985, when the new divi-
     sional management took over. Communication was improved, and a job evaluation
     was jointly undertaken after an employee survey revealed these sources of dissatisfac-
     tion. There were changes on the union side as well. After the 1985 strike, a more mod-
     erate union leadership was elected. The 1987 agreement was signed without recourse
     to a work stoppage, and the number of disputes going to arbitration declined from
     their normal level of ten a year during 1963–87 to two in 1988, and none in 1989 and
     1990.

Chapter

INDUSTRIAL RELATIONS IN THE CANADIAN MINING INDUSTRY: TRANSITION UNDER PRESSURE

Richard P. Chaykowski[1]

*T*he Canadian mineral industry as a whole has historically been a cornerstone of the Canadian economy in terms of its contribution to Gross Domestic Product (GDP), employment, and capital formation, and with respect to its role in Canadian export activity. In 1989, the value of Canadian mineral industry production, including minerals, mineral manufacturing, mining, and smelting and refining, reached $39 billion (roughly 4.5 percent of the economy); the value of exports, including smelted and refined metals, exceeded $27 billion; and employment in the entire mineral industry was approximately 390 000 (Pilsworth, 1990). The mining industry proper is a key component of the mineral industry, since it is the source of inputs for the entire industry.

Along with the United States, the USSR, Australia, and several other geographically smaller countries, Canada enjoys the unique position of being heavily endowed with significant deposits of accessible, high-grade mineral ores, giving it a natural comparative advantage in the production of these reserves, and offering the potential for the large-scale smelting and refining of minerals. Historically, Canadians have mined a variety of minerals, such as coal and metals, and the industry has consistently supplied the Canadian economy with sizable employment opportunities. The industry soon became equally significant for its role in the development of some of the major unions in Canada, including the United Mine Workers of America and the United Steelworkers of America.

This study will concentrate on the mining of metals, nonmetals (e.g., potash), and coal, and related smelting and refining. The oil and gas industry is sufficiently distinct to warrant a separate analysis. The industry consists of a large number of firms, and while there have been some studies of the larger companies, little is known about the industrial relations and human-resource practices of smaller, typically nonunionized, operations. This analysis concentrates on the major developments affecting the larger, "trend-setting" companies such as Noranda Minerals Inc., Inco Limited, and Falconbridge Limited, which are largely unionized. On the labour side, the analysis focusses on the major unions that have led the organization of labour in this industry, including the United Steelworkers of America and the United Mine Workers of America. The organization of labour in mining dates back to the origins of the labour movement in Canada. The often tumultuous course of industrial relations in mining has, therefore, had an important influence on the general development of union–management relations in Canada.

In assessing the challenges confronting Canadian and U.S. industrial relations in the coming decades, Kochan (1990) identifies several major developments affecting industry generally that have also had a significant impact on the Canadian mining industry. In particular, the globalization of markets and the commensurate increase in international competition, the resultant pressures to reduce labour costs, and the introduction of new technologies have significantly affected employment levels in the mining industry and the fortunes and goals of the union movement, and, importantly, appear to have affected the strategic response of some firms in the industry.[2] Industrial relations in the Canadian mining industry has recently begun to be influenced in important ways by each of these factors. The likelihood for the future is that the course of industrial relations in the industry will continue to be shaped by these developments.

However, generalizations across firms are difficult, since many characteristics of mining operations are unique to firms in the industry. In turn, those aspects of mining that set it apart have also shaped the development of industrial relations and the human-resource issues confronted by firms and unions—sometimes in exceptional ways. For example, harsh working conditions in remote areas have often resulted in high employee turnover and, at times, a poor image for the industry. Consequently, the remote location of many deposits has given rise to issues related to firms' ability to attract and retain workers, and, more recently, the prospects for a "commuting work force." Further, the production time horizon of a given operation is tied to the extent and quality of the mineral deposit.[3] Consequently, the desirability of making a large-scale capital investment in technologically advanced machinery, once a mine is in operation, is likely to depend on such underlying factors as the size and grade of an ore body. The diversity of types and sizes of operations is also considerable: giant multinationals such as Noranda Minerals Inc. and Inco Limited operate extensive mining, smelting, and refining operations, while small firms may mine only a single deposit, and for only a relatively few years.

Many of these industry characteristics have also affected the ability of unions to organize workers. Once organized, workers may be confronted with mine closures either as deposits are exhausted or as the declining quality of ore renders extraction uneconomical. Furthermore, the wide range of minerals extracted, which are associated with different extraction and processing technologies, a variety of markets, and, consequently, different types of firms, make the industry very heterogeneous and dynamic. Nevertheless, an analysis of the major developments surrounding the leading firms and unions can yield important guideposts to the course of industrial relations in the industry.

The Role of Mining in the Canadian Economy [4]

MINING PRODUCTION AND TRADE

While the Canadian mining industry has experienced modest growth over the last several decades, it remains an important component of the Canadian economy. The value of GDP for the entire mineral industry, including fuels, has fluctuated between 1970 and 1989: GDP declined in the late 1970s, with some recovery around 1980, followed by a decline with the recession of the early 1980s. But growth has been modest since 1982, reflecting a progressively more robust industry. Nevertheless, relative to the entire manufacturing sector, in which GDP nearly doubled over the 1970–89 period, mining's share of total GDP declined during this period (Statistics Canada 1989). In 1989, the value of GDP for the mining industry, excluding oil and gas, reached $8.9 billion; in addition, the value of GDP in the nonferrous smelting and refining manufacturing industry was $2.3 billion.[5]

Canada is a leading producer of a wide variety of minerals and an exporter of significant quantities of minerals in a variety of forms. For example, Canada exports raw materials, such as iron ore, potash, and coal, as well as refined minerals, including nickel, iron, gold, and copper. Major consumers include the United States, Japan, and Europe (Koepke, 1990). As Table 4.1 reports, Canada ranks as a top-five world producer of seventeen minerals, and produces over 15 percent of world uranium, zinc, potash, asbestos, nickel, titanium, and sulphur. Canada's major competitors include the United States, the USSR, Australia, and South Africa.

Canada's internal distribution of mineral resources is uneven. Except for Alberta and the individual Atlantic provinces, most provinces have a significant share of the value of total metal production, although the provinces of the Atlantic region, taken together, would rank at roughly the same level as British Columbia (see Table 4.2). Ontario, British Columbia, and Quebec rank as the top three in terms of the total value of metal production, whereas Ontario, Saskatchewan, and Quebec rank as the top three industrial mineral producers. Not surprisingly, then, Ontario and Quebec rank highest in terms of the total values of mineral production. Alberta's low combined-total-value ranking is attributable to the exclusion of oil and gas from the analysis.

Table 4.1
Canadian World Production Ranking, Selected Minerals, 1988

Mineral	World Rank	Canadian Production as % of World	Largest World Producer
Uranium[a]	1	33.6	Canada
Zinc	1	19.2	Canada
Gypsum	2	9.9	USA
Potash	2	26.3	USSR
Asbestos	2	16.3	USSR
Nickel	2	23.5	USSR
Titanium	2	18.1	Australia
Lead	3	10.3	USSR
Aluminum	3	8.8	USA
Suphur	3	15.3	USA
Platinum	3	4.6	South Africa
Molybdenum	3	14.1	USA
Copper	4	8.7	Chile
Cobalt	4	9.3	Zaire
Gold	5	7.1	South Africa
Silver	5	10.1	Mexico
Cadmium	5	7.7	USSR

Note: a Includes only Western World.
Source: "Canada's World Role as a Producer of Certain Important Minerals, 1988," in Energy Mines and Resources Canada, *1989 Canadian Minerals Yearbook: Review and Outlook* (Ottawa: Minister of Supply and Services Canada, 1989), Table 16b, page 70.29.

Finally, it is important to emphasize the international character of trade in minerals. Since the locations of mineral deposits are typically geographically dispersed, many industrialized nations must import a large proportion of their mineral consumption needs. Consequently, trade has, in some sense, always been global, but with several important constraints. First, trade in minerals, as with many other commodities, between Eastern bloc countries and Western industrialized nations has been subject to restrictions (Tilton 1989), partially for (strategic) political reasons. Second, the nationalization of some Western mining subsidiaries located in developing countries, coupled with the ascendancy of the newly industrializing countries, have affected mineral development patterns and trade patterns (Tilton 1989).

However, several developments in the 1980s likely will reshape further international mineral trade. Notable among these are the elimination of the Warsaw Pact and the resultant liberalization of East–West trade, as well as the emergence of powerful trading blocs—formally in Europe and North America, and less formally in the Pacific Rim. While the slowing growth of metal demand has already created a climate for increased competition, future general intensification of international competition among these blocs may spill over into mineral markets. In turn, the potential expansion of trade links with Eastern Europe, and ultimately,

Table 4.2
Regional Ranking by Value of Mineral Production, 1989

Province	% of Total Value of Metal Production[a]	% of Total Value of Industrial Mineral Production[a]	Ranking by Combined Total Value[b]
B.C.	14.4 (2)	7.0 (5)	4
Alberta	Nil	13.7 (4)	5
Saskatchewan	4.5 (7)	19.5 (2)	3
Manitoba	10.5 (4)	2.2 (8)	6
Ontario	38.4 (1)	28.5 (1)	1
Quebec	12.2 (3)	18.8 (3)	2
N.B.	4.4 (8)	4.9 (6)	8
Newfoundland	5.8 (6)	1.4 (9)	9
Nova Scotia	0.3 (9)	3.5 (7)	10
P.E.I.	Nil	Nil	11
NWT & Yukon	9.5 (5)	0.5 (10)	7

Notes: [a] Regional rank in parentheses.
          [b] Combined total value of metal and industrial mineral production.
Source: "Canada, Value of Mineral Production by Provinces, Territories and Mineral Classes, 1988," *Canadian Minerals Yearbook: Review and Outlook* (Ottawa: Minister of Supply and Services, 1989), Table 4, page 70.11.

the Soviet Union and China, may result in both further expansion and integration of markets (Tilton 1989).[6] These developments underscore the importance of "competitiveness" for Canadian mining firms.

THE STRUCTURE OF THE MINING INDUSTRY

A large number of firms operate in the mining industry. Important differences among the production activities of firms in the industry exist and, given the sometimes complex ownership interrelationships among firms, there may be alternative ways of viewing a corporate entity. It is also useful to distinguish between the various products produced.[7]

Between 1978 and 1987, the number of coal mines increased modestly, from 24 to 28, with slight fluctuations throughout the decade. During this same period, coal production doubled.[8] Importantly, the total number of employees remained between roughly 10 300 and 13 100.

During the 1978–87 period, the number of both nonmetal and metal mine establishments increased only modestly: nonmetal mines increased from 120 to 137, and metal mines from 107 to 108.[9] While the production levels of nonmetal and metal mines fluctuated during this period, net changes were modest.[10] Between 1978 and 1987, employment levels in nonmetal mining establishments dropped, from 16 035 to 12 181 and, significantly, employment levels in metal mining establishments dropped, from 56 447 to 45 496. Overall, the trend is toward declining employment levels in mining.

Importantly, with the exception of coal, there has been a trend toward decreasing the number of paid person-hours for industry "production" workers over the same time period. Further, metal mines data reveal a steady increase in tonnes mined per person-hour paid, from 2.92 in 1978 to 3.55 in 1987.[11] This trend suggests a long-run improvement in productivity.

In contrast to the more narrowly defined mine establishments, the number of corporations in the mining industry is much larger and the overwhelming majority of firms are Canadian.[12] For example, in 1986, the total number of "metal mine" corporations was 206 (172 Canadian and 34 foreign), or twice the number of metal mine establishments.[13]

Rank-ordered according to 1989 sales, the top five mining firms include Inco Limited (nickel and copper), Falconbridge Limited (nickel, copper, and zinc), Rio Algom Limited (uranium and potash), Cominco Limited (zinc), and Placer Dome Limited (gold); notably, Inco, Falconbridge, Rio Algom, and Cominco are also among the top 500 Canadian firms according to 1989 sales (*Financial Post* 1990).[14]

Each of these top five mining firms had total 1989 assets in excess of $2 billion, and Inco's total assets exceeded $4 billion; Inco Limited also ranked twenty-fifth in assets and *second* in income among the top 500 companies in 1989 (the high profit ranking was the result of exceptionally high nickel prices)(*Financial Post* 1990). The size of these multinational firms, contrasted with the smaller, single-operation mining companies, highlights the diversity that characterizes the industry.

In recent years, the number of firms operating in the industry has increased, and corporate relationships have become more complex.[15] A large number of smaller mining interests, which are identified as separate organizations, are partially or wholly owned by larger corporations.[16]

Corporate takeovers have also had a role in the process of corporate consolidation in the industry. In 1986, Falconbridge Limited completed the acquisition of the Kidd Creek operation (owned by the Canada Development Corporation since 1981), thereby adding a major zinc- and copper-production capability to its existing nickel (mining and smelting) production. However, Noranda Minerals Inc. (in conjunction with Trelleborg AB [Sweden], acquired 50 percent of Falconbridge in 1989, thereby consolidating their position in the mining industry (Noranda Inc. 1990). Placer Dome Inc., an international gold mining firm, was created through the amalgamation, in 1987, of Dome Mines Limited, Cambell Red Lake Mines Limited, and Placer Development Limited (Placer Dome Inc. 1988). In 1991, two gold-mining giants, Newmont Mining Corporation of the United States and American Barrick Resources of Canada, announced their joint intention to merge in a deal estimated to be worth approximately $5.6 billion (Robinson 1991). While the number of firms in the industry grows, consolidation among the largest firms appears to be a significant feature of the mining industry.

It is important to distinguish firms such as Falconbridge, which owns both operating mines and extensive smelting and refining capabilities, from smaller firms that may operate only mines, engage in exploration, contract for specific functions, develop mining equipment, or offer services incidental to primary mining. Thus, there is great diversity in the size, activity, and organization of firms in the industry. While smaller firms may concentrate in a particular market, larger firms are also continuing to expand into areas related to their core business. For example, Inco Limited has developed a successful unit that develops and markets automated mining machinery (see Till 1988), while continuing an overall strategy of focussing on basic mining operations. These strategies complement each other, since Inco Limited has become a world leader in developing many technologies associated with mining as part of a long-run strategy of using technology to increase productivity and reduce costs (Scales 1988).

*H*istorical Industrial Relations and Labour Developments in the Mining Industry: The Pre-1980 Era

EMPLOYMENT TRENDS IN THE INDUSTRY

A traditional view of product demand for mining firms is that it is closely tied to the business cycle.[17] Consequently, since the viability of individual mining operations is susceptible to variations in the demand for output that are induced by changes in aggregate demand, industry employment levels are significantly affected by major changes in aggregate-demand levels.[18]

While aggregate-demand factors are likely to affect individual firms differentially, the most striking trends in the aggregate employment levels throughout the pre-1980 era have occurred with respect to the ratio of "administrative and office" workers to "production and related" workers. Table 4.3 provides trends in employment levels by broad occupational group for metals, nonmetals, and coal.

During the 1970-to-1979 decade, the number of production workers in metals declined by approximately 10 000 employees (20 percent); the number of production workers in nonmetals remained steady, at approximately 16 500 employees; and the number of production workers in coal increased by approximately 2800 employees (46 percent). In contrast, the number of administrative and office employees increased in each mining activity during the same period.

Taken together, total employment in these three areas decreased, from 94 213 in 1970 to 90 691 in 1979. However, during the 1970-to-1979 period, while total "production" employment levels declined modestly, from 73 380 to 66 988, total "administrative and office" employment levels increased, from 20 833 to 23 703 workers. This trend toward a higher relative proportion of nonproduction workers is an extension of a trend evident throughout the 1948-to-1973 period (see

Table 4.3

Employment by Detailed Mining Activity and Employee Group for the Canadian Mining Industry, 1970–1987[a]

Year	Metals			Nonmetals			Coal		
	Prod. + Related	Admin. + Office	Total Workers	Prod. + Related	Admin. + Office	Total Workers	Prod. + Related	Admin. +Office	Total Workers
1970	51 102	15 488	66 590	16 245	4 415	20 660	6 033	930	6 963
1971	50 121	15 891	66 012	16 155	4 278	20 433	6 167	1 017	7 184
1972	46 257	15 737	61 994	15 911	4 109	20 020	6 952	1 752	8 704
1973	47 984	18 150	66 344	16 344	4 335	20 679	6 448	1 408	7 856
1974	50 886	19 152	70 038	17 767	4 628	22 395	6 601	1 541	8 142
1975	50 319	18 842	69 161	15 397	4 688	20 085	6 747	1 669	8 416
1976	49 834	18 435	68 269	16 447	4 877	21 334	7 862	1 134	8 995
1977	49 414	17 831	67 245	16 812	4 986	21 798	8 582	1 199	9 781
1978	39 977	16 470	56 447	16 133	4 749	20 882	9 060	1 513	10 573
1979	41 541	17 419	58 960	16 633	4 829	21 462	8 814	1 455	10 269
1980	47 592	18 526	66 118	16 645	4 795	21 440	9 598	1 818	11 416
1981	49 586	19 126	68 712	15 666	4 908	20 574	9 359	1 823	11 182
1982	44 261	17 242	61 502	12 848	4 323	17 171	10 548	2 055	13 113
1983	37 270	14 924	52 194	12 768	3 805	16 573	9 648	2 036	11 684
1984	39 181	13 502	52 683	13 008	4 250	17 258	9 892	2 013	11 905
1985	36 618	12 054	48 672	12 535	4 380	16 915	10 037	2 030	12 067
1986	34 941	11 546	46 487	12 376	4 887	17 263	9 078	1 667	10 745
1987	34 329	11 167	45 496	12 989	4 930	17 919	9 008	1 398	10 406

Note: [a] Does not include cement and lime or clay products (domestic clays) manufacturing.

Sources: "Canada: Employment, Salaries, and Wages in the Mining Industry," *Canadian Minerals Yearbook Review and Outlook* (1989, 1981, and 1977 reports) (Ottawa: Minister of Supply and Social Services); "Employment and Payroll, Coal Mines, by Province," Statistics Canada, *Coal Mines*, Catalogue 26-206 (Ottawa: Minister of Supply and Services, Annual 1978–88).

MacMillan, Gislason, and Lyon 1977, 12–16). While MacMillan and colleagues (1977) attribute this trend to the "professionalization" of the industry, the decline in relative production worker employment is also likely to be the result of two other factors: first, increasing usage of process technologies that, on the one hand, reduce the need for production workers, but, on the other hand, may increase the need for technicians and professionals; and, second, the effects of union wage increases on unionized firms' strategic planning with regard to the optimal capital–labour ratio.

THE HISTORICAL DEVELOPMENT OF TRADE UNIONISM

The current stance adopted by organized labour toward mining management, in general, appears to be shaped by an historical adversarial relationship.[19] Unions have had a long and turbulent tradition in the Canadian mining industry. Importantly, international unions, such as the United Mine Workers of America (UMWA) and the United Steelworkers of America (USWA), have consistently dominated the organization of labour in the mining industry.

Since the turn of the century, the UMWA, an international union based in the United States, has been the dominant organization in the Canadian coal industry. Williams (1986) describes the development of the United Mine Workers in Eastern Canada during the 1900–1920 period as the union worked to supplant the existing Canadian-based Provincial Workmen's Association in Nova Scotia. Palmer (1983, 156) identifies the difficult 1906 strike by the UMWA at Lethbridge, Alberta, as a major development among organized miners in the West, since the eventual agreement more firmly established the UMWA in this area.[20]

In the noncoal mining industry, MacMillan, Gislason, and Lyon (1977) describe the long struggle between the Mine, Mill and Smelter Workers Union, which had been a major union in mining, and the United Steelworkers of America. The rivalry resulted in the decline of the Mine Mill union, and, in 1967, culminated in the merger of the two unions. The United Steelworkers thus emerged as the dominant union in the Canadian metal mining and refining industry. The period up to the late 1960s demonstrated the successive amalgamation of unions and the growing dominance of the USWA.

The mining industry has, therefore, been dominated by international unionism. Table 4.4 provides national-based total union membership, total female union membership, and union membership by major mining group, and Table 4.5 presents the comparable international-based union membership statistics. While membership levels in international unions clearly dominated national membership levels throughout the pre-1980 period, important differences in trends exist. Overall, international union membership peaked in 1970, at more than 61 000, but experienced a significant decline in the early 1970s. By 1979, international membership had recovered somewhat, regaining the level that had prevailed in the late 1960s.[21] Total national union membership levels similarly declined in the early 1970s, rebounding in the late 1970s.

Table 4.4
National Union Membership in Mining in Canada, 1966–1988[a,b]

Year	Total Mines, Quarries, & Oil Wells		A Metal Mines		B Mineral Fuels		C Other Mines	
	Total Membership	Female Membership	Total Membership	Female Membership	Total Membership	Female Membership	Total Membership	Female Membership
1966	11 116	28	UP[c]	UP	UP	UP	UP	UP
1967	8 847	10	5940	0	387	0	2520	10
1968	5 530	4	348	0	322	0	4860	4
1969	5 612	17	0	0	355	0	5257	17
1970	5 811	251	492	0	509	47	4810	204
1971	6 068	231	506	0	488	15	5074	216
1972	3 184	17	627	0	478	17	2079	0
1973	6 750	204	1486	21	474	15	4790	168
1974	7 160	210	1948	50	636	36	4576	124
1975	8 291	202	2382	51	1004	27	4905	124
1976	9 183	419	3219	216	767	51	5197	152
1977	9 340	503	3149	294	769	62	5422	147
1978	9 218	199	2757	113	812	64	5649	22
1979	11 199	199	4622	94	856	66	5721	39
1980	12 639	322	5291	145	863	53	6485	124
1981	12 441	255	4948	104	924	39	6569	112
1982	10 513	230	4072	46	959	40	5482	144
1983	11 502	297	5025	51	1575	71	4902	175

Table 4.4 (continued)

Year	Total Mines, Quarries, & Oil Wells		A Metal Mines		B Mineral Fuels		C Other Mines	
	Total Membership	Female Membership	Total Membership	Female Membership	Total Membership	Female Membership	Total Membership	Female Membership
1984	10 764	291	5208	41	1404	39	4152	211
1985	11 011	494	5262	81	1453	42	4296	371
1986	13 957	565	7575	89	1567	40	4815	436
1987	12 994	596	7076	156	1320	38	4598	402
1988	13 567	511	7444	144	1384	43	4739	324

Notes: [a] National Unions may include "public" or "quasi-public" sector unions.
        [b] Does not include mineral manufacturing (smelting and refining).
        [c] Unpublished data.

Sources: Statistics Canada Corporations and Labour Unions Returns Act, Part II, "Labour Unions" (Ottawa: Minister of Supply and Services, 1966–67, Table 25C; 1968–69, Table 27C; 1970, Table 3; 1971–77, Table 27C; 1978–82, Text Table XLIII; 1983–84, Table 42; 1985–88, Appendix 1.6).

Table 4.5
International Union Membership in Mining in Canada, 1965–1988 [a]

Year	Total Mines, Quarries, & Oil Wells		A Metal Mines		B Mineral Fuels		C Other Mines	
	Total Membership	Female Membership	Total Membership	Female Membership	Total Membership	Female Membership	Total Membership	Female Membership
1966	50 598	42	UP [b]	UP	UP	UP	UP	UP
1967	55 475	527	37 386	95	9 883	135	8206	297
1968	53 494	465	37 740	102	9 084	70	6670	293
1969	57 740	223	37 249	102	12 259	74	8232	47
1970	61 291	375	48 411	189	7 171	2	5709	184
1971	40 583	70	27 853	46	7 038	0	5692	24
1972	40 008	175	25 216	139	7 691	0	7101	36
1973	43 112	314	27 170	234	7 257	3	8685	77
1974	44 568	665	28 965	478	7 763	67	7840	120
1975	46 748	829	28 725	557	9 181	76	8842	196
1976	48 410	979	30 150	627	9 299	138	8961	214
1977	48 131	1061	30 617	760	9 552	138	7962	163
1978	48 061	1169	29 886	823	9 278	137	8897	209
1979	50 059	1255	31 438	787	9 601	219	9020	249
1980	50 140	1457	32 611	1056	11 102	242	6427	150
1981	57 786	1656	35 449	1159	13 391	295	8946	202
1982	38 887	1236	23 569	900	8 198	204	7120	132
1983	35 810	1093	21 974	841	6 934	165	6902	87

Table 4.5 (continued)

Year	Total Mines, Quarries, & Oil Wells		A Metal Mines		B Mineral Fuels		C Other Mines	
	Total Membership	Female Membership	Total Membership	Female Membership	Total Membership	Female Membership	Total Membership	Female Membership
1984	37 027	1160	23 117	880	6 251	170	7659	110
1985	38 809	1116	22 341	743	8 690	238	7778	135
1986	37 514	1318	22 629	807	8 018	391	6867	120
1987	38 256	1405	22 696	813	9 253	513	6307	79
1988	38 513	1519	23 258	852	8 486	563	6769	104

Notes: [a] Does not include mineral manufacturing (smelting and refining).
[b] Unpublished data.

Sources: Statistics Canada. Corporations and Labour Unions Returns Act, Part II, "Labour Unions" (Ottawa: Minister of Supply and Services, 1966, Table 25B; 1967–77, Table 27.B; 1978–82, Text Table XLII; 1983–84, Table 41; 1985–87, Appendix 1.5; 1988, Appendix 1.7).

In the 1970s, international unions experienced significant membership declines in the "metal mining" group, where the greatest proportion of union members are employed.[22] International union membership in metal mining plummeted, by roughly 48 percent, between 1970 (the membership peak in the 1970s) and 1972 (the lowest membership level in the 1970s), before recovering to approximately 30 000 members for the remainder of the decade. In contrast, by the latter half of the 1970s, national union membership was trending upward in "metal mining," increasing steadily, from approximately 500 to more than 4600 members (i.e., over 800 percent) between 1970 and 1979.[23] International unionism was thus experiencing a long-run decline in the Canadian mining industry, while national unions started from a modest base but grew at a rapid rate.

A LEGACY OF STRIKE ACTIVITY

Strikes in the mining industry have traditionally been both frequent and bitter. Strikes have typically centred on attempts to organize workers and to consolidate union footholds in various regions, as well as on the terms and conditions of employment—particularly, wages. For example, in the coal mining industry, a violent organizational strike by the UMWA against Canadian Collieries Limited of Vancouver Island, involving 7000 miners, ended in defeat in 1914 (Palmer 1983, 155). Strikes remained frequent in the post–First World War period, despite the decline in coal production as a result of the shift to oil and electricity, and the closing of mines; Palmer (1983, 199) notes: "Coal mining accounted for almost 17 percent of all strikes in the 1920s, 49 percent of strike participants, and 52.5 percent of striker-days lost across the country."

Clement (1981, 34) describes the important conflict between workers represented by the Mine Workers' Union of Canada and the firms operating in the Souris coal fields of Saskatchewan; the conflict ultimately resulted in the infamous Black Tuesday clash of 1931, which resulted in the breaking of the union.

Aside from the conflicts noted in the coal industry, major strikes have occurred in metal mining. For example, the Mine Mill union and Inco engaged in a major strike in 1958 that ultimately resulted in the loss of the Sudbury Inco local to the USWA. Replacing Mine Mill at Inco in 1962, the USWA then engaged in bitter and costly strikes with the firm in 1969 and 1975. The 1969 strike, lasting 128 days and involving approximately 15 000 employees, remains one of the most significant strikes of recent Canadian labour history.

Mining strikes were thus often bitter, protracted confrontations that involved the use of scab labour by firms, violence, and riots. The legacy of strike activity from these earlier years has continued to influence the conflictual approach to union–management relations in the current era.

Table 4.6 presents a time series of data concerning strike and lockout activity in the Canadian mining industry since 1960.[24] The trend over the 1960–79 period was an increasing frequency of stoppages, increasing numbers of workers affected, and, particularly in the late 1970s, a significant increase in person-days lost.

Table 4.6

Strikes and Lockouts in Mining in Canada, 1960–1989[a]

	Strikes and Lockouts		Strikes and Lockouts in Existence	
Year	Beginning	In Existence	Workers Affected	Person-Days Not Worked
1960	18	18	4 806	20 780
1961	11	11	5 944	31 740
1962	11	12	9 788	130 520
1963	17	18	6 955	101 870
1964	12	13	10 721	82 120
1965	26	26	8 752	57 730
1966	41	43	49 713	533 770
1967	21	24	7 781	32 780
1968	24	24	6 007	114 550
1969	29	30	33 507	2 236 560
1970	14	15	6 876	53 680
1971	18	18	7 555	192 250
1972	31	33	16 770	372 240
1973	36	37	19 831	247 020
1974	64	65	37 211	701 560
1975	46	47	34 011	1 187 100
1976	48	52	35 582	1 564 210
1977	26	29	13 250	122 400
1978	42	43	37 172	1 719 240
1979	38	44	36 533	2 084 590
1980	33	33	21 460	417 390
1981	42	44	24 514	586 320
1982	8	11	15 084	405 100
1983	13	14	13 118	183 930
1984	11	12	4 329	60 180
1985	14	15	6 568	92 600
1986	18	18	12 019	451 730
1987	14	16	12 324	436 010
1988	15	16	6 444	163 270
1989	18	18	7 179	192 750

Notes: [a] Includes mineral fuels, and smelting and refining, but excludes all other mineral manufacturing.
Source: Strikes and Lockouts Database, Bureau of Labour Information, Labour Canada.

These trends unambiguously suggest a dramatic increase in labour strife up to the point of the recession of the early 1980s.

The period up to 1980 reflected a traditional industrial relations environment in which firms confronted the persistent challenges of strong and increasingly militant unions, while the union movement pursued the largely "business unionism" goals associated with international unions. The continual "crises" of adversarial labour relations, and the after-effects of the recession of the early 1980s that adversely affected major mining firms, coupled with the increasing pressures of international competition, would have a profound effect on industrial and labour relations developments in the 1980s.

Challenges to Traditional Industrial Relations in the 1980s: A Changing Environment and Altered Responses[25]

EMERGING DEVELOPMENTS IN THE INDUSTRY

While it was noted above that business cycles can be an important determinant of mineral demand and, hence, production levels, a recent analysis of demand in the Canadian metals industry suggests that changes in structural factors, such as the development of "metal-saving" technologies and shifts in the metal composition of products, may also have a significant impact on demand (see Nappi 1989, 111). In fact, Nappi (1989) examines how these factors have resulted in a general "atrophy" in the demand for many metals. The generally slow growth of GDP in the industry suggests that market expansion will continue to be modest.[26]

This market condition, in the presence of the increasing globalization of product markets, has put significant pressure on firms to reduce costs. In addition, labour-related public-policy developments in the areas of pay equity, workers' compensation, and the implementation of enhanced health and safety standards (e.g., the Workplace Hazardous Materials Information System) have added significantly to costs. Since labour costs have traditionally been a key aspect of the total cost structure, firms would be expected to develop several strategies to achieve labour-cost reductions.[27] First, we would expect firms to modernize in order to increase productivity and reduce labour costs. Second, independent of any capital-for-labour substitution, firms may downsize their labour forces. Third, unionized firms may choose to alter their relationship with the union.

While there is no available evidence that such strategies were explicitly developed by firms throughout the industry, an examination of the output trends, capital expenditure levels, and the employment and industrial relations indicators for mining does suggest a significantly altered role for labour in the production process, with consequences for the labour relations climate in the industry in the post-1980 period.

Between 1970 and 1988, the output of coal and coke increased by 367 percent. Among nonmetallic minerals, shipments of gypsum, lime, and salt and brine increased, asbestos shipments declined, and cement and potash production also increased during this period. The production of most metals declined sharply during the recession of the early 1980s, but the production of major metals recovered throughout the latter half of the 1980s, and in many cases record levels were achieved (see Tables 4.7A and 4.7B). Overall, across the range of major minerals (with the exception of asbestos), production has either increased or remained steady over the past twenty years.

Between 1983 and 1989, which is the period of recovery in mineral production levels, capital machinery expenditures in the metal mining industry increased by roughly 75 percent, whereas capital machinery expenditures in nonmetal mining declined by 28 percent. During this period, the combined capital and repair expenditures on machinery in metal mining increased by about 52 percent, and comparable nonmetal mining expenditures rose by approximately 11 percent (refer to Table 4.8).[28] Notably, while metal mining has undergone far greater employment losses than has nonmetal mining, it has correspondingly experienced far greater increases in capital expenditures on machinery.

The recession of the early 1980s had a significant impact on industry employment. After peaking early in the 1980s, production worker employment (in metals, nonmetals, and coal) had fallen, by 1987, below its 1980 level (see Figures 4.1 and 4.2). But disaggregated employment trends differed, depending on the subsector of the industry considered.

Figure 4.1
Metals Mining Employment—Production and Nonproduction

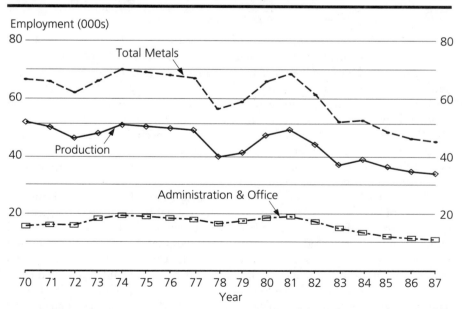

Source: Table 4.3.

Table 4.7A
Nonmetallic Mineral and Coal Production, 1970–1988 (000s tonnes)

Year	Asbestos Shipments	Gypsum Shipments	Cement Production	Potash Production	Coal Production	Coke Production
1970	1507	5733	8 014	3108	15 064	5144
1971	1483	6081	9 169	3558	16 723	4629
1972	1530	7349	10 022	3495	18 789	4725
1973	1690	7610	11 081	4454	20 470	5372
1974	1644	7226	11 727	5776	21 267	5450
1975	1056	5746	10 735	4726	25 258	5279
1976	1536	6003	10 910	5215	25 476	5286
1977	1518	7231	10 950	5764	28 519	4907
1978	1422	8074	11 374	6344	30 476	4968
1979	1493	8099	12 127	7074	33 200	5773
1980	1291	7285	11 408	7225	36 688	5292
1981	1122	7025	10 151	6549	40 082	4657
1982	837	5986	8 381	5309	42 811	3999
1983	858	7507	7 814	6294	44 906	4121
1984	837	7775	8 660	7527	57 401	4900
1985	750	7761	9 581	6661	60 681	4685
1986	662	8802	10 379	6753	56 608	4553
1987	665	9095	11 881	7668	61 212	4635
1988	705	8989	11 927	8190	70 607	4665

Source: Statistics Canada, *Canadian Economic Observer: Historical Statistical Supplement, 1988/89,* Catalogue 11-210, Vol.3 (Ottawa: Minister of Supply and Services, July 1989), Tables 8.5, 8.7.

Overall employment in the nonmetals group declined slightly between 1980 and 1982, and then remained steady through 1987. In contrast, between 1980 and 1987, overall metals employment declined by more than 13 000 employees. Importantly, while the employment losses in metals occurred primarily among production workers, administrative and office-worker employment also steadily declined over this period, by almost 8000 workers. This decline reversed (for the first time) the essentially uninterrupted increase in the relative employment of non-production workers in mining (see Table 4.3).[29] Clearly, the severe employment downsizing in the metals has been comprehensive.

These output and capital expenditure trends, taken together with significant employment reductions, suggest an increase in the capital-to-labour ratio, particularly in metal mining. Further, in a study of productivity trends in the Ontario metal mining industry, Green and Green (1991, 18) found that the industry adapted itself to new economic pressures in part by changing the capital-to-labour ratio: "it did respond by adjusting its inputs to help it meet changing demand and foreign competition. The basic approach has been to substitute capital (technology) for labour. This has been especially pronounced since the early 1980s." The development and introduction of new technologies by mining firms are particularly important and

Table 4.7B
Metals Production, 1970-1988a

Year	Copper[a,d]	Nickel[a]	Lead[a,d]	Zinc[a,d]	Aluminum	Gold[b]	Silver[b]	Uranium[c]
1970	610	278	353	1136	3469	74 928	1 376 329	3 723
1971	654	267	368	1134	3388	70 325	1 431 507	3 726
1972	720	235	335	1129	3295	64 632	1 427 525	4 428
1973	824	249	342	1227	3507	60 777	1 477 043	4 274
1974	821	269	294	1127	3598	52 813	1 331 510	4 350
1975	721	240	315	1004	3181	50 511	1 234 642	4 238
1976	731	241	256	982	2137	52 621	1 281 437	6 635
1977	759	233	281	1071	3586	53 923	1 313 684	6 824
1978	659	128	320	1067	3491	53 966	1 266 927	8 211
1979	636	126	311	1100	3103	51 143	1 146 908	6 530
1980	710	188	280	920	4489	48 975	1 129 416	6 481
1981	691	160	269	911	3755	47 046	1 129 394	7 526
1982	613	89	272	966	3515	64 736	1 313 630	7 643
1983	653	125	272	988	3394	73 512	1 197 031	6 823
1984	722	174	264	1063	3801	83 445	1 326 720	10 272
1985	739	170	268	1049	3619	87 561	1 197 072	10 441
1986	699	164	334	988	3838	102 900	1 087 989	11 502
1987	794	189	373	1158	4088	115 818	1 374 946	13 122
1988	756	199	352	1278	2351	130 487	1 371 474	12 325

Notes: a Thousands of metric tonnes.
b Thousands of grams.
c Thousands of kilograms.
d Metal content of production of the metal.

Source: Statistics Canada, Canadian Economic Observer: Historical Statistical Supplement, 1988-89, Catalogue 11-210, Vol 3. (Ottawa: Minister of Supply and Services, July 1989), Table 8.8.

Table 4.8

Total Capital and Repair Expenditures in Canadian Mining and Mineral Manufacturing Industries[a]

Year	Metal Mining Expenditures				Nonmetal Mining Expenditures[b]			
	Capital Construction	Repair Construction	Capital Machinery	Repair Machinery	Capital Construction	Repair Construction	Capital Machinery	Repair Machinery
1983	839.1	93.3	312.0	728.0	1123.3	25.5	433.9	401.5
1984	942.2	99.6	372.7	861.1	658.6	47.2	521.7	454.8
1985	1053.5	104.5	322.4	846.4	573.6	39.3	350.1	529.5
1986	979.7	99.6	319.4	811.3	502.4	31.2	256.6	565.4
1987	1328.2	109.8	372.9	880.8	421.7	23.2	251.6	608.8
1988[c]	1361.6	120.1	538.7	1003.8	379.0	26.2	263.8	601.7
1989[c]	1247.4	128.2	546.8	1037.5	350.4	31.0	311.3	612.1
1990	1076.2	117.2	533.4	1117.5	404.4	27.9	357.5	692.5

Notes: a Does not include smelting or refining, or cement, line, and lay manufacturing.
b Includes coal, asbestos, gypsum, salt, potash, quarrying, and sand pits.
c Preliminary or estimated.

Source: Energy, Mines and Resources Canada, 1989, *Canadian Minerals Yearbook Review and Outlook* (Ottawa: Minister of Supply and Services, June 1990), Statistical Table 84, page 70.105.
Energy, Mines and Resources Canada, 1990, *Canadian Minerals Yearbook Review and Outlook* (Ottawa: Minister of Supply and Services, June 1991). Statistical Table 86, page 72.104.

Figure 4.2
Nonmetals Mining Employment—Production and Nonproduction

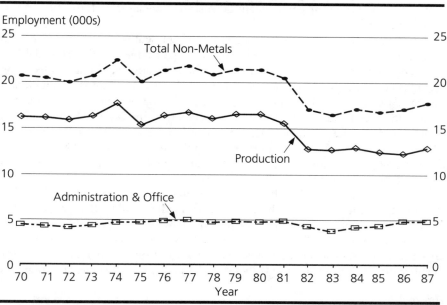

Source: Table 4.3

suggest a new strategy for competitiveness (Statistics Canada 1990b; Green and Green 1991).[30] In this regard, larger international metal mining firms, such as Inco Limited or Noranda Minerals Inc., are likely to be industry trend setters.[31]

MEMBERSHIP IN THE 1980s: THE STAGNATION OF INTERNATIONAL UNIONISM

In 1968, union density in the mining industry was approximately 50.9 percent; but, by 1978, union density had declined to 37.4 percent, and, by 1988, coverage stood at only 28.6 percent (Kumar and Coates 1991). An examination of membership trends further suggests that the union movement experienced increased difficulty in the industry. Overall, national unions in mining experienced a modest increase in membership throughout the 1980s, whereas the international unions suffered a membership decline from their peak in 1981. The key observation here is the apparent inability of the international unions to recover (see Tables 4.4 and 4.5).

Despite the sizable decline in metals employment, national union membership in metals has continued to increase throughout the 1980s; given the massive employment losses in the industry, the international unions have suffered the greatest membership losses. In fact, after peaking at close to 35 000 members in 1981, international union membership in metal mining dropped precipitously in 1982, and stood at approximately 23 000 in 1988. International membership essentially never recovered from the employment downsizing associated with the 1982 recession (see Figure 4.3).

The major international unions that currently represent workers in the Canadian mining industry include the United Steelworkers of America, the United Mine Workers of America, and, to a lesser extent, the International Union of Operating Engineers (Coates, Arrowsmith, and Courchene 1989). The largest mining union in Canada is the United Steelworkers of America. National unions active in the mining industry include the Canadian Association of Industrial, Mechanical and Allied Workers; the Canadian Association of Smelter and Allied Workers; the Fédération de la Métallurgie (Coates, Arrowsmith, and Courchene 1989); as well as distinctly regional unions, such as the Canadian Union of the Mine, Mill and Smelter Workers, Local 598 (Sudbury, Ontario).[32]

Membership levels in Canadian mining are presented in Table 4.9 for several of the major mining unions for the period from 1981 to 1989. Each experienced some loss of membership during this period. However, the two largest mining unions, the United Mine Workers and the United Steelworkers, have both experienced substantial membership losses. The USWA lost over 50 percent of its 1981 membership in mining and the UMWA over 85 percent.[33] Membership increases

Figure 4.3
Metal Mining Union Membership—International Versus National Unions

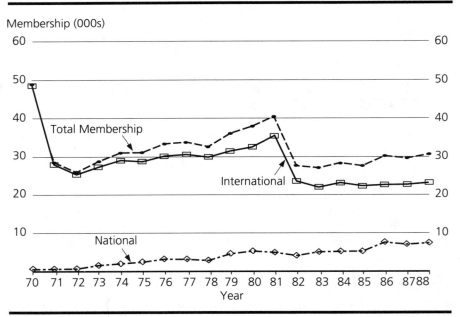

Table 4.9
Coverage in the Canadian Mining Industry by Major Union, 1981–1989

Union	Year								
	1981[a]	1982[a]	1983[b]	1984	1985[b]	1986[b]	1987	1988[b]	1989[b]
United Steel Workers	45 752	45 960	33 655	NA	30 785	25 825	NA	23 926	20 933
United Mine Workers	7 580	6 590	7 275	NA	4 900	6 145	NA	3 700	955
Mine, Mill & Smelter Workers (Local 598)	NA	NA	NA	1 740	1 720	1 720	1 720	1 550	1 550

Notes: a Unions covering bargaining units of 200 or more employees.
b Unions covering bargaining units of 500 or more employees.

Sources: Wood, W.D. and P, Kumar, eds., The Current Industrial Relations Scene in Canada, Volumes 1981 through 1985, Kingston, Ontario: Industrial Relations Centre, Queen's University, Table: Union Representation Within Industry Groups." (1981: 231-237; 1982: 250-253; 1983: 262-265; 1984: 270-272; 1985: 261-263). Kumar, P., with M.L. Coates, and D. Arrowsmith, The Current Industrial Relations Scene in Canada, Volumes 1986 through 1988, Kingston, Ontario: Industrial Relations Centre, Queen's University, Table: Union Representation Within Industry Groups in Canada." (1986: 329-331; 1987: 412; 1988: 517-523) Coates, M.L., D. Arrowsmith, and M. Couchene, The Labour Movement and Trade Unionism Reference Tables, 1989 volume, Kingston, Ontario: Industrial Relations Centre, Queen's University, Table 30: Union Representation Within Industry Groups in Canada, 1989." pp. 82-88. Mine, Mill & Smelter Workers (Local 598): Labour Canada, Directory of Labour Organizations in Canada (Ottawa: Minister of Supply and Services, 1984, 1985, 1986, 1987, 1988, 1989).

in national unions occurred at the same time that international unions experienced a relative decline in the industry.

Not surprisingly, the 1980s have been a period of relative calm in terms of work stoppages. The number of stoppages has declined to its lowest level since the early 1960s. Consequently, both the number of workers affected and person-days not worked have also declined.

Few negotiations with the major employers ended in a work stoppage in the 1988 to 1990 bargaining rounds.[34] However, the recession of the early 1990s will likely give rise to additional pressures at the bargaining table as employees seek real wage increases and protection against job loss.

CURRENT BARGAINING DEVELOPMENTS IN THE INDUSTRY

Bargaining developments in the industry have reflected environmental influences as well as changes in the goals of management and unions in response to new pressures confronting the industry. For example, while we would expect wage gains to reflect trends in the business cycle and, consequently, firm profitability and employment pressures, we also expect changes in production processes and the long-run downsizing of firms to have an impact on the types of clauses negotiated.

Monetary gains and improvements in a broad range of health and safety concerns continue to be key long-run goals for unions. However, in 1990 negotiations, unions have sought and, in many cases, have obtained major improvements in other non-wage items, including pensions, early retirement plans, severance pay, and contracting-out (Kendall, Kokkinos, and Porter 1991). Clearly, in the face of layoffs during the past decade, job security has become an issue of some importance for many unions. Consequently, any plans that reduce the impact of layoffs (e.g., severance pay or retraining) or that circumvent the need for layoffs (e.g., early retirement schemes) have gained in importance and are likely to remain high on union agendas.

For contracts pertaining to bargaining units of at least 500 employees, average annual wage increases in union contracts in the industry declined from the very high levels of 1980 (at 14.5 percent) to the very low level of 1.5 percent in 1986.[35] This trend likely developed in response to economic pressures in the industry. However, average annual wage increases grew from 3.7 percent in 1987 to 5.9 percent in 1990. This trend toward higher wage settlements has likely reflected the effects of the prolonged economic expansion of the mid to late 1980s.

Table 4.10 summarizes a panel of wage-settlement and unit-size information for contracts concluded by major mining firms during the 1980–90 period. Most firms in the panel signed three or four collective agreements during this period. Wage settlements declined into the mid-1980s, and recovered in the latter half of the 1980s for only some of the firms. For example, while the coal industry settlements remained low, wage recovery in the metals industry was most likely facilitated by the increase in base-metal prices, which, in turn, led to record profit levels at firms such as Inco Limited. However, the recession of the early 1990s will likely dampen

Table 4.10

Panel of Bargaining-Unit and Wage-Settlement Changes in Major Bargaining Units in Mining a

	1980	1981	1982	1983	1984	1985	1986	1987	1988	1989	1990
1. Brunswick Mining & Smelting United Steel Workers New Brunswick											
Employees	1280			1325				1170			
Contract Duration	39			24				36			
Ave. Annual Increase	14.9			6.3				3.3			
COLA	YES			YES				YES			
2. Cape Breton Develop. Corp. United Mine Workers New Brunswick											
Employees		3400		3200	3200	3200		2745			2200
Contract Duration		24		12	12	24		24			48
Ave. Annual Increase		7.1		6.0	5.0	6.4		3.8			3.4
COLA		NO		NO	NO	NO		NO			NO
3. Rio Algom Mines United Steel Workers Ontario											
Employees		2400			2500			1800			1800
Contract Duration		36			36			36			12
Ave. Annual Increase		10.4			5.0			3.7			5.9
COLA		YES			YES			YES			YES
4. Denison Mines United Steel Workers Ontario											
Employees		1675			1800			1505			1470
Contract Duration		36			36			36			12
Ave. Annual Increase		10.4			5.0			3.7			5.9
COLA		YES			YES			YES			YES

(continued)

Table 4.10 (continued)

	1980	1981	1982	1983	1984	1985	1986	1987	1988	1989	1990
5. Falconbridge Ltd. Mine Mill, Ontario											
Employees				1880	2570	1845			1845		
Contract Duration				19	17	36			36		
Ave. Annual Increase				0	4.2	5.5			6.2		
COLA				NO	YES	YES			YES		
6. Inco Limited United Steel Workers Ontario/Manitoba											
Employees		1900[b]	10 000[c]		1500[b]	7150[c]		1300[b]	6300[c]		1500[b]
Contract Duration		36	36		36	36		36	36		36
Ave. Annual Increase		9.8	5.0		0	4.0		5.1	12.0		7.6
COLA		YES	YES		YES	YES		YES	YES		YES
7. Fording Coal Ltd. United Steel Workers British Columbia											
Employees		1000		1350			1200				
Contract Duration		24		24			48				
Ave. Annual Increase		10.2		7.5			2.0				
COLA		YES		YES			NO				
8. Iron Ore Co. of Canada United Steel Workers Newfoundland											
Employees		1200			700			1268		895	1550
Contract Duration		36			36			36		36	36
Ave. Annual Increase		8.0			4.3			3.4		5.9	8.2
COLA		YES			YES			YES		YES	YES

Note: [a] Includes fuels.
[b] Manitoba Operations
[c] Ontario Operations

Source: Data provided by the Bureau of Labour Information, Labour Canada, 1991.

further wage increases. Notably, most firms downsized their work forces throughout the period; while employment levels in some firms fluctuated, the trend is toward lower levels. Again, employment declines are likely attributable to the continuing impact of technological changes on labour requirements.

While most contracts contain a cost-of-living-adjustment (COLA) clause, one of the most important developments was the negotiation of pension indexing by the USWA at Inco Limited in 1988 (Ontario Ministry of Labour 1988). A similar agreement was reached between the Mine Mill and Falconbridge Limited (at Falconbridge, Ontario), also in 1988. While pension indexing remains relatively uncommon (Kendall, Kokkinos, and Porter 1991), it is reasonable to expect an increasing number of contracts to contain such provisions in the future.

In a study of the determinants of private-sector nonwage bargaining outcomes during the 1975–84 period, Chaykowski (1991) finds that, relative to those of manufacturing firms, collective agreements in the mining industry are associated with lower measures of total nonwage contract outcomes, total nonwage pecuniary outcomes, and total nonwage nonpecuniary outcomes that are "favourable to the union." Table 4.11 provides a selected list of nonwage clauses and their prevalence in major mining contracts (covering 500 or more employees) that were in effect from 1986 through 1989. Importantly, roughly half of these contracts contain clauses dealing with the impacts of technological change (e.g., advance notice; retraining; income guarantees; severance), but there exist very few provisions for joint committees to deal with technological change. Interestingly, in an analysis of contracts negotiated from 1975 to 1984, Chaykowski (1991) finds that, relative to those in the manufacturing sector, collective agreements in the mining industry are associated with lower levels of technological-change bargaining outcomes that are "favourable to the union."

Other clauses we would expect to (and, in fact, do) find to be prevalent in mining contracts, given the long tradition of structured work rules, include on-the-job training and seniority provisions (e.g., promotion, transfers, layoffs, recall, bumping; see Table 4.11). The prevalence of clauses to restrict contracting out may be a union reaction to management attempts to reduce labour costs. Importantly, few incentive plans are observed—unions appear to demand guaranteed annual wage increases and to resist contingent-pay schemes.[36] An important development in this area again occurred at Inco Limited in 1988, and subsequently at Falconbridge in 1988, where "nickel bonuses" were negotiated.[37] In 1990, a new profit-sharing plan was negotiated at the Hudson Bay Mining and Smelting Co. in Manitoba. The negotiation of contingent-payment schemes in such key agreements suggests that the frequency of these plans may increase in the future.

These contract results are interesting in light of the findings of a 1991 survey of management goals in unionized and nonunionized firms in mining (see Table 4.12). Whereas (on average) lowering wage costs was cited as being of moderate importance, lowering benefits costs was (on average) rated as the most important goal of unionized firms. Interestingly, neither wage nor benefit costs were rated as being of particular importance to nonunionized firms, perhaps suggesting that

Table 4.11
Prevalence of Selected Collective-Bargaining Agreement Outcomes in Canadian Mining[a,g,h,i] (Contracts with at least 500 employees)

	1986	1987	1988	1989
Category 1: *Union Security*				
Supervisors and nonbargaining unit not to perform bargaining unit work	10 (4)[a]	13 (3)	9 (6)	5 (5)
Contracting-out restriction	7 (7)	11 (5)	10 (5)	5 (5)
Labour–management Committee to deal with CBA	5 (9)	10 (6)	7 (8)	4 (6)
Category 2: *Employee Security*				
Technological change:				
— Advance notice	9 (5)	11 (5)	11 (4)	6 (4)
— Notice to lay off	1 (13)	2 (14)	2 (13)	0 (10)
— Right to retraining	2 (12)	5 (11)	7 (8)	1 (9)
— Reference to retraining	8 (6)	7 (9)	6 (9)	5 (5)
— Joint Committee[b]	0 (14)	2 (14)	6 (9)	0 (10)
— Relocation allowance	0 (14)	1 (15)	0 (15)	0 (10)
— Employment guarantee	0 (14)	1 (15)	0 (15)	0 (10)
— Income guarantee	5 (9)	9 (7)	9 (6)	4 (6)
Employment guarantees — Qualification[c]	0 (14)	1 (15)	0 (15)	0 (10)
Employment guarantees — Duration[c]	0 (14)	1 (15)	0 (15)	0 (10)
Income guarantees	0 (14)	0 (16)	2 (13)	0 (10)
Training on the job[d]	11 (3)	11 (5)	13 (2)	7 (3)
Training — Outside course[d]	6 (8)	5 (11)	6 (9)	4 (6)
Training — Apprenticeship[d]	12 (2)	13 (3)	12 (3)	8 (2)
Category 3: *Seniority and Related Provisions*				
Seniority on promotion	13 (1)	13 (3)	15 (0)	9 (1)
Seniority on transfer	10 (4)	11 (5)	11 (4)	5 (5)
Seniority on layoff	14 (0)	13 (3)	15 (0)	8 (2)
Seniority on recall	11 (3)	13 (3)	15 (0)	6 (4)
Bumping	10 (4)	10 (6)	11 (4)	7 (3)
Job posting	13 (3)	12 (4)	13 (2)	7 (3)
Category 4: *Termination of Employment*				
Notice of layoff	7 (7)	11 (5)	6 (9)	3 (7)
Severance pay and/or SUB	12 (2)	11 (5)	10 (5)	8 (2)
Types of severance pay:				
— Layoff due to lack of work	3 (11)	3 (13)	6 (9)	3 (7)
— Technological change	7 (7)	9 (7)	7 (8)	5 (5)
— Resignation	1 (13)	0 (16)	1 (14)	0 (10)
— Retirement	2 (12)	1 (15)	2 (13)	1 (9)

Table 4.11 (continued)

	1986	1987	1988	1989
— Disability	1 (13)	0 (16)	0 (15)	1 (9)
— Incapacity	0 (14)	0 (16)	0 (15)	1 (9)
— Incompetence	0 (14)	0 (16)	0 (15)	0 (10)
— Discharge for cause	0 (14)	0 (16)	0 (15)	0 (10)
— Plant closure	3 (11)	2 (14)	1 (14)	1 (9)
— Plant merger	0 (14)	0 (16)	0 (15)	0 (10)
— Involuntary group termination	1 (13)	0 (16)	0 (15)	1 (9)
— Death	1 (13)	0 (16)	1 (14)	0 (10)
— Other (e.g., transfer)	0 (14)	0 (16)	0 (15)	1 (9)
Category 5: *Pay Guarantees*				
Wage Incentive Plans:				
— Plan A: Piece rate	0 (14)	4 (12)	1 (14)	0 (9)*
— Plan B: Group	0 (14)	2 (14)	1 (14)	0 (9)*
— Plan C: Productivity bonus	3 (11)	5 (11)	1 (14)	0 (9)*
— Plan D: Profit sharing	1 (13)	0 (16)	0 (15)	0 (9)*
— Plan E: Market-value bonus	1 (13)	2 (14)	2 (13)	0 (9)*
Wage change	14 (0)	16 (0)	15 (0)	10 (0)
Cost-of-Living adjustment[c]	7 (7)	10 (6)	11 (4)	3 (7)
Category 6: *Employee Benefits*				
Pension-benefit indexing[f]	0 (14)	1 (15)	2 (13)	1 (9)
Category 7: *Part-Time Workers*				
Ratio of part-time to full-time workers	0 (14)	0 (16)	0 (15)	0 (10)
Total number of collective agreements	14	16	15	10

Notes: a Figures in parentheses are numbers of collective agreements negotiated without the given clause.
 b Joint Committee to address training.
 c Employment guarantees with regard to technological change or contracting-out.
 d Fully, partially, or unpaid leave provisions.
 e May include nonoperative COLA clause.
 f May include clause indicating "consideration" of indexing.
 g Includes three observations from the crude petroleum and natural gas industry.
 h Includes smelting and refining.
 i Includes fuels.
 * Numbers only add up to 9.
Source: Collective Bargaining Agreement Database, Bureau of Labour Information, Labour Canada.

direct labour costs are of less concern to nonunionized companies.

Also important to unionized firms were the goals of improving flexibility in introducing new technologies and increased employee involvement (EI) in the workplace. The technology result is expected in light of the growing significance

Table 4.12

Importance of Industrial Relations Goals to Unionized and Non-unionized Mining Firms, 1985–1990[a, b, c]

	Unionized Establishments			Nonunionized Establishments		
	Not At All Important	Somewhat Important	Extremely Important	Not At All Important	Somewhat Important	Extremely Important
Lower wage costs	4	4	8	2	4	1
Lower benefits costs	2	5	9	2	4	1
Reducing "restrictive" work rules	1	9	6	2	3	2
Increasing contracting-out	6	6	4	4	1	2
Reduction of the number of job classifications	6	5	5	4	2	1
Obtaining wage flexibility (e.g., profit sharing; lump-sum payments)	3	8	5	2	0	5
Obtaining increased flexibility in assigning employees[d]	2	8	6	2	1	3
Improved labour–management co-operation (programs)	3	5	8	0	4	3
Improved flexibility in introducing new technologies	2	6	8	0	5	2
Increased employee involvement in the workplace	0	10	6	0	2	5

Notes:
a   Unionized firms were asked to consider their bargaining experience with their largest bargaining unit.
    Nonunionized firms were asked to consider the goals of their firm with regard to their largest operating unit.

b   Smallest bargaining unit was fewer than 100 employees; the largest unit was more than 5000 employees. Smallest operating unit (nonunionized firms) was fewer than 10 employees; the largest operating unit was fewer than 500 employees.

c   For unionized firms: number of missing =1; number of respondents indicating "Not Applicable" = 2.
    For nonunionized firms: number missing = 2; number of respondents indicating "Not Applicable" = 6.

d   Number missing = 3 for nonunionized firms.

Source: Richard P. Chaykowski, *IR/HR Practices in the Mining Industry: A Survey of Current Developments in North America* (Kingston, ON: Industrial Relations Centre, Queen's University, 1991).

of production and process technologies in the industry. The significance of the result for EI begs the question of whether management in unionized firms actually views EI as having potentially productivity-enhancing effects or as a way of sharing decision making with the union, or, rather, as a "generally desirable" objective.[38]

The goal of increased EI was, on average, rated highest by nonunionized firms. Significantly, no nonunionized firms rated improved labour–management cooperation programs, improved flexibility in introducing new technologies, or increased employee involvement in the workplace as unimportant goals, thereby underscoring the importance of these initiatives in nonunionized firms. Further, management of nonunionized firms tended to rate the goal of obtaining wage flexibility (e.g., through profit-sharing) as particularly important.

Finally, relative to other goals, contracting-out was (on average) rated as relatively unimportant to the management of both unionized and nonunionized firms. In the case of unionized firms, the contract data (see Table 4.11) suggest that unions have achieved a large measure of control in this area, so that it may no longer be a key goal of firms to seek this outcome as a method of labour-cost reduction. Instead, both unionized and nonunionized firms attach high importance to goals that relate to the relationship of management with their own work force.

BROADER LABOUR-FORCE AND EMPLOYMENT CONDITIONS

MacMillan, Gislason, and Lyon (1977) identify two chronic problems associated with industry employment: labour shortages, and turnover and the retention of employees. The major human-resources issues that appear to have traditionally occupied the attention of industry practitioners include work-force skilling and labour supply.

Employment issues relating to labour supply and training remain at the forefront of industry concerns in the 1980s and 1990s.[39] Skill shortages and training in the trades pose significant problems that, while recognized as persistent and long-run in nature, promise to be particularly pressing into the next century. These are problems that can dramatically affect individual firms, because many operations are located in northern or remote areas with little access to the larger labour markets of southern cities. Furthermore, as employees broaden their range of lifestyle concerns, living conditions in mining communities are rising to prominence on firms' agendas. Firms are now exploring new approaches to these problems, such as the prospects for long-distance commuting, and are attaching greater importance to the needs of dual-earner families.

In addition to the broader labour-force issues, health and safety has been of central concern to management and employees, because of the dangers inherent in the industry.[40] While the trend in the fatality rate (per 1000 workers) in mining has improved over the 1980s, the rate of 0.44 in 1988 means that mining, along with fishing and forestry, are among the most dangerous of industries; the rate in mining is far above the 1988 rate of 0.06 in manufacturing.[41] Aside from immediate risks of injury, a large number of occupational diseases are associated with mining, including silicosis, cancer, and other respiratory diseases linked to environmental hazards such as particulates, noise, vibrations, coal dust, asbestos, toxic gases, and radiation. Federal and provincial legislation regulating occupational health and safety includes workers' compensation, which provides benefits to accident victims, and a variety of standards legislation. Specific legislation is also enacted with respect to particular diseases or conditions (e.g., silicosis and dust exposure), or with respect to specific industries (e.g., coal mining).[42]

In 1988, the Workplace Hazardous Materials Information System (WHMIS) became effective in all jurisdictions. The legislation provides for the identification of hazardous materials, training and instruction of workers exposed to hazardous materials, labelling of hazardous materials, and provision of data sheets regarding the hazards of controlled products.[43] WHMIS constitutes a major legislative effort that is expected to have a significant impact on the broader mining industry, since there are a large number of potentially hazardous substances in use in the extraction, smelting, and refining processes of the industry. One of the ongoing challenges to employers will be the administration of this legislation in the workplace.

A combination of factors has led to considerable health and safety improvements since the Second World War: unions and firms have given these issues a high priority; firms have committed greater resources to improving working conditions; many of the new technologies have considerable safety-enhancing benefits; and policy makers have placed increased emphasis on this area. The long-standing importance of health and safety to workers in the mining industry, and the ongoing attention placed on health-related legislation by policy makers, promises to keep health and safety high on the agendas of unions and firms.

Environmental Change, Globalization, and Evolving Firm and Labour Strategies

Mining firms have exhibited a number of reactions to emerging economic and industrial relations developments. The impacts of increased international competition and changing demand patterns have induced significant firm responses. In turn, changes in management strategies, particularly with regard to the transformation of production processes, have profoundly affected the future prospects for unions in the industry, and consequently the role of the nonunion sector.

While employment growth is stagnating in the industry, this situation is not attributable to the type of North American industrial restructuring or "deindustrialization" characteristic of the heavy "rust-belt" industries, such as steel. Nevertheless, since changes in the structure of demand and competition from low-cost producers also affect employment trends in the mining industry, it is possible that mining operations (e.g., metals) would have suffered a similar fate had major firms not embarked on programs to transform production processes and capabilities through research and development, and investment in new technologies. While the introduction of new technologies is directly related to the decline in production employment levels, it is also related to greater cost competitiveness, and, hence, the survival of firms in the industry.

Underlying trends in employment levels in subsectors of the mining industry may vary, depending upon whether one considers metals, nonmetals, or coal. Further, employment trends in individual firms depend upon whether the firm is small or large, and whether it engages in a single activity or is vertically integrated with operations that include mining as well as smelting and refining. Recognizing that employment levels, therefore, vary according to firm-specific product and market conditions, the key development with respect to production worker employment may be the impact of new technologies.

The efficiency of mineral production and processing is closely tied to state-of-the-art engineering at each stage in the production process, including extraction, milling, smelting, and refining. Larger firms that have the resources for large-scale capital expenditures, and long-established operations based on a long-run mineral supply, are often in a unique position to engage in extensive mine or refinery modernization programs. For example, in the early 1990s, Inco Limited began rebuilding its Copper Cliff (Ontario) smelter complex, which will decrease smelter emissions; at the same time, Inco is continuing its long-run modernization program of its mines.[44] A smelter modernization plan is being considered by the Hudson Bay Mining and Smelting Company at its zinc operations in Flin Flon (Manitoba), which is expected to result in an employment downsizing of approximately 25 percent, significant cost reductions, and a major reduction in sulphur-dioxide emissions ("Bringing Flin Flon into the '90s" *Canadian Mining Journal* 1990, 56–58).

Common benefits resulting from such modernization programs include cost reductions, productivity improvements, and, of increasing importance, enhanced pollution abatement. Environmental considerations are often a key aspect of refining and smelting modernization programs, as governments establish increasingly stringent pollution standards (e.g., relating to acid rain resulting from sulphur-dioxide emissions). While employment losses are often a substantial side effect of modernization programs, jobs that remain are typically much safer, since new tasks often involve computer-assisted equipment control, remote control, and other systems that typically involve less physical contact with machinery or materials. With few exceptions, there has been little research concerning the reasons for adoption and the incidence of new technologies in mining and mineral manufacturing, or the impacts of new technologies on workplace outcomes, such as work organization, skilling requirements, and labour–management relations. Studies across establishments are also needed to gain an understanding of the impacts of such factors as unionization, organization characteristics, and type of operation, on the effects of new technologies.

A recent analysis of the diffusion of new computer-based technologies in Canadian mining and smelter operations, based on a survey by Statistics Canada, has provided important new evidence on the extent of use of, and the impacts of, new technologies related to automated material-handling systems, communications and networks, automated processing systems, and control systems.[45] The results reinforce the importance of new technologies throughout the industry: first, 52 percent of the operating mines (covering 85 percent of mining employment) used at least 5 of the 25 technologies; second, with regard to the impacts of the technologies, approximately 66 percent of the mines experienced improved output, approximately 50 percent achieved improved product quality, and approximately 66 percent obtained cost reductions; third, increased usage of technology was found to be positively correlated with positive effects on costs, quality, and output (Statistics Canada 1990b). Clearly, widespread adoption of these technologies will enable firms to enhance their competitive positions.

In the area of mineral manufacturing, a recent analysis of the extent to which work practices have been affected by the introduction of new production technologies was conducted at a Canadian metals refinery in which the work force was unionized (Chaykowski and Slotsve 1992). The new technologies resulted in redefinition of the job structure, in which some jobs were eliminated or changed, and new jobs created. While there was some evidence of a skilling effect, there was no evidence of deskilling. Importantly, while the union was largely reactive throughout the process, the firm did not engage in new human-resources strategies to accommodate the change:

> Interviews with various levels of management suggested that planning associated with the recapitalization program was directed only towards achieving technical efficiency (i.e., optimizing the technical subsystem) and neglecting planning adjustments aimed at adapting the social system (i.e., work organization and practices) that could be required to achieve joint optimization. Furthermore, traditional human resource and industrial relations practices were maintained in the transformed workplaces. (Chaykowski and Slotsve 1992, 327)

Given the pervasiveness of new technologies in the mining industry, as well as the positive productivity impacts for firms, the future challenge for mining firms may be to adjust their traditional human-resource strategies and organizational structures to achieve a new sociotechnical system that more fully captures the gains from new technologies.

Perhaps the leading example of the technological revolution in mining occurred at Inco Limited during the 1980s.[46] Described by Till (1988) as a reaction to low productivity, excessive labour-force sizes, and labour-costs pressures, the development and introduction of production technologies was a strategic choice by corporate management to correct what was clearly perceived as a competitive disadvantage in the market, particularly in the face of the weak product markets of the early 1980s. The result has been a discrete shift in corporate-investment and human-resource strategies.

The increased emphasis on investment in production technologies at existing facilities at Inco Limited has led to several positive outcomes, including industry leadership as an innovator, increased productivity, and lower production costs (see Till 1988; Scales 1988). But the effect on industrial relations outcomes at Inco Limited has also been significant. The production labour force has been cut from 10 000 in 1981 to 6300 in 1988. For the USWA, the decline in membership has been accompanied by a transition in posture. Once viewed as perhaps one of the most militant USWA locals in the country, the Sudbury local has adopted a stance of reaction to and acceptance of the impacts of technological change, including the effects on employment levels, work arrangements, and skill levels.[47] Gretton (1988) points to the development of ongoing "In-Term" and "Face-to-Face" meetings with the union and employees, and the consideration of union concerns regarding technological changes through a joint "Technological Change Committee," as developments that support an improved labour–management relationship.

In terms of positive outcomes for employees, two important benefits of implementing new technology include an improvement in mine safety (see Till 1988) and a dramatic increase in productivity levels that, in turn, facilitate high employee-compensation levels. Recent high-profit levels and compensation settlements at Inco Limited support this conclusion.

While Inco Limited has aggressively pursued a strategy of pushing the frontiers of technological change in the industry, accompanied by major labour-force downsizing, the traditional union–firm relationship has been preserved, albeit with a less confrontational stance between management and union. Relative to the pre-1980 era, the USWA appears to have become less militant and more accepting of changes occurring at Inco Limited.

Given the dramatic downsizing occurring at many large unionized firms, mining unions are challenged to expand coverage to the nonunionized portion of the industry. But several factors mitigate against union efforts to organize nonunionized firms, including industry characteristics that are unique to mining. For example, the remote locations of some mines and the limited life of some operations, which are ultimately associated with some degree of worker mobility, can result in a high cost of union organizing.

Further, the advanced level of human-resource management practices at some nonunionized firms may prove to be a decisive factor in efforts to organize workers. An important example of an organization that has remained nonunion is the Kidd Creek operation in Ontario. Amsden (n.d.) reports that the firm resisted four attempts at organization by the USWA (with the Steelworkers mounting a particularly intensive campaign in the early 1980s), as well as efforts by the International Brotherhood of Electrical Workers and interest by the Mine Mill union of Sudbury Originally owned by Texasgulf, Kidd Creek was purchased by the Canada Development Corporation in 1981, and was subsequently purchased by Falconbridge in

1986. Cawsey and Richardson (1979) describe the employee relations program at Kidd Creek as it originated at Texasgulf, including the following key components: a concern for management attitudes; the visibility of executives, and communication (e.g., through a grievance procedure and employee meetings); a competitive salary, with extensive benefits and merit increases; an employee share-ownership plan and safety bonus plan; and attitude surveys of employees. The program was credited with lower turnover, lower absenteeism, a low accident rate, and productivity performance that meets the "expectations" of management.

Cawsey and Richardson (1979, 55, Table 3) also identify a number of the root factors that gave rise to these strong results, including the availability of resources (e.g., to facilitate expenditure on working conditions and benefits), the availability of a skilled work force, firm growth, and the philosophy of management. This last factor, and in particular management emphasis on strong first-line supervision, is credited as being the most important contribution to the success of the employee relations program. While offered by Cawsey and Richardson (1979, 59) as a potential model for other firms, it is likely that the Kidd Creek approach to labour relations may be most relevant to growing and nonunionized mining operations.

A further challenge confronting unions is whether they can move beyond their traditional base among production workers to organize the large pool of white-collar employees in the industry. A major step in this direction was taken in 1991, when the 1200 salaried employees at Inco Limited (Sudbury) were organized by the USWA. This was the third attempt to organize these workers (Pender 1991). However, given the limited inroads to date among white-collar employees in the industry, it is uncertain whether the USWA, or other traditional mining unions, can repeat this success.

Is there potential for human-resources policies in nonunion firms to lead changes in human-resources management among unorganized firms, but also challenge the traditional approaches to industrial relations in unionized settings? Can changes in human-resources strategies affect the fortunes of the union movement, as has occurred in the United States? Kochan (1990, 215) concludes that the pace of innovation among Canadian management generally is less pronounced than in the United States: "...the nonunion sector seems to be less of a source of human-resource management innovation that is pressurizing unionized firms to match their lead. Second, where changes are occurring in union firms, the changes are coming through the normal bargaining and contract administration process." Given the deeply entrenched "traditional approach" to union–management relations in the industry, it is unlikely that innovation will be either marked or widespread in the unionized portion of the mining industry. Therefore, despite the tremendous competitive pressures confronting all firms, it is most likely that innovation, if it does develop, may occur first with the human-resource practices of nonunionized firms.

With regard to the United States, Kochan, Katz, and McKersie (1986) suggest that broad-based employer resistance to unions (e.g., resistance to organizing efforts or strategies of union avoidance) has been a major factor underlying the declining fortunes of unions. However, Chaison and Rose (1991, 182) note that this phenomenon is likely to be less of a factor in Canada. In the mining industry, the fortunes of the major unions appear to be most closely related to the economic well-being of firms and the accelerating drive to increase the usage of labour-saving technologies.

Strategies for Change and Prospects for Industrial Relations

Many aspects of the mining industry, by definition, continue to be hostage to the natural location and extent of the mineral resources. Human-resource issues can be unique to the frontier character of the industry, as whole work forces are created and laid off with changes in the condition of the natural resource. These unique conditions exist in addition to the market forces that affect other industries. In particular, labour shortages in certain occupational groups, turnover, and the skilling of the work force have been, and will likely remain, key issues.

In the realm of labour relations, the experience at Inco Limited demonstrates a corporate-level strategic business decision affecting two levels of the organization. First, the practice of collective bargaining has been characterized as changing from confrontation to accommodation, in the context of union "reaction" to changes in employment levels that were considered to be beyond the scope of bargaining. Second, as a consequence of the pervasive introduction of new technologies, the workplace has also been fundamentally transformed through increased skill requirements and new work relationships.

These changes are important since Inco Limited is often viewed as an industry trend setter. It is uncertain whether or not this experience has been replicated in other unionized firms, and whether or not work relationships in nonunionized firms have been altered by similar environmental influences. There is no evidence regarding this matter, and there is clearly a need for increased research on the impacts of the environmental pressures on collective-bargaining outcomes, union–management relations, and work organization in both unionized and nonunionized firms.

Since most large mining firms are unionized, organized labour is the central force in industrial relations. Employment trends throughout the 1980s, the increasing influences of international competition, and continued technological advances, taken together, have had a far-reaching effect on the union movement in mining. Each of the major unions in the industry has suffered successive membership losses that can largely be attributed to employment downsizing.

What is the future likely to hold for organized labour? The importance of new technologies in the industry appears to have permanently transformed the composition of the work force in terms of skill levels, production worker employment levels, and the white-collar/blue-collar mix. With the relative levels of white-collar labour remaining high, the challenge to unions will be to organize these groups of typically unorganized workers.

However, since the major unions remain "traditional" in their orientation, inroads in white-collar organization appears unlikely. Among larger firms, the blue-collar employment is likely to further decline. Employment of production workers will likely grow in smaller firms (which may introduce fewer labour-saving technologies into their operations as they expand, relative to larger firms), or in entirely new operations. While some union growth may be achieved through the organization of new mining operations, white-collar workers hold out the greatest potential.

Among unions, the traditional strength of the UMWA and the USWA in the industry is being eroded. While national union membership is increasing, this growth has, so far, been modest. The future of both major international unions in mining may be of immediate concern, but particularly, for the USWA, successes or failures in mining will have implications for the occupational composition and orientation of the USWA in Canada as a whole.

Whether or not the tenor of labour–management relations has been permanently transformed into a less confrontational relationship requires study at the firm level, of which there is a virtual absence of research. What is apparent is that unions appear to be largely reactive to the environmental changes imposed on the relationship between organized labour and management. It is equally evident that, given the renewed long-run prospects of many major firms, management is favourably positioned to take new initiatives on a wide range of human-resource and labour–management issues.

REFERENCES

Amsden, Michael P. n.d. "Management and Employee Relations in a Non-union Organization," Address at Queen's University (mimeo).

Barnacle, Peter. 1989. *The Current Industrial Relations Scene in 1989: Labour Legislation and Public Policy Reference Tables*. Kingston, ON: Industrial Relations Centre, Queen's University.

Canadian Mining Journal. 1990. "Bringing Flin Flon into the '90s." Don Mills: Southam Business Information and Communications Group Inc. (November).

Cawsey, T.F., and P.R. Richardson. 1979. "Employee Relations at the Kidd Creek Operations of Texasgulf." In *Employee Relations Initiatives in Canadian Mining*, Proceedings No. 5. Kingston, ON: Centre for Resource Studies, Queen's University. 45–60.

Chaison, Gary N., and Joseph B. Rose. 1991. "Continental Divide: The Direction and Fate of North American Unions." In D. Sockell, D. Lewin, and D. Lipsky, eds., *Advances in Industrial and Labor Relations*, Vol. 5. Greenwich, CT: JAI Press Inc. 169–205.

Chaykowski, Richard P. 1991. "The Analysis of Nonwage Bargaining Outcomes: Evidence From the Canadian Private Sector." In D. Sockell, D. Lewin, and D. Lipsky, eds., *Advances in Industrial and Labor Relations*, Vol. 5. Greenwich, CT: JAI Press Inc. 237–291.

Chaykowski, Richard P., and G. A. Slotsve. 1992. "Organizational Work Practices and the Impacts of Plant Modernization: A Canadian Case Study." *Industrial Relations*, Vol. 31, No. 2 (Spring 1992). 309–329.

Clement, W. 1981. *Hardrock Mining: Industrial Relations and Technological Changes at INCO*. Toronto: McClelland and Stewart Limited.

Coates, Mary Lou, David Arrowsmith, and Melanie Courchene. 1989. *The Current Industrial Relations Scene in 1989: The Labour Movement and Trade Unionism Reference Tables*. Kingston, ON: Industrial Relations Centre, Queen's University.

Financial Post. 1990. *Financial Post 500*. Toronto.

Gibbs, Graham W., and Paul Pintus. 1978. *Health and Safety in the Canadian Mining Industry*. Kingston, ON: Centre for Resource Studies, Queen's University.

Green, Alan G., and M. Ann Green. 1991. "Response to Crises: The Ontario Metal Mining Industry 1975–1985." Working Paper No. 45. Kingston, ON: Centre for Resource Studies, Queen's University.

Gretton, Wallace T. 1988. "Case Study: Canada-Inco Limited–United Steelworkers." In *New Perspectives in Industrial Relations: Developments in the U.S., U.K., and Canada*. Washington, DC: British-North America Committee, April. 57–61.

Jackson, Moira. 1990. "Human Resource Planning for the Mining Industry." *CRS Perspectives* 33 (July): 12–15.

Kendall, Glenn, Yiota Kokkinos, and Nancy Porter. 1991. "Collective Bargaining Outcomes in Canada's Minerals and Metals Industry, 1990." In Energy, Mines and Resources Canada, Mining Industry Employment Update. Ottawa: Minister of Supply and Services, January. 29–33.

Kochan, Thomas. 1990. "Looking to the Year 2000: Challenges for Industrial Relations and Human Resource Management." In K. Newton, T. Schweitzer, and J. Voyer, eds., Perspective 2000: Proceedings of a Conference Sponsored by the Economic Council of Canada, December 1988. Ottawa: Minister of Supply and Services. 203–17.

Kochan, Thomas, Harry Katz, and Robert McKersie. 1986. The Transformation of American Industrial Relations. New York: Basic Books.

Koepke, W.E. 1990. "International Scene." In Energy, Mines and Resources Canada, 1989 Canadian Minerals Yearbook: Review and Outlook. Mineral Report No. 38. Ottawa: Minister of Supply and Services. 2.1–2.6.

Kumar, Pradeep, and Mary Lou Coates. 1991. Industrial Relations in 1991: Trends and Emerging Issues. Kingston, ON: Industrial Relations Centre, Queen's University, in press.

MacMillan, J.A., G.S. Gislason, and S. Lyon. 1977. Human Resources in Canadian Mining: A Preliminary Analysis. Kingston, ON: Centre for Resource Studies, Queen's University.

Nappi, Carmine. 1989. Metals Demand and the Canadian Metal Industry: Structural Changes and Policy Implications. Kingston, ON: Centre for Resource Studies, Queen's University.

Noranda Inc. 1990. 1989 Annual Report.

Ontario Ministry of Labour. 1988. Collective Bargaining Settlements in Ontario. Toronto: May.

Palmer, Bryan D. 1983. Working-Class Experience. Toronto: Butterworth and Co. Ltd.

Pender, Terry. 1991. "Steelworkers Bid to Organize Inco Office Employees." Sudbury Star, March 22.

Pilsworth, D. 1990. "General Review" In Energy, Mines, and Resources Canada, 1989 Canadian Minerals Yearbook: Review and Outlook. Mineral Report No. 38. Ottawa: Minister of Supply and Services. 1.1–1.11.

Placer Dome Inc. 1988. 1987 Annual Report.

Robinson, Allan. 1991. "Gold Goliath Brewing in Mining Merger Talks." The Globe and Mail, May 29, B1.

Scales, Marilyn. 1988. "Primary Metals: Inco's Biggest Business." Canadian Mining Journal. Don Mills: Southam Business Information and Communications Group Inc., June: 23–27.

Statistics Canada. 1989. Canadian Economic Observer: Historical Statistical Supplement 1988/89, Vol. 3, Catalogue 11-210. Ottawa: Minister of Supply and Services, July.

——. 1990a. Gross Domestic Product by Industry, Vol. 4, No. 1, Catalogue 15-001. Ottawa: Minister of Supply and Services, April.

——. 1990b. Survey of the Diffusion of

Technology in the Mining Industry. Ottawa: Minister of Supply and Services, June.

Till, Larry. 1988. "Breaking New Ground." *Office Management Automation*, October: 50–54.

Tilton, John E. 1989. "Changing Patterns of Mineral Trade." In L. M. Jackson and P. R. Richardson, eds., *Marketing of Nonferrous Metals: Proceedings No. 19.* Kingston, ON: Centre for Resource Studies, Queen's University. 15–25.

Williams, C. Brian. 1986. "International Trade Unionism: The United Mine Workers in Eastern Canada, 1900–1920." *Relations Industrielles/Industrial Relations* 41/3: 519–40.

ENDNOTES

1. This essay is based on a larger study of industrial relations in the Canadian and U.S. mining industry, which is supported by grants from the Donner Canada Foundation and the Ontario Ministry of Labour. The author gratefully acknowledges this financial support. Subject to the usual disclaimer, the author gratefully acknowledges the helpful comments and suggestions of Moira Jackson, George Slotsve, Terry Thomason, and the participants of the Industrial Relations in Canadian Industry conference held at Queen's University in 1991. The author thanks the firm officers who participated in the survey, and also acknowledges the research assistance of Michael Shannon, Josée Voizard, Rahul Kumar, and Margaret Murphy. The author also thanks Labour Canada for generously supplying data needed to facilitate this analysis.

2. The notion of a strategic response to such pressures is discussed in Kochan (1990), but also in Kochan, Katz, and McKersie (1986).

3. In particular, long time horizons of operation exist at the Cape Breton Development Corporation coal operations and the Inco Limited nickel operations in Manitoba and Ontario, whereas a very short time horizon often exists at many of the precious-metals (e.g., gold) mines operating in remote areas of western or northern Canada.

4. The establishment and production level data discussed in this section were obtained from the following Statistics Canada publications: *Coal Mines*, Catalogue 26-206, Annual: 1978–88. *Non-metal Mines*, Catalogue 26-224, Annual: 1978–88; and *Metal Mines*, Catalogue 26-223, Annual: 1978–88.

5. Here GDP = Gross Domestic Product at factor cost in 1981 dollars. At $2.3 billion, these industries account for approximately 2.7 percent of total economic GDP. Note that this figure does not include "crude petroleum and natural gas" or "services related to mineral extraction," but does include the quarry and sand-pit industries: see Statistics Canada (1990a).

6. Tilton (1989) discusses the effects of these important changes in world patterns of demand, and the potential for growth in Eastern Europe, China, and the USSR for patterns of mineral trade.

7. The product classifications vary depending on the source of the data. For example, Statistics Canada distinguishes coal, nonmetal, and metal mines, but the *Canadian Mineral Yearbook* reports the total number of corporations involved with metal mining, mineral fuels, and other mining. The approach taken here is to discuss both types of data in order to convey a sense of the total mining activity.

8. Coal production increased from 30 477 kilotonnes in 1978 to 61 211 kilotonnes in 1987.

9. The number of metal mine establishments peaked in 1981 and 1982, at 128, but subsequently declined.

10. Nonmetal production levels were 67 087 kilotonnes in 1978 and 64 931 kilotonnes in 1987, while metal production levels were 248 056 kilotonnes in 1978 and 266 172 kilotonnes in 1987.

11. Data are from Energy, Mines, and Resources Canada, *Canadian Minerals Yearbook: Review and Outlook*, 1986 and 1988 reports. (Ottawa: Minister of Supply and Services.

Tables: Canada, Person-Hours Paid for Production and Related Workers, and Tonnes of Ore Mined in Rock Quarried in Metal Mines and Other Mineral Operations).

12. Data are from Energy, Mines, and Resources Canada, *Canadian Minerals Yearbook: Review and Outlook* 1972–89 reports (Ottawa: Minister of Supply and Services) (Table: Canada, Financial Statistics of Corporations in the Mining Industry, By Degree of Non-Resident Ownership.) Note that these data include corporations as considered under the Corporations and Labour Unions Returns Act. Specifically, "corporations" include all firms that conduct business in Canada and whose gross revenue or assets exceed the minimum levels specified in the Corporation and Labour Unions Returns Act. Thus, a "corporation" is to be distinguished from a mine establishment.

13. The total number of "mineral fuel" corporations was 2559 (2343 Canadian and 216 foreign), and the total number of "other mining" corporations was 5376 (5124 Canadian and 152 foreign). It is not known how many corporations classified under "other mining" are, in fact, related to the mineral fuel industry.

14. In addition, Noranda Minerals Inc., a unit of Noranda, is a major producer of zinc and copper.

15. See Energy, Mines, and Resources Canada, *Canadian Minerals Yearbook: Review and Outlook,* 1972–89 reports (Ottawa: Minister of Supply and Services), Table: Canada, Financial Statistics of Corporations in the Mining Industry, By Degree of Non-resident Ownership.

16. Refer to the *Canadian Mines Handbook 1990–91* (Toronto: Northern Miner Press Inc., 1990) for examples of major corporations having a significant shareholder interest in other mining sector firms.

17. See Nappi (1989, 19). Importantly, Nappi's (1989) analysis also examines other factors, which have been particularly important determinants of metals demand in the 1980s.

18. On the "supply" side, mining operations are also dependent on the extent, quality, and availability of the resources/deposits.

19. MacMillan and colleagues (1977, 91) describe the union–management relationship as fundamentally adversarial: "History illustrates that past union–management relations in mining have been characterized by economic and physical strife." Also, refer to Clement (1981).

20. Palmer (1983, 157) notes that the 1906 miners' strike also had a particularly significant impact on industrial relations public policy: "Indeed, the 1906 confrontation laid the foundations for the Industrial Disputes Investigation Act."

21. Changes in total mining international union membership levels were dominated by underlying changes in international membership levels in the metals.

22. International unions slightly increased their membership levels in the "mineral fuels" and "other mines" groups in the 1970s.

23. National membership levels also trended upward in the "mineral fuels" and "other mining" areas in the 1970s.

24. Note that Table 4.6 data include the fuel sector.

25. Note that aggregate figures covering, as examples, strikes, wages, or contract outcomes, includes the mineral fuels sector. However, as the data in Tables 4.5 and 4.6 indicate, union membership in the mineral fuels sector comprises a minority (approximately 22 percent in 1988) of total membership, so that aggregate trends for the industry are likely representative of the predominant nonfuels portion of the industry.

26. This depends, as noted above, on whether or not a significant expansion of trade with Eastern Europe or the Soviet Union takes place, and whether the economies of the newly industrializing countries demonstrate strong growth.

27. In the case of metals producers, such strategies as focussing on creating closer links between producers and consumers (Nappi 1989) would complement any labour-cost reduction strategies.

28. Capital expenditures on machinery is of particular interest in considering the potential employment effects associated with capital expenditures, because of the direct implications for capital-for-labour substitution.

29. Consider the relative employment of production (blue-collar) versus administrative and office (white-collar) workers in metal mining (Table 4.3). The ratio of white-collar to blue-collar employees increased from approximately 0.30 in 1970 to a steady ratio of around 0.39 in the early 1980s, and then declined in the late 1980s to roughly 0.33. However, the longer-run shift toward a higher relative proportion of white-collar workers that was established in the industry through the 1948–73 period appears to be continuing.

30. Green and Green (1991, 27) also note the key role of technology in firms' competitive strategy, specifically in the Ontario metal mining industry: "Apparently, the basic strategy of the metal mining industry was to meet rising costs and Third World competition by widespread adoption of best-practice technology; to meet the competition's subsidized production with sophisticated capital-intensive techniques."

31. While the use of new computer-based technologies appears to be broad (see Statistics Canada 1990b), it is important to note that the introduction of new technologies may be limited in situations where the economic viability of the operation is insufficient to warrant the investment—for example, because of the limited grade and size of an ore body. Consequently, there may be variance in the use of technologies, depending on the particular circumstances of a given firm.

32. It is also important to note that a broad range of unions whose primary membership base is not in mining are also active in some aspect of mining (e.g., the Canadian Brotherhood of Railway, Transport and General Workers, and the International Brotherhood of Boilermakers, Iron Ship Builders, Blacksmiths, Forgers and Helpers).

33. The trend in mining membership losses is even more significant when one considers that, in 1974, as reported by MacMillan, Gislason, and Lyon (1977, 94, Table 17), the United Steelworkers had a "mineral" industry membership of 60 898 and the United Mine Workers had a membership of 5800. (Note that no information is available regarding the size of the bargaining units included in these estimates.)

34. A major settlement was achieved at Inco, followed by a one-week stoppage and settlement at Falconbridge; the Cape Breton Development Corporation settled at its Atlantic Canada coal operations; new settlements were reached at Denison Mines

Limited and Rio Algom Limited in Elliot Lake in the face of layoffs in uranium mining; the Hudson Bay Mining and Smelting Co. Ltd. settled in Manitoba; and agreement was reached at Noranda Mines Limited in Quebec. In contrast, work stoppages occurred at Fording Coal Ltd. and Quintette Coal Limited in British Columbia: See Bureau of Labour Information, Labour Canada, *Collective Bargaining Review* (various issues), and Ontario Ministry of Labour, *Collective Bargaining Settlements in Ontario* (various issues).

35. The average annual wage increase was typically in the range of 3 to 4 percent during the 1983–87 period, with the 1986 increase being unusually low. During the 1980–90 period, from 7 to 19 contracts were negotiated in a given year, and most contracts included a COLA clause. These data were provided by the Bureau of Labour Information, Labour Canada.

36. An important exception to a reliance on guaranteed fixed wages would involve underground "bonus" systems for miners.

37. The "nickel bonus" is linked to the amount by which the "average realized price per pound of nickel" exceeds an agreed-upon base nickel price level, times employee hours worked: see Ontario Ministry of Labour (1988).

38. This is a strong result given that none of the unionized firms ranked increased employee involvement in the workplace as an unimportant bargaining goal.

39. As recently as 1990, as expressed at the "Human Resource Planning for the Mining Industry" Conference, these issues remain at the fore for many firms. Jackson (1990, 12) states: "It is becoming increasingly difficult for a mining organization to attract and retain an adequate number of properly trained people at all levels of its operations." The conference focussed on issues relating to concerns regarding recruitment, skill mix, training, and education.

40. Historically, the potential for fatalities in mining has presented a significant risk to miners. While all aspects of the industry are considered particularly dangerous, coal mining stands out with its legacy of loss of life: "Between 1871 and 1939, more than 1600 men were killed in Nova Scotia mines, while in Alberta, over 1000 died in the years 1905–45" (Palmer 1983, 198). Further, Palmer (1983, 296) notes the terrible coal mine tragedies at Springhill, Nova Scotia, where 125 died in 1891 and 114 died in 1956–57. Fatalities are also a feature of metal mining operations.

41. See Energy, Mines, and Resources Canada, *Canadian Minerals Yearbook: Review and Outlook*, 1979, 1981, 1987, and 1989 reports (Ottawa: Minister of Supply and Services).

42. Refer to Gibbs and Pintus (1978) for a thorough discussion of all aspects of mining health and safety issues.

43. See Barnacle (1989, 229–33, Table 63) for a complete summary of the legislation.

44. General examples of this technology includes automated equipment to handle ores or slurries, automatic material conveyor systems, and vehicles that are computer controlled (see Statistics Canada 1990b).

45. The survey covered all 324 known mines in Canada. Inactive mines or exploration mines were then excluded from the analysis, leaving 235 mines. The survey response rate was 97 percent.

46. In a feature article focussing on Inco Limited, Till (1988, 52) describes the extent of the introduction of new technologies: "And it's not just underground work that's being automated. From telephone switch-board functions through to accounting, inventory control and warehousing, seismic plotting, shaft design, and blasting to the end processes, milling and smelting—everything is being computerized."

47. Gretton's (1988) discussion of the USWA–Inco Limited industrial relations climate reveals the generally militant stance of the USWA during the pre-1980 period, as demonstrated by the 128-day strike in Sudbury in 1969, and the 1978 strike, which lasted over 8 months. In contrast, Till (1988) notes the current union attitude of acceptance of the necessity of the technological changes, despite the significant employment implications.

Chapter

5

INDUSTRIAL RELATIONS IN THE CONSTRUCTION INDUSTRY IN THE 1980s

Joseph B. Rose[1]

*T*his essay examines the effect of structural change on industrial relations in the construction industry in the 1980s. Specifically, it considers the impact of environmental changes (e.g., economic, political, and legal) on unions, employers (and their associations), and government during a decade in which collective bargaining has been under tremendous stress.

After providing an overview of the industry and its industrial relations system, we review union–management relations in the 1960s and 1970s. This period, which was characterized by fundamental changes in labour law and collective bargaining, provides a historical backdrop to the 1980s. Our chronicle of the 1980s covers such developments as: (1) the turbulent economic and political environments; (2) the organizational and structural changes in the unionized sector of the industry; (3) the rise of nonunion competition; (4) trends in construction wages and other bargaining outcomes; and (5) strike activity and the development of alternative dispute-settlement procedures.

The primary focus of this study is industrial relations in major building construction, i.e., the industrial, commercial, and institutional sector.[2] The findings are based on a broad range of published economic and collective-bargaining data as well as unpublished reports and documents provided to the author by employers, unions, and government agencies. These materials were supplemented by interviews with 34 persons familiar with construction developments in seven provinces (British Columbia, Alberta, Saskatchewan, Ontario, Quebec, Nova Scotia, and Newfoundland). Although the interviewees may not constitute a representative sample in a strict sense, they represent a cross-section of opinion within the industry.

Industry Overview

The construction industry contributes significantly to the overall performance of the Canadian economy. In 1989, total construction activity amounted to $100.1 billion, or 15.4 percent of Gross Domestic Expenditures (Statistics Canada 1990). In December 1989, the construction labour force stood at 876 000 workers, or 6.5 percent of the civilian labour force (Statistics Canada 1989b).

The construction industry features local product markets and a substantial degree of specialization. In contrast to that of many other industrial sectors, the construction product is immobile and dispersed geographically, and varies in size and composition. Product diversity is revealed in the number of sectors that make up the industry, e.g., residential, industrial, commercial, road building, and sewers and water mains. Government is a large consumer of construction services, accounting for upwards of one-third of construction expenditures (Statistics Canada 1978–90). The industry structure is characterized by ease of entry, a large number of small undercapitalized firms, competitive bidding, and a high rate of business failures. Construction instability reflects the industry's sensitivity to fluctuations in the business cycle and seasonality.

The construction labour market is casual, skilled, and seasonal, and experiences unemployment rates substantially above the national average. The labour force is predominantly male and organized into twenty or so trades and subtrades. Because of variations in product demand, the labour force is mobile across job sites within local markets, among geographic areas, and to other industries and occupations. The primary sources of skilled tradespeople include apprenticeship and other training, immigration, and institutional arrangements, e.g., the closed shop and the hiring hall.

Market and technological factors have significantly influenced the characteristics of employer and union organizations and the structure and substance of collective bargaining. Historically, contractors established local employers' associations to conduct their labour relations with craft-union locals. Construction has been one of the most heavily unionized sectors of the economy; union density was estimated at 70 percent in 1975 (Bain 1978). The construction unions are organized along craft lines, with each union carving out a work jurisdiction that defines its claim to act as the exclusive source of workers employed by contractors. Separate locals were chartered to represent members in each local market. Accordingly, multi-employer bargaining by craft, sector, and local area was the predominant structural arrangement. Employment insecurity and industry requirements for a highly skilled pool of labour underscored the importance of wages, the closed shop, the hiring hall, work jurisdiction, subcontracting, and selected work rules (e.g., staffing requirements and travel provisions) as bargaining issues.

*H*istorical Perspective

*D*uring the 1960s, labour relations in construction were characterized as unstable, even chaotic. It was a period in which economic expansion and decentralized bargaining structures produced a sharp increase in strike activity and wage settlements. For example, person-days lost due to strikes increased by almost 200 percent between the periods 1960–64 and 1965–69, and the construction–manufacturing wage differential widened from 19 percent in 1965 to 42 percent in 1970 (Rose 1980).

Most observers were persuaded there was an imbalance of bargaining power in favour of the building trades. As a result of the highly fragmented bargaining structures (by trade, sector, and geographic area) and the absence of employer solidarity (i.e., the lack of cohesion within and co-ordination among employer associations), unions were able to whipsaw weak employer associations and leapfrog wage settlements within and among labour markets. Bargaining outcomes were routinely passed on to the purchasers of construction in the form of higher costs, and, ultimately to consumers in terms of higher prices.

There were several reasons why employers lacked effective countervailing power. First, and foremost, there was no legal equivalent to trade-union certification that enabled associations to exercise effective direction and control over members. The building-trades unions were adept at exploiting such weaknesses, often by reaching interim settlements with individual contractors and applying pressure tactics on others (e.g., selective strikes). With some association members operating and others struck, the association's bargaining position was undermined. Second, association membership was voluntary, and business survival did not depend on membership in an association. Accordingly, associations did not represent all of the unionized contractors in a locality, and separate bargaining arrangements often existed for independent firms and for large industrial and megaprojects (with project wages pegged to local wage rates). When coupled with the narrow geographic scope of bargaining and the casual nature of the construction labour market, workers had little difficulty finding alternative employment during strikes. Organizational instability and the proliferation of contractor associations contributed to a third problem: the inability to establish interassociation alliances to co-ordinate bargaining (Rose 1986).

The rise in strike activity and wage inflation in the 1960s focussed public attention on the industry. In response to intense lobbying led by the Canadian Construction Association, the 1970s became a decade of legislative change. There was a broad recognition that many of the general principles embodied in collective-bargaining legislation were ill suited to the unique features of the construction industry. Accordingly, most provincial labour codes were amended to promote stronger employer associations, broader-based bargaining, and, ultimately, stable labour–management relations.

One fundamental change was the introduction of employer accreditation, i.e., a system of multi-employer certification. Although various systems of employer accreditation were adopted, they all conferred exclusive bargaining rights on the association (Rose 1986). By prohibiting individual bargaining, accreditation provided legal cohesion for multi-employer bargaining. Supplemental legal reforms often were required to facilitate broader-based bargaining. These included the creation of a province-wide bargaining council of building-trades unions in British Columbia and mandating province-wide bargaining on either a single-trade basis (Ontario) or a multitrade basis (Quebec).

Legislative interdiction resulted in profound changes in employer and union organizations and a rationalization of fragmented bargaining structures. By the end of the decade, local bargaining ceased to be the dominant bargaining structure. It was replaced by province-wide negotiations co-ordinated by province-wide employer and union bargaining agents. This shift significantly improved the collective-bargaining process.

> By providing legal underpinnings for multi-employer bargaining, accreditation has enabled employers to establish more effective associations and reduce their vulnerability to union divide-and-conquer tactics. The consolidation of bargaining structures also reduced the frequency of strikes and an important source of wage inflation, namely the ability of construction unions to leapfrog wages within and among labor markets. (Rose 1986, 17)

Despite these improvements, broader-base bargaining did not produce stable bargaining outcomes. As a result of strong demand and inflationary pressures, wages rose faster in the 1970s than in the 1960s, and the industry experienced larger and more protracted work stoppages than in the previous decade (Rose 1986). Consequently, the perception remained that wage settlements and strike activity were unacceptably high. Concerns about bargaining outcomes and the competitive position of unionized construction intensified in the early 1980s.

The 1980s: Economic, Political, and Legislative Developments

ECONOMIC UPHEAVAL

The 1980s are best characterized as a decade of economic upheaval and uncertainty. It began with a surge in demand, rising interest rates, and inflationary pressures, and then the economy plunged into the worst recession since the 1930s. Indeed, the economy experienced extremely high rates of both inflation and unemployment.

In October 1981, the Consumer Price Index recorded the largest one-year increase (12.9 percent) in more than 30 years. The recession lasted eighteen months (from June 1981 to December 1982), and the peak-to-trough decline in Gross Domestic Product (GDP) was 8 percent (Milner 1990). Employment fell by 5 percent in the same period, and unemployment climbed to 12.8 percent, the highest level since the Great Depression (Bank of Canada 1983–84). Economic recovery was accompanied by a sharp deceleration in inflation. The Consumer Price Index fell from 9.3 percent in 1982 to 4.5 percent in 1983, and annual inflation rates averaged between 4 and 5 percent thereafter (Statistics Canada 1982–90).

The depth of the recession and the pace and magnitude of economic recovery varied across Canada. As reported by the Bank of Canada (1983–84, 15):

> Goods-producing industries in central Canada have benefited particularly from expanding demand, after an especially pronounced contraction during the recession. . . .Provinces other than Ontario and Quebec have thus far been relatively less affected. The particularly weak performance of Alberta and British Columbia reflects continuing low prices for resource-based products following after a long period of high prices and very strong economic expansion.

Differences in regional economic recovery are reflected in provincial shares of national GDP. Ontario's share of national GDP rose from 37.1 to 41.9 percent, whereas Alberta's and Saskatchewan's shares fell from 13.9 to 10.2 percent and from 4 to 3 percent, respectively. The introduction of the National Energy Program, low oil prices, and high interest rates had a devastating impact on provincial economies dependent on energy production (Alberta) and agriculture (Saskatchewan) (Fagan 1991).

The 1981–82 recession had a significant adverse impact on construction activity, as the total value of construction work purchased (in constant 1981 dollars) declined for three consecutive years (1982–84) (Statistics Canada 1980–90a). This led to a dramatic rise in joblessness as the seasonally adjusted unemployment rate climbed from 11.9 percent in January 1981 to 23.8 percent in December 1982. Unemployment rates remained above 20 percent until mid-1985 (Statistics Canada 1989a). There was a strong recovery in 1985 (a 17.2 percent increase in the dollar value of construction purchased), followed by more modest growth rates the remainder of the decade (Statistics Canada 1980–90a).

These aggregate figures obscure interregional differences in demand for construction. For Canada, the value of new construction (in current dollars) rose by $41.7 billion, or 104 percent, between 1980 and 1989. In Ontario, new construction increased from $9.9 billion in 1980 to $32.5 billion in 1989, or by 230 percent. In contrast, the value of new construction in Alberta (in current dollars) went from $13 billion in 1981 to $8.2 billion in 1984, before recovering to $10.3 billion in 1989 (Statistics Canada 1980–90a). As a result of variations in the demand for new construction, there was substantially higher joblessness in western Canada than in Ontario and Quebec.

THE RISE OF NONUNION COMPETITION

The 1981–82 recession also altered the competitive structure of major building construction. Although the rise of nonunion construction is evident in all regions of Canada, western Canada experienced the strongest competitive shocks. In Newfoundland, which is a relatively small market, nonunion construction nearly doubled in the 1980s, and its share of commercial work reached an estimated 75 percent (industrial work remains predominantly union). With work commencing on the Hibernia project, union construction can be expected to capture a significantly larger share of total construction volume.

As discussed below, the pervasiveness of nonunion competition was influenced by political and legal factors, as well as the severity of the economic downturn. Thus, where provincial governments embraced free-market economic policies, one often found a shrinking and more competitive construction product market and the decline of the institution of collective bargaining. The emergence of nonunion competition can also be linked to employer dissatisfaction with collective-bargaining outcomes. Specifically, employers and construction clients were dismayed by the magnitude of wage settlements in the 1982 bargaining round, and the long-run compression of intertrade wage differentials. For example, Strand (1986) reports the labourers–plumbers wage differential narrowed from 31 to 11 percent between 1970 and 1983.

Unfortunately, there are no authoritative and impartial surveys of the rise of nonunion construction in the marketplace. There are, nevertheless, what appear to be reasonable estimates of market penetration. The swing away from unionized construction occurred rapidly (over two years) in Saskatchewan and Alberta as union employers found legal ways to operate on a nonunion basis. In Saskatchewan, the nonunion market share climbed to between 70 and 90 percent of total construction volume following the economic downturn and the repeal of the Construction Industry Labour Relations Act in 1983.[3] In Alberta, the union share was approximately 80 percent of the industrial and commercial construction in 1980. Today, 70 to 80 percent of commercial work and 40 to 60 percent of industrial work is nonunion. In both provinces, virtually all of the general contractors operate nonunion, and the only remaining union stronghold at the close of the decade appeared to be large industrial projects.

In British Columbia, the transition has been more gradual and, although nonunion penetration is significant, it is lower than in Alberta and Saskatchewan. In commercial and institutional construction, nonunion work increased its market share from about 20 percent in 1980 to between 40 and 60 percent at the end of the decade. Nonunion penetration of industrial construction is considerably lower. One estimate suggests it has remained at 5 percent throughout the 1980s, whereas another estimate places it at between 20 and 25 percent.

POLITICAL–LEGAL DEVELOPMENTS

The economic crisis of the early 1980s posed a challenge to governments of all political stripes. It was a decade in which governments espoused fiscal restraint. One of the earliest manifestations of the new fiscal conservatism was the adoption of public-sector wage-restraint programs in the early 1980s. As well, economic uncertainty, a sharp drop in oil prices, and high interest rates combined to reduce the political will to undertake many energy-related megaprojects. This trend is noteworthy because a number of megaprojects were under construction, e.g., James Bay, Syncrude, and Ontario's nuclear construction program, and projects estimated to cost in the tens of billions of dollars were being planned to deal with the energy crisis (Weiler et al. 1981). The expectation that construction megaprojects would assume a larger share of construction spending diminished as many proposed megaprojects were cancelled. The significance of this development is that such projects are normally undertaken by the unionized sector.

A review of construction spending in the 1980s reveals there was a steady decline in public investment in new construction. Prior to the 1980s, public investment in construction was relatively stable and constituted approximately one-third of the dollar value of construction activity. In 1980, public investment stood at 30.6 percent. It climbed to 35.3 percent in 1982, and then decreased annually, reaching 24.4 percent in 1989 (Statistics Canada 1978–90). Disaggregated figures also reveal that expenditures on engineering construction, including such government-sponsored projects as roads, dams, and electric-power construction, declined as a percentage of total construction expenditures (from 45.1 percent in 1980 to 28.8 percent in 1989). Once again, declining government support in these heavily unionized sectors contributed to the contraction of unionized construction.

The dawn of the new economic reality of the 1980s also signalled the emergence of greater government support for deregulating markets. Although all political parties have supported intervention in markets and the establishment of public or Crown corporations in the past, the 1980s witnessed the adoption of a broad array of policies aimed at promoting free enterprise (Tupper and Doern 1981, 1988). This situation was most prevalent in western Canada, where privatization ranked high on political agendas and the virtues of free enterprise were extolled. The ideological commitment to such policies was not unbridled. Indeed, it was occasionally tempered by the pragmatism associated with a resource-dependent regional economy. Nevertheless, it is difficult to dismiss the embrace of market deregulation as one factor that contributed to or sustained the rise of nonunion competition and the decline of unionism in the construction industry.

Other political decisions adversely affected the position of unionized construction. For one thing, there was a retreat from fair-wage policies. Fair-wage laws, such as the federal Fair Wages and Hours of Labour Act, establish fair wage and hour schedules for construction projects financed or subsidized by government. Given the considerable volume of publicly financed construction, such laws have been justified as ensuring "government contracts do not undermine the wage rates paid in the locality where work is done" (Foster and Strauss 1972, 304). These schedules were based on prevailing wages, and normally reflected union wage rates in major building construction and in urban labour markets. As such, fair-wage schedules insulated the unionized sector from nonunion wage competition.

The retreat from fair wages was signalled by the federal government's decision to cease producing wage schedules in the wake of its "Six and Five" wage-restraint program, introduced in 1982. Dismayed by large construction wage settlements in Nova Scotia and the belief that a fair-wage policy was inflationary, the federal government ceased publishing schedules and undertook a policy review. In 1987, it formally announced it would not produce wage schedules for three years, and that it would monitor the effects of this change. Although the federal government maintained that it was not abandoning the concept of fair wages and that it would retain existing enforcement mechanisms to deal with workers' complaints, the fact remains that fair-wage schedules would no longer form part of government contracts. Thus, with the exception of the decree system in Quebec and Manitoba's Construction Industry Wages Act, there was the prospect that collectively bargained rates might no longer serve as the fair-wage standard on federally supported projects.

Whereas the federal government abandoned fair-wage schedules, the practice at the provincial level varied. Historically, most provinces had enacted laws or orders-in-council regulating construction wages on government contracts (Hébert 1968; Strand 1986). However, there are indications that adoption of fair-wage schedules was spotty at best. In some jurisdictions (e.g., Nova Scotia and Newfoundland), fair-wage schedules were not revised and remained out of date. British Columbia, Alberta, and Saskatchewan are noteworthy because they do not produce fair-wage schedules. With the collapse of collective bargaining in the latter two provinces and the rapid ascent of the nonunion sector, there were no institutional mechanisms for determining a fair-wage standard. In the mid-1980s, construction wage rates plummeted in response to market forces and, in the resulting chaos, various Statistics Canada surveys were unable to report wage rates in these provinces. In Ontario, there was no change in policy, and fair-wage schedules were revised regularly to reflect prevailing wages.

Even more dramatic have been developments on the legislative front, particularly in western Canada. In December 1983, the newly elected Progressive Conservative government in Saskatchewan repealed the Construction Industry Labour Relations Act (CILRA). This law, which was passed by the NDP government in 1979, followed the lead of other Canadian provinces by introducing a system of province-wide bargaining (by trade) through designated employer and union organizations. It also outlawed the doublebreasted or dual-shop form of employer organization. This practice allows firms not only to simultaneously operate union and open-shop subsidiaries, but "to straddle subsectors of construction market" and to transfer "potential volume to its open-shop subsidiary" in order to remain competitive (Bourdon and Levitt 1980, 112). Although the aim of the CILRA was to promote labour relations stability, stiff union resistance to employer efforts to standardize employment conditions across trades led to a sharp upturn in the severity of conflict in the 1982 bargaining round. Following the steep downturn in construction activity brought on by the recession, the building-trades unions steadfastly opposed employer attempts to gain major wage rollbacks in response to the expanding open-shop sector.

The repeal of the CILRA, brought the construction industry under the general provisions of the Trade Union Act. Although this change appeared to have the support of the unions and employers (for different reasons), its ramifications may not have been fully understood.

> Repeal of Saskatchewan's accreditation legislation coincided with a sharp and sustained decline in the demand for construction. The effect of shattering the statutorily-imposed multi-employer units has been further amplified by the profuse growth of unionized companies operating double-breasted, and of nonunion companies. The demand for union labour and the power of unions has declined in tandem. With 70 to 80 percent of union members being unable to find union jobs, the unions' capacity to engage in effective job action is very limited. The nonunion employers have been reluctant to hire union members for fear of becoming unionized. (Rose and Wetzel 1986, 270)

In retrospect, the repeal of the CILRA was the most significant legislative development affecting collective bargaining in construction in the 1980s. Indeed, over the course of the remainder of the decade, collective bargaining became comatose. The thrust of union activity shifted to pitched legal challenges of doublebreasting under the successor-rights provisions of the Trade Union Act. Certification and the negotiation of renewal collective agreements became extremely difficult following the removal of legal restrictions on doublebreasting. As a result, bargaining was sporadic, except for the occasional industrial project agreement, as the decade drew to a close.

In Alberta, the economic downturn and increased nonunion competition stimulated a two-pronged strategy by unionized contractors to fight legal restrictions on doublebreasting. The first initiative was an intense lobbying campaign to repeal Section 133 of the Alberta Labour Relations Act, which prohibited the creation of "spin-off" firms. This effort resulted in the passage of Bill 110. Although Bill 110 was never proclaimed (it was rescinded in 1984, as a result of union lobbying), it nevertheless sent a signal to the industry, namely, that the government was sympathetic to the employers' plight. Another facet of the employers' strategy was to test the limits of Section 133 through the restructuring of construction firms. For example, the conversion of union firms to project-management operations (ostensibly to subcontract all work on an open-shop basis) was held not to violate Section 133 by the labour board. Since a project-management operation was not an "employer of employees," it could not be subject to a collective agreement. As well, a labour board ruling minimized the risk associated with establishing a "spin-off" firm by virtually eliminating an employer's liability for retroactive damages. It is, therefore, hardly surprising that 1983 was characterized as "the year of the nonunion contractor" (Fisher and Kushner 1986, 789).

By the early 1980s, there was increased evidence of nonunion penetration in British Columbia's construction industry. In 1984, a number of amendments were made to the Labour Code. For the construction industry, they included mandatory certification votes and project-specific certification (i.e., contractors would be certified only for the duration of the project), protection of nonaffiliation clauses (i.e., the right of building-trades members to refuse to work on projects with workers who are not members of an affiliated building-trades union), and the recognition of "economic development zones." As described by Strand (1986, 203), the latter change provided that

> the Lieutenant Governor in Council can declare specific projects, or parts of these projects he considers to be of special economic importance, to constitute an "economic development project" for a specified period. Once . . . so designated, then the exercise of a non-affiliation clause is limited to the site of the designated economic development project.

A major concern of the building-trades unions was Premier Bennett's declaration that Expo 86—the first major project to come on stream following the recession—would be an open site. These concerns erupted into a major confrontation when J.C. Kerkhoff and Sons became the first nonunion firm to be awarded an Expo 86 contract. Eventually, Cabinet carved the Expo site into a number of separate union and nonunion economic-development sites and thereby nullified the application of nonaffiliation clauses. Although an estimated 90 percent of the work at the Expo 86 site eventually was performed by union contractors (Strand 1986) and economic-development zones were not created elsewhere, there is no question the unionized sector was legitimately concerned about its possible application to Expo 86, and construction sites generally.

Shrinking markets and intensified nonunion competition prompted contractors to lobby for changes to the doublebreasting provisions in British Columbia (successfully) and Ontario (unsuccessfully). Conversely, in Newfoundland, where no common employer provisions were in place, union contractors and the building-trades unions proposed introducing legal restrictions on doublebreasting. This lobbying effort was unsuccessful. In general, legal developments outside of the three western provinces were relatively modest and, for the most part, involved fine-tuning of the centralized bargaining systems introduced in the preceding decade.

*C*hanges in Structure and Organizational Characteristics

*A*s noted above, the 1970s produced the consolidation of fragmented bargaining structures and the accreditation of employers' associations. The emergence of construction employer organizations devoted exclusively to labour relations (known as Construction Labour Relations Associations or CLRAs) was the dominant organizational change of the decade. The turbulent 1980s have led to additional organizational changes for CLRAs as well as a decline in the numerical strength of the building-trades unions and the ascendancy of merit shop organizations to serve the interests of both nonunion and doublebreasted construction firms.

UNIONIZED EMPLOYERS

Organizational stability and maturity appear to characterize CLRAs in central and eastern Canada. In these provinces, union acceptance and accommodation has been the norm, and systems of province-wide bargaining and broad regional bargaining (e.g., Nova Scotia) remained intact or were improved. For example, whereas efforts to formalize multitrade bargaining have not produced lasting structural realignments in Ontario, single-trade, province-wide bargaining has not been unwieldy. Indeed, there appears to be increasing evidence that the Construction Employers Coordinating Council of Ontario (CECCO) has successfully facilitated the co-ordination of negotiations across trades during the 1980s. In Nova Scotia, the Construction Management Bureau Limited successfully moved to stem intraorganizational conflict by transferring control over bargaining from its trade divisions to its board of directors.

A very different pattern emerges in western Canada. In Saskatchewan, membership in the Saskatchewan Construction Labour Relations Council (SCLRC) fell to 70 members, or about one-third of its strength, in 1984. For all intents and purposes, the SCLRC exists in name only, in that it laid off its staff and has not been engaged in collective bargaining since 1984. As well, the Alberta Construction Labour Relations Association (ACLRA) saw its membership decline by nearly 50 percent, from approximately 300 to 160 members, after bargaining collapsed. Even though the CLRA of British Columbia remained actively engaged in and committed to collective bargaining throughout the 1980s, it too underwent important changes. Under British Columbia's accreditation system (which permits opting-out by individual contractors), the CLRA was particularly vulnerable to increased nonunion competition. Facing strong internal pressures, the CLRA applied to de-accredit itself in 1988 in order to pursue bargaining on a purely voluntary basis. Although membership fell sharply (from 815 to 450 members), there seems to be general agreement within the industry that the CLRA is a smaller but stronger employer bargaining agent (described below).

UNION MEMBERSHIP

There is evidence that the economic downturn and intensified nonunion competition profoundly influenced construction union membership. Table 5.1 summarizes the trend in union membership for Canada and the provinces between 1980 and 1988. Overall, there was an increase in union membership of about 34 000 members (or 12 percent). At the same time, union density fell from 57.7 to 52.8 percent. The overall decline in union penetration is noteworthy because density levels in the construction industry ranged from 60 to 70 percent in the 1970s. Although Statistics Canada density figures show tremendous year-to-year volatility, and therefore should be interpreted cautiously, these figures appear to be broadly consistent with the trends reported in interviews with industry representatives.[4]

From 1980 to 1988, union losses were greatest in Alberta (44 percent), followed by Newfoundland (28 percent), Saskatchewan (23 percent), and British Columbia (15 percent). Indeed, the peak-to-trough erosion of union membership exceeded 50 percent in Alberta (1981 to 1987), Saskatchewan (1981 to 1987), and Newfoundland (1980 to 1984). In contrast to the Atlantic provinces, the three western provinces have not experienced as great a rebound in union membership since 1984. Elsewhere, union membership either has returned to a level roughly comparable to 1980 (e.g., Manitoba) or is significantly higher (e.g., Ontario and Quebec).

Some indication of the extent of membership decline for individual building-trades unions was revealed by Saskatchewan government statistics covering the period from 1980 to 1989.[5] The steepest membership losses were among the civil trades, e.g., bricklayers (80 percent), carpenters (62 percent), and labourers (46 percent). These figures are broadly consistent with our interview results, which indicate nonunion penetration has been greatest in the civil trades and less pronounced among mechanical trades (e.g., pipefitters).

The decline in unionism in western Canada has not led to concerted organizing campaigns by the building-trades unions to recoup members. There appear to be several explanations for the absence of an effective organizing strategy. First, the prolonged economic slump meant there were diminished opportunities to organize. The nonunion work force (including unemployed union members or former union tradespeople) appeared to place a higher value on maintaining gainful employment than on union representation. There also may have been a reduced demand for union services, reflecting identification with open-shop employers or disenchantment with unionism. Second, union financial resources were strained by the drop in dues revenue and protracted legal skirmishes before labour boards and the courts. Third, the ability of many firms to operate doublebreasted made it increasingly difficult to get certified and negotiate a collective agreement. Fourth, changes in certification procedures may have curtailed organizing activity. In

Table 5.1
Union Membership in Construction Industry, by Province, 1980–1988

	1980	1981	1982	1983	1984	1985	1986	1987	1988
Canada	274 731	278 003	271 243	272 965	211 377	228 643	271 754	284 376	308 106
Newfoundland	5 839	5 262	5 121	5 064	2 156	3 734	4 408	4 357	4 220
Prince Edward Island	454	918	469	590	194	201	264	281	273
Nova Scotia	9 074	9 371	12 223	4 795	3 600	6 545	7 429	7 158	8 385
New Brunswick	6 260	6 705	6 565	8 686	3 792	4 915	5 655	6 917	6 425
Quebec	50 868	45 160	42 109	56 036	57 353	69 185	77 294	77 588	92 011
Ontario	95 277	94 508	96 813	87 510	71 255	75 946	100 247	111 665	119 086
Manitoba	4 809	4 236	3 627	3 182	3 074	3 119	4 163	4 779	4 346
Saskatchewan	5 613	5 581	5 367	4 330	3 040	2 348	2 687	3 691	4 286
Alberta	43 236	47 996	45 845	44 315	24 344	18 843	22 743	23 314	24 142
British Columbia	53 002	57 972	52 832	57 847	42 227	43 745	46 817	44 579	44 858

Source: Unpublished data provided by Statistics Canada (CALURA).

British Columbia, there were 1102 construction certifications, accounting for 46.2 percent of total certifications between 1980 and 1983. In the period following changes to the Labour Code (1984 to 1989), there were 331 construction certifi-cations, which accounted for 23.2 percent of total certifications.[6]

Several of the employer representatives that were interviewed in western Canada criticized the building trades for failing to recruit new members aggres-sively. Even union representatives conceded that their reliance on traditional organizing methods (i.e., top-down organizing) were ineffective, and that they failed to respond to the problem by developing alternative organizing strategies. Whatever the shortcomings in union recruiting practices, it appears the opportu-nity to organize was hampered by market conditions and the legal environment. Because construction certification data are sparse, it is not possible to compare organizing activity in different regions of Canada systematically. Nevertheless, data exist that reveal that the building-trades unions actively recruited new members outside of western Canada. For example, construction certification activity increased following the economic recession in both Ontario and Nova Scotia (Ontario Labour Relations Board 1981–82 to 1988–89; Nova Scotia Department of Labour and Manpower 1979–80 to 1988–89). This trend stands in marked contrast to the decline in British Columbia.

UNION STRUCTURE

Historically, building tradespeople have been organized into seventeen internation-al unions, jointly affiliated with the American Federation of Labor–Congress of In-dustrial Unions (AFL–CIO) and the Canadian Labour Congress (CLC). As well, in 1978 the Building and Construction Trades Department of the AFL–CIO chartered the Canadian executive board of the Building and Construction Trades Depart-ment (hereafter referred to as the Executive Board) to co-ordinate the activities of international construction unions in Canada (Rose 1983). Quebec is the only province where rival unions have seriously challenged the predominance of the in-ternational building-trades unions. Indeed, escalating tensions between pro-auton-omy and pro-international local unions prompted the Quebec Federation of Labour to establish its own building-trades department (known as QFL–Construction). The Executive Board unsuccessfully protested this action as a breach of the CLC consti-tution. Subsequently, the situation deteriorated to the point that the AFL–CIO building-trades unions were suspended from the CLC in 1980.

Two structural realignments emerged from this situation in the 1980s. In Que-bec, the international building-trades unions lost their majority status. Prior to 1980 (when QFL–Construction was first recognized in law as one of the five union bargaining agents in the industry), international unions represented two-thirds of the industry (Ryan 1986); in 1990, they represent about one-third of the industry. Meanwhile, QFL–Construction now represents the largest bloc of the province's construction workers, at 42 percent. At the national level, the Executive Board established a new labour federation in 1982 (the Canadian Federation of Labour, or CFL) to house its craft and industrial unions. Three building-trades unions, the Carpenters, the Labourers, and the Structural Iron Workers, chose not to affiliate with the CFL, but retained affiliation with the AFL–CIO. The CFL's membership increased modestly between 1982 to 1989 (from 202 494 to 213 901) (Labour Canada 1982–89). Although international unions remain dominant in the industry, their share of construction union membership fell from 91 percent in 1980 to 72 percent in 1988 (Statistics Canada 1980–88).

MERIT-SHOP EMPLOYER ASSOCIATIONS

The rise of nonunion competition has led to the establishment of associations to represent the interests of open- or merit-shop contractors. Although some advocates of merit-shop organizations maintain they are not anti-union or exclusively nonunion, the purpose of the organizations is to represent the interests of firms without a labour affiliation.

Table 5.2 provides a summary of the major characteristics of these organizations in four provinces. The Newfoundland and Labrador Non-Union Contractors Association (N&LNUCA) is best characterized as a "limited-purpose" organization, formed for defensive reasons (i.e., in response to a Building Trades Council of Newfoundland and Labrador plan for long-term stability in construction labour relations and, in particular, the Hibernia project). This proposal became the basis for the Memorandum of Understanding (MOU), a unique tripartite agreement between the Building Trades Council, the Newfoundland CLRA, and the provincial government. Briefly, the MOU called for a province-wide, multitrade bargaining structure, a no-strike/no-lockout agreement for a minimum of five years, development of a jurisdictional disputes plan, and legislation prohibiting doublebreasting and updating the construction fair-wage schedule pursuant to the Industrial Standards Act. Perceiving the MOU as a threat to the interests of nonunion contractors, the N&LNUCA opposed its adoption. As a result of good organization, an intense lobbying effort, and good political timing (an impending election), the MOU failed to gain the approval of the provincial Cabinet. This campaign was the only major activity of the N&LNUCA.

In comparison to merit-shop associations in Alberta and Saskatchewan, the Independent Contractors and Business Association (ICBA) of British Columbia is older, larger and represents employers within and outside the construction industry. As well, its philosophic origins differ from those of other merit-shop organizations. Although its roots are in construction, it is morally committed to the establishment of an open-shop or right-to-work movement rather than being largely a response to economic crisis and opportunism. It is noteworthy that merit-shop association membership in Alberta and Saskatchewan includes numerous contractors that operate doublebreasted or nonunion within these provinces, whereas, in British Columbia, the same firms operate union and do not belong to the ICBA. As outlined below, the ICBA provides a range of services similar to those of other merit-shop associations.

Table 5.2

Merit-Shop Associations

Organization	Year Formed	Estimated Membership	Purposes/Objectives
Independent Contractors & Business Association of British Columbia	1975	400+	Provides a range of services for nonunion contractors, including training, a portable benefits program, and an employment referral plan. Acts as spokesperson for the open-shop movement.
Merit Contractors' Association (Alberta)	1986	110	Establish a cost-effective alternative to union construction and promote the interests of nonunion and doublebreasted firms. It provides numerous employment services, including wage surveys, employee registry and referral training, and a portable benefits plan.
Merit Contractors' Association Inc. (Saskatchewan)	1988	unavailable	Same objectives as the Merit Contractors Association (Alberta)
Newfoundland and Labrador Nonunion Contractors' Association	1987	400	Opposition to a tripartite agreement between the building-trades unions, union contractors, and the provincial government to stabilize construction labour relations.

The Merit Contractors Association Inc. (Saskatchewan) was founded in 1988 by those contractors who were instrumental in forming MCA–Alberta. Given its relatively recent formation and the fact it is virtually a carbon copy of the Alberta group, the latter group will be the focus of the discussion here. MCA–Alberta promotes the merit-shop concept as a cost-effective alternative for construction users and legislators. In co-ordinating and promoting the interests of its members, it provides a broad range of services, including liaison with business and government, and the development of employment policies and practices. It has encouraged members to develop pay-for-performance systems (e.g., bonuses) and established what might be characterized as "union substitutes," e.g., employee registry and referral and training. A computer-based registry system has been established to develop a pool of labour from which contractors can recruit skilled tradespeople and apprentices. In terms of apprentice training, MCA–Alberta participates in government/industry committees, and certified apprentices have been indentured by merit-shop contractors. As well, it offers a number of "union-like benefits," including a portable benefits program (e.g., life insurance, extended health care, and group retirement savings plan) and a grievance procedure. Such benefits and procedures differ from those normally provided by collective bargaining. For example, benefits coverage is less comprehensive, and, in the case of the retirement savings plan, employer participation is voluntary. The grievance procedure anticipates that MCA–Alberta will act as a mediator to resolve disagreements between employees and their employers. Although these differences are not insignificant, merit-shop contractors have attempted to establish competitive employment conditions to attract and retain skilled tradespeople.

Sufficient data are not available to judge the effectiveness of these organizations. To some extent the problem may be market-driven. The depressed construction market and generally slow recovery in western Canada have afforded nonunion and doublebreasted firms access to a large pool of tradespeople. Thus, even though registry and referral systems have been set up, some are not fully operational, and recruiting efforts generally appear to be more informal than in the unionized sector. Training largely consisted of skills upgrading and training for helpers, civil tradespeople and supervisors rather than preparing new journeymen/journeywomen. Given the larger government involvement in training in Canada, contractors and their associations have not been required to mount formal training programs comparable to the open-shop movement in the United States (Northrup 1984). There also are doubts about the willingness of open-shop firms to provide union-like benefits. An ICBA survey (1991) revealed that 56 percent of nonresidential contractors provided a medical plan, 16 percent provided a pension plan, and 19 percent provided no fringe benefits.

At this stage, it can reasonably be stated that nonunion penetration is dominant for specified trades, sectors, projects, and regions, and is likely to retain that position in the near future. The ultimate test for the merit-shop organizations and their members may be their ability to supply workers when faced with a strong and sustained demand for new construction. An economic upturn will test not only whether open-shop firms can continue to retain and attract skilled tradespeople, but the loyalty of doublebreasted firms to their merit-shop associations.

PEAK ORGANIZATION RELATIONS

The predominant national employers organization in Canada is the Canadian Construction Association (CCA). It represents more than 20 000 firms and acts as an industry spokesperson with the federal government and the business community. Because a substantial share of its membership is drawn from the traditionally unionized industrial, commercial, institutional, and engineering sectors of the industry, it has maintained a labour relations department to compile and disseminate legislative and collective-bargaining information. Relations with the building-trades unions were formalized in 1980, when the CCA and the Executive

Board established the Joint National Building Trades/CCA Labour–Management Committee (hereinafter referred to as the Joint Committee). It served as a forum for discussing issues of mutual concern, e.g., training and worker mobility. With the threat of nonunion competition looming larger, the Joint Committee prepared a report outlining recommendations to ensure the future of the unionized sector of the industry (National Joint Committee 1985). Specifically, it suggested ways in which unionized construction could be made more cost-effective (e.g., standardization of hours of work and overtime premiums, improving job-site practices, and eliminating jurisdictional disputes). The response to the report was not enthusiastic among provincial building-trades councils.

The spirit of co-operation evaporated in 1986, when the Executive Board withdrew from the Joint Committee, citing significant philosophical differences with the CCA. It was particularly concerned about prominent CCA members operating spinoff companies and the CCA's tacit support of merit-shop advocates. This development coincided with increased demands from nonunion members to establish a "nonunion contractors section" within the CCA similar to the section for union contractors. Notwithstanding the demise of the Joint Committee, the parties have jointly participated in the construction sector committee of the Canadian Labour Market and Productivity Centre.

*B*argaining Process and Outcomes

WAGES AND RELATED ISSUES

As noted above, the introduction of accreditation legislation and broader bargaining structures were expected to moderate wage settlements in the 1970s, but failed to do so. In the 1980s, there was a significant deceleration in construction wage settlements. Statistics Canada produces a "composite union wage index" and a "composite union wage index, including selected pay supplements." The trend in wages (and wages plus supplements) between 1971 and 1989 is summarized in Table 5.3. In the 1970s, double-digit increases predominated, whereas, in the 1980s, such increases were the exception. Overall, the increase in union wage indexes in the 1980s was less than half the increase reported in the previous decade.

Another perspective on wage trends involves comparisons of negotiated increases in base wage rates in construction with other industries. Since 1983, increases in construction base wages were slightly lower, but broadly consistent with the Canadian wage pattern (Labour Canada 1983–89). This situation represents a marked departure from that in the 1970s, when construction wage increases exceeded increases in manufacturing wages (Rose 1986). A further indication of construction wage stabilization is found in comparing the construction–manufacturing differential in gross average hourly wages. Whereas the construction wage

Table 5.3
Annual Indexes of Construction Union Wage Rates and Wage Rates and Benefits, 1971–1989

Year	Wage Rate Index (1986 = 100)	Percent Change	Wage and Benefit Index (1986 = 100)	Percent Change
1971	29.6	–	27.8	–
1972	32.6	10.1%	30.8	10.8%
1973	35.8	9.8	34.1	10.7
1974	39.2	9.5	37.7	10.6
1975	44.7	14.0	43.4	15.1
1976	51.1	14.3	49.7	14.5
1977	56.8	11.2	55.4	11.5
1978	60.5	6.5	59.2	6.8
1979	64.2	6.2	63.0	6.4
1980	69.2	7.8	68.1	8.1
1981	75.5	9.1	74.4	9.3
1982	82.5	9.3	81.4	9.4
1983	92.6	12.2	91.6	12.5
1984	95.6	3.2	94.9	3.6
1985	97.6	2.1	97.3	2.5
1986	100.0	2.5	100.0	2.8
1987	102.4	2.4	102.7	2.7
1988	105.8	3.3	106.5	3.7
1989	110.2	4.2	111.4	4.6
Increase: 1971–80	39.6	133.8%	40.3	145.0%
Increase: 1980–89	41.0	59.2%	43.3	63.6%

Source: Unpublished data provided by Statistics Canada.

advantage steadily increased between 1965 and the late 1970s, it fell from 147.2 percent in January 1980 to 119.3 percent in December 1989 (from $3.69 to $2.69 per hour) (Statistics Canada 1980–90b).[7]

Aggregate wage data obscure the upheaval in collective bargaining. In the aftermath of the large wage settlements reached in the 1982 bargaining round and changes in the economic and competitive climate, the mid-1980s were characterized by concession bargaining. The most significant bargaining outcomes included wage freezes and rollbacks, discontinuation of historical wage relationships (notably the creation of separate wage structures for industrial and commercial construction), standardization of work schedules (hours of work and overtime), and reductions in or the elimination of pay provisions for time not worked, e.g., travel time. Although there was evidence of some concessionary bargaining in all of the provinces, it was most pronounced where nonunion penetration was greatest, i.e., in western Canada and in Newfoundland (see Table 5.4).

Alberta

To fully appreciate the turbulent 1984 bargaining round, it is necessary to briefly review events leading up to these negotiations. The 1982–84 collective agreements provided for monetary increases that averaged about $4.70 per hour (or 28 percent) and increased the union–nonunion wage differential to about $6.60 per hour by late 1983. Confronted by a depressed market and rising nonunion competition, the Alberta Construction Labour Relations Association (ACLRA) unsuccessfully sought changes to the 1982–84 agreements, including deferral of scheduled wage increments and a contract extension through 1985. Subsequently, the ACLRA tried and failed to negotiate a comprehensive package that would provide labour-cost relief and greater flexibility.

In the 1984 talks, the ACLRA demanded wage rollbacks of $5 to $6 per hour to ensure the future of unionized construction. When the unions refused on the ground that agreeing to rollbacks would only prompt nonunion firms to cut their wages and perpetuate a downward spiral in wages, the ACLRA adopted a strategy of 24-hour lockouts, followed by the termination of collective agreements. Subsequently, unionized contractors unilaterally reduced wages to reflect current market conditions (generally, the rates that prevailed at the expiry of the 1980–82 collective agreements) and eliminated other employment conditions, e.g., benefits, travel pay, and room and board allowances. Union legal challenges were largely ineffective (Fisher and Kushner 1986). However, a few trades did achieve settlements with the ACLRA and other employer associations. The terms of settlement varied widely (from large wage rollbacks to a status quo agreement, with an enabling clause providing wage flexibility).

With the exception of isolated trade and project agreements, collective bargaining remained dormant until 1988.[8] There were several unsuccessful attempts to revive negotiations. The passage of the Construction Industry Bargaining Act (CIBA) in 1987 failed to overcome the acrimony left from the abortive 1984 talks. Following an upturn in the construction market (notably industrial work) in 1988, the CIBA was repealed, and amendments to the Alberta Labour Code were adopted to facilitate collective bargaining in construction. With the active support of the Minister of Labour, bargaining got back on track and resulted in agreements with almost all trades in 1989.

A number of changes in bargaining outcomes, besides wage reductions, have occurred. For example, separate wage structures were established for commercial and industrial construction in northern Alberta, and enabling clauses were adopted in the south to permit modified wage scales on individual projects. In commercial construction, benefits packages were reduced or curtailed, and travel pay and room and board allowances for out-of-town work were eliminated. In addition, daily and weekly hours of work were standardized, and the overtime premium was

Table 5.4
Major Examples of Concession Bargaining, 1984–1989

Province	Wages	Other Issues
Alberta	— Following the termination of the 1982–84 collective agreements, employers unilaterally rolled back wages by up to $5 per hour. — Separate wage structures for most trades for industrial and commercial/institutional construction.	— Numerous changes in commercial and institutional construction, including the reduction and elimination of benefits, expanded travel-free zones, tightening of room and board allowances, standardizing hours of work, and reduction of some overtime premiums.
Saskatchewan	Following the collapse of collective bargaining in 1984, wages are estimated to have fallen $3 to $4 per hour.	— Data not available.
British Columbia	— A wage freeze in the 1984–86 agreement and the first year of the 1986–88 agreement. — A lower residential wage rate (1986–88 agreement). — A separate wage structure for basic trades in commercial and institutional construction (1988–91 agreement).	— A broad range of provisions were modified to promote labour-cost savings in residential, commercial, and institutional construction, e.g., hours of work, overtime premiums, and travel pay.
Newfoundland	— Wages were effectively frozen for over four years (1985–89).	— No significant changes.
Nova Scotia	— Wage rates in the 1982–86 collective agreement were extended two years.	— Expanded travel-free zones, and increased flexibility in hiring and through enabling clauses.
Quebec	— Government decree established a wage freeze in 1984.	— No significant changes.
Ontario	— A wage freeze in first year of the 1984–86 collective agreement.	— No significant changes.

set at time and one-half for the first two hours of overtime per day.

But, the most dramatic outcome remains wage levels. One survey suggests construction wages have not significantly rebounded in the second half of the decade. Average hourly earnings (excluding overtime) for general contractors went from $13.90 in January 1984 to $12.34 in July 1984, to $14.63 in December 1989. For specialty trade contractors, average hourly earnings went from $16.29 in January 1984, to $13.89 in July 1984, to $15.44 in December 1989. Overall, the index of average hourly earnings for all contractors in 1989 was the same as in 1984 (Statistics Canada 1989–90).

Saskatchewan

In 1984, bargaining in Saskatchewan also involved contractor demands for large wage rollbacks and union resistance. However, unlike the case of Alberta, the repeal of the construction bargaining law obviated the need for contractors to formulate a sophisticated bargaining strategy. Slack demand and the opportunity to operate doublebreasted removed the necessity to enter into renewal agreements and, as a result, collective bargaining became inactive, with the exception of the odd contract extension and several project agreements. The legal status of expired collective agreements produced conflicting judgments by arbitrators and the Labour Relations Board. Although the Court of Appeal held that these agreements were enforceable, the matter has been appealed to the Supreme Court of Canada. Regardless of their legal status (and the validity of any claims for back pay), the fact remains there were only very limited opportunities to work for union contractors following the collapse of collective bargaining in 1984. As a result, there was an immediate and sharp drop in wages to reflect new market realities, and an erosion of union benefits packages and other conditions of employment.

Unfortunately, there are no precise figures depicting the decline in construction wages. Our interviews suggest that base wages fell by an estimated $3.00 to $4.00 per hour following the collapse of collective bargaining. According to Statistics Canada (1989–90), average hourly earnings (excluding overtime) for general contractors went from $11.06 in January 1984 to $9.25 in July 1984, to $11.13 in December 1989. For specialty trade contractors, average hourly earnings went from $12.25 in January 1984 to $11.22 in July 1984, to $12.44 in December 1989. Overall, the index of average hourly earnings for all contractors in 1989 was 2.8 percent higher than in 1984.

British Columbia

On the surface at least, some aspects of bargaining in British Columbia resembled the pattern in other western provinces. However, owing to the pragmatism and maturity of the parties the commitment of union contractors to collective bargaining, and the absence of political interference, the experience demonstrates the capacity of collective bargaining, to respond to economic and competitive shocks. In the 1984 bargaining round, contractors sought major concessions in response to the rise in nonunion competition. These included "an unspecified rollback in wage rates, an increase in straight-time weekly hours from 37 1/2 to 40, a reduction in paid travel time, increased discretion in the selection of work crews and deletion of the non-affiliation clause" (Strand 1986, 199). The unions opposed any wage cuts. The final result was a wage freeze for the 1984–86 collective agreement. In the 1986 bargaining round, the CLRA threatened to terminate the collective agreement after imposing a 24-hour lockout. This tactic failed to attract membership support and was quickly abandoned. The 1986–88 settlement resulted in a wage freeze in the first year, a temporary suspension of travel pay provisions, the establishment of a "clause and condition" standardization committee (to study issues such as hours of work and travel), and a residential construction addendum to the master agreement providing for labour-cost savings and improved flexibility on wages, travel, hours of work, and overtime premiums.

The 1988–91 collective agreement resulted in several breakthroughs. It represented the first three-year agreement, and it was achieved without a work stoppage. Additionally, it differentiated working conditions in commercial and institutional construction from those in industrial construction. It also contained enabling clauses to promote flexibility in regard to wages, hours, and travel provisions. Moreover, our interviews indicated that the building-trades unions have taken a more flexible approach in applying nonaffiliation clauses.

The CLRA and the Bargaining Council of Building Trades Unions also recognized the need to jointly promote unionized construction. Under the 1986–88 agreement, they adopted a joint action program to promote "fair wages" on all government-sponsored projects, to encourage all levels of government to award contracts to unionized contractors, to market unionized construction to major owners and clients, and to seek labour-law amendments. Because the development of a market recovery program is in its early stages, it is too soon to determine whether it will reduce the erosion to the open-shop sector, let alone improve union market share.

If, as suggested, collective bargaining responded (albeit belatedly) to changing market conditions in British Columbia, how do we account for the absence of a similar response in Alberta and Saskatchewan? Although the economic and legal climate in the latter provinces can be distinguished, environmental factors alone fail to provide a satisfactory explanation. Bargaining history and attitudinal structuring are quite different in the provinces. For example, in British Columbia, the CLRA and the building-trades unions have demonstrated they are strong and militant organizations. Their relationship has moved from "hyper adversarialism" in the 1970s to maturity in the 1980s, featuring mutual respect and accommodation. No similar transformation took place in Alberta or Saskatchewan. In Alberta, the ACLRA never garnered complete support from contractors; nor did it establish a good relationship with the unions. From its inception, the ACLRA was viewed as hostile to unions. Personality and bargaining conflicts were pervasive, and the unions' lack of trust in the ACLRA was reinforced by the latter's 1984 bargaining strategy and the formation of MCA–Alberta by a former retired official of ACLRA.

Considering that MCA–Alberta and the ACLRA operate out of the same building, the government is perceived as providing encouragement for nonunion construction, and the building trades are not as strong as their counterparts in British Columbia; it is hardly surprising that mistrust prevails, and there is considerably less evidence of bipartite or tripartite solutions to the problems confronting unionized construction. Similar, but less severe problems existed in Saskatchewan.

Newfoundland

The 1986–88 collective agreement imposed a construction wage freeze. Taking into consideration the elapsed time between the final pay increment in the 1982–85 agreements and the achievement of renewal agreements in 1989, construction wages were effectively frozen for longer than four years. Other conditions of employment, notably the hiring hall, travel arrangements, and hours of work and overtime, remained virtually unchanged.

Nova Scotia

Expectations about offshore oil development enabled the plumbers and three other trades on the mainland to negotiate an increase of $8 per hour in the 1982 bargaining round (other trades received $5 to $6). The four-year agreements, some of which called for annual increases of 11 percent, upset federal finance minister Marc Lalonde to the point that he suspended fair-wage schedules in the province. With the collapse of oil prices and mounting concerns over possible nonunion competition, contractors sought to reopen contract negotiations. This effort led to the extension of contracts, with the 1986 wage adjustments spread over an additional two years. Negotiations also resulted in the expansion of travel-free zones, increased flexibility in hiring (e.g., name hiring), and enabling clauses permitting union contractors to compete more effectively on designated projects and in specified geographic areas. As well, lower wage rates have been negotiated for journeymen/journeywomen, apprentices, helpers, and pre-apprentices for specified trades and smaller projects.

Quebec and Ontario

Although there was a wage freeze in both provinces in 1984 (one decreed, the other negotiated), the status quo largely prevailed in each. In Quebec, decrees were imposed in 1982 and 1984 and, in other years, there was strong government pressure to extend the decrees. Bargaining has taken place within the framework of the decree with no indication of major changes, in the form of either rollbacks or breakthroughs.

Ontario also has not experienced major rollbacks or improvements in flexibility. Some trades have adopted enabling clauses, but there have been only a few isolated cases where they have led to rollbacks. In response to nonunion competition, the sheet metal trade has introduced an industry recovery fund whereby hourly contributions by workers are used to subsidize unionized contractors bidding on "cost-sensitive" jobs. In the areas of hiring, travel, hours of work and overtime, and subcontracting, there is little evidence of increased flexibility.

The biggest change in bargaining has been the transition to province-wide negotiations. This change has required two forms of adjustments: (1) the consolidation of a large number of local craft agreements into individual provincial agreements by trade, and (2) the multitrade co-ordination of wage talks to promote standardized increases in monetary packages. Although centralized bargaining appeared to work reasonably well, employers in northern Ontario complained that province-wide bargaining imparted an upward bias on wage settlements, while unions in southern Ontario (primarily Toronto) maintained it had the opposite effect. In 1988, there was a movement away from across-the-board wage increases to two-tier settlements (a provincial rate and a higher rate for Toronto). The expansion of two-tier settlements in the 1990 bargaining round suggests a greater willingness to tie wage adjustments to local market conditions.

WORK STOPPAGES

A primary reason why policy makers supported legislation promoting employer accreditation and centralized bargaining structures in construction was to reduce industrial conflict. Table 5.5 reveals such a reduction was not realized in the short run, but construction strike activity did decline sharply in the 1980s. In comparison to the 1970s, strikes fell from 833 to 373 (55 percent), workers involved fell from 669 545 to 416 504 (38 percent), and days lost fell from 12 473 640 to 6 652 450 (47 percent). Even though aggregate strike activity declined during the 1980s, the magnitude of the reduction was greater in the construction industry. For example, days lost in construction dropped to 12.1 percent of the all-industry total (from 17.1 percent in the 1970s).

Perhaps the most noteworthy aspect of the construction pattern was the change in the relative severity of work stoppages (days lost per 1000 paid workers). The relative severity of construction strikes increased sharply between the 1960s and 1970s (from 1117 to 2612 days idle per 1000 workers), and then plummeted in the 1980s (to 1253 days idle per 1000 workers). In the process, the relative severity of construction work stoppages declined to 2.3 times the all-industry average (compared to 2.8 times the all-industry average in the 1970s).

Developments in Dispute Settlement

The 1980s were not only characterized by a decline in strike activity, but also featured the development of new dispute-settlement mechanisms. Both Nova Scotia

Table 5.5
Number of Strikes, Workers Involved, and Days Lost, in Construction and All Industries, 1960–1989

Period	Number of Strikes			Workers Involved			Days Lost		
	Const.	All Industries	Const. % All Industries	Const.	All Industries	Const. % All Industries	Const.	All Industries	Const. % All Industries
1960–69	1 054	4 364	24.2%	316 234	1 771 370	17.9%	5 108 000	30 326 782	16.8%
1970–79	833	8 772	9.5	669 545	5 296 325	12.6	12 473 640	73 211 280	17.0
1980–89	373	7 519	5.0	416 504	3 629 047	11.5	6 652 450	54 972 217	12.1
1960–89	2 260	20 655	10.9	1 402 283	10 696 742	13.1	24 234 090	158 510 279	15.3

Sources: Labour Canada, *Strikes and Lockouts in Canada,* 1960–85 (Ottawa: Minister of Supply and Services) and unpublished strike data (1986–89) provided by Labour Canada.

and Alberta adopted legislation providing for the final and binding resolution of interest disputes. In Newfoundland, the MOU constituted a major proposal to ensure long-term labour relations stability. Innovative disputes procedures developed in the 1970s, e.g., British Columbia's jurisdictional assignment plan, continued to be effective in preventing labour disputes.

INTEREST ARBITRATION

During the 1970s, it was increasingly recognized that fragmented bargaining in integrated industries was a recipe for protracted labour strife. Accordingly, British Columbia developed a system whereby the Labour Relations Board could impose a trade union council to prevent "minority" strikes and promote labour peace.

> We had the worst of both worlds in British Columbia: the disadvantages of centralization in C.L.R.A. (which could not afford to give a single union such as the Plumbers, a special concession it had not offered other building trades unions) and the disadvantages of fragmentation (since any one union such as the Plumbers could legally pull the rug out from under a shaky industry-wide package). (Weiler 1980, 202)

The establishment of a building-trades council meant that strike and ratification decisions must be supported by a two-thirds majority of the unions and a simple majority of all employees.

The introduction of interest arbitration in Alberta and Nova Scotia represents an alternative approach to "minority" strikes. The Alberta system, which was introduced in 1988, stipulates that, once settlements have been agreed to by 75 percent of the employers' organizations and trade unions in a sector, any remaining disputes shall be referred to a construction industry disputes board. Following a referral to arbitration, any work stoppage in progress must be terminated. The board has the power to issue a binding award and may choose its own method of arbitration, including final-offer selection. Although the statute does not specify arbitration criteria, it presumably recognizes that the majority of settlements reflect a pattern to be followed. The first referrals to arbitration under this provision were in 1990.

The Nova Scotia system was adopted in 1986 and provides that, where settlements have been reached with all but two or fewer unions, a work stoppage is restricted to a maximum of 21 days (beyond the settlement date for all but the two or fewer unions). If the two or fewer unions fail to reach a settlement, a Construction Industry Conciliation Board shall be appointed and the work stoppage shall be terminated. According to the Trade Union Act, the board has the power to impose a binding settlement and its award is to be consistent with the other settlements reached in the particular bargaining round and with due regard to historic relationships in the construction industry for that union or unions. This provision has been used on four occasions.

THE MEMORANDUM OF UNDERSTANDING (1987)

Although the MOU was not approved by the Newfoundland government, it did represent a comprehensive plan for the prevention and settlement of labour disputes. Specifically, it would have (1) taken wages out of competition by linking wage adjustments to a multicity index, (2) provided for no work stoppages for a minimum of five years and (3) established a new procedure for the resolution of jurisdictional disputes. Some aspects of the MOU have been incorporated into the Hybernia Project Agreement to provide stable labour relations.

JURISDICTIONAL DISPUTES

Although jurisdictional disputes have been a pernicious source of conflict in construction, only British Columbia has developed an expedited procedure for dealing with them. Developed by the CLRA and the provincial building-trades council in 1977, the Jurisdictional Assignment Plan provides for the referral of disputes to an impartial umpire for settlement and the issuance of work assignment guidelines. The plan was adopted as an alternative to other jurisdictional disputes procedures, notably the Impartial Jurisdictional Disputes Board in Washington, D.C.; labour boards; and the courts. Between 1978 and 1989, there were nearly 1200 applications under the plan. There has been a marked decline in applications in recent years; the number of applications fell from 223 in 1982 to 94 in 1985, to fewer than 30 per year after 1986. This trend has been attributed to the economic recession, the deceleration of innovation, declining union aggressiveness in pursuit of jurisdictional claims in response to increased nonunion competition, a greater tendency by the building-trades unions to settle claims on their own, and a natural consequence of years of decision making under the plan (Jurisdictional Assignment Plan 1987–89).

The consensus within the industry is that the plan has had a dramatic impact on the incidence of jurisdictional disputes. Unfortunately, data on the frequency of such disputes prior to the adoption of the plan are quite sparse. The available evidence reveals that, in the first five years of the plan (1978–82), there were 41 work stoppages and, in the next five years, there were 15 work stoppages. There was only one work stoppage per year from 1985 to 1988, and 1989 was the first year in which a jurisdictional work stoppage was not recorded. In light of the experience in British Columbia, it is somewhat surprising that other jurisdictions have not adopted alternative procedures, particularly given the overwhelming sentiment that jurisdictional disputes remain a serious labour relations problem.

*C*onclusions

*T*he past decade has been a period of adjustment for construction labour relations. The increase in demand for new construction in the 1960s and 1970s and expectations of further expansion in the 1980s gave way to a deep economic recession. The contraction of the product market and the increase in nonunion competition profoundly affected construction labour relations. The new competitive mix gave purchasers of construction, private and public, greater choice, and the industry became increasingly conscious of the need for cost containment.

In provinces experiencing the strongest competitive shocks, i.e., Alberta and Saskatchewan, legal support for collective bargaining was undermined, and employer strategies emphasized union replacement and suppression. In this environment, nonunion and doublebreasted firms became the dominant force in the marketplace, merit-shop associations emerged to represent their interests, and collective bargaining ceased to be the primary mechanism for regulating the employment relationship in construction. As the demand for new construction increased in the late 1980s and some normalization of bargaining returned (primarily in Alberta), there was clear evidence that contractors had achieved labour-cost savings and improvements in flexibility.

Outside of these two provinces, collective bargaining has adapted to market pressures. This trend was particularly evident in British Columbia, where the economic downturn was severe and nonunion competition intensified. Rather than attempting to browbeat the building-trades unions into submission with inflexible demands for large wage rollbacks, the CLRA and the unions pursued what might be described as a strategy to protect their mutual interests, i.e., the survival of the unionized sector. As befits a mature bargaining relationship, they recognized that survival would require greater flexibility and pragmatism. This goal was reflected in the bargaining outcomes, a less rigid application of the nonaffiliation clause, and a commitment to a market recovery program.

Generally, other regions of Canada did not experience economic and competitive shocks similar to those that occurred in the three western provinces. In these provinces, construction labour relations was characterized by either relatively modest changes (Nova Scotia) or maintenance of the status quo (Ontario and Quebec). Where change did occur, it often was temporary (e.g., a wage freeze) or involved the adoption of more flexible working conditions to achieve labour-cost savings. There was little evidence of change with respect to such institutions and practices as the closed shop, the hiring hall, subcontracting, and staffing requirements.

An important question for the 1990s is whether the dramatic shift toward nonunion construction will continue. In western Canada, nonunion construction appears to have carved out a secure niche, particularly in commercial and institutional construction. Future expansion will likely require breakthroughs on major industrial projects. Interestingly, such projects continue to be built exclusively or predominantly by union forces, even in Alberta and Saskatchewan. Decisions by construction users and governments regarding such projects continue to reflect the view that union contractors possess the expertise to undertake large, complex projects and the building trades unions have the capacity to readily supply the workers. Even though the union sector remains dominant in industrial construction, its position is by no means secure. A number of spokespersons pointed to the increasing ability of nonunion contractors to capture larger and more complex jobs and observed that large U.S. nonunion firms could enter the market in the future.[9]

In other parts of Canada, there has been an expansion in nonunion construction, but market penetration is relatively modest (except in Newfoundland). In the absence of an economic crisis or major changes in labour law, these regions are not as likely to experience significant increases in nonunion competition in the near future.

At the same time, the ability of the union sector to retain its position in industrial construction and recapture commercial and institutional work will require even greater flexibility in future bargaining. Even though collective bargaining has demonstrated its adaptability to market shifts, it has often been a lagged and incremental response. Moreover, no data exist that unambiguously show that negotiated labour-cost savings and increased flexibility have slowed or reversed the growth of nonunion construction. The success of any market recovery program will depend not only on emphasizing the attributes of the union sector, but on demonstrating that it is cost competitive. As for the building-trades unions, they will have to develop a coherent and co-ordinated strategy to meet the nonunion challenge. This strategy will undoubtedly require more sophisticated organizing campaigns, a comprehensive assessment of collective-bargaining priorities, and a strong commitment to market recovery programs. Such activities were not pursued aggressively or co-ordinated among building-trades unions in the 1980s.

REFERENCES

Alberta Labour. 1980–81 to 1988. *Negotiated Working Conditions in Alberta Collective Agreements*. Edmonton.

Bain, George Sayers. 1978. *Union Growth and Public Policy in Canada*. Ottawa: Labour Canada.

Bank of Canada. 1983–84. *Annual Report of the Governor to the Minister of Finance and Statement of Accounts*. Ottawa.

Bourdon, Clinton C., and Raymond E. Levitt. 1980. *Union and Open-Shop Construction*. Lexington, MA: Lexington Books.

Fagan, Drew. 1991. "Ontario Finishes Decade with Greater Share of GDP." *Globe and Mail*, February 2, B3.

Fisher, E.G., and Stephen Kushner. 1986. "Alberta's Construction Labour Relations During the Recent Downturn." *Relations Industrielles/Industrial Relations*, 41/4: 778–801.

Foster, Howard G., and George Strauss. 1972. "Labor Problems in Construction: A Review," *Industrial Relations*, 11/1 (October): 289–313.

Hérbert, Gerard. 1968. "Labour Standards Legislation." In H. Carl Goldenberg and John G.H. Crispo, eds., *Construction Labour Relations*. Ottawa: Canadian Construction Association. 230–303.

Independent Contractors and Business Association of British Columbia. 1991. *1990 Open Shop Construction Industry Survey*. Vancouver.

Jurisdictional Assignment Plan. 1987–89. *Annual Report*. Vancouver.

Labour Canada. 1960–85. *Strikes and Lockouts in Canada*. Ottawa: Minister of Supply and Services.

———. 1982–89. *Directory of Labour Organizations in Canada*. Ottawa: Minister of Supply and Services.

———. 1983–89. *Major Wage Settlements*. Ottawa: Bureau of Labour Information.

Milner, Brian. 1990. "Canada in Its First Homemade Recession." *Globe and Mail*, October 11, B1.

National Joint Committee. 1985. *Union Construction in Canada: Ensuring Our Future*. Ottawa.

Northrup, Herbert R. 1984. *Open Shop Construction Revisited*. Philadelphia: Industrial Research Unit, University of Pennsylvania.

Nova Scotia Department of Labour and Manpower. 1979–80 to 1988–89. *Annual Report*. Halifax: Queen's Printer.

Ontario Labour Relations Board. 1981–82 to 1988–89. *Annual Report*. Toronto.

Rose, Joseph B. 1980. *Public Policy, Bargaining Structure and the Construction Industry*. Toronto: Butterworths.

———. 1983. "Some Notes on the Building Trades–Canadian Labour Congress Dispute." *Industrial Relations*, 22 (Winter): 87–93.

———. 1986. "Legislative Support for Multi-Employer Bargaining: The Canadian Experience." *Industrial and Labour Relations Review*, 40/1 (October): 3–18.

Rose, Joseph B., and Kurt Wetzel. 1986. "Outcomes of Bargaining

Structures in the Ontario and Saskatchewan Construction Industries." *Relations Industrielles/Industrial Relations*, 41/ 2: 256–79.

Ryan, Dennis. 1986. "Division in the House of Labour: An Analysis of the CLC–Building Trades Dispute." *Proceedings of the 22nd Annual Meeting of the Canadian Industrial Relations Association*. Quebec: CIRA, 182–95.

Statistics Canada. 1978–90. *Private and Public Investment in Canada— Mid Year Review*. Ottawa: Statistics Canada.

——. 1980–90a. *Construction in Canada*. Ottawa: Statistics Canada.

——. 1980–90b. *Employment, Earnings and Hours*. Ottawa: Statistics Canada.

——. 1980–88. *The Corporations and Labour Unions Returns Act Annual Report*. Ottawa: Statistics Canada.

——. 1982–90. *Consumer Prices and Consumer Price Indexes*. Ottawa: Statistics Canada.

——. 1989a. *Historical Labour Force Statistics, 1989*. Ottawa: Statistics Canada.

——. 1989b. *The Labour Force, December 1989*. Ottawa: Statistics Canada.

——. 1989–90. *Construction Price Statistics*. Ottawa: Statistics Canada.

Strand, Kenneth. 1986. "Non-Union Construction in British Columbia." *Proceedings of the 22nd Annual Meeting of the Canadian Industrial Relations Association*. Quebec: CIRA, 196–213.

Tupper, Allan and G. Bruce Doern, eds. 1981. *Public Corporations and Public Policy in Canada*. Montreal: The Institute for Research on Public Policy.

——. 1988. *Privatization, Public Policy and Public Corporations in Canada*. Halifax: The Institute for Research on Public Policy.

Weiler, Paul 1980. *Reconcilable Differences*. Toronto: Carswell.

Weiler, Paul C., G. Hébert, R. Mitchell, J. Rose, and K. Strand. 1987. *Mega Projects: The Collective Bargaining Dimension*. Ottawa: Canadian Construction Association.

ENDNOTES

1. Financial support for this study was received from McMaster University, the Canadian Construction Association, the Provincial Building and Construction Trades Council of Ontario, the Labour Relations Bureau of the Ontario General Contractors' Association, the Ontario Erectors Association, and the Ontario Masonry Contractors' Association. The author wishes to acknowledge the valuable research assistance provided by David Hemphill.

2. This sector includes such construction projects as manufacturing facilities, office buildings, schools, and hospitals.

3. This law established a system of single-trade, province-wide bargaining and required unions and employers to establish bargaining agents compatible with the new bargaining structure.

4. Data provided by Statistics Canada (1980–88). One indication of the concern with the Corporations and Labour Unions Return Act (CALURA) data is revealed by the Quebec figures. In 1988, CALURA reports there were 92 011 construction union members in Quebec, and union density was 65.9 percent. The Quebec Construction Office reports 112 317 union members in 1988, and all construction workers are required to be union members by law. Although the source of this and perhaps other discrepancies is unclear, the Canadian Construction Association is attempting to reconcile CALURA data with those of its affiliates.

5. Data provided by Gerry Meier, Deputy Minister of Human Resources, Labour and Employment in Saskatchewan.

6. Data compiled by the Industrial Relations Council.

7. Some of the erosion in the construction–manufacturing wage differential is attributable to changes in sampling procedures in 1983 (the inclusion of smaller firms). The April 1983 survey reports a decline in the average hourly wage rate from the previous month (from $15.95 to $14.00 per hour in construction, and from $10.83 to $10.44 per hour in manufacturing). As a result, the construction–manufacturing wage differential fell from 147.3 to 134.1 percent. Nevertheless, over the remainder of the decade, the construction wage advantage continued to decline.

8. The number of construction collective agreements went from 81 (1981–82) to 41 (1984), to 13 (1986), to 26 (1988) (Alberta Labour 1981–82 to 1988).

9. Historically, U.S. contractors have been able to undertake construction work in Canada, provided they employ Canadian workers. The prospect of increased U.S. participation reflects changing market conditions rather than the adoption of the free-trade agreement.

Chapter

6

INDUSTRIAL RELATIONS IN THE CLOTHING INDUSTRY: STRUGGLE FOR SURVIVAL

Michel Grant[1]

*F*rom January to October 1990, 46 employers in the Quebec clothing industry declared bankruptcy, a 44 percent increase in plant closings compared to the same period in 1989. Of bankruptcies in the Canadian clothing industry, 70 percent have occurred in Quebec (Les Affaires, December 8, 1990). The purpose of this essay is to describe the tremendous pressures suffered by the clothing industry and to examine the adaptative strategies designed by management and unions caught up in a hostile economic and commercial environment. Here, the focus is on the Quebec situation, because of the concentration of the industry in that province, and we will more specifically examine the two main sectors in that industry where the greatest bulk of employment is located: men's and ladies' wear.

Characteristics related to the organization of clothing production and to its labour force have combined with factors stemming from an extremely competitive market to shape a unique industrial relations system. Labour–management relations have evolved in a particular institutional and legal context, on which historical references may shed some light. Market pressures and institutional arrangements in the Quebec clothing industry have contributed to creating an awareness of mutual interests between employers and unions and, when compared to other sectors, to promoting more co-operative strategies in collective bargaining and in labour–management relations. Preoccupations with industrial survival and with job protection have interacted in a reinforcement process. Those factors must also be taken into account in understanding the lower strike-propensity in that industry.

In this essay, we, first, present the industry in terms of its regional distribution in Canada and of the organization of production, stressing the importance of pressures from garment manufacturers in low-wage countries and imports into Canada, and their impact on plant closing and on job losses. Second, we look at industrial relations in ladies' and men's clothing, and of the decree system under which both labour and management in ladies' and men's wear have been bargaining for decades in Quebec. We also look at the collective-bargaining structure, the level of industrial strife, and the main issues challenging both parties inside and outside of the collective-bargaining area.

The Clothing Industry

*I*n his seminal book *Competitive Strategy*, Michael Porter charaterizes a fragmented industry as one in which no firm has a significant market share or can influence the industry outcome. Usually, fragmented industries are populated by a large number of small- and medium-sized companies (Porter 1980,191). According to this definition, the clothing industry is one such industry. Further, industrial fragmentation is characterized by low overall entry barriers to potential entrants; we will see that there exist a very high level of entry and exit movements in the apparel industry, particularly in ladies' wear. Smallness can sometimes become an advantage under certain conditions. The apparel industry is subject to competitive pressures stemming from the fashion market. Porter (1980, 198) stresses that rapid product and style changes require quick reactions: "Where frequent new product introductions and style changes are essential to competition, allowing only short lead times, a large firm may be less efficient than a smaller one, which seems to be true in women's clothing and in other industries where style plays a major role in competition."

Production is also fragmented, being undertaken by manufacturers, contractors, subcontractors, and homeworkers, and thus provides a very particular environment for the shaping of industrial relations institutions and practices.

CONCENTRATION IN QUEBEC

Traditionally higher unemployment rates in Quebec reflect the province's weaker and less diversified industrial structure when compared to that of Ontario, its neighbour. Quebec's economic origins lie in the fur trade during the French colonial period. Then, the economy began to convert to timber and agriculture. The growth in demand for consumer goods provided an impetus for light consumer-goods industries, with such products as garments, furniture, boots and shoes. The province developed a dependency on low-growth and low-technology industries, which are subjected to fierce competition from low-wage countries, whereas Ontario, because of its closer geographic proximity to U.S. industrial centres, was experiencing growth in steel-and automaking.

The clothing industry mainly consists of the following components, according to the Standard Industrial Classification from Statistics Canada: men's and boys' clothing; other clothing; women's clothing; children's clothing. Table 6.1, constructed from census data, shows that, historically, the clothing industry has been heavily concentrated in the province of Quebec and that, in national terms, its relative importance remains greatest in that province.

Table 6.1
Employment in Manufacturing and Clothing Industries

Region	Manufacturing	Clothing	Regional Distribution of Labour Force in Clothing(%)	Labour Force in Clothing as % of Total Labour Force in Manufacturing
1951				
Ontario	615 358	39 489	32.8	6.4
Quebec	453 073	67 706	56.1	14.9
Other provinces	292 231	13 350	11.0	4.6
Canada	1 360 662	120 545	100.0	8.9
1961				
Ontario	643 284	23 762	25.8	3.7
Quebec	466 443	57 940	63.3	12.4
Other provinces	295 138	10 226	11.1	3.1
Canada	1 404 865	91 928	100.0	6.5
1971				
Ontario	819 335	21 210	22.4	2.6
Quebec	501 825	61 695	65.1	12.3
Other provinces	386 175	11 795	12.5	3.0
Canada	1 707 335	94 700	100.0	5.5
1981				
Ontario	1 031 890	30 080	24.0	4.7
Quebec	642 035	79 475	63.5	12.4
Other provinces	545 450	15 615	12.5	2.9
Canada	2 219 375	125 170	100.0	5.6
1986				
Ontario	1 069 590	40 305	28.2	3.8
Quebec	613 295	84 920	59.4	13.8
Other provinces	513 860	17 805	12.4	3.5
Canada	2 196 745	143 030	100.0	6.5

Source: Census data for the mentioned years.

Those data indicate, for instance, that, in 1986, almost 60 percent of employment in the industry was located in Quebec and that, while 3.8 percent of manufacturing employment in Ontario is in clothing, in Quebec that proportion increases to 13.8 percent. We notice, however, that there has been a certain transfer of activities from Quebec to Ontario from 1971 to 1986. In 1971, 65 percent of employment in garments was situated in Quebec, and its relative importance, in terms of the province's manufacturing sector in general, was 12.3 percent. The major impact of imports has thus been mainly felt in Quebec, where the apparel industry is mainly concentrated in Montreal. By comparison, the apparel industry is more widely scattered throughout Ontario, "and adjustments in the face of imports have not caused localized income and employment set-backs to the same degree as in Quebec" (Matthews 1983, 159).

ORGANIZATION OF PRODUCTION

Although the invention of the sewing machine in the nineteenth century opened the way to large-scale production in clothing, initial production was carried out in homes, and growth led the way to the industrialization of production; the availability of cheaper industrial homework even slowed down, at times, the establishment of factories. Industrial homework and the "sweating system" became the prevailing production modes during the late 1890s (Rose and Grant 1983, 7–9). Homeworkers' enterprises often expanded into tenement workshops as additional hands entered the workforce. The fragmentation of production allowed manufacturers to farm out garments to contractors, some of whom manufactured clothing in their own factories, and others of whom distributed work to homeworkers and to "sweaters" (International Ladies' Garment Workers' Union [ILGWU] 1981, 8). Seamstresses were jammed into the contractor's home or in a small, unsafe, and unhygienic rented "sweatshop." Others worked in their homes with members of their family, including children. Industrial homework declined in the beginning of this century, when better ways to subdivide the work were developed, while apparel production and the use of electrical power increased, and other technological improvements, such as the button-hole machine, were introduced into factories (ILGWU 1981, 9). But homework has never however completely disappeared from the industry, and its importance has varied according to business cycles. The Great Depression of the 1930s witnessed a resurgence in homework in an industry characterized by the decentralized features of its production and by its high labour-intensiveness. We shall see later the conditions under which union and management responded to the persistent presence of homework in the clothing industry.

That industry remains labour-intensive, and what still counts in the fashion trade "is the hand that guides the pieces of limp cloth through the classically simple sewing machine" (B. Campbell, quoted in Coyle 1982, 15). The sewing machine itself has become a sophisticated piece of equipment. Straight seams can be stitched automatically, and there are machines for attaching buttons, zips, and trimmings, and making button holes: "Ideally the machine paces production, but, in clothing, machine processes are mostly not automated processes; they still rely on labour to operate them and piecerate incentive payments and time and motion study become vital forms of control" (Coyle 1982, 15).

Fragmentation of the production process makes it possible for the assembly of garments in a series of short and simple operations that can be spatially rearranged between different locations or contractors. The distribution of workers and shops in an increasing number of small units reflects the conditions of production and the division of labour. Outsourcing to contractors and to homeworkers can become an attractive management practice in a labour-intensive industry subjected to competition from low-wage countries. There has been an increasing trend in the last ten years to keep production in the shop at a designated minimum level and to outsource production above that level. Other employers have laid off the majority of workers and limited their production activities to design, cutting, and finishing. Some have decentralized their operation or have moved outside the city to smaller towns:

> The quality and brand image, if and when it is necessary, can be main-
> tained by adequate supervision of the pre-assembly and finishing stages
> of production on the main factory floor. The roles of the sweatshop
> economy, of artisan firms and homeworking become crucial in this
> scheme of subcontracting by domestic manufacturers, where access to
> a captive and disposable workforce becomes an essential strategy for
> reducing the unnecessary overhead costs. (Miller 1986, 47)

Phizacklea (1990, 14–15) notes, for instance, that Benetton subcontracts all the labour-intensive stages of production and combines a strategy of just-in-time systems in production and in distribution.

Even though labour-intensive, the men's wear industry is less vulnerable to fashion and style changes than the ladies' garment industry. Thus, the former has longer production runs and has experienced conditions more conducive to mechanization. Consequently, a greater level of mechanization in assembling men's wear and of investment required for equipment has not allowed homeworking to proliferate to the same extent in that sector. Production runs are much shorter in the ladies' clothing industry where technological development has been slower. A research report published in 1983 suggested that there were 30 000 homeworkers in the clothing industry in Quebec and that the great majority of them were primarily involved in the manufacture of ladies' and children wear   (Grant and Rose, 1985, 474).

Production organization and competitive pressures, both international and domestic, favour contracting-out. Table 6.2 indicates the increasing relative importance of units with fewer than 20 employees during the 1975–85 period; these units are comprised of subcontractors in most cases. In February 1988, three-quarters of employers in the ladies' garment industry had fewer than 20 workers, and only 8.3 percent of employers had more than 50 employees. Data for men's apparel for June 1988 suggest that 60.5 percent of employers had fewer than 25

Table 6.2

Distribution of Employers According to Size, Quebec and Ontario, 1975–1985

	0–19 Employees	20–49 Employees	50–99 Employees	100 and More Employees	Total
Quebec					
1975	672 (45.7%)	412 (28%)	210 (14.3%)	178 (12%)	1472
1985	828 (50.8%)	423 (26%)	216 (13.2%)	161 (9.9%)	1628
Ontario					
1975	207 (47.6%)	103 (23.7%)	61 (14%)	64 (14.7%)	435
1985	315 (49.8%)	117 (18.5%)	107 (16.9%)	93 (14.6%)	632

Source: Brief presented to the Quebec Minister of Labour, December 21, 1988, by the three principal union–management Joint Committees in the clothing industry (men's wear; ladies' garments; shirts and gloves).

employees, and 23 percent had more than 50 employees.

In ladies' apparel only, from 1983 to 1987, 1590 factories were created (421 manufacturers and 1169 contractors), while 1839 closed down (579 manufacturers and 1260 contractors). This trend fits into a general pattern, particularly in ladies' clothing, where the proportion of manufacturers decreases, while the proportion of contractors increases; even if the number of employers becomes higher in a sector, the number of employees does not increase, thus reflecting a downsizing of production units through contracting-out. For 1989, the proportion of contractors in men's wear jumps from 42 to 49 percent when we include the jeans sector. Waldinger (1986, 189) captures, at least partly, the essence of investors' reasoning supporting their strategic choices:

> The large apparel company, while well suited to make staple goods, is too cumbersome an entity to respond efficiently to sudden and unanticipated fluctuations. . . . Because apparel is a product very much subject to the vagaries of fashion change and the volatility of consumer spending, there is a role for a spot market that specializes in making up market changes and overruns on more standardized goods and for the small facilities that are best suited to producing small quantitites of short-lived fashions.

Finally, highly decentralized production in clothing allows more concentrated retailers to enjoy greater bargaining power when setting prices and delivery specifications with manufacturers.

IMPORTS

One of the main challenges facing the clothing industry originates from the increasing volume of imports manufactured in low-wage countries. The industry profited from the economic boom that occurred in the 1960s while a new division of labour was shaping up at the international level. Imports from countries whose principal competitive advantage rested on low labour costs rose significantly enough to induce the federal government to design a national policy for textile and clothing in 1970. In 1973, the Canadian government negotiated a Multifibre Arrangement (MFA) within the General Agreement on Tariffs and Trade (GATT). The purpose of this arrangement for the Canadian government was to provide companies with a certain protection through the imposition of quotas on imports while they restructure production in a more competitive fashion. The MFA was renewed in 1977, 1981, and 1986, and expired in July 1991. The Uruguay Round of negotiations undertaken in the 1990s is likely to result in further liberalization of multilateral trade, particularly in light of the gradual implementation of the Canada–U.S. Free Trade Agreement, and in view of the prospect of an eventual Mexico–Canada–United States trade pact.

The MFA regulates trade in textile and clothing on a bilateral basis. Each deal is struck country by country *and* product by product. The system does not allow for the control of imports from countries not party to the arrangement. If an agreement is made with one country on a specific product, there may be an increase in imports from another country for that specific product. Under these conditions, imports may unpredictably fluctuate. The deterioration of the Canadian trade balance in clothing eloquently shows that the MFA has not lived up to original expectations. Table 6.3 presents data on the trade balance in the clothing industry for 1980 and 1987.

Eighty percent of import value originates from low-wage countries. The situation is not significantly different in the United States, where 85 percent of imports in 1987 came from Asian countries, and 7 percent from South America (ILGWU 1988, 12). The increasing volume of imports during the 1980s has created enormous pressures on the clothing industry to develop strategies fostering flexibility in the organization of production and of work, and to look for new alternatives in minimizing costs.

Another factor affecting the clothing industry's competitiveness is the tariffs companies have to pay for imported fabric. According to representatives from the industry, approximately 50 percent of the apparel fabric used in Canada is imported because of the limited variety of fabric manufactured in Canada (Kurt Salmon Associates Inc. 1984, 6; Canadian Apparel Manufacturers Institute 1988, 1). In an

Table 6.3
Trade Balance in Clothing, 1980 and 1987 ($ millions)

Year	Imports	Exports	Balance
1980	777.5	230.2	- 547.3
1987	2261.3	451.8	-3930.4

Source: Commission du textile et du vêtement, *Rapport sur les textiles et les vêtements, 1988* (Ottawa: 1989).

industry dependent on the vagaries of fashion, and exposed to heavy offshore competition, the instant availability of material is vital for survival. Canadian apparel manufacturers are tied to mill prices in the United States, Europe, Japan, and the Far East, and to freight and import tariffs, thus adding costs and, according to them, affecting their competitiveness.

CHARACTERISTICS OF THE LABOUR FORCE

The labour force in the apparel industry is predominantly female, and when compared to the whole manufacturing sector, is more heterogeneous ethnically, older, and less educated. Data from the 1986 Census for Canada indicate that women represented more than 75 percent of the labour force in clothing, and that that proportion fell to 25 percent for the other manufacturing industries. The cutting rooms are a male stronghold. Men lay the cloth and the pattern on the fabric, and mark and cut the fabric; women sew the parts together. Immigrants comprised almost half the work force in the clothing industry, compared to close to one-quarter in other manufacturing industries.

Over half (53.9 percent) the female labour force in the clothing industry in 1986 had not gone beyond grade 10 in their education, as compared to 34.3 percent of women in manufacturing. One-quarter of the female labour force in manufacturing was 45 years old and over, and that proportion increased to 30 percent for apparel (Seward 1990, 29–30).

The competitive nature of the market requires that more effort be deployed to increase productivity and that the labour force be able to adapt to technological changes. Unions and management must also take into account labour-force characteristics when they determine work conditions and when they design their respective bargaining strategies.

Labour–Management Relations System

The main feature of industrial relations in the clothing industry in Quebec is the existence of a multi-employer voluntary structure for the bargaining of the collective agreements in each sector. Another original feature pertains to the existence of a legal context under which there is a partial extension of the agreement settled at the multi-employer level to nonunionized workers. We shall look at those features in the context of pressures from the labour and product markets, and in the context of the organization of production, to shed light on bargaining outcomes and issues.

THE DECREE SYSTEM

In 1934, the Quebec Legislative Assembly adopted a law, now called the Act Respecting Collective Agreement Decrees, allowing government to extend certain collective-agreement provisions to nonunionized workers in specific sectors. The purpose of that legislation, adopted during the Depression, was to provide workers with decent work conditions by keeping wages out of competition; according to the government's intentions, competition could not exist at the expense of work conditions. The Quebec Legislature was not the only elected body trying to adjust to the economic hard times and to deal with the potential social upheaval such economic conditions could generate. Before being repealed for its unconstitutionality by the U.S. Supreme Court in 1935, the National Recovery Act contained similar provisions that allowed the president of the United States to ratify private agreements and standardize work conditions in industrial branches; at the time of this Supreme Court decision, 400 orders had been implemented and another 300 were waiting for the presidential signature of President Franklin D. Roosevelt (Dubé 1990, 16).

In 1935, the Ontario Parliament adopted the Industrial Standards Act, by which both employers and employees' representatives could petition the Minister of Labour for the establishment of a schedule comprising such conditions as minimum wages, hours of work, vacations and other practices prevailing in the industry, these provisions of the law remaining in effect to this day. The minister may convene a conference of industry members, who will then develop a schedule for submission. The minister may then approve the schedule, with such changes he or she considers appropriate, provided the submission reflects a "proper and sufficient" representation of employers and employees. Three such schedules, presently covering approximately 220 employers and 6600 employees, are still in effect in the clothing industry in Ontario: Ladies' Cloak and Suit Industry (1981), Ladies' Dress and Sportswear Industry (1982), Men's and Boys' Clothing Industry (1988).[2] The first two schedules are now outdated and irrelevant, and in some cases specify conditions that fall below the minimum provided for in the general Employment Standards Act. Information obtained from the Ontario Ministry of Labour suggests that the ladies' garment rates are presently under review.

Interestingly, these laws were passed in the United States, Ontario, and Quebec at about the same time and under similar economic and social conditions. By resorting to a decree system, the Quebec government was opting for a compromise between a general minimum-wage law and a law establishing collective-bargaining rights. The recognition of the latter came in Quebec in 1944. Some decrees are regional (e.g., those for garage employees), others are provincial (e.g., all decrees in the clothing industry), and some are occupational (e.g., those for security guards). The decree system still exists today and regulates work conditions for approximately 140 000 workers in specific sectors,[3] even though the legislators have made no attempts to rejuvenate one of the oldest labour laws in the province. Article 2 stipulates: "The Government may order that a collective agreement respecting any trade, industry, commerce or occupation shall also bind all the employees and employers in Québec or in a stated region of Québec, within the scope determined in such decree."

The provisions of the collective agreement, whether amended or not by the parties or by the government, are those respecting wages and hours. The decree may also contain items related to holidays, social security, classification of operations, the determination of classes of employees and employers, and such provisions as the government may deem to be in conformity with the spirit of the act (Article 9). This law renders "null and void all agreements violating or coming in conflict with its dispositions" (Justice Taschereau, quoted in Dubé 1990, 15).

Article 6 stipulates that the minister may recommend to government the partial extension of a collective agreement "if he deems that the provisions of the agreement have acquired *a preponderant* significance and importance for the establishing of conditions of labour, without serious inconvenience resulting from the competition of outside countries or the other provinces [emphasis added]."

The criteria to be used to establish the preponderance of conditions of work to be decreed are not defined in the statute or in regulations. The Minister of Labour thus has sole discretion to evaluate the situation.

Sectors under decrees are usually characterized by the presence of a great number of small-size employers competing heavily among themselves. Thus, we find eight decrees in the clothing industry, the most important ones being in ladies' and men's clothing.

The administration of the decree is not done by a governmental agency but by the parties to the collective agreement. Articles 16 and 17 thus regulate the composition of the joint or parity committee:

> Art.16: The parties to a collective agreement rendered obligatory must form a parity committee to supervise and ensure the carrying out of the decree, its amendments and renewals.
>
> Art.17: The Minister may, at any time, upon such conditions and for such term as he deems proper, add to the committee such members, not exceeding four, as are submitted to him in equal number by the employers and employees who are not parties to the agreement.

The downsizing of production, particularly in ladies' apparel, and the drop in the unionization rate have been accompanied by an increase in the number of employers and employees covered exclusively by a decree, thereby creating the necessity of having representation from nonunionized shops. Some of these nonunion representatives are even involved in discussion pertaining to collective-agreement extension. Joint committees impose a financial levy on all employers and on all employees within their industrial jurisdiction to support their activities; the most important levy pertains to inspection.

INDUSTRIAL PEACE AND THE DECREE SYSTEM

Workers and their unions are aware of the clothing industry's predicament. More-over, both union and management are engaged in common endeavours beyond the traditional collective-bargaining forum. Participation in joint committees brings them into a common problem-solving process and is conducive to co-operative strategies and tactics. The Canadian director of the Amalgamated Clothing and Textile Workers Union (ACTWU), John Alleruzzo, stresses this point: "The parity committee has proved to be an ideal forum for a continuous dialogue . . . where management and labour can meet on a nonconfrontation basis . . . and such a rela-tionship has helped a great deal the collective bargaining process" (L'Aiguille, June–July 1985).

Joint committes have, for decades, been a permanent industrial relations fixture in the clothing industry. Depleted market conditions, the growing presence of nonunionized shops, and co-operative activities in joint committees probably account for the low level of labour strife in the garment industry. Co-operation with employers to help them meet the competition from nonunion plants was already a definite characteristic of the Amalgamated Clothing Workers in 1924 in the United States (Slichter 1941, 504). Hard times were more conducive to co-operation than to confrontation. During the slump in the clothing business in 1933:

> The policy by which the Amalgamated sought to maintain the em-ployment of its members against the competition of non-union plants had five principal parts:
> 1. The avoidance of strikes in union plants.
> 2. An attempt to organize non-union plants.
> 3. Temporary wage concessions on all rates and permanent conces-sions on specific rates.
> 4. Extension and enforcement of wage payments by results.
> 5. Abandonment of restrictive rules and policies which tended to raise the operating costs of employers and were of benefit to only small parts of the union membership. (Slichter 1941, 507)

This policy formulated by the international union still appears relevant in Quebec decades later. From the ACTWU's newspaper in the province, the aware-ness of interdependence between industrial survival and job protection is strong. The following statement does not originate from a union that has shown compla-cency toward management. In fact, despite conditions that are not conducive to strikes in the industry, the ACTWU struck in the mid-1970s and in the mid-1980s:

> Labor unions and workers should not deal with employers as belliger-ent beings continuously on the war-path but as partners jointly re-sponsible for the destiny of the same business establishment. . . . Private enterprise is the prominent producer of jobs. . . . To the pio-neers of the clothing industry in our province . . . which for more than

a century have provided jobs to many generations, we present the expression of solidarity and esteem of those who have worked as well as those who are still working in the industry (*L'Aiguille*, December 1982–January 1983).

The propensity to work stoppages[4] has been much lower in the clothing industry (3.4 percent) than in the manufacturing industry (9.4 percent). For example, when the International Ladies' Garment Workers' Union went on strike in August 1983, the previous strike had been called in 1940! The frequent work stoppages that occurred in the 1930s sought primarily to protect the existence of the union and of the collective agreement at a time when there was no labour code providing legal foundations for unions. The implementation of decrees to the clothing sectors allowed the union to concentrate on gaining recognition from employers (Copp n.d., 16–17).

The decree system came under heavy attack in 1987, when the much-publicized Scowen Report presented by business representatives appointed by the provincial government urged the latter to expand deregulation, and to thus abolish the decree system. Members of that committee were also voicing the objections of nonunionized employers in industries under decrees who increasingly resisted the extension of collective agreements to their businesses. During the months following the publication of this report, the provincial government seemed to move toward the proposal; the delays between the time deals were struck for collective-agreement extension and the times the minister gave approval were getting longer, as the government increased its attention to nonunionized employers' objections. As unionized employers had to abide by the rates stipulated in the new collective agreement, delays in extending these rates by decree increased the competitive advantage of nonunionized employers; these employers could go on implementing the lower wage schedule included in the unchanged decree during the elapsed time before the latter's renewal. Thousands of workers and union representatives marched alongside employers' representatives in the streets of Montreal in the spring of 1988 to support the decree system. It seems that this demonstration was helpful in encouraging the province to maintain the regime.

UNIONIZATION RATES

The closing of important unionized shops; the proliferation of nonunionized contractors and of homeworking, particularly in ladies' apparel; the downsizing of factories; the pressures from imports; the increasing resistance from employers to unionization—all have significantly contributed to a substantial drop in the clothing industry's unionization rate in Quebec, from 56.3 percent in 1968 to 33.3 percent in 1990 (Ministère du travail et de la main-d'oeuvre, n.d., 34; Racine 1990, 26). In the ladies' garment industry, the unionization rate was still at 50.1 percent in 1981, but fell to 24.3 percent in September 1990. That drop was caused by a reduction in the number of jobs, from 22 713 to 14 624. During that same period, the number of unionized shops in ladies' garments went from to 308 to 103, and the number of nonunionized contractors jumped from 338 to 631. In men's wear, the smaller percentage of contractors prevented a dramatic fall in the rate of unionization, which went from 60 percent in 1983 to 57 percent in September 1990.[5]

Moreover, unions have been experiencing enormous difficulties in initiating and sustaining organizational drives among nonunionized workers ever since the recession began in the early 1980s. Smaller units are also much harder to organize, and certain union representatives claim that the decree system hinders unionization because unorganized workers benefit from working conditions negotiated by the union and extended through the decree. Some labour organizers suggest that a widening gap in wages between unionized and nonunionized shops could create an incentive for workers to sign union membership cards. But, this strategy would probably be counterproductive. Because of the labour-intensive character of the industry, nonunion shops would be in a better competitive position to obtain more business, and the unionized employers would be at a competitive disadvantage because of their higher labour costs. The likely result would be the transfer of more jobs from the unionized to the nonunionized sector and a greater pressure to decrease union wages.

BARGAINING STRUCTURE AND ISSUES

As in the rest of Canada, the prevailing pattern of collective bargaining in Quebec is to negotiate at the plant level. Negotiations in the clothing industry, however, are done voluntarily, on a multi-employer basis, in both Quebec and Ontario. Workers in men's wear are represented by the Montreal Joint Board of the Amalgamated Clothing and Textile Workers Union (ACTWU). The master contract is negotiated with the following employer associations: Associated Clothing Manufacturers of the Province of Quebec; Montreal Clothing Contractors Association; Quebec Council of Odd Pants Employers. Each member authorizes his or her association, in writing, to enter into agreement on his or her behalf and accepts that the contract terms will be legally binding. Wage and other benefits for Quebec are then extended to the men's wear sector in Ontario. In ladies' clothing, the master agreement is negotiated by the Montreal Joint Board of the International Ladies' Garment Workers' Union (ILGWU) and the Quebec Fashion and Apparel Manufacturers Guild. The latter represents manufacturers, contractors, and jobbers.

Wages

In order to keep labour costs as low as possible in order to compete, the clothing industry has relied on a relatively inexpensive pool of labour, including a large proportion of immigrant women for whom the industry has been the port of entry into the labour market. Table 6.4 shows that estimated weekly earnings (including overtime) for employees paid by the hour are, relative to manufacturing, much lower in the clothing industry. Earnings in the clothing industry in December 1990 (see Table 6.4) were slightly over one-half of earnings in the manufacturing sector, and the gap seems to be widening: in January 1988, that ratio was closer to 60 percent (Statistics Canada 1988).

The general recession that Canada has suffered since autumn 1990 has brought a contraction of the domestic market, and buyers have reduced their consumption of goods produced by the garment industry. Workers in the industry face an additional dilemma. Even though they are at a disadvantage when their earnings are compared to those of other workers in the manufacturing sector, they "enjoy" a competitive disadvantage on an international basis. Table 6.5 indicates, for spring 1987, the relative position of several countries in terms of labour costs in the clothing industry. Canadian labour costs were the fourth-highest after those of Sweden, Japan, and France.

Although those numbers must be interpreted with reservation, they still eloquently illustrate the competitive advantage enjoyed by low-wage countries in a labour-intensive industry such as garments. It is not likely that, even in the long run, the labour-cost gap could be reduced significantly. The abrogation of the decree system, or even the disappearance of unions in the industry, would not substantially narrow international differentials.

Wages paid in the nonunionized sector are often effectively superior to those stipulated in the decree; decreed wages seem to address lower-paid personnel (Bellemarre 1986, 116). For example, the average hourly wage in the garment industry in 1990 was $11.17 for unionized workers and $9.14 for nonunionized workers.[6] This gap cannot be attributed to a violation of the decree provisions by employers in the nonunion sector, but rather to a different occupational distribution between the two sectors, and to the piece-rate system, which allows greater differentials between individuals and covers half the labour force in many sectors and occupations in the industry.

Piece rates are determined through bargaining in the union sector, and the procedure is grounded in the provisions of the collective agreements. Except for cutters in ladies' apparel, who are paid by the hour, employees may be paid by time-work or piece-work, and any changes made in the payment method must have the consent

Table 6.4

Estimated Weekly Earnings in the Clothing Industry, as of December 1990

	Canada	Ontario	Quebec
Manufacturing	$549.32	$563.65	$527.47
Clothing	288.03	297.01	294.80
Men's clothing	294.94	296.12	305.72
Women's clothing	NA	NA	NA
Children's clothing	266.94	NA	269.44

Source: Statistics Canada, Employment, Earnings and Hours, Catalogue 72-002 (Ottawa: Minister of Supply and Services, December 1990).

Table 6.5
Hourly Labour Costs in Selected Countries, 1987

Country	(U.S. dollars) Labour Costs	Index
Sweden	13.69	148
Japan	11.99	130
France	9.99	108
Canada	9.85	107
United States	9.24	100
United Kingdom	7.09	77
Spain	4.78	52
Venezuela	2.35	25
Taiwan	2.09	23
Hong Kong	1.93	21
South Korea	1.77	19
Mexico	.83	9
South Africa	.82	9
India	.65	7
Thailand	.58	6
Philippines	.57	6
China	.23	2

Source: Textile Asia, August 1987.

of both parties in ladies' and men's wear. The ILGWU's contract determines a price-setting procedure for piece-work rates in the making of complete garments. Article 24.01 stipulates: "Shop employees making complete garments shall, during a meeting convened at the instance of the Union, elect a Price Committee which shall settle prices with the employers for piece-work rates on all garments and new styles." For the manufacturing of section of garments, Article 25.01 indicates: "In calculating piece work rates in section work shops, management shall set piece-work rates so as to yield to the employees of average skills and ability an earning opportunity commensurate with an average hourly rate of at least twenty percent (20%) above the minimum scales provided in this agreement."

In both situations, the collective agreeement provides for binding arbitration when parties disagree on piece-rates. As in the case of the ILGWU, the ACWTU's contract guarantees that piece rates cannnot drop below the minimum wage. Article 5.1 of the collective agreement requires that: "fixing of prices for new piece-work rates . . . shall be made only through the collective bargaining between the representatives of the parties hereto." Article 5.11 seeks to protect the employee against a loss in earnings: "An employee paid on a piece rate or incentive basis who is required to wait for work due to a machine breakdown or other cause beyond his control shall be compensated at the rate of his average hourly earnings."

The decree and the collective agreements provide for *minimum* wage rates. Thus, an employer can grant rates above that minimum. The ILGWU's wage-bargaining policy for the last decade, that is, since the continuous drop in unionization rates in its sector, has focussed on trying to gain higher increases for lower-paid members. The purpose of this strategy is not only to conform to traditional egalitarian principles but, more importantly, to raise labour costs in the nonunion sector and thus prevent the transfer of jobs from the union sector to that sector. This example shows how job protection remains *the* priority, even when bargaining for better wages! Table 6.6 presents average wages in ladies' apparel for the more heavily populated occupations; the numbers are broken down according to union (U) and nonunion (NU) status.

The recourse to piece or incentive rates is often referred to as an avenue to productivity improvement. It is not, then, surprising that piece rate is so widespread in the clothing industry, and that, even for hourly paid workers, there remains a degree of flexibility in determining wages and in adapting to market forces.

Productivity and Technology

Porter (1990, 84) states that the only meaningful concept of competitiveness is *productivity*. Cline (1987, 109–10) identifies the following modes of adjustment in the clothing industry: increased scale and concentration, wage moderation, product and market shifts, foreign assembly and subcontracting, foreign investment, exit and diversification, and technical change.

The clothing industry was able to take off and develop a century ago because of federal protectionist policies. As pointed out earlier, the national policy has not produced expected results in raising significantly the level of competitiveness through greater management commitment to technological innovation. The historical trend toward the globalization of markets, of which free trade is an expression, has led the federal government to de-emphasize protectionist practices and to move toward trade liberalization. Many representatives from the industry even suspect that the Canadian government has decided to write off the garment industry. It is obvious that the industry has to increase its efforts and investments to survive in an environment that will become even more competitive. The only way to compensate for a wage disadvantage is to increase productivity, "which can be done through superior management and advanced technology" (Marshall 1987, 69). The ability of a high-wage country to compete in low-wage manufacturing industries, such as textile and clothing, "depends on producing products that cannot readily be copied in low-wage countries" (Marshall 1987, 69).

In 1981, the Canadian government created the Canadian Industrial Renewal Board with a $ 250 million budget, aimed at revitalizing and restructuring the textile and clothing industries, while the MFA was supposed to offer protection from imports and thus to create conditions conducive to industrial restructuring and to increased investments that could generate profitable returns. That program was set for five years and ended in 1986. Table 6.7 compares the evolution of the productivity index per employee and per hour of work relative to 1981.

The production of long runs has allowed greater technological changes in men's wear. Production time required for the sewing and pressing of fine clothing has dropped from 190 minutes per unit in 1960 to 110 minutes in 1990 because of the increasing production of engineered garments.

Preparing for the 1983 bargaining round, the ACTWU's director for Canada was reminding workers that the union had lost 20 percent of its members in the previous three years. He stressed that the priority had to be saving jobs. Management had asked for amendments that would allow employers to introduce new equipment without guaranteeing jobs to those affected. Members tended to perceive technological changes as a threat to jobs, while their bargaining committee saw them as a means to industrial survival in a competitive environment. Before the implementation of the new system, the collective agreement provided constraints on the introduction of technological changes by stipulating that "such changes shall not cause, directly or indirectly, a reduction in wages to the employees concerned or result in workers being thrown out of employment to the condition that such workers accept other available compatible work." The parties finally agreed upon an elaborate engineered incentive system with union involvement at the shop level. To increase productivity and, consequently, to improve competitiveness, the union agreed to remove harsher restrictions on management rights to introduce technological changes. Article 6.21 ultimately acknowledges that job termination can occur following the introduction of said changes:

> The Employer shall assign the employees affected (unless they are eligible for pension or unless they accept prepension), according to level of skill, productivity, adaptability, capacity to meet the normal requirements of the job and seniority, either to the newly introduced or changed machinery or to a substantially equivalent operation with the opportunity for substantially equivalent earnings. If such job assignment is not available, then the employee shall be assigned to any other available job. If no other such job is available or accepted, the Employer shall proceed with the termination of employment. Any retraining period shall be determined by mutual agreement but will not exceed four (4) weeks.

Table 6.7
Productivity Index (April 1988)
(1981 = 100)

	Per Employee	Per Hour of Work
Manufacturing	122.3	108.3
Textile	121.5	118.1
Clothing	103.7	118.8

Source: Commission du textile et du vêtement, *Rapport sur les textiles et les vêtements 1988* (Ottawa: 1989), 9.

The collective agreement stipulates, in Article 6.22, that employees for whom employment is terminated are to receive a "technological change indemnity"; the amount varies according to seniority. Outside observers not familiar with the crisis the industry has been experiencing may suggest that the union caved in. This opinion does not take into consideration actual market pressures causing plant closures and the prospect for more extensive job losses if firms are not allowed to adopt the appropriate measures in improving their production methods.

Article 6.3 stipulates that the proposed system be defined in accordance with established engineering practices in the industry and conform to decree minimums plus 10 percent for a complete performance by the employee. New rates can be challenged by the union and are arbitrable. Article 6.13 provides that "where a plant applies an engineered incentive system, it is understood that the union shall employ accepted engineered practices applicable to the case to resolve differences which may arise."

Article 6.7 states that a piece rate is subject to change when there is a change in machinery, method of production or technology, or any other element upon which the rate or standard is based; such change may include, among other things, job content or volume, machine pace or cycle, and equipment. Workers who are red-circled under the new system are eligible for subsidies that are gradually phased out as general wage increases are implemented in accordance with the collective agreement.

This collective agreement article was not an "easy sell" to the members, and the union spokesman told the members that it was better to negotiate technological change or re-engineering of a shop than to confront closure (*L'Aiguille*, July 1984). Summing up the impact of the new system three years later, the Canadian director recalled that it was accepted with a lot of criticism and skepticism. Twenty shops were applying the engineered incentive system, and all shops had witnessed an increase in hourly earnings of workers and, contrary to shops with traditional systems, an increase in the number of employees (*L'Aiguille*, April–May 1986).

Traditional piece-rate systems link remuneration to performance and may increase productivity. But the ACTWU went further in designing, with management, a scheme involving industrial restructuring. This approach can be enforced in an environment where the organization and the length of production runs permit mechanization, and where the union experiences substantial losses in membership. Even though those reforms will make the Quebec men's wear industry more competitive with industrialized countries, as well as with other Canadian provinces, they cannot counter the very low wage factors in the newly industrialized countries (Canadian Apparel Manufacturers Institute 1988, 1).

Unionized Job Protection

We have seen that a collective agreement can contain proactive measures designed to protect, and even to create jobs. The importance of outsourcing to contractors and to homeworkers has led unions to adopt protective measures in collective agreements and in decrees. Agreements in both ladies' and men's wear included closed shops, that is, where a worker is a member of the union *before* he or she is hired through the union hall. This procedure is to be found in industries, such as garments, where production is organized on a craft basis.

Both master agreements provide that, unless permitted by the union, employers cannot send work out to contractors when their own employees are not working full time. Manufacturers may use the services of contractors, under circumstances stipulated in the agreement, if they are unionized. This implementation of the contracting-out provisions is particularly difficult to apply in ladies' garments because of the increasing number of contractors during the 1980s, and because of the number of unionized manufacturers that have closed down. Moreover, the increasing downsizing of units and the short career of many contractors in the industry make union control extremely difficult.

Collective agreements in men's wear and in ladies' wear prohibit homework. Homework in men's clothing is much less important because the greater degree of mechanization does not render it practical or profitable. The decree in the men's clothing industry also prohibits homework, but the decree in ladies' garment allows it, if it is reported to the joint committee by the employer, who must conform to decreed rates. The Decree Respecting the Women's Clothing Industry provides that "no homework shall be given to a shop employee who already works in an establishment governed by this Decree." This means that a former employee could work at home—a situation that is theoretically possible—but most homework done by former factory employees is unreported, despite decreed provisions.

For section work in the ladies' garment, where the sewing machine is the standard piece of equipment, homework is a sensible alternative for contractors trying to reduce their labour costs. The greater variety in styles and shorter delivery schedules do not encourage longer production runs in ladies' clothing and investments in technology. Only 600 homeworkers were reported at the Joint Committee in 1990, and 400 were identified as homeworking on a casual basis. Work usually lands in homes through contractors, subcontractors, or jobbers. As mentioned before, an estimated 20 000 or more homeworkers manufactured ladies' wear in 1982 (Rose and Grant 1983). Those women were paid at piece rates below the decree provisions and both the legal minimum wage law in the province. The structure of employment and the organization of production in the industry have always been ideally suited to a shift from the open to the hidden economy (Miller 1986, 44). As Johnson and Johnson (1982, 102) points out:

> The employment of homeworkers in Canada is subject to regulation by provincial employment standards legislation. But the combination of a high proportion of employers who ignore requirements for registration of homeworkers and the failure of governments to impose fines or other penalties on employers . . . means that the practice of homework is, for the most part, unregulated.

This situation presents a great challenge because homework is situated outside the realm of labour–management relations within the shop context, thus raising the problem of control, as well as contributing to the transfer of jobs from the union sector to an unregulated sector.

Conclusions

More than anywhere else, industrial relations issues in the clothing industry are determined by the crisis suffered in the industry over the previous ten years. The overwhelming pressures of domestic and foreign competition, particularly from low-wage countries, have not been conducive to industrial restructuring and technological dissemination. Gloomy market prospects cannot generate long-term investment prospects that would increase productivity and competitiveness. We have seen, in the men's wear sector, for instance, that union resistance to technological changes is not a fundamental obstacle. On the contrary, the ACTWU's leadership has demonstrated support for those managerial strategies that would revitalize the industry and thus allow it to survive and maintain a certain level of employment.

The legal and institutional arrangements in the clothing industry have generated a high degree of industrial peace and have fostered co-operative attitudes and tactics. Unfortunately, those conditions were not sufficient to overcome other challenges of a hostile environment. The organization of production and the industry's labour-intensive features provide short-term opportunities to gain a partial competitive advantage. In the ladies' garments sector, the adaptative measures adopted by employers to cut costs include increasing the decentralization of production by outsourcing to contractors and to homeworkers. The continuous downsizing of production units has made it extremely difficult for the ILGWU to control the provisions of the collective agreement relative to the prohibition of contracting-out and of homework.

In addition to market pressures that intensified during the 1980s, in January 1991 garments became subject to the the 7 percent Goods and Services Tax and to a 8 percent provincial tax from which it had been exempt for many years in Quebec. Considering that consumers first reduce their expenses for clothing in recession periods, the combination of the growing liberalization of trade and of less protectionist federal policies can only render more pessimistic and more insecure employers, unions, and their members. We have seen that employees' earnings in the clothing industry are among the lowest among manufacturing industries. One cannot expect the union to allow working conditions to worsen and to reach the minimum legal standards without putting its own credibility in question. Moreover, the legal minimum standard for wages remains substantially superior to that of low-wage countries; as a result, even if Canadian employers had to abide by those standards, the labour-cost advantage of newly industrialized countries would not be significantly hampered.

The survival of employers and workers in the apparel industry depends on the ability of employers and unions to obtain government support for industrial restructuring and professional training. Conditions must be established so that employers are encouraged to make strong financial commitments to technological innovation and product specialization. Unions are very much aware that their own future is intimately connected with industrial survival, and that such survival can be achieved only through greater competitiveness and greater productivity.

Management and unions in the clothing industry were successful at the end of the 1980s in resisting the winds of deregulation aimed at the abrogation of the decree system. This system could, however, disappear if the unionization rates continue to decline. The task ahead is difficult, and the challenges involved lie both at and beyond the bargaining table. Managers and unions must convincingly express their will to revitalize and restructure the industry, and governments must be aware that a lack of support for the industry will incur economic, social, and political costs.

REFERENCES

Bellemarre, Guy. 1986. "L'impact économique de l'application des décrets au Québec: relevé critique des principales études empiriques." In Jean Bernier, *L'extension juridique des conventions collectives au Québec*. Quebec: Commission consultative sur le travail. 105–16.

Canadian Apparel Manufacturers Institute. 1988. *Brief to the Advisory Council on Adjustment from the Canadian Manufacturers Institute*. May 9.

Cline, William R. 1987. *The Future of World Trade in Textiles and Apparel*, Washington, DC: Institute for International Economics.

Copp, Terry. n.d. *La formation des syndicats industriels à Montréal de 1935 à 1945*.

Coyle, Angela. 1982. "Sex and Skill in the Organisation of the Clothing Industry." In Jackie West, ed., *Work, Women and the Labour Market*. London: Routledge and Kegan Paul. 10–26.

Dubé, Jean-Louis, 1990. *Décrets et comités paritaires*, Sherbrooke: Les Editions Revue de droit, Université de Sherbrooke.

Grant, Michel, and Ruth Rose, 1985. "L'encadrement du travail à domicile dans l'industrie du vêtement au Québec," *Relations Industrielles/Industrial Relations*, 40/3: 473–94.

International Ladies' Garment Workers' Union. 1981. *Statement of the ILGWU in Opposition to the Removal of Restriction on Industrial Work, before the US Department of Labor, Employment and Standards Administration, Wage and Hours Division*.

——. 1988. *Conditions in the Women's Garment Industry*. New York: June 21.

Johnson, Laura C., and Robert E. Johnson. 1982. *The Seam Allowance*. Toronto: Women's Educational Press.

Kurt Salmon Associates Inc. 1984. *Report on Technology versus Imports for the Sub-committee on Technology of the Lumley Task Force on the Canadian Textile and Clothing Industries*.

Marshall, Ray. 1987. *Unheard Voices*. New York, Basic Books.

Matthews, Roy A. 1983. *Canada and the Little Dragons*. Montreal: The Institute for Research on Public Policy.

Miller, Swasti. 1986. "Industrial Restructuring and Manufacturing Homework: Immigrant Women in the UK Clothing Industry," *Capital and Class*, 27: 37–80.

Phizacklea, Annie. 1990. *Unpacking the Fashion Industry*. London: Routledge and Kegan Paul.

Porter, Michael. 1980. *Competitive Strategy*. New York, The Free Press.

——. 1990. "The Competitive Advantage of Nations." 90/2 *Harvard Business Review*, 73–93.

Racine, France. 1990. "La Syndicalisation au Québec," *Le Marché du Travail*, 11/12: 21–28

Robert, Denis. 1989. *L'ajustement structurel et le fédéralisme canadien: Le cas de l'industrie du textile et du vêtement*. Kingston, ON: Institute of Intergovernmental Relations, Queen's University.

Rose, Ruth, and Michel Grant. 1983. *Le travail à domicile dans l'industrie du vêtement au Québec*. Montreal: Protocole UQAM–FTQ.

Seward, Shirley B. 1990. *Challenges of Labour Adjustment: The Case of Immigrant Women in the Clothing Industry*, Discussion Paper 90.B.1. Ottawa: The Institute for Research on Public Policy.

Slichter, Sumner H. 1941. *Union Policies and Industrial Management*. Washington, DC: The Brookings Institution.

Statistics Canada. 1988. *Employment, Earnings and Hours*, Catalogue 72–002. Ottawa: Minister of Supply and Services, April.

Waldinger, Roger D. 1986. *Through the Eye of the Needle: Immigrants and Enterprise in New York's Garment Trades*. New York: New York University Press.

ENDNOTES

1. The author wishes to express his appreciation to the following persons whose contribution and help were essential in preparing this essay on the clothing industry: John Alleruzzo, Canadian Director of the Amalgamated Clothing and Textile Workers Union; Sydney Cohen, Executive Director, Men's Clothing Manufacturers Association Inc.; Daniel Dubuc, Executive Director, Ladies' Clothing Joint Commission; Jésus Falcon, Vice-president, Quebec Joint Council of the International Ladies' Garment Workers' Union; Jacques Mossé, Executive Director, Men's Clothing Parity Committee. The author remains, however, solely and exclusively responsible for the content of this essay.

2. Information obtained from the Ontario Ministry of Labour. The dates in parentheses indicate the time of the last amendments brought to the schedules.

3. The following sectors are under decrees: bread distributors in the Montreal region; building materials industry; building service employees in the Montreal region; building service employees in the Quebec City region; cartage industry in the Montreal region; casket industry; corrugated paper industry; flat glass industry; furniture industry; garage employees in nine different regions, with each one having its own decree; hairdressers in five different regions, with each one having its own decree; handbag industry; installation of petroleum equipment; leather glove industry; men's and boys' shirt industry; men's clothing industry; metal trades industry in the Montreal and Quebec City regions, with each region having its own decree; musicians in the Montreal region; nonstructural metal work industry in the Montreal region; paper box industry; security guards; solid waste removal in the Montreal region; wholesale fur industry in the Montreal region; women's clothing industry; women's millinery industry; woodworking industry.

4. Propensity to work stoppages is a measure of the ratio of all work stoppages, including strikes and lockouts, to all collective agreements. Our data covers all work stoppages and all signed collective agreements under the Quebec labour jurisduction between April 1983 and December 1989. The total number of stoppages for that period was 1331, and the number of collective agreements 16 258, thus a proportion of 8.2 percent for the general population.

5. The respective unionization rates for ladies' and men's wear was provided by the respective joint committees.

6. These data were supplied by the ILGWU.

Chapter

7

LABOUR RELATIONS IN THE CANADIAN TEXTILE INDUSTRY

Terry Thomason
Harris L. Zwerling
Pankaj Chandra[1]

*D*ating from as early as 4000 B.C., the manufacture of textiles is an ancient industry, which played an instrumental role in the inauguration of the Industrial Revolution.[2] As such, textile fabrication is commonly perceived to be a mature industry, with a relatively static technology. However, the past four decades have witnessed significant advances with respect to both textile products and the manufacturing process. This recent progress was provoked, in part, by heightened competitive pressure from low-wage manufacturers located in newly industrializing nations. Since the Second World War, increased import penetration has induced a major restructuring of the Canadian textile industry. The result has been long-term reductions in employment, a trend that may continue or even accelerate in the wake of the recent abatement of trade barriers and further adoption of labour-saving technology. Canadian textile manufacturers have been forced to alter their product-market positions through mergers, foreign acquisitions, and the rationalization of domestic operations. Domestic operations have been streamlined through a combination of plant closings and investment in labour-saving technologies.

Global competition and increased mechanization have had two related impacts on textile labour relations. First, while traditionally one of the most conflict-ridden industries in North America, for the past twenty years, industry labour relations have been relatively pacific; the threat of foreign competition has led to joint efforts to influence Canada's international trade policy, which have established a pattern of labour–management co-operation in the industry. Second, the textile labour movement, historically divided among three unions, has become increasingly weak and fragmented in recent years. Labour has been forced to accept the necessity of restructuring within the industry and concomitant job loss; textile unions have acted more as observers than participants in this process. Their efforts have primarily been limited to ameliorating the ill effects of rationalization. Consequently, the collective-bargaining agenda is limited to the same bread-and-butter issues that have been negotiated for the past 30 years.

The remainder of this essay is divided into four sections. In the first, we discuss the basic economic dimensions of the industry, including its size, location, scale, and profitability; characteristics of the labour market; the impact of government trade and industrial policy; and, finally, recent technological developments, trends in capital investment, and productivity. A brief history of textile labour relations is presented in the second section. The third section reviews the current state of industry labour relations, including union density, the strike record, the bargaining structure, and the bargaining agenda. The final section contains our conclusions and predictions concerning the future of labour relations in the industry.

*I*ndustry Overview

*T*he textile industry encompasses a number of distinct manufacturing processes producing a wide variety of goods. These processes and products are partitioned into two major groups by the Standard Industrial Classification System: primary textiles and textile products. Primary-textiles manufacturers include those engaged in the production of fibres, yarns, and fabrics. Goods produced by establishments in the textile-products group include carpet, mats, and rugs; braids, laces, labels, cords, and ribbons; canvas and related products, including awnings, canopies, tents, and canvas bags; household products, such as blankets, towels, and curtains; hygiene products, such as dressing and bandages, sanitary napkins, diapers, and surgical gauze; tire cord fabrics; and other textile products, such as twine, fire hose, flags, hammocks, and tassels. Also included within the textile-products category are dyeing and finishing firms, as well as firms engaged in natural-fibre processing and the manufacture of felt products. Natural-fibre processing includes the preparation of natural fibres for spinning and the processing of textile waste.

Textiles have experienced a long-term decline in significance in the Canadian economy, partially because textile consumption has not increased proportionately with increased income, and partially because foreign competitors have captured a substantial share of the Canadian market. In 1950, textile industry production was valued at approximately $741 million, representing about 5.4 percent of all manufacturing shipments; in 1986, textile manufacturers produced nearly $7 billion, accounting for approximately 2.3 percent of total manufacturing shipments.

Between 1930 and 1945, the import penetration ratio for all textile products fluctuated between 18 and 23 percent of the domestic market (National Industrial
Conference Board 1956); since that time, it has increased dramatically.

Panel A of Table 7.1 reports data with respect to recent trends in Canada's international textile trade. Overall, these data indicate a substantial trade deficit in
textiles throughout the period, which grew from over $1.6 billion in 1975 (in
1981 constant dollars) to almost $2.1 billion in 1988. The higher deficit is princi-
pally a result of the expansion of the Canadian market, which grew at about 2.6
percent annually during the period. This growth has accelerated since 1983, increasing about 4 percent annually. Data further suggest that foreign producers
have increasingly penetrated the Canadian market, while Canadian manufacturers
have likewise been successful in expanding their export market.

Data in Panel B of Table 7.1 show that there is substantial variation between
subsectors with respect to both market size and international trade. For example,
while industry shipments were approximately equally divided between primary
textiles and textile products in 1986, foreign manufacturers controlled nearly 40
percent of the Canadian primary-textiles market but less than 30 percent of textile products. Sectoral variation in production and imports may be attributed, in
part, to two complementary trends: (1) increased domestic production of capital-
intensive, high-value-added product lines, and (2) increased import penetration
of low-value-added lines (Ahmad 1988).

INDUSTRY STRUCTURE

In 1986, there were 1096 establishments engaged in textile manufacture; 214 of
these were primary-textile firms, and 882 were in the textile-products sector.
While, on average, these establishments employed approximately 54 workers, this
figure is somewhat misleading. The largest 100 firms accounted for the bulk of industry production. Over 76 percent of textile plants employ fewer than 50 workers, but account for only 15 percent of total textile production, while less than 7
percent employ more than 200 employees and account for nearly 50 percent of total production. Finally, historical data reveal that, while per-establishment employment has declined in recent years, production scale has increased. Average
employment fell from approximately 75 employees in 1975 to 54 in 1986; during
this same period, the value of shipments per establishment increased by 15.9 percent, from $4.4 million to $5.1 million in 1981 constant dollars.

Ownership in certain subsectors is highly concentrated. Data from 1980 indicate that cotton yarn and cloth mills, man-made-fibre and filament plants, automobile fabric firms, thread mills, and cordage and twine firms were all closely
held, with at least 70 percent of domestic production controlled by the four leading enterprises in the sector. Data also indicate that primary-textile ownership
has become increasingly concentrated in recent years, as industry restructuring
and rationalization have eliminated smaller producers. Dominion Textile, the
largest firm in the industry, has been particularly active in this trend toward

Table 7.1
Shipments, Exports, and Imports, 1975–1988[a]

Year	Canadian Shipments	Exports	Domestic Shipments	Imports	Apparent Canadian Market (AMC)	Exports/ Canadian Shipments (%)	Imports/ AMC (%)
			Panel A: Total Industry (1986 Constant Dollars)				
1975	4433.9	193.0	4240.9	1815.4	6056.3	4.4	30.0
1980	5099.6	428.3	4671.3	1828.9	6500.2	8.4	28.1
1981	5146.6	472.2	4674.4	1847.7	6522.1	9.2	28.3
1982	4353.6	426.1	3927.5	1493.7	5431.2	9.8	27.6
1983	5104.9	419.3	4685.6	1848.7	6534.3	8.2	28.3
1984	5102.5	471.1	4631.4	2138.9	6770.3	9.2	31.6
1985	5140.2	507.7	4632.5	2335.9	6968.4	9.9	33.5
1986	5585.8	559.5	5026.3	2553.7	7580.0	10.0	33.7
1987	5970.5	645.3	5325.2	2777.5	8102.7	10.8	34.3
1988	6029.9	843.2	5186.7	2899.5	8086.2	14.0	35.9
			Panel B: By Subsector, 1988 (Current Dollars)				
Synthetic fibres	974	274	700	368	1068	28.1	34.5
Wool yarn & cloth	406	52	354	188	542	12.8	34.7
Other spun yarn	1418	163	1255	1075	2330	11.5	46.1
Broad knit. fabric	513	8	505	124	629	1.6	19.7

Table 7.1 (continued)

Year	Canadian Shipments	Exports	Domestic Shipments	Imports	Apparent Canadian Market (AMC)	Exports/ Canadian Shipments (%)	Imports/ AMC (%)
Primary Textiles	3311	497	2814	1755	4569	15.0	38.4
Nat. fibres & felts	142	49	93	145	238	34.5	60.9
Carpet, mat, & rug	1083	90	993	227	1220	8.3	18.6
Canvas & related	152	3	149	24	173	2.0	13.9
Narrow fabric	132	7	125	60	185	5.3	32.4
Dyeing & finishing	214	0	0	0	214	0	0
Household products	586	105	481	192	673	17.9	28.5
Hygiene products	386	12	374	22	396	3.1	5.6
Other textiles	658	102	556	263	819	15.5	32.1
Textile Products	3353	367	2986	933	3919	10.9	23.8

Note: [a] Due to changes in the Standard Industrial Classification, the data reported for years prior to 1983 are not fully compatible with the data reported in 1983 and thereafter. In 1988, industrial and trade statistics were collected on the basis of a new product classification, resulting in another break in historical continuity.

Sources: Statistics Canada, *Manufacturing Industries of Canada: National and Provincial Areas*, Catalogue 31–203 (Ottawa: Minister of Supply and Services Canada, various years).

Textile, Clothing, and Footwear Directorate; Service Industries and Consumer Goods Branch; Industry, Science, and Technology Canada. January 1990. Textile Industry Statistical Data. Ottawa. Mimeo.

consolidation. In 1985, the firm purchased Wabasso Inc., a bedding and towel manufacturer and the second-largest Canadian firm in the primary-textiles sector (Hunter 1985); in 1990, the company bought Textiles Dionne Inc., a Quebec yarn manufacturer and the ninth-largest Canadian textile producer (Dominion Textile 1990).

There is also evidence that some Canadian firms are increasing their foreign-investment portfolios. In 1975, Dominion Textile became the sixth-largest textile producer in North America when it purchased DHJ Inc. of New York (Colgan 1985). More recently, the company unsuccessfully attempted to take over Burlington Industries, Inc., an American company with assets approximately three times greater than those of Dominion Textile. The takeover would have given Dominion Textile control over 30 percent of the U.S. denim market (Gray 1987).[3] Foreign plants, which accounted for 40 percent of Dominion Textile's sales in 1985 and 60 percent of their income (Bell 1988), accounted for nearly 70 percent of sales and 85 percent of income in 1990 (Dominion Textile 1990). Indications are that this trend will continue; in response to a government proposal to cut tariffs, company president Charles Hantho said that "if the Canadian government provides less protection against non-U.S. imports than the American government, our obligations to our shareholders will force us to consider increasing future investments in the United States rather than in Canada in order to serve the emerging FTA North American market" (Enchin 1989). Furthermore, former company president Thomas Bell told shareholders at the 1988 annual meeting that Dominion Textile would be increasing its position in the Third World through joint ventures and importing–exporting services (Enchin 1988).

The industry has displayed considerable and growing financial strength throughout the 1980s. Return on investment (the ratio of after-tax profits to equity) ranged between a low of 1.7 percent in 1982 to 13.8 percent in 1988, averaging 10.4 percent annually during the period 1978–87, compared to 10.3 percent for all Canadian manufacturers. At the same time, the ratio of long-term debt to equity for textile firms fell from 28.83 percent in 1981 to 13.61 percent in 1988. In comparison, the ratio of long-term debt to equity for all manufacturing firms declined from 31.53 to 26.22 percent during that same period.

THE TEXTILE LABOUR FORCE

Canadian textile manufacturers have tended to locate in rural, relatively isolated areas with a large and comparatively unskilled work force that has few alternative employment opportunities. Location decisions were influenced by two factors: first, proximity to water, which provided power to the mills, and, second, a low-wage strategy. In addition, as indicated previously, the implementation of labour-saving technology and the pressures of international competition have induced a rationalization of the industry, which has led to a reduction in employment from more than 80 000 in 1950 to a little more than 60 000 today.

Nearly 95 percent of industry employment is located within Quebec and

Ontario. Furthermore, while textiles represent a more significant portion of Quebec's manufacturing base, there has been a steady migration of textile employment from Quebec to Ontario since 1961. In addition, there are substantial sectoral differences between the two provinces; in general, Ontario firms are in high-value-added sectors, whereas Quebec firms continue to service the apparel industry with lower-value-added product lines. Man-made fibre production is located primarily in Ontario. In contrast, a larger share of wool yarn and cloth manufacture is located in Quebec, as is the manufacture of spun yarn, broad knitted fabrics, and narrow fabrics, and the dyeing and finishing sector.

Within both provinces, the industry is concentrated in small to mid-size cities, where it often dominates the economic life of the community.[4] However, the importance of textiles for these communities may be diminishing as their economies diversify. For example, in Magog, textile employment as a share of all manufacturing activity declined 10.7 percentage points, from 80.5 percent in 1971 to 69.8 percent in 1981. The trend toward diversification creates nontextile employment alternatives, putting upward pressure on textile wages.

The textile industry has traditionally employed a larger proportion of women than have manufacturing industries generally. Census data show that more than 75 percent of these women are married. In addition, 1981 Census data indicate that the work force is low-skilled and relatively uneducated,[5] suggesting that the textile work force is relatively immobile, with few alternatives outside the industry, a claim frequently asserted to justify the necessity of special adjustment assistance measures. However, there are indications that recent technological change has raised skill requirements: labour-saving technology has eliminated many unskilled positions, while computer technology and an emphasis on flexibility in manufacturing have increased the complexity of many of remaining jobs (Bailey 1988; Employment and Immigration Canada 1988).

Table 7.2 presents wage rates and labour-cost data. Column IX shows that the wage rate for textile production workers has averaged between 73 and 81 percent of the manufacturing wage rate. Column III shows that real wages for textile production workers declined during the 1980s, as they did for Canadian manufacturing as a whole. Other data suggest that fringe benefits represent a smaller portion of total labour costs for textile firms than for other manufacturing industries (Courchene 1989): in 1989, fringes accounted for 29.4 percent of gross payroll for textile employers, compared to 32.2 percent for all manufacturers. At the same time, the ratio of wage and salary costs to the value of shipments in the textile industry, although declining from 1955 to 1986, was consistently higher than that for other manufacturing industries.

TRADE POLICY AND TEXTILES

Two events have dominated the development of the Canadian textile industry in recent years: the penetration of domestic markets by foreign producers, particularly those from low-wage countries, and the implementation of high-capital, process-

Table 7.2
Textile Employment, Wages, and Salaries, 1955–1986[a]

Year	Total Textile Employees	Textile Prod. Workers' Hourly Wage (Curr. $)	Textile Prod. Workers' Hourly Wage (1986 $)	Textile Admin. Employee Annual Salary (Curr. $)	Textile Admin. Employee Annual Salary (1986 $)	Textile Labour Costs As Share of Shipments %	All Mfg Prod. Workers' Hourly Wage (1986 $)	All Mfg Admin. Employee Annual Salary (1986 $)	Hourly Wage Textiles/ All Mfg %
	I	II	III	IV	V	VI	VII	VIII	IX
1955	69 144	1.12	5.22	4 027	18 739	25.6	6.46	18 568	80.9
1960	61 756	1.35	5.72	4 997	21 121	25.5	7.24	21 938	79.0
1965	76 676	1.66	6.48	6 068	23 676	24.7	8.21	24 132	79.0
1970	69 714	2.34	7.57	8 279	26 749	24.9	9.55	28 407	79.3
1975	71 030	3.74	8.47	12 262	27 805	25.2	11.01	31 340	77.0
1976	68 209	4.30	9.08	14 052	29 639	25.3	11.65	32 597	78.0
1977	65 514	4.80	9.38	15 374	30 029	24.6	12.00	32 861	78.3
1978	67 808	5.21	9.34	16 489	29 559	24.0	11.82	32 260	79.1
1979	69 217	5.76	9.46	18 196	29 889	22.7	11.82	32 324	80.1
1980	68 241	6.41	9.56	20 079	29 929	22.7	11.89	32 431	80.4
1981	67 493	7.00	9.28	22 380	29 653	21.8	11.81	32 236	78.6
1982	59 416	7.52	8.99	24 619	29 439	23.2	11.74	32 361	76.6
1983	60 790	7.65	8.65	26 439	29 883	21.7	11.87	32 793	72.9
1984	60 072	8.08	8.75	28 359	30 702	22.1	11.87	33 255	73.8
1985	57 868	8.56	8.91	30 327	31 570	22.6	11.84	34 133	75.3
1986	59 189	8.82	8.82	32 204	32 204	21.7	11.61	34 272	76.0

Note: [a] Due to changes in data collection methodology and the Standard Industrial Classification in 1969, 1970, and 1983, the data are inconsistent over time. See note in Table 7.1.

Source: Statistics Canada, *Manufacturing Industries of Canada: National and Provincial Areas*, Catalogue 31–203 (Ottawa: Minister of Supply and Services Canada, various years).

based technologies. Taken together, these events led to a restructuring and ratio-nalization of the industry and, consequently, a reduction in industry employment. The threat of foreign competition in the 1960s was at least partially responsible for unprecedented labour–management co-operation efforts, discussed later in this chapter. These co-operative efforts provided the impetus for government initiatives that shaped the course of rationalization and industry development.

High tariffs and other trade barriers implemented in the Great Depression re-duced the flow of imports to approximately 20 percent of the domestic market, a reduction that lasted until the end of the Second World War (National Industrial Conference Board 1956). However, the 1947 General Agreement on Tariffs and Trade (GATT) inaugurated a new era of international trade liberalization. By the mid-1950s, despite relatively high tariffs, Canadian textile and clothing manufac-turers began to experience an erosion of domestic markets attributable to in-creased imports from low-wage manufacturers in newly industrializing nations such as Japan and Hong Kong. Led by the United States, industrialized nations re-sponded to this import surge by negotiating the Long-Term Cotton Arrangement (LTA) in 1962. The LTA was a multilateral agreement that permitted importing na-tions experiencing "market disruption" because of cotton textile imports to unilat-erally limit imports without compensatiing exporting nations.[6]

By 1970, Canada had negotiated bilateral export-restraint agreements with sev-enteen importing nations under the terms of the LTA. Nevertheless, these agree-ments failed to reduce significantly the flow of low-cost imports. Dissatisfaction led to the joint submission of a report requesting a trade policy to reduce import levels through quotas by the textile unions and the industry trade association, the Canadian Textiles Institute (CTI). The result was the introduction of a national textile policy in 1971.

The 1971 textile policy had the objective of providing "a sense of direction and conditions within which the textile and clothing industries can plan, invest, and develop with a greater degree of confidence."[7] A twofold approach was used. First, the policy sought to provide temporary protection from imports when those im-ports "cause or threaten to cause serious injury to the production in Canada of any textile and clothing goods." An independent administrative body, the Textile and Clothing Board (TCB), was established to investigate the effects of imports on Canadian textile and clothing production. Unlike the situation prior to 1971, do-mestic manufacturers were able to initiate TCB inquiries that could result in rec-ommendations that the government negotiate a voluntary export-restraint agreement or impose a unilateral quota. Second, the policy attempted to encour-age the adjustment of Canadian manufacturers and their workers to international competition. Adjustment assistance to firms took two forms: (1) programs de-signed to aid industry restructuring and rationalization through the provision of funds for the expansion and modernization of capital equipment, and (2) programs to develop and strengthen domestic producers' export capabilities.[8]

Recent years have seen the progressive liberalization of textile trade policy. This trend is, in part, the result of a deterioration of domestic apparel producers' market position following removal of global quotas in 1978, as well as the relative strength of the domestic textile industry. As previously noted, textile firms showed considerable and increasing financial strength during the 1980s. By 1975, import penetration in textiles had stabilized at approximately 30 percent. Based on these data, policy makers argued that the textile industry no longer needed the same level of trade protection it had previously enjoyed. However, from 1979 to 1985, apparel imports increased from about 30 to over 40 percent of the domestic market. Since apparel manufacturers are consumers of textiles, clothing firms incur higher raw material costs when textiles are protected from foreign competition. Policy makers claimed, therefore, that the declining apparel industry could be aided through a reduction of textile tariffs.

In 1988, the Canadian government introduced a trade program that substantially favoured apparel manufacturers at the expense of textiles (Jennish 1988). The 1988 policy had three components, including tariff reductions on certain textile items not made in Canada, duty remissions, and a study of textile tariffs intended to reduce textile tariffs to levels comparable with those of other industrialized nations.[9] On January 1, 1989, the Canada–U.S. Free Trade Agreement (FTA) came into effect, further derogating textile protection. The FTA introduced a phased elimination of tariffs on trade in textiles between Canada and the United States over a ten-year period. On that same date, the TCB was dissolved, and its functions, along with the functions of the Tariff Board and the Canadian Import Tribunal, were assumed by a new agency, the Canadian Import Trade Tribunal (CITT). This latter event was significant since the TCB had long been seen as subservient to textile interests (Mahon 1984). Finally, in February 1990, the CITT issued a report that found that Canadian textile tariffs were substantially higher compared to other industrialized nations;[10] it recommended across-the-board tariff reductions upon completion of the Uruguay Round of GATT negotiations.[11]

TEXTILE TECHNOLOGY

While basic manufacturing processes date back to ancient times, the textile industry has undergone tremendous technological change in recent years, including product advances, such as the use of high-polymer chemistry in the development of new fibres, and process changes, such as the utilization of microcomputers for production control. These developments have begun to transform the industry from one that is low-technology and labour-intensive into a process-based, technologically intensive sector.

In turn, these technological changes have transformed the market environment. Product life cycles have become shorter as firms introduce new products at an increasing rate, a problem exacerbated by the industry's vulnerability to the whims of fashion. In this environment, firms compete on the basis of quality, product diversity, and quick response to markets. Production management is now seen as a source of competitive advantage for manufacturers. In other words, markets created by technological innovation are forcing firms to institute more "flexible" manufacturing systems.

Industry technological developments have taken two forms. Innovation prior to the mid-1980s principally involved improvements in machine speed and the elimination of labour inputs. Two examples are open-end spinning and the shuttleless loom. Open-end machines are up to four times faster than the ring-spinning machines that they have substantially replaced. In addition, open-end spinning simplifies production, reducing the number of discrete production stages and, consequently, labour input. Shuttleless looms are both faster and able to weave wider fabrics, thereby increasing effective speed. More recently, the industry has witnessed the introduction of microelectronic computer technology. Computers were first used to monitor production performance; more recently, they have been utilized in production control and as a means of integrating design and manufacturing. Both computer-aided design (CAD) and computer-aided manufacturing (CAM) have shortened design-to-production time, allowing the firm to quickly respond to market shifts. These systems have only recently been introduced into the industry, however; it is unclear whether textile firms have yet to take full advantage of this new technology.

INVESTMENT IN TECHNOLOGY

To sustain current market share, Canadian textile firms must compete on the bases of quality, delivery, and flexibility, which are a function of improved technology. One factor that may impede Canadian textile competitiveness is the absence of a domestic textile machinery industry. There are practically no manufacturers of textile machinery and equipment in Canada; nearly all machinery is imported from abroad. Several major competitor nations in textiles, such as Japan and some European countries, are also the primary innovators and producers of textile machinery. Because of their proximity to machinery manufacturers, textile firms in those countries have the opportunity to develop significant links with those suppliers, which allow them to make process enhancements more rapidly and, consequently, to generate better and more diverse products. In addition, close co-operation between textile makers and machinery suppliers permits the simultaneous development of new products and processes, reducing the time required to introduce new products into the market.

Table 7.3 shows that total capital expenditure (excluding repair) increased by almost 30 percent in constant 1981 dollars from 1980 to 1988. Most of this increase (81 percent) purchased enhanced productivity (machinery and equipment) rather than increased capacity (construction). The industry modernized rapidly during this period, with total capital and repair expenditures of $2.56 billion in constant 1981 dollars. Surveys of textile firms in 1980 and 1984 show that firms substantially invested in newer, process-based technologies, such as shuttleless looms and open-end spinning (Textile and Clothing Board 1981; 1985). In part, the modernization of the industry was supported by Canadian Industrial Renewal

Table 7.3
Textile Industry Capital and Repair Expenditures and Productivity, 1982–1988 (millions—of 1981 dollars)

	1982	1983	1984	1985	1986	1987	1988
Panel A: Capital Expenditures							
Construction	20.8	22.7	22.9	23.6	28.7	26.6	31.2
Machinery & Equipment	114.9	120.4	146.3	156.8	192.7	191.3	194.7
Subtotal	135.7	143.1	169.2	180.4	221.4	217.9	225.9
Panel B: Repair Expenditures							
Construction	14.4	13.9	14.7	13.9	14.7	13.3	14.2
Machinery & Equipment	78.6	81.8	88.1	97.1	99.5	95.8	91.9
Subtotal	93	95.7	102.8	111	114.2	109.1	106.1
Total	228.7	238.8	272.0	291.4	335.6	327.0	332.0
Panel C: Productivity							
Manufacturing							
Value Added Per Person-Hour Paid	26.28	28.40	29.74	29.56	30.03	—	—
Value Added/ Production Worker	53 619	58 381	61 923	61 938	63 385	—	—
Primary Textiles							
Value Added Per Person-Hour Paid	19.43	23.26	23.96	26.30	30.27	—	—

Table 7.3 (continued)

	1982	1983	1984	1985	1986	1987	1988
Value Added/ Production Worker	40 409	48 613	50 108	54 674	62 981	—	—
Textile Products							
Value Added Per Person-Hour Paid	17.50	18.93	18.64	18.69	17.93	—	—
Value Added/ Production Worker	35 871	39 510	38 909	39 646	38 642	—	—

Source: Statistics Canada, *Manufacturing Industries of Canada: National and Provincial Areas*, Catalogue 31–203 (Ottawa: Minister of Supply and Services Canada, various years).
Statistics Canada, *Public and Private Investment in Canada*, Catalogue 61–205 (Ottawa: Minister of Supply and Services Canada, various years).
Statistics Canada, *Capital and Repair Expenditures, Manufacturing Sub-industries, Canada*, Catalogue 61–214 (Ottawa: Minister of Supply and Services Canada, various years).

Board (CIRB) subsidies, although these subsidies accounted for less than 10 percent of total investment. Of the total, 55 percent was invested in new machinery, compared to 31 percent for machinery and equipment repair.[12] On the whole, investment expenditures indicate strong growth in the technological base of the textile sector.

INDUSTRY PERFORMANCE

The capital investment incurred by textile firms in the 1980s led to considerable improvements in productivity. As may be seen from Panel C of Table 7.3, productivity (measured in terms of value added per person-hour paid) in primary textiles increased by approximately 55 percent between 1982 and 1986, compared to a growth rate of 18 percent for all manufacturing during that period. In contrast, textile products experienced a below-average productivity growth rate of 2.5 to 8 percent. The exceptional productivity growth of primary textile firms is principally attributable to the adoption of labour-saving technology.

The explosion of technology in the textile industry has had two important impacts on textile workers. Most immediately, productivity increased much faster than the size of the market, which led to significant employment reductions and consequent unemployment. Second, widespread introduction of computer technology has changed work-force skill requirements. As we shall see, textile unions have had only limited success in coping with these problems. Unlike other industries, where union resistance to rationalization forced significant *quid pro quos* from management, such as some form of codetermination, the textile labour movement has limited its efforts to alleviating the ill effects of industry restructuring.

*H*istory of Textile Labour Relations

*I*nitial efforts to organize trade unions in the Canadian textile industry date back to the 1800s.[13] These early attempts were sporadic, isolated, and short-lived. Local organizations spontaneously emerged in relatively prosperous times, with little or no assistance from central organizing bodies such as the American Federation of Labor (AFL) or the National Trades and Labour Congress (NTLC). After experiencing limited success, they would disappear during the first recession, usually after a wage cut had provoked an ill-fated strike.

A number of factors explain the labour movement's failure during this period (Renner 1977). First, ownership was concentrated in few hands, particularly in the cotton sector; employers had substantial market power, which gave them the financial resources necessary to withstand strikes without risking loss of market share. Second, employers typically operated several mills, each located in a relatively isolated, small town. This fact had a number of negative implications for union organizing: (1) employers could shift production from struck mills during labour disputes, (2) isolated locations required relatively greater union organizing resources, (3) employers were better able to identify and fire union activists, and (4) employees in these one-industry towns lacked alternative employment opportunities and were consequently more reluctant to risk discharge for union activism or temporary unemployment during a strike. Third, the textile labour force included a disproportionately large number of young people and women, two population groups that were only peripherally attached to the industry or mill, and, therefore, not particularly receptive to union organization. Fourth, piece-rate incentive systems, prevalent in the industry, impaired worker solidarity. Finally, the textile mills employed a large number of semi-skilled and unskilled workers, who were easily replaced during a strike (Rouillard 1974) and who were ill-suited for craft-based organization as practised by the AFL and NTLC.

Several attempts were made during this period to establish a national or international textile union. The organization of the Hochelaga Mill of Dominion Cotton in 1905 led to eventual affiliation with the United Textile Workers of America (UTWA), a central formed by the AFL in 1901. As the result of a successful strike at Hochelaga in 1906, thirteen additional locals with a membership of 3000 were organized. The campaign succeeded despite a lack of support from the UTWA, which was preoccupied with organizing firms that had recently migrated from New England to the southern Piedmont. Paying substantially lower wages, these southern mills represented a much greater competitive threat to the New England workers that constituted UTWA's base than did Canadian plants.

Increased demand for textile products and labour shortages resulted in increased union activity during the First World War. By 1920, the UTWA had organized 14 locals with a total of 2534 members. In addition, the Quebec-based Confédération des travailleurs catholiques du Canada (CTCC) organized locals in Montreal, St-Hyacinthe, and Sherbrooke, from which the Fédération catholiques nationale du textile (FCNT) was formed. However, by the end of the 1920s, both unions had dwindled beyond the "relatively minor importance" they attained during the previous decade (Rouillard 1989).

Several institutional changes occurred during the Depression that paved the way for the more enduring organization of textile workers. Perhaps the most important was the formation of the Committee of Industrial Organizations (CIO) in 1935. In 1937, the CIO formed the Textile Workers Organizing Committee (TWOC), launching an organizing campaign in the U.S. industry. While a founding member of the CIO, the UTWA was made a subordinate body to the TWOC. Sidney Hillman, president of the Amalgamated Clothing Workers of America (ACWA), was appointed chairman of the TWOC; much of the TWOC's finances were contributed by the ACWA and the International Ladies' Garment Workers' Union (ILGWU). Similar to earlier efforts, the TWOC concentrated its resources on an unsuccessful attempt to organize mills in the southern United States. In 1938,

Emil Rieve, leader of the Hosiery Workers Union and a Hillman lieutenant, replaced Hillman as chairman of the TWOC, which led to the UTWA's exodus from the CIO. The UTWA reaffiliated with the AFL in 1939.[14] That same year, the TWOC formed the Textile Workers Union of America (TWUA).

Five major strikes occurred in the Canadian textile industry in 1936 and 1937: Wabasso in Trois-Rivières, Courtaulds in Cornwall, Canadian Cottons in Cornwall, Dominion Woolens and Worsteds in Peterborough, and several Quebec mills of Dominion Textile. With the exception of the Dominion Textile dispute, these strikes were similar to previous textile strikes: spontaneous and initially organized by local workers with little help from international or national bodies.[15] In each case, the strikers met fierce resistance by the employer;[16] firms refused to negotiate with union leadership and, in particular, with representatives from an international union such as the UTWA. Typical of employer attitudes was the official statement by Dominion Textile published in *La Tribune* (Royal Commission on the Textile Industry 1938, 183–84):

> Our employees are free to join a Labour organization if they desire to do so, and if there is any choice in the matter, it seems more fitting that they should join an organization which is not dominated and controlled by foreign elements. . . . The company will not permit any third party to interfere between the management and the employees or to take away from the employees their rights as individuals to deal with the company.

Textile firms urged employees to join company-sponsored work councils, sometimes arranging for an election among the membership. In face of this resistance, local unions were short-lived; most were eliminated during the return of the depression in 1938. However, with the exception of those employed by Wabasso, workers were able to secure gains in wages and working conditions through the assistance of newly established agencies charged with enforcing minimum labour standards, such as Quebec's Office des salaires raisonnables.

Many labour leaders active in the 1937 strikes attributed their failure to the absence of a unified Canadian textile labour union. In 1939, following a meeting between Paddy Draper (president of the Trades and Labour Congress), William Green (president of the AFL), and Sidney Hillman, the UTWA and the TWOC withdrew from Canada. Former UTWA and TWOC locals affiliated with the National Textile Council (NTC), an organization created by the TLC. Arthur Laverty, a UTWA organizer who had emerged from the rank and file during the Courtaulds strike, was named president of the new organization. The NTC dissolved in 1940, apparently as part of a plan by the newly formed Secretariat of Canadian Textile Workers Unions to amalgamate the textile unions (Renner 1977). While the secretariat was able to generate some interest in this plan, even among the leadership of the FCNT, the unity movement ultimately failed. As noted by Renner (1977, 122), "the fact that an attempt was made indicated that some unionists recognized that disunity was harming the effort to unionize textile workers."

While textile union membership declined during the recession of 1938, the Second World War produced two conditions favourable to union organization. For the first time, the labour movement was able to form enduring organizations in the textile industry. However, the continued failure of one union to become dominant within the industry established the pattern of fragmentation that is characteristic of the textile labour movement today.

In 1941, the TLC and Congress of Canadian Labour (CCL) began separate organizing campaigns in the textile industry. Following dissolution of the NTC, textile locals directly chartered with the TLC formed the United Textile Workers of Canada.Concurrently, the CCL formed a Canadian version of the TWOC and organized locals in Hamilton, Kitchener, St. Catharines, Stratford, and Toronto. One year later, the UTWA reappeared in Canada, attempting to organize Quebec mills.

In 1943 the TWOC leadership split between a faction advocating affiliation with the Textile Workers Union of America (TWUA) and a faction favouring the formation of an independent national union. Consequently, the national-union faction left the TWOC to form the National Union of Textile Workers, while other locals affiliated with the TWUA. Within five years of the drive for unity within the textile labour movement, as embodied in the NTC and the secretariat, five competing unions were active in the industry.[17] Of these, three unions emerged as the dominant textile labour organizations in the post–Second World War period: the TWUA, the FCNT, and the UTWA.

As discussed earlier, since the Second World War, foreign competitors had increasingly displaced Canadian textile firms from the market. As a result, jobs were lost. From 1965 to 1975, employment dropped by 7.4 percent. At the same time, membership in the three largest textile unions fell by 14.5 percent (see Table 7.4 below). Unions became increasingly concerned with the impacts of automation, greater workloads, and the reclassification of jobs (Hamelin and Harvey 1976). In this atmosphere, in 1966, the old FCNT (which was renamed the Fédération canadienne des travailleurs du textile [FCTT] in 1965) launched a series of massive strikes against three Dominion Textile plants in Quebec.[18] These strikes were a watershed in the history of labour–management relations in the industry. According to the retrospective view of one FCTT official, the strike was decisive because the union was seeking to transform its relationship with Dominion Textile from one of highly adversarial bargaining and rigid legalism to one where the union would be treated more like an equal partner in the enterprise.[19] The company made an unsuccessful appeal directly to the strikers in the hopes of catalyzing a return to work (Centrale des Syndicats Démocratiques [CSD] 1979a). The strike lasted for six months and crippled the company.[20] Afterwards, Dominion Textile undertook a study of its work force, subsequently overhauling its human-resource practices (Sexton, Leclerc, and Audet 1985).

The 1966 strike, which was the culmination of highly contentious labour–management relations in the industry, was a motivating force behind the formation of the Canadian Textile Labour–Management Committee (CTLMC) in 1967 (Sexton, Leclerc, and Audet 1985). The CTLMC was created to provide a forum in which the heads of the textile companies could meet with top officials of the three major unions to improve communications and to establish co-operative approaches to influence governmental trade and other policies affecting the industry (Sexton, Leclerc, and Audet 1985).

Since the mid-1960s, membership in the three largest unions has steadily declined. Two of these experienced significant organizational changes. The FCTT had become disenchanted with the increasingly radical political posture of the Confédération des Syndicats Nationaux (CSN), the resources that were being expended on political matters, and the growing dominance of public-sector affiliates within the federation (CSD 1979a). In 1972, the FCTT left the CSN to help form the Centrale des syndicats démocratiques (CSD). Four years later, the TWUA followed its U.S.–based international into a merger with the Amalgamated Clothing Workers Union, forming the Amalgamated Clothing and Textile Workers Union (ACTWU). The ACTWU had about 35 000 Canadian members in 1976, 40 percent of whom came from the TWUA.

Despite organizational changes and increasing attempts to organize nontextile workers, the major unions have not been able to stanch the continued loss of membership. The cumulative effects of industry rationalization, experienced by workers in the form of plant closures, permanent layoffs, and displacement resulting from technological change, has diminished the combined membership in these organizations, from almost 33 000 in 1970 to around 18 000 in 1988.

Textile Labour Relations In The 1980s

UNION DENSITY

Household surveys conducted by Statistics Canada as a part of their monthly Labour Force Survey indicate that 54.1 percent of the textile labour force was unionized in 1984 and that 56.7 percent was covered by a collective-bargaining agreement. By 1986, membership had declined to 47.2 percent, while collective-agreement coverage had risen to 57.2 percent of textile workers (Coates, Arrowsmith, and Courchene 1989).

Table 7.4 presents membership data for the three major textile unions for selected years between 1915 and 1988. The ACTWU is the largest of the three, with a total 1988 Canadian membership of 24 160 workers. Although a precise figure is unavailable, the ACTWU's textile membership probably exceeds 10 000 workers. Almost 61 percent of the ACTWU's overall membership is in Ontario, and nearly 30 percent work in Quebec (1991 personal communication with Efre Giacobbo of the ACTWU). The ACTWU's textile industry members are overwhelmingly concentrated in Ontario, although the union does represent employees at Consoltex in

Table 7.4
Membership, Major Textile Unions, 1915-1988

Year	UTWA	CTCC FCTT	TWUA ACTWU
1915	50	—	—
1920	2 534	—	—
1925	351	?a	—
1930	100	?	—
1935	28	?	—
1940	—	8 558	—
1945	9 000	6 789	6 000
1950	15 000	15 500	10 000
1955	5 000	7 440	16 750
1960	9 200	8 114	18 000
1965	10 977	10 121	14 399
1970	9 826	7 881	15 289
1975	8 969	8 918	12 470
1976	8 035	8 288	30 127
1977	6 771	8 672	29 291
1978	6 243	9 496	30 269
1979	6 910	9 461	31 935
1980	6 824	8 732	30 973
1981	6 644	8 055	28 762
1982	5 896	8 070	26 320
1983	5 793	7 187	26 531
1984	5 604	6 451	25 935
1985	4 288	5 567	25 317
1986	4 371	4 567	25 169
1987	4 263	4 425	24 906
1988	4 004	4 115	24 160

Note: A ? denotes that the information was unavailable for that year.
Source: Labour Canada, *Directory of Labour Organizations,* various years.

Cowansville and Peerless Carpets in Actonvale, Quebec. The ACTWU is a conglomerate union, increasingly organizing in nontraditional domains such as printing and electronics. Given employment trends in the textile and clothing industries, one would expect this trend to continue, if not accelerate.

The FCTT had 4115 members in 1988, making it the second-largest textile union (Statistics Canada 1991). In contrast to the memberships of the ACTWU and the UTWA, the FCTT is found exclusively in the Quebec textile industry. The union's largest units are at various Dominion Textile facilities. The UTWA's membership has declined steadily, from approximately 11 000 in 1965 to 4000 in 1988. By 1988, almost 54 percent of its membership was in Ontario, and 30 percent worked in Quebec. Like the ACTWU, the UTWA has also organized workers in numerous industries outside textiles.[21]

In recent years, the textile sector, particularly outside Quebec, has seen the entry of unions not traditionally active in the industry. Table 7.5 presents Ontario data on collective-bargaining coverage in 1984 and new certifications during the 1982–90 period disaggregated by union affiliation. Over 50 percent of textile employees covered by collective agreements in Ontario in 1984 were represented by unions other than the ACTWU or UTWA. Furthermore, the Steel Workers and the Auto Workers are the most dynamic unions with respect to new organizing and are significantly more active than the UTWA.

Many of these nontraditional unions began organizing textile workers as a result of linkages between their original jurisdictions and the textile industry. For example, the link between the textile and apparel industries is responsible for the entry of the ILGWU and the United Garment Workers. The largest textile bargain-

Table 7.5

Ontario Textile Industry, Collective-Bargaining Coverage and New Certifications, by Union, 1985–1990

Union	1985 CB Coverage		1985–1990 New Certifications	
	Locals	Employees	Locals	Employees
ACTWU	35	5 253	5	244
UTWA	11	1 635	2	73
Auto Workers	3	1 618	3	273
Electrical, Radio & Machine	1	32	—	—
Novelty Workers	—	—	1	7
Operating Engineers	5	29	—	—
United Garment Workers	1	101	—	—
ILGWU	1	18	—	—
Leather Workers	1	165	—	—
Labourers' International Union	1	408	—	—
Textile Processors	1	36	3	71
Machinists & Aerospace Workers	2	103	—	—
Energy & Chemical	1	639	1	88
Food & Commercial	4	426	3	116
Can. Paperworkers	1	18	1	21
Rubberworkers	6	646	—	—
Steel Workers	3	641	5	245
Retail & Wholesale	—	—	1	23
Teamsters	2	17	2	208
Can. Operating Engrs.	—	—	1	4
Graphics Commun.	—	—	1	2
Textile & Chemical	2	375	1	81
Independent	8	2 302	0	0
Total	88	14 399	30	1 456

Source: Ontario Ministry of Labour, Collective Agreement Data.

ing unit in Canada is a Chrysler auto fabrics plant represented by the Canadian Auto Workers that employs approximately 2000 employees. However, unions such as the Steel Workers and the Teamsters have organized textile workers on the basis of a conglomerate union strategy. Finally, in many instances, these unions did not actively seek to organize textile workers; such unions were approached by textile workers desiring organization because they were the most visible labour organizations in their communities.

These data indicate that the textile labour movement is becoming increasingly fragmented, while the three major unions have become less significant actors in the industry. The UTWA and FCTT have been especially hard hit in recent years. In part, the decline may be the result of the same structural factors cited by Renner (1977) as an explanation for the inability of unions to organize at the beginning of this century, including a high proportion of secondary wage earners and a lack of alternative employment opportunities. In addition, the decline is, at least in part, attributable to the unions' perceived weakness in the face of employment losses caused by restructuring and rationalization. This perception, and the inability of a single, dominant union to assume a leadership role, have induced nontextile labour organizations to organize in the industry. Finally, while there does not appear to be an active nonunion movement among textile employers, data from Ontario indicate that firms may be closing large (and presumably older) facilities, previously organized by the major textile unions. It is likely that organizing may become more, rather than less, difficult if the industry trend toward smaller (in terms of employment) plants continues.

TEXTILE STRIKE RECORD

Labour relations in the Canadian textile industry have been highly contentious since unions first appeared at the beginning of this century. Strike levels were similarly high in 1937, 1946–47, 1952, 1956, and 1959. According to Sexton, Leclerc, and Audet (1985, 16), "in number and scale, the textile industry had one of the worst strike records in Québec between 1946 and 1959." Table 7.6 presents work-stoppage data for the period 1960–1990. As this table shows, the industry suffered a high level of conflict in the early 1960s. Although textiles accounted for only 4.4 percent of manufacturing employment from 1960 to 1966, it accounted for 12.5 percent of person-days lost as a result of strikes and lockouts during that period.

Substantial labour conflict, in particular the 1966 Dominion Textile strike, provided the impetus for the formation of the Canadian Textile Labour–Management Committee (CTLMC) in 1967. The CTLMC was created so that the union and management could regularly meet to improve communications as well as establish co-operative approaches toward influencing governmental policies (particularly those regarding trade) that affect the industry (Sexton, Leclerc, and Audet 1985).[22] Eighteen members sit on the committee, with equal representation from management and labour. The Canadian Textiles Institute selects management

Table 7.6

Work Stoppages in the Textile Industry, 1960–1990

| Year | Textiles | | | Manufac-turing Person-Days Lost (000s) | Textile Days Lost as a Percent of All Mfg. |
	Number of Strikes	Number of Workers Involved	Person-Days Lost (000s)		
1960	1	1725	53.5	432.2	12.4
1961	5	1101	13.3	383.7	3.5
1962	7	2927	83.5	778.7	10.7
1963	8	113	8.3	498.7	1.7
1964	5	1474	3.7	1190.8	0.3
1965	7	1868	30.4	1470.8	2.1
1966	16	9145	651.3	1987.8	32.8
1967	8	2034	70.8	1976.3	3.6
1968	12	2568	28.3	3746.2	0.8
1969	15	7620	63.9	2690.3	2.4
1970	7	795	10.1	3630.7	0.3
1971	8	784	16.9	1541.5	1.1
1972	7	2725	33.9	2042.5	1.7
1973	9	2418	93.9	3361.5	2.8
1974	29	6608	101.7	4782.4	2.1
1975	15	4057	139.3	5351.8	2.6
1976	10	4021	255.8	4483.8	5.7
1977	9	1677	56.8	1636.9	3.5
1978	9	1944	18.6	2473.6	0.8
1979	13	2896	25.5	3117.2	0.8
1980	13	4159	105.6	3151.9	3.4
1981	9	1445	32.6	4621.1	0.7
1982	10	5839	36.7	1652.4	2.2
1983	5	528	6.3	1370.3	0.5
1984	7	1549	38.4	2373.2	1.6
1985	7	1709	97.8	1510.2	6.5
1986	8	1124	12.3	1378.7	0.9
1987	9	1120	13.2	1717.4	0.8
1988	6	850	16.9	1307.1	1.3
1989	6	496	14.6	1166.1	1.2
1990	5	903	17.0	2451.0	0.7

Source: Unpublished data, Labour Canada.

representatives from among its membership.[23] An attempt is made to achieve balanced representation, both sectorally (wool, knits, cotton, etc.) and geographically (between Quebec and Ontario). Union representatives come from each of the three textile unions—the ACTWU, the UTWA, and the FCTT.[24]

As moderator, the Reverend Gérard Dion played a critical role from 1967 until his death in 1990. In their study of the committee, Sexton, Leclerc, and Audet (1985, 61) comment that

> The Moderator was praised by all. His moral influence, great reputation, impartiality, good contacts, expertise, availability, independence and freedom of thought and action were all acknowledged without hesitation. . . . He is seen as a moderator, catalyst and chairman who forestalls confrontation, makes contact, interprets and gives permanence to the Committee while maintaining the quality of its work.

While concern has been expressed over the future viability of the committee without Reverend Dion's leadership, others believe that the committee will continue to serve an important function in the industry.

Although at its inception the CTLMC adopted a rule prohibiting its involvement in collective bargaining or specific grievances, it has apparently had a salutary effect on negotiations.

> Through the intermediary of the Committee, the parties concerned in labour relations are constantly kept aware of the real state of the industry. This inside information source colours labour relations by ensuring that at least the parties share an understanding of objective facts. This makes labour relations more realistic, and conflicts may thus be avoided or tempered. (Sexton, Leclerc, and Audet 1985, 70)

The CTLMC has also dealt with general problems of industrial relations such as absenteeism and various means by which to help the work force adjust to restructuring, such as early retirement, retraining, or reclassification. An analysis of the minutes from the 74 committee meetings held between 1967 and 1982 reveals that the most frequently discussed subject was Canadian and foreign trade policies (54 meetings). Productivity issues were discussed at 27 meetings, occupational safety and health at 12, education and training at 3, and absenteeism at 2 (Sexton, Leclerc, and Audet 1985).

The establishment of the CTLMC has been associated with a reduction in the number of confrontations. Table 7.6 also reports the ratio of person-days lost as a result of strikes and lockouts in the textile industry to person-days lost in all manufacturing (the conflict ratio). A comparison of this ratio with the industry's share of manufacturing employment (the employment ratio) reveals that industrial conflict has diminished markedly since 1967. Since 1966, days lost as a result of strikes in the textile industry accounted for only 1.5 percent of total workdays lost, substantially less than the industry's share of employment (about 4 percent).

Examination of the industry's strike record indicates that there has been a diminution in the frequency and intensity of labour disputes. An exception is the 1985 Dominion Textile strike. In that year, Dominion Textile renegotiated eight contracts at six of its Quebec plants (Rheault 1989). These negotiations occurred in the midst of the dramatic restructuring of the textile industry. Since the recession of 1981–82, the industry had experienced a series of plant closures (Colgan 1985), most notably, the cessation of operations by Wabasso, announced in January 1985. The Wabasso closures resulted in the loss of approximately 1300 jobs (Hunter 1985). From 1981 to 1984, Dominion Textile closed eight plants, eliminating 1700 Canadian jobs (Rheault 1989).

In 1985, Dominion Textile reorganized its structure and operations. As part of this reorganization, the company sought to end centralized bargaining with a common front of the eight FCTT locals representing 2700 employees at six Quebec mills (Rheault 1989). Instead, the company wanted to negotiate on a plant-by-plant basis, since each plant was considered to be a separate profit centre.[25] By March 1985, Dominion Textile had reached agreements with the UTWA, representing employees at two Ontario plants and a third in Nova Scotia (Rheault 1989). However, the FCTT refused to agree to a similar settlement at the Quebec facilities.

Two Dominion Textile bargaining positions were unacceptable to the FCTT: the addition of a weekend shift and wage offers that would not be rolled into base salaries (Rheault 1989; Rouillard 1989).[26] In April 1985, after Dominion Textile tabled its "final offer," workers at St-Jean and Valleyfield responded with slow-downs and, it is alleged, sabotage and vandalism (Rheault 1989). The company locked out employees at both plants. On May 5, union members voted overwhelmingly to reject the company's offer and authorize a strike. However, after Dominion Textile revised its final offer, the two Magog locals agreed to the company's terms and then disaffiliated from the FCTT (Rheault 1989).[27]

On August 15, 1985, the company announced that it was permanently closing the St-Jean and Valleyfield plants. Part of the plants' production and machinery had already been successfully shifted to the company's Drummondville plant, which was represented by an independent local union (Rheault 1989). The company maintains these closures were motivated by a reduction in demand as a result of increased imports, and by the fact that the Drummondville facility was able to make up for the lost production during the lockout. However, FCTT officials and some outside observers view these actions as an attempt to discipline a militant union (Rheault 1989; Rouillard 1989).[28] These observers argue that, otherwise, it is difficult to understand why the company would close the St-Jean mill, one of its most modern facilities.

The 1985 Dominion Textile strike illustrates the risks of union militancy in a climate of industry rationalization and corporate restructuring. Furthermore, it exemplifies differences in militancy between two major textile unions, the UTWA and the FCTT. These differences are not lost on employers.

Table 7.7 presents work-stoppage data disaggregated by union. These data indicate that there are considerable differences with respect to labour militancy. To a certain extent, these numbers reflect differences in the number of bargaining units represented by the three unions. The ACTWU represents three to four times as many units as does the UTWA, and approximately twice as many as does the FCTT. Nevertheless, it appears that both the FCTT and the ACTWU are significantly more militant than the UTWA. As one union official put it, the UTWA "does not have

Table 7.7
Textile Work Stoppages, by Union 1980–1990

Year	ACTWU			UTWA			FTCC			OTHER		
	Number	Workers	Person-Days Lost	Number	Workers	Person-Days Lost	Number	Workers	Person-Days Lost	Number	Workers	Person-Days Lost
1980	3	901	8 910	1	353	1170	3	448	10 540	6	2 457	85 010
1981	4	681	1 690	—	—	—	1	350	12 950	2	241	5 760
1982	3	538	5 530	—	—	—	1	77	2 190	6	5 142	24 900
1983	—	—	—	—	—	—	3	301	5 680	2	227	610
1984	1	140	330	1	356	1140	—	—	—	4	573	6 660
1985	2	386	6 430	—	—	—	2	1158	84 940	2	88	480
1986	2	700	5 210	—	—	—	—	—	—	5	317	3 980
1987	1	558	1 400	—	—	—	1	35	1 590	5	420	8 120
1988	2	440	2 430	1	80	110	1	130	7 410	2	200	6 970
1989	1	112	1 040	—	—	—	—	—	—	5	384	13 530
1990	1	290	7 830	—	—	—	—	—	—	4	613	9 140
	20	4 746	40 800	3	789	2420	12	2499	125 300	42	10 662	165 140

Source: Work Stoppage Master File Database, Labour Canada.

the numbers . . .[or] . . . the money." In addition, while the ACTWU conducted a greater number of strikes during this period, the average duration of the FCTT's job actions was significantly longer, suggesting more contentious relations between labour and management. Interestingly, the "nontextile" unions were far more militant than any of the major textile unions, accounting for nearly 57 percent of the total number of strikes and more than 50 percent of person-days lost, while representing less than 50 percent of all textile workers.

BARGAINING STRUCTURE

As might be expected, given the fragmentation of the labour movement, collective bargaining in the textile industry is highly decentralized. Agreements are negotiated on a single-plant basis, except where the employer has two or more plants in a single location covered by the same certification. According to Corporations and Labour Unions Reporting Act data, the UTWA and FCTT had 59 agreements, covering 57 employers, in 1988.[29] As noted earlier, until the 1985 round of negotiations, Dominion Textile bargained with a common front of eight FCTT locals. Currently, the company conducts separate negotiations with four of these locals.

Pattern bargaining in the Canadian textile industry is insubstantial. According to one union official, "thirty years ago Dominion Textile set the pattern, but this is no longer the case." Employers appear to initiate most of the pattern bargaining that does occur. When asked if there was an attempt to establish patterns across collective agreements with the same or with different employers, one official stated: "Employers push this more than the unions do." Some union officials believe that employers attempt to set patterns regarding fringe benefits, using the Canadian Textiles Institute as a forum for discussion, although this allegation is denied by representatives of the institute.

Bargaining priorities are set by the locals. The central offices of the three major unions limit their involvement to providing support and expertise to the locals.[30] Professional union staffs keep abreast of industry negotiations and study developments in labour-standards regulation with the intention of improving upon both.[31] Numerous obstacles prevent unions from establishing favourable industry patterns. Foremost is the decentralized bargaining structure, which is advantageous for employers who are able to whipsaw fragmented and divided unions, as Dominion Textile demonstrated in its 1985 negotiations with the FCTT. Given limited competition among domestic producers and intense foreign competition, there is little incentive for employers to acquiesce to union-instigated patterns in order to "take wages out of competition." Neither side can accomplish that feat.

COLLECTIVE-BARGAINING TRENDS AND ISSUES

Kochan, Katz, and McKersie (1986) argue that the collective-bargaining agenda for many manufacturing industries in the United States changed in the 1980s as a result of the globalization of international trade and the development of nonunion competition. Computer-based technologies made short production runs economically feasible, while the competitive advantage of "niche marketing" induced firms to shift from mass production to flexible manufacturing systems. Effective implementation of flexible manufacturing systems has required that firms reorganize work and adopt complementary human-resource practices.

Specifically, labour and management in the United States introduced changes at three different levels. At the workplace, these changes involved the introduction of mechanisms designed to increase worker participation and involvement, such as quality circles and worker-attitude surveys, and the elimination or simplification of work rules to lower costs and increase managerial flexibility. Job classifications were broadened; work rules preventing employers from reorganizing work and introducing team-based production were eliminated. Management began to base compensation on the work group's performance and on the employees' breadth of skills ("pay-for-knowledge"). Concomitantly, formerly adversarial bargaining relationships became more co-operative. Unions became more directly involved in areas traditionally considered to be the exclusive domain of management, such as employee training and production planning. Management began to share confidential business information with employees and the union. Finally, in return for a relaxation of work rules, unions were able to secure new guarantees of employment security for their members.

Despite substantial global competition and the introduction of computer-based technologies, there is little evidence of similar developments in the Canadian textile industry. These environmental forces have not transformed workplace relations or the bargaining agenda in this industry, as they have in others. There are a number of possible explanations as to why this has not occurred. First, employers have yet to widely implement flexible manufacturing systems requiring a more flexible work force. The industry has traditionally perceived the problem of meeting foreign competition as one of increasing productivity rather than increasing manufacturing flexibility. Second, since technology is imported and increasingly process-based, production personnel are not involved in machinery design. Workers adapt to the technology rather than vice versa. Consequently, there is little opportunity for workers to participate in production decisions. Third, much of the work force is low-skilled and relatively uneducated, with a tenuous attachment to the industry; team production would require substantial investment in human capital. Finally, because textile unions are weak, management has been able to introduce workplace changes with little or no opposition. The industry has been able to restructure without granting concessions to the unions.

Union officials interviewed for this study unanimously agreed that foreign competition, technological change, and plant closures are the most significant issues confronting textile unions and their members today. Given the dramatic employment losses since 1980 and continued efforts to rationalize, this is hardly surprising. Textile unions have generally accepted the necessity of mechanization and restructuring and the consequent job loss, as reflected in the comments of Vernon Mustard, president of the UTWA:

By way of long standing principles, there is a natural inclination to protect the old values and standards. Unions, not unlike companies, must recognize change when it arrives and must adapt to the new economic environments.

One would have to be an idiot not to realize the disastrous consequences if Canadian industry or any other individual country were to ignore this new age of microelectronics and robotics as this new revolution unfolds over the rest of the world. (1985, 26)[32]

As a consequence, the major unions have all co-operated with employers in efforts designed to influence government trade policy.

However, textile unions differ with respect to their approaches to the challenges of automation and foreign competition. The UTWA perceives its role as "minimizing the on-the-job psychological and emotional trauma" of job loss, ensuring that there is an "equitable sharing between non-management and management personnel of the cost and sacrifices of productivity change," and protecting members "against abuse or lack of fair treatment as the change unfolds" (Mustard 1985, 26). While Mustard contemplates increased union participation in the implementation of new technology in the industry, this participation is limited:

> Management is responsible for targeting and scheduling the implementation of equipment. Management has established goals for maximizing the new equipment. The union becomes a carry-along participant, monitoring and possibly recommending departures from the standard format or change in method or direction, to further expedite the introduction and/or more sensitively deal with the psychological, emotional, or stress elements within the workforce. (Mustard, 1985, 26)

There is little desire to involve the union in the decision of whether or how to implement rationalization, restructuring, or technological change. Nor have unions been able to secure employment guarantees in exchange for a relaxation of work rules.

The FCTT, in contrast, has endorsed more fundamental changes in workplace relations in order to improve industry productivity. It has advocated implementation of Quality-of-Work Life (*qualité de vie au travail*) programs that emphasize greater worker participation and more flexible work arrangements. In their estimation, "une approche syndicale nouvelle et globale" is required:

> Le défi de l'augmentation de la productivité, duquel dépend la survie de l'industrie mais aussi l'augmentation du niveau de vie des travailleurs qui y oevrent, doit dorénavant élargir son champ d'application traditionnel à un nouveau mode d'action: l'amelioration de la qualité de vie au travail. (CSD, 1979b, 38)

Unlike the UTWA, the FCTT and the ACTWU have historically perceived production decisions as being within their scope. As noted earlier, the 1966 Dominion

Textile strike represented an effort by the FCTT to change the fundamental labour–management relationship to make the union an equal partner in the enterprise. Similarly, the ACTWU has long been involved in co-operative labour–management efforts in the clothing industry, an industry composed of many small employers also under considerable pressure from foreign competition.[33] While both unions may wish to become more involved in production decisions, neither has the strength to negotiate rights of participation or consultation.

In recent years, textile management has been increasingly concerned with work rules that limit its ability to fully utilize the substantial capital investment of the 1980s (Colgan 1985). Specifically, as early as 1979, management sought to implement continuous production, 24 hours a day, seven days a week. In place of five-day work weeks, Dominion Textile has sought to substitute five-day operations of three shifts, with weekends covered by two twelve-hour shifts, or a two-week cycle of six days one week and four days the next. The FCTT has resisted these demands, which were the central issue in the 1985 strike.

Table 7.8 provides data on contract clauses negotiated by unions in Ontario between 1984 and 1990. An examination of the data reported in Panels B through D shows that textile agreements are consistently less likely to contain provisions protecting employees against the effects of technological change, providing employees with training or retraining, requiring advance notice of layoff or plant closure, or mandating various forms of financial assistance for displaced workers, than are other manufacturing agreements. In contrast, data in Panel G indicate that textile firms are more likely to negotiate seniority-based restrictions on managerial discretion to promote, transfer, lay off, or recall employees than are other manufacturing employers. A straightforward interpretation of these data is that textile unions are unable to obtain expensive or highly restrictive protections that limit management's ability to restructure operations. The relatively greater incidence of seniority-based protection seems to indicate that textile unions settled for the only protection they could obtain.

Technological change is particularly troublesome for textile workers and their unions. While unions recognize the need for continuous modernization, they are critical of textile firms' management of the human aspects of technological change. Despite union appeals in contract negotiations and in joint committee work, textile firms have largely resisted involving the unions in the decision-making process.[34] The data in Panel C of Table 7.8 bear this out; anecdotal evidence is even more convincing.

Although unions have sought prior notification of new machinery, typically none is received. Instead, firms typically lay off employees, install new machines in their absence, and then recall the employees, who first find out about the new equipment upon their return. One union official stated, "Often . . . employees only find out about this [new technology] when they see the new machinery being shipped into the plant." The belief that employers are mishandling the human aspects of technological change is not limited to labour leaders. James Robertson, former vice-president, human resources, at the Canadian Textiles Institute and

Table 7.8

Contract Provisions, Ontario Collective Agreements, Covering 200 or More Employees, 1984–1990

Provision	All Manufac- turing	Percent Textiles
Panel A: Employee Participation & Quality-of-Work Life		
Labour–Management Committee on industrial relations issues	36.02	12.90
Compensation for Joint IR Committee	12.55	0.00
Joint Productivity Committee	6.66	3.23
Safety and Health Committee	78.78	66.13
Compensation for Safety & Health Committee	40.26	45.16
Quality-of-Work Life Plan	1.70	0.00
Childcare program	1.28	3.23
Profit -sharing plan	2.48	1.61
Panel B: Employee Training Programs		
Company training and education plan	53.29	45.16
Apprenticeship training programs	43.92	14.52
Panel C: Technological Change		
Advance notice of technological change	13.87	1.61
Advance notice of layoff due to tech change	3.87	0.00
Joint consultation prior to tech change	31.76	12.90
Arbitration of tech-change disputes	2.09	4.84
Training opportunities and/or benefits for displaced employees	36.17	14.52
Income protection for displaced employees	20.76	0.00
Transfer arrangements for affected employees	26.72	14.52
Relocation allowance for affected employees	1.47	0.00
Reduction of work force through attrition	8.83	0.00
Severance pay for displaced employees	9.30	3.23
Special benefit fund for employees affected by technological change	2.87	0.00
Joint Automation Committee	8.75	0.00
Panel D: Layoff Notice		
Advance notice of layoff to union	19.68	4.92
Advance notice of layoff to employees	52.67	47.37
Advance notice of permanent layoff	18.28	1.61
Panel E: Layoff Compensation		
Severance pay or layoff allowance	35.86	14.52
Supplemental unemployment benefits	15.80	0.00

Table 7.8 (continued)

	Percent	
Provision	All Manufac- turing	Textiles
Panel F: Plant-Closure Provisions		
Advance notice of plant closure	18.95	0.00
Advance notice of layoff in plant closure	4.53	1.61
Consultation with union prior to plant closure	12.32	11.29
Transfer arrangements for employees affected by plant closure	20.68	12.90
Income maintenance for employees affected by plant closure	3.49	0.00
Retaining of employees displaced by plant closure	5.11	4.84
Severance pay	21.84	6.45
Relocation allowance	7.36	0.00
Panel G: Employee Deployment and Seniority		
Role of seniority in promotions		
Sole or primary factor	36.49	53.23
Equal or secondary factor	34.70	29.03
No provision	28.81	17.74
Role of seniority in transfer		
Sole or primary factor	37.18	40.32
Equal or secondary factor	19.98	37.10
No provision	42.84	22.58
Role of seniority in layoff		
Sole or primary factor	78.32	88.71
Equal or secondary factor	17.74	11.29
No provision	3.95	0.00
Role of seniority in recall from layoff		
Sole or primary factor	74.90	82.26
Equal or secondary factor	15.26	14.52
No provision	9.84	0.00
Bumping provision	66.90	75.81
Panel H: Other Restrictions on Managerial Discretion		
Layoff prohibited or restricted	16.81	12.90
Subcontracting restricted or prohibited	35.47	14.52
Restrictions on work performed by non– bargaining unit employees	74.75	83.87
Union participation in classifying jobs	38.03	41.94
Union participation in setting wage rates	45.46	62.90

Source: Ontario Ministry of Labour, Collective Agreements Data.

secretary to the CTLMC, elaborated on this perspective: "Once the labour force knows that new machinery is coming in, its members start to worry about whether or not they will have a job. I have seen too many cases where retooling resulted in prolonged production losses for the employer" (Meyer 1989). Robertson urged that employees be informed during the planning stage of technological change. Efre Giacobbo of the ACTWU suggested that companies should also consult their employees regarding the choice of machinery. He asserted that the companies consider only mechanical production in choosing machinery: "The company doesn't look at the feasibility of having someone keep up with the machine, or how it will affect employees working downstream."

To date, textile unions have had their most substantial impact in helping members who have been displaced by the restructuring process. When confronted with a plant closure, the union typically forms a local committee (comité d'adaptation) responsible for advising displaced workers of their eligibility for various forms of provincial and federal assistance. These committees also attempt to place unemployed textile workers in new jobs.

PLANT-LEVEL CO-OPERATION

Recent years have seen the proliferation of joint labour–management committees in the industry, undoubtedly encouraged by the CTLMC. As noted by Madeleine Olivier of the UTWA, the CTLMC provides the unions with a forum in which to "teach company presidents what is going on in their plants." Others have questioned whether these efforts have an impact on the shop floor, as communication problems exist between the executives who sit on the committee and plant management (Sexton, Leclerc, and Audet 1985). Nevertheless, it seems likely that the spirit of top-level labour–management co-operation has at least provided an example to, and a climate for, similar innovations in the workplace.

In addition to the co-operative efforts of the industry-level CTLMC, a substantial number of plant-level joint committees are in operation. Plant committees fall into two categories: first, joint health and safety committees, which are mandated by law, and, second, other general or specialized committees created voluntarily by the parties. General committees address a wide range of industrial relations problems that fall outside the scope of collective bargaining or the jurisdiction of existing grievance procedures. For example, some UTWA locals have created "Bonne Entente" committees that serve as a forum for criticizing plant management concerning matters such as the organization of work, e.g., the layout of work stations. Other committees more narrowly focus on specific issues such as productivity or product quality.

While labour–management committees have existed in the industry for at least twenty years, these older committees were "mostly on paper," not becoming active until the late 1980s. There are few consistent patterns in these co-operative efforts. Sometimes the employer is the moving force; on other occasions, either the firm's employees or the union is. However, union officials are unanimous in asserting that the committees are only as successful as management allows them to be. Although most committees operate by consensus, ultimate decision-making authority rests with the employer. Employee representatives may be union officials, department representatives, activists, or volunteers. They may be nominated by union officers, selected by departmental employees, or elected at local meetings. The union's professional staff monitors the committees and advises members to ensure that the committees are functioning properly in fulfilling their mandates. As might be expected, these voluntary committees vary widely in effectiveness. Nevertheless, textile unions are generally supportive of these efforts. Even in cases where employee members were initially suspicious, they often became interested in and enthusiastic about the committees, once convinced of their effectiveness.

It is difficult to obtain a precise estimate of the incidence of the voluntary committees. An examination of Table 7.8 indicates that, in Ontario, for the years 1984–90, only 12.9 percent of collective-bargaining agreements negotiated in the textile industry contained a provision for labour–management committees on industrial relations matters. Three percent had a provision for joint productivity committees, and none had a provision for a joint automation committee. However, officials from the FCTT and the ACTWU estimate that between 40 and 50 percent of the plants they represent have voluntary committees of various types. With regard to the lower number of formally negotiated committees, one union official suggested that "a lot goes on that isn't in the contract," and added that items are frequently left out of the contract for fear that the employer will not consult concerning the matter.[35]

There are signs that textile industry management is becoming increasingly concerned with human-resource issues and that the industry may now be confronting the strategic choices described by Kochan, Katz, and McKersie (1985). In 1987, the industry, in co-operation with the federal government, formed the Textile Technology Centre in St-Hyacinthe, Quebec. Among other activities, this centre is engaged in the development and implementation of new technologies (*Montreal Gazette*, October 18, 1989). In 1988, Employment and Immigration Canada commissioned a report examining human resources in the textile industry. It emphasized that the textile sector's current challenge is "ensuring that it has the human resources necessary to maintain and build on its competitive position" and noted that

> having the latest technology does not provide a competitive edge. Instead that edge comes when a company's employees are trained and motivated to obtain the optimal performance from the technology. . . . . Human resources development in turn must be part of a company's longer-term strategy for capturing those markets where its products can compete most successfully. (Employment and Immigration Canada 1988, iv)

Building on this work, the Joint Human Resource Committee, a tripartite group, was formed in March 1990. This committee is charged with reporting recommendations with respect to four issues: (1) industry image and the improvement of industry communications with government, educational institutions, and the public; (2) education, training, and development within the industry; (3) the implementation of new technology and the adaptation of human resources to new technology; and (4) textile worker adjustment to job loss in the context of continued industry rationalization.

Conclusions and Prognostications

Since the Second World War, the health of the textile industry has largely been dependent upon its ability to cope with the threat of foreign competition. This ability has been substantially enhanced by the technological developments of the 1980s. However, as Dertouzos, Lester, and Solow (1989) argue with respect to the American textile industry, the industry's success in a global market hinges on certain strategic choices. In particular, these authors suggest that, to succeed, the industry must (1) emphasize "technological innovation, a commitment to research and development, and mechanisms for rapid and sophisticated technology transfer",[36] (2) implement flexible production systems and niche marketing; and (3) develop interfirm linkages, such as the Quick Response Program, in order to respond quickly to market changes.[37] There are some indications that the industry is beginning to address these issues.

It is likely that management will continue to introduce changes in personnel practices as it takes advantage of new computer-based technologies and implements flexible production systems. In addition, textile wages are likely to increase relative to other industries as productivity increases and as skill requirements increase. However, it is unlikely that the labour movement will play more than a minor role in this process. Labour is too weak and too divided to have an effective voice.

REFERENCES

Ahmad, Jaleel. 1988. "Trade-Related, Sector-Specific Industrial Adjustment Policies in Canada: An Analysis of Textile, Clothing, and Footwear Industries." Discussion Paper No. 345. Ottawa: Economic Council of Canada.

Bailey, Thomas. 1988. "Education and the Transformation of Markets and Technology in the Textile Industry." Technical Paper No. 2. Teachers College, Columbia University, New York, NY. National Center on Education and Employment.

Bell, Thomas R. 1988. "Dominion Textile Reaches into Global Markets." *Canadian Textile Journal*, February: 29–31.

———. 1979a. *Lutte de travailleurs du textile du Québec*. Montreal.

———. 1979b. *Productivité et qualité de vie au travail dans le textile*. Montreal.

———. 1985. *La Base*. Montreal, Octobre.

Coates, Mary Lou, David Arrowsmith, and Melanie Courchene. 1989. *The Current Industrial Scene in Canada: The Labour Movement and Trade Unionism Reference Tables*. Kingston, ON: Industrial Relations Centre, Queen's University.

Colgan, Fiona. 1985. "The Regional Impact of Restructuring in the Canadian Manufacturing Sector 1960 to 1982: The Case of the Quebec Textile and Clothing Industries." M.A. Thesis, Department of Geography, McGill University.

Courchene, Melanie. 1989. *The Current Industrial Scene in Canada:*

Wages, Productivity, and Labour Costs Reference Tables. Kingston, ON: Industrial Relations Centre, Queen's University.

Dertouzos, Michael L., Richard K. Lester, and Robert M. Solow. 1989. *Made in America: Regaining the Productive Edge*. Cambridge, MA: MIT Press.

Dominion Textile Inc. 1970. *Annual Report*. Montreal.

———. 1990. *Annual Report*. Montreal.

Employment and Immigration Canada. 1988. *Canadian Textiles Industries: Human Resources Study*. Ottawa: Minister of Supply and Services.

Enchin, Harvey. 1988. "Import Policy Forcing Domtex to Invest in U.S. and Europe," *Globe and Mail*, October 8, B7.

———. 1989. "Domtex Talks of Rise in U.S. Stake," *Globe and Mail*, June 20, B1, B6.

Gray, Alan D. 1987. "Domtex Aims at the Top in Burlington Bid," *Financial Times of Canada*, May 4, 1, 6.

Hamelin, Jean, and Fernand Harvey. 1976. "Les conditions de travail dans le filatures de coton." *Les travailleurs Québécoises 1941–1971*. Quebec: L'Université Laval 401–57.

Hunter, Nicholas. 1985. "1,300 workers Lose Their Jobs as Wabasso Throws in Towel," *Globe and Mail*, January 17, B1, B6.

Jennish, D'Arcy. 1988. "New Relief for the Rag Trade," *Maclean's*, April 4, 26–27.

Kochan, Thomas A., Harry C. Katz,

and Robert B. McKersie. 1986. *The Transformation of American Industrial Relations*. New York: Basic Books.

Mahon, Rianne. 1984. *The Politics of Industrial Restructuring: Canadian Textiles*. Toronto: University of Toronto Press.

Meyer, Noel. 1989. "Jim Robertson Launches New Career." *Canadian Textile Journal*, August, 16–17.

Morton, Desmond, with Terry Copp. 1984. *Working People: An Illustrated History of the Canadian Labour Movement*. Toronto: Deneau.

Mustard, Vernon. 1985. "Productivity in Textiles: The Labour Perspective. Who are the Winners and Losers?" *Canadian Textile Journal*, November: 21–26.

National Industrial Conference Board. 1956. *The Canadian Primary Textile Industry*. Prepared for the Royal Commission on Canada's Economic Prospects.

Renner, Roland. 1977. "The Development of Unions in the Canadian Primary Textile Industry." M.A. Thesis, Department of Economics, McGill University.

Rheault, Denis. 1989. "Labour Conflict at Dominion Textile From March 1985 to August 1985." Unpublished mimeo, McGill University.

Rouillard, Jacques. 1974. *Les travailleurs du coton au Québec 1900–1915*. Montreal: Presses de l'Université du Québec.

——. 1989. *Histoire du syndicalisme Québécois*. Montreal: Boréal.

Royal Commission on the Textile Industry. 1938. *Report of the Royal Commission on the Textile Industry*. Ottawa: Minister of Supply and Services.

Sexton, Jean, Claudine Leclerc, and Michel Audet. 1985. *The Canadian Textile Labour–Management Committee, Lessons From Experience, 1967–1982*. Ottawa: Minister of Supply and Services.

Textile and Clothing Board. 1981. *Textile and Clothing Inquiry: Report to the Minister of Regional Industrial Expansion*, Vol. 1. Ottawa: Minister of Supply and Services.

——. 1985. *Textile and Clothing Inquiry: Report to the Minister of Regional Industrial Expansion*, Vol. 1. Ottawa: Minister of Supply and Services.

Thomas, Hugh. 1979. *A History of the World*, Revised and augmented edition. New York: Harper and Row.

ENDNOTES

1   Our thanks to the following individuals for the donation of their time and expertise in helping us to better understand the industry: Eric Barry, Marc Beaulieu, Pierre Gagnon, Efre Giacobbo, Yvon Jacques, Eva Kutasi, Madeliene Olivier, Maurice Pepin, Jean Richard, Jacques Savoie, Elizabeth Siwicki, Gilles Thibodeau, Michael Timmons, and Paul Villeneuve. We also extend our appreciation to Len Haywood and Doris Phillips of the Ontario Ministry of Labour, Jane Hansen of Labour Canada, and Michael Caplan of Industry, Science and Technology Canada for providing some of the data used in this study; to Michel Greiche, Carole Michelucci, Lissa Poggi, and Serge Silberman for their able research assistance; and to Michel Grant, Joseph Rose, and the other participants of the Canadian Industry Conference at Queen's University for their helpful comments and suggestions. All, of course, are absolved of responsibility for any remaining errors. This research was partially funded by a grant from the REPAP Foundation.

2   Two inventions in the early eighteenth century, the flying shuttle and the spinning jenny, paved the way for the mechanization of textile production. While a water-powered spinning jenny was patented and built by John Wyatt and Lewis Paul in 1738, their invention was not fully exploited until 1771 when Richard Arkwright coupled it with a new form of social organization, the "factory," which combined mechanization and centralized production with an authoritarian system of workplace discipline. As a result, Arkwright is generally and mistakenly credited with the invention of the spinning jenny (Thomas 1979). Textile manufacture began in Canada with the construction of a cotton mill in Sherbrooke, Quebec, in 1844. This event is particularly significant since the mill was built by the first Canadian limited-liability company (Royal Commission on the Textiles Industry 1938).

3   Dominion Textile did purchase Burlington's Erwin denim plant, making it the world's largest denim producer (Bell 1988).

4   Census data reveal that, for such Quebec cities as Magog, Drummondville, and Cowansville, textiles accounted for over 50 percent of manufacturing employment and for over 20 percent of total employment (Textile and Clothing Board 1985).

5   Only 28 percent of all textile workers have a trade certificate or some university education, compared to 41 percent of workers in other manufacturing industries; 27 percent of textile workers have less than a grade 9 education, compared to 17 percent for other manufacturing.

6   The LTA was superseded in 1974 by the Multifibre Arrangement, which extended coverage to fibres other than cotton.

7   Statement of the Hon. Jean-Luc Pepin to the House of Commons on the Textile Policy, May 14, 1970.

8   These programs underwent a major change in 1981 with the establishment of the Canadian Industrial Renewal Board (CIRB), which became responsible for coordinating assistance for the textile, clothing, and footwear industries. The CIRB significantly increased funding to textile firms for capital investment and implemented programs specifically designed to encourage rationalization.

9   This program was at least partially the result of a political alliance between the Mulroney government and clothing interests who had supported the Progressive Conservative government's agenda of liberalized trade and the FTA.

10   Industry spokespersons argue that such comparisons are misleading. The United States has significantly greater nontariff barriers to protect textile products than does Canada.

11   There are indications that the government may be retreating from this position. In March 1990, Trade minister John Crosbie announced that, in the MTM textile negotiations, the Canadian government would insist on protection equivalent to that available to Canada's major trading partners, and, in particular, the United States. In July 1990, Finance minister Michael Wilson announced that tariff reductions would be made within the context of GATT. In December 1990, GATT negotiations broke down.

12   The remainder represents investment in building construction.

13   The first textile unions appeared in two Ontario cotton mills organized by the Knights of Labour in the 1880s (Rouillard 1974).

14   The UTWA along with the other CIO unions had been expelled from the AFL in 1938.

15   However, in the Courtaulds, Canadian Cottons, and Dominion Woolens and Worsted strikes, the local organizations affiliated with the UTWA soon after the strike began.

16   Commenting on these strikes in their history of the Canadian labour movement, Morton and Copp (1984, 163) indicate that, "in Canada and the United States, no industry fought unionism more consistently or more brutally. By fleeing to low-wage, one industry towns, textile plants had secured favourable ground. Government reports of starvation wages and long hours did nothing to soften their attitude."

17   These include the FCNT, the TWUA, the UTWA, the UTWC, and the National Union of Textile Workers.

18   The name change marked the Fédération's transformation from a Catholic to a secular union. The parent CCCT underwent a similar metamorphosis when it became the Confédération des syndicats nationaux (CSN).

19   According to Jean-Paul Hétu of the CSD, "La grève de 1966 a été décisive. . . . Cette grève n'était pas seulement une question d'avoir plus d'argent mais une question d'être. Le syndicat voulant être reconnu en toute plénitude, comme agent privilégié, dans les rapports sociaux avec la compagnie et non plus être considéré comme un étranger et un fauteur de trouble. La compagnie reconnaissait légalement le syndicat, mais par obligation. . . . La notion de partenaires égaux dans l'entreprise n'avait pas de signification pratique, c'était pour le syndicat un objectif à atteindre" (CSD 1979a, 50).
   The concrete manifestation of this desire to be "partenaires égaux dans l'enterprise" was the union's demand for greater control over time-and-motion studies that formed the basis of company incentive plans. Among other things the union succeeded in obtaining a clause that allowed the union to verify piece rates, using their own time-study engineer (CSD 1979a).

20   Between 1966 and 1967, sales revenue fell by over 27 percent; sales did not again reach their 1966 levels until 1971. The company reported a loss of income from opera-

tions in excess of $10 million in 1967 and a loss of nearly $2 million in 1968 (Dominion Textile 1970). After this strike the company altered its approach to labour–management relations (Sexton, Leclerc, and Audet 1985).

21   The UTWA represents employees in industries as diverse as dairy products, metal products, mining, pharmaceuticals, and industrial paper products.

22   Indeed, the committee was instrumental in the creation of the joint labour–management submission to the Ministry of Industry, Trade and Commerce in 1968, which eventually led to the 1971 National Textile Policy.

23   From the beginning, the committee decided that only designated representatives could attend committee meetings; they could not send substitutes. Sexton, Leclerc, and Audet (1985) credit this rule for significantly contributing to the committee's success.

24   Despite attempts to balance representation among various interests, Sexton, Leclerc, and Audet (1985, 64) report that some members believe that the committee has been overly concerned with the relationship between Dominion Textile and the CSD, to the point that those members may eventually leave the committee.

25   Dominion Textile was able to splinter the common front and bargain on a plant-by-plant basis following 1985 negotions.

26   Significantly, seven-day operations were already in effect in the Ontario mills.

27   Yvon Jacques, spokesman for the FCTT in these negotiations, claims that the Magog locals were less militant than the Montreal locals and therefore susceptible to the blandishments of company officials who, he believes, negotiated privately with Magog workers. Jacques believes that, in return for a settlement that included the seven-day operation, the company offered to guarantee that the Magog mills would remain open (Rheault 1989).

28   According to both union and company officials, the St-Jean plant had the highest grievance rate of any Dominion Textile plant (Rheault 1989).

29   One can interpret this inability to consolidate bargaining units as an additional sign of labour's weakness in the industry.

30   One official asserted that textile unions vary in the extent to which they consult their membership during negotiations.

31   Apparently, the FCTT is the strongest practitioner of pattern bargaining among the unions. Comparing comments made by the FCTT's chief negotiator with those of officials of the ACTWU and UTWA, one would conclude that the FCTT takes the most proactive approach to pattern bargaining. One management official of Dominion Textile expressed some admiration for the FCTT's broad perspective regarding labour conditions within the industry (Rheault 1989).

32   Mustard (1985) also believes that the union must help prepare workers for technological change. Such beliefs are not limited to the UTWA. Arguing that increasing industry productivity is essential to the survival of the industry, the FCTT has commented that "On peut donc dire que 'la productivité est plutôt une affaire de généraux que de chefs' bien que cela demeure l'affaire de tout le monde. Tous doivent y contribuer, ce que

suppose que tous doivent y trouver un avantage" (CSD 1979b, 32).

33 The ACTWU has provided technical assistance to clothing manufacturers since the early 1900s; and, in recent years, has been instrumental in the Tailored Clothing and Technology Corporation [(TC)^2]program, a research-and-development effort to mechanize garment production.

34 In the last three and one-half years, the FCTT has adopted a policy favouring "participative management programs." As part of this approach, the union is attempting to induce management to "implicate the employee from the very beginning" of the process of changing technology. However, interviews with other union officials indicate that the tradition of autocratic management in the textile industry remains quite strong.

35 Beyond that, he suggested that demanding the contractual codification of co-operative undertakings might be considered antithetical to the spirit of co-operation. In fact, the demand to put such matters into writing and resort to legalistic enforcement could be counterproductive.

36 Importantly, Dertouzos, Lester, and Solow (1989) distinguish between capital investment and technological innovation. They believe that capital investment is not enough to be competitive since the technology is equally available to foreign competition.

37 Quick Response is a program that was originated by apparel manufacturers and retailers, whereby data on clothing sales at the retail level (recorded at the point of sales using bar-code technology) are fed back to manufacturers through computer links. This immediate feedback is designed to allow manufacturers to quickly respond to market changes. More recently, Quick Response programs have been extended backward through the supply chain to textile producers.

Chapter

8

RESTRAINT, PRIVATIZATION, AND INDUSTRIAL RELATIONS IN THE PUBLIC SECTOR IN THE 1980s

Mark Thompson
Allen Ponak[1]

*T*he period between 1965 and 1991 marked the emergence of public-sector collective bargaining in Canada. Employee relations changed from regimes dominated by unilateral management decision making to systems of collective bargaining. This transition inevitably was accompanied by experimentation and difficulty for the parties and the public. Because the systems that exist today were created in the late 1960s and 1970s, these earlier decades were characterized by more significant events than were the 1980s. However, important changes did occur in the period after 1980 that may well presage the course of public-sector industrial relations for the rest of the century.

This essay will focus on developments that had the most substantial impact on public-sector industrial relations in the 1980s, in particular, wage controls and privatization. To understand these forces, it is necessary to appreciate the extent of the changes that came before them. The first section of this essay outlines the basic elements of public-sector industrial relations as they emerged by 1980 and identifies major trends in the 1980s. These trends, while important, did not provoke fundamental change in the system. The second section concentrates on wage-restraint programs and privatization, the two major forces the industrial relations systems faced. It will also include a brief discussion of back-to-work legislation, an issue some predicted would become more significant after the early 1980s.

Before discussing industrial relations in the public sector, it is well to recall the role of the public sector in Canadian life. In many respects, this country was built by public and "parapublic" agencies, i.e., branches of government or private agencies acting as extensions of government policies. Initially, the "public sector" was the colonial government in central and Maritime Canada. In the West, private trading companies assumed many governmental functions under charter from the British Crown. After Confederation, the federal government adopted policies to shape the development of the Canadian economy and to preserve national independence from an expansionist neighbour to the south. Later, an array of public institutions was created to further these and other public ends, including transportation systems, cultural organizations, social-service agencies, and other elements of the infrastructure of economic development.

As a consequence, Canada has never displayed the kind of suspicion of the public sector that is evident in the United States. At a recent conference on privatization in Saskatoon, the keynote speaker, an American executive in the United Nations system charged with promoting privatization, stated the principles of privatization: "Firstly, in every country, governments run enterprises. Secondly, in every country, governments run enterprises badly. Thirdly, it is in everyone's interest to move enterprises from the hands of bureaucrats into the hands of entrepreneurs" (Faoro 1990, 14). It is safe to assert that these remarks do not reflect the traditional view of the public sector held by the majority of Canadians. This tradition does not mean that Canadians hold all public institutions in high regard or that some members of the public would not endorse those sentiments. However, when conservative governments proclaim their intentions to reduce the importance of the public sector, it is well to recall the extent to which these initiatives depart from long-standing national traditions. In contrast, public resistance to higher taxes, as shown by opposition to the Goods and Services Tax, may demonstrate opposition to extension of the public sector. This combination of a traditionally high regard for the role of the state and hostility to increased taxes to pay for public goods may affect public-sector industrial relations in the remainder of the decade, as governments try to maintain levels of service while cutting (or not increasing) public spending.

*P*ublic-Sector Employment and Unionism

*I*n this essay, the public sector is defined as including: (1) federal, provincial, and local government; (2) health care; (3) education; and (4) government enterprises. While statistical data are available on the first three categories, it has proved far more difficult to collect information on government enterprises (Thompson and Ponak 1984). Thus, government enterprises are included in the discussion where information is available.

Table 8.1
Public-Sector Employees, 1986 and 1991, and Percentage Change (000s)

	1986	1991	% Change
Education	784.7	889.2	13.3
Health and Welfare	865.9	1029.7	18.9
Local government	179.9	202.8	12.7
Provincial government	210.8	227.0	7.7
Federal government	256.6	261.8	2.0
Total Public Sector	2297.9	2610.5	
Total Public and Private	8882.1	9582.0	
Public-Sector Proportion (%)	25.8	27.2	

Source: Statistics Canada, *Employment, Earnings and Hours,* Catalogue 72–002 (Ottawa: Minister of Supply and Services, various years). Table 1.1. Figures are for January of reporting year.

EMPLOYMENT

According to Table 8.1, employment in the public sector, excluding government enterprises, stood at 2.7 million workers in 1991 and accounted for 27.2 percent of total paid employment in the Canadian economy. This ratio (public sector to the entire economy) has been increasing slowly over time. In 1986, the public sector accounted for 25.8 percent of total employment, and in 1975 it was estimated that the public sector employed 23.7 percent of workers in Canada (Bird 1978). Inclusion of government enterprises would likely raise the public-sector proportion to approximately 30 percent of the overall work force (Thompson and Ponak 1991).

Within public employment, the health and welfare sector now contains the most employees and has been growing significantly in size. Between 1986 and 1991, employment in health and welfare increased by close to 20 percent. By comparison, employment growth in the other parts of the public sector in the same period has been more modest, ranging from 13 percent in education to 2 percent in the federal government. Table 8.1 shows, perhaps contrary to general belief, that employment in federal, provincial, and local governments combined is less than employment in either the health or the education sector.

UNIONISM

It is not the size of the public sector that has attracted the attention of the industrial relations community: it is the degree of unionization. Table 8.2 shows that, in 1988, public administration had by far the highest union density in Canada, with over three-quarters of employees belonging to unions. Transportation, communication, and utilities—a category that includes many public employees in government enterprises (e.g., Radio-Canada, Ontario Hydro) and local transit—has the next-highest union density (57 percent). In contrast, the union density in

Table 8.2
Union Members as a Percentage of Paid Employees, by Sector, 1988

Forestry	47.3
Mines, quarries, oil wells	28.6
Manufacturing	36.8
Construction	52.8
Transportation, communication, utilities	56.6
Trade	10.4
Finance, insurance, real estate	3.4
Service	33.4
Public administration	76.8
Overall Economy	33.7

Source: Statistics Canada, *Corporations and Labour Unions Returns Act, Annual Report,* Catalogue 71–202 (Ottawa: Minister of Supply and Services, 1988).

manufacturing (the traditional focus of industrial relations research) is under 40 percent.

In Table 8.3, data from 1986 are used to show disaggregated public-sector union density. The figures in this table are derived from a labour-force survey and show generally lower levels of union density than Corporations and Labour Unions Returns Act (CALURA) data provided in Table 8.2. The provincial government is the most unionized part of the public sector, followed by education and the federal government. The health sector has the lowest union density, but it is still higher than 50 percent.

The high levels of union membership in the public sector were mainly achieved in the 1970s. As Table 8.4 indicates, public employees accounted for only 10 percent of unionized workers in 1965, but, by 1975, this proportion had tripled, and it continued to rise through 1986. If public enterprises were included, it is likely that more than half of all union members in Canada are in the public sector.

It is no surprise, therefore, that the two largest unions in Canada are public-sector ones—the Canadian Union of Public Employees (CUPE) and the National Union of Provincial Government Employees (NUPGE). Moreover, were teachers'

Table 8.3
Union Members as a Percentage of Paid Employees, by Sector, Disaggregated, 1986

Education	66.7
Health and Welfare	55.2
Local government	63.9
Provincial government	70.7
Federal government	64.6

Source: Mary Lou Coates, David Arrowsmith, and Melanie Courchene, *The Labour Movement and Trade Unionism Reference Tables* (Kingston, ON: Industrial Relations Centre, Queen's University), 51–53.

Table 8.4
Public-Sector Union Membeship Growth,[a] *1965–1986*

	Union Membership (000s)				
Sector	1965	1970	1975	1984	1986
Education	14	36	313	535	539
Health and Welfare	64	121	232	500	525
Local Government	75	86	107	153	157
Provincial Government	16	116	150	174	206
Federal Government	3	125	176	188	184
Total Public Sector	172	484	978	1550	1611
Overall Economy	1589	2173	2884	3651	3527
Public Sector as Percentage of Total	10.8	22.3	33.9	42.5	45.7

Note: [a]Figures were not available for government enterprises, which, generally, are highly unionized. With government enterprises included, it is likely that public-sector unionism would have accounted for half the Canadian union total in 1986.

Sources: Figures for the overall economy were obtained from Labour Canada, *Directory of Labour Organizations in Canada* (various issues). Public-sector union membership figures obtained as follows: 1965—Canada Department of Labour, Economics and Research Branch, *Industrial and Geographic Distribution of Union Membership in Canada*, 1965; 1970—"Industrial and Geographic Distribution of Union Membership in Canada, 1970," *The Labour Gazette*, August 1971: 557–62; 1975—"Industrial and Geographic Distribution of Union Membership in Canada, 1975," *The Labour Gazette*, May 1977: 224–26; 1984—Statistics Canada, *Survey of Union Membership,* conducted as a supplement to the 1984 *Labour Force Survey*, Catalogue 71–001 (Ottawa: Minister of Supply and Services, 1984). 1986—Statistics Canada, *Labour Market Activity Survey,* conducted as a supplement to the 1986 *Labour Force Survey* (Ottawa: Minister of Supply and Services, 1986). Mary Lou Coates, David Arrowsmith, and Melanie Courchene, *The Labour Movement and Trade Unionism Reference Tables* (Kingston, ON: Industrial Relations Centre, Queen's University 1989), 51–53.

and nurses' unions to form national unions, these groups would rank among the largest labour organizations in Canada. CUPE and NUPGE continue to experience solid growth (see Table 8.5). In contrast, Canada's fifth-largest union, the Public Service Alliance of Canada (PSAC), has seen its membership decline slightly in the 1980s. Based almost exclusively in the federal civil service, PSAC has lost members as the federal government reduces its overall employment levels.

Many explanations have been offered for the rapid transition of public employees from nonunion to union status (Goldenberg 1988; Ponak 1982; Rose 1984). Certainly, favourable legislation enacted in the 1960s and 1970s was a powerful influence promoting unionization. An important element in the growth process was the history of employee organization in the public sector. Although government employees did not become unionized until the mid-1960s, they had long been organized into employee and professional associations. Dating in some cases to the First World War, these associations engaged in consultation with public-sector employees on subjects as diverse as training, educational opportunities, social functions, and compensation.

Unionism in most of the public sector emerged when these organizations

Table 8.5
Public-Sector Unions

Union	Level of Government	Annualized Change in Members			
		Members 1990 (000s)	1971– 80 (%)	1981– 85[a] (%)	1986– 90 (%)
Canadian Union of Public Employees (CUPE)	Local/ Health	376.9	17.1	2.1	4.8
National Union of Provincial Government Employees (NUPGE)	Provincial	301.2	21.3	3.3	3.7
Public Service Alliance of Canada (PSAC)	Federal	162.7	5.3	3.5	-2.1

Note: [a]In 1954, Labour Canada figures began including all Rand formulae in calculations, which provides a misleadingly high rate of growth.

Sources: Mary Lou Coates, David Arrowsmith, Melanie Courchene, *The Labour Movement and Trade Unionism Reference Tables* (Kingston, ON: Industrial Relations Centre, Queen's University, 1989), 27–30; Mary Lou Coates, *Industrial Relations in 1990: Trends and Emerging Issues*, (Kingston, ON: Industrial Relations Centre, Queen's University, 1991), p. 48.

transformed themselves from associations into unions and exchanged consultation for collective bargaining. Important factors in this transformation included: (1) rising employee expectations and militancy, which characterized society in general during the 1960s; (2) the demonstration effect of successful action by existing public-sector unions; (3) increasing evidence of the inadequacies of traditional consultation mechanisms (Frankel 1960), and (4) a shift in public policy from a position of hostility toward public-sector unions to one of positive support.

It is likely that the period of high union growth within the public sector is over, and these unions cannot be counted on as sources of growth for the labour movement, as they were in the 1970s and 1980s, unless nurses and teachers affiliate with the mainstream labour organizations (e.g., the Canadian Labour Congress and the Confederation of National Trade Unions). The reasons for this stability are, first, that many areas of the public sector are almost saturated in terms of union density. Most school boards, hospitals, and civil services are already unionized. While a few nonunion pockets remain, such as research hospitals in a few provinces, opportunities for organizing several thousand workers in one campaign seldom exist.

Second, the public sector itself is not growing as quickly as it did during the 1970s. Indeed, during the 1980s, governments began to focus on reducing their services, and the concept of privatizing government services and government enterprises (discussed below) gained currency.

For the public-sector unions themselves, a period of consolidation may actually prove useful. Rapid growth also gave rise to structural problems. Organizations originally designed for consultation activities were not necessarily well adapted to collective bargaining. Large increases in membership and numerous new locals were difficult for most organizations to digest. Analyzing a strike conducted by CUPE, one observer pointed to the following as factors contributing to the strike:

> (a) a multiplicity of elected positions barren of power, (b) powerful staff positions, notably the regional directors, unaccountable to an electorate, (c) dues paid to locals and rebated to the central organization, leaving it preoccupied with fiscal survival and debt collection rather than policy and leadership functions; and (d) in the hospital sector, a national servicing staff stretched very thinly, unsupported by any locally paid officers. (Deverell 1982, 181)

Looking at the PSAC, another observer commented that the union "continues to cling to an antiquated structure . . . incompatible with the occupational bargaining units which cut across government departments" (Rose 1984, 110). The 1990s, accordingly, may provide public-sector unions with an opportunity to carefully evaluate their organizational structure and prepare for the challenges that lie ahead.

*P*ublic-Sector Legislation

*M*ost jurisdictions have separate statutes for at least some of their public-sector employees (see Table 8.6). In the federal jurisdiction, for instance, the Public Service Staff Relations Act (PSSRA) governs the civil services and certain government enterprises (e.g., the National Film Board), while most Crown corporations are governed under the Canada Labour Code. In Ontario, the tendency toward special statutes for public employees is more pronounced; separate laws exist for school teachers, hospital workers, police, fire fighters, college teachers, and provincial civil servants.

The multiplicity of statutes reflects an absence of consensus on important aspects of public-sector labour policy. Whereas private-sector legislation is guided by a generally accepted underlying set of policy considerations derived from PC 1003 in 1944, no such model exists for the public sector. Thus, each jurisdiction has experimented and devised its own solutions to the issues posed by public-employee unionism.

The result has been considerable variation, both within jurisdictions and across jurisdictions. In Alberta, for example, teachers, municipal employees, and liquor board workers have the right to strike, while hospital workers, police and fire fighters, college and university staff, and civil servants do not. Civil servants, hospital employees, police and fire personnel in Ontario cannot strike; teachers from elementary school through university, and some liquor distribution employees

Table 8.6
Public-Sector Labour Legislation

Jurisdiction	General Private Sector	General Municipal	Police	Fire Fighters	Hospitals	Teachers	Civil Service	Government Enterprises	Additional Comments
Federal	Canada Labour Code	Canada Labour Code	Canada Labour Code	Public Service Staff Relations Act (Canada Labour Code)	Public Service Staff Relations Act	Public Service Staff Relations Act	Public Service Staff Relations Act	Canada Labour Code	Royal Canadian Mounted Police excluded from Public Service Staff Relations Act and Canada Labour Code
British Columbia	Industrial Relations Act	Industrial Relations Act	Industrial Relations Act	Industrial Relations Act	Industrial Relations Act	Industrial Relations Act	Public Service Labour Relations Act	Industrial Relations Act	
Alberta	Labour Relations Code	Labour Relations Code	Police Officers Collective Bargaining Act	Labour Relations Code	Labour Relations Code	Labour Relations Code	Public Service Employees Relations Act	Labour Relations Code	Right to strike removed from hospital workers in 1984
Saskatchewan	Trade Union Act	Trade Union Act	Police Act	Fire Department Platoon Act	Trade Union Act	Education Act	Trade Union Act	Trade Union Act	Earliest comprehensive public-sector labour legislation in Canada (1944)
Manitoba	Labour Relations Act	Labour Relations Act	Labour Relations Act; City of Winnipeg Act; Police Act	Labour Relations Act; Fire Department's Arbitration Act	Labour Relations Act	Public Schools Act	Labour Relations Act; Civil Service Act	Labour Relations Act	1986 pay-equity legislation applied to public sector
Ontario	Labour Relations Act	Labour Relations Act	Police Act; Ontario Provincial Police Public Service Act	Fire Department's Act	Labour Relations Act; Hospital Labour Disputes Arbitration Act	School Boards and Teachers Collective Negotiations Act; Colleges Collective Bargaining Act	Crown Employees Collective Bargaining Act	Crown Employees Collective Bargaining Act	1987 pay-equity legislation to apply to public sector

Table 8.6 (continued)

Jurisdiction	General Private Sector	General Municipal	Police	Fire Fighters	Hospitals	Teachers	Civil Service	Government Enterprises	Additional Comments
Quebec	Labour Code	Labour Code	Labour Code Div. II; Civil Service Act; Police Force Surete du Quebec	Labour Code Div. II	Labour Code Public Service Act	Labour Code Public Service Act	Labour Code Civil Service Act Public Service Act	Labour Code Civil Service Act Public Service Act	Frequent revision of public-sector labour laws
New Brunswick	Industrial Relations Act	Industrial Relations Act	Industrial Relations Act (Police Act)	Industrial Relations Act	Public Service Labour Relations Act	Public Service Labour Relations Act	Public Service Labour Relations Act Civil Service Act	Public Service Labour Relations Act	Public Service Labour Relations Act modelled closely on federal Public Service Staff Relations Act
Nova Scotia	Trade Union Act	Trade Union Act	Trade Union Act	Trade Union Act	Trade Union Act	Teachers' Collective Bargaining Act	Civil Service Collective Bargaining Act	Trade Union Act	Police have the right to strike
Prince Edward Island	Labour Act	Labour Act	Labour Act Police Act	Labour Act	Labour Act	School Act	Civil Service Act	Civil Service Act	Registered nurses recently included in Labour Act
Newfoundland	Labour Relations Act	Labour Relations Act	Labour Relations Act The Royal Newfoundland Constabulary Act	Labour Relations Act St. John's Fire Department Act	Public Service Collective Bargaining Act	The Newfoundland Teachers Collective Bargaining Act Canada Labour Code	Public Service (Collective Bargaining) Act Public Service Act Public Service Staff Relations Act	Public Service Collective Bargaining Act	Ban on strikes by civil servants aggressively challenged by unions in 1986
Northwest Territories		Canada Labour Code							
Yukon Territory									

Source: Table compiled as of April 1991 through a statutory review of each jurisdiction; Peter Barnacle, Labour Legislation and Public Policy Reference Tables (Kingston, ON: Industrial Relations Centre, Queen's University, 1989).

have the right to strike. Police in several provinces are prohibited from joining associations affiliated with the general labour movement; no such restrictions are in place elsewhere. Six jurisdictions place government enterprises under general private-sector statutes; in the remaining five, civil service statutes govern. There are also notable public- and private-sector differences with respect to bargaining-unit determination and union recognition (Ponak and Thompson, 1989).

The diversity of approaches does not mean that some important commonalities do not exist. The freedom of employees to engage in union activity without employer interference is well entrenched. Employers are obliged to recognize and engage in meaningful negotiations with unions enjoying majority support. Grievance procedures for the resolution of rights disputes through binding arbitration are provided almost universally, whatever the statutory framework (Swinton 1984). In all jurisdictions, municipal workers (police and fire fighters excepted) are governed by the general private-sector legislation and enjoy the same rights as private-sector workers.

During the 1980s, the statutory framework remained relatively stable, with the exception of two important areas—compensation and ad hoc strike legislation, both discussed later. Statutory changes affecting dispute-resolution procedures were not widespread. In British Columbia, teachers were put under general labour legislation in 1988 (the Industrial Relations Act) and acquired the right to strike. Alberta legislation removed the right to strike from hospital workers (workers struck anyway), but gave employees of the liquor commission the right to strike for the first time. Early court decisions under the Charter of Rights had little impact on public-sector labour relations.

The most important permanent change in the legal regime of public-sector labour relations occurred in the Supreme Court of Canada in 1982. In 1980, the federal government, acting under a provision of the PSSRA, attempted to designate all air-traffic controllers as essential. Previously, the parties had agreed that all commercial flights would be cancelled in the event of a strike by controllers, leaving 10 to 15 percent of that bargaining unit to be designated as essential to service military and other emergency flights. The union objected to the government's 1980 designation proposal and was upheld by the board responsible for administering the Act. The government took the case to the Supreme Court, which ruled that, contrary to the practice followed for fifteen years, the board did not have the authority to determine the necessary level of service. Instead, the government would determine the necessary level of service, leaving to the parties or the board only the determination of the number of employees necessary to maintain that service.

Following this decision, the federal government maintained its intention of requiring air-traffic controllers to service all commercial flights, with the result that 100 percent of the bargaining unit were designated as essential. Another dozen bargaining units, ranging from aircraft operations to nurses to stationary engineers, were put in the same position, effectively nullifying their right to strike. An additional nine bargaining units had 60 percent or more of their members designated, which virtually eliminated any hope of mounting an effective strike (Swimmer 1987).

One response of the PSAC the union most directly affected by this decision, was to make an agreement with the federal government to negotiate simultaneously for virtually all of its bargaining units, thus raising the spectre of a government-wide strike should negotiations break down. By early 1991, the parties had not even approached such a point in their relations, but the union did issue such threats in response to a government proposal to limit wage increases to 3 percent in 1991.

In 1989, the federal government announced a new set of policies ("Public Services 2000") for the management of the public service (Tellier 1990). The goal of Public Services 2000 was to strengthen the authority of public-sector managers in order to improve the efficiency of the public service. The implications of these policies for collective bargaining were not immediately clear. However, in June 1991, the government introduced legislation to facilitate job transfers, allow wider discretion for the hiring of part-time and casual workers, and simplify dismissal procedures. Public-sector unions immediately announced their opposition to these proposals. In the summer of 1991, it was difficult to predict the fate of this legislation, in light of the government's preoccupation with the constitution and other issues.

Apart from these changes in the federal government's industrial relations policies, however, there were no significant new policy initiatives with respect to dispute resolution.

COLLECTIVE BARGAINING AND COMPENSATION

The years after public employees gained the right to bargain collectively were also notable for rising government expenditures and increases in the number of employees in the public sector. Many workers in industries such as health care, education, and social services were traditionally paid very low wages on the grounds that their clients could not afford compensation equivalent to that paid in the rest of the economy. As these agencies became integrated into the public sector, this argument disappeared. Thus, the combination of market conditions, the changing nature of the public sector, and newly gained employee bargaining power produced generous negotiated settlements from the late 1960s through the mid-1970s, ranging from 7.2 percent in 1969 to 19.1 percent in 1975 (Maslove and Swimmer 1980), giving rise to concerns that public-sector bargaining favoured union interests so much so that settlements there would inevitably exceed settlements in the private sector. Simultaneously, public-sector settlements also provoked complaints that public-sector workers, once paid less than their counterparts in the private sector, had moved ahead so far that they enjoyed a wage premium over workers in other industries.

Both fears proved largely groundless. While public-sector settlement levels did exceed private-sector levels occasionally between 1967 and 1975, over the 1970s and late 1980s, public- and private-sector wage settlements were fairly similar at the aggregate level (Wilton 1986; Gunderson and Riddell 1991). The large settlements that attracted special attention in the early 1970s reflected agreement between the parties that public-employee groups needed to "catch up" with wages paid elsewhere in the economy.

A public-sector wage premium relative to the private sector does exist. However, it seems to have been highest in the late 1970s and has been dissipating since then. By the late 1980s, it was between 5 and 10 percent, occasionally reaching 15 percent, depending on the specific group and the time considered. Much of that premium is accounted for by the higher incidence of union membership in the public sector (since union membership is associated with a wage premium for workers in both the public and private sectors) and tends to favour women and lower-paid public-sector workers. The largest public-sector wage advantage is at the municipal and provincial levels, and the smallest is at the federal level (Gunderson and Riddell 1991).

DISPUTES AND THEIR RESOLUTION

Whether, and under what circumstances, public employees should be legally permitted to withdraw their services has been a policy concern since public-sector laws were first debated. The pros and cons of giving public employees the legal right to strike have been extensively reviewed elsewhere (see, for example, Swimmer 1984; Ponak and Thompson 1989; Weiler 1980). For purposes of this discussion, it is sufficient to note that the debate over the public-sector right to strike has not been resolved. As shown in Table 8.7, there is a diversity of treatment for various groups of public employees.

Where the right to strike has been substantially restrained, interest arbitration has been substituted. Police and fire fighters are most frequently governed by arbitration. Arbitration as a dispute process has been the target of much criticism, focussed on the ground that its use decreases the likelihood that the parties will reach a settlement at the bargaining table. The criticism receives limited support by empirical studies showing public-sector settlement rates under arbitration of between 65 and 70 percent, compared to more than 90 percent under a right-to-strike system (Ponak and Falkenberg 1989). Despite these findings, there have been few policy shifts within those jurisdictions that rely upon arbitration.

A compromise policy approach referred to as a "choice-of-procedures" was first introduced under the federal PSSRA in 1967 and has gained acceptance elsewhere, although such acceptance is not widespread. Under this dispute-resolution procedure, labour can choose between arbitration or the strike as the mechanism for resolving any bargaining disputes. One study across several Canadian and American jurisdictions with choice of procedure found that few strikes actually occur, and that unions are more likely to choose arbitration over the strike option (Ponak and Wheeler 1980). However, since the party with the right to select a dispute mechanism may gain a strategic advantage over its opponent, choice of procedure

Table 8.7
Dispute Procedures by Jurisdiction, 1990

Jurisdiction	General Municipal	Police	Fire Fighters	Hospitals	Teachers	Civil Service	Government Enterprises
British Columbia	RTS[a]	RTS	RTS	RTS	RTS	RTS	RTS
Alberta	RTS	ARB[b]	ARB	ARB	RTS	ARB	RTS
Saskatchewan	RTS	COP[c]	COP	RTS	COP	RTS	RTS
Manitoba	RTS	ARB[d] COP	ARB	RTS	ARB	COP	RTS
Ontario	RTS	ARB	ARB	ARB	RTS	ARB	ARB
Quebec	RTS	ARB	ARB	RTS	RTS	RTS	RTS
New Brunswick	RTS	RTS COP	ARB	RTS	RTS	RTS	RTS
Nova Scotia	RTS	RTS	RTS	RTS[e]	COP or RTS[f]	ARB	RTS
Prince Edward Island	ARB	ARB	ARB	ARB	ARB	ARB	ARB
Newfoundland	RTS	ARB	ARB	RTS	RTS	RTS	RTS
Federal	RTS	COP	COP	COP	COP	COP	COP[g] or RTS
Yukon Territory					ARB	COP	COP[g] or RTS
Northwest Territories	RTS	RTS	COP	COP	RTS	ARB	

Notes:
a Right to strike
b Compulsory arbitration (choice of procedures: one party may choose arbitration, forcing it on the other. The award is binding.)
c Choice of procedures
d City of Winnipeg
e Some large hospitals (e.g., Victoria General) do not have RTS.
f COP for matters bargained with individual school boards; RTS for matters bargained province-wide
g COP for some units under the Public Service Staff Relations Act (e.g., National Film Board); RTS under the Canada Labour Code (e.g., Atomic Energy)

Sources: Table compiled as of April 1990 through a statutory review of each jurisdiction; Peter Barnacle, *Labour Legislation and Public Policy Reference Tables* (Kingston, ON: Industrial Relations Centre, Queen's University 1989).

has not spread much beyond the federal sector. Indeed, British Columbia, which used this approach in the 1970s, later abandoned it.

One measure of the effectiveness of Canadian public-sector dispute-resolution policy can be seen in Tables 8.8, 8.9, and 8.10, which summarize time lost as a result of strikes. Annual totals of public-sector work-days lost as a result of work stoppages are presented in Table 8.8. There is substantial annual fluctuation, with respect to both total time lost and the public-sector proportion of overall strike activity in the economy. In any given year, one or two disputes account for a significant proportion of the time lost, a normal pattern for Canadian strikes generally. Usually six to eight large strikes of long duration account for one-half of the total working days lost in any year, a pattern that holds for the public sector.

It can be seen from Table 8.8 that total strike volume (i.e., working days lost) decreased during the 1980s. Between 1976 and 1980, the public sector lost 1.5 million working days to work stoppages; from 1981 to 1985, this figure declined to 1.3 million; and, from 1986 to 1990, strike volume further declined to slightly fewer than 1.0 million working days lost.

When contrasted with the rest of the economy, however, the pattern becomes more complex. Overall strike activity throughout the Canadian economy declined during the 1980s—thus, the decline in public-sector work stoppages was part of a more general trend. Between 1981 and 1985, the proportion of working days lost attributable to the public sector (versus the private sector) actually rose from 20 percent (1976–80) to slightly more than 25 percent. In the latter half of the 1980s, the trend was again reversed. Between 1986 and 1990, the public sector accounted for only 18 percent of overall strike volume, comparable to the 1976–80 time period.

These data are noteworthy for several reasons. First, the downward trend in the absolute volume of the public-sector strikes may mean that the issue of public-sector disputes will decline in importance. To the extent that the incidence of these strikes continues to drop, political pressure to make changes should also decline. In fact, the relative stability of dispute-resolution policy during the 1980s may well reflect reduced public concern about government strikes.

Disaggregated analysis of public-sector strike activity by province and industry is presented in Tables 8.9 and 8.10. With respect to jurisdiction, it is clear that the province of Quebec, with less than one-quarter of Canada-wide public-sector employees, continues to be the most strike-prone jurisdiction. Strike volume in that province was stable from 1973 to 1990, accounting for just under 40 percent of total public-sector strike volume in Canada. British Columbia also experienced a disproportionately high volume of public-sector strikes; with 10 percent of total employment, the province accounted for 20 percent of total public-sector strike losses.

Conversely, the provinces of Ontario, Alberta, and Manitoba experienced less public-sector strike activity relative to their shares of total employment. It is interesting to note that, while public employees in British Columbia and Quebec have wide latitude to engage in legal strikes, their counterparts in Ontario,

Table 8.8

Public-Sector Strike Loss, by Jurisdiction, 1973–1990

Year	Working Days Lost (000s)	As Percentage Overall Economy	
1973	773	13.4	
1974	631	6.8	
1975	1873	17.2	
1973–75 (Mean)	<u>1092</u>	<u>12.6</u>	
1976	2226	19.2	
1977	428	12.9	
1978	849	11.5	Nation-wide postal strike
1979	1801	23.0	Quebec public sector, Saskatchewan civil service
1980	2426	27.0	Quebec teachers' strike 40 percent of total
1976–80 (Mean)	<u>1546</u>	<u>19.8</u>	
1981	2657	29.9	Nova Scotia health care, B.C. municipalities, postal dispute account for two-thirds of total
1982	823	14.2	Alberta nurses, B.C. civil service, 40 percent of total
1983	2,072	46.6	Quebec teachers, B.C. general strike, two-thirds of total
1984	638	16.5	Recession and public-sector wage controls reduced total
1985	531	16.7	Ontario Hydro and Air Canada flight attendants half the total
1981–85 (Mean)	<u>1344</u>	<u>25.7</u>	
1986	701	9.8	
1987	756	19.8	B.C. General Strike 38 percent of total
1988	445	9.1	
1989	1678	45.1	Quebec public sector 46 percent of total
1990	775	15.0	
1986–90 (Mean)	<u>871</u>	<u>17.6</u>	

Source: Labour Canada, *Strikes and Lockouts in Canada, 1973–1990* (Ottawa: Minister of Supply and Services, 1984). Note that, because of definitional differences, the totals in this table are not identical to totals calculated by Labour Canada.

Table 8.9
Public-Sector Strike Loss, by Jurisdiction, 1973–1990

Jurisdiction	1973–85		1986–90	
	Percentage of Public Sector Total Working Days Lost[a]	Percentage of Total Public Employment[b]	Percentage of Public Sector Total Working Days Lost[c]	Percentage of Total Employment[c]
British Columbia	13.4	10	21.2	10.5
Alberta	4.9	7	5.4	9.2
Saskatchewan	3.3	3	2.2	2.9
Manitoba	1.0	5	0.1	3.7
Ontario	12.3	29	19.0	40.1
Quebec	38.9	21	41.5	24.2
New Brunswick	0.9	2	0.1	2.0
Nova Scotia	5.1	3	1.8	2.7
Prince Edward Island	0.0	1	0.0	0.3
Newfoundland	1.7	2	6.3	1.4
Northwest Territories	NA	—	>0.01	0.2
Federal	18.5	17	2.2	2.7
Total	100.0	100.0	99.71[d]	100.0

Sources: [a] Labour Canada, *Strikes and Lockouts in Canada,* 1973–85 and unpublished data from Labour Canada.
[b] Ponak, Allen. 1982. "Public-Sector Collective Bargaining" in John C. Anderson and Morley Gunderson, eds., *Union-Management Relations in Canada,* Don Mills, ON: Addison-Wesley, 343–378.
[c] Statistics Canada. *Employment, Earnings and Hours,* Catalogue 72–002, Table 1.2, 1986–90.
[d] Total is less than 100 percent due to rounding errors.

Alberta, and Manitoba are much more likely to be governed by compulsory arbitration. Although rigorous analysis has not been carried out regarding the relationship between strike legislation and strike volume in Canada, common sense dictates that a relationship should exist.

Finally, Table 8.10 presents a sectoral breakdown of strike volume. Education, health care, and the federal public administration are underrepresented in terms of work stoppages compared to their respective shares of total government employment. Local and provincial employees, in contrast, are overrepresented. Such is especially the case with respect to provincial government, which, although accounting for less than 10 percent of total public-sector employment, was responsible for 30 percent of the overall strike volume. The provincial government share of strike activity increased sharply during the last part of the 1980s compared to previous time periods.

Only one study has systematically examined factors possibly associated with Canadian public-sector strike variation. Smith (1984) tested a model in which strike activity was posited as a function of unanticipated inflation, unemployment levels, wage guidelines, contract expirations, and a time trend line. Dependent variables were strike frequency, working days lost, and workers involved, each

Table 8.10
Public-Sector Strike Loss, by Component, 1973–1990

Component	1973–85		1986–90	
	Percentage of Public Sector Total Working Days Lost	Percentage of Total Government Employment	Percentage of Public Sector Total Working Days Lost	Percentage of Total Government Employment
Education	29.8	24.6	26.6	36.5
Health & Welfare	16.5	17.8	24.9	35.6
Local government	14.7	11.5	15.2	8.1
Provincial government	12.5	16.4	31.3	9.2
Federal government	2.8	15.2	1.9	10.6
Government Enterprises	23.7	14.5	NA	NA
Total	100.0	100.0	98.0	100.0

Source: Labour Canada: *Strikes and Lockouts in Canada,* 1973–85, and unpublished data from Labour Canada.

measured on a quarterly basis inclusively from 1972 to 1980. The only independent variable that was statistically significant in any of the equations was the time trend variable (i.e., strike activity in the public sector increased over time). None of the other variables were statistically significant, regardless of the dependent variable, and estimated coefficient signs were often in opposite directions from the hypotheses. The explanatory power of the equations was weak, particularly when working days lost and workers involved were used as dependent variables. The results were similar when Quebec data were treated separately.

Two comments can be made about Smith's findings. First, the data end at the fourth quarter of 1980. The data in this paper show (Table 8.8) that strike activity (expressed as working days lost) decreased after 1980. Thus, extending Smith's analysis through 1990 might produce somewhat different results with respect to the time trend line. Second, the model that Smith used in his study was developed largely on the basis of private-sector models, an explicit and deliberate aspect of the research. An important objective of the study was to determine whether factors that account for private-sector strike variation could also explain public sector-strike activity. The answer appears to be "no." Smith's model provided adequate results for the private-sector, but not for the public sector.

These results reinforce what most observers of the public sector have long suggested—namely, that the underlying dynamics of collective bargaining and dispute resolution are different for the two sectors. In particular, there exists a political dimension to decision making and the costs of agreement and disagreement in the public sector that is largely absent in the private sector. Moreover, unlike in the private sector, where dispute mechanisms are similar across jurisdictions and industries, in the public sector a great deal of variation in dispute procedures is evident. Models of public-sector strike activity that fail to adequately capture such forces will, in all likelihood, continue to produce disappointing results.

Reactions to the Spread of Collective Bargaining

In many ways, the rapid spread of collective bargaining represented one of the most dramatic changes in the public sector in recent Canadian history. The substantial gains made by public-sector unions stimulated a number of reactions from management and governments.

MANAGEMENT STRUCTURES

Perhaps the most urgent task for public-sector employers in the immediate aftermath of the unionization of their work forces was to establish appropriate structures for dealing with their unionized employees. Union victories in the early rounds of bargaining are partial testimony of the difficulties that management encountered in attempting to meet this challenge. By the end of the 1970s, several patterns of management organization for collective bargaining had emerged.

The federal and provincial governments established de facto labour relations departments to represent them in dealings with their own employees. These agencies often report to "treasury board," the secretariats established to serve cabinet committees charged with controlling expenditures. Treasury board representatives, together with line managers from ministries or departments concerned, typically form negotiating committees.

At the level of municipalities, school boards, and other agencies of local government, practices vary widely. Elected officials are reluctant to cede bargaining authority to unelected parties, thus inhibiting the development of professional bargaining agents. Larger municipalities typically have specialized labour relations departments to represent them in negotiations with labour organizations. Elected officials occasionally sit on negotiating committees, but seldom play a prominent part in bargaining, and play almost no role in contract administration. In smaller municipalities, elected officials and general managers are likely to represent the employer.

Hospitals are typically represented by employer associations, which essentially negotiate province-wide agreements, although individual hospitals can opt out of those structures in some jurisdictions. Provincial governments bear the ultimate financial responsibility for negotiated settlements in the health sector, and they generally favour some form of centralized bargaining to assist them in monitoring and controlling costs. School boards in a number of provinces follow similar practices. In provinces where local government bodies bargain individually, pattern bargaining appears to be very strong, especially for teachers and uniformed security services.

In Quebec, a system of highly centralized bargaining covering most of the major elements of the public sector exists. The parties negotiate over economic matters on a provincial basis, often in a highly politicized atmosphere. The Minister of Finance is often directly involved in negotiations. Each bargaining round in Quebec has become a major political event in the life of the province, and virtually every large set of negotiations has entailed the passage of at least one piece of special legislation (Hébert 1984).

PUBLIC-SECTOR WAGE CONTROLS

The industrial relations system established for virtually all public-employee groups was based on "free collective bargaining" modelled on the private sector. That is, the parties were to be free to bargain to an impasse with the possibility either of a work stoppage or of compulsory interest arbitration as the mechanism for resolving disputes. The results of bargaining or arbitration were to be based on the relative bargaining power of the parties or a combination of economic and industrial relations factors considered by arbitrators (see Swan 1984). In the rounds of bargaining in the late 1960s and early 1970s, this system operated as the legislation had intended.

Beginning in 1975, however, public-sector wage controls severely limited the right of the parties to negotiate settlements. In addition, the authority of arbitrators to award increases above stipulated levels was effectively abolished. The nation's first peacetime wage-control program was imposed by the federal government in 1975 and was to last for three years. The Anti-Inflation Program covered both the public and private sectors, and prices as well as wages, but its primary target was public-sector compensation (Maslove and Swimmer 1980). This was a period of accelerating inflation, and the Trudeau government acted on the belief that public-sector settlements stimulated price increases by imposing greater costs on the taxpayer as well as encouraging higher wage demands by private-sector unions. In response to these pressures, the federal government imposed a series of limits on compensation increases for the federal departments and Crown corporations. Several provincial governments passed legislation to bring their own public sectors under the federal program. Other governments, most notably Quebec's, established parallel systems for restraining increases in compensation.

The inclusion of both the public and private sectors in the Anti-Inflation Program united the Canadian labour movement against it. The Canadian Labour

Congress (CLC) backed a constitutional challenge to the actions of both the federal and the provincial governments. The CLC also organized a one-day work stoppage by more than 800 000 workers, labelled a "National Day of Protest," to show its opposition to the government action.

In the end, labour's action did not deter the government. The constitutional challenge failed, and political pressures were insufficient to bring about any change in the original program. The rate of increase of both wages and prices moderated slightly while the Anti-Inflation Program was in effect, although the rate of wage increases declined more than prices, and public-sector wages were restrained more than private-sector wages (Maslove and Swimmer 1980). Doubts remained about the relative importance of the Anti-Inflation Program and a weakening economy, but public opinion enabled the government to continue the program until its scheduled demise in 1978.

Whatever the uncertainty about the effects of the Anti-Inflation Program, the lesson for governments of the 1975–78 period was that wage controls aimed at the public sector were popular politically and might have some influence on wages and prices generally.

Public-Sector Labour Relations at the End of the Growth Phase

As noted above, the golden age of public-sector industrial relations lasted from the mid-1960s to about 1982. By 1982, the basic outlines of the system were in place. The dominant legislative regime was several statutes dealing with specific elements of the public sector. These statutes permitted bargaining over a wide range of issues, though not to the same extent as in the private sector. All provinces permitted strikes by municipal employees not in police and fire departments. In addition, virtually every jurisdiction had extended the right to strike to other groups in the public sector. Perhaps most importantly, these statutes uniformly removed the employer's right to determine wages and most conditions of employment unilaterally by providing for compulsory arbitration where strikes were prohibited.

Public-sector employers had established formal structures to deal with unionized employees, but among politicians, at least, there were serious doubts about management's ability to withstand the pressures these unions could bring to the bargaining table. While there was little evidence of unions dealing directly with politicians instead of management negotiators ("multilateral bargaining"), the Anti-Inflation Program and ad hoc back-to-work legislation were clear indicators that politicians were prepared to intervene directly in the bargaining process from time to time.

Unionism in the public sector had grown rapidly throughout the period, but the rate of increase had already begun to diminish by the end of the 1970s. The sheer size of pubic-sector unions did not completely offset their structural weaknesses, however. The three major public-sector unions resulted from mergers that left them with weak central authority and a lack of experienced leadership. Furthermore, large elements of their membership lacked experience in militant action in either bargaining or political arenas. These organizations had grown under relatively benign conditions and were not well equipped to cope with adversity.

Apart from the internal dynamics of the large national organizations, public-sector unions lacked cohesion. Two large and militant groups of public employees, teachers and nurses, had no national organization committed to collective bargaining. Non-nursing health workers were divided among several different unions, and police unions did not extend beyond provincial boundaries. Finally, public-sector workers in Quebec were predominantly represented by provincial bodies heavily engaged in Quebec politics.

Despite these weaknesses, public-sector unions had been extremely successful at the bargaining table in the 1960s and 1970s. By the end of the 1980s, it was apparent that national linkages were much less important for public-sector unions than for their private-sector counterparts, since most of the relevant comparisons in bargaining and power centres are provincially based. In addition, the early successes of public-sector unions seem to have been the result of public sympathy for expanding the public sector and improving the conditions of employment there and not the skill or power of public sector unions.

Collective-Bargaining Issues in the 1980s

For public-sector industrial relations, the decade of the 1980s really began in 1982. As outlined above, the previous fifteen years had been marked by the process of conversion from consultation to bargaining, expanded bargaining rights for public employees, rapid growth in unionism, and generous collective-bargaining settlements. This pattern changed abruptly in 1982. First, the Trudeau government enacted wage controls limited to public employees. Later, most of the provinces followed suit. When the Mulroney government was elected in 1984, privatization of elements of the pubic sector appeared on the federal political agenda. Again, several provincial governments echoed the same theme. It appears that contracting-out of public services to the private sector, a variation of privatization, became more common in the 1980s. Finally, back-to-work legislation was a severe form of limitation on public-sector bargaining rights.

The sum of these developments represented substantial shifts in the climate of public-sector industrial relations, leading some to wonder if they constituted the beginning of a fundamental reversal in Canadian social policy, which had emphasized greater protection for workers and expansion of the welfare state since the end of the Depression of the 1930s (Panitch and Swartz 1988). We will address each of these issues and then draw some conclusions about structural changes in public-sector industrial relations.

Compensation Controls

Perhaps the first major development in public-sector labour relations in the decade of the 1980s was the enactment of the federal government's "Six and Five" wage control program in 1982. In June of that year, the Minister of Finance announced legislation that limited wage increases in the federal public service and Crown corporations to 6 percent in 1982–83 and 5 percent for the following year. Moreover, all collective agreements were extended through the life of the program, effectively removing the right to bargain and strike from all public employees in the federal jurisdiction (Swimmer 1984).

Although the federal program naturally attracted widespread interest, it was, in fact, part of a series of such measures. In February 1982, the government of British Columbia announced its own "Six and Five" program, similar in structure to the federal program that came later, although it did not extend existing collective agreements. Quebec and Newfoundland introduced their own control legislation prior to the federal government's doing so. Ultimately, every province, except New Brunswick, Manitoba, Saskatchewan, and Alberta, enacted statutory control programs between March 1982 and April 1983. Perhaps the most severe controls were imposed by Quebec, which actually reduced salaries already negotiated in the public sector. The other programs were generally in the "Six and Five" range, though there were many individual variations (Kumar 1985).

The economic environment in which this second round of wage-control programs occurred differed from the 1975–78 period. Both periods were marked by historically high rates of inflation, with energy prices being an important stimulus to rising prices. Simultaneously, labour productivity was falling, while wage settlements remained relatively high. The divergence of Canadian wage and price trends from the those in the United States was also a matter of concern to the government (Kumar 1985).

Controls were introduced in 1975, during a period of economic recovery. In 1982, the economy was moving into the most severe recession since the 1930s. The rate of inflation, while high by historic standards, was beginning to decelerate by 1982. The increase in the Consumer Price Index fell from an annual rate of

12.7 percent in the third quarter of 1981 to 11.5 percent in the second quarter of 1982. By the second quarter of 1982, the effects of the recession were also beginning to become apparent in bargaining. Wage increases in public-sector settlements without cost-of-living adjustment (COLA) clauses fell from a high of 14.1 in the fourth quarter of 1981 to 11.9 percent in the second quarter of 1982, while unemployment rose from 7.5 percent in 1981 to 11.0 percent a year later.

In all cases, governments declared publicly that their wage-control programs were being established to fight inflation and reduce government spending in a period of declining revenues. Ministers of finance were also careful to state that they did not attribute current economic problems to public-sector wage increases (see Kumar 1985; Thompson 1988), although it was clear that at least some policy makers privately blamed public-sector wage settlements for inflation (see Swimmer 1984).

Academic reviews of wage-control programs have not been kind to the authors of these measures. The announced rationale for the federal Six and Five program was to restrain wages in both the public and the private sector and to reduce government expenditures. In fact, federal public-sector wage increases had lagged other public-sector settlements and the private sector prior to the introduction of the Six and Five program, and there was no evidence that wages in the federal government influenced levels in the private sector. Moreover, the savings by restraining wage increases were minuscule as a proportion of federal spending. These findings led to the conclusion that the real objectives of the program were political, i.e., to demonstrate the will of the federal government to hold down wage increases and thereby serve as an example for other employers, both public and private (Swimmer 1984).

Table 8.11 provides information on major contract wage settlements in the private and public sectors between 1978 and 1989 for the economy as a whole. These data support the proposition that there was no convincing economic rationale based on private–public wage differentials to support the imposition of controls. From 1978 to 1980, private-sector settlements were ahead of public-sector settlements, in some cases by substantial margins. This trend was reversed in 1981 and 1982, just prior to the introduction of controls, but the public-sector advantage in these years was less than 1 percent. Overall, Table 8.11 shows no clear pattern with respect to private–public wage differentials between 1978 and 1989; in fact, on a compounded basis, the private sector had a slight (4 percent) wage-settlement advantage over the twelve-year period.

Moreover, during the control period, with the exception of 1983, public-sector wage settlements continued to be higher than those in the private sector by a small margin. This suggests that the settlement cap in several restraint programs had been set too high, so that settlements would have been lower in the absence of controls (Kumar 1985).

An analysis of collective-bargaining settlements in Ontario between 1978 and 1983 found that the provincial control program "slightly dampened wage-rate increases in the education, local-government, and provincial government subsectors" (Auld and Wilton 1985, 104). At the same time, the controls seemed to

Table 8.11

Average Annual Wage Increase in the Public and Private Sectors, 1978–1989

	1978	1979	1980	1981	1982	1983	1984	1985	1986	1987	1988	1989
Public Sector	7.1	9.2	10.9	13.2	10.5	4.6	3.9	3.8	3.7	4.2	3.9	5.3
Private Sector	8.7	10.9	11.6	12.8	9.6	5.4	3.2	3.3	3.0	3.9	4.9	5.3

Source: Labour Canada, Major Wage Settlements, 4th Quarter 1985, 1986, 1989.

have increased the size of wage settlements in the health subsector, while only slightly reducing wages in the private sector. In particular, the impact of public-sector settlements on the private sector was "minimal," and there was no strong case for permanent public-sector wage controls because public-sector wages (except for the health subsector) responded to much the same economic variables as did the private sector (Auld and Wilton 1985).

A review of the impact of restraint programs in four provinces (British Columbia, Manitoba, Ontario, and New Brunswick) revealed no direct relationship between provincial economic growth (or decline) and the degree of restraint. There also was substantial variation in settlements across subsectors within each province. In every province, the number of provincial employees rose, despite claims by several governments that the size of the public service had to be reduced. On balance, it appeared that the four control programs were driven by political priorities, not economic pressures (Thompson 1988).

If governments did not heed economic imperatives to implement control programs, they were generally accurate in their political judgments. Public-sector unions protested vigorously when controls were implemented, but took direct action only in Quebec and British Columbia, the two provinces known for their especially militant labour movements.

In British Columbia, the initial restraint program was expanded and made more restrictive after its introduction. In July 1983, the provincial government announced a wide-ranging restraint program, which included a 25 percent reduction in government employment and substantial reductions in the bargaining rights of public-sector unions, plus other measures to reduce social services. The combination of measures enabled the major public-sector unions in the province to form a coalition of groups opposed to the government's program. After a series of major demonstrations and a threatened general strike, the government and the coalition agreed to restore most of the public-sector bargaining rights, while leaving other government cutbacks and wage controls in place (Thompson 1985).

Several Quebec public-sector unions struck in January 1983 in opposition to restraint legislation. The government forced an end to the stoppages through legislation that threatened severe penalties for further strikes. Additional strikes did occur, and the labour movement and the government eventually agreed on a compromise restraint program (Thompson 1986).

In hindsight, these protests seem isolated and fundamentally ineffectual. Strikes, slowdowns, and other types of economic action were usually illegal, and were neither large enough nor sufficiently long lasting to bring meaningful pressure against governments. Labour's political protests were generally muted and not very effective. Despite rhetoric of solidarity, it appears that private-sector unions were not willing to support economic action by public-sector groups against controls.

Both governments and labour learned important lessons from this experience. Politicians understand that a moderate program of wage restraints in the public sector is relatively easy to implement. Labour came to realize that confrontations were unlikely to be successful. A more promising strategy is political pressure, including public-relations campaigns, high-profile lawsuits, and efforts to win sympathy from nongovernmental public-sector employers.

In the first half of 1991, first the federal government and then five provinces (British Columbia, Newfoundland, Quebec, New Brunswick, and Nova Scotia) announced yet another round of wage controls. The rationale for these measures (except for British Columbia's) is governments' fiscal problems, since inflation is at around 5 percent range and public-sector wage settlements have been equal to or lower than the private sector in most cases, nurses being the most notable exception. In British Columbia, the only large group that had negotiated settlements much higher than those in the private sector were teachers, who were bargaining for only the second time over many nonsalary issues with the right to strike.

After threats of retaliation at the bargaining table and politically by labour, major unions and the Quebec government agreed on compensation limits. The British Columbia labour movement explicitly denied any intention to form another coalition to oppose the government, preferring legal challenges while waiting for a change in government.

With rare exceptions, such as the 1991 agreement between the Quebec government and major public-sector unions, there were no initiatives from public employers to find co-operative solutions to the problems arising from financial restraints. Perhaps the unions concerned would have rejected such overtures had governments extended them, but political factors overrode sound industrial relations practices. In addition, the restricted scope of public-sector bargaining inhibits negotiations over such subjects as job security (Thompson 1989).

Privatization and Contracting-Out

Wage controls were sporadic and often dramatic events in public-sector industrial relations. The erosion of the public sector itself was a more gradual, but equally profound, development that affected public-sector industrial relations.

During the 1960s and 1970s, the public sector grew steadily in Canada. Not only did the number of government employees increase, but nongovernmental organizations became part of the public sector in various ways. For example, hospitals opened and operated by charitable or religious organizations became dependent on public funding. While they legally remained under the control of their owners, these institutions were affected by the extension of collective bargaining outlined above and came to be considered public or "parapublic" employers. In several jurisdictions, private electrical utilities were purchased by provincial governments, in keeping with a Canadian tradition of public ownership of utilities. Finally, the expansion of education and the welfare state created thousands of new schools, universities, and social-welfare agencies to serve a growing population.

This process was reversed in the 1980s. Through a variety of measures, governments sought to reduce their size. In a few cases, functions once performed or funded were abandoned. A more common process was the transfer of activities or entire agencies to the private sector. Apart from a general philosophical preference for reducing the public sector by conservative governments, the motives for privatization and contracting-out were varied and not always stated explicitly. In a few cases, such as Air Canada, governments sought to avoid large capital expenditures required to maintain the firm's competitive position. Other governments evidentally believed that turning functions over to the private sector would increase efficiency (Stanbury 1991a). Governments did not publicly state that their motives included weakening public-sector unions, though it is reasonable to assume that was an objective in several jurisdictions. To appreciate the implications of the privatization process for public-sector industrial relations, it is necessary to consider the mechanisms by which divestiture occurred.

PROCESSES FOR REDUCING THE PUBLIC SECTOR

The industrial relations impacts of divestiture vary considerably according to the means by which a government transfers activities or agencies from the public to the private sector. Most attention has been given to privatization, the sale of government assets to the private sector. However, there exist several important variations of this process. First, it is necessary to consider the nature of the public organization according to its function and proximity to the private sector.

At one end of the continuum, public enterprises (usually referred to as "Crown corporations") often perform functions that generate revenue and may be found in the private sector in other jurisdictions. Telecommunications, electric power, and airlines are common examples of Canadian public enterprises. Many jurisdictions have government publications bureaux and recreational facilities in this category. Government agencies are also responsible for other functions that do not generate revenue per se, but are similar to the activities of private businesses. Catering, building maintenance, and computer services are typical examples. Finally, there are the core functions of government, including public security, tax collection, and the like, which have few parallels in the private sector.

Another area of distinction is the nature of the transfer from the public to the private sector. Publicly owned entities can be sold intact in a single transaction to the private sector, shares can be sold in several instalments, or only parts of these organizations can be sold. The sale of whole organizations can be to a single private firm, usually to be incorporated into existing operations. An alternative technique is to sell shares in a public enterprise to the public, perhaps with some preferential treatment for purchases by employees of the organization affected. In a number of cases, small operations have been sold to their employees.

Finally, specific functions in existing public agencies can be contracted out to private enterprises. Maintenance and catering are the most common examples, but computer services, hospital pharmacies, and educational-film lending services have been treated in this way. Examples of privatization of each of these organizational types and mechanisms for the transfer occurred in the 1980s.

EXTENT OF PRIVATIZATION AND CONTRACTING-OUT

There is no authoritative register of the extent of privatization in the 1980s, and there are problems of definition, but one estimate through December 1990 identified more than 80 such events (Stanbury 1991b). The federal government, Quebec, Saskatchewan, and British Columbia were most active in this area. For the federal government, the most notable transactions have been the sale of Air Canada, Canada Development Corporation, Teleglobe Canada, and two aircraft-manufacturing firms. Of less significance were the sales of Nanisivik Mines and the Northern Canada Power Commission. Among the more significant examples in the provinces were the sale of Québécair, and majority control of Donohue and SOQUEM by the Quebec government. In Saskatchewan, the government sold the provincial oil and gas corporation, the Prince Albert Pulp Company, and the Potash Corporation. Although the Alberta government has not been particularly active in privatizing its assets, its sale of Alberta Government Telephone was second in size only to SOQUEM among sales of provincial assets, and the sale of Pacific Western Airlines was one of the five biggest transactions. The British Columbia government sold the natural gas distribution systems in the Vancouver and Victoria metropolitan areas and the maintenance facilities for the provincial highway system (Stanbury 1991b).

Much less is known about the importance of contracting-out in the public sector. Often responsibility for specific services passes to the private sector, while the main functions of an organization are unaffected. It is not known if the pace of contracting-out accelerated in the 1980s, though it would be logical to expect such developments, given the economic and political climates.

A handful of studies indicates that contracting-out of support services, such as catering or janitorial functions, is quite common in the public sector. The provincial government of British Columbia has contracted-out some laundry services for hospitals in the Vancouver area, janitorial services for provincial government buildings, and catering for provincial penal institutions (Stanbury 1991b). Janitorial services already had been contracted-out in public administration generally in the 1970s (McFetridge and Smith 1988). A study of 124 municipalities in British Columbia in 1989 revealed that 21 percent of all services were carried out exclusively by private contractors, and 32 percent of all services were performed by both contractors and civic employees; the author estimated that these figures would be higher for Ontario (McDavid 1990). The Ontario government contracted-out the operation of a number of provincial parks (although the Liberal government decided not to renew these contracts in the late 1980s). A national survey in the early 1980s found that 41 percent of all municipalities with 10 000 or more residents rely on private contractors to collect residential solid waste (McDavid and Schick 1987). Several major firms have aggressively sought contracts to supply meals to universities, schools, and hospitals. A 1989 study of 68 British Columbia hospitals reported that 67 percent relied on contractors for some functions (West 1988).

UNION REACTIONS

Public-sector unions almost universally oppose both privatization and contracting-out. They typically claim that public employees can be as efficient as the private-sector employees when permitted to function under the same conditions. They also point to the social importance of many governmental functions and the need to run them without pressures from the profit motive.

The reaction of unions based primarily in the private sector is different. Generally, these unions are found in public enterprises with private-sector counterparts. By and large, unions in these circumstances have not opposed privatization. Thus, the Canadian Air Line Pilots Association did not oppose the sale of Air Canada or Pacific Western Airlines shares (although the Canadian Auto Workers, which represents ticket agents, attacked the privatization of Air Canada), and the International Brotherhood of Electrical Workers supported the sale of B.C. Hydro's gas divisions to a private firm. This support may be linked to the nature of the privatization, as discussed below, or the unions' belief that their members may prosper under private ownership, removed, for instance, from the coverage of public-sector wage controls.

When labour has opposed privatization and contracting-out, its strategy has operated at three levels. Politically, unions seek allies from outside the labour movement who will support their stand against a reduction in government services. Unions and their partners use advertising, joint lobbying campaigns, demonstrations, publicity campaigns, letters to politicians, and the like to convince politicians and the public to oppose divestiture.

The second level of the strategy is to bargain for contract language that limits the ability of public employers to eliminate parts of the public sector or that makes such actions more expensive. The master agreement for the Province of British Columbia, for instance, contains a clause banning the contracting-out of any work "presently performed by employees" covered by the agreement that would result in a layoff of these employees. The same agreement provides for elaborate layoff procedures whereby employees displaced by privatization or contracting-out can bid for jobs in the government service. There is also a provision requiring the union to be notified of plans for privatization and to be given the opportunity to suggest alternative mechanisms for reducing the cost of the services the employer proposes to privatize (Fryer 1989). None of these measures has deterred the government from its strategy of reducing employment levels, however.

The third union strategy has been litigation. The legal ramifications of privatization and contracting-out can be formidable, touching on successor rights and the union's bargaining authority. The Canadian Union of Postal Workers has launched a series of actions before the Canada Labour Relations Board and arbitration tribunals, seeking to stop the employer's proposals to establish postal substations in private businesses, such as drugstores. The B.C. Government Employees' Union launched a suit to guarantee employees in operations subject to privatization the right to bump back into the government service in lieu of retaining their former positions.

IMPACT OF PRIVATIZATION AND CONTRACTING-OUT ON INDUSTRIAL RELATIONS

The impact of government and employer strategies on industrial relations is still difficult to estimate. It is clear that governments have been able to proceed with privatization in the face of union opposition in virtually every case. Almost the only known example of a government rescinding its plans to privatize an operation because of union pressure was in Quebec, where the government abandoned an announced initiative to sell its retail liquor stores after the union involved mounted an intense publicity campaign. Union efforts to stop privatization by reliance on collective-agreement clauses have seldom borne fruit (Fryer 1989). What are not known, however, are cases in which governments have avoided privatization because of union opposition or fear that private firms would not buy the government operations in the face of union opposition. In British Columbia, the government announced plans to sell several branches of the Hydro Authority and its own public service, and later abandoned these initiatives.

The nature of the privatization process seems to be an important factor in determining its industrial relations impact. When whole enterprises have been sold to the public, there has been relatively little union opposition, and successor-rights provisions in relevant labour codes ensure that union representation and the applicable collective agreements are not disturbed. The same principles seem to apply when entire enterprises are sold to existing private firms. In the cases of the larger sales, Canadair to Bombardier, Teleglobe to Memotec, B.C. Hydro's gas distribution system to Inland Natural Gas, the purchasing companies were unionized and comfortable with assuming collective-bargaining obligations. This is less likely to be the case in the sale of small operations to employee-owned firms or nonunion companies in the private sector. Several small unionized operations, which were sold by the B.C. government to employee-owned companies, were subsequently decertified when the law permitted.

When small elements of government services have been privatized or contracted-out, the results have been highly variable. When the language of the applicable collective agreement is sufficiently strong, the impact of contracting-out can be the substitution of private-sector managers for public employees who were never in a union bargaining unit, or were a small fraction of a bargaining unit. In other cases, the contract or privatization statute has given public-sector workers preference for jobs in the private-sector operations that take over government functions. A result of such conditions may mean that the public-sector union moves with its members to the private sector. If the private-sector employer has its own bargaining unit that is larger than the group of employees coming from the government, the most likely outcome seems to be that workers move from one union to another. If the private employer is nonunion, then some labour organization must attempt to organize the entire bargaining unit resulting from the transfer of government workers.

There seem to be no published data on the impact of privatization and contracting-out on the employment, wages, and working conditions of the employees affected. Where collective agreements cover employees in the private sector, several bargaining rounds may have to occur before the impact of the new economic and managerial environment becomes apparent. Supporters of privatization assert that private employers will be able to pay wages on a par with the private sector, and may even expand employment opportunities by seeking new markets. Opponents point to cases such as maintenance workers in a Toronto plant of Canada Post who were forced to strike against their private employer to achieve standards well below those enjoyed by Canada Post employees (Gutstein n.d.). Contracting-out of solid-waste collection services almost invariably results in job losses.

On balance, the least disruption to industrial relations seems to occur when a public enterprise is sold to the public or to a private firm that will maintain it as a separate entity. At the other extreme, the greatest change seems likely to follow the sale of part of a government operation to a private-sector firm that seeks to integrate its purchase with existing operations or the contracting-out of public functions to firms with quite different terms and conditions of employment than prevail in the element of the public sector losing the functions.

*B*ack-to-Work Legislation

*D*uring the development of public-sector collective bargaining between 1965 and 1973, every jurisdiction legalized strikes by at least some elements of the public sector. By including all organized workers, public- and private-sector, under common legislation, Quebec and Saskatchewan established the most permissive legal regimes. Other jurisdictions had long permitted strikes by municipal workers, and gradually moved to legalize stoppages by other public-sector bargaining units, including teachers, hospital workers and provincial government employees.

In the face of these statutory developments, the incidence of "back-to-work" legislation also grew. These laws were passed to end specific disputes, generally with provision for compulsory arbitration to resolve the items in dispute. The passage of such legislation, which occurred more frequently as wage-control programs were implemented, led some observers to declare that public-sector workers, the last group of employees to receive legally sanctioned bargaining rights, were being stripped of those rights incrementally less than a decade later (Panitch and Swartz 1984; Sack and Lee 1989). To others, back-to-work legislation was a welcome relief from public-sector stoppages, which had prevailed since the 1960s (Macdonald 1985).

There is no question that the incidence of back-to-work legislation rose in the 1970s, as Table 8.12 indicates. During the 1950s, there were no such laws recorded for the public sector. The first examples of this legislation occurred in 1965 in Ontario and Quebec. On an annualized basis, the average occurrence of back-to-work laws rose from 0.6 per year in the 1960s to 2.1 per year in the 1970s, to 2.6 per year in the 1980s. However, to fully appreciate governments' reliance on back-to-work legislation, it is useful to analyze the data further.

The data in Table 8.12 show that Quebec was by far the jurisdiction most prone to such legislation, although its proportion of the statutes (39 percent) is almost identical to its share of time lost in public-sector labour disputes. The Quebec experience also should be viewed in the context of an industrial relations climate prone to legislative intervention. Between 1965 and 1983, for instance, a total of 84 bills bearing on labour relations were enacted by the Quebec National Assembly (Morin and Leclerc 1986). However, essential-services legislation also reduced the need for *ad hoc* legislation, while effectively restricting the right to strike.

Between 1960 and 1990, Ontario accounted for 24 percent of all back-to-work laws. Five of its fourteen laws were enacted to end strikes by teachers in 1976, the first year of a comprehensive statute to regulate bargaining and disputes by teachers. The two federal statutes ended strikes by air-traffic controllers and postal workers.

Despite predictions to the contrary (Panitch and Swartz 1984), back-to-work

Table 8.12
Back-to-Work Legislation in the Public Sector, 1950–1990

Years	Federal Jurisdiction	Quebec	Ontario	British Columbia	Saskatchewan	Other Provinces	Total
1950–54	—	—	—	—	—	—	0
1955–59	—	—	—	—	—	—	0
1960–64	—	—	—	—	—	—	0
1965–69	—	4	1	—	1	1	7
1970–74	—	2	2	1	—	—	5
1975–79	2	5	6	4	1	—	18
1980–86	—	9	4	2	3	3	21
1987–90	2	3	1	—	2	—	8
Total	4	23	14	7	7	4	59

Source: Unpublished data, Labour Canada.

legislation did not grow in importance in the 1980s. Two federal statutes dealt with the post office (although the right of the federal government to designate essential employees has made major strikes less likely in the federal civil service). Quebec continued to legislate frequently, despite general essential-services legislation that lessened the need for *ad hoc* laws. In contrast, Ontario virtually ceased to enact such laws, perhaps because the system of collective bargaining for teachers provides a variety of dispute-settlement mechanisms (see Chapter 9, this volume). Other provinces, except for Saskatchewan, also had little interest in back-to-work laws.

Conclusions

On balance, the decade of the 1980s were difficult ones for public-sector unions and their members, but there were strong currents of stability that benefited labour. Settlements frequently lagged both the private sector and increases in living costs. Government enacted wage controls at the end of the prosperity of the early 1980s, and then held the line on wage increases during the aftermath of the recession of the 1980s. Viewing wage controls from 1975 through 1991, it is hard to escape concluding that the rationales that governments offered for these measures grew weaker with each new round of controls. In 1975, the country was facing double-digit inflation, and the Supreme Court upheld the federal government's action on the grounds that an emergency situation prevailed. By 1982, inflation had abated, but public-sector wage increases were running slightly ahead of those in the private sector. In 1991, governments simply argued that deficits or cutbacks in federal transfer payments made restrictions on public-sector compensation necessary. In all three rounds of wage controls, the federal government played a leading role in setting the political agenda for provincial governments.

Viewing the decade from the perspective of the industrial relations system, however, change seems less profound. The "transformation" of industrial relations in the 1970s remained in place. The basic elements of statutory frameworks enacted by 1975 remained in effect in 1990. While there was no expansion in collective bargaining comparable to that which occurred in the 1970s, public employees remained committed to collective bargaining, and no government substantially withdrew bargaining rights extended in the 1970s. The declining incidence of strikes and lower wage settlements presumably removed some public pressures for drastic restrictions on bargaining procedures. Several jurisdictions restricted the right of "essential services" workers to strike, but *ad hoc* back-to-work legislation was relatively rare outside of Quebec.

Perhaps the greatest long-term threat to the stability of public-sector industrial relations would be the change in the role of the public sector itself. In many juris-dictions, especially the federal government, fiscal pressures and a conservative po-litical ideology combine to create a consensus that the level of government must be reduced. If the trend toward privatization and contracting-out continues, then a number of the basic elements of public-sector industrial relations will be under-mined. For instance, the structure of bargaining, patterns of union representation, the relevant legal regimes, compensation levels, and labour disputes are all affect-ed by the transfer of enterprises and services from the public to the private sector. Reductions in the size of government undermine the bargaining power of public-sector unions, but do not necessarily alter the structures of public-sector industrial relations. However, there is no evidence that large numbers of employees wish to forgo the protections of collective bargaining.

REFERENCES

Auld, Douglas, and David Wilton. 1985. "Wage Settlements in the Ontario Public Sector Controls Program." In David W. Conklin, Thomas J. Courchene, and William A. Jones, eds., *Public Sector Compensation*. Toronto: Ontario Economic Council. 80–109.

Bird, R.M. 1978. "The Growth of the Public Sector in Canada." In David K. Foot, ed., *Public Employment and Compensation in Canada: Myths and Realities*. Scarborough, ON: Butterworths and Co. (Canada) Ltd. 19–44.

Deverell, John. 1982. "The Ontario Hospital Dispute, 1980-81." Paper presented to the Canadian Industrial Relations Association Annual Meeting, June 3.

Faoro, Louis R. 1990. "Global Trends in Privatization." In O. Yul Kown, ed., *International Privatization: Global Trends, Policies, Processes, Experiences*. Saskatoon: The Institute for Saskatchewan Enterprise. 13–22.

Frankel, S. 1960. "Staff Relations in the Canadian Federal Public Service: Experience with Joint Consultation." In J.E. Hodgetts and D.C. Corbett, eds., *Canadian Public Administration*. Toronto: Macmillan. 369–385.

Fryer, John. 1989. "Privatization, Outsourcing and Subcontracting: The Canadian Public Sector: A Union Viewpoint." In Gladys W. Gruenberg, ed., *Arbitration 1988: Emerging Issues for the 1990s. Proceedings of the Forty-First Annual Meeting of the National Academy of Arbitrators*.

Washington, DC: The Bureau of National Affairs. 132–46.

Goldenberg, Shirley. 1988. "Public Sector Labour Relations in Canada." In Benjamin Aaron, Joyce N. Najita, and James Stern, eds., *Public Sector Bargaining*. 2nd ed., Washington, DC: The Bureau of National Affairs. 266–313.

Gunderson, Morley, and W. Craig Riddell. 1991. "Provincial Public Sector Payrolls." In Melville McMillen, ed., *Provincial Public Finances, Benefits, Problems and Prospects*. Toronto: Canadian Tax Foundation. 164–92.

Gutstein, Donald. n.d. *Privatization in Canada*. Mimeo. Ottawa: Canadian Labour Congress.

Hébert, Gérard. 1984. "Public Sector Bargaining in Quebec: A Case of Hypercentralization." In M. Thompson and G. Swimmer, eds., *Conflict or Compromise: The Future of Public Sector Industrial Relations*. Montreal: The Institute for Research on Public Policy. 229–82.

Kumar, Pradeep. 1985. "Recent Public Sector Wage Restraint Programs: The Economic and Labour Market Rationale?" In Bryan M. Downie, ed., *Proceedings of the 21st Annual Meeting of the Canadian Industrial Relations Association*. Quebec: CIRA. 40–60.

McDavid, James C. 1990. "Contracting Out Public Works Services in B.C." In O. Yul Kwan, ed., *International Privatization: Global Trends, Policies, Processes, Experiences*. Saskatoon:

The Institute for Saskatchewan Enterprise. 281–96.

McDavid, James C., and Gregory K. Schick. 1987. "Privatization Versus Union–Management Cooperation: The Effects of Competition on Service Efficiency in Municipalities." *Canadian Public Administration*, 303 (Fall): 472–89.

McFetridge, Donald G. and Douglas A. Smith. 1988. *The Economics of Vertical Disintegration*. Vancouver: The Fraser Institute.

Macdonald, Donald. 1985. *Royal Commission on the Economic Union and Development Prospects for Canada*. Ottawa: Minister of Supply and Services.

Maslove, Allan M., and Gene Swimmer. 1980. *Wage Controls in Canada 1975–78: A Study of Public Decision Making*. Montreal: The Institute for Research on Public Policy.

Morin, Fernand, and Claudine Leclerc. 1986. "The Use of Legislation to Control Labour Relations: The Quebec Experience," In Ivan Bernier and Andrée Lajoie, eds., *Labour Law and Urban Law in Canada*. Toronto: University of Toronto Press. 67–166.

Panitch, Leo V. and Don Swartz. 1984. "From Free Collective Bargaining to Permanent Exceptionalism: The Economic Crisis and the Transformation of Industrial Relations in Canada." In Mark Thomson and Gene Swimmer, eds., *Conflict or Compromise: The Future of Public Sector Industrial Relations*. Montreal: The Institute for Research on Public Policy. 403–36.

———. 1988. *The Assault on Trade Union Freedoms*. Toronto: Garamond Press.

Ponak, Allen. 1982. "Public-Sector Collective Bargaining." In John C. Anderson and Morley Gunderson, eds., *Union–Management Relations in Canada*. Don Mills, ON: Addison-Wesley. 343–78.

Ponak, Allen, and Loren Falkenberg. 1989. "Resolution of Interest Disputes." In Amarjit Sethi, ed., *Collective Bargaining in Canada*. Toronto: Nelson. 260–93.

Ponak, Allen, and Mark Thompson. 1989. "Public Sector Collective Bargaining." In John C. Anderson, Morley Gunderson, and Allen Ponak, eds., *Union–Management Relations in Canada*. 2nd ed. Toronto: Addison-Wesley. 373–406.

Ponak, Allen, and Hoyt Wheeler. 1980. "Choice of Procedures in Canada and the United States." *Industrial Relations* 18/3 (Fall): 292–308.

Rose, Joseph B. 1984. "Growth Patterns of Public Sector Unions." In Thompson and Swimmer, eds., *Conflict or Compromise: The Future of Public Sector Industrial Relations*. Montreal: The Instutite for Research on Public Policy. 83–119.

Sack, Jeffrey, and Tanya Lee. 1989. "The Role of the State in Canadian Labour Relations." *Relations Industrielles/Industrial Relations* 44/1: 195–223.

Smith, Douglas A. 1984. "Strikes in the Canadian Public Sector." In Thompson and Swimmer, eds., *Conflict or Compromise: The Future of*

Public Sector Industrial Relations, 201–228. Montreal: The Institute for Research on Public Policy.

Stanbury, W. T. 1991a. "Controlling the Growth of Provincial Governments: The Role of Privatization." In Melville McMillan, ed., *Provincial Public Finances Plaudits, Problems and Prospects.* 371–96. Toronto: Canadian Tax Foundation.

——. 1991a. "Summary Data on Federal and Provincial Privatization Efforts in Canada, 1979–1990." Unpublished manuscript, Faculty of Commerce and Business Administration, University of British Columbia.

Swan, Kenneth P. 1984. "Grating Expectations: The Limitations in the Development of Normative Criteria in Interest Arbitration." In Thompson and Swimmer, eds., *Conflict or Compromise: The Future of Public Sector Industrial Relations.* Montreal: The Institute for Research on Public Policy. 315–37.

Swimmer, Eugene. 1984. "Six and Five." In Allan M. Maslove, ed., *How Ottawa Spends 1984: The New Agenda.* Toronto: Methuen. 240–75.

——. 1987. "Changes to Public Service Labour Relations Legislation: Revitalizing or Destroying Collective Bargaining?" In Michael J. Prince, ed., *How Ottawa Spends 1987–88: Restraining the State.* Toronto: Methuen. 293–316.

Swinton, Katherine. 1984. "Grievance Arbitration in the Public Sector." In Thompson and Swimmer, eds., *Conflict or Compromise: The Future of Public Sector Industrial Relations.*

Montreal: The Institute for Research on Public Policy. 339–72.

Tellier, Paul M. 1990. "Public Service 2000: The Renewal of the Public Service." *Canadian Public Administration* 33/2 (Summer): 123–32.

Thompson, Mark. 1986. "The Future of Voluntarism in Public Sector Labour Relations." In Geoff England, ed., *Essays in Labour Relations Law.* Toronto: CCH Canadian. 103–29.

——. 1988. "Public Sector Industrial Relations in Canada: The Impact of Restraint." In Barbara Dennis, ed., *Proceedings of the Annual Spring Meeting, 1988 of the Industrial Relations Research Association.* Madison, WI: IRRA. 502–8.

——. 1989. "From Compromise to Resistance: Public Sector Industrial Relations in Canada." In Alan Gladstone, Russell Lansbury, Jack Stieber, Tiziano Treu, and Manfred Weiss, eds., *Current Issues in Labour Relations: An International Perspective.* New York: Walter de Gruyter. 307–18.

Thompson, Mark and Allen Ponak. 1984. "Industrial Relations in Canadian Public Enterprises." *International Labour Review* 123/5 (September–October): 647–63.

——. 1991. "Canadian Public Sector Industrial Relations: Theory and Practice." In D. Sockell, D. Lewin, and D. B. Lipsky, eds., *Advances in Industrial and Labor Relations,* Vol. 5. Greenwich, CT: JAI Press Inc. 59–93.

Weiler, Paul C.1980. *Reconcilable Differences: New Directions in Canadian Labour Law Reform.* Toronto: Carswell.

West, Denise. 1988. "Contracting Out in B.C. Health Care Facilities." Unpublished paper written for Commerce 422, Faculty of Commerce and Business Administration, University of British Columbia.

Wilton, David A. 1986. "Public Sector Wage Compensation." In W. Craig Riddell, ed., *Canadian Labour Relations*. Toronto: University of Toronto Press. 257–84.

ENDNOTES

1.   The authors are, respectively, William M. Hamilton Professor of Industrial Relations, Faculty of Commerce and Business Administration, University of British Columbia, and Professor, Faculty of Management, University of Calgary. We wish to acknowledge the valuable assistance of Ms. Corliss Olson in the preparation of quantitative data for this study.

Chapter

9

INDUSTRIAL RELATIONS IN ELEMENTARY AND SECONDARY EDUCATION: A SYSTEM TRANSFORMED?

Bryan M. Downie[1]

*T*his essay focusses on collective bargaining by teachers in Ontario elementary and secondary education. Ontario education presents an interesting example of a public-sector industrial relations system that has undergone major stresses and pressures. Ontario also has the largest system of education in Canada, and one of the most decentralized industrial relations systems. In Quebec, Newfoundland, New Brunswick, and Prince Edward Island, industrial relations are centralized at the provincial level. In Quebec, bargaining is centralized at the provincial level, but with some issues negotiated regionally or locally. In Saskatchewan and Nova Scotia, too, bargaining structure is a blend—monetary issues are negotiated at the province-wide table, but certain issues may be bargained at the school-board level. In Ontario, Manitoba, Alberta, and British Columbia, bargaining is conducted at the school-board level.

In Ontario, collective bargaining for all staff takes place at the local level. Despite differences in bargaining structure and labour legislation across the provinces (see Tables 9.1 and 9.2), Ontario's developments in teacher/school-board bargaining are *not* atypical. The issues that have found their way to the bargaining table are very similar to those in other provinces. The demographic and economic factors that have influenced teacher bargaining also have been remarkably similar across the country. In a recent study, Grant (1991) compares the Quebec and Ontario industrial relations systems in education, and, while it is clear that there are major differences with respect to bargaining arrangements and public policy, the issues and pressures confronting the two systems have been very similar.

While trends in teacher bargaining have been similar across Canada, the degree

Table 9.1
Bargaining Arrangements in Ontario Education

	A Separate Elementary Agreement	and	A Separate Secondary Agreement	or	A Common Elementary–Secondary Agreement
Boards of Education	FWTAO OPSTF AEFO		OSSTF AEFO		
Roman Catholic Boards	OECTA AEFO		OECTA AEFO		OECTA AEFO

to which teachers have made inroads, and their capacity to do so, have undoubtedly varied. For example, there is much more bargaining activity in Ontario than elsewhere (there are now approximately 280 collective agreements in Ontario education) and, therefore, more opportunity for innovation and change. Also, there is considerable variation in dispute-resolution procedures across the country, and not all teacher unions have the right to strike (see Table 9.2). In Ontario, however, the unions (officially referred to as teacher federations) have retained the capacity and the opportunity to conduct lengthy strikes when necessary to make new breakthroughs or protect established gains.

Major developments in collective bargaining took place in Ontario education in the 1980s. But, unlike the private sector, the public sector experienced a transformation in the industrial relations system in the 1970s. Such was the case in education in Quebec and the other provinces, as well. The decade of the 1970s was a period of turmoil and change not only in collective bargaining, but also in education policy, school-board structure, and teacher attitudes. In addition, during that period, bargaining was impacted by the federal government's anti-inflation program. The 1980s saw further pressures for adaptation in Ontario, which will be discussed later.

This essay has been organized into four sections. In the first, we discuss the organizational and financial aspects in Ontario education that have shaped the industrial relations system. In the second, we examine the configuration of bargaining, the bargaining representatives, the history of key industrial relations developments, the legislative framework governing collective bargaining, and the use of strikes and other sanctions. In the third, forces influencing negotiations in the late 1970s and 1980s are set forth, along with developments regarding teacher sanctions. The substantive issues in collective bargaining are presented with emphasis on the changes that have occurred during the decade of the 1980s. The major trends and developments in teacher–board collective agreements are examined, and conclusions are drawn with regard to whether and how the provisions of the collective agreement restrict management and enhance worker control. Finally, we address whether and how the industrial relations system has been

Table 9.2
General Aspects of Teacher Collective Bargaining

Province	Type of Bargaining	Notice to Bargain	Commencement of Bargaining	Time Limit for Bargaining (if applicable)	Normal Expiry Date of Collective Agreement(s)
Nfld.	Provincial	Within the 3 months preceding the expiry of the current agreement	Within 3 days of notice to bargain	NA	August 31
P.E.I.	Provincial	Within the period of 3 months and 14 calendar days, excluding July and August, preceding expiry of current agreement[a]	Within 14 calendar days of notice to bargain.	When negotiations have continued for 45 calendar days and a conciliation officer is appointed on written request of either party or at the discretion of the Minister of Labour.	August 31
N.S.	Provincial and Local	Within the 2 months preceding the expiry of the current agreement.	Within 20 days of notice to bargain.	NA	July 31 (for Provincial Agreement)
N.B.	Provincial	Within the 2 months preceding the expiry of the current agreement.	Within 20 days of notice to bargain, unless later date is mutually acceptable.	45 days, unless extension of the period is mutually agreed to.	August 31

Table 9.2 (continued)

Province	Type of Bargaining	Notice to Bargain	Commencement of Bargaining	Time Limit for Bargaining (if applicable)	Normal Expiry Date of Collective Agreement(s)
Que.	Provincial and Local or Regional	At least 8 days' written notice of the commencement of negotiations is provided by either party; such notice may be given within 90 days of the expiry of the current agreement, unless another delay is provided for.[b]		NA	December 31 (for Provincial Agreement)
Ont.	Local	Within the month of January in the year in which the current agreement expires.	Within 30 days of notice to bargain.	NA	August 31 (Sec. 50[c], Bill 100)
Man.	Local	Within the 90 to 30 days preceding the expiry of the current agreement, excluding July and August.	Within 14 days of notice to bargain, unless later date is mutually acceptable.	NA	December 31 (could change to June 30 after 1989, due to change in fiscal year)
Sask.	Provincial and Local		Not later than 100 days before expiry of existing agreement (by September 22 for agreements expiring December 31).	NA	December 31 (for provincial agreement)
Alta.	Local	Within the 120–60 days preceding the	Within 30 days of notice to bargain.[c]	NA	December 31 or August 31

Table 9.2 (continued)

Province	Type of Bargaining	Notice to Bargain	Commencement of Bargaining	Time Limit for Bargaining (if applicable)	Normal Expiry Date of Collective Agreement(s)
		expiry of the current agreement.			
B.C.	Local	Within the 4 months preceding the expiry of the current agreement.[d]	Within 10 days of notice to bargain.	NA	June 30

Notes: [a] *Prince Edward Island* (as per Schools Act—Regulations). (a) Not later than 6 months (excluding July and August) preceding expiry of current agreement the parties meet to determine data and information that each should make available to the other; (b) Not later than 4 months (excluding July and August) preceding expiry of current agreement the parties meet to present and analyze the data and information that each has collected; (c) Prior to the commencement of formal negotiations, the parties attempt to resolve as many issues as possible through mutual consultation.

[b] *Quebec* (as per amendments to the Quebec Labour Code—Special Provisions Applicable to Public and Parapublic Sectors). (a) The negotiation stage begins 180 days before the expiry date of the collective agreement; (b) The bargaining agent for the certified association must present written proposals on all matters negotiated at the provincial level except salaries and salary scales not later than 150 days before the expiry date of the collective agreement; (c) Within 60 days of receipt of these proposals the management negotiating committee presents written counter-proposals on all matters negotiated at the provincial level except salaries and salary scales. Within 30 days of the publication of the report of the Institut de recherche et d'information (by November 30 of each year), both parties submit their proposals on salaries and salary scales.

[c] *Alberta* (as per Bill 22). The parties shall exchange bargaining proposals within 15 days of their first meeting.

[d] *British Columbia.* If notice is not given by either party 90 days or more prior to the expiry of the agreement, both parties are deemed to have given notice 90 days prior to the expiry.

Source: Canadian Teachers' Federation.

transformed, and conclude by assessing the likely direction of industrial relations in the future.

Sector Overview

The industrial relations system in Ontario education is a reflection of the organizational structure, and the financing, of the province's education system. Since its inception, the structure of the education system in Ontario has been composed of: a central department or ministry, local school boards, with provision for local board autonomy; and a system of legislative grants to supplement local taxes to finance education (Harris 1967). Some other features which have shaped the system as well.

Schools are officially described as either elementary or secondary. In most provinces, both elementary and secondary schools are included in a single system. However, a ratepayer in Ontario is informed of the amount of his or her elementary school taxes and secondary school taxes as separate figures and in total. There are two types of publicly supported elementary schools, the public or non-sectarian and the separate, normally Roman Catholic. All ratepayers in the province are public school supporters unless they declare themselves to be separate school supporters. In such a case, the ratepayer's share of the property taxes collected for support of the elementary schools goes to the local separate school board. Until 1986, there were no publicly supported Roman Catholic *secondary* schools. In that year, public funding was extended to the secondary school level.

All of the schools are owned and operated by the local school boards. Responsibility for the schools, however, is shared by the local school board and the Ministry of Education. Final responsibility for education rests with the ministry under the Education Act. The ministry's responsibilities include such things as training and certifying teachers, authorization of text books, and defining the course of study. The school board is responsible for many aspects, including the building and maintaining of schools, the provision of supplies, and other operational issues. From the beginning, public education in Ontario has been based on shared responsibility between central and local authority. Today, the Director of Education, who co-ordinates the administrative aspects of a board, also functions as liaison between the board and the ministry.

Education in each school board is financed by a combination of local taxes and legislative grants. The legislative grant to each school board is administered by the ministry according to a formula (based on student enrolment) issued annually before the local tax rate is established. The local school board determines the amount of money it requires for capital expenditure and maintenance and, taking into account the amount available to it from a grant, works out the amount to be raised from the local property tax. It reports this amount to the municipal council each spring.

The ministry has the authority to apportion legislative grants, stipulate the conditions for payment of those grants, and define approved capital and operating costs. For example, grants can be withheld if the ministry's regulations are not fulfilled. Moreover, the ministry is able to encourage school boards to undertake certain programs and measures by offering additional grants.

The school board, in most cases, is free to reject a grant and, hence, not introduce a proposed change. The grant system is simply designed to provide educational opportunities up to a minimum level. That is, regardless of the local tax base, there is a minimum standard of facilities, and so on. School boards may raise additional funds to provide better facilities, pay higher salaries, and so on, through additional property taxes.

The significance of the financing system, for the purposes at hand, is that there is a large measure of local autonomy. In most cases, local boards pay for a large proportion of education costs. Therefore, there is a high degree of local financial autonomy. As well, school boards are responsible for hiring and appointing principals and teachers, and determining their terms of employment, including salaries. As a result, collective bargaining, which takes place at the school board level, is both viable and logical.

The most significant changes in education came, not in the 1980s, but in the period from the mid-1960s to the mid-1970s. A combination of circumstances provided an uncertain environment for teacher–board negotiations. The most important factors were: (1) a rapidly changing educational system; (2) changes in the composition and philosophy of the teaching professional, reflected in changing leadership and a developing professional militancy; (3) a social climate conducive to teacher militancy; (4) the formation of the county board system, which resulted in the consolidation of local boards into much larger units; and (5) ceilings on school board spending imposed by the Ministry of Education.

These changes and forces resulted in great turmoil in relations between school boards and the teacher federations. First, prior to the early 1960s, education in the province was very strictly structured by the Department of Education. The body of knowledge within course content had remained more or less stable. At that time, course content and educational philosophy began to change—a result induced by Sputnik, a decentralization policy by the Department of Education, and a different philosophy of education held by many of the new, more highly qualified, teachers and administrators. To changing curriculum must be added the philosophy reflected in the Hall–Dennis report, which had been commissioned by the provincial government—abolition of grade 13, nongraded learning, and a much more liberal and nonstructured system than previously. Although the report did not come out until 1968, its philosophy was manifested in many ways beforehand.

A mood of instability in much of the teaching profession was created by the speed with which many of the changes were introduced, without, in many cases, sufficient understanding of the ramifications, proper preparation, and above all, sufficient education of students, parents, and teachers. Therefore, it must be remembered, when considering the phenomenon of sudden teacher militancy in the 1960s and 1970s, that even the mechanics of teaching—what is taught, how it is taught, and the environment in which it is taught—were going through a period of rapid change. The changes tended to widen the gap between the principal and the classroom teacher and, by adding new layers of administrators and consultants, between the teacher and the school board.

At the same time, there was a substantial increase in the proportion of young teachers in the profession. Facilitating that change was a huge increase in teacher demand and a severe shortage of teachers in the province in the late 1960s and early 1970s. For example, many boards had to resort to recruiting to temporary contracts individuals who had not yet completed their university training. As well, teachers, like many other groups, were affected by the dramatic social changes that took place in the 1960s.[2] It had become acceptable to break tradition or, in some cases, the law, and teacher attitudes had shifted in this direction.

Another element that increased teacher–board friction was added at about the same time. The *county board* system, effected in 1969, reduced the number of school boards by a factor of seven, to less than 200.[3] At the time the change resulted in two side effects. The reorganization increased the distance, as well as the level of mistrust, between the individual teacher and school trustees.

A significant change in financing occurred in 1971, when the ministry introduced spending ceilings on school board expenditures. The ministry's assessment was that it had increased grants to ease the burden on the local taxpayer, but municipalities simply spent the difference, and taxes continued to climb. Up to this time, the only obligation placed on a school board was to provide a minimum level of education. A board could go beyond the level based on community needs and other considerations and fund additional initiatives through local taxation. However, spending ceilings put an absolute limit on what could be spent, regardless of the source of funding. The ministry's power to withhold grants for violation of regulations ensured board compliance. The ceilings increased by a flat percentage amount each year.

The ministry's influence in salary determination, while indirect, was therefore considerable. Boards, if faced with teacher salary demands beyond what the increase in ceilings would allow, were forced to cut back in other areas of their educational program. Or, teacher salaries had to be restrained. Therefore, the ceilings simultaneously affected teacher expectations and reduced salary demands. These effects continued until 1975.

The above changes and conflicting forces resulted in increased militancy by the teachers and fierce confrontation between the teacher federations and school boards. There was no period quite like it before or since in Ontario education. During this period, negotiations were conducted, but they had no official status. In late 1975, labour legislation regulating collective bargaining was enacted. The School Boards and Teachers Collective Negotiations Act (hereafter referred to as

Bill 100) was conceived, spending ceilings were lifted, and industrial relations in the sector entered a very different format. Bargaining under that regime will be discussed below. There were very significant industrial relations developments prior to that time, however, and these are the subject of the next section.

Industrial Relations Profile up to 1980

BARGAINING STRUCTURE

Industrial relations in Ontario education was shaped by all of the factors mentioned above. For example, the teacher unions in the province are a reflection of the structure of the education system. It should be noted first that, originally, they were *not* unions, but professional associations. In 1944, the Teaching Profession Act established the Ontario Teachers' Federation (OTF). In addition to providing statutory membership, the act also established the automatic deduction of dues by school boards. While membership in the OTF is compulsory, power has always resided with the affiliate federations. There were, and are today, five affiliates, each representing a different teacher constituency. The conditions were present early, therefore, for local, segmented bargaining.

The roots of this balkanized system of collective bargaining are contained, in part, in the province's system of education. It was noted that, at the *elementary* level (generally grades 1 through 8), there are two types of publicly supported schools, the "public" or nonsectarian and the "separate" (normally Roman Catholic). The teachers' affiliate in the *separate* schools is the Ontario English Catholic Teachers' Association (OECTA). There have been, and continue to be, two affiliates in the *public* elementary schools, one for women and one for men— the Federation of Women Teachers' Associations of Ontario (FWTAO) and the Ontario Public School Teachers' Federation (OPSTF); the latter had been known for many years as the Ontario Public School Men Teachers' Federation.

In the public secondary school system, there is a teacher affiliate—the Ontario Secondary School Teachers' Federation (OSSTF)—representing nearly all *secondary* school teachers. Finally, a number of school systems in the province have bilingual programs and, in the late 1980s, French language school boards have been formed and funded. There is a separate affiliate—l'Association des enseignants franco-ontariens (AEFO)—representing French-language teachers in both the elementary and secondary schools.

Over time, the typical bargaining patterns saw the OSSTF negotiating with a public school board for its *secondary* school teachers, the FWTAO and Men's Federation (OPSTF) negotiating together with a public school board for all *elementary* school teachers, and the OECTA negotiating for elementary teachers with the separate school boards. The AEFO almost always negotiated together with one of the other four federations. For example, in the public secondary schools where it had secondary school members, the AEFO would negotiate jointly with the OSSTF.

These bargaining arrangements predated by many years any labour legislation governing teacher–board collective bargaining and resulted in separate collective agreements for elementary and secondary school teachers.

In the separate school system, there were no publicly funded secondary schools; hence, no collective bargaining occurred in that sector. This situation changed slightly in 1986. In that year, Bill 30 extended full funding to Roman Catholic school boards for *secondary* schools and, there, the OECTA negotiates for the secondary teachers. At some boards in that system, the elementary and secondary teachers negotiate together as one unit, and, in some cases, the two groups negotiate separately, even though they are both represented by the OECTA and separate collective agreements are signed for the elementary and secondary bargaining units. In cases where there are French-language teachers in a Roman Catholic school board, the AEFO negotiates for those teachers, often jointly with the OECTA. Indeed, the branch affiliates generally do negotiate jointly, and the typical bargaining configurations are depicted in Table 9.1.

Unlike the case of private-sector labour relations, nonunion competition does not exist in Ontario education. By statute, all teachers in publicly funded schools must belong to a teachers' federation. Every teacher in Ontario is automatically a member of the OTF and automatically becomes a member of one of the affiliates. Each affiliate is organized on a provincial basis, and each has its own board of directors, executive, and provincial staff. They have their own local, regional, and provincial organization. Concurrently, in theory, the Ontario Teachers' Federation is the official professional organization of all the teachers in the province. In practice, however, the OTF has been a loose and weak confederacy of the five, demonstrably more powerful, affiliates. The affiliates have always been autonomous organizations with their own constitutions, and they, in turn, are represented on the governing body of the OTF.

The balkanization of teacher groups in the province is firmly established. The teachers have, for decades, been segregated on a male–female, elementary–secondary, Catholic–Protestant, and English–French basis. Not only are the affiliates autonomous, but their separation has been fortified by system attributes and attitudes that still prevail. Secondary school teachers, for example, have consistently eschewed negotiating with elementary school teachers. There was a feeling among the former that the latter were less professionally committed. The elementary school teachers had been less militant, and the phenomenon of "coattailing" had always been fairly widespread. That is, the charge was levied that elementary school teachers within a board would wait for the secondary school teachers to negotiate an agreement and then sign for similar terms. Another complaint was that elementary school teachers, if they did not "coattail," would sometimes negotiate a lower agreement in the middle of the secondary school negotiations. Either way, secondary school teachers had always felt that elementary teachers reduced their bargaining power. In contrast, secondary school teachers, and in particular the

OSSTF, have always been considered elitist and aloof by the other affiliates.

Then, too, there are differences between elementary and secondary school teachers. Almost all of the latter have at least a Bachelor's degree, and some hold graduate degrees. Despite the requirement that elementary school teachers hold a university degree, the proportion who do so is not as high as in the secondary schools. This status difference has, in the past, maintained a sharp distinction between the two groups. As well, there are different organizational arrangements in the two systems. There is a lower pupil/teacher ratio (PTR) in the secondary schools, and the work day is not the same. Elementary school teachers have more classroom contact hours, whereas secondary school teachers require and, in most cases, have more spare periods for preparing lessons and performing other non-classroom duties.

The separation of elementary and secondary school negotiations is further justified by the existence of somewhat different salary structures in many boards. A single salary schedule is one that pays the same salary to teachers with equivalent qualifications, regardless of whether they are teaching in elementary or secondary schools. The typical schedule contains seven categories, with all seven applying to elementary teachers and only the highest four applying to secondary school teachers. In Ontario, however, there have been and still are separate salary schedules for elementary and for secondary school teachers. The salary schedule or grid is a scheme that reflects two dimensions—training and experience. The grids combine increments (generally yearly and almost always automatic) for years of experience up to a maximum number, say, ten years, and four category levels (seven in the elementary schools) for different levels of educational attainment. In addition to the existence of three more category levels to encompass those teachers who do not have a university degree, placement on the elementary school grid in Ontario is governed by a different category certification plan from that in the secondary schools. The degree of provincial uniformity provided by the classification plans depends on acceptance of the affiliates' certification chart by school boards. Boards have generally adopted these systems voluntarily, but are under no compulsion to do so. Even if elementary and secondary school teachers had the same certification plan and salary grid, a case can be made for separate negotiations. The desired allocation of available dollars within the grid may be quite divergent in the two groups.

Among the elementary school teachers, as well, there is little or no inclination to close ranks and form one affiliate. For example, the FWTAO, nourished by feelings of discrimination and a desire to protect women's rights, has shown little desire to merge with the OPSTF. The latter, long dominated by principals and, of course, entirely male, has demonstrated an interest in amalgamation, but to date these overtures have been rejected by the FWTAO.

Things are equally decentralized on the trustees' side. In 1949, the existing provincial trustees' organizations formed an umbrella organization. For our purposes, their names are not important, but, in 1953, they incorporated into the Ontario School Trustees' Council (OSTC). Nevertheless, co-ordination among the

That's history now!

local school boards, at the best of times, has been extremely difficult. The protection of local board autonomy is one of the most salient features in Ontario education, and this in itself makes co-ordination in collective bargaining difficult. If anything, conflict rather than collaboration has been a recurring theme among various trustee groups.

HISTORICAL SKETCH OF INDUSTRIAL RELATIONS

Up to the early 1970s, there had never been a school closing in Ontario as a result of an impasse in teacher–board negotiations, despite the fact that teacher bargaining in the province predates Bill 100 by many years. The bargaining, of course, had been of a more genteel nature than that typically found in the private sector. Limited in scope, in terms of the substantive issues dealt with at the bargaining table, it was referred to as "collective negotiations"—a term still preferred by many teachers and trustees in place of the more militant-sounding "collective bargaining." Nevertheless, the historical record is clear; collective bargaining of a sort was well established in Ontario by the 1950s and 1960s (Muir 1968). Collective bargaining occurred in cases where school boards voluntarily agreed to negotiate with the federations.

The character and nature of teacher–board conflict, however, changed dramatically in the late 1960s and, from 1969 to 1975, negotiations were more combative than ever before. Mistrust permeated the system, to the extent that the Ontario government felt the need to set up a special commission in late 1970 (The Reville Commission) to examine teacher–board relations. A new era began, and teacher–board relationships continued to deteriorate over time.

The emphasis in negotiations to that point was on negotiating salaries. Until the 1970s, working conditions were *not* negotiated, and settlements would take the form of school board resolutions or jointly signed memoranda. Negotiations were between the local board and the local teachers of one of the teachers' associations. The provincial bodies of the teachers' associations, throughout time, played an advisory role.

Also, until the mid- and late 1960s, the exercise of power was rarely an important part of teacher–board negotiations—or, more accurately, power was unilaterally applied by the school boards. Nevertheless, in rare cases, sanctions were set up by teacher groups in order to apply pressure on an intransigent board. The predominant sanction up to the early 1970s was "pink listing." When a particular set of negotiations broke down, an "in dispute" designation by one of the provincial affiliates would take the form of a letter—on pink paper, in the case of the OSSTF. The letter would be sent to all members of the affiliate. Typically, it would advise members that, while it would not be considered unprofessional to accept a position with the school board "in dispute," any teacher who did so would not receive support from the affiliate in the future.

Pink listing had a stronger impact when accompanied by the threatened mass resignation of teachers employed by the board in dispute. Under the individual teachers' contract (signed by all teachers when hired), resignation may only occur on December 31 or August 31, and notice to this effect must be given by November 30 or May 31. Hence, resignations of all or most of the teachers could be collected in advance by an affiliate in negotiations and held as a pressure tactic up to the November 30 or May 31 deadline.

Mass resignations were threatened frequently, but, up to 1970, had taken place only once. From 1970 to 1975, in addition to pink listing and *threatened* mass resignations, teachers used study sessions (which amounted to one-day strikes), work-to-rule in various forms, political pressure, and lobbying. Then, in 1973, secondary school teachers at a number of public school boards used *actual* (not threatened) mass resignations. In the fall, a mass work-to-rule of Metro Toronto's 8000 secondary school teachers took place. There were many other activities as well, and the year culminated in a one-day general strike across the province in December.

In late 1973, the government introduced legislation (Bill 275) that would give teachers the statutory right to bargain collectively. Negotiations were to be at the local level. Teachers were not given the right to strike, but the bill did provide for compulsory binding arbitration of any unresolved disputes. The bill, however, died on the order paper.

As a consequence, while there was a reasonably sophisticated and well-developed system of negotiations by the mid-1970s, many aspects were missing. Teachers did not have the *statutory* right to bargain. Recognition of the teachers' bargaining committee by a school board was voluntary. A board could withdraw from negotiations at any time and unilaterally change conditions of work. The mechanisms had simply grown up without definition of the rights and responsibilities of either party. The scope of negotiable items was not clear. As well, an appropriate bargaining unit had never been specified, and, therefore, the precise coverage of an agreement or memorandum was not certain. The question, for example, of whether principals and vice-principals should be in the bargaining unit was an important one, and at some point would have to be clarified. The essential question of the teachers' right to strike had never been confronted. A specific prohibition did not exist in any legislation, but the right to strike and the legality of other sanctions were very much uncertain. The giving of notice to bargain, contract expiry dates, and related procedures were murky as well.

Then, in late 1974 and early 1975, about 660 high school teachers in Windsor went on strike, *without* submitting their resignations. The strike lasted eight weeks. The issue of the legality of teacher strikes was clearly drawn. The Windsor Board of Education asked the Ontario Supreme Court for an interlocutory injunction restraining the teachers from continuing their strike and picketing. Mr. Justice Osler denied the application of the Windsor board. His decision was not a clear victory for the teachers, however. He found that the teachers were in breach of their contracts and pointed out that the board did have civil remedies, including the right to discharge without notice. Nevertheless, while the decision did not totally clarify the right of teachers to strike, it did make clear the futility of trying to prevent strikes through court action. This development, in addition to all of the conflict between teachers and school boards, led the government to pass Bill 100, which resulted in *bona fide* collective bargaining and the right to strike. More than any other development, Bill 100 has changed the system of industrial relations.

TEACHER STRIKES PRIOR TO BILL 100

From 1970 to 1975, there were numerous collective-bargaining marathons. The teachers would insist that nonsalary items (i.e., working conditions and, more specifically, the pupil/teacher ratio) be negotiated. The pupil/teacher ratio (PTR) determines the number of teachers who will be employed in a school system. This decision had always rested with the school board, and was not a shared or negotiated decision. Most boards resisted teacher demands in this and other working-conditions areas, such as instructional load (the number of daily teaching periods per teacher) in secondary school negotiations, or noontime supervision in elementary negotiations.

A review of these confrontations reveals unmistakably that the real issues at stake were *decision making* and *power*. That is, the procedural matters regarding working conditions that were discussed over and over again in teacher–board negotiations were ones of teacher input versus real decision-making power or influence in the area of working conditions. Teachers were making some progress, but it was gradual at best. Just prior to the introduction of Bill 100, for example, York County secondary school teachers (after a lengthy strike) had won only the right to be *consulted* on a range of policies, but not the right to negotiate them. In Windsor, the settlement of the secondary school teachers' strike mentioned above required the Windsor trustees to consult on some policy issues, although other policy changes would be subject to agreement by the teachers. Occasionally, some boards had agreed to put the PTR in the collective agreement, but this practice was by no means widespread.

The existence of strikes, as well as the other sanctions used by teachers, made it absolutely clear that a comprehensive piece of legislation was necessary that would provide a legal framework for collective bargaining. Teachers, if they did not have the right to strike on a *de jure* basis, did have it in practice. In the three years prior to the enactment of Bill 100, there were 28 teacher strikes in the province. The incidence of economic sanctions demonstrated that teacher discontent would be manifested, in a tangible and overt manner, with or without legislation. Other reasons also caused ministry officials to totally rethink their original approach to the problem.

PUBLIC POLICY

In Bill 100, the government opted for a separate, and essentially conservative, piece of legislation, the main provisions of which are congruent with the autonomy of local school boards (the locus of decision making in the Ontario educational system), current teacher and trustee institutions, and the system of bargaining. In large measure, teacher and trustee institutions, their joint dealings, and Bill 100 are a reflection of important aspects of the educational system outlined earlier. Bill 100 legitimizes overt teacher–board conflict, but, at the same time, it rigorously regulates negotiation disputes through a rather revolutionary (for that particular time) set of dispute-settlement procedures.

The stated purpose of Bill 100 is to some extent similar to that of the National Labor Relations Act (Wagner Act) in the United States. The major labour problems facing that country in 1935 were bitter, and organizational and recognition strikes were common. The sanctions imposed by Ontario teachers were also often for recognition purposes. In passing the Wagner Act, the U.S. Congress decreed that the best way to move beyond such disputes and dampen labour–management conflict in general was to provide *bona fide* collective bargaining. The National Labor Relations Act, therefore, provided the protected rights of employees to organize and to bargain collectively. In somewhat similar fashion, the Ontario Ministry of Education came to the conclusion that authentic collective bargaining with sanctions would bring about a greater degree of harmony between the parties.

Quite unlike the Wagner Act in the United States and similar labour legislation in Canada, Bill 100 does *not* provide for the certification of teacher unions. Instead, those who designed Bill 100 hoped to promote stable relationships by simply recognizing the existence of the prevailing and predominant institutions. This very different approach demonstrates the extent to which the existing institutions and institutional arrangements shaped and determined Bill 100.

Both parties wanted negotiations to remain at the local level, and Bill 100 so provides by specifying that negotiations take place between a board and a branch affiliate.[4] With respect to the scope of the bargaining unit, the bill included principals and vice-principals. In section 64, it affirms that principals and vice-principals must be members of the branch affiliate, and included in the negotiating unit. However, Bill 100 provides that in the event of a strike, a lockout, or a closing of the schools, both principals and vice-principals must remain on duty.

Prior to Bill 100, the teachers had taken the position that all matters involved in the teacher–board relationship should be subject to bargaining. They argued that teachers, as professionals, were more qualified to determine educational policies than were trustees, and that there is a close relationship between the quality of education and their demands with respect to such things as class sizes and the pupil/teacher ratio. Therefore, these and similar demands were not only legitimate, but also bargainable issues helpful to the educational system. There were, and are, a vast array of subjects that teachers desire to negotiate—teacher classification, general working conditions, sick leave, maternity leave, reduction in staff and job security, class contact hours, preparation time, the use of itinerant teachers, the use of paraprofessionals, and the establishment and improvement of grievance procedures. The list is by no means exhaustive, and the issues are ones that affect teachers directly. The trustees had consistently argued that to expand the scope of bargaining beyond salary and other forms of compensation would be to infringe upon their management rights.

The matter was resolved under section 3(1) of Bill 100: "The Act applies to all collective negotiations between boards and teachers in respect of *any term or condition of employment* put forth by either party for making or renewing any agreement (emphasis added). Section 8 reiterated this point: "Negotiations shall be carried out in respect of *any term or condition of employment* put forward by either party (emphasis added). These stipulations constituted a major victory for the teachers' federations.

However, Bill 100 provides for collective bargaining, but not unfettered collective bargaining. The legislation provides for tightly controlled collective bargaining, with considerable third-party assistance (mediation and fact finding) and a separate commission (the Education Relations Commission, or ERC) to administer the act, oversee negotiations, monitor strikes, and advise the government when a strike places in jeopardy students' courses of study. The commission acts as a buffer between the government and the negotiating parties, and much of the success of Bill 100 depends on keeping ministry intrusion into collective bargaining to a minimum.

In addition to voluntary or, in some cases, imposed mediation, there are elaborate procedures outlined in Bill 100 that must be followed before a strike (or a lockout) can be called. That is, before there can be a legal strike several things must transpire:

1. Notice of desire to negotiate must have been given, in January of the year of contract expiry, by at least one of the parties.
2. The dispute must have been referred to a fact-finder, and fifteen days must have elapsed after the ERC has released the fact-finder's report to the public.
3. The school board's last offer must have been submitted to and rejected by the teachers in the branch affiliate.
4. The teachers must also have voted (at the same time as, or after, the last-offer vote) in favour of strike action. This vote must not take place until fifteen days have elapsed after the release of the fact-finder's report.
5. After a majority vote in favour of a strike, written notice of the strike, and the date on which the strike will commence, must be given by the branch affiliate to the school board. This must be given five days before commencement of the strike.
6. The current collective agreement must have expired. Because all collective agreements must expire on August 31, no matter how fast the parties go through negotiations, a strike cannot take place until September 1.

A board lockout can occur only after the teachers introduce a sanction. In any case, by the time sanctions by either side take place, the hurdles and possible interventions are considerable. Many avenues for settlement will have been suggested and/or tried. All else failing, as noted, there is one more measure the ERC may use to end a strike or a lockout. Bill 100 makes it a duty of the ERC to:

advise the Lieutenant Governor in Council when, in the opinion of the Commission, the continuance of a strike, lockout or closing of a school or schools will place in jeopardy the successful completion of courses of study by the students affected by the strike, lockout or clos-ing of a school or schools. (Bill 100, Section 60[1][h])

The government, of course, at its own initiative, has the option of presenting legislation to end a strike or lockout, regardless of the recommendations of the commission.

In summary, while collective bargaining was to be somewhat more regulated than in the private sector, the teachers' federations had won three major victories in Bill 100—the statutory right to bargain collectively, the right to strike, and open-scope negotiations.

Developments from the Late 1970s through the 1980s

THE COLLECTIVE-BARGAINING ENVIRONMENT

In the ensuing years, the following factors have had an impact on collective bar-gaining by teachers in Ontario: (1) the lifting of provincial spending ceilings in late 1975, and provincial spending restraint ever since that time; (2) the Anti-Inflation Program of the federal government, which ran from late 1975 through 1978; (3) provincial wage controls, introduced in 1982 and lifted in 1984; (4) the extension of full provincial funding to Roman Catholic school boards for sec-ondary schools in 1986; and (5) falling enrolment throughout much of the period. Each of these will be discussed briefly.

It was noted above that, in 1970, the Ministry of Education imposed spending ceilings on school board spending. A few months after Bill 100 was passed, the ministry announced the removal of ceilings. This shifted the major responsibility for resisting teacher demands back to the local level. Teacher salary increases and other collective-bargaining cost increases, which, in turn, result in increases to a school board budget beyond provincial government grants, have to be met through local tax increases. Since that time, the year-to-year increases in provin-cial government grants have been sharply curtailed. The major onus for restraint has been on school trustees.

Second, negotiations began under Bill 100 during a turbulent period in Canadi-an industrial relations, a period marked by a great deal of uncertainty. The federal government passed the Anti-Inflation Program, which imposed wage and price controls. Enabling legislation was enacted in Ontario that placed education under the restraint program. Therefore, bargaining during the first three years under Bill

100 took place under the influence of wage and price controls. When the schools opened after Bill 100 was enacted, there were 122 sets of negotiations where the existing collective agreement had expired and no settlement had been reached by September 1, 1975. Few of these had reached agreement by the time the prime minister made his surprise announcement in mid-October of mandatory wage and price controls. Collective bargaining in most sectors of the economy became—particularly, in the first six to nine months of the controls program—immensely complex and uncertain because of the unsettled, desultory, and sluggish nature of Anti-Inflation Board (AIB) decisions. Salaries were determined by an AIB formula, which caused numerous problems, and the teachers' federations demanded major changes in working conditions. In light of these developments, it is not surprising that there were six teacher strikes in the first year under Bill 100.

Third, teacher–board negotiations were also significantly impacted when a second round of wage controls for the Ontario public sector was enacted in 1982. Briefly, Bill 179 (the Inflation Restraint Act), introduced in the Ontario Legislature in late 1982, limited compensation increases in the public sector to up to 9 percent in the first year of the program (the "transitional" year) and to 5 percent in the second year (the "control" year). Unlike the Anti-Inflation Program, this legislation, in effect, removed the right to strike and also provided for the formation of the Inflation Restraint Board (IRB) to administer the act and to monitor wage and price increases in the public and private sectors. For all intents and purposes, collective bargaining was suspended during 1983 and 1984.

Fourth, the Education Amendment Act (Bill 30) received Royal Assent on June 24, 1986. The act extended full funding to separate school boards that elect to perform the duties of a secondary school board. Bill 30, because it resulted in enrolment shifts to the Roman Catholic system, had both financial and job-security implications for both sectors and, as a consequence, it continues to have collective-bargaining ramifications. Bill 30 resulted in the transfer of a large number of secondary school students from schools operated by boards of education (public boards) to secondary schools operated by the newly created Roman Catholic school boards. As a result, it was necessary to build into the legislation safeguards for those teachers of a public board of education whose positions would disappear as a direct result of the transfer of students. The legislation provided for the transfer of teachers from the public system to the Roman Catholic system, and the legislation went to considerable lengths to protect the rights of such teachers (including the transfer of the teacher's contract).

Bill 30 did not specify the collective-bargaining arrangements for the newly funded boards. A decision of the ERC granted bargaining rights to the OECTA for secondary teachers at Roman Catholic school boards and gave them separate branch-affiliate status. The decision was an important one for the stability of bargaining rights and relationships. It meant that secondary school teachers who are members of OECTA and AEFO in the Roman Catholic system have the same rights as secondary school teachers who are members of OSSTF and AEFO in the public system. If they so chose, they could (and can) sign a separate collective agreement

Table 9.3
Number of Pupils and Teachers in Ontario Secondary Schools, 1976–1988

Year	Pupils	Teachers	PTR
1976[a]	611 820	33 954	17.03
1977[a]	612 730	36 174	16.86
1978[a]	608 351	36 206	16.73
1979[a]	596 963	35 750	16.55
1980[a]	582 332	35 137	16.37
1981[a]	564 321	34 610	15.99
1982[a]	556 038	34 260	15.89
1983[a]	548 563	34 353	15.56
1984[a]	537 882	34 296	15.27
1985	473 436	30 706	15.03
1986	464 131	30 216	14.88
1987	456 317	29 967	14.67
1988	453 922	30 234	14.46

Note: [a] All secondary schools (public and Roman Catholic).
Source: Data provided by the Education Relations Commission.

covering secondary teachers only. Those teachers who were transferred to a Roman Catholic school board because of Bill 30 had enjoyed that right prior to their transfer from the public system. Following the decision by the ERC, new legislation covering French-language schools in the province explicitly provided for separate elementary and secondary negotiations in those school systems, as well.

Fifth, student enrolment through most of the period was falling. Such was particularly the case in public secondary schools (see Table 9.3), and the problem was amplified in the public system because of the extension of funding to Roman Catholic school boards for secondary school education. Consequently, the number of teachers was reduced over the period in both elementary and secondary education, but the attrition was particularly severe in the latter. Therefore, up to the mid-1980s, a major issue for the federations was job security. As a result, the relative decline in teachers was significantly less than the relative decline in students.

Table 9.4
Number of Pupils and Teachers
in Ontario Roman Catholic Secondary Schools, 1985–1988

Year	Pupils	Teachers	PTR
1985	58 440	3479	16.24
1986	77 733	4580	15.86
1987	97 905	5900	15.54
1988	106 897	6837	15.02

Source: Data provided by the Education Relations Commission.

In Roman Catholic secondary schools, of course, enrolment increased significantly in the late 1980s (see Table 9.4).

THE STRIKE RECORD

The strike record before and after Bill 100 is an interesting one. It was noted above that, in the three years prior to Bill 100, there were 28 teacher strikes. One of the characteristics of bargaining since that time has been the low level of strike activity. Excluding 1982–83 and 1983–84, when wage controls effectively pre-empted collective bargaining, there were 2206 sets of negotiations over twelve rounds of bargaining from 1975 to 1989. Of these, a total of 2152 ended in a negotiated settlement without sanctions. During the twelve bargaining rounds, there have been only 53 strikes.[5] Therefore, only 2.4 percent of the situations wound up in sanctions; or, put another way, 97.6 percent of all cases were negotiated without sanctions.

However, strikes have occurred in every sector (elementary, secondary, and separate schools), and there has been considerable variety in the length and the type of sanction: some have been work-to-rule sanctions, others a total withdrawal of services, and some a combination of the two. In some cases, there have been both a teacher sanction and a school board lockout. Typically, the parties in a sanction situation have been allowed to pursue their bargaining strategies relatively unimpeded by government intervention. This situation is positive from an industrial relations perspective and unusual in the public sector. The Education Relations Commission has consistently taken the position with the parties, with the public, and, most importantly, with government officials that lengthy sanctions must be allowed to occur. Eighteen strikes lasted a minimum of 30 school days, or six weeks. Eight lasted at least 40 school days, or two months. By any standards, these are lengthy strikes.

When discussing specific ERC interventions, it is useful to divide the period into two parts: first, commission policy in the first year of Bill 100; and second, commission policy thereafter. As noted earlier, the first year after Bill 100 was enacted was particularly conflictual because of the Anti-Inflation Program and this situation led to some policy determinations peculiar to that specific period. From 1975 through 1989, teachers' strikes have been terminated through legislation on only eight occasions, five of these occurring during the first year the statute was in force. Since that time, there have been only three advisements from the ERC. In two of those cases, a voluntary resolution of the dispute was reached by the parties before back-to-work legislation was passed. As a consequence, for the past thirteen rounds of bargaining, there has been only one case where back-to-work legislation has been enacted. In one other case, legislation was drafted and presented in the legislature, but it was not enacted.

In their classic work on the transformation of industrial relations during the 1980s, Kochan, Katz, and McKersie (1986) note that the nature of the strike weapon has changed. They argue that strikes are often called today for defensive reasons—to prevent concessions or, in some cases, for the survival of the union. In many cases, strikes have been a losing proposition for unions. Such has not been the case in Ontario education. It is true that sanctions often occur because of a deteriorating teacher–board relationship, a lack of trust between teachers and administrators, an autocratic director of education, and/or other related problems. The outcome, however, has often been the insertion in the collective agreement of a provision(s) to remedy the situation. While it cannot be said that the federations have been the clear victors in all or even a majority of strike situations, rarely have they been clear losers. Today, in Ontario, teacher strikes remain a viable weapon, and there has not been a downward trend in either the frequency or the length of teacher strikes.

THE SUBSTANTIVE BARGAINING ISSUES

Unlike the case of private-sector collective bargaining, change in Ontario education has been driven, not by the employer, but by the unions (federations). Collective bargaining has produced many changes. Since 1975, a significant number of important matters have found their way into collective agreements. Progress for teachers, however, has been evolutionary and not revolutionary. In the late 1970s and throughout the 1980s, the issues in teacher bargaining were in the areas of salary and working conditions. This continues to be the case, and significant breakthroughs have been made, particularly in the working-conditions area.

In what follows, both wages and fringe benefits, and working conditions, will be discussed.

Wages and Fringe Benefits

Teacher salaries have always been an issue in negotiations—just how contentious generally depends on the rate of inflation and the degree of spending restraint imposed on the system. Since the enactment of Bill 100, however, salaries have not been a great bone of contention. The ERC acts as an information system for the federations, school boards, and third-party neutrals, and its data are widely respected and utilized by the parties. Therefore, in the early stages of each bargaining round, a "range of reasonableness" for salary *increases* becomes evident. While there have been exceptions, salary increases have generally not been the most difficult item to resolve.

A number of salary-related items were issues in the late 1970s and early 1980s, but these have now been resolved. For example, there was pressure from the federations to shorten the salary grid so that teachers would reach the maximum salary in a shorter period of time. The matters of teacher certification and placement on the salary grid were settled by 1975 in secondary schools, and by the mid-1980s in the elementary and separate schools. With respect to salary *levels*, Ontario teachers over the past decade have fared as well as or better than any group of teachers in Canada. Table 9.5 presents salary scales for teachers in the ten provinces for the period 1980–90. Ontario salaries have remained at, or close to, the top throughout the period.

Over that period, as well, there was major progress with respect to fringes. Indeed, fringe-benefit issues are now relatively straightforward, particularly in light of the fact that pensions are provided for in provincial legislation rather than subject to collective bargaining. In 1990, there was a major disagreement between the provincial government and the teacher federations with respect to pension funding and related issues, but these differences were resolved outside of collective bargaining.

A survey of 256 collective agreements by the ERC for the year 1989–90 revealed that, today, many other fringe benefits are provided in collective agreements, and the provisions are extensive. In 90 percent of the collective agreements, a group life insurance plan is provided, with the board paying 80 to 100 percent of the cost. The board pays for less than 50 percent of the cost in only 4 percent of the cases. Dental plans have been established in 255 of 256 collective agreements. In 85 percent of the agreements, at least 80 percent of the cost is paid by the board. In 1989–90, over 90 percent of the agreements included a provision that the board would subsidize over 80 percent of the Ontario Hospital Insurance Premium. In 90 percent of the agreements, boards subsidized at least 80 percent of the cost of providing semiprivate coverage. All of the agreements provided extended health care, and 95 percent of them had the board paying at least 80 percent of the cost. Vision care was provided for in three-quarters of the agreements, and, in two-thirds of the boards, at least 80 percent of the cost was paid for by the board. Long-term disability (LTD) plans were included in 90 percent of the agreements. Where an LTD plan exists, at least 50 percent of the cost is subsidized by the board in one-third of the agreements. The above are provisions reported by the ERC. Most collective agreements provide other benefits, including sick-leave and sabbatical-leave plans.

Bargaining has not been all one-sided, especially during the 1980s. The teachers have accused many boards of "contract stripping," what in the private sector would be called "concession bargaining." But unlike the case in the private sector, these efforts have generally not met with a great deal of success. For example, in the 1980s, a few school boards tried to roll back or eliminate a retirement gratuity. The latter is a lump-sum payment teachers collect from a board upon retirement. As noted, in addition to receiving this lump-sum payment, teachers are covered by a provincial pension plan. While the costs of the retirement gratuity were minimal during the 1980s, they are an unfunded liability, and will now be very significant because of the high retirement rate. Many boards tried to be proactive and limit the payout through collective bargaining. The teachers' federations strongly opposed this negotiating stance, and, as a consequence, the issue was often a very contentious one. Most boards had very limited success in this endeavour, although there are now many agreements that have "grandfathered" and/or capped the benefit.

Table 9.5
Teacher Salary Scales, Ten Provinces, 1980–1990[a]

Year	B.C.	Alta.	Sask.	Man.	Ont. Secondary	Ont. Elementary	Que.	N.B.	N.S.	P.E.I.	Nfld.
1980	$25 563	$28 775	$26 670	$25 988	$27 512	$26 114	$26 735	$21 851	$25 268	$21 376	$23 583
1981	28 670	31 795	29 806	28 899	29 943	29 475	30 489	24 582	28 503	24 112	26 498
1982	33 254	36 245	33 976	32 656	32 189	32 128	33 726	30 974	30 839	27 005	29 214
1983	34 255	38 420	36 354	36 020	33 798	33 734	31 384	30 974	33 997	27 005	30 383
1984	34 255	38 605	37 662	36 901	35 316	35 421	32 341	32 523	35 016	28 134	30 383
1985	34 255	40 565	37 662	37 639	36 870	36 838	33 072	33 499	37 508	28 837	30 383
1986	35 280	41 340	39 128	38 768	38 669	38 694	34 230	34 169	38 258	30 740	32 962
1987	36 383	42 995	39 128	40 319	40 462	40 644	35 599	36 236	39 406	33 199	34 825
1988	38 206	42 995	40 308	41 569	42 315	43 119	37 259	37 685	41 007	34 527	36 574
1989	40 920	46 135	41 930	43 003	45 054	45 965	38 749	38 439	43 059	34 527	38 446
1990	43 932	48 440	43 608	NA	47 875	48 999	40 737	40 776	45 214	37 252	NA

Note: [a] Province-wide scales are shown for the four Atlantic provinces, Quebec, and Saskatchewan; the Alberta, Manitoba, and B.C. scales are for Calgary, Winnipeg, and Vancouver, respectively. The Ontario elementary salary scales are for Ottawa, and the secondary salary scale is for Toronto. The salary category used in each case is the lowest bachelor degree category requiring at least sixteen years of schooling, including four years of post-secondary education.

Source: Data provided by the Canadian Teachers' Federation.

Growth in Working-Conditions Provisions

The major legacy of collective bargaining has been in the area of working conditions and job security. Given the broad scope of negotiable issues in Ontario, it is not surprising that such is the case. Nor is it surprising in light of some of the evidence elsewhere. A 1970s U.S. study (Flango 1976) indicated that the major gains to teachers from collective bargaining were centred in the domain of working conditions. More recently, Woodbury (1985) found that lower class sizes under collective-bargaining regimes in the United States are related to the legal scope of bargaining and to the right to strike. It was found, for example, that legal restrictions on the negotiability of class size were related to *higher* pupil/teacher ratios, and vice versa. In Ontario, of course, there are no restrictions and, in light of the Woodbury study, it is not surprising to find that the number and type of provisions in collective agreements, with respect to working conditions, are diverse and impressive.

At the same time, it should be noted as well that new clauses in this realm are by far the most difficult to negotiate into a collective agreement, because of the perceived, and perhaps actual, threat to management rights, and the potential long-run cost implications. Trustee and administrator resistance peaks on items in the working-conditions area. The issues of PTR and/or maximum class sizes are directly connected to educational policy.[6]

Class size is a more realistic indicator than PTR of the load a teacher is likely to have and, consequently, of the amount of personal attention the individual student is likely to receive. PTR is only indirectly related to class size. A lower PTR means more teachers in the system, which should result in small class sizes. However, that is not always the case, if the teachers added by a reduced PTR are not allocated to teaching positions. For example, new personnel could be allocated nonclassroom teaching assignments, such as guidance counsellors, librarians, and special education resource teachers. For this reason, in the 1980s, the teachers' federations have concentrated more on negotiating class-size provisions or reducing existing maximums rather than trying to reduce PTR.

In any case, at stake in both issues is the amount of potential teacher–pupil contact. Teachers argue that close and personal attention of a teacher are positive factors in a student's development. Therefore, PTR and class size are two-sided issues. The school board and the public are likely to call them "working conditions." Teachers are just as likely to note that they involve the "quality of education." For the trustees, they involve "management rights," for the teachers they are areas for "shared decision-making responsibility," and so on. At any rate, both issues do involve both professional and job-security concerns for the teachers.

When Bill 100 was enacted, the federations continued to focus on working conditions. After the second round of bargaining, there were 47 collective agreements (out of a total of 185) with a pupil/teacher ratio provision. In 39 of these cases, the clause was a mandatory provision. The incursion with respect to class size was similar. Thirty agreements in 1977 contained a class-size provision.

Nevertheless, in the early years, there was a great deal of flexibility in collective-agreement provisions on working conditions. This flexibility was achieved through "best efforts" clauses and/or by using "guidelines" only. Some collective agreements combined two variables—number of periods (instructional load) and number of students (class size) to be taught—into one variable, which also allowed more discretion for the administration. Another system used to minimize the importance of negotiating working conditions was a letter of intent appended to the collective agreement.

Class Size

There has been a truly remarkable growth of class-size provisions over the years (see Table 9.6). From 1977–78 through 1988–89, class-size provisions in collective agreements increased in frequency, from 22.7 percent to 61.5 percent. The increase in class-size provisions has taken place in all sectors—elementary, secondary, and Roman Catholic. While initially public secondary teachers led the way, today elementary and Roman Catholic panels have caught up. Indeed, the growth has been the most spectacular in Roman Catholic boards. Less than 10 percent of the agreements contained provisions related to class size in 1977–78, and by 1988–89, the proportion had increased to 58.2 per cent.

While their incidence has increased, the larger development has occurred in the content of the provisions. As noted, class-size provisions in the collective agreement directly attack the prerogatives of management by specifically limiting the size of classes. Limits may be achieved in a number of ways, including specifying ranges, maxima, or averages. There are two types of collective-agreement provisions—direct and indirect. An example of a direct class-size provision is an article in a 1989–91 secondary school agreement that states, "by the thirtieth day of September the following class sizes shall not be exceeded." Mandatory class-size maximums are listed, which reduce any board flexibility on the matter.

Table 9.6

Class-Size Provisions, by Year and Panel

Year	Elementary		Secondary		RCSS		Total	
	%	No.	%	No.	%	No.	%	No.
1977–78	25.8	17	28.4	19	9.3	4	22.7	40
		63		67		43		176
1982–83	32.0	21	42.0	23	24.0	10	33.6	54
		66		53		41		160
1988–89	67.1	53	63.0	51	49.0	29	64.7	133
		79		81		59		219
1989–90	64.6	42	61.3	38	58.2	32	61.5	112
		65		62		55		182

Source: Data provided by the Education Relations Commission.

Indirect provisions provide greater flexibility for school boards in determining class sizes. The following clause in a 1987–88 collective agreement is an example: "the board agrees to maintain the current practice of staffing schools based upon the needs of the system. In determining these needs the following factors will be taken into consideration: a) class size as it relates to the programme and levels offered . . ." Obviously, this provision gives the board more latitude in administering class sizes.

In a study of class-size provisions, Fraser (1990) analyzed a random sample of twelve public secondary school collective agreements. In 1977–78, four contained class-size provisions. By 1988–89, ten agreements had class-size provisions. Of the agreements with such provisions, three in 1977–78 and six in 1988–89 had direct provisions. Moreover, in this sample of agreements, class-size maximums decreased or remained the same over the period. In sum, over time, class-size provisions have clearly increased in frequency and have become more restrictive.

Pupil/Teacher Ratio

Negotiated PTR provisions rose in all sectors during the period 1977–78 and 1988–89 (see Table 9.7). In 1977–78 and 1982–83, secondary panels had a substantially higher percentage of agreements with a specified PTR than either elementary or Roman Catholic boards. By 1988–89, provisions in secondary agreements had declined, and percentages across panels had converged. The greatest percentage increase in provisions was between 1977–78 and 1982–83. Since that time, there has been a levelling off. One reason may be the fact that much more emphasis is now placed by the federations on class-size provisions.

There may be other reasons as well, however. For example, the federations may have realized that the PTR would decline (because of the declining trend in enrolment) without the benefit of negotiations. Certainly, all else being equal, reduced numbers of students will result in a reduction in the PTR. However, the observed rate of decline in enrolment was substantially greater than the decline in

Table 9.7
Pupil/Teacher Ratio Provisions, by Year and Panel

Year	Elementary		Secondary		RCSS		Total	
	%	No.	%	No.	%	No.	%	No.
1977–78	31.8	21	47.8	32	16.3	7	34.1	60
		66		67		43		176
1982–83	53.0	35	72.0	38	29.0	12	53.1	85
		66		53		41		160
1988–89	46.8	37	56.8	46	57.6	34	53.4	117
		79		81		59		219
1989–90	50.8	33	56.5	35	54.5	30	53.8	98
		65		62		55		182

Source: Data provided by the Education Relations Commission.

the number of teachers employed, which suggests that other factors may be working to limit the reduction of teachers in the face of declining secondary enrolment. In line with this observation is the fact that PTR at Roman Catholic secondary schools has declined steadily at a time when enrolment has dramatically *increased*.

It seems likely, therefore, that lower PTRs have been the combined result of the federations' success in negotiating class-size provisions, and lower PTRs in collective agreements, and declining enrolment. A factor not related to collective bargaining probably accounts for some of the decline, as well: special education programs, which expanded in secondary schools in the 1980s, require a very low pupil/teacher ratio. Therefore, the PTR would have declined, at least to some extent, regardless of collective bargaining. Over the years, the actual system-wide PTR (as distinct from the negotiated PTR) has consistently decreased in both systems by more than the negotiated PTR.

Many agreements now include provisions on the PTR that give teachers more control. By 1989, all but two of the sampled public secondary agreements in Fraser's (1990) sample contained a specifically defined PTR but, in addition to a system-wide PTR, four agreements defined PTRs for specific instructional areas. For example, one agreement stipulated separate PTRs for each secondary school as well as library, guidance, and gifted programs. In earlier years (1977–78 and 1984–85), separate PTRs were not present in the agreement.

Moreover, with the passage of time, the definition of the PTR has been tightened up, which also reduces board flexibility. Thus, by 1989, eight of ten agreements in Fraser's (1990) sample contained provisions excluding certain school personnel from system-wide PTR calculations. As an example, agreements might exclude principals, guidance teachers, teachers on leave, special education teachers, and others from its calculations. There have been other advances as well. By 1989, several agreements had provisions requiring boards to hire additional teachers if the negotiated PTR was exceeded.

Component Staffing

Next to the negotiation of specific class sizes in the collective agreement, the most important breakthrough for the teacher federations has been the negotiation of component staffing. Component staffing is a staff-*allocation* mechanism. Its attraction to teachers is that it determines the number of teachers in a school system on the basis, not of system-wide student enrolment, but of position and program area in each school. That is, it considers separately each defined position and program area (or component) at the individual-school level. Unlike systems based on PTR (which are often related to the number of students on a *global* basis and do not necessarily mandate new staff), component staffing provides for teachers in designated positions and program areas. As a consequence, it reduces management's flexibility in the allocation of staff.

Fixed teacher quotas in some component-staffing systems can create overstaffing situations. Where there is a reduction in student enrolment, the teacher

Table 9.8

Component Staffing, by Year and Panel[a]

Year	Elementary		Secondary		RCSS		Total	
	%	No.	%	No.	%	No.	%	No.
1988–89	40.5	32	70.4	57	26.6	16	47.7	105
		79		81		39		199
1989–90	35.4	23	67.7	42	26.7	12	43.7	77
		65		62		33		160

Notes: [a] The most comprehensive component staffing provisions cover all major areas in one location. Other agreements have several-staff allocation features that are effectively the same as component staffing. Where there are five or more of these, credit is recorded for component staffing.

Source: Data provided by the Education Relations Commission.

quota given in the collective agreement does not change. The result, from the board's perspective, is excess staff, and hence a staffing mechanism that does not accommodate significant changes in student population. Perhaps not surprisingly, where component staffing is found a comprehensive system is rarely called for. Most component staffing formulas simply mandate the allocation of personnel to positions of responsibility in each school (i.e., principal, vice-principal, and department heads). Rather than employing a comprehensive staffing formula, they rely on negotiated PTR to determine the number of teachers required in the school system.

Component staffing is a recent development. Less comprehensive component-staffing mechanisms (i.e., those that simply allocate personnel to positions of responsibility in each school) were negotiated into agreements in the Metro Toronto area in the mid-1970s. Comprehensive component-staffing provisions first appeared in the early 1980s, and data from the ERC on the issue are not available before the period 1988–89. However, by 1989–90, 43.7 percent of agreements on file at the ERC (as indicated in Table 9.8) contained component-staffing provisions. They were far more prevalent in secondary agreements (67.7 percent in 1989–90) than in elementary and Roman Catholic agreements (35.4 percent and 26.7 percent in 1989–90, respectively).

One additional breakthrough has been in the area of recourse and due process if working-conditions provisions are breached by a board. In some agreements teachers have been given the right of individual appeal, which is outside of the grievance process. For example, one agreement now gives teachers formal recourse where class-size maximums have been exceeded. An extensive five-step process, initiated prior to any grievance, seeks to provide teachers with suitable compensation (i.e., reduction of various supervision duties) for violation of class-size provisions. If the offer of compensation is not acceptable to a teacher, the grievance process may then be initiated.

PTR, class size, and workload will continue to be major issues throughout the province in future negotiations. There is always potential for a continuing battle with respect to each of these. For both sides, "principle" is involved. From the teachers' viewpoint, the first step was to obtain a provision in the collective agreement, and the next was to lower the pupil/teacher ratio, the maximum class size, and so on. And there will always be numerous permutations on each issue. At the same time, school boards will always be reluctant to change because of the cost and control implications.

PTR, class size, and instructional load can be referred to as "militant" issues. They are all important to teachers, but, of the three, the one issue that stirs teachers at large is class size. While a class size of, say, 20 or 30 may not seem large on the face of it, the difficulties of managing, helping, and teaching this number of students depends to a great extent on the facilities, the subject, and the characteristic of the students. It is an issue that directly affects the individual teacher and his or her effectiveness.

Joint Committees

Another avenue for teacher influence on a wide range of issues is through joint committees in any number of areas. Collective bargaining has encouraged teacher participation in decision making through the inclusion of such consultative committees in the collective agreement. The growth of committees has been spectacular since the passage of Bill 100. Once established in the agreement, the parties can take future action to ensure that they represent important mechanisms for participation and shared responsibility and influence. To the degree that committees represent genuine attempts at consultation by school boards, and if they are carefully conceived to ensure at least a modicum of *joint* action and power, the committee approach does make a contribution to teacher power.

Charles and Humphreys (1985) analyzed the degree of teacher involvement in decision making prior to and under Bill 100. They examined the degree of teacher involvement in decision making through joint committees established in the collective agreement in four areas: instructional programs (e.g., curriculum development); working conditions (e.g., instructional load); personnel policies/practices (e.g., professional development); and job security (e.g., transfer policies). They conducted a content analysis of each collective agreement in their stratified sample of boards in order to determine the degree to which control was held by teachers or the board/administration. They found there was a significant gain by teachers of control in all four areas during the period examined, and particularly while negotiating under Bill 100. Charles and Humphreys (1985, 508) concluded that teachers and school boards have entered a period of shared decision making, and that collective bargaining had "paid off with a substantial gain in the role teachers play in decision-making about the working place."

Other Provisions

Another form of teacher participation is provided through compulsory grievance machinery under section 52 of Bill 100. Almost all agreements provide for a grievance committee, and all must, of course, provide for grievance procedures. These are often taken for granted, but no other collective-agreement provision transforms industrial relations quite like the due process that flows from the grievance process. This has been particularly the case in the Roman Catholic system where, during the 1980s, "just cause" clauses have been negotiated for the first time by the OECTA in some agreements.

Also related to working conditions is the matter of job security, particularly in the public school system. Student enrolment declined during the late 1970s and the 1980s. The decline was severe until the early 1980s in elementary schools and continued to be a problem through the 1980s in public secondary schools because of enrolment shifts to Roman Catholic secondary schools when the latter were fully funded in 1986. During the period, the federations argued that declining enrolment presented an opportunity to reduce class size rather than lay off teachers. In addition, however, as soon as Bill 100 was enacted, job-security clauses that gave teachers protection from layoff became an important issue in collective bargaining. By the 1980s, the vast majority of collective agreements included some provision to deal with the job-security problems caused by falling enrolment, and today the problem of teacher surplus/redundancy is largely resolved. Most contracts provide some system for transferring surplus teachers within the school board and then provide a series of options that a redundant teacher may select.

It is worth noting, too, that collective bargaining has gone beyond mainline working conditions and job-security matters. The reach in education negotiations is far greater than normally seen in private-sector bargaining. For example, school staffing is often negotiated. This used to be a fundamental issue of school board policy—how many principals, vice-principals, librarians, and so on, should be included in a school. Some school boards have attempted to rationalize the organization of the school system (e.g., the number and type of department heads) and have had to negotiate such change with the branch affiliate. The definition of the school day and the definition of extracurricular duties have also been negotiated in a few cases.

What has occurred in Ontario is very similar to what has occurred in the United States. A major study on U.S. public-sector bargaining (Coleman 1990, 290) commented on the direction of bargaining in education:

> Education is now probably in an era of "negotiated policy." Bargaining still emphasizes the conditions under which work is performed, but it now also focuses on securing more teacher participation in determining educational policy and in deciding how schools are to be run. Conflicts over money and security are still present, but added to these are (1) intensified conflicts over teacher participation in managerial decision-making, and (2) the use of the collective bargaining agreement to limit the exercise of discretionary judgement by the people who run the schools.

Without question, collective bargaining in Ontario education has influenced how schools in the province are run; it has impinged on the prerogatives of school boards and school administrators. This, of course, is not surprising. It is the purpose of collective bargaining and workplace democracy. Collective bargaining has given the teachers considerable control and influence over the conditions under which they work. At the same time, school boards and their management have coped well with these changes.

Analysis and Inferences

Kochan, Katz, and McKersie (1986) note that traditional industrial relations theory treats management as reacting to union demands, pressures, and initiatives. They have argued for a new theory of industrial relations, one that is grounded in strategic choice. According to Kochan, Katz, and McKersie, it is the interaction of market pressures with union, management, and public-policy choices that determines industrial relations outcomes. This model is useful in explaining what has occurred in Ontario education. However, the model was put forward because management as an actor in industrial relations has been ignored in academic analysis, and Kochan, Katz, and McKersie argue that the causal flow has now been reversed; that is, unions have, over the 1980s, been forced to react to management's agenda.

This does not seem to have been the case in Ontario education. In the 1970s, the federations adopted a traditional trade union strategy, i.e., progress through adversarial collective bargaining. This strategy has remained remarkably consistent through the 1980s. More importantly, the federations have been the driving force for change in both the 1970s and the 1980s. It is true that the provincial government (as ultimate employer and holder of a large share of the purse strings) has had an impact on the system through funding and wage-restraint policies, and through the public-policy framework ultimately adopted to regulate collective bargaining. But the federations clearly played a major role in two of the major provisions of public policy (i.e., open-scope bargaining and the right to strike), and federation strategy on workload, PTR, class size, and staffing have shaped the main industrial relations outcomes. The federations have been more successful than most unions in Canada in directly exercising control over their conditions of work. In short, the major story in Ontario education has been the degree to which collective bargaining has paid off for the federations.

During the 1980s, in the private sector, major economic and organizational restructuring took place, which have, in turn, driven industrial relations outcomes. Such restructuring did not occur in education and, of course, there is no nonunion competition, which has also been a major cause of change in the private sector. Nevertheless, the parties in education have faced pressures and changes during the 1980s of a similar nature to those faced in the private-sector, and, in this light, it is surprising that the federations continue to be proactive and school board management reactive. School board management has not had an identifiable industrial relations strategy in the sense that Kochan, Katz, and McKersie use it. There is a major reason for this. Unlike private-sector management, they cannot follow a union-avoidance policy. The unions are mandated by statute. Therefore, at best, and with rare exceptions, they have only been able to react to the federations' collective-bargaining agenda. By the late 1970s, however, they were doing so in a more sophisticated and professional manner. After Bill 100 was enacted, trustees and school administrators gradually improved their effectiveness at the table by hiring staff who are specialists in industrial relations, or by hiring professional negotiators. Today, the industrial relations function within school boards is handled far better than it was in the 1970s.

There have been occasions when boards have tried to take the initiative in bargaining by making demands to change the collective agreement. For example, it was noted above that there was a minor amount of concession bargaining in the 1980s, which the federations refer to as "contract stripping." For the most part, however, these demands have "fallen off the table" at the end of bargaining. Unlike the case in the private sector, few work-rule and staffing-level changes have been forced through by school board management to reduce costs. While the bargaining agenda has been expanded, it has generally been driven by the federations. At the same time, some boards have tried to introduce change by suggesting shifts in the process to facilitate a more co-operative relationship with a branch affiliate. These initiatives to introduce a "new" industrial relations, generally through relationships by objectives (RBO) or by "single-team bargaining," have been sporadic and not widespread.

However, Kochan, Katz, and McKersie's framework is useful in another respect. They suggest three levels of activities for the analysis of industrial relations at the firm (school board) level: strategic activities at the top of the firm (school board); collective-bargaining activities at the middle level; and workplace activities. They note that collective-bargaining activities may become intertwined with changes at the lower and higher levels. Most changes in Ontario education have taken place at the collective-bargaining level, but the federations have influenced top-level decision making through such mechanisms as negotiated class sizes and component-staffing formulas, and by forcing boards to negotiate organizational changes in the schools which, at one time, would have been the subject of unilateral board policy. Collective bargaining has impacted the workplace as well through negotiated provisions related to lunch-time supervision, preparation time, job postings, and transfer policies.

On the public-policy front, school boards have consistently and vociferously argued that the *scope* of bargaining should be narrowed by changes to Bill 100. They have consistently lost that argument. The employer not at the bargaining table (i.e., the provincial government) has had only mixed success. It has followed a strategy of restricting the salary and fringe-benefits package through the introduction of various measures, including provincial ceilings (1970–75), the Anti-Inflation Program (1975–78), wage controls (in the 1982–83 and 1983–84 negotiation rounds), and through a strategy of providing provincial grants that do not cover the increasing costs of education. Therefore, the government has been able to introduce some restraint and control as far as its own costs are concerned, but it has been unable to wrest from the federations their considerable influence, and it has been unable to control the bargaining agenda as the provincial government has been able to do in Quebec (Grant 1991).

Clearly, it is accurate to say that there is *not* a "new" or "transformed" industrial relations system in Ontario education. Kochan, Katz, and McKersie would have predicted such an outcome. The parties operate in a *relatively* stable environment with all employers unionized, and, therefore, it is not strange that school boards continue to relate to the federations and their teachers in a traditional way. Rather than being "new," the industrial relations system is traditional, but evolving toward greater degrees of worker (teacher) control. Over the next decade, industrial relations, in Ontario is unlikely to change dramatically. If there is to be a "new" industrial relations, it is likely to be directed by union, not management, strategic choice, perhaps in the area of teacher (or federation)–driven curriculum change. More likely, we will see continuing efforts by the federations to make further inroads into their traditional areas of interest (e.g., workload, instructional load, staffing, and job security).

One development could change the above scenario. The provincial government, in an effort to gain greater control over bargaining outcomes, might try to move to province-wide bargaining, perhaps through a change in funding provisions. If this were to occur, there would be major resistance from school boards and, quite likely, from the federations as well. The system in Ontario has been stable, but progressive, and one where, it should be reiterated, the right to strike is alive and well. This is unusual in the Canadian public sector, either provincial or federal. In this light, a move to province-wide bargaining would be a mistake. Bill 100 has been a success, at least in part, because policy makers consulted with, and listened to, the parties before Bill 100 was introduced (Downie 1978, 1984). The provincial government that enacted Bill 100 in 1975 was a minority government. Hence, it took pains to build Bill 100 from the ground up through extensive consultation with the parties. This, perhaps more than anything else, has been the strength of the system. It is a major lesson for policy makers.

REFERENCES

Charles, L., and E. Humphreys, 1985. "Bargaining to Achieve Teacher Control in Ontario." *Relations Industrielles/Industrial Relations* 40/3: 495–509.

Coleman, C. 1990. *Managing Labor Relations in the Public Sector*. San Francisco: Jossey-Bass Publishers.

Downie, B. 1978. *Collective Bargaining and Conflict Resolution in Education: The Evolution of Public Policy in Ontario*. Kingston, ON: Industrial Relations Centre, Queen's University.

———. 1984. "Collective Bargaining under an Essential Services Disputes Commission." In M. Thompson, and G. Swimmer, eds., *Conflict or Compromise: The Future of Public Sector Industrial Relations*. Montreal: The Institute for Research on Public Policy. 373–401.

Flango, V. 1976. "The Impact of Collective Negotiations on Education Policies." *Journal of Collective Negotiations in the Public Sector* 5/2: 133–54.

Fraser, D. 1990. "Trends in Working Conditions Provisions in Ontario Education." Master's Research Essay, School of Industry Relations, Queen's University.

Grant, M. 1991. *Collective Bargaining for Teachers in Canada: Centralization, Decentralization and State Control in Quebec and Ontario*. Westport, CT: Praeger.

Harris, R. 1967. *Quiet Revolution: A Study of the Educational System of Ontario*. Toronto: University of Toronto Press.

Kochan, T., H. Katz, and B. McKersie. 1986. *The Transformation of American Industrial Relations*. New York: Basic Books.

Muir, J.D. 1968. *Collective Bargaining by Canadian Public School Teachers*. Ottawa: Information Canada.

Woodbury, S. 1985. "The Scope of Bargaining and Bargaining Outcomes in the Public Schools." *Industrial and Labor Relations Review* 38/2: 195–210.

ENDNOTES

1. I would like to acknowledge the helpful comments of Robert Saunders, Ed Aim, Jim Breckenridge, and Jim Butler of the Education Relations Commission of Ontario.

2. There is no need to detail these other than to note the new disposition of low-power groups to challenge authority.

3. Consolidation of school jurisdictions had taken place at a rapid rate: in 1960, there were 3676 school boards managing 7482 schools, and in 1965, 1673 school boards operating 6206 schools. In 1968, just prior to the major consolidation, there were still 1446 school boards in Ontario.

4. The act defines "board" as a board of education, public school board, and Roman Catholic or Protestant board. A "branch affiliate" is a local affiliate of one of the federations.

5. One additional strike took place in 1982–83, so that there has been a total of 54 strikes over the period 1975 to 1989.

6. Class size and PTR are related but different. Class size refers to the number of students in a specific class; PTR refers to the number of students enrolled in a school or system divided by the number of teachers assigned to the school or system.

Chapter

CANADA'S AIRLINES: RECENT TURBULENCE AND CHANGING FLIGHT PLANS

E. G. Fisher
Alex Kondra[1]

*I*ndustrial relations in Canada's airlines have changed substantially in recent years, in the face of intense competition and substantial restructuring. Competition increased as a result of a combination of factors: deregulation, "globalization" (or market expansion), technological change, economic recession, and privatization. The fierce competition unleashed by these factors triggered a shaking-out process and set the stage for a major restructuring aimed at generating greater efficiencies.

Facing intense competition in a deregulated marketplace during 1978–91, carriers aggressively reduced fares and expanded routes; enhanced frequent-flyer programs; consolidated computer reservation systems; solidified new operating structures using feeder airlines; placed orders to replace aging aircraft and expand fleets with wide-body, fuel-efficient aircraft; and sought union concessions in collective bargaining. A spate of mergers and acquisitions accompanied these developments, as well.

Such restructuring culminated in the emergence of two dominant airlines. This new structure resembled Canada's pre-deregulation "friendly duopoly." In sharp contrast, though, both of today's major carriers are former government-owned enterprises and are nearly equal in size. Moreover, a major carrier formed during the 1980s, Canadian Airlines International Ltd. (CAIL), may be assuming the leadership role from the long-standing industry leader: Air Canada.

This essay examines union and management strategies and coping mechanisms under intense competition and substantial restructuring. Strategic decisions influence tactical measures at the bargaining table and in legal proceedings (Kochan,

Katz, and McKersie 1986). Hence, our focus is on collective-bargaining outcomes, including recent approaches to dispute resolution, and legal responses. As critical challenges are still being faced regionally, nationally, and internationally, it is argued that labour relations have yet to stabilize fully.

Industry Overview

Canada's airlines contribute substantially to the country's domestic economy and international trade. Today's two major regularly scheduled carriers are Air Canada (AC) and CAIL. In 1990, AC's operating revenue totalled $3.9 billion versus CAIL's $2.7 billion. However, their respective 1990 losses were $74 million and $15 million (Byfield 1991).

Including their subsidiary airlines, Air Canada and Canadian Airlines International accounted for 97.5 percent of all revenue passenger-miles on domestic airlines during the first quarter of 1990. Air Canada and CAIL each owned $2.3 billion in capital assets in 1989, and, respectively, flew 16.6 billion and 13.8 billion passenger-miles in 1990 (Byfield 1991; *Air Canada Annual Report 1990*; *PWA Corp. Annual Report* 1990; Statistics Canada 1990). While AC's fleet numbered 104 planes and CAIL's 83 planes in 1991, the latter fleet was roughly five years younger.

There is a high degree of union penetration at both major airlines. Roughly 80 percent of their work forces are unionized. Early in 1991, AC had about 19 000 employees, and CAIL had roughly 16 700 employees. Both work forces were to be trimmed. Slated for layoff in the spring of 1991 were as many as 2000 CAIL employees, and, at AC, up to 1000 unionized employees and 400 managerial employees, including 8 of 23 vice-presidents.

Today's airlines operate in a marketplace that is highly competitive, domestically and, especially, internationally. Not only have Canada's two major carriers put together supporting networks of feeder airlines, but they also have formed international alliances to compete with much larger, global airlines, such as British Airways and American Airlines.

In today's "hub-and-spoke configuration," connectors use smaller, often propeller-driven, aircraft to feed passengers along spoke routes to the hubs the major airlines have established across Canada (e.g., Halifax, Montreal, Toronto, Calgary, and Vancouver).[2] Passengers may transfer at the hub to a connector flight bound for nearby, regional destinations. In contrast, predominantly jet aircraft carry those passengers flying on the trunk routes connecting domestic hubs or on routes linked to international hubs.

Aside from such measures to realize economies of scale, discount fares prevail today, and extensive service competition exists. For instance, a fare war broke out

over the Atlantic during the Persian Gulf War early in 1991. By matching or un-
dercutting one another's discount fares, competing airlines sought to increase revenues by increasing load factors from their low levels during the military conflict
and recession. Of note, Canada's domestic market has experienced many more
"seat sales" under deregulation than prior to it. Following British Airways' lead,
both of Canada's major airlines have endeavoured to improve service, including
on-time performance, during the late 1980s and early 1990s.

In the 1970s and earlier, competition was limited as a result of the high degree
of industry regulation in most countries. The pre-1980 airlines environment also
lacked interwoven networks and alliances extending from regional markets
through domestic ones to international routes. Flights tended to be less carefully
planned or structured to realize economies of scale. Indeed, a number of flights
took place directly from one point to another without an intervening transfer at a
hub airport. The major restructuring of the 1980s and early 1990s resulted from
increased competition which began in the late 1970s and disrupted the relative
stability of the previous, highly regulated environment.

Clear Skies in a Highly Regulated Market: 1937–1978

International air traffic has been, and continues to be, regulated by international
agreements on the Freedoms of the Air, and bilateral agreements among nations.
As agreed to at a 1944 conference on civilian aviation, the Freedoms of the Air
agreement, which amounts to privileges accorded among contracting states, reaf-
firms the sovereignty of nations over their airspace. Within the framework of the
Freedoms of the Air, bilateral agreements among nations regulate access to foreign
markets on international routes. Each government retains the right to assign international routes to its domestic carriers.

A key issue is "cabotage" or a foreign carrier's privilege to serve the domestic
market of another country (Canadian Air Line Pilots Association [CALPA] 1988).
A sanction against unapproved cabotage is that the home state of the offending
carrier open its market to foreign airlines to offer point-to-point flights in its domestic market. Some nations have statutes prohibiting cabotage (e.g., the United
States). As a result, once passengers enter the cabin of a foreign carrier, they normally will be discharged only in another country.

Prior to 1978, all domestic routes in Canada were heavily regulated under federal law, with decisions being subject to scrutiny by the federal government. Regulation included domestic route structures, overseas destinations, and fares. It
tended to support federally owned Air Canada during 1937–78. As in other coun-

tries, this flag carrier had been established to meet the needs of the postal service, to consolidate a highly fragmented private air service, and to avoid foreign industry control (Langford 1981).

KEY CARRIERS

Being a "crown jewel," Air Canada was quickly established as the industry leader, a status perpetuated by the regulatory process. Formed in 1937 by an act of Parliament, and becoming Canada's first national air carrier in 1939, Air Canada immediately became Canada's largest airline. By 1977, it was still at least three times the size of any of its competitors by many industry measures (Langford 1981).

As a public-policy instrument until the 1980s, Air Canada received many prized routes, including international routes to Europe. In return, it operated a number of uneconomic domestic routes to meet its "social" obligations, although there has been some emphasis on profits in recent years (Langford and Huffman 1988). Air Canada's monopoly on transcontinental and international routes was maintained until 1957 (Langford 1981).

The second-largest airline, Canadian Pacific Airlines (CP Air), was the only other national carrier in the pre-deregulation Canadian marketplace. CP Air had been formed in 1942 by combining ten smaller airlines. It was allowed to operate mainly in western Canada and, as of 1948, on a few unlucrative Pacific Rim routes (Bain 1987). Commencing in 1958, minimal competition with Air Canada was allowed on certain transcontinental routes and, in 1965, across the Atlantic (Langford and Huffman 1988). In contrast, Air Canada was assigned lucrative routes to Britain, the Caribbean, and western, northern, and eastern Europe in 1965. Similarly, CP Air had no transborder routes between Canada and the United States until 1967, when it was granted the Vancouver–San Francisco route.

Operating in a regulated "division of the world," CP Air and Air Canada became dubbed the "friendly duopoly" (Gillen, Stanbury, and Trethway 1988). The two airlines matched air fares in head-to-head competition, and discount fares were limited in coverage and were more infrequent than in the early 1990s. Moreover, Air Canada and CP Air flew 75.3 percent of all revenue miles and 91.2 percent of the total scheduled revenue miles in 1977 (Statistics Canada 1978).

There were five regulation-defined regions in southern Canada, each being served by its own airline. While the five regional carriers largely complemented existing transcontinental services, they were allowed to compete with the two major airlines on a limited basis after 1961 (Langford 1981).[3]

The largest of the five regionals, Pacific Western Airlines (PWA), had only 4.8 percent of the total revenue miles and a meagre 3.2 percent of the scheduled revenue miles in 1977 (Statistics Canada 1978). PWA was the only regional airline to mount credible competition on a national basis in the wake of deregulation. The remaining pre-deregulation airlines were all commuter, local service, and charter airlines, and flew only 10.3 percent of the total revenue miles (including charter services) and 1.0 percent of the scheduled revenue miles in 1977.

The highly regulated environment with a limited emphasis on competition re-sulted in a relatively stable, but somewhat inefficient industry. Management was not fully in tune with the demands of a competitive marketplace prior to deregula-tion. Such was especially the case at Air Canada, where the operation of "social" routes had been entrenched for decades as a corporate objective, emanating from the airline's role as a public-policy instrument (Langford 1981). The holding cor-poration that ran CP Air was also prepared to tolerate operating losses in its airline subsidiary, since it had several other profit-earning subsidiaries, including Canadian Pacific Rail. Management's incentives to resist labour's demands were further lim-ited, in that regulated pricing permitted passing on some of the costs to consumers. Aside from the relative stability of a regulated market, other forces, such as techno-logical change, influenced airline labour relations prior to deregulation.

*U*nion–Management Relations: 1945–1978

*I*nitially, unions met resistance throughout the airline industry. It was not until after the enactment of the Wartime Labour Relations Regulations in 1944 that these unions gained recognition from carriers to bargain collectively on behalf of their unit members. For instance, although the Canadian Air Line Pilots' Associ-ation (CALPA) was originally formed in 1937, it was not until the mid-1940s that CALPA gained exclusive bargaining rights at Air Canada's precursor and CP Air (Smith 1970).

Shortly after certificates were issued to the bargaining agents representing em-ployees at each of Canada's two major carriers in the 1940s, the first collective agreements were negotiated. The initial labour contracts were very basic, and short by today's standards. Aside from two exceptional circumstances, no single union has represented all employees at one airline.[4] Thus, there have been several labour contracts at a number of airlines. Carriers, though keeping one another in-formed, do not bargain jointly with the unions representing their employees.

Under this fragmented bargaining structure, bargaining is conducted tradition-ally on a company-wide basis with each of the several employee units, grouped along craft lines. Changes negotiated at one bargaining table often translate into changes at other bargaining tables, either at that particular airline or at a competi-tor. In other words, collective bargaining in the industry is characterized by "pat-terns." However, different craft units can, and often do, have differing sets of priorities in their bargaining agendas.

Because of its size and CP Air's policy to follow it, Air Canada became the pat-tern setter. It agreed to a number of labour breakthroughs in the industry (Newby

1986; Smith 1970). Air Canada's orbit of comparison, especially for pilots, tended to be the U.S. airlines with which it competed on transborder routes (Ford 1981; Smith 1970). Settlements at Air Canada were often adjusted subsequently to local labour-market conditions and the size and the ability of its competitors to pay.

In the face of a labour surplus in the labour market, strikes by individual crafts tended to be ineffective, since the employer could replace striking workers. Unions would seek to co-ordinate their strike activity, and employers would respond by adjusting the speed of negotiations at various bargaining tables to attempt to isolate the opportunity for each craft group to engage in a strike. Such actions would diminish the employer's vulnerability to a concerted effort by several unions to close down its operations through a strike. In contrast, tight labour markets tended to give unions more of an upper hand at the bargaining table. These conditions would tend to give rise to a "leapfrogging" of settlements, as the unions would co-ordinate bargaining activities to have a series of settlements, rather than all settle at once for roughly the same terms and conditions of employment (Ford 1981; Newby 1986).

A crucial development in airline agreements, from the perspective of industry mobility, was the adoption of seniority as the overriding criterion for work assignments. As rewards for length of service, seniority-based assignments foster employee loyalty to the firm. To go elsewhere in the industry means to start at the bottom of the new employer's seniority list. The seniority system also seems to have reinforced the rivalry between Air Canada's and CP Air's pilots within their common union, i.e., CALPA (Smith 1970).

FOUR MAJOR CRAFT UNITS

Employees normally have been split into four major craft units at the national and regional levels: (1) pilots, (2) flight attendants, (3) passenger (or ticket) agents, and (4) machinists: mechanics and related ground personnel (e.g., baggage handlers). The first two groups comprise the cabin crews of aircraft; the last two work on the ground. Machinists chiefly deal with and maintain planes. Pilots and machinists are predominantly male, and flight attendants and passenger agents mostly female.

As to relative bargaining power, pilots and mechanics have greater interdependence with carriers than do flight attendants and ticket agents. With their industry-specific training, pilots and mechanics possess a strong ability to shut down operations in the event of a work stoppage (O'Connor 1985). They are strategic workers, since carriers cannot fly safely, and therefore lawfully, without their services, unless properly qualified replacements are available. Replacement availability depends upon the type of aircraft and labour-market conditions, namely, how many qualified pilots or mechanics are unemployed. Airlines are dependent upon passenger agents and flight attendants, in that they interact directly with customers. But, it takes much less time and money to train replacements for them.

Cabin crews at both majors and passenger agents at Air Canada were represented by their own associations during 1945–78. These associations matured from being headquartered and run out of houses, sometimes in an admittedly amateurish manner, to having a full-time professional staff (Canadian Air Line Employees' Association [CALEA]) 1980; Newby 1986; Smith 1970). In contrast, a more traditional craft union, the Brotherhood of Railway and Airline Clerks (BRAC), represented ticket agents at CP Air. Union representation has changed over time at Canadian airlines. For instance, flight attendants were once represented by the machinists' union and CALPA at certain regional airlines, while the International Brotherhood of Teamsters represented them at Air BC in 1991.

Pilots

Pilots are the "aristocracy of labour" at the airlines, receiving the highest compensation packages paid by air carriers. Pilots fly very expensive capital assets, undergo very expensive training, possess skills idiosyncratic to the industry, and could inconvenience service delivery, for example, by staging a sick-in during the busy Christmas holidays. Mitigating against strikes by pilots is the fact that they must continue to fly in order to maintain their licences to fly.

Seniority-based work assignments are most pronounced for cabin crews. Seniority determines the route flown and the position filled (i.e., captain, first officer, or second officer).[5] Certain routes are highly prized by cabin crews in terms of destinations served, the equipment flown, and the corresponding compensation. Cockpit crews at major carriers are paid by a formula whose factors include: hours flown, time of day, mileage, speed, gross weight, location (land versus sea), position filled, and years of service.

The formula pay system, which had prevailed in the United States, was adopted at Air Canada in 1956 and at CP Air in 1961. Key reasons for adopting formula pay included being able to adapt pay scales more readily to new aircraft and to compare pilots' pay at major airlines in Canada with their U.S. counterparts. Previously, pilots received a monthly salary, which might later be adjusted for new equipment types (Smith 1970). Such flat-rate pay systems have continued to be the norm in lower tiers of the industry.

Because of pilots' importance to the airlines, their pay has generally kept abreast of that of other groups, if not set the pattern for them. Such is particularly the case for major carriers, since they fly long-haul routes, sometimes with aircraft types that few unemployed pilots are qualified to fly (see Table 10.1).

Pay and seniority-based scheduling matters comprise the bulk of pilot grievances, and they typically are resolved prior to arbitration. Pilots historically have submitted substantially fewer grievances to arbitration than have other airline units, and most of these arbitrations concern disciplinary actions or dismissals, often for alleged incompetence (Ford 1981; Smith 1970). Representing 12 percent of the industry's employees, pilots had 4 percent of grievances (see Table 10.2A and 10.2B).

Table 10.1
Pilots' and Co-Pilots' Salaries and Employment, 1977–1989

| | CP Air/CAIL | | | Air Canada | | |
	Employment	Nominal Average Wage $	% Increase	Employment	Nominal Average Wage $	% Increase
1977	1489	40 105		528	42 605	
1978	1482	42 087	4.94	526	42 613	0.02
1979	1676	48 496	15.23	569	52 080	22.22
1980	1879	50 918	4.99	638	56 772	9.01
1981	1887	58 373	14.64	668	63 848	12.46
1982	1857	64 656	10.76	636	74 501	16.68
1983	1820	66 250	2.47	569	82 125	10.23
1984	1794	71 538	7.98	511	86 213	4.98
1985	1767	82 272	15.00	525	84 121	-2.43
1986	1732	87 079	5.84	604	98 044	16.55
1987	1715	85 990	-1.25	963	98 601	0.57
1988	1733	92 972	8.12	1133	97 716	-0.90
1989	1755	98 302	5.73	1227	106 191	8.67

Source: Statistics Canada, *Air Carrier Operations in Canada*, Catalogue 51–002 (Ottawa: Minister of Supply and Serveces, 1967–90).

A key issue that pilots faced during 1945–72 was the conversion from propeller to jet aircraft. Chiefly implemented during the 1960s, this technological change altered pay scales and permitted the replacement of three-person crews with two-person crews. Pilots' unions generally accepted two seats in the cockpit, but there often was resistance by the junior pilots, who ultimately might bear the brunt of whatever layoffs resulted (Smith 1970).

Flight Attendants

Leading a rather nomadic lifestyle, flight attendants originally were nurses and were paid accordingly (Newby 1986). The high hourly wage rates they receive (e.g., roughly $28 per hour in 1991 for a flight attendant at the fourth pay step) are offered to attract them to accept the physical and mental demands of flying, dealing with the public, and providing emergency services, if necessary.[6] However, low monthly hours place their annual earnings near the bottom of the industry (approximately $26 000). Although seniority pay exists, it is not nearly as steep as for pilots, and turnover is high. Hence, flight attendants are not closely tied to their industry (Cappelli 1987).

A key issue flight attendants faced during 1945–72 was pay equality for stewards and stewardesses, and employment equity—namely, the merging of seniority lists—so that women also could become pursers (Newby 1986). Passenger agents faced similar issues (CALEA 1980).

Table 10.2A

Number of Rights Arbitration Awards Filed by Airlines with the Federal Mediation and Conciliation Service, 1978–1988

Year of Filing	1978	79	80	81	82	83	84	85	86	87	88	Total	% Total
Air Canada	17	25	15	29	20	24	14	25	16	18	23	226	51
	(47)	(72)	(47)	(69)	(50)	(58)	(43)	(64)	(50)	(50)	(30)	(54)	
Canadian Pacific/ CAIL (Feb. 87)	2	1	1	6	1	7	6	5	3	15	13	60	13
	(0)	(100)	(100)	(50)	(0)	(43)	(0)	(20)	(33)	(20)	(31)	(28)	
Eastern Provincial	2	5	11	9	7	2	8	2	2	0	0	48	11
	(0)	(40)	(64)	(33)	(43)	(50)	(25)	(0)	(0)	(-)	(-)	(38)	
Nordair	0	0	3	5	6	8	7	2	1	1	0	33	7
	(-)	(-)	(100)	(20)	(17)	(50)	(43)	(50)	(0)	(0)	(-)	(39)	
Pacific Western	3	2	11	9	7	7	1	0	3	5	0	48	11
	(66)	(0)	(0)	(66)	(57)	(43)	(0)	(-)	(33)	(20)	(-)	(35)	
Wardair	1	0	4	5	7	5	3	2	2	2	1	32	7
	(100)	(-)	(50)	(40)	(57)	(40)	(0)	(50)	(100)	(50)	(0)	(47)	
Totals	25	33	45	63	48	53	39	36	27	41	37	447	100
	(44)	(64)	(44)	(56)	(46)	(51)	(28)	(53)	(44)	(34)	(30)	(45)	

Note: Figures in brackets denote percentage of disciplinary cases.
Source: Federal Mediation and Conciliation Service, Arbitration Decisions: Canada Labor Code, Part V (Ontario: Labour Canada), 1978–88 Indexes and Summaries.

Table 10.2B

Number of Rights Arbitration Awards Filed by Union with the Federal Mediation and Conciliation Service, 1978–1988

Year of Filing	1978	79	80	81	82	83	84	85	86	87	88	Total	% Total
Passenger agents at CP Air/ CAIL (BRAC/TCU)	0 (-)	0 (-)	0 (-)	1 (0)	1 (0)	3 (0)	1 (0)	0 (-)	0 (-)	9 (11)	2 (50)	17 (12)	4
Passenger agents at others (CALEA/CAW)	9 (44)	15 (44)	26 (27)	25 (60)	17 (56)	9 (33)	8 (38)	3 (100)	3 (0)	4 (75)	2 (50)	120 (45)	27
Flight attendants (CALFFA/CUPE)	3 (100)	3 (66)	8 (50)	22 (55)	16 (31)	13 (31)	11 (27)	8 (25)	9 (67)	9 (33)	8 (13)	110 (41)	25
Pilots (except Wardair) (CALPA)	4 (0)	0 (-)	1 (100)	1 (100)	2 (50)	6 (50)	3 (33)	0 (-)	0 (-)	1 (0)	2 (50)	20 (40)	4
Machinists, baggage handlers, station attendants, etc. (IAM)	8 (50)	14 (86)	9 (89)	14 (50)	13 (54)	22 (77)	16 (25)	25 (56)	15 (40)	18 (39)	24 (33)	178 (52)	40
Other	1 (0)	0 (-)	1 (0)	0 (-)	0 (-)	0 (-)	0 (-)	0 (-)	0 (-)	0 (-)	0 (-)	2 (0)	0
Total	25 (44)	33 (64)	45 (44)	63 (56)	48 (46)	53 (51)	39 (28)	36 (53)	27 (44)	41 (34)	37 (30)	447 (45)	100

Note: Figures in brackets denote percent of disciplinary cases.
Source: Federal Mediation and Conciliation Service, Arbitration Decisions: Canada Labor Code, Part V (Ottawa: Labour Canada), 1978–88 Indexes and Summaries.

Table 10.3
Sales/Passenger Agents' Wages and Increases, 1978–1993

	Air Canada (Sales Agents)		CP/CAIL	
	Wage (Jan.1)	% Increase from Previous Year	Wage (Jan.1)	% Increase from Previous Year
1978	$4.62*		$3.99*	
1979	4.99*	8.0	4.60*	15.2
1980	5.39*	8.0	4.60*	0.0
1981	6.04*	12.0	5.13*	11.6
1982	6.67*	10.0	5.64*	10.0
1983	7.07*	6.0	5.99*	6.1
1984	7.42*	5.0	6.29*	5.0
1985	6.13*[a]	NA[a]	6.54*	4.0
1986	6.37*	3.9	6.80	4.0
1987	6.57	3.1	6.80	0.0
1988	6.76	2.9	7.36	8.2
1989	7.03	4.0	7.65	3.9
1990	7.39	5.1	8.03	5.0
1991	7.83[b]	6.0[b]	8.43	5.0
1992	8.22	5.0	9.02	7.0
1993			9.48	5.1

Notes: Wages are for entry-level positions.
Those followed by an asterisk (*) are based on wage-increase information from the Bureau of Labour Information.
[a] Notes the introduction of a two tier-wage system.
[b] There is a COLA clause that may allow this to rise to 7.5 percent.

Passenger Agents

While ticket agents receive the lowest hourly wages of the four major crafts (see Table 10.3), their pay tends to be higher than for comparable work elsewhere (Bailey, Graham, and Kaplan 1985). Their compensation includes other airline perquisites, such as free travel. Since seniority applies to transfers and layoffs, senior passenger agents have an influence over where they work and live, as do their counterparts in cabin crews.

Mechanics and Related Ground Personnel

This group is represented by the International Association of Machinists and Aerospace Workers (IAM). Members of the machinists' union are the second-highest paid group of employees in the industry with a first-year mechanic earning approximately $37 500 a year in 1991 ($18 to $20 an hour, depending on length of work week). While occupying strategic positions for service delivery like pilots, mechanics are somewhat less tied to the industry, as some of their skills are transferable elsewhere. But, a seniority pay system exists in which mechanics can advance through higher pay grades as they learn more of their trade, and they can shift into industry-specific areas like avionics (i.e., aircraft electronics).

The machinists' union, the IAM, has represented nearly equal segments of skilled workers—principally mechanics—and unskilled workers—including ramp (or station) attendants, catering employees, and clerical workers. This split has created political factions and dissention in the IAM.

The IAM is also the most militant of the unions representing airline employees, a fact that is reflected in the number of strikes they have undertaken (see Table 10.4)

Table 10.4
Lawful Work Stoppages at Canada's Three Major Carriers, 1945–1991

Carrier	Year	Union	Air Canada Duration	Notes
Air Canada	1968	IAM	13 days	Work to rule
	1969	IAM	29 days	
	1971	IAM	10 days	Rotating strike
	1973	CALEA	55.5 days	Finance department in Winnipeg; First-agreement strike.
		IAM	13 days	
	1974	CALEA	6 days	Rotating strike
	1975 –76	CALEA		Slowdown/Lockout
	1978	IAM	10 days	Airline failed to operate.
	1982 -83	CALPA	39 days	Failure to report for training on B767s.
	1985	CALEA	23 days	Workers were replaced.
	1985	CALFAA	46 days	Workers were replaced.
	1987	IAM	20 days	
CP Air	1973	IAM	63 days	Airline partially operated.
	1985	BRAC	3 hours	Co-ordinated action by the unions
		CALFAA		in the face of CP Air's somewhat
		IAM		precarious financial position.
PWA	1963	CALFAA	NA	Firm broke the Traffic Employees'
		TEU		Union (TEU), rendering it company-dominated.
	1978	CALFA	25 days	
	1985	CALFAA	119 days	Started as a coalition; broke
		CAW	89 days	down when the CAW signed an
		IAM	119 days	agreement ahead of the others. Airline operated in spite of strike.

and the number of disciplinary grievances they have been subject to (see Table 10.2A and 10.2B). Their two peaks in disciplinary arbitrations occurred during concession bargaining: 1983 and 1985. Their 1988 peak in interpretation arbitrations is associated with the amalgamated agreement at CAIL.

UNION AND MANAGEMENT RESPONSES

Labour legislation can have an impact on employers' acceptance of unions and on how collective bargaining is conducted (Kochan, Katz, and McKersie 1986). Labour law is more supportive of unionization and collective bargaining in the airlines industry in Canada than in the United States. U.S. legislation permits an employer to negotiate with various unions about which bargaining agent, if any, will represent its employees in the wake of a merger or acquisition of one airline by another (McKelvey 1988). In contrast, a successor bargaining agent is determined in Canada through majority choice in a representation vote administered by a labour relations board.

A U.S. holding company (e.g., Texas Air Corporation) can operate a nonunion subsidiary with a lower-cost work force (i.e., Continental) along with a unionized subsidiary (i.e., Eastern), and even have them flying the same routes (McKelvey 1988). This tactic of weakening the power of unions through "double-breasting" is generally not available in Canada. Under what is termed a "common employer declaration," a labour relations board would most likely declare that these operations were not separate employers, since the holding company ran them. It, then, would deem that the labour contract also applied to the nonunion operation, so that the nonunion arm could not undermine bargaining rights at the union arm. Similarly, the duty to bargain in "good faith" expires in the United States after an impasse has occurred (i.e., a lawful work stoppage), but continues during an impasse in Canada (Bemmels, Fisher, and Nyland 1986).

Major Carriers' Responses to Unions

Canada's major carriers have opted, though occasionally with some reluctance, for the strategic choice of union acceptance. The fragmented bargaining structure accounts for some of this choice. It meant that any one union, especially of pilots or machinists, could close down the airline, and that this could happen more frequently than if only one union represented all employees at a major carrier (Weiler 1980).

While limited outbreaks of labour strife occurred during 1945–78 at Air Canada and CP Air, a much different situation existed in the air than on the ground. Cabin crews were not involved in any bargaining strikes at the major carriers. But, there were periodic eleventh-hour settlements in the face of substantial votes in favour of strikes (Ford 1981; Newby 1986). In one such settlement in 1968, Air Canada's pilots successfully sought to catch up to a wage increase the IAM had achieved in the previous bargaining round (Ford 1981).

The most frequent set of major bargaining strikes during 1945–77 involved the

IAM and the industry's pattern setter: Air Canada. Strikes occurred in 1969 (29 days), 1971 (10 days, rotating), 1973 (13 days), and 1978 (10 days, in a strike/lockout that closed operations) (see Table 10.2B). The IAM also had a nine-week strike with CP Air in 1973, during which the airline partially operated. The 1973 strike ended when CP Air's board of directors ratified a tentative agreement they had previously refused to ratify.

The 1973 strike with the IAM made CP Air very reluctant to take strikes in the years to follow. In fact, it was CP Air's only bargaining strike during 1945–78, as CP Air generally waited for Air Canada to incur bargaining strikes and followed the pattern set by settlements at Air Canada (Smith 1970; Newby 1986).

The other set of bargaining strikes at Air Canada involved the passenger agents' bargaining agent, the Canadian Air Line Employees' Association (CALEA), especially when it represented Air Canada's finance department employees during 1972–76. There was a short strike by AC's ticket agents in 1974 (6 days, rotating), and a series of strikes involving the finance department. The latter commenced with a first agreement strike in 1973 (55.5 days) and involved a series of slow-downs during 1975–76, which ended in a five-day lockout in June 1976, and culminated in the replacement of the CALEA by the IAM as the certified bargaining agent (CALEA 1980).

Lower-Tier Carriers' Responses to Unions

In contrast, regional, local, commuter and charter airlines have had a long history of labour turmoil, reflecting actions to minimize the roles of unions or to keep them out. Pacific Western, for example, fired CALPA pilots from a newly acquired subsidiary and then rehired them as nonunion employees in the late 1950s. PWA also ignored certain contractual provisions (e.g., seniority-based work assignments) in its own pilots' agreement with CALPA until the early 1960s (Smith 1970).

Pacific Western later accepted its pilots' union (CALPA), but apparently attempted to suppress or replace two others. During its expansionary phase in the 1960s, PWA agreed to and implemented seniority-based work assignments for CALPA pilots, though with flat-rate pay scales (Ford 1981). PWA also replaced workers during a 1963 work stoppage involving its flight attendants, who later settled, and ticket agents, whose union (Traffic Employees' Association) it broke and transformed into a company-dominated association (CALEA 1980; Newby 1986, 35). Six of PWA's pilots had refused to cross picket lines during this dispute, even though their agreement was in force.[7]

Wardair engaged in similar practices in the charter market. Although it replaced the work force during a two-month first-agreement strike with its flight attendants in 1973, a settlement was reached. The settlement, however, reflected the relative bargaining advantage Wardair enjoyed vis-à-vis its Canadian Air Line Flight Attendants' Association (CALFAA) local (Newby 1986).

Wardair's replacement strategy involved establishing relations with three independent associations representing: pilots and flight engineers, supervisory personnel in maintenance and engineering (The Canadian Airline Supervisors and Inspection Association [CASIA]), and passenger agents. Baggage handling was subcontracted, so that the only traditional airline union at Wardair was the IAM, which represented the mechanics (Ford 1981). CASIA was set up to withstand a mechanics' strike, such as the stoppage that occurred in 1987.

Several factors explain such responses at lower-level carriers. Smaller and less widely dispersed bargaining units are more easily intimidated or replaced. The greater ease of entry into these smaller markets, because of reduced capital requirements, results in more competition and lower profit margins than on major routes. Also, a number of the founders of smaller airlines possessed a highly entrepreneurial or "bush-pilot mentality," which predisposed them toward resisting, subverting, or breaking unions (Newby 1986; Smith 1970). Reflecting this, smaller regional airlines account for a disproportionate number of arbitrations (see Table 10.2A) and Canada Labour Relations Board applications (CLRB 1978–89), apparently reflecting hard-line managerial approaches. Nearly all of these influences appear to remain at work today.

Tensions in the 1978 Bargaining Round

Many of the kinds of pressures experienced during the 1978 round of negotiations at PWA and Air Canada foreshadowed developments that accompanied deregulation. At issue were planned mergers and acquisitions, which apparently resulted from strategic moves by each airline to position itself for impending or possible deregulation.

Air Canada was about to purchase Nordair, a regional airline in Quebec. Nordair was unionized, but had a much lower (labour) cost structure. Air Canada planned to run Nordair as an independent, parallel operation and to focus it on the charter market. Air Canada's pilots sought a merged seniority list with Nordair's pilots, so that they would not lose work to the cheaper work force at Nordair. Air Canada ultimately did not acquire Nordair.

PWA did acquire TransAir, a regional airline based farther east on the Canadian prairies, and integrated the two systems. This enabled PWA to position itself from the Pacific coast to western Ontario. In its negotiations with pilots, PWA insisted that pilots from both airlines integrate their seniority lists before the 1978 round of bargaining could be completed and the two agreements could be consolidated. The arbitration award for both sets of CALPA members generated discord within the amalgamated unit, leading to unsuccessful court challenges to that award. PWA pilots viewed themselves as having lost out in that particular decision (Ford 1981).

*T*urbulence and Changing Flight Plans: 1978–1991

*A*irlines encountered much "turbulence" during the 1980s at all levels within the industry. Forces that shaped the industry during this period were: (1) deregulation, (2) economic recession and challengers, (3) globalization and alliances, (4) technological change, and (5) privatization. These forces created intense competition and provided a catalyst for the restructuring of industry operations, including fleet realignments and efforts to control labour costs.

DEREGULATION

Regulated pricing and the market domination by major airlines spurred cries for deregulation in both Canada and the United States, where North American deregulation first commenced in late 1978. This was the major catalyst for Canadian deregulation.[8] It created politically embarrassing spreads between Canadian and U.S. airfares, and saw the loss of business to U.S. air carriers (Barone et al. 1986). Canadian deregulation was not as stressful as the rapid U.S. deregulation as it was gradually phased in in Canada. Nonetheless, a substantial shaking out and subsequent settling in took place in both countries.

The federal government began its long road to full deregulation in 1978 by directing the Canadian Transport Commission (CTC) to license more domestic charter flights (Barone et al. 1986). The CTC followed in 1980 by shifting from a "public convenience and necessity" test to a policy with emphasis on public benefits and competition. This liberalization policy was accelerated gradually, and full deregulation was achieved on January 1, 1988.

Deregulation generally eased entry into and exit from the industry and relaxed controls on airfares and routes. Canada's two major carriers (AC and CP Air) experienced competition primarily from existing carriers in the regional (feeder), commuter, and local markets.

ECONOMIC RECESSION AND CHALLENGERS

The economic recession of 1981–83 focussed attention on labour costs and created cut-throat competition through fare cuts. The two trunk carriers found themselves at a major competitive disadvantage, as several smaller carriers had lower cost structures (Gillen, Oum, and Trethway 1987).

The biggest challengers to the national carriers were Pacific Western Airlines and Wardair. PWA was initially a regional airline, but it had always pursued a policy of vigorous expansion, and it continued to do so under deregulation (Arnold and Brown 1986; Tupper 1981). PWA essentially became the third national airline in Canada in 1981 when it was awarded a Toronto–Calgary route. Although PWA had a keen eye for cost control, which was beneficial under deregulation, it had relatively costly labour contracts at the onset of deregulation (Tupper 1981).

Wardair, an innovative and relatively new airline, emphasized service and operated primarily in the charter market until 1985, when it entered the regularly scheduled market. Having operated in the lower-revenue charter airline service, Wardair judiciously monitored cost and parleyed its reputation for high-quality service to find a market niche among regularly scheduled airlines. While operating only a handful of planes in 1982, Wardair enjoyed a substantial labour-cost advantage (16.2 percent of total operating costs) over its other major competitors, AC (32.9 percent), CP Air (29.3 percent), and PWA (41.4 percent) (Statistics Canada 1983).

GLOBALIZATION AND ALLIANCES

As markets expanded globally, it became increasingly clear that, in order to provide competitive service and realize appropriate economies of scale, consolidation and rationalization were essential to airline survival (Gillen, Stanbury, and Trethway 1988). The corresponding by–products of globalization were alliances and mergers and acquisitions. Alliances ranged from those among regional and trunk carriers to those among international carriers based in various countries.

Alliances and mergers and acquisition allowed for the formation of the hub-and-spoke configuration that predominated in the 1980s. Adoption of the hub-and-spoke configuration was a key form of restructuring that contributed to service rationalization. Commuter and feeder routes were shifted away from uneconomic jet service to turbo-prop aircraft.[9]

One form of alliance involves "code-sharing." There are two kinds of such commercial, seat-sharing arrangements. One permits a carrier to serve destinations it has no licence to serve, thereby extending its coverage. The other, older marketing scheme permits two or more airlines to alternate flying planes on a route for which both have a licence. In either case, the nonflying airline has first call to fill a certain number of seats on the other's planes. Codes for these flights and the connecting flights of each airline show up on the other's computer reservation system.

A major acquisition and merger took place in 1987 when CP Air was purchased by PWA Corporation, the holding company owning Pacific Western Airlines. This purchase resulted from CP's lack of profitability and PWA's cash-rich situation, as well as PWA's aspirations to grow in a deregulated environment. CP Air was integrated with PWA to form Canadian Airlines International. Eastern Provincial Airways (EPA) and Nordair, which had been previously purchased by CP Air, were also integrated into CAIL. CP Air had operated EPA (since 1984) and Nordair (since 1986) as separate, parallel business units. The formation of CAIL shrank the number of national carriers in 1987 from four to three: CAIL, AC and Wardair.

Problems were encountered in merging four distinct airlines, each having its own distinct culture, into an integrated airline system at CAIL. The rise in arbitrations at CP Air/CAIL in 1987–88 were a result of merging seniority lists, and, especially, amalgamating collective agreements. Language adopted from certain former agreements was being tested. Hence, more interpretation issues arose at CAIL in 1987 (12) and 1988 (9) than in 1986 (2) (see Table 10.2A). Nevertheless, the merger provided the unified, organized fleet needed to compete in a deregulated marketplace: a nation-wide hub-and-spoke configuration.

After the formation of CAIL, Wardair was the third-largest of three national carriers. Wardair was quite vulnerable in 1989 because: (1) fare and frequent-flyer competition had reduced operating earnings; (2) the airline was carrying a rather heavy debt load of $600 million; (3) it had no network of feeder airlines; and (4) it was listed in a computerized reservation system that was separate from those of CAIL and AC, thereby being less accessible to travel agents and others. Indicative of its financial problems, Wardair posted an operating loss of $57.7 million in 1988, compared with a $7 million profit in 1987.

The "friendly duopoly" became firmly entrenched in 1989 when PWA Corp. purchased Wardair. This capped the frenzy of mergers and acquisitions in Canada that had accompanied deregulation. By acquiring Wardair, PWA Corp. neutralized a trunk-line competitor and reduced the number of national carriers from three to two, the number that had existed prior to deregulation (Fisher and Kondra 1990).[10]

PWA Corp.'s acquisition of Wardair also improved its strategic market position, since it grew overnight to become virtually the same size as Air Canada.[11] It also gained a carrier with a much lower labour-cost structure and acquired landing rights at certain international destinations (e.g., Paris and Gatwick, England). Adversely, PWA Corp. inherited Wardair's debt load and a fleet of aircraft that was largely incompatible with its own fleet.

Canadian Airlines International also inherited Wardair's frequent-flyer program and its liabilities. Its liabilities comprised the rewards of, for example, free flights, car rentals, or hotel accommodations with affiliated firms for points that each customer accumulated while travelling with the airline or using the services of affiliated firms. On the positive side of the ledger, such programs were important forms of nonprice competition that also develop customer loyalty to the particular airline. Frequent-flyer programs had been first introduced in the early 1980s and remained in the 1990s, as a key means of nonprice competition after the industry had consolidated.

CAIL and AC purchased all or part of many regional airlines to provide co-ordination of feeder services in their hub-and-spoke structures (Gillen, Stanbury, and Trethway 1988). Code-sharing on computer reservations systems facilitated co-ordination. In 1991, the AC affiliate network consisted of the following "connectors": Air Nova, Air Alliance, Air Ontario, Air BC, and Northwest Territorial Airways. CAIL "partners" include Air Atlantic, Air St. Pierre, Calm Air, Canadian Partner, Inter-Canadian, and Time Air (National Transportation Agency of Canada 1991). Canada's north is served by Canadian Northern, and two partners more were added in 1991: Intair, serving routes in Quebec, and Air Toronto, with certain U.S. destinations.

Fleet Realignment

The outbreak of mergers and acquisitions during the 1980s occasionally led to the combining of fleets of aircraft from two or more different manufacturers. This meant maintaining at least two sets of repair facilities and spare parts. Reducing the types of aircraft in service minimizes training and inventory costs, creating substantial savings (Kubish 1990).[12] Exacerbating this compatibility problem was the replacement of aging fleets of less fuel-efficient aircraft with newer, more modern planes.

A number of airlines in the scheduled market, such as Wardair, had undertaken large expansions of their fleets to acquire new, more fuel-efficient aircraft, including Boeing 757s and 767s, and the Airbus 310s and 320s. Increased debt loads resulted. Rising interest rates added to the financial instability of airlines and helped to facilitate mergers. Liquidation of aircraft to rationalize merged fleets and the selling of contracted future new plane deliveries helped alleviate debt loads.

TECHNOLOGICAL CHANGE

The growth of computers facilitated code-sharing agreements and integrated computer reservation systems (CRSs). Integrated CRSs became a key strategic tool of market segmentation for carriers. Airlines not listed in another air carrier's CRS often encountered difficulties in gaining passengers who might transfer from another carrier. Flights of a carrier affiliated with one CRS did not show up automatically on the terminals at travel agencies or carriers that belonged to or were served by a different CRS.[13]

Computers also facilitated the development and introduction in the 1980s of "glass cockpits" with computerized navigation and flight control. Flight plans can be programmed into the computer, simplifying the work of pilots and perhaps ultimately, enabling future reductions in crew sizes. Flight plans can be selected, for example, to minimize fuel costs, subject to approval by air-traffic controllers (Melady 1989).

PRIVATIZATION

Both present trunk air carriers in Canada were once government corporations. PWA Corp., which owns and operates CAIL, was owned by the provincial government of Alberta, while Air Canada was owned in its entirety by the Canadian government. The Alberta government purchased 99.5 percent of PWA's shares in 1974 (Arnold and Brown 1986). Peter Lougheed, then premier of Alberta, was motivated by a need to ensure adequate air service in Alberta, which was undergoing tremendous growth during its oil boom of the 1970s (Tupper 1981).

With the exception of moving the head office from Vancouver to Calgary, PWA operated as an independent company with no interference from the provincial government. This allowed PWA to continue on its aggressive expansion path and keep its costs in line (Arnold and Brown 1986). The Alberta government eventually divested itself of all but 14.9 percent of the company in 1983.[14] Privatization did not create a major change in the direction of the firm.

The enactment of the Air Canada Act in 1978 paved the way for AC to become privatized roughly a decade later. The crucial words "in contemplation of profit" signalled that Air Canada was to become less of a Crown corporation (Langford 1981). To permit greater private-sector orientation, this act enabled AC to raise capital in private finance markets for the first time, although subject to government approval (Langford and Huffman 1988).

Air Canada was privatized in two stages over roughly one year, becoming fully privatized in July 1989.[15] AC was privatized, in part to spare the Canadian public, in a time of restraint, the debt load needed to finance the impending upgrading of its fleet. Air Canada's public and social role arguably had declined, especially in the wake of the formation of CAIL. The round of concession bargaining at Air Canada in 1985, which is explained later, was a key to lowering operating costs to position Canada's flagship strategically to compete in the private sector.

Privatization provided Air Canada with much more flexibility, allowing AC to more freely tap private financial markets to finance the replacement of its aging fleet. AC planned to add $1.5 billion worth of aircraft to its fleet during the 1990s (*Financial Post*, March 15, 1990). It was able to finance privately $1 billion in planned expenditures for airport improvements across its network, including upgrading maintenance facilities, during 1990–93. Related to privatization, Air Canada may no longer operate money-losing routes, previously operated for social and political purposes, and there should be less political pressure to deal with unions in a "fair" manner.

Privatization represented a significant change in course for Air Canada. It meant that the former Crown corporation sought to become a "lean and mean" private-sector enterprise. Initially, management was somewhat out of touch with the demands of a competitive marketplace. Even after its full privatization in 1989, social and political considerations lingered at Air Canada. Observers suggested that they hindered AC's attempts to adjust employment practices, especially to engage in layoffs to respond to changing economic circumstances. As an abrupt change in direction, privatization resulted in culture shock for many employees (Stockhouse 1991).

*T*urbulent Airline Labour Relations: 1978–1991

*T*he changed environment set the stage for the bitter turmoil that followed in the newly competitive market. The increased number of competitors and the flexible air fares stimulated by deregulation caused the major carriers to pay greater attention to labour relations, in order to lower their labour costs relative to those of their competitors.

Wages and work rules were a key focus of cost-cutting measures, as lucrative union contracts gained in the pre-deregulation market were targeted. While other items, such as interest and fuel costs, are relatively the same across all carriers, labour costs are the single largest controllable cost in the short run (Cappelli 1987). As such, they can differentiate costs among carriers, influencing profits (Thornicroft 1989).

Many bitter strikes and lockouts ensued throughout Canada and the United States, as air carriers tried to increase their competitive advantage by lowering labour costs. The pool of potential replacement workers had grown during the 1981–83 recession for all crafts, including pilots. Thus, contracting-out or hiring replacement workers became increasingly viable options during work stoppages. The majority of bargaining strikes during the 1980s in Canada involved connector or charter airlines, but major carriers also incurred lawful work stoppages (discussed later). Air Canada, for instance, took strikes in the mid-1980s to prepare for privatization.

Management at CAIL achieved some success in reducing labour costs, which, for instance, diminished from 35.1 percent in 1977 to 27.7 percent of operating expenses attributed to labour, and reached their nadir in 1985 (27.1 percent) (see Table 10.5). Hence, carriers emerged somewhat better positioned strategically to face intense competition.

CONCESSION BARGAINING

The first round of concession bargaining took place in the early 1980s and was confined primarily to the smaller carriers. Canada Labour Relations Board findings of bad-faith bargaining at regional airlines were common (CLRB 1978–89). Work forces often were replaced during lawful work stoppages to gain concessions from unions. For instance, in 1981, flight attendants were replaced during a long (13-week) and bitter strike at Wardair. Flight attendants were stranded all over the world and had to pay their own expenses to return home (Newby 1986). The fact that Wardair dictated the terms of settlement reiterated an experience of the past: the perils of going it alone in strike action.

Concessions gained by Wardair included longer duty days and the introduction

Table 10.5
Selected Operating Statistics for Air Canada and CP Air/CAIL, 1977–1989

		Operating Revenue ($ thousands)	Profit Before Tax ($ thousands)	Employment	Labour Cost Per Kilometre (cents)	% Operating Expenses Attibuted to Labour
Air Canada	1977	1 132 109	41 866	20 364	2.13	36.6
	1978	1 215 205	77 275	20 459	1.90	33.8
	1979	1 342 158	86 056	21 878	1.79	33.6
	1980	1 455 658	80 443	23 316	1.82	32.1
	1981	1 467 635	51 134	23 199	1.89	31.2
	1982	1 330 404	(31 928)	22 943	2.05	32.9
	1983	1 242 690	(895)	21 287	2.02	34.2
	1984	1 296 228	6 326	21 552	1.89	33.6
	1985	1 345 331	(25 989)	21 086	1.82	32.1
	1986	1 352 077	31 194	21 743	1.79	33.3
	1987	1 318 885	29 230	21 644	1.81	32.9
	1988	1 345 310	67 431	21 999	1.73	33.9
	1989	1 385 733	72 023	22 676	1.70	33.4
CP Air/CAIL	1977	393 585	7 378	6 855	1.67	35.1
	1978	428 008	36 413	6 989	1.50	33.4
	1979	451 759	23 293	7 573	1.48	33.1
	1980	519 707	8 503	8 501	1.44	30.6

Table 10.5 (continued)

	Operating Revenue ($ thousands)	Profit Before Tax ($ thousands)	Employment	Labour Cost Per Kilometre (cents)	% Operating Expenses Attibuted to Labour
1981	555 897	(19 860)	8 920	1.50	29.4
1982	520 427	(39 600)	8 831	1.56	29.3
1983	500 473	(13 735)	7 957	1.46	29.9
1984	517 940	8 405	7 555	1.23	28.8
1985	537 529	(13 708)	7 746	1.21	27.1
1986	564 253	(1 973)	8 385	1.28	29.6
1987	905 679	40 614	13 039	1.40	28.6
1988	1 008 638	7 214	14 337	1.28	26.0
1989	953 011	(64 507)	15 082	1.42	27.7

Note: All dollar values are expressed in constant 1977 dollars. Total passenger kilometres for 1981–87 are estimates based on available data.
Source: Statistics Canada, Air Carrier Operations in Canada, Catalogue 51–002 (Ottawa: Minister of Supply and Services, 1976–90).

of a nonunion in-flight service manager, thought to be a key service element. The 1981 experience softened the CALFAA local of Wardair flight attendants. They agreed to a nonmerged two-tier wage system in 1983 without a work stoppage (Newby 1986, 100–101).[16] This meant that new hires would receive lower wages than the existing work force, and that they could not reach the same pay level the existing work force would enjoy for the duration of the contract.

The Major Round in 1985–86

The largest round of concession bargaining occurred in 1985–86, spreading to Air Canada, CP Air, and Pacific Western. Lump-sum bonuses, two-tier pay scales, no wage increases, more flexible work rules, golden lists (guaranteeing no layoffs to certain current employees), and bitter strikes were common features of the 1985–86 bargaining round (see Table 10.4). In the final analysis, current employees kept their jobs and often retained their pay levels. In return, employers received (1) productivity gains from the loosening of work rules, (2) cost savings from rollbacks to other forms of compensation (e.g., premium rates or fringe benefits), and (3) the ability to hire workers at lower pay scales than current workers.

CP Air experienced a three-hour strike by machinists, ticket agents, and flight attendants in July 1985 when negotiations inadvertently slid past the strike deadline. Of note, productivity and wage concessions (or freezes in certain contract years) were forthcoming. Although each labour contract had certain unique features, each one also took into account CP Air's somewhat precarious financial position at this time (Verma 1987).

CP Air and the IAM agreed in 1985 to assign certain tasks, such as aircraft pushbacks, to lesser-skilled station attendants. To achieve greater work force flexibility, a procedure was set up that culminated in arbitration, to decide what tasks were common to several mechanical trade classifications. All full-time workers as of a specified date were guaranteed employment in their trade for as long as productivity improvements affecting them remained in effect. Those mechanics who would be required to move to promote greater work-force flexibility were eligible to receive either relocation assistance or enriched severance pay.

Like the CP Air–IAM agreement, the agreement between CP Air and its passenger agents (BRAC) also involved productivity gains and the guaranteeing of certain jobs in "golden lists," as long as such productivity gains were realized. Key features of the BRAC–CP Air agreement of 1985 included: (1) increased flexibility in the scheduling of ticket agents, (2) increased percentage and weekly usage of part-time agents, (3) reductions in the number of full-time agents, (4) a voluntary separation plan identical to the one made available to some IAM members, and (5) equal status for part-time agents with full-time agents regarding overtime assignments, as well as complete medical, dental, and extended health care benefits, and participation in the pension plan. The prorating of fringe benefits for part-time agents was an important way in which BRAC sought to make it difficult to substitute part-time agents for full-time agents.

Flight attendants at CP Air (CALFAA) agreed to a nonmerged two-tier wage structure. In return, there was an employment guarantee for all full-time flight attendants in full-time positions as of July 1985. Their entry-level hourly wage rate of $17 was later matched by their counterparts at Air Canada. Such a two-tier wage structure had been absent from the machinists' agreement of 1985.

The machinists' agreement was reopened in 1986 to avoid threatened subcontracting. Among other features, these negotiations yielded (1) stipulated limited changes to the shift schedule, (2) some cutbacks from full-time to part-time, and (3) lower rates of pay for new hires among unskilled workers. In exchange, extended job-protection guarantees were given to baggage handlers, and the minimum age for retirement with full pension was lowered from 60 to 58 (Verma 1987).

To establish merged two-tiered pay scales and effect greater flexibility and additional reductions in labour costs like those achieved at CP Air, Air Canada replaced passenger agents (23 days) and flight attendants (46 days) during two strikes in 1985. Air Canada succeeded in separating the timing of the two strikes, so that managerial personnel could replace each bargaining unit and greater concessions could be induced from each group. The length of the two strikes clearly reflects the reluctance of unions (CALEA and CALFAA) to agree at Canada's leading major carrier to deflate contractual provisions, some of which represented breakthroughs for airlines employees. Additionally, Air Canada's status as a Crown corporation with parliamentary backing and funding meant that AC might be able to pay more than, say, CP Air, and that political pressure might be exerted on Air Canada.

The ticket agents' settlement, reached in May 1985, was partially patterned after a settlement reached late in 1984 with the IAM, the bargaining agent for AC's finance department. The CALEA settlement extended the salary scale downwards by several steps, reducing the rate for new hires, by nearly 20 percent. As at CP Air, it increased the percentage of part-time ticket agents, increased the amount of work they could do per week, and provided them with fringe benefits (e.g., dental and pension plans) equivalent to those enjoyed by full-time employees. This agreement also established a fully integrated seniority list, expanded the amount of temporary hiring, and permitted managerial personnel to perform a greater amount of bargaining-unit work (e.g., work in Maple Leaf Lounges or to avoid passenger inconvenience). In exchange, full-time employees prior to a specified date were given job security: they would not be laid off or forced to become part-time as long as part-time employees were employed at the base.

The flight attendants' settlement, reached in September 1985, was partially patterned after the CALFAA–CP Air settlement of July 1985. The CALFAA–Air Canada contract lowered the new hire rate to match CP Air's, provided one-time signing bonuses similar to the one-time productivity bonuses at CP Air, increased the maximum monthly flying limitation from 75 hours to match CP Air's 80 hours (CP Air also had 85 hours' compulsory for three months of the year), and increased the duty day limitations to 14 hours on charter operations, as at CP Air. However, a guarantee of job security was removed from the second memorandum of agreement, which was ratified. The memorandum of agreement also addressed such issues as dropping disciplinary measures against employees for actions during the strike and dropping Canada Labour Relations Board actions, in order to smooth the adjustment into regular customer service.

The machinists' (IAM) agreement at Air Canada was reached in October 1985 and bore some resemblance to the machinists' agreement at CP Air. It introduced 58 years as the base for early retirement, established some new categories and classifications in avionics, raised a minimum qualification for an overtime premium, permitted the exercise of seniority in transfers in the light of the centralization of certain job functions (e.g., load dispatch), formally referred to the employee assistance program, simplified the grievance mechanism, and created a certificated classifications committee to make recommendations to management. Perhaps, the most important feature of this agreement was that it provided for new entry rates (at $7 per hour for all basic nontrade classifications). This new entry rate was 30 to 35 percent lower than the previous ones and undoubtedly played a role in CP Air's renegotiating its machinists' agreement in 1986 to lower new hire rates for unskilled workers.

The most important development, in our opinion, was that the cost reductions and productivity enhancements Air Canada gained in 1985 were crucial elements in AC's strategy to prepare for privatization and impending full deregulation. As a result of the 1985 bargaining round, Air Canada brought its labour costs into line with CP Air's, as well as those of larger U.S. competitors.[17]

The longest work stoppage during the mid-1980s took place at Pacific Western, which was still mainly a regional carrier. It lasted for four months during 1985–86 and involved a coalition of machinists (IAM), flight attendants (CALFAA), and passenger agents (the Canadian Auto Workers, or CAW). PWA contracted out mechanics' work, reportedly spending some $50 million to have its planes serviced abroad, and replaced the others to extract concessions (Macdonald 1986). The union representing passenger agents (CAW) cut its losses, opting to settle first, which caused some difficulties with the other two unions. In retrospect, this early settlement was arguably wise, for PWA could likely have extracted greater concessions than it did, since the regional market it served was in a severe economic decline (Macdonald 1986). Nevertheless, PWA enhanced its strategic position for a more fully deregulated environment.

SUBSEQUENT BARGAINING ROUNDS: 1986–1991

The formation of Canadian Airlines International, the expansion by Wardair, which rendered it vulnerable to unions and generally much improved market conditions, helped end two-tier wage schedules during 1987–89. These conditions also allowed for pay increases (see Table 10.1), since Air Canada, CAIL, and Wardair each sought labour peace to compete effectively on trunk and international routes.

Indicative of these changes is the fact that there were only two bargaining strikes at major carriers during 1986–91, and neither of them involved CAIL. Operations were closed at Air Canada by a 20-day strike with its machinists (IAM) in 1987 during a peak flying season. Commencing late in November and spreading into the early Christmas season, this strike ostensibly focussed on the indexing of pensions and the inclusion of past retirees under this plan, both of which had previously been agreed to (Downie 1991). The second strike took place at Wardair in 1987 and also involved the machinists (IAM). Supervisors belonging to an in-house association (CASIA) carried out maintenance during this eleven-day strike, thereby enabling Wardair to continue operations.

The first CAIL contracts were patterned after expiring CP Air agreements, but included employees from four merged airlines. In spite of factionalism and considerable tensions associated with merging seniority lists, pay rates, and job classifications, these contracts were peacefully renegotiated in 1988 with machinists and, in 1987, with pilots (CALPA), flight attendants (Canadian Union of Public Employees, or CUPE), and passenger agents (Transportation Communications Union, or TCU, formerly BRAC). They were multiple-year agreements, indicating that CAIL wanted to keep flying and was willing to pay for industrial peace. PWA Corp. would have faced much greater difficulties in attempting to replace a nation-wide bargaining unit, if it had wanted to extract further concessions from newly merged employee groups.

Aside from improved wage and benefit packages, another plum traded off for labour peace was greater employment security for certain employees (e.g., those listed in "golden lists"). Nevertheless, layoffs did occur after collective agreements were amalgamated. Ironically, the 1987–88 settlements at CAIL removed several of the concessions PWA had gained during its 1985–86 strike (Fisher and Kondra 1989; 1990).[18]

The 1990 Round

All four major groups at AC and CAIL signed new collective agreements during 1990 in a round of productivity bargaining. Pay increases were granted to each craft unit, partly to preserve industrial peace. In exchange, Canada's two major carriers received concessions generating greater productivity or cost savings. The 1990 settlements seemed to reflect the settling-in process, fleet realignments, and a noticeable shift from price competition to service competition.

Wage increases of roughly 6 percent per year were negotiated for each of the first two years of these agreements for machinists (IAM), flight attendants (CUPE), and passenger agents (CAW) (see Table 10.1). CAIL strenuously avoided cost-of-living adjustment (COLA) clauses like those agreed to at Air Canada, and backloaded its contracts, with relatively higher wage increases coming in subsequent contract years, rather than immediately (or up front).[19]

As a part of the apparent *quid pro quo* bargains that were struck, the 1990 settlements focussed on productivity gains and dealt with fleet realignments. For instance, the Air Canada–CALPA agreement increased monthly flying maximums, provided for training and pay for new equipment (e.g., Airbus 320s), and set up a committee to evaluate pilots' route assignments. It also established two offshore bases to be used to fly around the world, which were mothballed later in 1990.

At CAIL, flight engineers in former Wardair Airbus 310s were replaced by pilots (CALPA), and certain positions were protected on this newer equipment for former Wardair pilots until those planes could be sold. The protecting of positions limited the number of pilots who changed from one type of aircraft to another, thereby limiting the corresponding retraining costs. There were pay and benefits increases, and domestic pilot bases were reduced from seven to five.[20]

The 1990 CAIL flight attendants' contract may give the company an edge over Air Canada. It maintained a two-tier pay scale and incorporated some former Wardair operating efficiencies (e.g., a new in-charge position to be multi-aircraft qualified and a mandatory phone-in on designated operations to verify departure time). In exchange and in light of future plane deliveries, a no-layoff clause was agreed to, covering those bargaining-unit members on the day the contract was signed. Roughly 400 flight attendants were induced to take early retirement or voluntary leaves of absence, helping alleviate employee surpluses.

To ensure high-quality service, the 1990 CUPE–CAIL agreement, which amalgamated agreements at Wardair and CAIL, created the position of a customer service director (CSD), a bargaining-unit member or purser with added responsibilities. Perhaps, the most important feature of this new agreement, this initiative seems to reflect the shift from price to service competition under the re-emergence of the friendly duopoly. Making this innovation possible was the existence of the in-flight service manager (ISM) at Wardair, which was a managerial position. The ISM was eliminated in exchange for upgrading the CSD position, which had limited application.[21] A CUPE–Air Canada settlement later in 1990 reaffirmed the elimination of one level of in-flight bargaining-unit supervision on wide-body jets (which had been initiated in 1985) and, from a managerial perspective, continued to permit the possibility of managerial supervision on flights.

The 1990 CAIL–IAM contract continued the CP Air–IAM tradition of providing employment guarantees in return for productivity gains, especially in quality control, and reimplemented a binding procedure to broaden trade classifications. Its 1990 Air Canada–IAM counterpart increased monetary rewards for certain trade certificates and dealt with ground handlers' contracts by providing job security for employees rendered redundant by the transfer of such service to an Air Canada connector, and by permitting the deployment of employees as station attendants at entry-level pay scales to retain such work.

The 1990 contract for passenger agents (CAW) at CAIL promoted flexible shift arrangements; established parameters for subcontracting (e.g., to the United States), job security, staff reductions, recall, and employment protection; and continued restrictions on transfers after training to minimize subsequent productivity losses and the costs of training. Similarly, the 1990 Air Canada–CAW contract set parameters for base closures and job security, while increasing the minimum time between transfers.

The 1990 round of negotiations did not anticipate the subsequent, rapid increase in fuel prices or the war in the Persian Gulf during January and February 1991. In anticipation of war, air traffic declined substantially late in 1990, wiping out profits earned earlier that year. Losses in 1990 were reported as $74 million at AC and $15 million at CAIL (versus a $111 million profit and a $52 million loss, respectively, in 1989).[22]

In 1990–91, Air Canada shelved previous plans to fly around the world; cut back on domestic routes; and planned to sell various assets, including its office tower in Montreal. A similar set of retrenchment measures was implemented at CAIL, which used a videotaped newsletter by management in early 1991 to prepare its employees for further cuts and possible mid-contract concessions from its unionized employees. The machinists' union (IAM) responded that concessions would be granted only in return for a guarantee of no subsequent layoffs. However, negotiations with all four major groups were still being conducted in mid-1991.

THREATS AND OPPORTUNITIES

The 1980s were tense times. Associated with mergers and acquisitions was the rationalization of the work force, which was exacerbated by the poor economy during the late 1980s and early 1990s, resulting in the loss of thousands of jobs. Technological changes also threatened some jobs. Another consequence of mergers and acquisitions was that bargaining units had to be merged. Where different unions represented the same craft, representation votes were required. This meant that one union would grow and another would shrink, or even disappear. Although the fragmented bargaining structure continued to constrain those unions that remained, the major threats facing them in the early 1990s were, first and foremost, the major air carriers' huge debts and operating losses and, second, the existence of lower-cost work forces at the feeders of major carriers.

Employment

The restructuring following the formation of CAIL typically culminated in layoffs, transfers, or work-sharing arrangements. Recession in the early 1990s led to further downsizing and streamlining of major carriers' organizations.

Canadian Airlines International was viewed as being "upfront" and making "deep cuts early" (Aherne, Chemello, and Fedorus 1989). In 1989–90 the company undertook a substantial downsizing and wrote off the loss associated with the merger with Wardair in 1989. Former Wardair employees absorbed the brunt of layoffs associated with the Wardair integration into CAIL.

Air Canada's policy on layoffs changed as its mandate shifted from a mixture of social and economic goals to an exclusively commercial mandate. Although layoffs did occur at Air Canada during the 1980s, it had remained roughly the same size (23 000 employees). Some observers claimed that, as a Crown corporation, AC was characterized by the belief that large-scale layoffs demoralize staff, something a company should do only as a last resort as it enters a recession. However, Air Canada's new board of directors instructed it in 1990–91 to adopt the private-sector approach of responding quickly to market signals with the necessary cuts.

Aside from layoffs, the major carriers used early retirement incentives, voluntary leaves of absence, and work-sharing arrangements to flexibly carry out downsizing in 1990–91. Earlier, Air Canada had set an example by implementing work sharing, instead of furloughs, with its pilots in 1982–84. This meant that all pilots worked fewer hours, thereby sharing the lower demand for their services, and that junior pilots could maintain their licences by continuing to fly. Pay levels were preserved; morale was maintained or enhanced; trust was built; and Air Canada retained valuable human assets (i.e., junior pilots) for the upturn in passenger traffic that ensued. Work-sharing arrangements spread among the four major crafts at both major carriers during 1990–91. However, to minimize costs in a slumping air-passenger market, CAIL reverted in mid-1991 to the CP Air policy of using pilot furloughs to alleviate employment surpluses.

Technological Change

Technological change altered certain workplace relations in the 1980s and 1990s. Ground crews, for instance, were confronted with the advent of conveyer belts, laser scanners, and containerized cargoes, which eliminated a number of air-freight jobs (Thornicroft 1989).

Increasing automation continues to pose serious threats to ticket agents' jobs. This trend includes the advent of self-service machines—including via home computers—and integrated ticketing systems, like Gemini, which are available to travel agents. In response to automation, two pilot programs were negotiated at Air Canada in 1990 to jointly study the monitoring of agents' telephone calls by supervisors and video-display terminals and related matters (Canadian Auto Workers 1990).

Newer aircraft (i.e., Airbus 310s and 320s, and Boeing 737s, 757s, and 767s) reduced some flight crews from three to two persons, potentially threatening the job security of junior pilots.[23] Although this threat led to a 39-day refusal by CALPA pilots to report for training on 767s, two-pilot crews are now extensively deployed. As fleets are upgraded, those pilots who exercise their seniority to shift from older aircraft to the "glass cockpits" in modern aircraft require retraining, which can be expensive. However, "glass cockpits" permit effective on-the-job training using simulators, and simulators provide a less-expensive means to augment actual flying time, so that pilots can fly the requisite hours to maintain their pilots' licences (Melady 1989).[24]

New Bargaining Agents

Several unions merged and reorganized to gain strength, both financially and at the bargaining table. Shortly after their 1985 strikes at Air Canada, flight attendants merged with the Canadian Union of Public Employees (CUPE), and ticket agents at

Air Canada (CALEA) joined the Canadian Auto Workers (CAW).[25] The CAW replaced the Canadian Association of Passenger Agents at Wardair in 1988. Ticket agents at CAIL, who belonged to the Transportation Communications Union (TCU—the autonomous Canadian successor to BRAC), joined CAW just after Wardair was merged into CAIL late in 1989. Also, Wardair pilots, who belonged to a local independent union (Air Crew Association of Canada), voluntarily joined CALPA at this time.

Fragmented Bargaining Structure

When employers used divide-and-conquer tactics during concession bargaining in the 1980s, the fragmented bargaining units proved to be detrimental to the unions. It became more difficult to exact an economic toll on the employer who could more easily replace the smaller bargaining units (e.g., CALEA and CALFAA at Air Canada in 1985).

The alternative to going it alone, namely, co-ordinated bargaining efforts by union coalitions, is not without its perils. Such a union pact was not necessarily able to overcome labour-market gluts (e.g., PWA), or the poor financial performance of an air carrier (e.g., CP Air) in 1985–86. Indeed, the coalition at PWA ultimately broke apart. Co-ordinated bargaining efforts may have somewhat retarded the concessions that CP Air was able to gain from the IAM in 1985, as evidenced by the subsequent reopening of the resulting contract for renegotiation.

Debt Loads and Operating Losses

As of June 30, 1991, Air Canada and PWA had debt-to-equity ratios of roughly 2.3 to 1, which are relatively high, and were expected to lose some $500 million during 1991–93: $300 million for PWA and $200 million for AC. PWA's debt-to-equity ratio would have been even higher, if it had calculated its operating leases as debt (*Edmonton Journal*, August 10, 1991).

The critical issue appears to be whether each craft union can deliver the kind of productivity enhancements and other cost savings during mid-contract negotiations that will preserve its members' jobs at each major carrier. Mid-contract negotiations are quite a challenge, since mid-contract work stoppages are illegal, and the lack of an explicit deadline reduces some of the pressure on unions to settle.

Lower-Cost Work Forces at Feeders

The partial or complete ownership of feeder airlines by trunk carriers created problems for unions. Potentially, airlines could, and did, shift some of their services to their feeder airlines. This was an economy measure, since the connectors generally enjoyed lower cost structures. For instance, the basic contractual salary in 1990 for a Boeing 727 captain (CALPA) at Air Canada was $11 392 per month; the comparable salary for a Dash 8 captain was $3634 at Air Ontario (CALPA), $4194 at Air BC (CALPA), and $4200 at Air Nova (CALPA). Similar differentials applied to other terms and conditions of employment for pilots, as well as the other groups.

Similar differentials also applied to those connectors, such as Northwest Territorial and Air Alliance in the Air Canada system, which are not unionized.[26]

As to comparators, similar contractual provisions were negotiated for the four major groups at each AC connector and its CAIL partner counterpart in each regional labour market. Thus, Air BC (an AC connector) and Time Air (a CAIL partner) had very similar, if not the same, contractual provisions in the regional labour market of British Columbia and the Prairies.

The lower-cost work forces at connectors posed a major threat to employees at the major carriers. Trunk-carrier employees could lose their jobs, for instance, through a base closure. If they later gained employment with the connector now providing, say, passenger or baggage-handling service, they most likely would earn a lower wage, and might not be covered by a collective agreement.

LEGAL RESPONSES

The legal environment clearly has an effect on a union's or management's choice of strategies (Kochan, Katz, and McKersie 1986), and can constrain strategies undertaken. During restructuring, the limits of legislation may be tested, as unions or management seek to maximize gains in collective bargaining or in attempts to organize or consolidate employee groups. As the Canadian Labour Relations Board (CLRB), which administers the Canada Labour Code governing industrial relations in the airline industry, is an administrative body, it has the ability to change legal constraints over time without statutory changes, by the nature in which it interprets existing legislation. Consequently, legislation may be repeatedly tested, and case law can evolve.

CLRB Case Load

There was a dramatic upsurge in CLRB applications, reflecting the turbulence of deregulation (see Table 10.6). A number of breaches of the duty to bargain in good faith (three in 1980 and two in 1983) were found against regional carriers. Determinations of illegal strikes, often used to speed negotiations or express labour solidarity (e.g., by refusing to cross a picket line), also increased during 1978–89, peaking dramatically at eleven during the major round of concession bargaining in 1985. Indicative of the militancy of the IAM, the CLRB issued cease-and-desist orders at least twelve times against machinists, as compared with four times against ticket agents, and once against flight attendants.

The CLRB experienced increases in applications related to the consolidation of carriers, with several of the following matters often being raised simultaneously in one application: "sale of business," "single employer" declarations, and "reviews."[27] Merger and acquisition matters peaked before the CLRB in 1986.

Common Employer Applications

The acquisition of airlines enabled some unions to grow, and an important means to further this goal was a common employer declaration. A case in point involves

Table 10.6

Applications Received by the Canada Labour Relations Board for Air Transportation[a], 1973–1989[b]

	73–74	74–75	75–76	76–77	77–78	78–79	79–80	80–81	81–82	82–83	83–84	84–85	85–86	86–87	87–88	88–89
Certification	11	9	22	12	24	19	22	29	11	20	18	20	9	21	20	21
Review[c,e]	5	4	11	4	7	6	8	17	12	9	15	12	19	16	19	9
Relocation	0	0	1	2	1	3	2	2	3	4	2	4	7	0	5	1
Unfair[d]	3	10	6	9	10	9	16	47	46	39	55	64	42	54	42	34
Illegal strike	0	0	0	0	1	2	3	3	3	2	2	3	11	1	3	3
Sale of business[e]	0	0	0	0	1	1	3	4	5	1	3	5	1	20	7	4
Single employer[e]	0	0	1	0	2	0	2	0	1	0	5	2	4	16	8	3
Miscellaneous	2	1	1	4	3	2	5	8	4	6	8	18	6	17	10	6
Total	21	24	42	31	49	42	61	110	85	81	108	128	99	145	114	70

Notes: [a] Air transportation includes airlines, airport operations, servicing of aircraft, helicopters, and flying schools or clubs.

[b] Reports are for fiscal years from April 1 through March 31.

[c] Review applications can involve simple name changes on certificates, labour board reviews of bargaining writ(s) determination, and administrative proceedings (e.g., inclusions/exclusions or new technology).

[d] Unfair labour-practice complaints.

[e] Often filed jointly following a merger or acquisition.

Source: Canada Labour Relations Board, Annual Reports, 1973–89.

the Canadian Auto Workers (CAW) and PWA Corp. in mid-1989.

A single-employer ruling represented a strategic opportunity for CAW to represent ticket agents at both CAIL and AC. In 1989, the CAW represented passenger agents at both Wardair and Air Canada and had formerly represented passenger agents at PWA, but it had lost the representation vote to TCU in 1987, when the four bargaining units at EPA, Nordair, PWA, and CP Air were amalgamated to form one unit at CAIL.

A common employer declaration would lead to a new representation vote involving CAIL and Wardair employees. A lengthy hearing was obviated in October 1989 when, on the day before the CLRB was to hear this case, PWA Corp. announced that it was going to integrate Wardair operations into CAIL to reduce capacity and eliminate duplication of services (*Financial Post*, April 3, 1990). After the CLRB issued a common employer declaration, the CAW won the representation vote, and Wardair's pilots joined CALPA.[28]

At the connector level, both CAIL and AC have closed certain bases of operations. Feeder airlines have taken over such functions as passenger service, typically with a lower cost structure. This led to at least one application for a common-employer declaration between AC and its connectors, two of which were nonunion. If successful, unions could have substantially increased the size of their bargaining units.

Air Canada argued this was an arm's-length arrangement; the counterargument was that there was an illicit two-tier labour contract. A decision in this precedent-setting case with Air Nova, Air Ontario, and Air B.C. was rendered in December 1989. The CLRB decided that Air Canada and its connectors were not a common employer for labour relations purposes. This decision seems to reflect the fact that trunk carriers and their feeders have differing abilities to pay, and draw their work forces from somewhat different, though overlapping, labour markets.[29]

COPING MECHANISMS

The amount of change that Canada's two major carriers underwent during the mid- to late-1980s created tremendous stresses and strains, which were potentially debilitating. The assembling of five formerly independent airlines at CAIL into a trunk and international carrier with a feeder network within a short period of time was a unique experience. The privatization of Air Canada, coupled with a subsequent softening of the air-passenger market, forced a sharper focus in their operations and consequent restructuring—including layoffs. Both major carriers sought to promote productive flexibility and constructive union–management relations. A variety of coping mechanisms were developed or used to smooth these major transitions during the mid-1980s to the early 1990s.

Employee Assistance Programs

The two national airlines and their unions had developed employee assistance programs (EAPs) in the late 1970s. These programs, which included confidential

counselling, greatly assisted in easing the transition for both managerial and organized employees. Former Wardair employees who were displaced in 1989 layoffs
resulting from Wardair's integration with CAIL were allowed six months' access to
Wardair's EAP, introduced in 1987.

Contract Administration

Newly amalgamated agreements at CAIL required uniform administration across
each of the corresponding nation-wide bargaining units. Moreover, in the face of
the threat of layoffs and a drop in morale, a key goal was to maintain or improve
working relationships among professional practitioners in daily interactions and
between the company and its work force.

Dispute-resolution mechanisms were carefully revamped. CAIL and its unions
retained two standing mediator/arbitrators to assist in contract renegotiations and
grievance handling. The third parties ironed out "fence" agreements that provided for the merger of seniority lists for several unions at CAIL. CAIL and the IAM set
up an informal, expedited arbitration mechanism to solve problems better.

In short, the focus at both majors shifted to: (1) carefully managing relationships to minimize problems resulting from the upheaval (especially with regard to
technological change and the rationalization and reorganization in the industry),
(2) promoting the spirit over the letter of the law whenever possible, and (3) resolving labour relations problems at the lowest levels possible. Training of supervisors helped shift certain labour relations functions from staff to line functions in
newly streamlined organizations.

Fence Agreements

Since seniority determines work assignments for cockpit and cabin crews, seniority
lists had to be merged before collective agreements could be amalgamated. Where
an employee was placed on the merged list, it could mean losing or retaining a job.

The process of merging seniority lists was divisive, resulting in substantial legal
fees for the corresponding unions. It usually involved lengthy arbitration hearings, possibly preceded by lengthy mediation, and sometimes was followed by
court challenges. An extreme example is former Eastern Provincial Airways' pilots (CALPA), who challenged three fence-agreement awards during 1984–90. Two
were denied, and a third was pending in 1990 (Fisher and Kondra 1990).

A landmark decision in 1979 by arbitrator Paul Weiler sought to minimize the
destructive impact of a corporate merger on employees. It used a "rank ratio" to
combine the seniority lists for flight attendants at TransAir and Pacific Western.
There was a three-to-one ratio of flight attendants at PWA (347) to TransAir
(113). The rank-ratio rule put together blocks of four employees: three from PWA
and one from TransAir, starting from the top of both lists. Within each block,
seniority was determined by initial hiring date, regardless of airline. Then, blocks
were stacked in descending order to form the merged list (Newby 1986). Subsequent fence agreements were constructed along similar lines, also taking into

account the kinds of routes and planes flown by pilots (Munroe 1990).

In the wake of Wardair's absorption into CAIL late in 1989, pilots and flight attendants were rewarded for quickly merging their seniority lists by the fast-tracking of collective bargaining. Thus, CAIL concluded a new agreement with each group in the first half of 1990 (Fisher and Kondra 1990).

Scope Agreements

Several "scope" agreements have been struck to deal with the division of work between the national airlines and their affiliates. Such agreements establish, for example, an orderly progression of pilots in terms of training and routes when moving from connector airlines to trunk carriers. They also restrict feeders to certain kinds of aircraft, possibly precluding connectors from competing with Canada's two major carriers.

Negotiations in 1988–89 yielded three scope agreements at Air Canada. An agreement was reopened with Air Canada's pilots (CALPA) to reach a letter of understanding (#17) that limited aircraft size for Air Canada's feeders, and another (#18) that envisaged seniority-based progression from feeders to Air Canada. A memorandum of understanding was signed with the CAW, dealing with job-security issues raised by feeder alliances. AC's scope agreements are similar to CAIL's feeder contracts, which envisage regional carriers' not growing beyond a certain size.

At CAIL, the company and CALPA signed a letter of understanding in 1990 that committed the two parties to the negotiation of the scope issue. The result was the drawing of a "line in the sand." Regardless of the route it flew, any plane that seated 70 or more passengers was to be covered by the CAIL–CALPA agreement, and any plane seating fewer than 70 passengers was to be covered by the relevant CAIL partner–CALPA agreement.

Other Trust-Building Efforts

Presently, a good rapport between the CAW and management at Air Canada and Canadian Airlines International appear to have given the union a voice in managing the technological threats its members face. Technological threats appear to have contributed to previous strike action by ticket agents (CALEA 1980; CLRB 1973–89). Open dealings helped CAW ticket agents negotiate the two previously mentioned joint studies with management at Air Canada on monitoring and video-display terminals.

This illustrates the important point that some craft groups arguably made gains by accommodating change, while others tended chiefly to resist change. Ongoing negotiations with unions (e.g., with the IAM over reassigning commissary workers at Air Canada) are another example of the various measures instituted to keep employees and unions "on board." In contrast, flight attendants (CUPE) at Air Canada have pursued a policy of "negotiation through arbitration" (see Table 10.5). Some 300 grievances were awaiting arbitration in 1991. Such a log-jam shrouds this union–management relationship in uncertainty, eroding trust, and may adversely affect the individuals directly affected even more by delaying decisions over their contractual rights.[30]

1991 and Beyond

At the feeder level, Canadian Airlines International moved to place all its affiliate airlines under a single moniker: Canadian Regional Airlines. Air Canada indicated early in 1991 that it likely would consolidate its affiliated airlines into a similar, single entity, also to gain further economies (Stockhouse 1991).

A further rationalization process could ensue at such newly consolidated regional carriers. Some of the same issues were being addressed, and some of the same processes were being experienced as occurred with the formation of CAIL. Indeed, the IAM lodged an application in mid-1991 with the CLRB for a declaration that the Canadian Regional Airlines was the common employer of all the CAIL partner feeder airlines, and the CAW reportedly was interested in pursuing this strategy. A successful application could provide an opportunity for the IAM and other craft unions to consolidate regional bargaining units into nation-wide units. Some currently nonunion operations might be subsumed into the union fold along the way in representation votes. Such moves probably would improve the unions' bargaining power relative to carriers by posing the threat of nation-wide shutdowns at feeder airlines.

With regard to vertical integration, employees at some feeders (e.g., Air BC, an AC connector) probably will resist being folded into a vertically integrated bargaining unit for fear of losing regional autonomy and being bumped from their jobs by employees with greater seniority at the corresponding major carrier. These are some of the reasons why pilots at CAIL (CALPA) decided to opt for the previously explained scope agreement in which a threshold of 70 passengers separates CAIL flights from flights at its regional partners.

In contrast, CALPA members at Air Canada and its connectors decided in mid-1991 to amalgamate their locals into one large organization and have a fence agreement, with merged seniority lists, to determine the kind of equipment pilots were to fly. A fence agreement was avoided at CAIL for two additional reasons. First, having been through several rounds of creating fence agreements, pilots at CAIL were well aware of the bad feelings, future litigation, and substantial costs that such a process can generate. Second, junior pilots at CAIL mounted a successful lobby effort within CALPA to preserve the status quo.

At the international level, air routes and, therefore, jobs continue to be determined by bilateral agreements and carrier assignments to international routes by the federal government. In 1991, CAIL began to use a state-of-the-art terminal (Terminal 3 or "Trillium") at Toronto's Pearson Airport as a beachhead to the

American market, and has gained somewhat greater access to that market with its acquisition of Air Toronto. Air Canada has sought, but is yet to receive, greater access to the Orient, especially Japan, which CAIL traditionally has served. In 1991, Air Canada's ambitions to expand routes overseas remained uncertain, however, with the discontinuing of service on its routes to Bombay, Korea, Singapore, and several European destinations.

OPEN SKIES

"Open Skies" negotiations between Canada and the United States, which began in early 1991, were meant to overhaul the existing air pact, which has not changed since 1974. "Open Skies" hopes to completely deregulate air routes over Canada and the United States. It would permit cabotage, thereby enabling the carriers of one country to provide domestic service in the other.

The existing agreement was viewed in 1991 as being out of date, especially in the light of restructuring of the industry in the interim; and lop-sided, favouring the United States. It was estimated that Canada's share of lost benefits from not having open skies was in the order of $2 billion to $3 billion (*Edmonton Journal*, April 10, 1991). Competition policy reportedly also motivated Canada to participate in these talks. Concern about reduced competition stemmed from the re-emergence of the friendly duopoly, suggestions of a possible merger between AC and CAIL, and fears of a division of the marketplace between the two.

Should a merger of AC and CAIL take place before "Open Skies" becomes a reality, it could force the government's hand to either re-regulate the Canadian market or throw it open to foreign carriers, in order to increase competition. It was estimated that a merger would shrink the combined work force at the two major carriers from its present level of approximately 37 000 to 27 000 employees (*Financial Post*, February 7, 1991). A key factor against a possible merger was the millions of dollars it would cost the merged airline to buy out employees' contracts. Given the precarious financial position of Air Canada, and especially CAIL in 1991, another option was to increase the percentage of foreign ownership permitted in Canadian carriers to, say, 49 percent, to allow for larger financial alliances with foreign carriers.[31]

Airlines and labour groups in Canada generally opposed "Open Skies," although Air Canada's reaction might be described as lukewarm in the light of its greater penetration of the U.S. market. Both airlines have complained about factors limiting their ability to compete fairly with their larger U.S. counterparts. Higher labour costs, higher interest rates, higher fuel costs, and higher taxes were cited among the items placing Canada's airlines at a serious competitive disadvantage (*Edmonton Journal*, October 10, 1990). To further complicate matters, U.S. airlines have virtually complete control over their hubs. A key reason is that most U.S. airports are run by municipalities, and airlines can buy and sell privileges at them in private transactions, free from federal government regulation. This has made access to landing and takeoff slots and airport gates a serious impediment to the ability of any airline to compete with the major U.S. carriers on U.S. soil, irrespective of their country of origin. A key remaining question is the ability of the U.S. federal government to deal with such a serious barrier at the bilateral talks.

The most far-reaching outcome to the "Open Skies" negotiations would allow cabotage throughout Canada and the United States. Access by Canadian airlines to U.S. computer reservation systems, as well as airports, may be the largest barriers to achieving completely open skies. The other, limited outcome may be to maintain the status quo. It was not clear at the time of this writing that a middle ground could be reached. If attained, it presumably will involve a phasing in of bilateral deregulation along with attempts to preserve some of the integrity of Canada's airlines.

The key point is that a move toward open skies could lead to developments not unlike those associated with deregulation in each country. Should "Open Skies" become a reality, we may see the merger of the two Canadian airlines or mergers between the Canadian and U.S. airlines, followed by the loss of jobs. In a worst-case scenario, the current major carriers in Canada would become much smaller feeder airlines, chiefly flying passengers to U.S. hubs and mega-hubs (e.g., Denver and Chicago).

The scenario of alliances between major U.S. and Canadian carriers began to unfold in mid-1990 when Air Canada announced that it was negotiating a "strategic alliance" with U.S. Air that could see the two carriers buy equity in each other. By encompassing operations, marketing, and potential investment opportunities, an agreement in principle between AC and U.S. Air seemed to go beyond the more common loose agreement under which carriers exchange traffic and share frequent-flyer programs. U.S. Air, the sixth-largest carrier in the United States with 428 planes and 60 million passengers in 1990, represented a good match with Air Canada, since U.S. Air was chiefly a domestic carrier, having few international routes to siphon off AC's passengers through its U.S. hub airports.

Unlike American and Delta Airlines, who reportedly were lukewarm to overtures from CAIL for a similar alliance, U.S. Air had incurred losses during 1989–90, presumably making it more willing to grant Air Canada more than another major United States carrier might have.[32] Air Canada also announced its intentions to negotiate similar comprehensive deals, which could theoretically include sharing planes, staff, ordering equipment, and cross-ownership of shares, with carriers in Europe and Asia (*Financial Post*, August 20, 1991).

Conclusion

Crucial to understanding the strategic choices made by employers and unions are the history of union–management relations and the statutory framework surrounding labour negotiations. The parties' past history often constrains their ability to choose newer directions. Within the legal framework, successorship, common-employer, and bad-faith bargaining provisions in Canada have made it more difficult for Canadian airlines to resist or avoid unions than is the case in the United States.

Canadian airlines have undergone a major transition over the last thirteen years. Factors contributing to the upheaval were the challenges of competing in deregulated, global markets; an air-traffic market weakened by economic recession; the hub-and-spoke reconfiguration and a corresponding fleet realignment; and very lean (or red) bottom lines at various carriers.

Deregulation witnessed the rise of Pacific Western (PWA) and Wardair to increase the number of national carriers to four. In the wake of PWA's gaining effective or legal control of CP Air, Wardair, and three other regional carriers (TransAir, EPA, and Nordair), a "friendly duopoly" re-emerged, but with players of nearly equal proportions. The two carriers are now locked into a marketplace of limited size, or a "constant-sum game," which provides little incentive to compete on price except in a recession. Serious barriers to entry exist, and today's duopoly may provide even less competition than in the past, since it now extends from trunk carriers to feeders, and into the commuter market—a new development.

To remain competitive and survive during 1978–91, key labour relations responses included concession bargaining, productivity bargaining, and substantial downsizing (e.g., layoffs). Concessions, including zero wage increases and lower wages for new hires, were granted during the early and mid-1980s. To preserve labour peace and improve carrier competitiveness, especially in scheduling and service, the late 1980s and early 1990s witnessed productivity bargaining, in which union members received pay increases in exchange for productivity gains for carriers.

A variety of coping mechanisms were used during this transition. They included: (1) employee assistance programs, especially for dealing with mergers, acquisitions, and layoffs; (2) work-sharing arrangements in place of layoffs; (3) new employee representation and alliances among unions; (4) hearings before the Canadian Labour Relations Board (CLRB) and arbitration boards to clarify legal rights; (5) fence agreements to integrate seniority lists; (6) scope agreements to delimit work jurisdictions; (7) ongoing or fast-tracked negotiations; (8) honest, straightforward dealings; (9) carefully designed private dispute-resolution mechanisms, including mediation/arbitration; (10) shifting certain labour relations responsibilities from staff to line functions; and (11) an emphasis on the spirit, as opposed to the letter, of the collective agreement. Nevertheless, pockets of resistance to change remained among those with vested interests in preserving the status quo.

Although the parties worked together to modify the industrial relations system at the margin, there were no dramatic changes in the conduct of industrial relations. For example, greater employee involvement, profit-sharing plans, or giving unions a role in joint government (as in General Motors' Saturn plant)—ideas that have characterized the transformation of U.S. industrial relations—were not pursued in this industry. The changes were more evolutionary, rather than transformational in nature. The evolutionary changes seem to have resulted chiefly from the greater support of collective bargaining by Canadian labour law and the phasing in of deregulation in Canada. Both factors contrast sharply with the U.S. philosophical orientation and dampened the upheaval in Canada.

Canada's major carriers continue to accept the legitimacy of the unions representing the vast bulk of their employees. In contrast, union resistance or avoidance remains at certain regional airlines, and especially at charter operations where intense competition and highly entrepreneurial attitudes continue to prevail. In terms of applications for common-employer declarations in the wake of consolidations and restructuring, the legal battlefront has shifted from the major carriers to the division of regional feeders that was created at CAIL and being considered by AC.

The operative words may be "broken skies," which is a flying term for limited, clear visibility, interspersed with storm clouds. Collective agreements negotiated in 1990 were consistent with a shift from price competition to competition by a duopoly based on service. But, further turbulence and changing flight plans were being generated by the financial stress that Canada's major carriers experienced during the 1990–91 downturn in the economy and uncertainty about the outcome of Canada–U.S. "Open Skies" negotiations to deregulate North American trans-border routes.

Financial pressures and "Open Skies" negotiations helped clarify the direction the industry will take: global "strategic alliances." Encompassing operational, marketing, and potential investments, the comprehensive deal that was being negotiated between Air Canada and US Air in mid-1991 reportedly was a harbinger of similar developments in Europe and Asia, as well as North America. Paralleling developments observed during domestic deregulation, such carrier realignments could spark further rounds of rationalization, possibly costing thousands of additional jobs, while international deregulation could compound this situation.

In the face of impending environmental change, the challenge for the parties within industrial relations is to examine whether gradual change at the margin will be enough to cope with the potential changes in the workplace or whether they may have to consider changes that are likely to challenge the traditional foundations of our industrial relations system.

REFERENCES

Aherne, Michael, Sandra Chemello, and Anna Fedorus. 1990. "Canadian Airlines International: A Strategic Focus on Human Resource Planning and Change Management." Field research project, Faculty of Business, University of Alberta.

Air Canada Annual Report 1990.

Arnold, William L., and John L. Brown. 1986. "Tracking Strategy in the Airlines: PWA 1945–84." Canadian Journal of Administrative Science 3 (December): 171–203.

Bailey, Elizabeth, David Graham, and Daniel Kaplan. 1985. Deregulating the Airlines. Cambridge, MA: MIT Press.

Bain, D.M. 1987. Canadian Pacific Air Lines. Calgary: Kishorn Publications.

Barone, S.S., Mansour Javidan, G. B. Reschenthaler, and Dennis J.H. Kraft. 1986. "Deregulation in the Canadian Airline Industry: Is There Room for a Large Regional Airline?" The Logistics and Transportation Review 22: 421–48.

Bemmels, Brian, E.G. Fisher, and Barbara Nyland. 1986. "Canadian-American Jurisprudence on 'Good Faith' Bargaining." Relations Industrielles/Industrial Relations. 41: 567–621.

Bureau of Labour Information. 1989. Major Wage Settlements: Listing of Sic 501 (1978–89). Ottawa: Labour Canada.

Byfield, Mike. 1991. "Storms loom in the open skies." Alberta Report, March 18, 16–17.

Canada Labour Relations Board (CLRB). 1978–89. Annual Report. Ottawa.

Canadian Air Line Employees' Association (CALEA). 1980. "History of CALEA." Manuscript, 1–10.

Canadian Airline Pilots Association (CALPA). 1987a. "CALPA Member Airlines." The Canadian Air Line Pilot 43: 6–8.

———. 1987b. "Voices from the Past: Reminiscences and Comments from Past Presidents." The Canadian Air Line Pilot 43: 15–29.

———. 1988. "The Division of the World." The Canadian Air Line Pilot 44: 12–18.

Canadian Auto Workers (CAW). 1990. "GST Breakthrough at Air Canada." CAW Canada/Air Canada Report. June.

Cappelli, Peter. 1987. "Airlines." In David B. Lipsky and Clifford B. Donn, eds., Collective Bargaining in American Industry. Lexington, MA: Lexington Books. 134–86.

Downie, Bryan M. 1991. "When Negotiations Fail: Causes of Breakdown and Tactics for Breaking the Stalemate," Negotiation Journal 7: 175–86.

Edmonton Journal, October 10, 1990. "Transport experts raise open-skies warning," D9.

———. April 10, 1991. "Airlines promised access to U.S.," D9.

———. August 10, 1991. "Too many airplanes; too few passengers," A10.

———. August 21, 1991. "Air Canada,

US Air broaden horizons with alliance," D9.

Financial Post, October 2, 1989. "Air Canada prospering on private competition," 23.

——. March 15, 1990. "$1B in upgrades planned to keep Air Canada on top," 4.

——. April 3, 1990. "PWA faces 'hefty loss' for 1990 first quarter," 52.

——. June 12, 1990. "Air Canada told to look outside for leadership," 3.

——. February 7, 1991. "PWA ready to sell stake to U.S. Airline," 1.

——. August 20, 1991. "Air Canada looks to alliance with US Air," 36.

Fisher, E. G., and Alex Kondra. 1989. "Managing Change in North American Airlines." Unpublished manuscript, Edmonton, Faculty of Business, University of Alberta.

——. 1990. "Canada's Airlines: Flying Through Turbulence." In Allen Ponak, ed., Teaching and Research in Industrial Relations. Laval: Canadian Industrial Relations Association. 143–53.

Ford, Michael. 1981. "Collective Bargaining in the Canadian Air Transportation Industry." Field research project, Faculty of Business, University of Alberta.

Gillen, David W., Tae H. Oum, and Michael W. Trethway. 1987. Identifying and Measuring the Impact of Government Ownership and Regulation on Airline Performance. Ottawa: Economic Council of Canada.

Gillen, David W., W.T. Stanbury, and Michael W. Trethway. 1988. "Duopoly in Canada's Airline Indus-

try: Consequences and Policy Issues." Canadian Public Policy 14: 15–31.

Kochan, Thomas A., Harry C. Katz, and Robert B. McKersie. 1986. The Transformation of American Industrial Relations. New York: Basic Books.

Kubish, Glenn. 1990. "Unifying the Fleet." Alberta Report 17 (February 26): 16.

Langford, John W. 1981. "Air Canada." In Allan Tupper and G. Bruce Doern, eds., Public Corporations and Public Policy. Montreal: The Institute for Research on Public Policy. 251–84.

Langford, John W., and Ken Huffman. 1988. "Air Canada." In Allan Tupper and G. Bruce Doern, eds., Privatization, Public Policy and Public Corporations in Canada. Halifax: The Institute for Research on Public Policy. 93–150.

Macdonald, Derek. 1986. "Pacific Western Airline Strike." Unpublished MBA research paper, University of Alberta.

McKelvey, Jean T. 1988. Cleared for Takeoff. Ithaca, NY: New York State School of Industrial and Labour Relations, Cornell University.

Melady, John. 1989. Pilots: Canadian Stories from the Cockpit. Toronto: McClelland and Stewart.

Munroe, Donald R. 1990. "Canadian Air Line Pilots Association: The Canadian Airlines Master Executive Council and Air Crew Association of Canada and Canadian Airlines International." Unpublished arbitration award, February 8.

National Transportation Agency of Canada, 1991. *Annual Review of the National Transportation Agency of Canada 1990.* Ottawa: Minister of Supply and Services Canada.

Newby, N. Jill. 1986. *The Sky's the Limit.* Vancouver: Mitchell Press Limited.

O'Connor William E. 1985. *An Introduction to Airline Economics.* New York: Praeger Publishers.

PWA *Corp. Annual Report,* 1990.

Smith, F.E.W. 1970. *The First Thirty Years: A History of the Canadian Air Line Pilots Association.* Vancouver: Mitchell Press Limited.

Statistics Canada. 1976–90. *Air Carrier Operations in Canada,* Catalogue 51–002. Ottawa: Minister of Supply and Services.

Stevenson, Garth. 1987. *The Politics of Canada's Airlines from Diefenbaker to Mulroney.* Toronto: University of Toronto Press.

Stockhouse, John. 1991. "Hello Cruel World." *The Globe and Mail Report on Business Magazine* 7 (February): 34–47.

Taylor, Peter Shawn. 1990. "Flying into head winds." *Alberta Report* 17 (August 20): 20–1.

Thornicroft, Kenneth W. 1989. "Airline Deregulation and the Airline Labour Market." *Journal of Labour Research* 10 (Spring): 163–81.

Tupper, Allan. 1981. "Pacific Western Airlines." In Allan Tupper and G. Bruce Doern, eds., *Public Corporations and Public Policy.* Montreal: The Institute for Research on Public Policy, 285–317.

Weiler, Paul. 1980. *Reconcilable Differences.* Toronto: Butterworths.

Verma, Anil. 1987. "Case Study: CP Airlines Ltd. (1984–86)." Abstract in Joseph M. Weiler, *Report of the Port of Vancouver Container Traffic Commission: An Industrial Inquiry Commission under the Maintenance of Ports Operation Act, 1986.* Vancouver. 201–4.

ENDNOTES

1. We are indebted to those we interviewed: Capt. Haydn Acheson, Sam S. Barone, R.L. (Bob) Biggar, Lynn Brophy, Jim Callon, Dave Collins, Sandra Cronkright, Anne Davidson, Val Dufour, Kevin Howlett, Andrea Jolicoeur, Ron S. Keras, S.J. (Judi) Korbin, Marc Leblanc, Richard Nolan, August E. Pokotylo, M.S. (Sue) Singer, S. M. Smillie, George Smith, Kevin Smith, Sue Szczawinska, Tony Wohlforth, and Ron Young. Guy Lalonde and Catherine Green, Bureau of Labour Information, provided useful information. We greatly appreciate the support of the Social Sciences and Humanities Research Council and the Rice Fellowship.

2. In Canada, which has a population one-tenth that of the United States, hubs are much smaller than their U.S. counterparts. Since they are strung from east to west along the U.S. border, Canadian passengers, unlike their U.S. counterparts, rarely fly away from their ultimate destinations to a major hub.

3. This regional policy began to break down in 1969 when PWA purchased TransAir (Barone et al. 1986). It was in ruins after both Eastern Provincial Airways and PWA gained routes to Toronto in 1981 (Stevenson 1987). However, the regional airline policy was not officially removed until 1984 (Gillen, Oum, and Trethway 1987).

4. The exceptions were at Air BC and Eastern Provincial Airways. This situation no longer exists today.

5. When a pilot retires, leaving a seat vacant, he or she is replaced by a pilot of a smaller aircraft. This creates a need for training and creates an upward bumping process at each level of the fleet, each requiring the retraining of a pilot (Cappelli 1987).

6. Because of data incompatibility, a time-series analysis of wages for flight attendants and machinists is not included in Table 10.1 or 10.3.

7. An arbitrator substituted suspensions of several months for discharges (Smith 1970). After CALEA was certified as a bargaining agent for ticket agents at PWA in 1971, PWA became embroiled in a 25-day strike/lockout in 1978 (CALEA 1980).

8. Administrative deregulation in the United States was in full swing in 1977, and the Airline Deregulation Act was passed in 1978 (Cappelli 1987). Air service to Canada's far north was not deregulated.

9. Fuel costs are substantial in the industry, too, and consumption is influenced by aircraft choices (O'Connor 1985). Turbo-prop is more fuel-efficient on the shorter, lower-density, routes or where more frequent flights with smaller capacity are desired.

10. In gaining approval from the Bureau of Competition Policy to acquire Wardair, PWA Corp. made the commitment to operate CAIL and Wardair as distinct, separate units, but the airlines were integrated in 1989.

11. The exception is work force size. AC was expected to earn only half its profits in 1990 from passenger and freight service. AC also maintains other airlines' fleets, giving it a larger work force than CAIL's.

12. CP Air decided to standardize its fleet in 1985 to 737s and DC-10s and no longer fly its 747s (Bain 1987). PWA, which operated 737s almost exclusively (Arnold and Brown

1986), sold Wardair's entire fleet after the decision to fully integrate the two airlines (Kubish 1990). This was expected to increase profits by $12 million and increase aircraft utilization.

13. Although AC and CAIL share a CRS called Gemini, this practice was found not to be anti-competitive by a competition tribunal.

14. The Pacific Western Airlines Act limited any one shareholder to no more than 4 percent of the stock, with the exception of the Alberta government (Arnold and Brown 1986).

15. *Financial Post*, October 2, 1989, 23. A group representing 5000 AC employees had strongly advocated the privatization of the airline (Langford and Huffman 1988). Bill 129, which allowed for the privatization of AC permitted no one shareholder to own more than 10 percent of the company with a 25 percent foreign-ownership ceiling. AC is also required to comply with the Official Languages Act, preserve maintenance bases, and maintain its corporate headquarters in Montreal. Of note, some 18 000 of the 23 000 AC employees owned stock in the company in 1990. This may explain why AC's board of directors was pushing for cost cuts to boost stock prices (*Financial Post*, June 12, 1990, 3).

16. Two-tiered wage scales can be nonmerged in two ways. The ceiling rate for new hires can be below the floor for continuing employees, or, if these rates overlap, the rates of progression through pay steps may differ.

17. This assessment is based upon a compilation of contractual provisions that are confidential. They may be verified by checking the relevant collective agreements, in which the last round's changes are indicated by a vertical lines in the margins.

18. For instance, the first CAIL–IAM agreement reverted to the CP Air–IAM mechanical trade classifications. This and other contract language (i.e., article 7) substantially reduced PWA's 1985 gains to cross-utilize mechanics by restricting mechanics' work outside their classifications to temporary assignments.

19. For example, passenger agents at Air Canada received increases of 6 percent for 1990 and 5 percent plus a possible COLA addition of 2.5 percent for 1991 (CAW 1990). Their counterparts at CAIL agreed to 5 percent in 1990, 7 percent in 1991, and 5 percent in 1992.

20. The CAIL pilots' contract was extended for nineteen months.

21. Wardair had a nonunion in-flight service manager (ISM) since 1981, and Air Canada had negotiated a largely equivalent position in a memorandum of agreement that was rejected in 1985. Wardair considered ISM surveillance to be a key ingredient in providing superior cabin service. Indeed, during 1982–88 Wardair had more (10) disciplinary arbitrations with flight attendants than the much-larger Air Canada (8). Wardair employees viewed the ISM position as demeaning and unfair, indicating why this was an area of conflict in 1990.

22. In 1989, PWA experienced its first loss ($56 million) since 1970, which included a $73.8 million write-down associated with the Wardair purchase (Taylor 1990).

23. Canadian pilots initially resisted two-person crews but agreed to them for 737s early in

the 1970s (CALPA 1987b). DC-8s were retrofitted for three crew members, and a non-pilot seat was successfully resisted on the B-747 (CALPA 1987a).

24. Even though glass cockpits can fly and even land modern aircraft by themselves, various emergency conditions can be programmed into simulated training.

25. The official title of the CAW is the National Automobile, Aerospace, and Agricultural Implement Workers Union of Canada.

26. In 1990, a Dash-8 captain at Air Alliance received a basic monthly salary of $3986. At Northwest Territorial, which operates in Canada's north, which was not deregulated and generally has longer flights, a Dash-8 captain received $7377 a month.

27. Review applications involve, among other things, simple name changes on certificates; labour board reviews of bargaining-unit(s) determinations, and administrative proceedings, such as inclusions or exclusions from bargaining units.

28. Since the IAM represented machinists and CUPE represented the flight attendants at Wardair and CAIL, the amalgamation of these two bargaining units into one became an internal union matter.

29. CLRB files 530-1525 and 560-172, Decision No. 771, December 29, 1989.

30. Some observers claim that the CUPE policy of "negotiation through arbitration" is a carryover from public-sector bargaining to the private sector.

31. Both Canada and the United States restrict foreign ownership of domestic airlines to 25 percent, and no single shareholder can own more than 10 percent of Air Canada (*Edmonton Journal*, August 21, 1991). Similarly, the Province of Alberta increased the maximum portion of PWA Corp. that could be owned by a single shareholder to 10 percent in 1991.

32. U.S. Air lost $210 million in the first half of 1991 (*Edmonton Journal*, August 21, 1991).

Chapter 11

INDUSTRIAL RELATIONS IN THE CANADIAN TELEPHONE INDUSTRY

Anil Verma
Joseph M. Weiler[1]

*T*he industrial relations and human-resource policies in the Canadian telephone[2] industry developed and matured under the regulated monopoly regime that shaped the industry since its inception. In the 1980s, the regulatory system came under increasing legal, political, and economic challenges for reform. Telephone technology made large strides in its ability to connect subscribers more efficiently and to use the telephonic channels to communicate much more than just the human voice. Developments elsewhere—in particular, the dissolution of the Bell System in the United States—and increasing (domestic) competition also brought some pressures for change to labour relations in this industry.

But the pressures for change in industrial relations and human-resource practices, though present in the telephone industry, were moderate because any dilution of the regulatory context in which these practices exist proved to be slow and gradual. The absence of severe economic pressures is both an advantage and a detriment to the industry. With relative financial stability, telephone firms could afford to invest in initiatives such as employee involvement and training. However, experience tells us that the likelihood of change is always weaker in the absence of a crisis or cathartic event. In the absence of such a crisis, the challenge for the telephone industry in the 1990s lies in achieving change from an older paternalistic and authoritarian style to one that is more participative and egalitarian.

In this essay, we provide, first, an overview of the structure of the industry in light of the historical developments. This overview is followed by an analysis of the current economic, technological, and regulatory environment in which telephone companies must operate. The next two sections describe each of the parties to the employment relationship and the process and outcomes of collective bargaining. The last two sections discuss the emerging issues and challenges in industrial relations and human-resource practices for the industry.

The Canadian Telephone Industry

Canada has had a long and fruitful association with the telephone. Not only did its inventor, Alexander Graham Bell, live and work in Canada during his career, but his father, Melville Bell, owned the first Canadian telephone company, which was formed in 1877. To develop their economy, Canadians needed to communicate over large distances in a sparsely populated country. The telephone contributed to the unique needs and development of the Canadian economy. Today, Canada boasts one of the most advanced communication networks in the world. Canadians are also one of the most intensive users of the telephone anywhere. In 1987, there were 37 billion telephone conversations, for an average of 1436 calls per person (Statistics Canada 1988). Today, almost 99 percent of all Canadian households and businesses have telephones.

By 1988, the industry posted revenues of $11.88 billion and profits of $1.299 billion (see Table 11.1)—a growth of 70 percent in revenues and nearly 96 percent in profits since 1981, which is above the rate of inflation for the period and well above the average rate of growth in profits for most other industries. The industry employed 102 625 persons in 1981, which decreased to 96 146 by 1988. The number of calls, both local and long distance, increased nearly 36 percent over the period 1981–88. Clearly, significant gains in productivity were made in the 1980s, primarily through introduction of new technology.

In 1990, there were nearly 80 different telephone systems in the country, although the largest 16 accounted for more than 98 percent of the revenues. Table 11.2 lists eleven of the most prominent companies; their ownership; regulatory jurisdiction; major unions; and two indicators of size: number of employees and annual sales revenue. There are diversified owners of these companies. The largest, Bell Canada, accounts for roughly 55 percent of the industry. It is regulated federally and wholly owned by BCE Inc., a widely held Canadian company listed at the Toronto and Montreal stock exchanges. It employed 55 335 persons in 1989. It services almost all of Ontario, Quebec, and the Northwest Territories. Table 11.3 shows key performance indicators at Bell over the 1981–89 period. BCE Inc. also owns substantial parts of the following telephone companies: Maritime Telephone & Telegraph (MT&T) (33.7 percent); Télébec Ltée. (100 percent); NewTel Enterprises, owner of the Newfoundland Telephone Co. (53 percent); Bruncor Inc., owner of New Brunswick Telephone Co. (31 percent); Northern Telephone (99.8 percent); and NorthwesTel (100 percent).

Table 11.1

The Canadian Telephone Industry: An Historical Overview, 1981–1989

	1981	1982	1983	1984	1985	1986	1987	1988	1989
Revenues (millions)	6987	7865	8533	9292	9963	10 601	11 093	11 880	12 644
Profits (millions)	664	649	835	948	1028	1081	1157	1299	1450
Assets (millions)	18 623	19 923	20 414	21 275	22 017	23 199	24 356	26 027	28 030
Debt/equity ratio	1.21	1.20	1.15	1.08	1.06	1.00	0.93	0.98	0.97
Number of phones connected (thousands)	16 944	16 802	16 631	16 480	15 974	12 948	13 444	13 976	14 648
Number of residence phones (thousands)	11 751	11 758	11 746	11 745	11 338	9 701	9 952	10 228	10 578
Number of business phones (thousands)	5 193	5 044	4 885	4 735	4 636	3 247	3 492	3 748	4 070
Number of local calls[a] (millions)	27 186	27 554	28 944	31 205	32 926	34 673	34 831	NA	NA
Number of toll calls (millions)	1 453	1 475	1 541	1 641	1 792	1 959	2 207	2 534	2 487
% Revenue from long-distance	53.0	52.6	52.7	53.2	54.3	55.5	55.2	54.2	54.4
Capital spending/investment (thousands)	601 679	643 092	614 827	656 951	812 960	817 017	703 046	766 519	910 035
Total telephone plant (cost) (millions)	22 298	24 467	25 917	27 307	28 484	19 494	32 112	35 123	37 694
Number of employees	102 625	105 061	100 576	96 602	94 134	91 671	92 720	96 146	98 625

Note: [a] Number of local calls for small industry estimated by Statistics Canada, based on assumption that telephones are used by smaller companies to the same extent as those operated by larger telephone systems in each province. Larger telephone companies estimate own local calls.

Source: Statistics Canada, Telephone Statistics, Catologue 56–203 (Ottawa: Minister of Supply and Services, various years).

Besides their holdings in telephone companies, BCE Inc. has other substantial interests in the telecommunications industry. Tele-direct (Publications) Inc. publishes telephone directories and Yellow Pages (100 percent BCE-owned); Bell-Northern Research is a research and development company (30 percent); Telesat Canada provides satellite links (24.6 percent); Teleglobe Canada provides satellite and other links with overseas communication networks (30 percent); and Terra Nova Telecommunications (100 percent). BCE Inc. owns 55.2 percent of the telecommunication equipment manufacturer, Northern Telecom. In 1990, BCE Inc. was listed as the second-largest Canadian corporation in terms of sales by the *Financial Post 500* publication.

As Table 11.2 shows, not all telephone companies in Canada are private corporations. Notably, telephone companies in Manitoba and Saskatchewan are provincially owned and are regulated[3] Crown corporations. Alberta's telephone system (with the exception of Edmonton), initially owned by the Province of Alberta, was privatized in 1990. Several other telephone systems are owned by local governments; for example, the Edmonton telephone exchange is owned by the City of Edmonton.[4] Among other companies not shown in Table 11.2, it is important to mention that Northern Telephone Limited, which serves parts of northern Ontario, is owned almost completely by BCE Inc.[5] Ontario Northland Communications, owned by the Province of Ontario, provides long-distance services to portions of northern Ontario.

The diversity in ownership and regulation result largely from historical developments. Many observers hold that the present system of industry regulation (and, consequently, the industry structure that results from such regulation) is inadequate to respond to the demands of the modern economic environment (Janisch and Schultz 1989). The next section discusses the historical developments that shaped the industry and the current efforts to reshape it in light of new economic challenges.

*E*volution of the Regulatory Regime

EARLY DAYS

After Melville Bell founded the Bell Telephone Company of Canada in 1877 (it received its Royal Charter in 1880), three other companies began a variety of telephone services: The Canadian Telephone Company, another Bell subsidiary; Montreal Telegraph; and Dominion Telegraph.[6] By 1882, however, Melville Bell's original firm had managed to buy out all the others, establishing a virtual monopoly. The company ran into trouble, though, as its patents were declared void in 1885 and 1887. Tough times that followed prompted the crippled monopoly to divest operations in Prince Edward Island (1885), British Columbia

Table 11.2
Major Companies in the Canadian Telephone Industry

Company	Regulatory Jurisdicion	Ownership	Geographical Coverage	Sales C$ (millions) 1989	# of Employees 1989	Major Unions[a]	% Revenue from Toll Calls
AGT Ltd. (formerly Alberta Government Telephone)	Federal (Provincial till 1990)	Telus Corp. (40% by Prov. of Alberta; rest widely held)	Alberta (exc. Edmonton)	1 163	10 800	IBEW	66
Bell Canada	Federal	BCE Inc.; widely held	Most of Ontario, Quebec, NWT	15 253	55 335	CWC-Craft & Operators CTEA-Clerical	57
B.C. Tel	Federal	Anglo-Canadian Tel (owned 50.1% by GTE, U.S.A.)	Most of British Columbia	1 689	15 157	TWU	49
Island Tel (Is. Tel)	Federal	52.2% MT&T; rest widely held	P.E.I.	5.5	363	CWC	58
Manitoba Telephone System (MTS)	Provincial	Prov. of Manitoba	Manitoba	516	5 462	IBEW-Craft CWC-Operators	57
New Brunswick Tel (N.B. Tel)	Federal	Bruncor Inc.	New Brunswick	300	2 651	CWC	61

Table 11.2 (continued)

Company	Regulatory Jurisdiction	Ownership	Geographical Coverage	Sales C$ (millions) 1989	# of Employees 1989	Major Unions[a]	% Revenue from Toll Calls
Maritime Tel & Tel (MT&T)	Federal	33.7% by BCE Inc.; rest widely held	Nova Scotia	385	4 198	AC&TWU	60
Newfoundland Tel (Nfld. Tel)	Federal	NewTel Enterprises (53% by BCE Inc.)	Newfoundland	26	2 066	CWC	63
Québec Téléphone (Que. Tel)	Provincial	50.6% by Anglo-Canadian Tel (owned 50.1% by GTE, U.S.A.)	Gaspé; north of St. Lawrence; Labrador	22	1 971	Syndicat des employés d'exécution (SCFP)	60
SaskTel	Provincial	Prov. of Saskatchewan	Saskatchewan	513	4 400	CWC	61
Télébec Ltée.	Provincial	BCE Inc.	Parts of Quebec	143	1 230	Teamsters	73

Notes: [a] CWC—Communications & Electrical Workers of Canada
CTEA—Canadian Telephone Employees' Association (Independent)
IBEW—International Brotherhood of Electrical Workers
AC&TWU—Atlantic Communications & Technical Workers' Union (Independent)
TWU—Telecommunication Workers' Union (Independent)

Source: Annual Reports, Financial Post Cards

Table 11.3
Bell Canada: An Historical Overview, 1981–1989

	1981	1982	1983	1984	1985	1986	1987	1988	1989
Total operating revenues	3 845	4 359	4 710	5 140	5 499	5 795	6 164	6 372	6 989
Net income	476	521	588	625	629	651	709	787	871
Total assets	10 005	10 620	10 817	11 342	11 901	12 693	13 628	14 565	15 624
Total debt ratio	50.16	47.74	46.49	47.39	46.42	45.01	43.12	41.60	40.33
Total equity ratio	49.84	52.26	53.51	52.61	53.58	54.99	56.88	58.40	59.67
Rate of return on average total capital	10.86	10.90	11.45	11.77	11.63	11.36	11.41	11.46	11.43
Network access services	6 348	6 416	6 574	6 823	7 092	7 404	7 761	8 092	8 504
Number of local conversations	13 200	13 309	14 484	15 207	15 893	16 600	18 123	NA	20 743
Number of long-distance conversations	748	747	788	848	927	1 028	1 192	1 382	1 586
% Revenue from toll calls	48.4	49.5	49.9	50.5	51.9	53.6	48.9	49.1	48.5
Capital expenditures	1 401	1 417	1 139	1 285	1 368	1 638	1 981	2 197	2 326
Total Number of employees	57 869	54 927	53 119	49 807	48 807	49 459	52 159	53 448	55 942
—Clerical & associated empls.	18 400	17 600	16 900	15 900	16 000	16 100	17 000	17 500	18 500
—Communications sales empls.	600	700	800	800	800	700	700	700	700
—Craft & services empls.	15 600	15 000	15 000	14 200	13 800	13 900	14 900	15 500	16 000
—Operator services & dining service empls	6 800	6 000	5 500	5 100	4 700	4 700	5 000	4 500	5 000

Source: Data provided by Bell Canada upon request.

(1889), Nova Scotia (1888), and New Brunswick (1889). In Nova Scotia and New Brunswick, the company managed to acquire equity positions in the new companies that it still holds to this day. The nullification of the original patents allowed a variety of companies to enter the business in Ontario and Quebec, many of which are still operating as independents (Babe 1990, 74).

In the West, Bell Telephone had few challengers until 1892. Although several municipal systems had begun to operate in Manitoba as early as 1899, it was not until 1908–9 that the governments of Manitoba, Saskatchewan, and Alberta acquired the assets of Bell Telephone, after enacting a number of laws allowing for government control of their respective telephone systems. In British Columbia, the provincial government resisted pressures for public ownership and preferred to leave it in private hands (with the exception of municipal systems), subject to regulation. The provincial intent had been to bring telephone service under provincial regulation, but these plans were dashed in 1916 when Parliament enacted legislation to bring the B.C. telephone operations under federal regulation by the Board of Railway Commissioners.

GUIDING PRINCIPLES OF REGULATION

Telephone companies, like some other utilities, have always been argued to be "natural monopolies," a term used to convey two main ideas. First, the cost (to the economy) of providing telephone services would be too high if competition were allowed. Second, not everyone would be able to afford telephone services if its prices were determined by market forces. These two ideas have formed the historic basis of telephone regulation, although, as we discuss later, they are under gradual modification. A third principle supporting the regulatory regime in this industry is known as "system integrity." This notion, believed in the past to be essential for high quality standards, has been eroded considerably since 1975. Below we discuss each of these principles and the extent to which each is being modified in response to developments in technology and the global marketplace.

Economies of Scale

In its barest form, this argument evokes images of competing telephone companies digging up neighbourhoods to lay multiple sets of cables. The need to avoid this undesirable scenario has been used to grant monopoly coverage to the entire telephone system. Modern telephone systems, however, consist of several other components besides the cable that connects each subscriber with the exchange. There are exchanges, long-distance connections through cables or on radio waves, and multiple terminals, of which the telephone receiver is but one these days. The argument for economies of scale lacks appeal when considering radio links between large traffic centres, or a variety of terminal devices that may be linked to telephone networks.

Service Universality

This argument holds that, at prices determined by the market, not everyone would be able to afford the service. Limited subscription reduces the value of the service to the subscribers as well as to society as a whole. To achieve universal coverage, therefore, basic telephone service (i.e., local service) must be subsidized by allowing companies to charge a premium for other services such as long-distance and custom calling. Many studies, including some by the Canadian Radio-television and Telecommunications Commission (CRTC), show little support for this notion. For example, the evidence suggests that both local and long-distance services have been highly profitable for Bell Canada (Babe 1990, 146–48).[7]

System Integrity

This argument was used from the early days until the mid-1970s to allow telephone companies to maintain a total monopoly over all aspects of the system, including the once-ubiquitous black, rotary-dial telephone receiver set. The telephone companies argued that, unless they controlled every component of the system, they could not guarantee high-quality reception at the other end. This doctrine was challenged in 1975 in the case of Harding Communications and in 1977 by Challenge Communications Limited. In both cases, the courts and the CRTC rejected the argument that Bell Canada's monopoly practices were justified because of the need for system integrity. Since then, it has been widely accepted in the industry that competitors or subscribers can connect their own equipment into telephone companies' networks.

NEW DIRECTIONS IN INDUSTRY REGULATION

The economic and technological context for telephone companies in Canada changed rapidly during the 1980s. By 1991, rapid advances in technology along with regulatory developments abroad have brought considerable pressure on Canadian government and regulatory policy to recast telecommunications policy. Any shift from the regulated-monopoly regime that shaped the industry prior to 1980 will likely have significant consequences for industrial relations and human-resource practices. What follows, therefore, is a brief overview of the pressures for change and the potential policy responses to these pressures.

Technological Developments

In less than 25 years, telecommunications networks have almost completely switched processing signals from analog to digital. This change constitutes a large technological leap because it allows telephone companies to offer a large variety of services beyond simply carrying human voice. Digital processing allows telecommunication networks to be operated by computers, which can be programmed to receive, process, store, and transmit almost any signal that is digital in nature. Thus, not only is the range of services offered enhanced, but such services can all be done very efficiently at high speeds. Another technological advancement that is vastly increasing the capacity of networks to carry digital signals is the use of optic fibres in place of conventional cables. An optic fibre is a strand of fibreglass through which signals can be transmitted on laser beams. Since the frequency of light is much higher than that of sound, an optic fibre can carry thousands more signals than a conventional cable of similar thickness. The quality of transmission is also much better.

Janisch and Schultz (1989) suggest that this revolution in digital technology has converted POTS (Plain Old Telephone Service) into PANS (Pretty Amazing New Services). Telephone companies are now responsible, either directly or indirectly, for services as diverse as automated teller machines, electronic mail, video conferencing, and remote paging.[8] Even the telephone service has grown to offer a wide range of services such as forwarding, screening, and storage of calls in voice mailboxes. Cellular networks permit users to place a call from almost anywhere, for instance from a car, a boat, or an airplane.

Regulatory Developments in Other Countries

Driven, in part, by these technological developments and, in part, by business needs, a number of countries began to revise their regulatory policies in the 1980s. The most significant development for Canadians was the decision in the United States to deregulate long-distance telephone services and to recast regulatory policy for companies providing local services.[9] The Bell system was dissolved in 1984, and competition in long-distance service was allowed. Most U.S. consumers now have a choice of three long-distance operators: AT&T, MCI and U.S. Sprint. In addition, many businesses with large-volume traffic of their own have installed private networks. Deregulation has also allowed telephone customers to acquire unimpeded rights to use terminal equipment of their own choice, supplied by a large variety of domestic and overseas manufacturers. Although the merits of some effects of deregulation have been debatable, the telecommunication industry, in general, had prospered in the years following the dissolution of the Bell System and the accompanying partial deregulation.[10]

In the United Kingdom, Parliament privatized British Telecom and changed its policy to permit (regulated) competition in both local and long-distance services. Although only one competitor, Mercury Communications, had been permitted entry by 1991, there is pressure on the regulators to allow more entrants. Germany is moving more cautiously by allowing some competition in the manfacturing of communications equipment and in computer-enhanced end-user applications. In Japan, the government moved to permit greater competition in the end-user equipment segment of the industry. Nippon Telephone and Telegraph (NTT) was privatized. However, it retained the network monopoly.

Needs and Responses of Canadian Business

Advocates of regulatory revision suggest two implications of these developments abroad for Canada. First, the new technologies offer new opportunities to Canadian firms for improving operational efficiency. If the regulatory system does not allow Canadian businesses full and free access to these new services, the Canadian economy as a whole will be less efficient and, hence, less competitive. For example, conferencing can cut down the cost of travel. But this example, according to some users, is only the tip of the iceberg. Much greater efficiencies can be realized in connecting engineers and scientists who are working on similar problems, but may be separated by distance or location of certain facilities. For some innovation-paced companies, such as Hewlett-Packard, a six-month delay in introducing a product could make the difference between market success and failure (Janisch and Schultz 1989).

Second, if Canadian firms cannot access such services internally, they will increasingly bypass domestic networks and buy services from foreign (mostly U.S.) networks. According to industry sources, while the incidence of bypass is increasing in volume, it has been largely undocumented. In 1991, it was not uncommon for business users to use private lines running from Toronto to Buffalo and then switch from there to the U.S. or international networks. An indirect measure of this activity was available from the number of U.S. firms that established sales offices in Toronto. In a June 26, 1991, decision, the CRTC prohibited the routing of any overseas basic telecommunications traffic by way of the United States, when that traffic originates or terminates in Canada. Industry studies indicated, however, that "bypass" continues to erode market share for Canadian carriers.[11]

Telecommunications was one of the few service sectors included in the Canada–U.S. Free Trade Agreement (FTA). In the short run, its impact was considered to be minimal because the FTA "grandfathered" existing practices in both countries. Also, the scope of the agreement is limited to computerized services and "enhanced" communications services. However, its long-term effect could be substantial as it would constrain regulators on both sides from making regulatory policy based on internal considerations alone. The FTA, thus, moves telecommunications from being a narrow regulatory issue being to a much broader trade issue (Janisch and Schultz 1989).

Canadian telephone companies came under increasing pressure to cut rates in the 1980s. Bell Canada was found by the CRTC to have made "excess" profits of $206 million in 1988, and it was ordered to pay back this excess to its subscribers. In 1990, Canadian long-distance rates were 20 to 40 percent higher than in the United States. In response to these pressures, Bell Canada applied for and received permission to cut a number of rates during 1989–91. The company says its goal is to provide services that are competitive with those offered in the United States by cutting rates gradually over the next five years. These cuts, in terms of current rates and traffic volume, would amount to roughly $900 million.

New Directions in Regulatory Policy

By 1991, a number of developments were influencing the shape of new regulatory policies. First, there was the promotion by business users and acceptance by government policy makers of the competitive paradigm. Telephone companies and their trade unions oppose moves to introduce greater competition. Second, the Canada Supreme Court ruling in the case of *Alberta Government Telephones* (v.) *Canadian Radio-television and Telecommunications Commission*, [1989] 2 SRC 225, made it clear that the federal government had full authority under the constitution to regulate telecommunications, even the affairs of provincially owned companies. The court said, while these companies had "crown immunity," such immunity could be removed by federal legislation. This ruling put the onus on the federal government to come up with a new statute that will bring greater cohesion and purpose into telecommunications regulation in Canada. A bill is under preparation to be introduced to Parliament in late 1991. This bill is expected to allow the CRTC to promote greater uniformity in telecommunications policy across Canada.

The latest move toward deregulation/increased competition was being led by Unitel Communications (formerly Rogers/CNCP) and, following on their heels, by B.C. Rail/Lightel (BCRL). The Unitel application was filed with the CRTC on May 16, 1990, and sought approval to enter the long-distance market in seven provinces. Unitel requested that it be permitted to connect its private-line long-distance network into the local networks of Bell Canada, B.C. Tel, and other regional telephone companies. As part of its application, Unitel asked that it be billed for the installation of its own switches next to Bell's at a cost approximately 33 percent less than what Bell usually charges its customers. Unitel also asked the CRTC to let it charge its customers 15 percent less than the Bell rate, so that it could build up a client base and develop its network. In support of this application, Unitel argued that it will offer customers more choice, ultimately leading to lower prices and more services.

A CRTC decision in Unitel's favour would signal the introduction of competitive long-distance service in Canada. A similar application by Unitel's predecessor, CNCP, was denied in 1985. The CRTC did, however, state that it supports competition in principle. In preparation for the anticipated decision in their favour, Unitel completed its digital network from Victoria to Halifax. This would seem to be a rather expensive gamble on their part if they were not confident that the CRTC would decide in their favour, especially when the major telephone companies had just previously completed their fibre-optic link across the country. Cantel, a cellular-phone operator, has already announced that it will reroute its mobile communications traffic to Unitel if they succeed in their application. As part of the hearings on the Unitel/BCRL applications, the CRTC also considered further liberalization of the rules for resale and sharing, rate rebalancing, and entry of multiple long-distance voice competitors. CRTC hearings on Unitel's application began in April 1991, and a decision is expected by late 1991 or early 1992.

Although it is difficult to predict the outcomes of the new telecommunications legislation and the CRTC's ruling on the Unitel application, it is safe to surmise that greater competition will characterize the industry in the 1990s.[12] This means that there will be pressure on company profitability and an attempt by management to make their operations more productive. The next two sections describe the employment relationship and its response to the pressures of the 1980s, which are expected to intensify in the 1990s.

Unions in the Employment Relationship

Like other firms at that time, most telephone companies opposed early efforts by their workers to organize unions. At Bell Canada, there were numerous efforts to organize unions from the early 1900s until 1919. Although no union succeeded in forming a lasting organization, there were many instances of organized resistance against Bell, most notably the Toronto Operators' Strike of 1907.[13] From 1919 until 1944 (when the federal government adopted PC 1003), Bell sponsored its own employee organization called the Joint Conference Committees (Kuyek 1979). Soon after PC 1003 was passed by the federal government, Bell and others were obliged by law to create an arm's-length relationship with employee organizations. Consequently, a number of employee associations were registered in the years to follow: Plant Employees' Association (1944),[14] Traffic Employees' Association (1945), Accounting Employees' Association (1946), and Commercial Employees' Organization (1947). In 1949, the federal labour code was enacted, bringing labour relations in the federally regulated telephone companies under federal jurisdiction. At Bell, the various employee associations merged to form the Canadian Telephone Employee Association (CTEA) in 1949. Many of these employee associations evolved into certified unions that proved quite independent of management influence and assertive of their collective-bargaining rights. Eventually, some unions were raided, and others chose to affiliate themselves voluntarily with a national or international union. As shown in Table 11.2, independent unaffiliated unions still exist at B.C. Tel, MT&T, and Bell Canada.

The history of the Canadian Telephone Employees' Association at Bell Canada is illustrative of this pattern. The CTEA was formed in 1949 by the amalgamation of several employee associations, most of whom had their origins in Bell-sponsored employee committees under the Plan of Employee Representation (CTEA 1971). In 1949, the CTEA represented all of the operators, craft, technical, clerical, and sales workers at Bell. Despite its questionable lineage, the CTEA tried to pursue a stance independent of employer influence. This, however, has proved to be a difficult tight-rope walk for the CTEA. Unlike most other unions, the CTEA has adopted a "no strike" policy, which it has adhered to since its inception in 1949. The Communications and Electrical Workers of Canada (CWC—a Canadian breakaway from the Communication Workers of America [CWA]) successfully raided the technical employees' CTEA bargaining unit in 1975 and the operators' association, the Communications Union of Canada (itself a breakaway from the CTEA) in 1979–80. Clerical and sales employees continue to belong to two CTEA bargaining units. These units were the target of yet another (failed) raiding attempt by the CWC in 1986–87.

Apart from the independents, the major union in the industry is the CWC, with approximately 40 000 members across Canada in 1990. The International Brotherhood of Electrical Workers (IBEW), which has been active in organizing the industry since the turn of the century, currently represents some 9 000 telephone workers, mostly in western Canada. An account of early organizing efforts by the IBEW in British Columbia can be found in Bernard (1982).

Although most eligible employees are almost completely organized in the industry, there is a tiny nonunion sector that was born through the advent of cellular technology and may grow significantly in the 1990s. Two major cellular companies, Bell Cellular and CanTel, were unorganized in August 1991. Bell Cellular is a subsidiary of BCE, Inc., employing some 400 workers. The management in these companies is employing the approach used by large nonunion companies by paying wages similar to unionized wages and keeping employees excited about being part of the "team" (Foulkes 1980; Verma and Kochan 1985). This strategy to keep workers uninterested in unionization appeared to have succeeded in the first few years. At CanTel, a subsidiary of Rogers Communications, there are roughly 300 eligible employees, also without a union. At Unitel, the CWC mounted a campaign in 1987 to organize some 2000 workers, spread across the country and currently represented by an unaffiliated enterprise union. The CWC failed to get a majority of workers to sign cards, partly because, in having opposed Unitel's bid to enter the long-distance telephone business, it had not endeared itself to Unitel's workers. At N.B. Tel a large group of eligible employees are not unionized. These are the clerical support staff, sales and programmers, and engineering technicians, who, in total, account for 1000 out of a total of 2600 employees. The CWC says that it will continue to explore the possibility of organizing workers in these companies, which are likely to register strong growth in the 1990s. If the CWC or other unions fail to organize these workers, a growing part of the telephone industry could become nonunion or be represented by weak in-house unions.

Collective Bargaining—Structure and Process

BARGAINING STRUCTURE

Most telephone companies have separate bargaining units for operators, craft workers, and service employees (ie., sales and clerical). Collective bargaining by employee groups is decentralized across the country, but centralized within the firm, which in most cases coincides geographically with the province. There are more than 50 collective agreements in effect, covering more than 50 000 workers. Of these, 20 cover 500 or more workers, according to Labour Canada's collective-agreements file. The largest bargaining unit, a CTEA local, covers roughly 19 500 clerical workers in Ontario and Quebec. The CWC represents 20 500 craft and service workers in Ontario and Quebec in two bargaining units at Bell Canada, the largest group of workers within a company represented by a single union.

LABOUR-MANAGEMENT RELATIONS

The earliest managers were not only against unionization, but used tactics to oppose organizing that bordered on the illegal. Victimization, firings, "yellow-dog" contracts, and intimidation were used frequently. The organizing drives by the IBEW in the United States and Canada during the 1910s proved to be a turning point in the history of the relationship. In the United States, the IBEW led the operators in Boston in 1912 to demand better working hours (an end to split shifts and an eight-hour day). The company ultimately agreed to these demands. The IBEW's success in this context led to rapid unionization of telephone workers throughout New England. In Canada, the IBEW made a number of efforts to organize telephone workers between 1917 and 1921. Although the union failed in most of its attempts, the organizing drives influenced the companies to sponsor their own employee organizations.

The 1920s were also the decade of the rise of the *human-relations* school of management theory (Jacoby 1985). Management in the telephone companies began an era of paternalistic benevolence: employees could elect representatives who, in turn, discussed wages and working conditions with management to "mutual advantage." There was no right to strike or arbitration in the event of disputes. The company generally paid for all expenses incurred in running an employee association's office, including the salaries of its executive. Bell also set up a stock-purchase plan at the time that the Joint Conference Committees were instituted. The plan proved to be popular and helped the company increase worker identification with the company, and thus reduced the threat of unionization.[15]

Social and recreational activities that encouraged closer informal contracts between workers and first levels of management were promoted. Recognition programs, like the Distinguished Service Award (DSA), were instituted. The DSA was promoted as a badge of honour that employees were encouraged to display with pride. One of the prime objectives of the human-relations school was to prevent the formation of independent employee organizations. These policies succeeded well through the 1920s, a period of economic boom, and the 1930s, when enthusiasm for unionization was well tempered by the Great Depression.

These policies laid the foundation for management's relations with its employees for several decades to come. Even the legal requirement of PC 1003, and later the Canada Labour Code that required the employer to be at arm's length from employee organizations, did not substantially alter the paternalistic character of labour–management relations. At Bell, it was not until 1975, when the CWC succeeded in organizing the craft workers, that labour–management relations entered a new era of independent union representation.

In 1964, the IBEW started another organzing drive at Bell. This turned out to be a sustained effort that lasted three years. Though the drive was once again unsuccessful, it started a chain of events that ultimately led to the CWC victory. By the end of the IBEW drive, discontent with the CTEA had become widespread. A number of dissident organizations formed in both Ontario and Quebec. The New Union for Telephone Employees (NUTE) and Exodus were two such groups in Ontario; the Quebec movement called itself Bloc-Action. Thus when the CWC, whose forerunner, the CWA, had approached Bell workers as early as 1964, launched its organization campaign at Bell in 1975, it found a receptive audience for its appeal. The 1975 campaign moved with lightning speed for the company. Within four months, the CWC had been certified, and the company came face-to-face with an independent union for the first time in its history.

The CWC proceeded to negotiate into the collective agreement with Bell Canada a number of important changes in the terms and conditions of employment: a new grievance procedure providing the right to final arbitration of disputes; an increase in the number of shop stewards; and substantial improvements in wages and benefits. The presence of an independent union was in many ways a "shock" to Bell management. Bell responded by rationalizing its practices and professionalizing its management, a response similar to that which occurred in the United States—described by Slichter, Healy, and Livernash (1960)—after unionization's initial "shock-effect" on management. Training of managers in aspects of industrial relations became (and continues to be) a priority at the company.[16]

Telephone companies that became unionized after the regulated-monopoly regime came into place did not experience the same level of shock as did other firms operating in a more competitive environment. There is no evidence to suggest that regulatory agencies have scrutinized wages or benefits to the extent of questioning the outcomes of collective bargaining.[17] Thus, it is not clear if the regulatory process encourages management to be a "tough" bargainer. Of course, if profitability falls below the allowable rate of return, management will have some incentive to cut labour and other costs. For the most part, it appears that, in bargaining with independent unions, management was not unduly worried about its ability to pass on most of the increases in labour costs to the subscriber. This system of a bilateral monopoly set the tone for labour–management relations until the mid-1980s when the regulated monopoly system began to gradually unravel.

In 1991, labour–management relations in the industry are at a cross-roads. On the one hand, there are many positive forces helping the parties deal with each other's needs creatively. For example, most companies have years of experience in dealing with their unions. They have developed expertise and joint processes either to resolve differences or to formalize them. On the other hand, the understandings and structures they have developed over the years to deal with their problems and differences are under pressure for change occasioned by the new competitive climate and the regulatory process in the industry. Therefore, we submit that the institutionalized processes of collective bargaining and resolving labour–management conflict need to have the capacity to evolve and mature in response to changes in the competitive context of the industry. Technological change has altered the economics of the business, which, in turn, has altered the traditional balance of power between labour and management. These changes in the market and technology will require new understandings in labour–management relations if the industry is to prosper in the 1990s. In the next section, we describe the major outcomes of collective bargaining negotiated incrementally over the last twenty years.

Collective Bargaining Outcomes

WAGES

As discussed above, there are some reasons to believe that a regulated-monopoly regime may lead to higher-than-normal wages. First, both theory and some econometric evidence suggest that union wage gains under a monopoly are higher than they would be under conditions of greater competition (Freeman and Medoff 1984). Second, unless regulatory bodies rigorously question collective-bargaining outcomes, there may be a tendency for management not to bargain so "hard" and to pass on any "excess" costs to the customer.[18] It is very difficult to estimate the true monopoly effects on wages in the telephone industry because all telephone companies are regulated and, thus, there is no control group with which to compare them.

It is possible, however, to compare wages in the industry with other wages. As Table 11.4 shows, average wages for hourly paid employees in the communications industry (including other services, such as broadcasting) were $16.06 per hour— neither the highest nor the lowest in our economy. Wages in communications were roughly 23 percent higher than the average for all industries, at $13.08 per

Table 11.4
*Wages for Hourly Paid Employees in Selected Industries, 1983–1990
(dollars per hour)*

Industry	March 1983[a]	December 1990[a]	% Change
Mining	14.30	19.74	38.0
Utilities	13.66	19.37	41.8
Paper & allied	12.90	18.51	43.5
Primary metals	13.16	18.36	39.5
Petroleum & coal	14.86	17.79	19.7
Construction	14.08	17.66	25.4
Transportation equipment	11.89	16.86	41.8
Chemical	10.99	16.07	46.2
Communications	12.84	16.06	25.1
Health	11.02	15.80	43.4
Transportation	11.79	15.19	28.8
Machinery	11.16	14.94	33.9
Electrical	9.79	14.28	45.9
Services	8.63	11.57	34.1
Finance	7.58	10.95	44.5
All Industries	9.72	13.08	34.6
Consumer Price Index[b]	87.50	121.80	39.2

Sources: [a] Statistics Canada, *Employment, Earnings and Hours*, Catalogue 72-002 (Monthly) (Ottawa: Minister of Supply and Services, 1990 and 1983).
[b] Statistics Canada, *Consumer Prices and Price Indexes*, Catalogue 62-010 (Ottawa: Minister of Supply and Services, 1990 and 1983).

hour. Over the period 1983–90, the communications industry wages rose 25.1 percent compared to an all-industry averge of 34.6 percent. Only petroleum and coal industry wages rose slower than those in the communication sector.

Table 11.5 shows the maximum weekly wages for operators and craft workers in several telephone companies from 1986 to 1990. Bell Canada paid the highest wages in the industry. For operators, the other two companies in Quebec, Quebec Tel and Telebec, were trying to achieve parity with Bell rates. Newfoundland Tel was the only other company where wages rose faster over the period than those at Bell. Among the others, wages at B.C. Tel were closest to Bell's. For craft workers, the same general pattern held, except that AGT wages were closer to Bell's.

BENEFITS

Table 11.6 shows some benefits comparatively across the major telephone companies. For example, in 1990, cost-of-living adjustment (COLA) clauses were found in agreements at Bell and Quebec Tel only. In these two cases, the trigger was set around a 5.5 to 6.0 percent change in the consumer price index (CPI). The number of paid holidays was generally set at eleven except for Bell, Newfoundland Tel, and Quebec Tel where the collective agreements provide for twelve days. Overtime premium rates were typically paid at time-and-a-half, except for AGT, Manitoba Tel, and SaskTel, where it was twice the regular rate. Bell provides for a two-tier system where rates start at time-and-a-half and escalate to double rates after two hours of overtime or on weekends.

A recent trend has been to allow workers to apply for educational leave. In 1990, such provisions existed either in the collective agreement or through company policy at four companies: MTS, N.B. Tel, Newfoundland Tel, and Quebec Tel. Only in Manitoba is there a provision for the employer to reimburse the costs of education, provided that the education suits company skill requirements. While there is no contractual provision for payment of education costs at N.B. Tel and Bell, there is a long-established company practice that provides for 75 percent to 100 percent reimbursement for tuition and texts for education obtained outside the company. In most jurisdictions, however, there is no practice of the employer paying any educational-leave costs. With increasing emphasis on skill development in light of rapid changes in technology, it is likely that more companies may move to create opportunities for education in the future.

CONTRACTING-OUT

Few companies, including Bell, have negotiated any provisions with respect to contracting-out. While AGT, MTS, and SaskTel had some restrictions, at B.C. Tel, management agreed to its union's proposal to incorporate into its collective agreement a comprehensive procedural system to deal with contracting-out and technological change. The Committee on Contracting Out and Technological Change (COTC) was formed by the parties in 1978, and has been successful in reducing the number of disputes in this area going to grievance arbitration.

Table 11.5
Maximum Weekly Rates for Operators and Craft Workers in Selected Canadian Telephone Companies, 1986–1990 (expressed in dollars)

Employee Group Company	Operators						Craft					
	1986	1987	1988	1989	1990	%Change 1986–90	1986	1987	1988	1989	1990	%Change 1986–90
Bell Canada	458.07	484.82	517.09	542.94	577.80	26.1	709.03	750.44	784.21	823.42	868.71	22.5
B.C. Tel	449.05	449.05	462.35	476.35	520.10	15.8	680.90	680.90	701.35	722.40	772.95	13.5
Quebec Telephone	445.13	467.25	467.25	512.63	538.13	20.9	653.63	686.25	686.25	803.20	843.20	29.0
SaskTel	409.00	409.00	421.00	436.00	453.00	10.8	673.00	673.00	693.00	717.00	746.00	10.8
AGT	404.60	429.10	453.25	471.45	491.40	21.5	709.20	709.20	730.48	752.39	833.60	17.5
Maritime Tel and Tel	362.00	390.00	400.00	412.37	425.80	17.6	590.00	645.00	651.00	680.00	709.00	20.2
New Brunswick Tel	357.00	369.25	376.75	403.20	430.50	20.6	576.00	620.50	633.00	674.99	710.05	23.3
Manitoba Telephone System	347.90	362.95	399.70	436.45	435.01	25.0	663.50	690.46	711.35	732.65	764.55	15.2
Newfoundland Tel	338.00	354.00	372.00	393.00	436.45	29.1	565.00	592.00	623.00	658.00	697.48	23.4
Telebec Ltée.	–	–	478.46	497.60	517.50	–	–	–	741.08	770.72	801.55	–
Island Tel	–	–	–	403.95	418.55	–	–	–	640.00	672.00	704.95	–

Note: Since collective-agreement expiry dates do not coincide, wages shown here in a given year may understate or overstate the "true" differentials across firms. This may be further exacerbated by some agreements that expired in 1990, but were not renegotiated by the end of the year.

Source: Collective Agreements, various years.

TECHNOLOGICAL CHANGE

In 1991, most collective agreements contained some provisions on technological change, which was to be expected given the impact of technology in this industry. As Table 11.6 shows, the general approach was to negotiate in the area of job security (usually immunity from layoff for reasons of technological change), training and retraining rights to move to a new job, and income security in the form of severance pay, moving expenses, etc. Only B.C. Tel, AGT, and Quebec Tel had a joint committee to consider technological change issues. Of these, the B.C. Tel committee (COTC) was most involved in making decisions.

PART-TIME WORK

Part-time workers, although not new in the industry, became more formalized within the employment structure in the 1980s. Most unions negotiated benefits such as vacations and holiday pay to be paid on a prorated basis. Limitations (maximum indicated as 'Hi' and minimum indicated as 'Lo' in Table 11.6) on the working hours of part-time workers were negotiated. At SaskTel, part-time workers could not exceed 10 percent of the full-time work force, and only ex-operators could be hired for part-time work. At N.B. Tel, the cap at 35 percent was the most generous for management purposes.

ELECTRONIC MONITORING AND VDT WORK

As Table 11.6 shows, electronic monitoring of operators was conducted at most companies, though the conditions under which such surveillance could be conducted were restricted. At Bell, employees must be informed that they are being monitored. They are reported at the group level to both managers and employees. At MTS, as described later, routine monitoring was ended pursuant to the recommendations of a joint labour–management task force.

Most agreements provided for relief from long hours at computer consoles (video-display tube or VDT). In most companies, unions had also negotiated temporary reassignment for pregnant women. At MTS, VDT use along with a number of other ergonomic issues became the subject of a joint labour–management effort in 1988. This is described later in greater detail.

EMPLOYMENT EQUITY

Joint committees on employment equity existed at Bell, MTS, and SaskTel. At B.C. Tel, the union was formally consulted, but the joint-committee format was not used. In most other telephone companies, there was some degree of consultation with the union. This issue appears to be moving toward greater importance in labour–management relations coincidental with its new prominence in provincial politics.

Table 11.6
Comparison of Industrial Relations and Human-Resource Management Practices in Telephone Companies (Operators)

Practices	AGT	Bell	B.C. Tel	Is. Tel	MTS	MT&T	N.B. Tel	Nfld. Tel	Que. Tel	SaskTel
Contracting-out										
—General restrictions	Yes	—	—	—	—	—	—	—	—	—
—Specific restrictions	Notice	—	Yes	—	Yes	—	—	—	—	Yes
—Joint Committee	—	—	Yes	—	—	—	—	—	—	—
Technological Change										
—Job security	—	Yes	Yes	Yes	Yes	—	—	—	Yes	Yes
—Training/retraining	Yes	Yes	Yes	Yes	Yes	Yes	—	Yes	Yes	Yes
—Income security	Sev Pay	Many	Some	Many	Some	Mov Exp	Some	Some	Some	Some
—Joint Committee	Yes	—	Yes	—	—	—	—	—	Yes	—
Part-time Work										
—Limitation on hours	Hi	Hi/Lo	Hi	Hi/Lo	Hi/Lo	Hi/Lo	Hi/Lo	Hi/Lo	Hi	—
—Cap: % of work force	—	—	—	—	—	—	35% max	—	—10%	max[a]
—Vacation/H'day Pay	Prorata	—	Prorata	—	% pay	—	—	—	Prorata	Prorata
Electronic Monitoring	Yes	Yes	Yes	—	—	—	—	Yes	Yes	Yes
—Frequency	Quart'y	Daily	Monthly	—	—	—	—	Monthly	Daily	Daily
VDT Work: Relief	—	Yes	Yes	Yes	Yes	Yes	Yes	—	—	Yes
—Pregnancy relief	—	Yes	—	Yes	Yes	Yes	Yes	Yes	—	Yes
—Joint Committee	—	—	—	—	Yes	—	—	—	—	—

Table 11.6 (continued)

Practices	AGT	Bell	B.C. Tel	Is. Tel	MTS	MT&T	N.B. Tel	Nfld. Tel	Que. Tel	SaskTel
COLA : trigger (%CPI)	—	5.5-6%	—	—	—	—	—	—	6.0%	—
No. of Paid Holidays	11	12	11	11	11	11	11	12	12	11
Overtime premium	2X	1.5X[b]	1.5X	1.5X	2X	1.5X	1.5X	1.5X	1.5X	2X
Employment Equity										Joint
—Joint Committee	—	Yes	Consult only	—	Yes	—	—	—	—	Aff.Act.
Educational Leave	—	—	—	—	Yes	—	—	Yes	Yes	—
—Paid	—	—	—	—	Some	—	—	No	No	—

Notes: [a] Only ex-operators may be employed.
[b] Premium increases to two times regular pay for weekends and in any week in excess of two hours of overtime.
Sources: Collective agreements as of November 1990.

OTHER TERMS AND CONDITIONS

The number of paid holidays at most companies was either eleven or twelve days a year. Overtime premium in the West was generally twice the regular rate, whereas it was 1.5 times elsewhere. At Bell, the premium started at 1.5 times but went up to twice in any week that overtime exceeded two hours. Paid educational leave was almost nonexistent. Only MTS allowed some kinds of education to be on paid time. Others, such as Quebec Tel and Newfoundland Tel, allowed unpaid leave for educational purposes.

STRIKES

Historically, the industry has not been strike prone, with a few exceptions. In the 1980s, there were only a few strikes. Some companies such as AGT have not had a major strike for the last 85 years. However, B.C. Tel has had a long history of conflict, both in its early years and over the 1960–81 period (Bernard 1982). The conflict at B.C. Tel peaked in 1981 when workers occupied a number of telephone exchanges throughout the province. Part of the conflict at B.C. Tel could be attributed to conflictual labour–management relations within the firm and to the polarized nature of politics and collective bargaining generally in British Columbia. As described later, the parties attempted to build a better relationship in the 1980s and succeeded in reducing strikes (to none in the 1980s) and using arbitration and mutual negotiations to settle differences.

Labour–management relations at SaskTel saw many upheavals in the 1980s. In the early 1980s, there were no major strikes, except for some "study sessions" that lasted a day or half-day. A Progressive Conservative government was elected in 1982 and re-elected in 1986 after a twelve-year stint of NDP governments between 1971–82. The labour movement has been allied very closely with the NDP (and its predecessor, the CCF) in Saskatchewan ever since the Social Democrat party was founded by Tommy Douglas in 1932. When the contract at SaskTel expired in 1986, both sides were poised for a fight. There followed a two-year period, during which there were strikes, lockouts, violence on the picket lines, and numerous unfair-labour-practice and other statutory charges filed with the Labour Relations Board. The number of grievances going to arbitration was very high. A two-year collective agreement was signed, followed by a year during which there was no contract. In 1988, a new three-year contract was concluded. In late 1990, with the contract due to expire in 1991, the parties negotiated a new agreement. It was ratified by the workers but rejected by the company's board of directors as unacceptable. This unprecedented action on the company side was another indication of the political conflict in which labour relations at SaskTel had become entangled. In the meantime, the chairman, who was also the chief executive officer, along with two other vice-presidents, left the company. As of August 1991, the company had no chairman and no collective agreement. The attempts of both parties to put their relationship back on a professional track received a boost with the election of a more centrist NDP government in the fall of 1991.

Bell experienced two major strikes in recent years. In 1979, there was a one-month strike by craft workers. It was a rotating strike and, hence, the company had little trouble in maintaining full operations throughout the strike period. The operators went on an all-out strike at about the same time (late 1979 and early 1980) for four months. The second strike, by two CWC bargaining units representing craft workers and operators, lasted for seventeen weeks. Despite this lengthy strike, the employer managed to keep operations near normal with the help of managers and supervisors. Two factors helped the company in maintaining services to the public. First, the rapid computerization of exchanges and other equipment has made it easier for a replacement crew to take over the operations. Second, Bell's tradition of long-term service and promotion from within has created a managerial cadre familiar with skills in most jobs in the company. During the strike, managers worked long hours to install phones, climb up telephone poles, and staff operator services.[19] (Although managers kept services near normal, their ability to sustain this performance in the long run is doubtful because of the fatigue that sets in with time.) The CWC acknowledged the ability of management to operate during a strike. But rather than using the strike as an economic weapon, the union's strategy was to inflict public-relations damage on the company, a goal it achieved to some extent.[20]

*E*merging Issues in the Employment Relationship

EMPLOYEE INVOLVEMENT

Some telephone companies have taken the cue from their counterparts in other industries by introducing employee involvement (EI) programs. Although these programs take a variety of forms in practice,[21] they share some common elements. First, they all aim to increase identification with the organization and its strategic goals of increasing quality and productivity, and, thereby, competitiveness. Second, most of them exhort employees to become directly involved in solving quality and production problems on the shop floor. Third, many of these programs attempt to reorganize individual workers into teams as the unit of work, though this is not nearly as common as the preceding two features. Fourth, EI implementation almost always begins with some training in problem-solving skills, an experience for workers that is unprecedented in the history of Canadian industry. Last, some form of employee recognition, monetary or otherwise, is also an integral part of these programs, though this aspect is neither new nor universal.

As well documented in the literature, EI initiatives emerged as one of the most potent and controversial initiatives at the workplace in the 1980s (Cutcher-Gershenfeld, Kochan, and Verma 1991). For management, EI holds the prospect of enhanced productivity, which is grounded in workers' ideas and ingenuity. For many unions, though, EI is considered an attack on the independence of labour organizations, because EI programs have the potential to dilute, if not destroy, the pluralist system (Verma and Gallina 1991). Many unions fear that EI programs facilitate the dominance of corporate values that could gradually weaken labour organizations and collective bargaining. Consequently, many unions have adopted polices opposing EI programs in the workplace.[22]

The CWC, the largest union in the industry, has taken a somewhat different stance on this issue. Their approach has been to accept the principal goals of EI as a step toward achieving greater worker control over the workplace. However, they disagree with management (and agree with other unions) about who should control and direct EI efforts. Their support for worker participation and involvement is similar to that of the Communication Workers of America (CWA), which has an even longer tradition of supporting some forms of EI in the United States (Kochan, Katz, and Mower 1984). In Canada, the CWC adopted a policy statement on "work reorganization" at their annual convention in June 1990 that effectively endorses EI efforts in principle. It also identifies other guidelines that EI programs must follow if they want union involvement and support.

Bell Canada and the CWC

At the 1990 round of bargaining between Bell and the CWC, the union got its first chance to implement some of these ideas at the bargaining table. The following initial proposal was tabled by the union.

CWC Proposal on Reorganization of Work

Should the Company undertake a program of work reorganization it will be done under the following principles:

1. Full recognition of the provisions of the Collective Agreement.
2. Employees will not be laid off as a result of improved productivity resulting from the reorganization.
3. No reorganization to be undertaken without the agreement of the Union.
4. Committees dealing with reorganization to have equal Union/Management representation and decisions arrived at will be by consensus only. Where no consensus is arrived at no workplace change will take place.
5. All bargaining unit employees are to be eligible to membership on workplace committees on a rotational basis.
6. Employees serving on workplace committees to be given adequate training. Training to be paid for by the Company.

7. Wages and expenses for employees on workplace committees to be paid by the Company.
8. Certain aspects of workplace reorganization may require membership approval by a referendum vote.
9. Establishment of a jointly administered Sectoral Training Fund based on the program established between CWC and the electronic and electrical manufacturing industry.
10. A commitment to equal opportunity for employees to take advantage of training.
11. A commitment to job enrichment to give employees more meaningful jobs as well as enhanced employment opportunities.
12. Recognition that certain aspects of workplace reorganization may require membership approval in a similar manner to the collective agreement.

By this time, Bell had already put in place at least two different EI programs, called "EQUIPE" and "IMPACT." (These are described below.) During negotiations, the union found stiff resistance from the company over their proposals because they deviated from the company's view of the future in two important respects. First, these proposals would give the union a veto over EI implementation. The company viewed this provision as an unacceptable limitation on its right to manage the workplace. Second, these proposals ask for joint governance of the EI process. Management at Bell felt that, while some degree of joint governance may be possible in the future, the proposals went too far at the time. In other words, these proposals were seen as too much change in too short a time.

Bell countered the union's EI proposals by suggesting that a joint committee be struck with a mandate to explore further co-operation in this area. The final agreement was to sign a Letter of Intent (as opposed to a clause in the agreement):

> A Consultative Committee, composed of three (3) representatives of the Company and three (3) Officers of the CWC or their delegates, will be established to provide a forum for discussions on various concepts of training and workplace reorganization.
>
> The Committee will meet within three (3) months following the signing of the two above-mentioned Collective Agreements and will thereafter jointly determine the frequency of its subsequent meetings.

Clearly, this initiative is a slow start relative to labour–management EI programs elsewhere. However, this could yet prove to be a significant development at Bell, as well as in the telephone industry. Both the company and the union are leaders within the industry, and their patterns are often emulated in a variety of other contexts.

The management of Bell Canada on its own has investigated a variety of employee-involvement initiatives since 1985. Working with many consultants, including the American Productivity Centre, the company introduced a program called IMPACT (Innovative Methods and Plans in ACTion). This project was focussed exclusively on addressing the issue of white-collar productivity. EQUIPE (Excellence through Quality, Initiative, and Participation of Everyone),[23] which put groups of employees through training in problem-solving skills, was a subsequent initiative that grew out of the experience with IMPACT. More than 150 districts throughout the company participated in some form of productivity- or quality-improvement process.[24] The EQUIPE groups achieved the stated goals in many ways, although they never spread completely through the organization.

These employee-involvement initiatives were complemented by other efforts. A suggestion scheme, implemented in 1985, generated over 22 000 suggestions in the first five years, of which some 6 percent were accepted, resulting in a net benefit of $27 million to the company. Bell initiated a Productivty College in 1985, and the Bell Quality Institute in 1987, to provide intensive training in the area of productivity and quality. The company also implemented a variety of employee-recognition programs in various regional departments.

By 1991, as the company continued its efforts in this area, it could look back to some progress as well as some looming challenges. After five years of experience with employee involvement, management appeared committed to move further in this direction. In moving ahead, though, it had to decide whether employee involvement would retain the format of a program such as EQUIPE, or whether its features should be integrated into the job itself to create self-supervising, autonomous, work teams.[25] In addition, given the developments in collective bargaining, further progress would mean some degree of union involvement, and likely more power sharing with the union. In that event, both management and union would have to grapple with the structure and process of joint "ownership" of the employee-involvement process.

Manitoba Telephone System (MTS) and the CWC

The Manitoba Telephone System (MTS) is owned by the Province of Manitoba and provides telephone services to all parts of the province. Its employees are represented by two different unions in three locals. The operators are represented by Local 5 of the Communication and Electrical Workers of Canada (CWC), the clerical and sales employees by Local 7 of the CWC, and the technical employees by the IBEW. A co-operative joint effort of the company and the CWC has attempted to address concerns for better working conditions, as well as better customer service.

The operators are a distinct group within the company. Their numbers rose slightly, from 687 in 1981 to roughly 700 in 1990. Almost half of the operators, who work full-time, part-time, and on a term basis, are located in Winnipeg. Among the Winnipeg operators, 90 percent are female. More than half of them are 20–40 years of age, and a similar number come from single-income families. Almost 80 percent of them have obtained at least a high school diploma, and 25 percent have a college diploma or some university education. About 40 percent have 0–4 years seniority, while 22 percent have more than fifteen years experience in the company.

In January 1986, telephone operators in the Directory Assistance office in Winnipeg reported experiencing "shock"-like incidents in the days and months following an electrical power failure and surge. The "shocks" were felt as sudden tingling sensations in the operators' arms and on one side of their bodies. There were also reports of numbness, acute onset of headache, dizziness, and extreme soreness in facial and neck areas.[26] In June 1986, telephone operators in the Winnipeg Long-Distance Toll (TOPS) office reported similar experiences. In September 1986, TOPS operators exercised the right to refuse work that they considered to be unsafe, and they walked off the job. By October 1986, the government again issued a stop-work order, and operator offices were closed, telephone traffic was rerouted to other regions, while terminals and staff were relocated.

During 1986 and 1987, various investigations sought to determine the technical, ergonomic, and environmental causes of the "shock"-like incidents. Meanwhile, reports of incidents persisted, and managers and supervisors in Operator Services experienced their own morale problems and frustrations in dealing with an on-going situation exacerbated by the coinciding media attention and labour–management tension. In November 1987, a high-level Engineering and Medical Review concluded that the equipment and electrical systems were not a source of the "shock"-like incidents; however, some of the incidents were likely the result of the effects of the accumulation of electrostatic charge. Nevertheless, the primary cause was seen to be occupational stress.

Documentation of similar investigations confirmed for MTS management and for CWC union representatives that the symptoms reported by the operators were, for the most part, attributable to the stress inherent in operators' highly repetitive, closely measured, high-productivity tasks. During 1986 and 1987, this stress was increased by fears and poor communication associated with the initial "shock"-like incidents.

In February 1988, the CWC and MTS agreed to a series of immediate actions and a longer-term "Trial Change" project, aimed at reducing the sources of stress for telephone operators and managers. A Start-Up Committee of union and management representatives set up an Operator Services project, the purpose of which was:

> to [investigate] trial approaches to organizational and managerial systems that will improve the working environment by reorganizing work, improving communications and empowering employees and managers to be more directly involved in decisions, while maintaining and improving the level of customer service.

MTS Executive approval was given to the project, and the terms were specified in a Letter of Understanding signed by national officers of the CWC and the executive vice-president of MTS.

Following the Start-Up Committee's selection of an external consultant, a

Design Team of three union and three management representatives from Operator Services assumed responsibility for the design, implementation, and evaluation of the trial project. In June 1988, the Design Team began its work, and, in November, a "Trial Office" was opened within the Ft. Rouge building in Winnipeg. The "Trial Office" consisted of 40 operators and an assistant manager, randomly selected from volunteers, to put to trial a number of substantial changes in job design, work-procedures training, and participative management.

As the time neared for evaluation and decision making relative to the "Trial Change" project in Operator Services, MTS and CWC established a group of senior corporate and union representatives to act as trustees for this project; the Trustees' Action Statement stated that its mission was "to improve the Work Environment and the Quality of Customer Service, by Changing Approaches to Management and the Organization of Work in MTS Operator Services, in a cost-effective manner." In May 1989, the Design Team conducted an evaluation of the experience of the "Trial Office," and, in July 1989, they made recommendations for system-wide changes to the Trustee Group of senior CWC and MTS representatives.

Recommendations

1. Smaller work units be established at the Winnipeg Region Operator Services.
2. Each manager and operating staff member receive education for at least 5 days per year on the following aspects of performance management: industrial relations, employment equity, corporate strategic plan, new MTS services, MTS training courses, budgets, business operation and planning, annual report.
4. Operator training be given priority as a long term means of improving customer service.
5. Cross Training of operating staff on both TOPS and MIDAS throughout the Winnipeg operator service units. New operating staff will be hired on the expectation of being cross trained.
6. Remote monitoring in operator services be discontinued immediately. This does not preclude the necessity to conduct surveillance for security and/or service analysis reasons. Adjacent monitoring be utilized for development and training and as a means to provide operator feedback.
7. All operating staff receive education on what customer service really means in different areas.
8. Unlimited trading of shifts and partial shifts between operating staff including IOU trades be adopted on the following basis. All trades are to be entered in the trade book. In the event of a dispute, trades entered in the book will stand.
9. Information and exchange meetings be scheduled every month. Matters relating to collective agreement will not be discussed.

During the summer and fall of 1989, the union and management trustees reviewed the recommendations in detail. In January 1990, the trustees signed a Memorandum of Agreement on changes in Operator Services, which they recommended to their respective constituents. In February and March 1990, the recommendations were approved by the MTS Executive and ratified by the full membership of CWC Local 5.

The "Trial Office" has continued to function throughout this time of discussion and ratification, and will be transformed into a work group within the redesigned organizational structure of Operator Services in Winnipeg. The trustees played a key role in facilitating an agreement by their principals on a set of recommendations for changes in Operator Services. During the foreseeable future, the MTS–CWC trustees hope to continue to give *high-level visibility* and support to the ongoing change process, while ensuring that proper *evaluation* is made of the changes, and to facilitate *consultation* and participative processes for workplace reorganization in Operator Services.

Quality Circles at B.C. Tel

B.C. Tel has had a history of labour unrest dating back to the 1960s. This is demonstrated by the bitter dispute and long strike in which workers occupied a number of telephone exchanges across the province in 1981 (Bernard 1982). But, as technological advances during the 1970s and the 1980s gradually reduced the company's dependence on workers, management could increasingly maintain and operate most equipment and provide many customer services during a strike. This loss of economic power by the union contributed, in part, to the militancy of union members during those years.

In the 1980s, both sides made efforts to improve their relationship. As a result, there has been no strike in the company since 1981. By 1991, both company and union representatives agreed that labour relations had improved considerably, compared to those of the 1968–81 period. The relationship in 1991 was characterized by "friendly" rapport between union leaders and management, and some "agreements to disagree." There are some examples of areas in which the parties work together, such as a joint committee on jurisdictional disputes and the Joint Standing Committee on Contracting Out and Technological Change (COTC). The COTC was formed in 1978 to provide a co-operative forum for exchange of information on technological change and to allow for dialogue and problem solving in cases of contracting-out. The success of this committee, by 1991, was reflected in the very low incidence of arbitrations concerning technological change.[27]

After the 1981 strike, B.C. Tel introduced quality circles, which were becoming popular in the United States at the time. Membership in the circles was voluntary for employees. The circles grew gradually in number, to reach a peak of 90 in 1987. Each circle consisted of approximately ten employees. Thus, at its peak, the program covered roughly 10 percent of the work force at the company. The circles met once a week for an hour on company-paid time to discuss quality of service and other on-the-job problems. By 1991, the enthusiasm had waned some-what, and the number of circles still meeting every week had dropped to 60. The company was moving gradually toward task-specific teams, which were constituted and assigned by management. In addition to the circles, the company also ran the following programs: the Speak Out program, the Star Suggestion program, and a video newsletter to update employees on company plans and progress.

The Telecommunications Workers Union (TWU) opposed company initiatives in this area right from the beginning. The union felt that employee-involvement initiatives were management attempts to increase worker identification with the goals of the company and to get workers to accept management-initiated changes without scrutiny (Shniad 1983). The union held that the programs had the appearance of giving workers input rather than real say in decisions. When the management proceeded with its plans to introduce circles, the union set up a "Quality Circle Fightback Committee" with the mandate to educate workers in the dangers of getting involved in the circles. Although no systematic assessment of these efforts were made, the slow growth and later decline of the circles program suggested that the union countereducation plan had some negative impact on the success of the program.

Other Telephone Companies

Among other firms, AGT tried to introduce employee involvement without union support. To bring about greater awareness of quality and related problems, the company began training workers in a "total quality" program. The union, an IBEW local, was not ideologically opposed to such efforts, but wanted the company to negotiate its terms. AGT thus faced the choice of either proceeding on its own and thereby risking union opposition, or negotiating some accommodation that might include joint ownership of the employee-involvement initiatives.

At N.B. Tel, an employee-involvement program was started in 1988 in one of the smaller departments. Although the union is not formally a partner, it has been kept informed of the developments. The union's national representative and local president attended presentations on current status made by representatives of Design Teams to the Steering Committee, composed of the Executive and Department Heads. By mid-1991, the initiative had spread to parts of one of the larger operating departments, and management intends to extend its scope in the future. Management's intent is to keep the union informed of the developments, but it was unclear whether union support or involvement would be formalized in due course.

As further deregulation brings competitive pressures to bear on the industry, we may expect to see more EI initiatives. To the extent that management favours these EI programs, the prospect of implementing these systems is aided by the CWC's proactive and positive stance on the issue. There will be continuing pressure, though, on management to move EI toward joint governance, and on the union to concede on demands for veto rights or other methods of exclusive control.

Some researchers have argued that the EI process is not easily captured within the traditional mode of substantive rules in the collective agreement (Verma 1991; Cutcher-Gershenfeld 1991). Rather, they are best managed jointly through procedural arrangements like joint governance (Kochan and Cutcher-Gershenfeld 1988). Thus, companies and unions face two scenarios: move toward joint governance or risk losing the initiative either to labour opposition or to the worker apathy that can come with management dominance.

EMPLOYMENT SECURITY

Although there were no major contractual developments in collective bargaining, the telephone industry was one of the very few sectors to provide virtual employment security in the 1980s. Significant layoffs were rare among telephone companies, even as many other industries downsized their work forces. Any cuts were managed through attrition, voluntary separation packages, early retirements, or cuts in part-time and casual work. When these measures were insufficient, employees in the telephone industry were retrained and reassigned to another department or location.

There are two major factors contributing to employment security in the industry. First, demand for telephone and telecommunications services does not fluctuate very much with the business cycle. Overall, the demand has been increasing monotonically over time, along with the population. An economic recession in Canada, and fluctuating housing starts, affect demand for business use and home-subscriber services, respectively, but the variations are relatively small. Second, the paternalistic traditions of the early years have yielded a value system in which management puts a high priority on employment security. At Bell, it is a long-standing tradition to use layoffs as a last resort. At N.B. Tel, the policy is more explicitly committed to "no layoffs." As discussed above, job security is sometimes guaranteed in the agreement, such as at B.C. Tel, under conditions of technological change. At SaskTel, the union proposed to formalize a general employment guarantee in writing, but was turned down by the company. There was little pressure to formalize employment security in the contract in the 1980s, in large part because layoffs had not been a concern.

FLEXIBILITY

At a number of telephone companies changes were made in the collective agreement to increase flexibility in work assignment and hours. For example, at MTS, changes were negotiated to allow for cross-training within the craft classifications. The intent was to enhance customer services by responding quickly to service requests. At Bell, the collective agreement provides for home dispatch, which allows craft workers to proceed directly to a work site from home instead of commuting first to the employer's premises and thence to the work site. Also, some sales staff are "telecommuting" to work by connecting to firm computers from home. Overall, flexibility was not a major issue in the industry in the 1980s, as most jobs were not very narrowly defined.

SHARING PROGRAMS

Most unions remained either cool or opposed to the concept of profit-sharing and other such compensation plans that are contingent on performance, and hence variable over time (e.g., gain sharing). In 1991, there were no such plans in place in the industry for rank-and-file employees. Bell, among others, operates a gain-sharing plan for management employees. N.B. Tel operates a Team Share Plan, which rewards all non-union employees (for example, managerial, clerical, sales, computer programmers, and technical staff) when the company exceeds certain financial and customer-satisfaction objectives. The same plan was offered to the union during the last round of negotiations, but was rejected by the union's negotiation team. Despite the lack of developments so far, it appeared likely that this issue will remain on the collective-bargaining agenda in the 1990s.

COMMUNICATION AND FEEDBACK

The use of employee surveys to assess attitudes toward work, supervision, and the organization increased in the 1980s. In 1990, Bell asked 3000 of its employees to complete a survey, and 75 percent responded. The survey was not slated to be conducted periodically, but it is highly likely that more surveys would be taken in the future. At AGT, surveys are taken regularly. Company-wide surveys are conducted every three to five years, and departmental surveys are done almost once a year. N.B. Tel and SaskTel had not conducted a survey for the last five years. At B.C. Tel, surveys were taken every two years during much of the 1980s. Results were disseminated widely, and discussion among employees and managers was encouraged to develop corrective policy measures.

Most companies moved their communication programs to high gear during the 1980s. The spread of video technology made it common for companies to issue video newsletters. A typical newsletter would feature a message from the chief executive officer, followed by briefs about past results, current plans, and future outlook. The assumption underlying these efforts was that a visual medium would be more effective in increasing employee identification with the firm and its goals. Despite the fact that communication initiatives attracted substantial corporate budgets, there was no assessment of the efficacy of these new methods. In addition, all companies used the more traditional methods of publishing newsletters and brochures to inform employees. There was also an increase in the use of employee meetings as a way to keep employees informed and provide an opportunity for employees to ask questions of their own.

JURISDICTIONAL DISPUTES AT B.C. TEL

As outlined earlier, the telephone industry saw a great deal of automation and computerization over the last 25 years. One of the human-resource implications of technological advancements was that the distinctions between the work of many groups of employees became blurred. Digital switching brought the work of many bargaining-unit members (i.e., Technicians) close to a nonbargaining-unit person-nel. As these distinctions blurred, jurisdictional disputes both within and across the bargaining-unit boundaries became common. What follows is an account of a dispute at B.C. Tel, and its successful resolution within the procedures of collec-tive bargaining.

The trouble began in the mid-1960s, when the engineering assistants (who had previously been outside the bargaining unit) decided to join the union. The com-pany voluntarily accepted this decision of the engineering assistants, and there-after the engineering assistants were covered by the collective agreement. The problem was then, and still is, that much of the work done by engineering assis-tants (now called technicians) was the same or similar to work done by (graduate) engineers and other excluded employees. With the accelerating rate of introduc-tion of new technology in the last twenty years, a multitude of new jobs was creat-ed in the company—many of which were in excluded positions—doing work that resembled the work done, particularly, by technicians. Not surprisingly, the union became concerned about the "drain of bargaining-unit work" to management be-cause during the same era the number of Technician Positions decreased.

The other important development during the period 1969–81 was the fact that, when negotiations for renewals of the collective agreement broke down and the union went on strike, the company continued to operate during these work stop-pages. The fact that the company's operations had become increasingly automat-ed, coupled with the fact that a substantial number of workers were excluded employees, made it easier for the company to continue to operate during a strike or lockout. As a result, the union attempted to stop work from being "siphoned away" from the bargaining unit. Accordingly, the union made contracting-out and work jurisdiction key demands in the 1977 negotiations. The parties resolved the contracting out issue in 1977 when they agreed to the Joint Standing Com-mittee on Contracting Out and Technological Change (COTC) to regulate this practice. However, no such agreement was achieved about work jurisdiction. This issue remained a key union bargaining demand in 1979 and 1981. The union also pursued a vigorous litigation campaign in front of the Canadian Labour Rela-tions Board (CLRB) in an attempt to gain bargaining authority over many workers in excluded positions who were doing similar work to that being done in the bar-gaining unit. The union sought a declaration by the CLRB that the union's bar-gaining certificate covered these positions. The CLRB ultimately ruled against the union in a series of decisions, culminating in Decision #206 in August 1979.

When the union lost on the litigation front, it turned its attention back to the bargaining table and initiated a process that led ultimately to arbitration. But, at all times, the root of the problem from the union's side was its perception that bargaining-unit work was increasingly being done by excluded persons. The union's response to this perceived threat to its authority was to press for exclusive jurisdiction over what it claims to be "bargaining-unit work."

The arbitrator, in his award, proposed criteria that recognized the union's legitimate interests in preserving its authority over bargaining-unit work, while at the same time provided the company with a degree of flexibility in making work assignments that was not evident in the union's exclusivity proposal. Specifically, the award rejected the union's position that *all* elements, tasks, and duties contained in the bargaining-unit job descriptions should be considered job duties within the sole jurisdiction of the bargaining unit. The award held that a joint Work Jurisdiction Committee, with equal representation from both sides, would be struck and would have a permanent umpire, a mediator-arbitrator.

The award also outlined the criteria under which the committee and the umpire were to resolve disputes. The umpire and committee were to be guided by the principle that the core functions of work encompassed by the job descriptions referenced in the collective agreement shall be work that remains the exclusive work of bargaining unit members. For the more peripheral functions of bargaining-unit jobs, decisions about work assignments were to be guided by the need for the parties to make sensible judgments that reflect their mutual interests in preserving and enhancing the integrity of the bargaining unit, the skills of bargaining-unit jobs, the job security of bargaining-unit members, and the need for the company to make decisions about the deployment of human resources that will produce greater efficiency and competitiveness. Under the union's exclusivity proposal, the questions that the Work Jurisdiction Committee and the umpire would face include: the issue of whether there was *any* overlap between the elements, tasks, and duties in the job descriptions and the work being done by excluded staff. Under the award, the Work Jurisdiction Committee and umpire would focus on the nature, amount, and frequency of the work that is being performed by both bargaining unit and excluded personnel. The committee and umpire would then make a judgment of whether the assignment of this work was inconsistent with a sensible balance of the legitimate interests of the parties, as recognized in the award.

There was some latitude in these criteria to resolve work-jurisdiction issues. This degree of flexibility in the award could prove to be the virtue rather than the vice of this work-jurisdiction mechanism. The new mechanism was designed to recognize the essential jurisdictional constituency of the parties (i.e., their "jurisdictional rights"), and to channel decisions at the work-assignment level, where there is a potential conflict between the parties' bargaining authority (rights) to a process that identifies their essential interests and seeks to resolve them through the mechanisms of negotiation, mediation, and arbitration.

This dispute-resolution system was designed to be a quick and inexpensive tool where the emphasis is on problem solving and accommodation of interests, rather than on the adjudication of rights. The intent was to remove these disputes from the laps of third-party adjudicators and place the responsibility squarely on the shoulders of the parties to arrive at creative solutions to these problems. The experience of the parties since the Committee was struck in 1988 had been mixed. The Union continues to be frustrated by what it perceives to be the lack of compliance by the company in recognizing its jurisdiction over bargaining unit work despite the guidance of the award and the dispute resolution system that has been established to govern this issue. However, the parties continue to attempt to make the system work effectively and are not anxious to abandon the system in favour of other more confrontational means of resolving this issue.

*F*uture Directions

*I*n many ways the pressures for change in the telephone industry had only begun to intensify in the 1980s. The pace of change in technology was rapid, but these shocks were cushioned, to some extent, by the regulated monopoly regime. While there was erosion of the monopoly at the terminal end, and some "bypass" in long-distance communication, the bulk of the system remained sheltered from both deregulation and open competition.

Correspondingly, most features of the industrial relations system remained unchanged, and where change did take place it was gradual. Most firms maintained their system of virtual employment security. Labour–management relations remained at arm's length, with a relatively low level of strike activity. Some changes were negotiated to improve flexibility and to protect job and income security in the event of technological change. Tentative steps were taken toward greater employee involvement, communication, and feedback. MTS was the only company to invite substantive union participation in the process, while Bell agreed to investigate future projects within a joint committee. At other companies, employee involvement was mostly a management initiative with no (or negative in the case of B.C. Tel) input from the union. The dominant union in the industry, CWC, adopted a proactive and positive stance on employee involvement so long as EI did not undercut the union's collective–bargaining authority.

The 1990s are likely to bring greater pressures on the industry to change both its business and its industrial relations practices. In the aftermath of the Supreme Court of Canada ruling on the AGT case, the federal government's new communications bill is expected to unveil a policy framework for the 1990s. Although its contents are not known in mid-1991, it is expected that the framework would include an endorsement for greater competition. The Unitel and BCRL applications before the CRTC in 1991 are also expected to be successful—if not immediately and fully, at least gradually and in some aspects. Thus, telephone companies can expect to experience more competition in various parts of their operations.

However, more competition does not always have to signify threats to a business enterprise. For example, if the CRTC decides to dilute the monopoly regime, it may also create opportunities for the telephone companies to seek permission to enter new businesses made possible because of technological advances. In the United States, AT&T and other Bell companies have been permitted by the regulators to offer home-shopping and banking services over telephone lines. The advent of fibre optics would also allow telephone companies to offer video services at home. These new businesses would likely be more competitive than the phone business has been in the past. To enter these businesses successfully, phone companies would have to be more aggressive in the market and more innovative in product lines.

In the area of human resources and industrial relations, the telephone companies appear to be well poised to take advantage of the gradual increase in competition. Their strengths lie in a trained work force, high levels of job security, a generally forward-looking management, and a willingness to accept and work with unions. The gradual exploration and introduction of innovations, such as employee involvement and joint initiatives with the union, though slow in pace, are commendable because the industry is exploring them *without* an immediate crisis.

As discussed in Chapter 12, the common experience suggests that, until economic pressures build up to a crisis point, usually indicated by substantial loss of economic profits, it is difficult for a change process to set in. Given the regulated nature of the telephone industry, it is unlikely that most telephone companies would face the financial crises that firms experience in unregulated industries, such as steel or automobiles. The impetus for change, therefore, has to be proactive and generated from within, rather than under the coercive influence of external forces. If telephone companies continue the momentum for change, they could transform their human-resource management from an older paternalistic, hierarchical, and authoritarian style to a participative, self-governing, egalitarian organization, *without* going through a crisis. This could be called the "high road" or the "telephone route" to the 1990s.

The evolution of the "telephone route" is far from assured, though. Much depends on the choices that the parties make to nurture the seeds that have been sown in the 1980s. As the experience of B.C. Tel in the 1960s and 1970s and Sask-Tel in the 1980s shows, it is possible for any initiative, no matter how creative or needed, to be mired in labour–management conflict. As competition increases, the cost of such conflicts would be even higher than in the past. The comfortable alliance between paternalistic ideas and an assured business under regulation would also militate against any attempts to devolve management rights and power. Various programs to increase employee participation and to "empower" workers could remain as window-dressing for an inherently authoritative and directive organization. For most companies, partnership with the union (such as between Bell Canada and the CWC) is a strong possibility, despite the absence of a financial crisis. As competition increases, these opportunities would narrow as the parties would have more conflict on their agenda. The successful evolution of a "telephone route" would be a major achievement, as it would demonstrate that change and restructuring can be accomplished proactively, without going through the shock of a crisis.

REFERENCES

Babe, Robert E. 1990. *Telecommunications in Canada*. Toronto: University of Toronto Press.

Bernard, Elaine. 1982. *The Long Distance Feeling: A History of the Telecommunications Workers' Union*. Vancouver, BC: New Star Books.

Canadian Telephone Employees' Association (CTEA). 1971. *A History of Organization*. Toronto: January.

Cutcher-Gershenfeld, Joel. 1991. "The Impact of Economic Performance of a Transformation in Workplace Relations." *Industrial and Labor Relations Review*, 44/2 (January), 241–60.

Cutcher-Gershenfeld, Joel, Thomas A. Kochan, and Anil Verma. 1991. "Recent Developments in U.S. Employee Involvement Initiatives: Erosion or Transformation." In David B. Lipsky and David Lewin, eds., *Advances in Industrial and Labor Relations*, Vol. 5. Greenwich, CT: JAI Press Inc. 1–31.

Ehrenberg, Ronald G. 1979. *The Regulatory Process and Labor Earnings*. New York: Academic Press.

Foulkes, Fred K. 1980. *Personnel Policies in Large Nonunion Companies*. Englewood Cliffs, NJ: Prentice-Hall Inc.

Freeman, Richard B. and James L. Medoff. 1984. *What Do Unions Do?* New York: Basic Books.

Hendricks, Wallace. 1986. "Collective Bargaining in Regulated Industries." In David B. Lipsky and David Lewin eds., *Advances in Industrial and Labor Relations*, Vol. 3. Greenwich, CT: JAI Press Inc. 21–42.

———. 1987. "Telecommunications." In David B. Lipsky and Clifford B. Donn, eds., *Collective Bargaining in American Industry: Contemporary Perspectives and Future Directions*. Toronto: Lexington Books. 103–33.

Jacoby, Sanford M. 1985. *Employing Bureaucracy: Managers, Unions, and the Transformation of Work in American Industry, 1900–1945*. New York: Columbia University Press.

Janisch, Hudson N., and Richard J. Schultz. 1989. *Exploiting the Information Revolution: Telecommunications Issues and Options for Canada*. Montreal: Royal Bank of Canada, October.

Klein, Alice, and Wayne Roberts. 1974. "Besieged Innocence: The 'Problem' and Problem of Women— Toronto, 1896–1914." In Janice Acton, Penny Goldsmith, and Bonnie Shepard, eds., *Women at Work: Ontario 1850–1930*. Toronto: Canadian Women's Educational Press. 244–49.

Koch, Marianne, David Lewin, and Donna Sockell. 1987. "The Determinants of Bargaining Structure: A Case Study of AT&T." In David Lewin, David B. Lipsky, and Donna Sockell, eds., *Advances in Industrial and Labor Relations*, Vol. 4. Greenwich, CT: JAI Press Inc. 223–51.

Kochan, Thomas A., Harry C. Katz, and Nancy R. Mower. 1984. *Worker Participation and American Unions: Threat or Opportunity?* Kalamazoo, MI: W.E. Upjohn Institute for Employment Research.

Kochan, Thomas A., and Joel Cutcher-Gershenfeld. 1988. Institutionalizing and Diffusing Innovations in Industrial Relations. Washington, DC: U.S. Dept. of Labor, Bureau of Labor-Management Relations and Cooperative Programs.

Kuyek, Joan. 1979. *The Phone Book: Working at Bell*. Kitchener, ON: Between the Lines.

Sangster, Joan. 1978. "The 1907 Bell Telephone Strike: Organizing Women Workers." *Labour/Le Travailleur*, 3: 109–29.

Shniad, Sid. 1983. "We're All in This Together—Or Are We? An Alternate Perspective on Q.W.L., Tech Change and the Current Economic Crisis." Paper presented to the B.C. Worklife Conference "Bridging the Gaps," September 23, Vancouver, B.C.

Slichter, Sumner H., James J. Healy, and E. Robert Livernash. 1960. *The Impact of Collective Bargaining on Management*. Washington, DC: The Brookings Institution.

Statistics Canada. 1988. *Telephone Statistics 1987*, Catalogue 56-203. Ottawa: Minister of Supply and Services.

Verma, Anil. 1991. "Restructuring in Industrial Relations and the Role for Labor." In Margaret Hallock and Steve Hecker, eds., *Labor in a Global Economy: A U.S.–Canadian Symposium*, 47–61. Eugene, OR: University of Oregon Press.

Verma, Anil, and Mark Gallina. 1991. "Radical and Unionist Critiques of Direct Worker Participation." Presented to the Third European Regional Congress of the International Industrial Relations Association, September. Bari-Naples, Italy. 23–26.

Verma, Anil, and Thomas A. Kochan. 1985. "The Growth and Nature of the Nonunion Sector Within a Firm." In Thomas A. Kochan, ed., *Challenges and Choices Facing American Labor*. Cambridge, MA: MIT Press. 89–118.

ENDNOTES

1. We wish to acknowledge the assistance of many induviduals, although it is impossible to mention everyone who provided information contained in this chapter. The contributions of Steve Bedard, Raymond Buist, Herb Doucet, Jack Lax, Richard Long, Bryan Luce, Thomas Mullins, Tom Panelli, Michael Podovilnikoff, Denis Sutton, Sheila Whiteley, and participants in the Industrial Relations in Canadian Industry conference held at Queen's University in April 1991 were especially helpful. Timely and able research assistance was provided by Peter Seidl and Angela Zezza. Financial support from the Social Sciences and Humanities Research Council and the National Centre for Management Research and Development is gratefully acknowledged.

2. In this chapter, we limit our analysis to Canada's telephone companies. Our scope, therefore, is much narrower than the telecommunications industry, which includes a host of other groups such as telegraph, broadcasting, and some communication equipment-manufacturing firms. However, we do include the full range of services that telephone companies have come to provide (i.e., carrying signals, other than voice, such as data and pictures).

3. A recent Canada Supreme Court decision has ruled that such provincial Crown corporations fall under federal regulatory jurisdiction. *See Alberta Government Telephones* v. *Canadian Radio-television and Telecommunications Commission*, [1989] 2 SCR 225. The next section discusses the implications of this decision for future regulation of the industry.

4. Other municipally-owned systems include those in Thunder Bay, Kenora, Dryden (all from Ontario), and Prince Rupert (B.C.). In Ontario alone, there are 32 independent telephone systems.

5. Northern Telephone's principal exchanges are: Cobalt, Haileybury, Kapuskasing, Kirkland Lake, New Liskeard, and Timmins.

6. The historical account that follows is derived largely from Babe (1990), Chapters 6–10.

7. See Babe (1990, 140–43) for a more detailed description of the empirical evidence on profitability of local services.

8. To this list one may add computer-aided manufacturing, computerized inventory control, electronic funds transfer, voice mail, home information services, facsimile and electronic banking from home. This list is not exhaustive, as there are myriad services that are now possible through digital telecommunication networks.

9. For more detailed account of changes in regulation of the U.S. telephone system and its effect on industrial relations, see Hendricks (1986; 1987) and Koch, Lewin, and Sockell (1987).

10. The telecommunications industry accounted for 2.7 percent of the GNP in 1968. Twenty years later, it had increased its share to 6 percent (or US$4.9 trillion) of the GNP. The long-distance companies, both AT&T and most of the new ones, remained profitable and continued to invest heavily in long distance networks (Janisch and Schultz 1989, 7).

11. See "Teleglobe warns of 'bypassing' crisis," *Financial Post*, August 15, 1991.

12. In 1991, the Department of Communications announced new rules making it easier for individuals and companies to license low-cost microwave communication links that could connect telephones and other equipment over short distances, typically up to 30 km ("Rule changes may lower phone bills," *Financial Post*, August 21, 1991). Such connections could provide competition for the telephone companies in local services. If Unitel succeeds in its application, these local networks could plug into Unitel's long-distance network to fully bypass the telephone companies. This is yet another example of the gradual erosion of the monopoly regime.

13. The strike was short but newsworthy. Within days of the strike, a royal commission was appointed, with John Winchester and William Lyon Mackenzie King serving as commissioners. Their report indicted the company for creating an extremely stressful work environment for the operators and recommended a number of improvements. Largely as a result of the report, the company reduced the workday to seven-and-a-half hours and instituted more frequent and longer rest periods. For a more detailed description of the strike, see Sangster (1978) and Klein and Roberts (1974).

14. The PEA was first registered in 1943 under the Ontario Collective Bargaining Act. For further details, see CTEA (1971).

15. Kuyek (1979, 40) provides the following description of the Stock Purchase Plan:

> The Stock Purchase Plan for Employees gave the Bell worker the right to purchase, at par value, one share for each $300 of the workers' annual earning. There was a limit of 20 shares, each of which was paid for by deductions from the workers' paycheque. The company promoted the plan as an "encouragement of thrift and savings" and stated in its Annual Report for 1921 that "the possession of financial interest in the company by the employees appeared to the Board to be of mutual advantage." This was indeed true, although the advantage may have accrued more to the boss than the worker. The plan assured that employee savings could be used directly by the company, thus shoring up its capital base. It also did much to promote employee identification with company goals.
>
> By 1922, over 4,300 employees were subscribing and the par value of the shares being paid for by regular deductions was $1.4 million—money which in effect never left company coffers. The employees' investment continued to increase until 1930 when 11,659 employees out of a total of 14,509 were subscribing. With the onset of the Depression the rate of subscription fell off dramatically as the workers had no savings left which they could invest."

16. Among other initiatives, Bell contracted with the University of Toronto's Centre for Industrial Relations to hold seminars and conferences for its managers.

17. In the United States, Ehrenberg (1979) examined practices of 49 regulatory commissions to conclude that roughly half of the commissions accepted negotiated wages as fair and reasonable. Most commissions had not developed well-defined standards to analyze labour costs and, in cases where some analysis was attempted, it was quite simplistic. To our knowledge, no such study has ever been undertaken in Canada, although there are indications that the approach of Canadian regulatory bodies is to accept compensation outcomes of collective bargaining as a given, as long as they are

in line with comparable wage patterns.

18. The experience at B.C.Tel, however, suggests that management bargained hard prior to the introduction of competition in the early 1980s. The TWU mounted four strikes in 1969, 1973 (O.K.Tel), 1977 and 1981 in order to achieve contractual language and wages that were acceptable to its menbers.

19. Some 2000 managers were deployed in the first week of the strike. This number rose to 8000 in week four, and at the peak of the strike, some 10 000 managers and supervisors were filling in for workers. There were roughly 15 000 employees in managerial ranks at the time.

20. In one incident, the union urged the public to withhold $50 from each telephone bill as a form of protest. The company advertised an award for information leading to the arrest and conviction of anyone engaged in sabotage of company property. There were no claimants for the award. The company placed advertisements in the media to assure the public of uninterrupted phone service.

21. A common form of employee involvement that has been around for many years is the suggestion scheme operated in many companies in 1991, including MTS, Bell, and AGT. In this section, we restrict our discussion to those forms that involve workers in groups rather than individually.

22. See Verma and Gallina (1991) for a description of the policies opposing many forms of EI that have been adopted by major Canadian unions, such as the Canadian Auto Workers (CAW), Canadian Paperworkers' Union (CPU), the Canadian Labour Congress (CLC), and the British Columbia Federation of Labour, among others.

23. An "E" was added at the end to give it a bilingual touch; it translates in French to "team."

24. In addition to IMPACT and EQUIPE, there were other initiatives, such as the WCPIP (White Collar Productivity Improvement Process), 10 STEP, and 12 STEP. The main objective of all these efforts was the same—to get employees involved in problem solving in the area of quality and productivity.

25. For conceptual analysis and case-study data on the two forms of employee involvement, see Cutcher-Gershenfeld, Kochan, and Verma (1991).

26. The Provincial Workplace Health and Safety Division issued a stop-work order for the Directory Assistance office (MIDAS), which was subsequently rescinded. The Directory Assistance Office (MIDAS) work stations were staffed by management employees and volunteer operators.

27. Based on interviews conducted by Perry Armitage with company and union officials in January 1991.

Chapter

CANADIAN INDUSTRIAL RELATIONS IN TRANSITION

Richard P. Chaykowski
Anil Verma[1]

*T*he evidence gathered in the preceding chapters points to significant changes in the conduct of industrial relations over the last decade. A finding of changes having occurred over time is not, in itself, very instructive or interesting. In order to draw lessons for policy and research, these changes require interpretation in the context of Canada's current needs and aspirations for the future. The directions in which Canadian industrial relations are evolving are understood meaningfully only when they are set in a conceptual framework of the change process. To interpret the evidence from the previous chapters, we return in this chapter to some of the questions posed at the beginning of this book (in Chapter 1). What is the extent of changes in Canadian industrial relations practices over the last ten years and, further, do these changes signify that the industrial relations system is changing in its fundamental characteristics? If it is changing in fundamental ways, what are the characteristics of the "new" order? Lastly, what role can policy and research play in the context of such change?

Accordingly, this chapter has two primary objectives: first, we attempt to generalize from the experience of the ten sectors covered in the book. It is prudent for us as editors to, once again, point out that this generalization suffers from the exclusion of some important sectors of the Canadian economy. Nonetheless, the chapters do comprise a large sample, since they are based on the experiences of scores of firms, unions, and government agencies or departments. In this sense, some generalization can be made with a high degree of confidence in its validity and in its ability to provide the reader with an accurate overview of some of the directions in Canadian industrial relations practice. To this end, we sketch the process of change in a seven-stage model suggested by the industry studies, and summarize the evidence from the chapters by examining the pressures experienced by each sector and the responses of the parties to these pressures. We then relate the experiences of each sector in the 1980s to the seven-stage change process.

Our second primary objective is to consider the implications of these findings for policy making and practice, on one hand, and for theory construction and research, on the other. To the end, we consider the choices that each of the parties to the industrial relations system face in the 1990s, and conclude by discussing the implications for theories of change and restructuring in industrial relations and for the type of research needed to develop our understanding of this critical process.

A General Model of the Evolution Process

CHANGE IN CANADIAN INDUSTRIAL RELATIONS AND THE STRATEGIC-CHOICE FRAMEWORK

In their assessment of changes in U.S. industrial relations, Kochan, Katz, and McKersie (1986) provide a description of the traditional system, the transformed "new" system, and a detailed, institutionally rich description of the process by which the traditional system was transformed. We build around this work to adapt it to the Canadian context. First, we argue that Kochan, Katz, and McKersie's description of the traditional system in the United States is a reasonably good approximation of the dominant industrial relations system in Canada in the 1960–80 era. In the 1980s, the initiative in collective bargaining was assumed by management in both the United States and Canada. In many instances, strategic business decisions were made outside collective bargaining, with profound implications for industrial relations. Second, although substantial changes have occurred in Canada in the 1980s, it is clear that the Canadian system had not (yet) "transformed" to the same stage the U.S. system had reached by 1991. Third, the process by which changes were occurring in Canada in the 1980s was clearly different from the process by which the transformation of the industrial relations system had occurred in the United States.

Thus, we are left with a number of issues that must be addressed in proposing a model of the evolution process. First, if the process by which change is occurring in Canada is different from that in the United States, are there multiple paths that firms or industries can follow in their evolution or transformation? If so, then the different paths need to be specified. Second, if Canada had not reached the same transformational stage as that attained by the United States in 1991, what stage had it reached? Third, what are the other stages in this evolutionary process? Last, can the model help us place the Canadian evolutionary process on the path that would predict its future course?

STAGES IN THE EVOLUTION AND TRANSFORMATION OF INDUSTRIAL RELATIONS

The proposed model is both an extension and a modification of the transformation process described by Kochan, Katz, and McKersie (1986). Two important features are unique to this model. First, it considers an evolutionary path in the development of industrial relations, in which union power is a key component in explaining the potential outcomes. A central feature of the U.S. experience is the growth of the nonunion sector, which brought pressure on the system for transformation. Clearly, union power in the United States was substantially weaker than management's during the transformation process. In Canada, unions displayed greater willingness and ability to oppose the managerial agenda in collective bargaining. In the 1980s, even though management initiatives set the tone for collective bargaining, several changes initiated by labour were adopted in collective bargaining (e.g., pension indexing, income security). It is also generally unlikely that political, legal, or structural factors that contribute to union power will change substantially in the near future. Union power may decline in the longer term if certain conditions become unfavourable to unions, a possibility that the model incorporates.[2] However, a "new" system need not necessarily involve the growth and eventual dominance of the nonunion sector, as in the United States. Second, this model outlines a number of intermediate stages between the traditional system and the "new" system. This is important, since it enables us to characterize the developments of the 1980s, when changes did occur in Canada, albeit at a much slower pace than in the United States. The Canadian experience, by providing an opportunity to observe industries at various stages of transformation, is valuable in developing an understanding of the process of the evolution of industrial relations systems.

We outline seven stages that characterize the evolution of industrial relations in which the relative power between labour and management is an important factor determining change. The "traditional" system described in detail by Kochan, Katz, and McKersie (1986, Ch. 2 and 4) marks the first stage in our model (Figure 12.1). Under this system, the focus is on collective bargaining, because strategic survival of the firm and the industry is not in question. Markets are largely stable and domestic (free of foreign competition) in the United States, and continental for Canada. Unions "take wages out of competition" by organizing most firms in the industry. Bargaining outcomes focus on annual improvements in wages. Employment security is not a major concern, as layoffs are assumed to be cyclical. Work rules tend to be numerous and relatively rigid, restricting management prerogatives whenever possible to protect workers from arbitrary treatment and undue hardship at the hands of managers. Union policies in these circumstances have been described as "job control" unionism (Kochan, Katz, and McKersie 1986, 28).

Figure 12.1

Stages in the Evolution of Industrial Relations

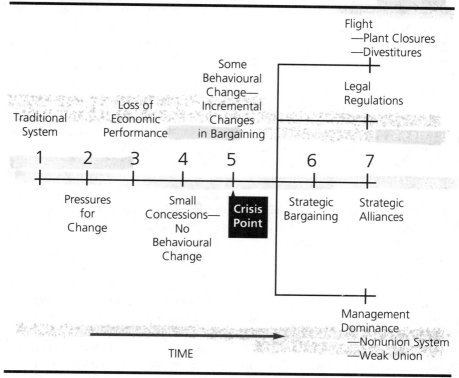

Labour–management relations are characterized by "arm's-length" transactions in which neither side trusts the other enough to enter into joint alliances of any significance. The principal mode of interaction is through bargaining and dispute-resolution mechanisms.

Stage two is characterized by the onset of new pressures for change. In Chapter 1, we outlined the pressures that began to intensify in the Canadian economy in the 1980s. Developments such as increased foreign competition, deregulation and privatization, changes in technology, and demographic shifts appeared at first as separate influences, but later intensified as the combined pressure forced firms to restructure many aspects of their operations. At stage two, firms can still make profits because of entrenched markets and specialized niches and, in some cases, efficient plants. At stage three, firms begin to experience loss of market share and profits as the margins are squeezed by the changing business environment. Plants may become relatively less efficient, and the need to adapt rapidly to changing product markets may become pressing. Many large firms, especially conglomerates with multiple product lines, can plateau at this stage for a period of time before being forced to take corrective action.

Stage four is reached when the firm initiates some corresponding changes in collective bargaining. Given the patterns of traditional arm's-length relationships, bargaining takes the form of management asking for concessions aimed at reducing costs and increasing productivity (e.g., wage moderation and changes in work rules). Since labour possesses enough power to oppose these demands for concessions, concessionary outcomes are usually muted. Thus, only minor changes take place in the substantive aspects of the relationship, even as the decline of economic performance continues. Patterns of labour–management relations remain virtually unchanged from stage one.

Stage five, which may be called the "crisis point," signals that the firm's long-run profitability, and, in some cases, survival, is threatened, unless substantial changes are made in the operations and in the relationship. The crisis can catalyze change at this stage, as the parties are forced to reconsider their traditional stance. However, to accept change, the parties must come to the conclusion that the present crisis is not another cyclical downturn that will reverse itself in time. The leaders on both sides must also convince their constituents that conditions have changed sufficiently to warrant significant policy shifts. A tendency toward minor concessions and accommodations may accompany this recognition process, but these changes are not sufficient to prevent the firm from experiencing further economic decline. At this stage, the firm and union may be maintaining a traditional system that is no longer well suited to the new economic and social environment.

At some time after stage five, the firm may take a variety of different paths, such as flight, management dominance,[3] and strategic alliances (Kochan, Katz, and McKersie 1986, Ch. 3; Verma 1991a; 1991b). For example, the firm may decide that business conditions have deteriorated beyond repair. These firms will decide to exit the market. They may do so by relocating, divesting, or simply closing the plant or business. Another possibility lies in some kind of legal or governmental intervention. Some firms may enter bankruptcy in order to reorganize. Others may seek government or labour relations board intervention, depending on the specific situation. Governments can mediate or legislate solutions, and labour boards can arbitrate a variety of disputes. We see these kinds of administrative interventions as a temporary solution that allows the parties some time to rethink their relationship. Eventually, they will have to confront the issue of transforming their relationship away from a traditional system toward one of the other possibilities of flight, management dominance, or strategic alliances.

Another possibility after stage five is the progressive weakening of the union. At one extreme, workers may decide to withdraw support for the union, although this was not a likely scenario in Canada in the 1980s. This can happen in a variety of ways, through aggressive employer action: the employer may orchestrate a decertification of the union, a possibility that is more likely in small and medium-sized units rather than in large ones; firms that bargain centrally with all of its locals can decentralize bargaining to deal with smaller groups, each of which will be weaker than the larger collective; firms can subcontract or doublebreast by opening nonunion subsidiaries and transferring business out of the unionized operations.[4] Greater use of technology can also reduce management's reliance on workers. Unions would lose power as their ability to shut down operations during a strike would decline. A more direct weapon that management may wield in extracting concessions is the threat of plant closure or relocation, or withholding new investments that may be essential to improve productivity and maintain plant life-expectancy. Each of these possibilities could result in a management-dominated system in which the union is either weakened or rendered ineffective.

However, if union strength does not wane immediately after the crisis point is reached, the parties may enter a phase of strategic bargaining, i.e., bargaining over terms that address business survival (Kochan, Katz, and McKersie 1986, Ch. 5). If the parties engage in bargaining over terms linked directly to new investments, jointly address productivity and employment-security issues, or engage in joint governance of initiatives aimed at addressing such issues, then they may be said to have reached stage six. Of course, the success of strategic bargaining is not assured simply by the parties' willingness to engage in such bargaining. In many cases, strategic bargaining fails because the parties have not modified their traditional stance toward each other in terms of trust or working relationships. If bargaining fails at this stage, the outcome may be one of those described above. If strategic bargaining succeeds, they may move toward stage seven, which may include a variety of new understandings across a broad range of issues. For example, investments may be promised by the company in new plant and equipment in exchange for wage moderation and employment guarantees. In other cases, it may include changes in work rules and work organization to make the workplace more flexible and productive. The parties may decide to work jointly in the governance of such integrative activities as training, communication, employee involvement, and work reorganization. The formation of such strategic alliances would signal stage seven (Kochan, Katz, and McKersie 1986, 237–42). Movement to this stage would also signify that industrial relations have been transformed from the traditional "job control" system to a new order characterized by strategic alliances and joint governance to achieve high flexibility and productivity, on one hand, and greater employment security and worker participation in decision making, on the other.

The alternative paths of management dominance and strategic alliances will have considerably different implications for unions, employees, and firms. On the employee side, management dominance implies a loss of job control, whereas a move toward strategic bargaining and alliances is likely to provide more secure employment and more interesting jobs than the traditional system can sustain in the economic environment of the 1990s. For firms, the two alternatives offer very different outcomes regarding management control and decision making, but either outcome may yield greater economic performance than is possible under the traditional system in the circumstances of the 1990s.

It is unlikely that every firm across diverse industries would evolve through all the stages on the evolutionary path shown in Figure 12.1. This path is suggested as a schema to map the differential and the common experiences of different industries and firms. It is likely, as pointed out in Chapter 11, that telephone companies may go directly from stage two or three to stage six and beyond, i.e., they may not experience the crisis point, given the system of regulation in the industry. Others may skip stage four, depending on the quality of union–management relations. The exact path taken by a given firm would depend on the responses of the parties to the outcomes at each stage. In that sense, this model does not sketch out the dynamic process of industrial relations that leads to transformation. The feedback loops in the system have been described well by others (Kochan, Katz, and McKersie 1986, 113; Kochan 1980, 25; Craig 1986, 3) and, therefore, are not included in Figure 12.1.

Industrial Relations Developments in Canadian Industry

As noted in the introductory chapter to this volume, Canadian industries experienced a wide range of internal and external pressures in the 1980s. The major external factors affecting Canadian industries included the increased levels of international competition and the economic and political realignments that gave rise to trading blocs and altered patterns of trade. The globalization of markets created long-run pressures for industrial restructuring in a number of industries. Macroeconomic conditions, such as interest rates and the rise in the value of the Canadian dollar, also affected the competitive position of Canadian firms (Chapter 1, Figure 1.5). In turn, firms responded to the need to increase their competitive capability by adopting new technologies. External competitive pressures added to the effects of important *internal* public-policy and economic developments such as deregulation, privatization of Crown corporations, changes in provincial legislation, and new trade agreements.

Each of the pressures for change affected the industries examined differentially. Consequently, the evolutionary process of change in the conduct of industrial relations has differed across industries and, thus, given rise to different outcomes.

PRESSURES FOR CHANGE IN THE 1980s

International Competition

The auto industry experienced significant competition from offshore producers, particularly from the Europeans and the Japanese. While the linkages between the Canadian and U.S. auto producers make offshore competition the major concern, there remains the threat that U.S. parent corporations can move production from

Canada to the United States to achieve lower production costs. Overseas competition was also intense in the mining industry, in which foreign producers often have financial advantages conferred by government sponsorship, and in the garment and textile industries, in which foreign manufacturers benefit from significantly lower labour costs. Since the United States is an important trading partner in steel, the rise of efficient minimills there has put pressure on Canadian producers to reduce costs and increase quality. The challenge in steel will be to meet rising competition from U.S. and offshore firms. The future growth of firms in both airlines and telecommunications will depend on the degree of further globalization of these industries and the extent to which domestic markets are opened to foreign firms. For example, as airlines in Canada emerge from the period of adjustment to privatization and deregulation, and as the government liberalizes opportunities for foreign companies to compete with Canadian firms (e.g., the "Open Skies" agreement with the United States), economic opportunity and competitive pressures will intensify. In the future, increased competition from U.S. construction firms may also emerge as an important factor for Canadian firms.

With the exception of mining, trade agreements figure prominently in most of the private-sector industries. In the auto industry, the Auto Pact has partially removed the direct threat of competition with U.S. producers.[5] The maintenance of the Auto Pact alongside the FTA has favoured stability in the development of industrial relations in this industry. However, the FTA and the appreciation in the Canadian dollar that took place in its aftermath, has made Canadian steelmakers' competitive position worse, thereby adding to the pressure to reduce labour costs and increase workplace flexibility, while threatening employment and income security. The general progressive liberalization of trade policy and the FTA have, together, increased competitive pressures on the textile industry; in the garment industry, the Multi-Fibre Agreement and tariffs on imported materials have been central to the competitive capability of the industry.

The Role of Technology

Technology has acted as a catalyst for organizational change in firms and created new pressures on unions by threatening employment and altering workplace organization. The role of technology in affecting the industrial relations system has been most pronounced in autos, steel, mining, telecommunications and textiles, with more specific effects in airlines.

Major investment decisions in the auto industry are typically made by the parent corporations in the United States, Japan, or Europe, and are therefore largely out of the control of Canadian subsidiaries.[6] Nonetheless, investment in the Canadian auto industry was substantial in the 1980s. Steel firms have also recognized the importance of technological innovation to their competitive capability. However, confronted by declining profits in the late 1980s and early 1990s, steel firms experienced increased difficulty in financing the required investments. In contrast, even while experiencing particularly difficult financial situations in the early 1980s, major mining firms led a technological revolution that has made the industry among the most competitive in the world. But it has been the larger mining firms that have had the financial capability to develop and implement new production technologies. The importance of new technologies in textiles also increased throughout the 1980s, and it may hold the key to the future competitive capability of this industry. The airline industry provides a useful example of a situation in which technologies can lead to changes that affect particular segments of the labour force, as in the cases of pilots and passenger agents.

Internal Pressures for Change

The federal government has pursued two related economic policies in the form of deregulation and privatization. In telecommunications, neither unions nor firms had experienced major pressures to change their relationship as the system of regulation had changed only at margin during the 1980s. The process of privatization affected airlines (Air Canada), and deregulation contributed to the restructuring of the airline industry, so that by the end of the 1980s, only two major carriers remained in Canada. The combined impact of deregulation and privatization on the airline industry has contributed to employment losses and intense pressures to reduce costs. With labour being such an important production input, the impact of these policies on collective bargaining in the industry has been significant.

Legislation has also had a direct impact on the conduct of industrial relations. In construction, government retreat from the Fair Wages and Hours of Labour Act created an environment less advantageous to unions. The resulting unfavourable legislative environment that developed in the western provinces through the 1980s was a major contributing factor to the deunionizaton of the construction industry. In contrast, the enactment of Bill 100 in Ontario in 1975 created teacher bargaining rights, the right to strike, and open-scope negotiations, thereby creating an environment that facilitated the complete unionization of education and the growth of union power. Throughout the 1980s, teacher unions made major gains through collective bargaining.

Layered over these developments were new issues arising from the evolving demographic composition of the labour force and new public-policy initiatives in the areas of human and employee rights. The increasing female labour-force participation rate continues to have an impact on firms and unions as they attempt to design programs and policies that will accommodate the changing patterns of employee needs. While industries such as steel, autos, and mining remain largely solitudes of male employment, there is a growing recognition in these industries that, as their work forces become increasingly professionalised, they need to alter their human-resource policies to address the needs and concerns of women. As the average age of many firm work forces increased in industries such as mining, autos, and steel, and as firms downsized during the 1980s, many unionized companies confronted the prospect of being unable to develop a cohort of skilled younger workers.

This situation gave rise to increased emphasis on early-retirement schemes. Finally, employment-equity legislation became an important human-resource issue in federal jurisdictions as the government increased its emphasis on this problem.

Fiscal Restraint and Restructuring in the Public Sector

In the public sector, the increased demands for government expenditures on public programs in which costs are escalating (e.g., health care), in conjunction with increasing deficits, have created an awareness and a (stated) desire on the part of public-policy makers to impose restraints. These pressures to cut spending in the public sector are analogous, in many ways, to competitive pressures in the private sector, as they both result in a search for greater productivity. In the 1990s, cutbacks in program expenditures have been imposed, along with reductions in civil-service employment levels and restraints on wage increases. Governments, as employers, are also exploring new initiatives to improve efficiency in the civil service (e.g., Public Service 2000, an initiative of the Federal Government to examine and improve service quality and efficiency in the federal civil service). Since the fiscal constraints appear unavoidable, it is likely that union resistance to spending cuts will intensify in the 1990s.

OUTCOMES AND RESPONSES

In order to become more competitive and productive, firms attempted to increase workplace flexibility, which effectively gave management greater control over the workplace. Another initiative to improve productivity has taken the form of technological innovation, which has had considerable impact on work organization, worker skills, and employment levels. Also, in response to competitive pressures, firms reduced labour costs, both by cutting employment (often accompanied by technological innovation) and by attempting to reduce the levels and alter the composition of remuneration to workers. Employment reductions, therefore, resulted from industrial restructuring within industries, as well as from the processes of reorganization and rationalization of firm operations.

Workplace Flexibility

The introduction of new technologies into the workplace often required work reorganization, new skills, and new forms of workplace flexibility. Work reorganization took the form of just-in-time work schedules or job rotation; retraining was required to facilitate the use of new production technologies; and flexibility was sought through a reduction in the number of job classifications, the cross-training of workers, flexible hours, and part-time work. There is modest evidence suggesting some innovations in workplace flexibility in many of the private-sector industries examined. However, human-resource and industrial relations innovations in the area of workplace flexibility have been, for the most part, limited both in terms of the extent of usage within an industry, as well as in terms of diffusion across industries (see Table 12.1). There was some increase in flexibility because of work-rule changes in autos; increased flexibility in working hours in steel, airlines, and construction; some cross-training in textiles and telecommunications; and multiskilling in airlines. There have also been a number of innovations particular to specific industries (e.g., telecommuting for sales staff in telecommunications and flexibility for travel allowances in construction). In contrast, reductions in job classifications have been prevalent and have occurred in automobiles, steel, mining, and textiles.

Employment and Income Security

Almost all of the private-sector industries and some parts of the public sector experienced employment cuts in the 1980s. Such costs resulted in a decline in union membership in most sectors. Not surprisingly, employment- and income-security concerns have been at the fore. A variety of innovations in employment- and income-security outcomes, some favourable to unions and some to management, were found across industries: advance notice was established in autos; contracting-out or outsourcing was prevalent in autos, construction, mining, and garments; breakthroughs in pension indexing were achieved in mining, autos, and steel; and severance pay was a feature in autos and mining, and to a lesser extent in garments (see Table 12.1). The construction industry in western Canada underwent a dramatic increase in subcontracting through "project-management" operations and in doublebreasting; similarly, outsourcing to contractors and homeworkers became a feature of the garment industry. In both of these cases, these changes led to the development of nonunion alternatives.

Where prevalent, outsourcing, in which parts are typically produced in nonunion shops, and nonunion subcontracting represent a growing menace to membership levels and the attainment of wage objectives. The use of these alternatives to union labour have been growing in construction and garments, and have become increasingly prevalent in mining. The ability of firms to subcontract was linked to the deunionization of the construction industry in western Canada. One of the key side effects of this deunionization process in construction was a significant drop in labour costs through wage concessions and rollbacks. In garments, outsourcing has resulted in a diminished role for unions. The use of homework in garments remains a threat to unionized employment. By the 1990s, major mining firms contracted-out for many of the repair and small-scale projects previously carried out by in-house workers. While subcontracting is not currently prevalent among Canadian steel firms, the intense competitive pressures in the industry may make this option increasingly more attractive to employers.

Joint Union–Management Initiatives and Employee Involvement

While joint initiatives showed some spark in a few industries in the 1980s, the overall contribution of such efforts to change and restructuring in industrial

Table 12.1
Recent Innovations in Human Resources and Industrial Relations[a,b]

Industry	Workplace Flexibility	Employment and Income Security	Joint Union–Management Initiatives	Flexible Compensation
Automobiles	—increased flexibility in work rules —some job-classification consolidation	—some advance notice (e.g., plant closures) —improved severance —pension indexing (e.g., 1988 Chrysler agreement) —outsourcing restrictions	—some joint initiatives —strategic-level initiatives (e.g., CAW membership in GM Quality Council) —some teamwork	None
Steel	—some increased flexibility through changes in working hours and job classifications	—pension indexing (e.g., Stelco) —some improvements in income security	—None at firm level —CSTEC at industry level	—gain sharing (e.g., value-added-based plan at Stelco, 1991)
Mining	—decrease in job classifications	—contracting-out restrictions —some severence for technological change —pension indexing (e.g., Inco)	None	—profit sharing (e.g., Inco and HudBay)
Construction	—inclusion of "enabling" clauses in collective agreements —improved work scheduling	In Western Canada: —increased subcontracting (e.g., through project-management operations)	None	None

Table 12.1 (continued)

Industry	Workplace Flexibility	Employment and Income Security	Joint Union–Management Initiatives	Flexible Compensation
	—relaxation of overtime penalties —greater flexibility for travel allowances	—increase in double-breasted firms		
Garments	—reduced restrictions on the introduction of technological change (e.g., "engineered incentive system")	—increased outsourcing (e.g., to contractors and homeworkers) —some severance (e.g., technological-change indemnity)	None	None
Textiles	—some decrease in job classifications —some cross-training	None	—long-standing joint Labour-Management Committees become effective in the 1980s	None
Public Sector	None	—increased contracting-out	None	None
Education	—reduction in management flexibility (e.g., class size, PTR and component-staffing provisions)	—increased job security (e.g., increased job transfer rights by the 1980s)	—increase in joint committees since Bill 100 (1975)	None

Table 12.1 (continued)

Industry	Workplace Flexibility	Employment and Income Security	Joint Union–Management Initiatives	Flexible Compensation
Airlines	—increase in part-time work —changes in work hours —required call-in for departure time (attendants) —multiskilling	—some employment guarantees for workers affected by restructuring subject to productivity gains —worksharing (e.g. pilots)	None	None
Telephone	—more homework —use of home dispatch —increased cross-training —telecommuting for sales staff	—downsizing managed through attrition	—joint program to improve working conditions at MTS —management-run quality circles (e.g., B.C. Tel) —movement to joint process (e.g., Bell)	None

a *Sources for this table*—Chapters 2 through 11, this volume.

b This table provides examples of innovations. Note that the prevalence of these innovations can vary considerably within an industry. Specifically, while most innovations occur at only some firms in an industry, they nonetheless constitute a new and important development. Refer to each of the respective chapters for discussion of these developments.

relations was minor. On the positive side, the parties co-operated through CSTEC at the industry level in steel and the Canadian Auto Workers (CAW) participated in the GM Quality Council. Both education and textiles saw a strengthening of the role of joint committees. At the firm level, a few telephone companies began experimenting with joint committees to oversee co-operative efforts at the workplace. However, these advances were almost invisible in many other industries. In steel, the success of CSTEC did not translate into firm-level joint initiatives. In much of mining, construction, garments, airlines, and the public sector, there were no significant developments in joint initiatives, despite the mounting economic pressures. Many companies took unilateral steps to implement a variety of employee-involvement (EI) plans. The unions, in most cases, remained either opposed or indifferent to employee-involvement initiatives. In a small number of cases where the union was open to discussions on employee involvement, management preferred not to involve the union.

Changes in the Composition of Compensation

Reductions in wage costs and flexibility in employee compensation have became important firm objectives through the 1980s and into the 1990s. Confronted with relatively high labour costs and volatile profit levels, many firms have sought to link compensation levels to the fortunes of the firm. While wage concessions, the use of lump-sum payments, and wage freezes have occurred in a number of industries, the incidence of these outcomes is increasingly linked to the financial circumstance of individual firms and is less frequent in Canada than in the United States. Firms in the steel, airline, and construction industries provide examples of these bargaining outcomes.

The Canadian Auto Workers, among others, strongly opposed both concessions as well as contingent compensation schemes throughout the 1980s. In fact, the position of the CAW leadership on these issues played an important role in the formation of the CAW. Despite the union's opposition to management initiatives on flexibility, changes in job classifications and the use of work teams on the shop floor were negotiated in some parts of the auto industry. Also, a growing number of key bargaining settlements in mining and steel resulted in innovative flexible compensation schemes, including profit sharing and gain sharing plans (see Table 12.1).

THE EXTENT OF CHANGE ACROSS CANADIAN INDUSTRY

In the 1960–80 era, each of the private-sector industries developed a traditional industrial relations system characterized by a high degree of unionization, arm's-length union–management relations, and the centrality of collective bargaining to industrial relations. By the 1980s, each of the competitive, public-policy, and technological pressures combined to bring about changes described above. In some cases, the pressures for change had begun the process of transforming industrial relations. The emerging picture is one of considerable variance in the responses of the actors, and differing degrees of evolution of the industrial relations systems of various industries.

Downsizing employment put pressure on unions in mining, steel, textiles, and construction. In some cases, downsizing contributed to the gradual process of deunionization, as in the cases of mining, textiles, and construction. Across the private-sector industries analyzed, unionization had either stagnated or begun to decline by the early 1990s. In some of these industries, new union organizing had obviously made few inroads, so that, on balance, organizing efforts were insufficient to stem the gradual decline in union density. In addition, the levels of strike activity in the 1980s had declined relative to those of the 1960s and 1970s; important strikes occurred; but, in automobiles, mining, construction, garments, textiles, airlines, and telecommunications, the level of conflict was relatively low throughout the 1980s. In marked contrast, the level of conflict was relatively high in steel, and this situation contributed to some degree to the crises in the industry in 1990–91.

Evolution in the Private-Sector Industries

The traditional industrial relations system in the telephone industry began to change very slowly in the 1980s. Although subject to some of the same pressures as other industries, unions and management in telecommunications were to a significant extent buffered from external pressures by virtue of operating in a regulated environment. The lack of competition in the industry allowed firms to maintain their "profitability," thus avoiding shocks to the union–management relationship (e.g., rapid and large downsizing). The parties began introducing some innovations in the areas of workplace flexibility and joint union–management initiatives, such as quality circles (see Table 12.1), more so in anticipation of increasing deregulation and competition than in response to any immediate crises.

Textiles and garments, as related industries, were subjected to very similar pressures, the most important of which have been international competition and technological change. Firms in these industries experienced lower economic performance, and unions suffered membership losses and weakened bargaining positions. While concessions have not been a defining characteristic of collective bargaining in either industry, unions were both reactive and defensive in collective bargaining.

Unions and management in textiles had not engaged in any fundamental behavioural change by the beginning of the 1990s. The industrial relations system was probably best characterized as approaching but not reaching a point of crisis. While long-standing joint labour–management committees became more effective in the 1980s, no major new joint labour–management initiatives were undertaken (see Table 12.1). The traditional system has remained intact but has not evolved;

nor had it deteriorated, probably in large part because of such mechanisms as the bipartite Canadian Textile Labour–Management Committee.

Unions are perhaps in a more tenuous position in garments, where employers have increased the outsourcing of work to contractors and homeworkers. Employers have begun to incorporate the nonunion option more openly and explicitly in their strategic plans. The shift toward the employment of nonunion workers, coupled with the sharp decline in union density, suggests that the garment industry has passed through a turning point beyond stage five, and toward the nonunion system rather than toward the strategic-bargaining route.

Employers and unions in steel and airlines are at a turning point (close to stage five) in the development of their industrial relations systems. At various times during the 1980s and early 1990s, major firms in these industries have experienced intense pressures from competitors, a loss of economic performance, and, consequently, some behavioural changes. In steel, declining profits of firms in the late 1980s (i.e., financial crisis at Stelco and Algoma) made for an uncertain future for the industry. These trends resulted in membership losses for the United Steelworkers union in their traditional base. The long-run process of corporate rationalization in airlines, and the financial difficulties confronting both Air Canada and Canadian Airlines International in the early 1990s resulted in successive rounds of employment losses, and ultimately weakened the bargaining positions of unions in the industry.

Management and unions in steel and airlines have begun the search for a new equation in their relationship, but it was not clear by mid-1991 if they would move to strategic bargaining in the near future. Unions in these industries, weakened by considerable membership losses, also began to look for new arrangements to address such issues as employment security, contingent compensation, and flexibility. Signs of any evolution in the direction of joint union–management governance of the restructuring process were still feeble. However, conditions were ripe in both industries for the parties to move toward more bargaining over strategic issues. If this does not happen in the near future, the industry may decline further, losing market share to foreign competition. The nonunion option remained unlikely as an alternative in both industries (with the exception of Dofasco in steel), at least for the immediate future.

In mining, the recession of the early 1980s exacerbated already stagnating product-demand conditions. Major firms such as Falconbridge and Inco adopted a strategy of heavy investment in new technologies that resulted in drastic cuts in employment and union membership. By the end of the 1980s, the traditionally conflictual union–management relationships at these firms gave way to greater accommodation as firms pushed for workplace changes and the adoption of flexible compensation schemes, while unions negotiated some forms of employment and income security. However, these accommodations were not indicative of greater mutuality and equality in the bargaining relationship. The introduction of flexible compensation plans and new technologies signalled a shift of power in favour of management. The long-run decline in union density further corroborates the view that mining industrial relations have evolved in the direction of management dominance.

The evolution of the construction-industry industrial relations system became sharply bifurcated along regional lines during the 1980s. In central and eastern Canada, where the economic pressures were significant but less severe than in western Canada, the centrality of collective bargaining to the industrial relations system was maintained. Unions were clearly in a disadvantageous bargaining position relative to the 1960s or 1970s, but their effectiveness remained unchanged. Thus, while the pressures for change existed, they were apparently insufficient to induce substantial changes in the behaviour of unions and firms. This portion of the construction industry, particularly in Ontario and Quebec, remained traditional.

In marked contrast, a combination of legal, economic, and political factors, in conjunction with the rise of active employer resistance to unionism, led to the deunionization of the industry in western Canada. In the 1980s, the industrial relations system had moved to a point of crisis: bargaining was characterized by wage rollbacks, freezes, and concessions; industrial relations received diminished legal support; employers turned to subcontracting and doublebreasting and nonunion firms became dominant; management strategy regarding unions involved resistance and replacement; union density was in sharp decline, and union organizing campaigns were ineffective in reversing the trend. Unions and firms in this segment of the industry failed to arrive at industrial relations initiatives that could have led to new strategic alliances within the framework of collective bargaining. Instead, driven by employer initiatives, the industry evolved along a path of deunionization.[7]

The automobile industry was not subjected to the same intensity of economic and institutional pressures experienced in other industries in the 1980s. The maintenance of the Auto Pact, the rise in Canada of manufacturing plants owned by offshore producers, the continued acceptance of unionism by the major employers, and a robust union have combined to yield a mature but dynamic industrial relations system. The CAW has achieved important gains in employment and income security, while successfully opposing attempts to introduce any forms of flexible compensation. Management has, in turn, obtained some improvements in workplace flexibility. Together, some workplace joint initiatives and teamwork have been introduced, but only limited strategic-level joint initiatives have been undertaken (see Table 12.1). Collective bargaining remains the centrepiece of the system and mutual acceptance is deeply rooted, but the parties' mutual trust has been diminished by the restructuring of the industry in the 1990s.

Public-Sector Developments

Public-sector industries may be distinguished from the private sector along several dimensions that also define key differences in the industrial relations systems. In the federal, provincial, and municipal public sectors, as in education, direct competition is not a factor. In each of these industries, the ability to provide services depends on the ability of the government to finance the expenditures. However, mounting deficits in the 1980s; high levels of taxation, which limit the acceptability of further tax increases; rapid escalation of the costs of social programs; and the declining economic growth of the early 1990s have combined to place intense financial pressures on governments.

Government response has been to restrain spending by reducing employment and introducing periodic wage controls or guidelines. More recently, governments have also privatized Crown corporations and subcontracted for services. The growth of public-sector unions has slowed down, largely as a result of the already high density levels. While wage guidelines or controls are, ultimately, enforceable through legislative fiat, it is not clear that such tactics have diminished union power in the long run. While these developments have put pressures on unions in the public sector, the traditional system of industrial relations has been maintained.

Driven by demographic trends, declining student enrolments have resulted in some modest employment losses in Ontario education. This has created demands for improved employment security, for example through transfer rights. Spending cuts in the government budget may result in further demands to reduce employment and moderate wage increases. The result will be increased pressure at the bargaining table. But, throughout the 1980s, teacher unions grew in strength, particularly in terms of their ability to bargain effectively. Among teachers in Ontario, there is no nonunion competition, so that there is no alternative (nonunion) industrial relations strategy available to management. Collective bargaining is firmly entrenched as the centrepiece of the industrial relations system. Neither have there been moves toward co-operative strategies; adversarial collective negotiation's have been the mechanism of change. Perhaps for these reasons, the government was considering moving to a province wide-bargaining structure. In their view, this would provide greater control over costs compared to the decentralized structure. It is likely that, despite any major pressures that may emerge in the 1990s, and barring any public-policy upheaval, the traditional system in education will certainly remain intact.

*S*trategic Choices, Policy Options, and Prospects for the Future

*U*nion membership and density in most broadly defined private-sector industries either declined or stagnated in the 1980s, and there exists little potential for further union growth in the public government sector (see Chapter 1, Table 7.1). Recent research suggests that, while the broader public sector remains vibrant, private-sector unionism is in decline. But the extent of the private-sector decline and the implications of this trend for the entire labour movement remain subjects of considerable debate and continued research (Chaison and Rose 1991; Meltz 1990; Troy 1991; Kumar 1991).

In the public sector, and particularly in the case of education, unions consolidated their positions throughout the 1980s. Collective bargaining remains the focus of industrial relations in the public sector, and while the period of significant membership growth is past, unions will likely remain strong. Despite increased efforts at contracting-out and privatization, the net effects on union membership have been marginal. Acceptance of unions by management remains high in education, and the ability of management to wish unions away remains low in the civil service.[8] The prospect is, thus, for the traditional industrial relations system to be maintained into the twenty-first century, with only incremental changes gradually modifying the traditional system.

In most private-sector industries examined, the prospects for unionism are in marked contrast to the public sector. The macro perspective of unions in decline or retrenchment is largely confirmed across industries, but to widely varying degrees. Unionism remains strong and vibrant in autos and telecommunications. But union membership in textiles has essentially stagnated; in mining, it plummeted at the turn of the 1980s, and then steadied at a much lower level. Both union membership and density have fallen in garments. While union densities remained stable in steel and airlines, unions in these industries are facing membership declines resulting from the difficult economic conditions in these industries, coupled with downsizing in operations. Most threatening to unions are the deunionization trends in construction in the West, and in garments, although further shifts in public policy in favour of unions could have a positive effect on unionization levels. In key industries, the picture of the 1980s and early 1990s is one of unions experiencing membership losses or stagnant growth, and increasing pressures at the bargaining table.

However, in industries where unions are under great pressures, so, too, are many of the leading firms. For the most part, collective bargaining remains central to the industrial relations system, but, increasingly, the 1980s produced signals that the traditional system was either coping poorly or changing very slowly to adapt to the requirements of the new economic realities.

The private- and public-sector industries analyzed in this volume are at disparate stages in the evolution of their industrial relations systems, largely because the pressures impacting different industries vary in intensity and form. In most cases, competitive pressures have had the most significant effects. Consequently, trade agreements have been, and will likely remain, of critical importance. The experiences with automobiles, garments, textiles, and steel suggest that different trade agreements can have a unique role in mediating or intensifying the impacts of competition, depending on the industry concerned. The Auto Pact and Multifibre Arrangement have mediated the impacts of competition considerably in autos and (less so) in garments, respectively, whereas the FTA has heightened pressures in textiles and steel. The successful negotiation of bilateral trade agreements can be an important component of a government strategy to improve competitiveness across industries.

Independent of institutional trade arrangements, the long-run trend toward the globalization of markets requires that both managers and unions carefully examine their strategic options. Production-cost reductions have become a major management objective in virtually every industry. Although under pressure, unions may adopt collective-bargaining strategies that increase firm productivity and consequently permit real wage increases for employees without sacrificing cost competitiveness (Freeman 1990). Unions and management may also further explore new methods of increasing productivity through workplace flexibility, flexible compensation, and joint union–management initiatives at both the workplace and strategic levels. Many unions have resisted changes in each of these areas, particularly in cases where organized labour fears that the purpose of such innovations is to weaken or supplant the union. The challenges for managers and unions here are twofold: first, to learn from the "best practice" in human-resource and industrial relations innovations in these areas; and, second, to develop a joint strategy. That will allow these innovations to be implemented without unduly compromising the interest of either party.

The importance of well-functioning industrial relations systems to the well-being and prosperity of firms and whole industries has been well demonstrated by the experiences of mining firms in the early 1980s, textiles firms through the 1980s, and steel firms in the early 1990s. The challenge is to develop industrial relations initiatives that will promote the interests of both labour and management while improving the competitive capability of the industry. In most cases, this may require a movement away from the traditional systems that evolved in the 1960s and 1970s, toward systems that allow for greater joint governance of the restructuring process.

The emerging roles of collective bargaining and unions across the industries examined in this book suggest that the types of systems that develop will increasingly differ across industries. Several alternative paths are available, and the choices made by the parties will be a decisive factor in determining the prospects for the future. First, systems may evolve along the path of deunionization, largely as a consequence of aggressive management actions in the context of a favourable environment, as in the case of construction, or through less-aggressive management initiatives, as has occurred in garments. The collective-bargaining framework in construction has the ability to adapt (as did the B. C. construction industry), but the active pursuit of the nonunion path by management in western Canada suggests that the most likely challenge to unions in the rest of the industry will continue to be the nonunion option. Second, systems may evolve more gradually along the path toward deunionization, as a consequence of strategic business decisions and efforts to alter the tenor of the relationship, e.g., as in mining. For mining unions, one viable strategy is to increase the level of organizing activity in order to reverse the long-run trend toward declining density. Third, the parties may adopt new joint initiatives at the workplace and strategic levels, with collective bargaining continuing to act as the basis of the system. This course requires that both management and unions hold sufficient power so that the system outcomes do not compromise one party's interests in favour of the other party. The path of industrial relations in autos most closely approximates a movement along this course, although the progress made toward a new order is quite limited. The CAW and auto management have opted for accommodation, and have pursued joint initiatives that may ultimately move the industrial relations system toward more formal strategic alliances. An opportunity exists for the parties to shape the system in this direction.

In industries such as textiles, airlines, and steel, which are at a potential turning point in the development of their industrial relations systems, the parties face similar choices. Confronted with increasingly difficult economic prospects in the 1980s and early 1990s, there is a tendency among unions to adopt a reactive posture to management initiatives. But Canadian unions remain well entrenched, so that any further decline may be slow. As yet, there is no indication that the large unionized firms in these industries are considering nonunion options, and, in some cases, flight of investment capital from Canada is not a reasonable alternative. Management and unions could maintain the *status quo*, which would perpetuate existing adversarial union–management relationships in difficult economic circumstances, but which could ultimately contribute to further losses in economic performance. While the pressures in the 1990s to adapt may be greater for the unions, in order to achieve many of its productivity and strategic objectives, management must work with organized labour. Since any path toward deunionization will be gradual, evolution toward a more mature collective-bargaining system characterized by greater accommodation and strategic alliances may ultimately be the most viable strategy for the 1990s. The latter path would require a fundamental change in the philosophy, direction, and objectives of both labour and management.

In industries in which the economic and social pressures for change have been the least, such as telecommunications, the parties remain committed to a system in which collective bargaining is central. At the outset of the 1990s, telecommunications remained relatively shielded from the major competitive pressures confronting other industries. However, if changes in government policies increase competition in the industry, as it is widely expected (even within a regulated structure), then the industrial relations experiences of the airline industry may provide valuable lessons for unions and firms.

In order to maximize opportunities for successful strategic business planning in increasingly competitive markets, management can either achieve more direct unilateral control, as in the case of construction or garments, or attempt to develop alliances with organized labour, particularly at the workplace and strategic levels. In a unionized setting, a joint commitment to achieving objectives could potentially increase the likelihood of making both parties better off. This, however, is unlikely in cases where the union sees the job of making its members well off as a distributive issue, i.e., any improvements in wages and working conditions have to be "fought for."

The type of industrial relations system that emerges in each of these industries depends on the decisions made by the parties themselves. Overall, the long-run prospect is for increased diversity among industries. In the short run, the further decline of private-sector unions will likely continue. Consequently, the objectives and relative roles of management and labour in many relationships may further shift. These changes are likely to occur because the economic and internal systemic pressures that took root in the 1980s, and the consequent process of industrial restructuring, are expected to intensify throughout the 1990s.

Implications for Policy, Theory, and Research

The findings discussed in this book suggest that change in the industrial relations system, though underway in the 1980s, was not substantial. By 1991, the traditional system remained largely entrenched because the parties continued to adhere to their traditional roles in industrial relations. The vision and political will that are needed to develop new solutions to the economic and social challenges were evident only in isolated cases. It may be inferred, at the risk of errors that come with such generalizations, that most responses in the 1980s were reactive in nature. This may explain why the parties in many industries have failed to explore more innovative approaches, despite sharp increases in competitive pressures.

One possible explanation is that, given historical developments, bilateral relations are too fragile to experiment with new arrangements. The delicate power balance that existed between labour and management *circa* 1980 was developed, after all, over 50 years of gradual accretion under the Wagner Act model. Now, neither party wants to be the first to move in a new direction, lest they lose ground to the other. Canada has also had a long and continuing tradition of government intervention in industrial relations. It is possible that labour and management may be more amenable to considering new arrangements if government would provide some assurance that public policy would continue to strive to maintain the power balance that has served Canada well in the past. Government, in its leadership role, can use influence and moral suasion to orchestrate new arrangements between the parties. As discussed in Chapter 3, the Quebec government has been trying to catalyze a joint restructuring process with labour and management in a few cases. While it is too soon to say whether the Quebec approach will be successful, there is a strong argument for a new role for public policy in industrial relations for the 1990s, when demands for restructuring will likely be even more intense. Of course, government initiatives in the 1990s will have to be more creative and ingenious than in the past. The large budget deficits accumulated over the last twenty years mean that public-policy proposals that involve large budgetary outlays are unlikely to be greeted with enthusiasm.

For building theories of industrial relations, these studies suggest that the strategic-choice framework can be useful if it is suitably modified to fit the Canadian context. Compared to the United States, Canada lacks the sizable nonunion sector that inspired the research leading to the strategic-choice framework. At the same time, the growth of the nonunion sector in western construction and the weakening of unions in several others is well captured by the framework. Most importantly, the strategic-choice framework provides an analytical basis for guiding labour and management policy. The framework also needs to account for greater activity at the sectoral level in Canada. Policy at this extra-firm level can have a significant impact on firm-level outcomes. Lastly, there has always been a substantial role for public policy in industrial relations in Canada. Our findings suggest that, if public policy is to play an effective role in the restructuring process, it will have to move away from the old-style interventions (e.g., back-to-work legislation, wage controls, etc.) toward more innovative interventions, such as the orchestration of bilateral arrangements to share power and responsibility for economic performance. The strategic-choice framework appears useful in guiding public policy toward this new role.

These studies suggest a variety of directions for further research. We have identified the move toward strategic bargaining and alliances as a key path to future prosperity. Future research needs to improve our understanding of the conditions under which strategic bargaining takes place and succeeds. Such research would greatly assist other parties in moving more quickly and directly from the exploratory steps to strategic bargaining. Second, further research could focus on providing new directions in public policy to facilitate the restructuring process. Since this is relatively a new role for the government (on such a large scale), our knowledge of the ways in which the government can facilitate strategic bargaining among the parties remains inadequate. Third, these studies could be well complemented with more firm-level studies of the restructuring process. A better understanding of the linkages between industry and firm-level changes is needed if sectoral initiatives continue to gain momentum during the 1990s. If there are certain conditions under which sectoral initiatives complement and support firm-level efforts, we need to develop an understanding of these conditions.

The evidence gathered in these studies at the industry level reinforces the view that the choices that parties make in their industrial relations strategies are critical to the evolution of the industrial relations system. Despite intense competitive pressures from the global marketplace, the future course for Canadian industry, in terms of meeting both equity and efficiency objectives in the 1990s, is not inevitable in any sense. Much depends on the responses of the parties to these challenges. For example, labour and management could move toward joint governance, which will facilitate greater productivity and prosperity, or they could strive to maintain the status quo, which would make it more difficult to maintain social and economic progress. Thus, the evolutionary process is, in part, determined by the actors themselves. At each stage, the industrial relations outcomes are mediated by the responses and choices of the parties as the outcomes of one stage become inputs for the next stage. The evolutionary path can be altered at every stage by the policy choices of the parties. This suggests that there is an urgent need for all parties to think and act strategically. Otherwise, the course of industrial relations, determined by reactive responses of the parties, will leave policy makers everywhere ineffective in guiding the evolution of Canadian industry.

REFERENCES

Chaison G.N. and Joseph Rose. 1991. "Continental Divide: The Direction and Fate of North American Unions." In D. Sockell, D. Lewin, and D. Lipsky, eds., *Advances in Industrial and Labor Relations*, Vol. 5. Greenwich, CT: JAI Press Inc. 169–205.

Craig, Alton W.J. 1986. *The System of Industrial Relations in Canada*. 3rd ed. Scarborough, ON: Prentice-Hall Canada Inc.

Freeman, Richard. 1990. "Canada in the World Labour Market to the Year 2000." In K. Newton, T. Schweitzer, and J. Voyer, eds., *Perspective 2000*. Proceedings of a Conference sponsored by the Economic Council of Canada, December 1988, 187–98.

Kochan, Thomas A. 1980. *Collective Bargaining and Industrial Relations*. Homewood, IL: Richard D. Irwin, Inc.

Kochan, T.A., H. Katz, and R. McKersie. 1986. *The Transformation of American Industrial Relations*, New York: Basic Books.

Kumar, Pradeep. 1991. "Industrial Relations In Canada and the United States: From Uniformity to Divergence." Queen's Papers in Industrial Relations 1991–2. Kingston, ON: Industrial Relations Centre, Queen's University.

Meltz, Noah. 1990. "Unionism in Canada, U.S.: On Parallel Treadmills?" *Forum for Applied Research and Public Policy*, 5/4 (Winter): 46–52.

Panitch, Leo V., and Don Swartz. 1984. "From Free Collective Bargaining to Permanent Exceptionalism: The Economic Crisis and the Transformation of Industrial Relations in Canada." In Mark Thompson and Gene Swimmer, eds., *Conflict or Compromise?: The Future of Public Sector Industrial Relations*. Montreal: The Institute for Public Policy. 403–35.

Troy, Leo. 1991. "Convergence in International Unionism Et Cetera: The Case of Canada and the US." Queen's Papers in Industrial Relations, 1991–3. Kingston, ON: Industrial Relations Centre, Queen's University.

Verma, Anil. 1991a. "Restructuring in Industrial Relations and the Role for Labor." In Margaret Hallock and Steve Hecker, eds., *Labor in a Global Economy: A U.S.–Canadian Symposiun*. Eugene, OR: University of Oregon Press.

———. 1991b. *The Prospects for Innovation in Canadian Industrial Relations in the 1990s*. Ottawa: Canadian Federation of Labour.

ENDNOTES:

1. Author names are listed in alphabetical order to reflect the equal contributions made. We want to thank Bryan Downie, Morley Gunderson, Pradeep Kumar, and Joe Rose for helpful comments received on an earlier version of this manuscript.

2. The decline of private-sector unionism relative to the public sector in Canada may indicate an underlying long-run weakening of the power of private-sector unions.

3. In the context of our framework, this term refers to a system characterized by either no union or a severely weakened union.

4. This option, though limited by law, or the ability of unions to organize new nonunion companies, or by labour-market conditions, was available, particularly to the construction industry, in the 1980s.

5. Indirect competition still exists due to "captive imports" (see Chapter 2) and the potential transfer of production from Canadian to U.S. plants of the Big Three automakers.

6. Canadian subsidiaries can bid internally for new investments on the basis of cost and quality.

7. The exception to this in western Canada was British Columbia, where the collective-bargaining system adapted to the pressures, although it was subjected to nonunion competition.

8. In contrast, Panitch and Swartz (1984) argue that government employers became increasingly committed to weakening union power in the early to mid 1980s.

KEY WORD INDEX

Absenteeism, 72, 75, 85n
   at Dofasco, 120
AC, *see* Air Canada (AC)
Accounting Employees' Association, 417
Act Respecting Collective Agreement
      Decrees, 228
Act to Restrict Smoking in Workplaces, 23
Adjusted gross margin (AGM), 113
Adjusting to Win, 30
Adversarial culture
   in automobile industry, 75, 78, 79
   in mining industry, 149
Advisory Council on Adjustment, 30
Affirmative action plans, 27
AFL-CIO, *see* American Federation of
      Labour–Congress of Industrial
      Organizations (AFL–CIO)
AGM, *see* Adjusted gross margin (AGM)
AGT, 436
AIB, *see* Anti-Inflation Board (AIB)
AIF, *see* Annual improvement factor
Air BC, 389
Air Canada (AC), 18, 311, 359, 362–63,
      372, 377, 379–80, 383, 386, 456
Air Crew Association of Canada, 388
Airline industry
   common employer applications in,
         389–91
   competition in, 358
   concession bargaining in, 378
   contract administration in, 392
   craft units of, 363–70
   deregulation of, 360, 372, 397
   fare wars in, 359–60
   fence agreements in, 392
   fleet realignment in, 376
   flight attendants in, 365
   globalization and, 374
   open skies negotiations in, 395–96
   pilots in, 365
   privatization of, 376–77
   salaries in, 365
   scope agreements in, 393
   strikes in, 369
   technology in, 376, 387
   union-management relations in, 362–72

   wages in, 368
AISI, *see* American Iron and Steel Institute
Alberta Construction Labour Relations
      Association (ACLRA), 197, 206
Alberta Labour Relations Act, 195
Algoma Steel Corporation Ltd., 87, 98,
      121-24
   historical overview of, 122
Amalgamated Clothing and Textile
      Workers Union (ACTWU), 230,
      236
American Federation of Labour–Congress
      of Industrial Organizations
      (AFL–CIO), 103, 200, 257
American Iron and Steel Institute (AISI),
      97
An Act to Amend the Unemployment
      Insurance Act, 30
An Act to Provide for Pay Equity, 24
Annual improvement factor (AIF), 53, 64,
      65
Anti-Inflation Board (AIB), 340
Anti-inflation Program, 302, 303, 339
APTA, *see* Canada-U.S. Automotive
      Products Trade Agreement
Arbitration, 295
AT&T, 414
Atlas Specialty and Stainless Steels, 90,
      127-29
Automobile industry, *see also* Canadian
      Auto Workers (CAW)
   absenteeism in, 72, 75, 85n
   assembly plant practices in, 67–71
   average earnings in, 46–47
   bargaining in Canada vs. U.S. in, 77
   effect of Auto Pact on, 53–54
   effect of 81/82 recession on, 64
   employment security issue in, 65–66
   evolution of, 52–59
   free trade and, 81
   income security in, 66
   international competition and, 39
   labour relations characteristics of, 45–52
   layoffs in, 55, 65, 66
   management strategy in, 59
   membership, 45, 49

mergers in, 54
overcapacity in, 80
profile of, 40–52
profit sharing in, 64
rationalization in, 53, 57, 58
strikes in, 49, 50–51
structure of, 42–45
supply/demand imbalance in, 79
team systems in, 66
transplant companies, 39, 42, 43
U.S.-Canadian divergence in, 59–76
as value-added industry, 45
vertical integration in, 54
work rules in, 72
Auto Pact, 6, 53–54
    Canadian Value Added percentages
        and, 81

Back-to-work legislation, 314
Base wage rates, 64–65
Basic oxygen furnaces (BOFs), 97
BCE Inc., 406
B.C. Tel, 435–36, 439–41
Bell Canada, 406, 411, 412, 415, 417, 420,
    429, 430–32
Big Three, the, 39, 42, 48
    agreements of with CAW/UAW, 60–63
    free trade and, 81
    job losses in U.S., 65–66
    recent initiatives of, 58
    response of to Japanese competition, 57,
        66
    work stoppages in, 51–52
Big Two, the, 90
Bill 30, 340
Bill 100, 336, 337–39, 340, 456
Bill 110, 195
Bloc-Action, 420
BOFs, *see* Basic oxygen furnaces
Bonne entente committees, 275
BRAC, *see* Brotherhood of Railway and
    Airline Clerks (BRAC)
Brotherhood of Railway and Airline Clerks
    (BRAC), 364
Bruncor Inc., 406
Business unionism, 155

Cabotage, 360

CAD, *see* Computer-aided design (CAD)
CALEA, *see* Canadian Air Line Employees'
    Association
CALPA, *see* Canadian Air Line Pilots'
    Association
CALURA, *see* Corporations and Labour
    Union Returns Act
CAM, *see* Computer-aided manufacturing
    (CAM)
CAMI, 48
Canada
    economic growth in, 9–11
    employment in, 12–14
    productivity in, 12
    trade and, 11–12
Canada Development Corporation, 311
Canada Labour Market and Productivity
    Centre (CLMPC), 30
Canada-U.S. Automotive Products Trade
    Agreement (APTA), 53
Canada-U.S. Free Trade Agreement, 1, 4,
    30, 86n
    automobile industry and, 81
    clothing industry and, 226
    labour cost and, 14
    as shift in public policy, 17
    steel industry and, 87, 96–97
    telephone industry and, 415
    textile industry and, 253
Canadian Air Line Employees' Association
    (CALEA), 364
Canadian Air Line Pilots' Association
    (CALPA), 371, 394
Canadian Airlines International Ltd.
    (CAIL), 358, 375, 385, 386
Canadian Airline Supervisors and
    Inspection Association (CASIA),
    372
Canadian Automotive Repair and Service
    Council, 29
Canadian Auto Workers (CAW), 22, 40,
    72–74, 393
    agreements of with Big Three, 60–63
    collective agreement coverage in, 45
    contingent compensation and, 462
    contrasted with UAW, 77, 78
    divergence of from UAW positions, 58,
        59, 74–75

guidelines for management relations, 73–75
legislative lobbying of, 78
Master Agreement of, 49–52
NDP ties of, 78
organization of, 49
reaction of to recent Big Three strategies, 58, 59
relation of union to locals, 77
union density in, 45
vs. USWA, 104
view of Saturn model, 75
Canadian Collieries Limited, 154
Canadian Construction Association (CCA), 189, 203–204
Canadian dollar
decline of, 14
value of, 16, 97
Canadian Electrical and Electronics Manufacturing Industry, 29
Canadian Federation of Labour (CFL), 200, 201
Canadian Industrial Renewal Board (CIRB), 254–57, 280n
Canadian Labour Congress (CLC), 104, 200, 302–303
Canadian labour movement, vs. U.S., 3–4
Canadian Labour Relations Board (CLRB), 378, 389, 439
Canadian Motor Vehicles and Automotive Parts Industry, 49
Canadian Pacific Airlines (CP Air), 361, 374–75, 381, 382
Canadian Paperworkers, 104, 447n
Canadian Radio-Television and Telecommunications Commission (CRTC), 413, 416, 441–42
Canadian Steel Producers Association (CSPA), 97
Canadian Steel Trade and Employment Congress (CSTEC), 29, 124–25, 130, 131
Canadian Telephone Employee Association (CTEA), 417–18
Canadian Textile Institute (CTI), 252
Canadian Textile Labour-Management Committee (CTLMC), 29, 260, 264, 266

Canadian Transport Commission (CTC), 373
Canadian Union of Public Employees (CUPE), 22, 287, 387
CASIA, see Canadian Airline Supervisors and Inspection Association (CASIA)
CAW, see Canadian Auto Workers (CAW)
CCA, see Canadian Construction Association (CCA)
CECCO, see Construction Employers Coordinating Council of Ontario (CECCO)
CFL, see Canadian Federation of Labour (CFL)
Challenge Communications Limited, 413
Chapparel Steel, 101
Choice-of-procedures, 295
Chrysler Corporation, 64
modern operating agreements of, 66
CILRA, see Construction Industry Labour Relations Act
CIO, see Committee of Industrial Organizations (CIO)
CIRB, see Canadian Industrial Renewal Board (CIRB)
CLC, see Canadian Labour Congress
CLMPC, see Canada Labour Market and Productivity Centre
Clothing industry
components of, 222
decree system in, 228–31, 238
deregulation and, 240
as fragmented, 221
GST and, 240
homework in, 223, 238, 239
imports and, 225–27
joint committees in, 230
multi-employer structure in, 227
in Quebec, 220, 221–23
trade balance in, 226
unionization rates in, 231–32
unionized job protection in, 238–39
wages in, 232–35
women in, 227, 232–33
CLRAs, see Construction Labour Relations Associations

CLRB, *see* Canadian Labour Relations
    Board (CLRB)
Code-sharing, 374
Cokeless steel, 100
COLA, *see* Cost-of-living adjustment
    (COLA)
Cold Metal Products, 90
Collective agreements, 24–30
    in CAW, 45
    in clothing industry, 233–38
    provisions, 25
Collective bargaining, 2, 3, 18, 31
    in Canada vs. U.S., 77
    CAW and, 48, 49, 58–59
    in construction industries, 189–90, 205,
        206–211
    decentralizing of, 105, 269
    in mining industry, 164
    vs. nonunion system, 3
    in Ontario education, 323–27, 339–42,
        343–44, 352–53
    public-sector, 284, 294–95, 304–305
    in steel industry, 104, 105–107
    in textile industry, 269–75
Cominco Limited, 146
Commercial Employees' Association, 417
Committee of Industrial Organizations
    (CIO), 258
Committee on Contracting Out and
    Technological Change (COTC),
    423, 439
Communications and Electrical Workers of
    Canada (CWC), 418, 430–35
Communications Workers of America
    (CWA), 430
Commuting work force, 142
Comparable-worth legislation
Competition (international), 16, 30,
    454–55
    in airline industry, 358
    in automobile industry, 39, 66, 82, 454
    FTA and, 455
    in mining industry, 173
    in steel industry, 87, 97, 115, 129
    in textile industry, 244
Competitiveness, 16
    in clothing industry, 235
    as productivity, 235

of steel industry, 90
    strategic choice and, 5
Computer-aided design (CAD), 254
Computer-aided manufacturing (CAM),
    254
Computer technology
    in automobile industry, 58
    in textile industry, 254, 270
Concession bargaining, 207
    in airline industry, 378
Congress of Industrial Organizations, 59
Connective bargaining structure, 53
Construction Employers Coordination
    Council of Ontario (CECCO),
    197
Construction industry
    bargaining in, 189–90, 205–211
    deregulation and, 193
    effect of 1981 recession on, 191, 192
    Expo 86 and, 196
    fair-wage schedules and, 194
    megaprojects, 193
    nonunion competition in, 192, 196, 201
    public investment in, 193
    sectors of, 188
    strikes in, 189, 211
    union density in 188
    union membership in, 198–200
    wage issues in, 204–206
Construction Industry Bargaining Act, 206
Construction Industry Labour Relations
    Act (CILRA), 194–95
Construction Industry Wages Act, 194
Construction Labour Relations
    Associations (CLRAs), 197, 215
Construction Management Bureau Limited,
    197
Contingent compensation, 58, 64, 64–65
Contingent pay, 27, 170
Continuous casting, 97–98, 99
Contracting out, 26, 169, 170
    public sector and, 311–12
    in telephone industry, 423–24
Contract stripping, 344, 354
Corporations and Labour Unions Returns
    Act (CALURA), 287
Cost-of-living adjustment (COLA), 53
    in mining industry, 166

in public sector, 306
in steel industry, 104, 111, 112
in telephone industry, 423
COTC, *see* Standing Committee on
        Contracting Out and
        Technological Change (COTC)
County board system, 330
Courtice Steel, 90
CP Air, *see* Canadian Pacific Airlines
Craft-union locals, 188
Crown corporations, 310
CRTC, *see* Canadian Radio-Television and
        Telecommunications Commission
        (CRTC)
CSPA, *see* Canadian Steel Producers
        Association
CSTEC, *see* Canadian Steel Trade and
        Employment Congress
CTC, *see* Canadian Transport Commission
        (CTC)
CTEA, *see* Canadian Telephone Employee
        Association (CTEA)
CTI, *see* Canadian Textile Institute (CTI)
CTLMC, *see* Canadian Textile
        Labour-Management Committee
CUPE, *see* Canadian Union of Public
        Employees (CUPE)
Customer service director (CSD), 385
CWA, *see* Communications Workers of
        America (CWA)
CWC, *see* Communications and Electrical
        Workers of Canada (CWC)

Decree system, 228–31, 238
De facto free trade, 81
Deindustrialization, 173
Deregulation, 1, 456
    of airline industry, 360, 373
    effect on clothing industry, 240
    effect on trade unions, 18
    impact of on construction industry, 193
    as shift in public policy, 18
    of telephone industry, 416
Digital processing, 413
Discrimination, 27
Dispute-settlement mechanisms, 211–14
Distinguished Service Award (DSA), 420
Divergence/convergence debate, 22–23

Dofasco, 88, 98, 116–20
    absenteeism at, 120
    employee relations policy of, 116, 118
    historical overview of, 117
    job security at, 120
    nonunion strategies, 119
    profit-sharing plan at, 119
    suggestion scheme used by, 118
Dominion Textile, 246, 264, 266–67, 269
Doublebreasted organizations, 194, 196
Dual-shop organizations, 194

EAPs, *see* Employee Assistance Programs
        (EAPs)
Economic growth (Canada), 9–11
Education Relations Committee (ERC),
        338, 340
EEC, *see* European Economic Community
Efficiency, 3
EI, *see* Employee involvement (EI)
Employee Assistance Programs (EAPs),
        391–92
Employee benefit plans, 52
Employee discipline rates, 75
Employee involvement (EI), 28–29, 66
    in mining industry, 170
    in telephone industry, 429–37
    in textile industry, 270
Employee relations, at Dofasco, 118
Employer accreditation, 190, 197
Employer associations, 232
Employment
    in goods- and service-producing
        industries, 14
    government promotion of, 30
    male vs. female rates of, 12
    mix, 13
    part-time, 19
    shift toward service sector, 13
Employment rate, annual change in, 13
Employment security, 458
    in automobile industry, 65–66
    in telephone industry, 437
EQUIPE, 431
Equity, 3
ERC, *see* Education Relations Committee
        (ERC)
European Economic Community (EEC), 11

Fairness and equity, 27–28
Fair-wage policies, 193–94
Fair Wages and Hours of Labour Act, the, 193
Falconbridge Limited, 147
FCTT, *see* Federation catholique national du textile (FCTT)
Federal Mediation and Conciliation Service, 366, 367
Fédération catholique national du textile (FCTT), 262, 271
Fédération de la Metallurgie, 164
Federation of Women Teachers' Associations of Ontario (FWTAO), 331
Fence agreements, 392
Flexibility,
    in automobile industry, 76, 77
    in mining industry, 170
    in steel industry, 93, 104
    telephone industry, 437
    in textile industry, 270
Flying shuttle, 280n
Focus 2000, 29
Ford Motor Company of Canada, 52
Formulaic wage rules, 53
Fragmented bargaining structures, 197
Fragmented industry, 221
Free collective bargaining, 302
Freedoms of the Air, 360
Free Trade Agreement, *see* Canada-U.S. Free Trade Agreement
Frequent-flyer programs, 375
Friendly duopoly, 358, 375
FTA, *see* Canada-U.S. Free Trade Agreement
FWTAO, *see* Federation of Women Teachers' Associations of Ontario (FWTAO)

Gain sharing, 27
    in steel industry, 104
GATT, *see* General Agreement on Tariffs and Trade
GDP, *see* Gross Domestic Product (Canada)
General Agreement on Tariffs and Trade (GATT), 226, 252

General Motors of Canada, 52, 53, 54, 74,
    see also Big Three, the
    Saturn subsidiary of, 74–75
    world-class contract of, 66
General Preferential Tariff, 124
Global marketplace, 2, 358
    airline industry and, 374
    effect of on Canadian economic performance, 8
Goods and Services Tax (GST), 240, 285
Grievance rates, 75
Gross Domestic Product (Canada), 8, 9–11
    exporting and importing and, 17
    mineral industry and, 141
GST, *see* Goods and Services Tax (GST)

Hall-Dennis report, 329
Harris Steel, 90
HEAT program, 124–25
Hilton Works, 107, 109
Honda of Canada, 42
Hub-and-spoke configuration, 359
Hudson Bay Mining and Smelting Co., 170
Hyundai Auto Canada, 42

IAM, *see* International Association of Machinists and Aerospace Workers (IAM)
IAS, *see* Industrial Adjustment Service (IAS)
ICBA, *see* Independent Contractors and Business Association
ILGWU, *see* International Ladies' Garment Workers' Union
Immigration, 2
IMPACT, 431–32
Inco Limited, 26, 142, 154, 170, 173, 175, 176, 177
Income maintenance, 30
Income security, 26, 458
    in automobile industry, 66
    vs. employment security, 26
Income sharing, 113
Independent Contractors and Business Association (ICBA), 201
Industrial Adjustment Service (IAS), 29, 124, 125
Industrial homework, 223, 238, 239

Industrialism and Industrial Man, 3
Industrial relations
    in Canada vs. U.S., 3–4
    change in, 449–50
    effect of global market pressures on, 2
    equity and efficiency in, 3
    innovations in, 459–61
    pressures for change in, 1–2
    recent developments in, 18–24
    stages in evolution of, 450–54
    strategic behaviour in, 5
    traditional system of, 6
Industrial relations policy, 7
Industrial Standards Act, 228
Industry, as level of analysis, 6
Inflation Restraint Act, 340
Inflation Restraint Board (IRB), 340
In-flight service manager (ISM), 385
Interest arbitration, 213
International Association of Machinists and
    Aerospace Workers (IAM), 21,
    368, 370–71, 383
International Brotherhood of Electrical
    Workers (IBEW), 21, 418
International competition, *see* Competition
    (international)
International Ladies' Garment Workers'
    Union (ILGWU), 231, 258
International trade (Canadian), 11–12
    free trade and, 17
International Union of Operating
    Engineers, 164
International Woodworkers, 22
Ipsco, 90, 102
IRB, *see* Inflation Restraint Board (IRB)
Ivaco, 90

Job-bank program, 65
Job control focus, 53
Job control unionism, 450
Job Opportunity Bank, 65
Job security, 26
    at Dofasco, 120
    in mining industry, 164
Joint Committee, the, 204
Joint committees, 64
    in clothing industry, 230
    in construction industry, 204

industry-level, 29, 31
labour-management, 28, 113, 275,
    458–62
    in textile industry, 275
Joint Human Resource Committee, 276–77
Jurisdictional Assignment Plan, 214
Just cause clause, 352
Just-in-time systems, 72

Kaiser, 100
Kidd Creek, 176

Labour, cost of, 14–17
Labourers' International Union of North
    America, 21
Labour force
    participation of women in, 19
    part-time employment and, 19
Labour-management relations
    in automobile industry, 49
    code of conduct for, 29
    in steel industry, 109–114, 124–25
    at Stelco, 109–114
    U.S.-Canadian divergence in, 59–72
Labour movement
    Canada vs. U.S., 22–23, 37n, 77
    legislation affecting, 23–24
    relation of NDP to, 23, 77, 78
Lake Erie Works, 107, 109
Lasco, 90, 102, 127
Laurel Steel, 90
Layoffs, in automobile industry, 55, 65, 66
Leapfrogging, 363
Limited-purpose organizations, 201
Locals
    in automobile industry, 77
    in steel industry, 110
Long-Distance Toll (TOPS), 433, 434
Long-term Cotton Arrangement (LTA),
    252
Long-term disability (LTD), 344
Lower-tier carriers, 371–72
LTA, *see* Long-term Cotton Arrangement
    (LTA)
LTD, *see* Long-term disability (LTD)
LTV, 100, 123, 126
Lump-sum payments, 17, 64, 65

Management
    Canadian vs. U.S. in auto industry,
        78–79
    CAW guidelines for relations with,
        73–74, 75
    impact of Auto Pact on, 54
    recent strategy of in automobile
        industry, 58, 59
    in telephone industry, 420–21
    in textile industry, 271–72
    UAW position on, 64, 74, 76
    union involvement in, 49, 58, 59, 64
Manitoba Rolling Mills, 90
Manitoba Telephone System (MTS),
    432–35
Manufacturing, relative earnings in Canada
    vs. U.S., 15
Maritime Telephone & Telegraph
    (MT&T), 406
Master Agreement, 49-52
Master Contract, 77
MCAs, see Merit contractors associations
    (MCAs)
MCI, 414
McLouth, 100
Memorandum of Understanding (MOU),
    201, 214
Merit contractors associations (MCAs),
    202–203
Merit-shop employer associations, 201–203
Mine, Mill and Smelter Workers Union,
    149
Minimills, 100–102, 109
Minimum wage, 228, 235
Mining industry
    bargaining developments in, 165–70
    Canadian production ranking in, 144
    COLA and, 166
    effect of globalization on, 142
    employment statistics for, 148, 157
    flexibility in, 170
    frontier character of, 177
    international competition in, 173
    job security in, 164
    labour shortages in, 170, 172
    modernization programs in, 173–74
    professionalization of, 149
    recession of 1981 and, 157
    safety issues in, 172
    strikes in, 154–56, 164
    structure of, 145–47
    technological developments in, 142,
        166, 174, 175
    union density in, 162
    union membership in, 150–53, 164
Modernization
    in automobile industry, 53
    in mining industry, 173–74
MOU, see Memorandum of Understanding
MTS, see Manitoba Telephone System
    (MTS)
MultiFibre Arrangement (MFA), 6, 226
Multilateral bargaining, 303
Multiskilling, 66, 104
Multitrade bargaining, 197
Multiyear contracts, 53

N&LNUGA, see Newfoundland and
        Labrador Non-Union Contractors
        Association
National Collective Agreement, 72
National joint initiatives, 29–30
National Labour Relations Act, 337
National Steel, 98
National Textile Council (NTC), 259
National Trades and Labour Congress
        (NTLC), 257
National Training Board, 30
National Union of Provincial Government
        Employees (NUPGE), 22, 287
N.B. Tel, 438
NDP, see New Democratic Party (NDP)
Neelon Casting, 126, 139n
New Democratic Party (NDP), 23, 77, 78
    steel industry ties to, 104
Newfoundland and Labrador Non-Union
        Contractors Association
        (N&LNUGA), 201
NewTel Enterprises, 406
New Union for Telephone Employees
        (NUTE), 420
Nippon Steel, 102
Nippon Telephone and Telegraph (NTT),
        414
NKK Corporation, 98
Nonunion system, 3, 6, 48, 116

in Canada vs. U.S., 471
in construction industry, 192, 196, 201
in mining industry, 176
Nonwage provisions, 17
Noranda Minerals Inc., 142
Nordair, 372
North American Free Trade Zone, 81
Northern Telephone, 406
NorthwesTel, 406
NTC, *see* National Textile Council (NTC)
NTLC, *see* National Trades and Labour
 Council (NTLC)
Nucor Inc., 99, 101
NUPGE, *see* National Union of Provincial
 Government Employees (NUPGE)

OECTA, *see* Ontario English Catholic
 Teachers' Association (OECTA)
Ontario education
 Bill 100 and, 337–39
 class size issue in, 347–48
 collective bargaining in, 324–27,
  339–42, 343–44, 352
 component staffing in, 350
 legislation affecting, 336–39
 pupil/teacher ratios in, 333, 346, 348–53
 role of ministry in, 330
 salary schedules in, 333
 strikes in, 335, 336, 342–43
 wages in, 343–44
 working conditions as issue in, 346–47
Ontario English Catholic Teachers'
 Association (OECTA), 331
Ontario Nurses Association, 22
Ontario Public School Teachers' Federation
 (OPSTF), 331
Ontario School Trustees' Council (OSTC),
 333
Ontario Secondary School Teachers'
 Federation (OSSTF), 331
Ontario Teachers' Federation (OTF), 331
On-the-job training, 26
Open door policy, 119
Open-end spinning, 254
Open hearth steelmaking, 97
Open Skies agreement, 6, 18, 395
OPSTF, *see* Ontario Public School
 Teachers' Federation (OPSTF)

OSSTF, *see* Ontario Secondary School
 Teachers' Federation (OSSTF)
OSTC, *see* Ontario School Trustees'
 Council (OSTC)
OTF, *see* Ontario Teachers' Federation
 (OTF)

Pacific Western Airlines (PWA), 361, 372,
 373, 375
Parapublic agencies, 284
Part-time employment, 19, 26
Pattern bargaining, 114
Pay equity, 23–24
Pay-for-knowledge system, 66, 72, 270
Pension Benefits Act, 23
Pension indexing, 66, 113, 166
PEP, *see* Performance through Employee
 Participation
Performance through Employee
 Participation, 126
Piece rate incentive systems, 258
Placer Dome Limited, 146
Plant committees, 275
Potash Corporation of Saskatchewan, 18
Privatization, 1, 456
 of airline industry, 376–77
 public sector and, 310–14
 as shift in public policy, 17–18
 union reaction to in public/private
  sectors, 312
Productivity (in Canada), 12
 in clothing industry, 235–38
Profit sharing, 17, 27
 in automobile industry, 64, 65
 in steel industry, 101, 113, 116, 119
Project management, 458
PSAC, *see* Public Service Alliance of
 Canada (PSAC)
PSSRA, *see* Public Service Staff Relations
 Act (PSSRA)
PTR, *see* Pupil/teacher ration (PTR)
Public policy
 affecting Ontario education, 336–39
 shifts in, 17–18
Public sector
 back-to-work legislation and, 314–16
 collective bargaining and, 294–95,
  304–305

contracting-out and, 311–12
defined, 284–85
employment, 286
fiscal restraint and, 457
legislation affecting, 290–94, 291
privatization and, 310, 311–14
recent developments in, 465–66
reduction of, 310–311
strike loss in, 298–99
strikes in, 308
union density in, 287
unionization of, 286–90
union membership in, 287
unions, 289
wage controls, 302–303
wage increases in, 307
Public Service Alliance of Canada (PSAC),
     288
Public Service Staff Relations Act
     (PSSRA), 290
Pupil/teacher ratio (PTR), 333, 336, 346,
     348–53
PWA, *see* Pacific Western Airlines (PWA)

Quality Circle Fightback Committee, 436
Quebec Federation of Labour (QFL), 200
Quick Response Program, 277, 283n
QWL, 78

Rationalization
     in automobile industry, 53, 57, 58, 78
     in textile industry, 245
RBO, *see* Relationships by objectives
     (RBO)
Relationships by objectives (RBO), 354
Republic Engineered Steel, 123
Restraint programs, 308, 457
Restructuring, 1–32
Rio Algom Limited, 146
Roman Catholic separate schools, 328, 347

Saskatchewan Construction Labour
     Relations Council (SCLRC), 197
Sask Tel, 437
Saturn model (General Motors), 75
Scab labour, 154
Scanlon Plan, 126
School Boards and Teachers Collective

Negotiations Act, 330–31
Scope agreements, 393
Search for a Better Way, The, 29
Semi-autonomous work groups, 28
Service Employees International Union,
     21, 38n
Severance pay, 66
Sexual harassment, 27
Sharing programs, 438
Shuttleless loom, 254
Sidbec-Dosco, 90
Six and five wage controls, 305
Slater Steels, 90
Social unionism, 48, 79
SPC, *see* Statistical process control
Speak Out program, 436
Spinning jenny, 280n
Spin-off firms, 195, 196
Standing Committee on Contracting Out
     and Technological Change
     (COTC), 435
Star Suggestion program, 436
Statistical process control (SPC), 58
Steel industry, *see also* United Steelworkers
     of America (USWA)
     aggregate performance of, 90, 91
     average hourly earnings in, 94
     Canada-U.S. Free Trade Agreement
          and, 96–97
     Canada-U.S. market shares, 95
     Canadian vs. U.S. productivity, 92–93
     competitive strategy of, 101
     effect of 81-82 recession on, 90, 105
     flexibility in, 93
     foreign trade and, 95–97
     free trade and, 87, 130
     gain sharing in, 104
     governmental role in, 123–24
     Japanese investment in, 102
     large vs. minimills in, 100–101
     major companies, 89
     NDP ties to, 104
     output and employment in, 93
     pattern bargaining in, 114
     profitability of vs. U.S., 87
     recycling, 90
     safety in, 101–102
     specialization in, 100

SUB and, 112
technological developments in, 97–100
in U.S., 100–102
wages in, 101, 107
young workers in, 101
Steffco, 112–14
Stelco, 87, 97, 104, 107–16, 137–38n
    bargaining outcomes in 1980s, 110–11
    COLA and, 111
    historical overview of, 108
    PEP program of, 126
    profit sharing and, 111
    strikes, 105, 110
Strategic choice framework, 2–6
    relation of to Dunlop systems
        framework, 5
strategic choices
    defined, 4
Strikes
    in airline industry, 369
    in automobile industry, 49, 50–51
    in construction industry, 189, 211
    dispute settlement mechanisms for,
        211–14
    in mining industry, 154–56, 164
    in Ontario education, 335, 336, 342–43
    in public sector, 308
    in telephone industry, 428–29
    in textile industry, 259, 264–69
SUB, see Supplementary Unemployment
        Benefits
Suggestion schemes, 118
Supplementary Unemployment Benefits
        (SUB), 65, 66
    in steel industry, 112
Sweatshop work, 223
Sysco, 90
System integrity, 412

Taskforce on the Canadian Motor Vehicles
        and Automotive Parts Industry, 53
TCB, see Textile and Clothing Board
        (TCB)
Teacher federations, 324
Team Share Plan, 438
Teamsters, 264
Technological change indemnity, 237
Technology, 7, 31

advances in, 1
in clothing industry, 235–38
FTA and, 253
metal-saving, 156
in mining industry, 142, 166, 174, 175
role of, 455–56
in steel industry, 97–100
in telephone industry, 413–14, 425
in textile industry, 253–57
Telebec Ltée, 406
Telecommunications Workers Union
        (TWU), 436
Teleglobe Canada, 311
Telephone industry
    benefits in, 423
    cellular networks, 414
    collective bargaining in, 419–29
    contracting-out and, 423–24
    deregulation of, 416
    economies of scale in, 412
    employee involvement in, 429–37
    employment equity and, 425
    employment security in, 437
    flexibility in, 437–38
    FTA and, 415
    historical overview of, 407
    labour-management relations, 419–21
    major companies of, 409–410
    POTS and PANS, 414
    service universality and, 413
    sharing programs, 438
    strikes in, 428–29
    system integrity and, 413
    technological developments in, 413–14,
        425
    VDT use by, 425
    wages in, 421–23
Textile and Clothing Board (TCB), 252
Textile industry
    capital and repair expenditures in,
        255–56
    collective bargaining coverage in, 263
    collective bargaining in, 269
    exports/imports in, 247–48
    labour force in, 249–50
    performance of, 257
    strikes in, 259, 264–69
    structure of, 246–49

technology in, 253–57, 272
union density in, 261–64
union membership in, 260, 262
wages and salaries in, 251
women in, 250
Textile Workers Organizing Committee
  (TWOC), 258
Textile Workers Union of America
  (TWUA), 259
Time Air, 389
TOPS, *see* Long-Distance Toll (TOPS)
Toronto Operators' Strike, 417
Toyota Motor Manufacturing Canada, 42
Trade Union Act, the, 195
Traffic Employers' Association, 371, 417
Transplants, 39, 42, 43
Trial Change project, 433–34
Trial Office, 434–35
TWOC, *see* Textile Workers Organizing
  Committee (TWOC)
Two-tier systems, 58
TWUA, *see* Textile Workers Union of
  America (TWUA)

UAW, *see* United Auto Workers
UMWA, *see* United Mine Workers of
  America (UMWA)
Unemployment, problem of in Canada, 12
Union density, 18, 19–21
  in Canada vs. U.S., 3
  in CAW, 45
  in construction industry, 188
  in mining industry, 162
  in public sector, 287
  in textile industry, 261–64
Union Drawn Steel, 90
Union membership, 20, 21–22
  in automobile industry, 45, 49
  in construction industry, 198–200
  in manufacturing and primary industries,
    21-22
  in mining industry, 150–53, 162, 164
  in public sector, 287–88
  in steel industry, 103
  in textile industry, 260, 262
Unions, *see also* Canadian Auto Workers
  (CAW); United Steelworkers of
  America (USWA); etc.

automobile industry, 45–52
clothing industry, 231–32
management relations in auto industry,
  74–75
organization of, 49
participation of women in, 19
pay equity and, 24
public sector, 289
strength of in Canada vs. U.S., 22–23
view of FTA, 17
United Auto Workers (UAW), 22, 45, 52,
  53, 54, 66–72
  agreements of with Big Three, 60–63
  vs. CAW response to recent
    developments, 58, 59, 74–75
  contrasted with CAW, 77, 78
United Brotherhood of Carpenters and
  Joiners, 21
United Food and Commercial Workers
  International Union, 21, 22
United Mine Workers of America
  (UMWA), 141, 149, 178
United Steelworkers of America (USWA),
  21, 22, 26, 29, 90, 103, 125, 141,
  149, 178
  vs. CAW, 104
  CSTEC and, 124, 131
  dealings of with Steffco, 112–14
  dealings of with Stelco, 111–12
  Humanity Fund of, 104, 111
  typical worker in, 103
United Textile Workers of America
  (UTWA), 271
Unitel Communications, 416
U.S. Sprint, 414
USWA, *see* United Steelworkers of
  America (USWA)
UTWA, *see* United Textile Workers of
  America (UTWA)

VDT, *see* Video-display tube (VDT)
Video-display tube (VDT), 425
Visitation programs, 118
Voluntary restraint agreements (VRAs), 96
VRAs, *see* Voluntary restraint agreements

Wabasso, 267
Wage controls, 302–303

six and five, 305
Wage incentive plans, 27
Wage-progression systems, 58
Wage restraint programs, 193
Wages
    in airline industry, 368
    in automobile industry, 48, 54, 58
    base rates, 64–65
    in clothing industry, 232–35
    in construction industry, 204–206
    in Ontario education, 343–44
    in small communities, 101
    in steel industry, 105, 107
    in telephone industry, 421–23
    in textile industry, 251
    variable vs. fixed, 101
    in various industries compared, 106
Wagner Act, 2, 103, 109, 337
Wardair, 371, 375
Weirton Steel, 123
Wheeling-Pittsburgh, 100

WHMIS, *see* Workplace Hazardous
    Materials Information System
    (WHMIS)
Women
    in clothing industry, 227
    participation of in labour force, 2, 19
    pay equity legislation, 24
    in textile industry, 250
Woods Taskforce on Industrial Relations, 6
Worker ownership issue, 123
Work Jurisdiction Committee, 440
workplace
    innovations, 28
    privacy in, 2
Workplace flexibility, 27, 457
Workplace Hazardous Materials
    Information System (WHMIS), 23,
    156, 172
World-class contract (General Motors), 66

Z-line, 126

NAME AND AUTHOR INDEX

Adams, Roy, 105, 111, 113, 137n
Aherne, Michael, 386
Ahmad, Jaleel, 246
Allan, John, 112
Alleruzzo, John, 230
Amsden, Michael P., 176
Ansberry, Clare, 101
Armitage, Perry, 447
Arnold, William L., 373, 376
Arrowsmith, David, 45, 49, 164, 261
Audet, Michel, 29, 261, 266
Auld, Douglas, 306, 308

Babe, Robert E., 412, 413, 445
Bailey, Thomas, 250
Bain, Goerge Sayers, 188
Bain, Trevor, 93
Barbash, Jack, 3
Barnacle, Peter, 186n
Barnett, Donald F., 87, 100, 124, 136n
Bean, R., 21
Bedard, Pierre Marc, 139
Bell, Alexander Graham, 406
Bellemarre, Guy, 233
Bell, Melville, 408
Bell, Thomas, 249, 280
Bemmels, Brian, 370
Bernard, Elaine, 418, 435
Betcherman, Gordon, 28
Bird, R.M., 286
Bourdon, Clinton C., 194
Bourque, Rey, 139n
Broderick, Renae F., 27
Brown, John L., 373, 376
Byfield, Mike, 359

Campbell, B., 223
Cappelli, Peter, 365, 378
Cawsey, T.F., 176
Chaison, G.N., 3, 22, 23, 37n, 177, 467
Chaykowski, Richard P., 24, 166, 175
Chelius, James, 4
Chemello, Sandra, 386
Clement, W., 154, 183n
Clergue, Francis Hector, 121
Cline, William, 235

Coates, Mary Lou, 17, 18, 19, 22, 23, 38n, 45, 49, 162, 164, 261
Coleman, C., 352
Colgan, Fiona, 249, 267, 272
Copp, Terry, 231, 281
Coté, Michel, 45
Courchene, Melanie, 49, 164, 250, 261
Coyle, Angela, 223, 224
Crandall, Robert, 100, 136n
Crosbie, John, 281
Cutcher-Gershenfeld, Joel, 430, 437, 447n

de Grandpré, A. Jean, 30
Delaney, Ken, 29, 104
Dertouzos, Michael J., 277, 283n
Deverell, John, 290
Dion, Reverend Gerard, 266
Docquier, Gerard, 29, 131
Doern, G. Bruce, 193
Downie, Bryan, 384
Draper, Paddy, 259
Dube, Jean-Louis, 228, 229
Dunlop, John T., vi, 2, 3
Dworkin, James, 4

Ehrenberg, Ronald G., 446n
Enchin, Harvey, 249

Fagan, Drew, 191
Falkenberg, Loren, 295
Faoro, Louis, 285
Fedorus, Anna, 386
Fisher, E.G., 196, 206, 370, 392
Flango, V., 346
Fleming, James, 121, 122
Florida, Richard, 102
Ford, Micheal, 363, 364, 370, 372
Foster, Howard G., 194
Foulkes, Fred K., 116, 418
Frankel, S., 289
Fraser, D., 348
Freeman, Richard B., 16, 17, 421, 468
Fryer, John, 312, 313

Gallina, Mark, 104, 430
Giacobbo, Efre, 275

Gibbs, Graham W., 185n
Gillen, David W., 361, 373, 375
Gindin, Sam, 59, 64, 76
Gislason, G.S., 149, 170, 184n
Goldenberg, Shirley, 288
Grant, Michel, 223, 224, 239, 323
Gray, Alan D., 249
Green, Alan G., 161, 184n
Green, M.A., 161, 184n
Green, William, 259
Gretton, Wallace T., 175, 186n
Gunderson, Morley, 24, 295

Halpern, Norman, 28
Hantho, Charles, 249
Harris, R., 328
Harris, Vic, 112
Healy, James J., 420
Hébert, Gerard, 194, 302
Hendricks, Wallace E., 445
Heneault, Robert E., 138n
Herzenberg, Stephen, 49, 64, 65, 76, 78
Hetu, Jean Paul, 281n
Hillman, Sidney, 259
Hogan, Willam, 87, 100, 136n
Holmes, John, 53, 59, 65, 76, 85n, 86n
Howell, Thomas R., 90, 92, 136n
Huffman, Ken, 361, 377
Hunter, Nicholas, 249, 267

Ichniowski, Casey, 29

Jackson, Moira, 185n
Jacoby, Sanford M., 419
Jacques, Yvon, 282n
Janisch, Hudson N., 408, 414, 415, 445n
Jennish, D'Arcy, 253
Johnson, Laura C., 239
Johnson, Robert E., 239

Katz, Harry C., 2, 3, 4, 53, 65, 66, 72, 75,
    76, 85n, 86n, 113, 177, 269, 276,
    342, 353, 449, 450, 452, 453
Keeling, Bernard, 98
Kendall, Glenn, 164
Kenny, Martin, 102
Kerkhoff, J.C., 196
Klein, Alice, 446n

Kochan, Thomas A., 2, 3, 4, 17, 37n, 113,
    116, 126, 131, 142, 177, 182n, 269,
    276, 342, 353, 418, 449, 450, 452,
    453
Koepke, W.E., 143
Kokkinos, Yiota, 164
Kondra, Alex, 392
Kubish, Glenn, 376, 403n
Kumar, Pradeep, 18, 23, 37n, 45, 53, 59, 65,
    76, 77, 85n, 86n, 103, 162, 305,
    306
Kushner, E.G., 196, 206
Kuyek, Joan, 417, 446n

Langford, Hohn W., 361, 362, 377
Leclerc, Claudine, 29, 261, 266, 315
Lee, Tanya, 315
Lendvay-Zwickl, Judith, 14, 23, 94
Lester, Richard K., 277, 283n
Levitt, Raymond E., 194
Lewin, David, 4, 29, 445n
Litvak, Isaiah A., 90
Livernash, Robert, 420
Lougheed, Peter, 376
Lyon, S., 149, 170, 184n

McDavid, James C., 311, 312
Macdonald, Derek, 315, 383
MacDonald, Neil D., 81
McFetridge, Donald, 311
McKelvey, Jean T., 370
McKersie, Robert B., 2, 3, 4, 113, 177, 269,
    342, 353, 449, 450, 452, 453
McKitrick, Ross, 12, 19
MacMillan, J.A., 149, 170, 183n, 184n
McMullen, Kathryn, 28
Mahon, Rianne, 253
Mansell, Jacqui, 28
Marshall, Ray, 236
Maslove, Allan M., 294, 302
Matthews, Roy A., 223
Maule, Christopher J., 90
Medoff, James L., 421
Meier, Gerry, 219
Melady, John, 376
Meltz, Noah M., 3, 4, 30, 37n, 65, 66, 72,
    75, 76, 77, 85n, 86, 103, 467
Meyer, Noel, 275

Milbourne, Bob, 97, 114, 138
Miller, Swasti, 224, 239
Milner, Brian, 191
Mitchell, Daniel J.B., 27
Morin, Fernand, 315
Morton, Desmond, 281
Mower, Nancy R., 430
Muir, J.D., 334
Mustard, Vernon, 271, 282n

Nappi, Carmine, 156, 183n, 184n
Newby, N. Jill, 362, 364, 365, 372, 392
Northrup, Herbert R., 203
Nyland, Barbara, 370

O'Connor, William E., 363
Olive, David, 121, 122
Olivier, Madeleine, 275
Oum, Tae H., 373

Palmer, Bryan D., 149, 154, 183n, 185n
Panitch, Leo V., 305, 315, 474n
Paré, Terence, 101
Pender Terry, 176
Pepin, Jean-Luc, 280n
Perry, Ross, 85n
Perusek, G., 53, 65, 72, 77, 78
Petro-Canada, 18
Phizacklea, Annie, 224
Pintus, P., 185n
Ponak, Allen, 285, 286, 288, 293, 295
Porter, Michael, 221, 235
Porter, Nancy, 164
Preston, Richard, 101, 102

Rayback, Joseph G., 137
Renner, Roland, 257, 259, 264
Rheault, Denis, 266, 267, 282n
Richardson, P.R., 176
Riddell, Craig, 27, 295
Robb, Roberta E., 24
Roberts, Wayne, 446n
Roosevelt, Franklin D., 228
Rose, Joseph B., 3, 22, 23, 37n, 176, 189,
        190, 195, 204, 288, 290, 467
Rose, Ruth, 223, 224, 239
Rouillard, Jacques, 258, 267
Roy, Francine, 42

Rusonik, Anthony, 59, 76
Ryan, Dennis, 77, 200

Sack, Jeffrey, 315
Sangster, Joan, 446n
Scales, Marilyn, 147, 175
Schick, Gregory K., 312
Schorsch, Louis, 87, 124
Schultz, Richard J., 408, 414, 415
Sexton, Jean, 29, 261, 264, 266, 275
Sherman, Frank A., 116
Shniad, Sid, 436
Sichter, Sumner H., 230
Slotsve, George A., 175
Smith, Douglas A., 299, 300, 311
Smith, F.E.W., 362, 363, 364
Sockell, Donna, 445n
Solow, Robert M., 277
Stanbury, W.T., 310, 311, 361, 375
Stockhouse, John, 377, 394
Storey, Robert, 116, 119, 138
Strand, Kenneth, 192, 194, 196
Strauss, George, 194
Swan, Kenneth P., 302
Swartz, Don, 305, 315, 474
Sweeney, Vincent, 137n
Swimmer, Gene, 294, 295, 302, 305, 306
Swinton, Katherine, 293

Taylor, Cec, 110
Teller, Paul M., 294
Telmer, Fred, 111, 115, 138n
Thomas, Hugh, 280
Thompson, Mark E., 1, 4, 102, 285, 286,
        293, 308
Thornicroft, Kenneth W., 378, 387
Till, Larry, 147, 175, 186n
Tilton, John E., 144, 145, 182n
Trethway, Michael W., 361, 373, 375
Troy, Leo, 4, 23, 37n, 38n
Tupper, Allan, 193, 373, 374

Verma, Anil, 4, 27, 37n, 102, 103, 104,
        116, 126, 138, 381, 418, 430, 437

Waldinger, Roger D., 225
Warrian, Peter, 29, 131
Weiler, Paul C., 193, 213, 370, 392

Weiner, N., 24
West, Denise, 312
Wetzel, Kurt, 195
Wheeler, Hoyt, 295
White, Robert, 75
Wilkinson, Paul, 139n
Williams, Brian C., 149

Wilson, Michael, 281n
Wilton, David A., 295, 306, 308
Woodbury, S., 346

Yates, C., 49, 77, 78

Zeytinoglu, I., 105, 111, 138n

To the Owner of This Book:

We are interested in your reaction to *Industrial Relations in Canadian Industry*, by Richard P. Chaykowski and Anil Verma. With your comments, we can improve this book in future editions. Please help us by completing this questionnaire.

1. What was your reason for using this book?
    - _____ university course
    - _____ college course
    - _____ continuing education course
    - _____ personal interest
    - _____ other (specify)

2. If you used this text for a program, what was the name of that program?

3. Which school do you attend?

4. Approximately how much of the book did you use?
    _____ 1/4 _____ 1/2 _____ 3/4 _____ all

5. Which chapters or sections were omitted from your course?

6. What is the best aspect of this book?

7. Is there anything that should be added?

8. Please add any comments or suggestions.

fold here